Baptized in PCBs

Baptized in PCBs

Race, Pollution, and Justice
in an All-American Town

ELLEN GRIFFITH SPEARS

THE UNIVERSITY OF NORTH CAROLINA PRESS *Chapel Hill*

This book was published with the assistance of the
William R. Kenan Jr. Fund of the University of North Carolina Press.

The paper in this book meets the guidelines for permanence
and durability of the Committee on Production Guidelines for
Book Longevity of the Council on Library Resources.

The University of North Carolina Press has been a member
of the Green Press Initiative since 2003.

Library of Congress Cataloging-in-Publication Data
Spears, Ellen Griffith.
Baptized in PCBs : race, pollution, and justice in an all-American town /
Ellen Griffith Spears.
pages cm — (New directions in Southern studies)
Includes bibliographical references and index.
ISBN 978-1-4696-1171-6 (cloth: alkaline paper)
ISBN 978-1-4696-2729-8 (pbk.: alkaline paper)
ISBN 978-1-4696-1172-3 (ebook)
1. Polychlorinated biphenyls—Environmental aspects—Alabama—Anniston.
2. Polychlorinated biphenyls—Health aspects—Alabama—Anniston. 3. Anniston
(Ala.)—Environmental conditions. 4. Monsanto Company—History. 5. Environmental
justice—Alabama—Anniston. 6. Environmental health—Alabama—Anniston.
7. African Americans—Health and hygiene—Alabama—Anniston. 8. Working class—
Health and hygiene—Alabama—Anniston. 9. Anniston (Ala.)—Race relations.
10. Anniston (Ala.)—Social conditions. I. Title.
TD427.P65S68 2014
363.738'4—dc23
2013041122

Portions of this book have been adapted from "Making Illnesses Visible: The New-
town Florist Club and the Quest for Environmental Justice in Gainesville, Georgia," in
Emerging Illnesses and Society: Negotiating the Public Health Agenda, edited by Randall
M. Packard, Peter J. Brown, Ruth L. Berkelman, and Howard Frumkin, 171–90, © 2004
The Johns Hopkins University Press, reprinted with permission of The Johns Hopkins
University Press; and "Reducing Environmental Burdens: A Southern Agenda," in *American Crisis: Southern Solutions*, edited by Anthony Dunbar, 200–211, © 2008 NewSouth
Books, reprinted with permission of NewSouth Books.

For Brian

CONTENTS

MAPS AND ILLUSTRATIONS

PREFACE

What I am interested in are the strategies for maintaining the silence and the strategies for breaking it. —Toni Morrison, *Playing in the Dark*, 1992

Biologist and nature writer Rachel Carson opened her 1962 landmark study *Silent Spring* with a lovely, lyrical, but partly fictionalized parable that vividly anticipated mounting problems associated with chemical pesticides. Carson combined real examples from several distinct locales and melded them into one coherent and powerful narrative to demonstrate the detrimental impact of reckless commercial pesticide use on nature and human health, predicting the dystopia that might result if such chemicals remained unregulated. She was abundantly clear, each example of pesticide exposure was true, but not all of these problems beset any one place.[1]

Like Carson's account, *Baptized in PCBs* makes an argument for reforming how we manufacture, use, and regulate toxic chemicals in the United States. However, the city on which this story centers—Anniston, Alabama—is not fictional; portions of its landscape resemble Carson's vision of the future. Its streams were at one time declared "devoid of life" and remain off-limits to residents who depended on local fish or once enjoyed local swimming holes. The toxic exposures in the town have included not only pesticides such as parathion but also lead and mercury. Most significant, however, are levels of polychlorinated biphenyls (PCBs) in residents' bodies that rival the highest non-workplace human exposures around the world. The Anniston Army Depot hosts a Superfund site, where toxic levels of trichloroethylene (TCE) threaten the water supply. Until 2011, the depot was also home to a substantial cache of Army nerve gases—sarin and VX—and mustard agent, outdated and decaying weapons of the Cold War.[2]

Anniston has played a key role in two significant chemical dramas that arose in the twentieth century: the struggle to identify and contain persistent chemical pollutants and the need to determine the fate of the Cold War–era chemical weapons stockpile. Tracing the city's history from its founding in 1872 as a model for southern industrial development to its 2002 designation as "Toxic Town USA," this book documents residents' discovery of the extent of environmental pollution in their city and what they have achieved in reducing toxic harms. The toxic burden of the city's history continues to have resounding effects.

Anniston's history of civil rights activism proved crucial in orienting the contemporary fight for environmental justice. When the Monsanto Chemical Company's PCB contamination and the U.S. Army's planned chemical weapons incinerator made national headlines in the early 2000s, Anniston garnered more sustained national and international press coverage than it had in several decades. Not since Mother's Day, 1961, when local Klan sympathizers firebombed a Freedom Riders bus just four miles west of the Monsanto plant, had the city drawn so much attention. That story of violent repression of nonviolent civil rights protest is here, too, along with accounts of the indigenous civil rights movement that both predated and followed the 1960s.

I first visited Anniston in 1988 on an election year Super Tuesday swing through the South with the Reverend William Sloane Coffin. As a chaplain at Yale, Coffin had marched with civil rights workers in Selma in the 1960s. Coffin, who had recently been named president of a national peace organization, and I, as regional field organizer for the group, traveled through Georgia, Florida, and Alabama, pressing the case that any "peace dividend" realized at the end of the Cold War ought to be redirected to fight poverty. We spent an afternoon at the offices of the *Anniston Star* in lively conversation with the newspaper's publisher, H. Brandt "Brandy" Ayers. (This nationally recognized locally owned paper is at once information source, commentator, and major player in the Anniston story. Formerly called the *Hot Blast*, after the iron smelting method used by the town's first major industry, the paper has been a fixture in the city since 1882. Family patriarch Harry Mell Ayers, *Star* editor and publisher through much of the Jim Crow era, moved among Alabama's power brokers, helping to shape Anniston's fortunes by courting the chemical industry and the military. Under his son Brandy's leadership, the Democratic-leaning paper, nicknamed by opponents "the Red *Star*," has provided liberal commentary in conservative, now majority-Republican north Alabama.)[3] The passing of the Cold War era was especially consequential for this city. The two local military installations, Fort McClellan and the Anniston Army Depot, depended—even more than we then knew—on chemicals used in warfare, gaining or losing economically with each shift in U.S. defense policy.

I returned to Anniston many years later with a new set of tools and questions that emerged from academic interests in the origins of social inequalities in environmental public health and the movements that are working to end such disparities. Attending a community health fair in Zinn Park in downtown Anniston in 2002, I met David and Shirley Baker, activists with Community Against Pollution, an organization committed to addressing the PCB problems. I visited with Opal Scruggs, who lived nearby and whose grandfather had worked at the Monsanto plant. Later, I talked with Cassandra Roberts and other members of the Sweet Valley/Cobbtown Environmental Justice Task Force and learned more about the ongoing fight to redress the harm of seventy years of exposure to Monsanto's PCBs.

During the coming months and years, I interviewed people on all sides of the pollution debates, including Monsanto and Solutia officials in St. Louis, EPA and corporate remediation team staff on the ground, industry public relations consultants, military affairs personnel, and representatives of the Department of Homeland Security, which ran first responder "live agent" chemical training at the decommissioned Fort McClellan site. Acting on calls by historians for "community-based histories of resistance and struggle," I talked with dozens of residents who participated in court cases over PCB contamination and organized opposition to chemical weapons incineration, as well as their attorneys and allies. I attended numerous community meetings held by local environmental organizations, the EPA, the Army's Chemical Demilitarization public relations team, and others. I also began an informative association with members of the Anniston Environmental Health Research Consortium, researchers who conducted PCB health studies to determine the extent of PCB exposure and surveyed community perceptions of health and disease. Following the global pathway of PCBs led me to archives and experts from St. Louis to San Francisco to Stockholm. I pored over more than 7,000 pages of trial transcripts documenting the court cases brought by Anniston residents to hold Monsanto to account.[4]

In early summer 2003, to better understand community responses to plans to incinerate the chemical weapons stored at the Anniston Army Depot, I took part in the training being provided for residents of the "Pink Zone," those areas most at risk of exposure to toxic gases if an explosion occurred during incineration. Depot workers were to begin dismantling the Cold War chemical weapons stockpile stored in Anniston later that summer and were distributing protective equipment to residents in case of a nerve agent release at the site. (Ominously, the trainer who demonstrated the protective equipment that day was reading *Armageddon*, eleventh in the twelve-part "Left Behind" series of Christian pre-millennial apocalyptic novels.) When I finished donning a rudimentary gas mask along with Timothy and Kama Cherry and their children, the couple, both of whom worked in public health in Anniston, gave me a sense of how threatened local people felt. They would invite me to dinner, they said, but if the chemical alert "whoop siren" went off (indicating a release of nerve agent), they wouldn't have an extra mask for me. As permanent residents, they were being issued masks; though I often stayed in the city, I was not. Now, in 2013, the destruction of chemical weapons is complete. Although state environmental officials fined the Army and its contractors for several violations, the absence of a major obvious incident is due in no small measure to the diligence of advocates of safe disposal.[5]

Until environmental justice activism against Monsanto blew toxic secrets wide open in this southern town, the Anniston story was a problem of silences. However, Anniston's residents confronted a different kind of silence than the absence of birdsong that Carson described in *Silent Spring*. "A secret is not something unrevealed, but told privately in a whisper," wrote the French filmmaker Marcel Pagnol. The problem was not that nobody knew. In the 1930s, medical and professional journals reported links between PCBs, liver ailments, and the severe skin disease chloracne. Monsanto's internal memos and court testimony revealed that corporate representatives told state and federal agency staff in the 1960s and 1970s about the chemical load in their plant wastes—though they did so belatedly, deliberately understating the threat, and often only when pressed. On the chemical weapons front, U.S. negotiators notified the Russians of how many and what types of deadly nerve agents were locally stored but resisted sharing that information with local reporters. It wasn't that corporate and government authorities didn't tell anybody; they just never told the people who most needed to know.[6]

Upon learning of PCB contamination in the mid-1990s, nearly everyone in the factory neighborhood had personal health experiences to share. Some had been quite literally baptized in the chemicals. At her family's convenience store on Clydesdale Avenue, several blocks north of Monsanto, Shirley McCord kept an informal record of illnesses and deaths among neighbors and loved ones. The list eventually reached seventeen pages in length.[7]

Arthur Bowie's family had lived in West Anniston since the early 1940s, in the African American neighborhood just eight-tenths of a mile east of the Monsanto plant. When they first heard about the serious pollution, Arthur and Bettye Bowie had a nice home off Lincoln Park, near where Arthur had lived as a child. Forced to sink their retirement savings into moving, they left West Anniston, fearful of what playing in PCBs might do to their grandchildren. "It was poison," said Mrs. Bowie, "but we didn't know then about PCBs. Monsanto was too lowdown to tell us not to eat the fish, to [say] move, get away from the community because we have saturated your community with poison." Now they were saddled with toxic knowledge, knowing they carried in their bodies PCBs, but deeply uncertain about what that fact might mean. Opal Scruggs, of the predominantly white West End neighborhood, lived about four blocks west of Monsanto for most of her life and was over sixty when she learned she had very high levels of Monsanto's PCBs in her blood. Like the Bowies, what angers her most is the fact that Monsanto officials never told residents what they knew.[8]

In exploring how the chemical industry, the U.S. military, and racism altered the landscape and human bodies and how local people responded, I confront several questions: How are race and class and gender imbricated with geography in decisions about placing and monitoring polluting industries? How do we tackle documented concentrations of toxics in poor and minority communities when their disposition on the landscape seems so deeply entrenched? What reinvigorated conception of justice would better serve people who live and work in polluted places? More plainly stated, as one practiced observer put it, "I get it. You are trying to find out how we got into this mess and 'how do we get out of it?'"[9]

Thanks to numerous people who shared their perspectives, this study includes many voices. Where I anticipated reticence, people were forthcoming. Tell this story, was the general sentiment; if it helps one other community avoid what we have gone through, I am glad to share what happened to me. I have endeavored to do their story justice. Omissions, mistakes, and errors of interpretation are mine. There will always be more to tell.

MANY PEOPLE DESERVE THANKS. The Emory University Graduate Institute of the Liberal Arts provided a stimulating interdisciplinary launch for this research. Insights shared by Allen Tullos on the dynamics of power and justice in Alabama, Dan Carter on narrative southern history, Howard Frumkin on environmental health in Anniston, and Cris Levenduski on the texture of good writing grounded the project. Edna Bay, Kevin Corrigan, Amy Lang, Nathan McCall, Cindy Patton, and Jonathan Prude gave key insights at various stages. Rudolph Byrd and Regina Werum encouraged my research through an Andrew Mellon Foundation Teaching Fellowship. Chairs Uriel Kitron, William Size, and colleagues in the Department of Environmental Studies at Emory and Violet Johnson at Agnes Scott College provided welcoming and intellectually nurturing places to teach and write.

The Center for the Study of Health, Culture, and Society at Emory's Rollins School of Public Health and faculty members Randall Packard, Peter Brown, Howard Kushner, and Kate Winskell provided unique occasions for exchanging ideas through the Mellon-Sawyer Seminars. The A. Worley Brown Southern Studies Fellowship and the Ford Foundation Vernacular Modernities program and its director, Bruce Knauft, supported the project with research awards. A Reynolds Historical Collection Fellowship enabled my work in the Lister Hill Library at the University of Alabama at Birmingham. A Research Grants Committee award from the University of Alabama facilitated the project. The Columbia University Oral History Project, the Hambidge Center for the Creative Arts and Sciences, and the Lillian E. Smith Center for the Creative Arts provided places to explore documentary techniques and to write. My long association with the Southern Regional Council also informs this research.

Many thanks are due friends and colleagues who generously read, commented, suggested sources, and gave advice and support: University of Alabama faculty Jim Hall, Lynne Adrian, Natalie Adams, Heather Elliott, Jolene Hubbs, John Miller, Fred Whiting, and others; historians and writers Raymond Arsenault, Susan Ashmore, Craig Colten, Christine Cozzens, Constance Curry, Catherine Fosl, Matthew Klingle, Cliff Kuhn, Suzanne Marshall, Carolyn Merchant, Marie Price, Christopher Sellers, Gary Sprayberry, and Robert Woodrum; attorney Cleo Thomas; physician Henry Kahn; environmental engineers Wendy Pearson and Jack Matson; journalists Dennis Love and John Fleming; the Southern Studies seminar group and ILA colleagues Terry Easton, Kent Glenzer, Randy Gue, Emily Satterwhite, and Pat Wehner. Amy Benson Brown of the Manuscript Development Program at Emory and UA publisher-in-residence George Thompson shared advice. Thanks especially to Kamla Dutt, Marcia Klenbort, Virginia Shadron, Mary Anne Smith, and Bobbi Patterson for providing support and key insights. Special thanks go to Gerald Markowitz and anonymous reviewers.

Appreciation is due the Anniston Environmental Health Research Consortium, particularly principal investigators Howard Frumkin, Martha Lavender, Jane Cash, Scott Bartell, and Christie Shelton, along with Judy Simmons and Rhoda Johnson.

Historian Grace Hooten Gates passed away just as I began this research, but I gratefully encountered the detailed documentary record that she constructed of Anniston's past. Acknowledgment is due many archivists, including Teresa Kiser, Tom Mullins, Linda Dukes, and Diane Betts of the Alabama Room at the Anniston–Calhoun County Public Library; Jack Eckert at the

Center for the History of Medicine, Francis A. Countway Library of Medicine of the Harvard Medical Library; Laura Anderson at the Birmingham Civil Rights Institute; Jay Kempen at the Monsanto Archives in Special Collections at Washington University of St. Louis; Bill Tharpe at the Alabama Power Archives; Jennifer McClure at Gorgas Library and Jessica Lacher-Feldman of the W. S. Hoole Special Collections Library at the University of Alabama; Jamie Leonard, associate dean for Legal Information Services of the University of Alabama School of Law; Randall Burkett, Naomi Nelson, Kathy Shoemaker, and Randy Gue at the Manuscript, Archives, and Rare Book Library at Emory; and Michael Flannery, Tim Pennycutt, Peggy Balch, and Lachiecia Anderson of the Reynolds Historical Collection at the Lister Hill Library at UAB. German translation advice supplied by Stefan Lutz of the Emory Chemistry Department helped reveal more about the early history of PCBs.

I appreciate the conscientious work of research assistants Bonnie Applebeet, Emma Joan Bertolaet, Jamie Burke, Iman Folayan, Mary Heske, Kirsten Hesla, Juyeon Lee, Caitlin McClusky, William Tomlin, and Mary Tubbs. Louis T. Laverone checked legal citations. Lillia Callum-Penso, Rebecca Callum-Penso, Rebecca Groves, and Ryun Miller diligently retrieved and organized documents and duplicated audio interviews. Teresa Knight pitched in at various stages. Pat Williams, Lesly Fredman, and Rita Furman not only are superb transcribers but also shared a deep commitment to the project.

Thanks to Eric Francis and Brendan DeMelle for suggestions based on their extensive research into Monsanto's corporate history, and to Ken Cook and staff of the Environmental Working Group for making a vast array of internal Monsanto documents accessible online through the Chemical Industry Archives. Thanks also to Carol Williams, who first alerted me to outrage reduction strategies, and to Yomi Noibi of ECO-Action.

Charles Jones most generously shared his graphic design talents. Tips on mapping and demographics came from Michael Page and Annette Watters; assistance with photos came from Michael Schwarz and *Anniston Star* photographer Bill Wilson. *Anniston Star* journalists too numerous to name are cited in the text. Veteran news editors Nancy Albritton and Susan Wells kindly undertook thorough reads; and Lisa Moore and Liz Wheeler, whom I met through Georgia Volunteer Lawyers for the Arts, offered valued advice.

This manuscript was made immeasurably better by the keen perceptions of Jennifer Meares, compassionate editor and dear friend, with an impeccable ear for argument. Her editorial acumen is reflected throughout. Thanks to Rebecca Johnson, who proofread the text, and to Linda Webster, who prepared the index.

Editor-in-Chief David Perry, Editorial Director Mark Simpson-Vos, Series Editor Charles Reagan Wilson, Associate Managing Editor Paula Wald, Caitlin Bell-Butterfield, Alex Martin, and others at the University of North Carolina Press guided the manuscript with care and insight through every stage.

People from academic institutions, corporate affairs offices, government agencies, law firms, and nonprofit organizations who helpfully shared information and advice include Michael Abrams, Leah Rawls Atkins, Craig Branchfield, Stephanie Yvette Brown, Robert Bullard, Henry Caddell, David Cain, David O. Carpenter, Brooks Fahy, Alan Faust, Timothy Garrett, Edgar C. Gentle III, Melissa Hammonds, Larry Hansen, Mark Hermanson, Brian Holtzclaw, Ralph Knowles, John Lawry, Leslie Leahy, Charles Lee, Pam Tau Lee, Max McCombs, Max Michael, Peter Montague, Kirsten Moysich, Jim Olson, Robert B. Roden, Stephen B. Ross, Leslie Rubin, Carolyn Green Satterfield, Pamela Scully, Allen Silverstone, and Glynn Young.

Deepest thanks go to people in Anniston and beyond who opened their homes and their office doors and generously shared insights, documentary records, phone advice, meals, places to stay, and stories. The list includes H. Brandt Ayers, Josephine Ayers, Carrie Baker, David Baker, Scott Barksdale, Rev. George Bates, Betsy Bean, Kay Beard, Arthur Bowie, Bettye Bowie, Representative Barbara Boyd, Jacqueline Brown, Georgia Calhoun, Betty Carr, Shirley Baker Carter, Jeannette Champion, Wanda Champion, Lea Cheatwood, Kama Cherry, Timothy Cherry, David Christian, Judge U. W. Clemon, Pete Conroy, Elizabeth Crowe, Jimmy Curvin, Alice Donald, Joanne Finch, Dennis Gibson, Pollie Goodman, Linda Green, James Hall, Wayne Carmello-Harper, Sylvester Harris, Bert Haskew, former Anniston mayor Hoyt "Chip" Howell, Kathy Jackson, Bessie Jones, Myrtle Joshua, Rev. Randy Kelley, Rufus Kinney, Brenda Lindell, Rev. Thomas Long, Suzanne Marshall, Angela Martin, Shirley McCord, Hobson City mayor Rev. Alberta McCrory, Janie Forsyth McKinney, Eloise Mealing, Rose Munford, Betty Scott Noble, Rev. Phil Noble, Phil Noble Jr., Councilman Herbert Palmore, Lula Palmore, Katie Pyles, former Hobson City mayor Robert Pyles, Rev. Nimrod Q. Reynolds, Charity Richey-Bentley, Cassandra Roberts, Jerry Roberts, Gordon A. Rodgers Jr., Elise Ayers Sanguinetti, Phil Sanguinetti, Opal Scruggs, Rev. Henry Sterling, Donald Stewart, Edgar Stroud, Sherri Sumners, Carla Thomas, Cleo Thomas, Hank Thomas, Chris Waddle, Linda White, and Craig Williams.

All would not have been possible without the warmth and encouragement of my entire family, including Lelia and Ben, who ably assisted, and most of all, Brian, who welcomed this presence in our midst for many years.

ABBREVIATIONS

AAD   Anniston Army Depot
ACC   American Chemistry Council
ACEF   Anniston Community Education Foundation
ACS   American Chemical Society
ACWA   Assembled Chemical Weapons Assessment
ADEM   Alabama Department of Environmental Management
ADPH   Alabama Department of Public Health
AFL-CIO American Federation of Labor–Congress of Industrial Organizations
ANCDF Anniston Chemical Agent Disposal Facility
ANSI   American National Standards Institute
ASNE   American Society of Newspaper Editors
ATSDR Agency for Toxic Substances and Disease Registry (now combined with the National Center for Environmental Health, part of the U.S. Centers for Disease Control and Prevention)
AWIC   Alabama Water Improvement Commission
BRAC   Base Realignment and Closure
CAC   Community Advisory Committee of the Anniston Environmental Health Research Consortium
CAG   community advisory group
CAP   community advisory panel; Citizens Against Pollution; Community Against Pollution
CBR   Chemical-Biological-Radiological
CBTU   Coalition of Black Trade Unionists
CCC   Civilian Conservation Corps
CCHW   Citizens' Clearinghouse on Hazardous Waste
CCIA   Calhoun County Improvement Association
CDC   U.S. Centers for Disease Control and Prevention
CDCAC Chemical Demilitarization Citizens Advisory Commission
CDP   Center for Domestic Preparedness
CEJ   Citizens for Environmental Justice
CEQ   Council on Environmental Quality

CERCLA Comprehensive Environmental Response, Compensation, and Liability Act

CMA Chemical Manufacturers' Association; Chemical Materials Activity

CORE Congress of Racial Equality

COUL Committee of Unified Leadership

CRBI Coosa River Basin Initiative

CUE Calhoun County Clean Up the Environment

CWS Chemical Warfare Service

CWWG Chemical Weapons Working Group

DDT dichloro-diphenyl-trichloroethane

DEQ Department of Environmental Quality

EDF Environmental Defense Fund

EPA Environmental Protection Agency

EWG Environmental Working Group

FDA Food and Drug Administration

FEMA Federal Emergency Management Agency

FWPCA Federal Water Pollution Control Act; Federal Water Pollution Control Authority

GAO General Accounting Office (later Government Accountability Office)

GASP Greater Birmingham Alliance to Stop Pollution

GB sarin (nerve agent)

HAZMAT hazardous materials

HBCUs historically black colleges and universities

HCl hydrochloric acid

HHS U.S. Department of Health and Human Services

HUD U.S. Department of Housing and Urban Development

IARC International Agency for Research on Cancer

IBT Industrial Bio-Test Laboratories

ICWU International Chemical Workers Union

MACs maximum allowable concentrations

MADPCH Mothers and Daughters Protecting Children's Health

MASA Medical Association of the State of Alabama

MCC Monsanto Chemical Company

MECSI Monsanto Enviro-Chem Systems Inc.

MICC Monsanto Industrial Chemicals Company

NAACP National Association for the Advancement of Colored People

NAPCA National Air Pollution Control Administration

NASCAR National Association for Stock Car Auto Racing
NBAF National Bio and Agro-Defense Facility
NBUF National Black United Fund
NCEH National Center for Environmental Health
NEJAC National Environmental Justice Advisory Council
NEPA National Environmental Policy Act
NHANES National Health and Nutrition Examination Survey
NIOSH National Institute for Occupational Safety and Health
NPL National Priorities List
NRC National Research Council
NRDC National Resources Defense Council
NWF National Wildlife Federation
OCAW Oil, Chemical, and Atomic Workers International Union
OECD Organization for Economic Cooperation and Development
OREPA Oak Ridge Environmental Peace Alliance
OSHA Occupational Safety and Health Act; Occupational Safety and
Health Administration
PCBs polychlorinated biphenyls
PIC product of incomplete combustion
POP People Opposing Pollution
POPs persistent organic pollutants
ppb part(s) per billion
ppm part(s) per million
PRP Potentially Responsible Party
RCRA Resource Conservation and Recovery Act
REACH Regulation, Evaluation, and Authorisation of Chemicals
(European Union protocol)
SAFE Serving Alabama's Future Environment
SCHW Southern Conference on Human Welfare
SCLC Southern Christian Leadership Conference
SNCC Student Nonviolent Coordinating Committee
SOC Southern Organizing Committee for Social and Economic
Justice
SOCMA Synthetic Organic Chemical Manufacturers Association
SPRING Supporters of Proven Reliable Incineration of Nerve Gas
SSSMA South Soil Staging and Management Area
STP Stop the Pollution
TAG Technical Assistance Grant
TCDDs tetrachloro-dibenzo-dioxins, or dioxins

TCDFs tetrachloro-dibenzo-furans, or furans
TCE trichloroethylene
TRC Truth and Reconciliation Commission
TRI Toxic Release Inventory
TSCA Toxic Substances Control Act of 1976
TSP trisodium phosphate
UNCED United Nations Conference on Environment and Development
USPHS United States Public Health Service
VA Veterans Affairs
VX nerve agent
WAC Women's Army Corps
WAF West Anniston Foundation
WARF Wisconsin Alumni Research Foundation
WPA Works Progress Administration

INTRODUCTION

Toxic Knowledge

As things worked out, there was—and is—a lot of American symbolism in the
Monsanto story. —Monsanto public relations director Dan J. Forrestal, 1977

On February 22, 2002, an Alabama jury unanimously held the global agrochemical giant Monsanto and its corporate partners legally responsible for
PCB contamination in the land and in the bodies of people who had lived
near the company's Anniston, Alabama, plant. The state court jury found
Monsanto and its partner companies liable on six counts—"suppression of
the truth, negligence, trespass, nuisance," "wantonness," and "outrage."
Alabama law interprets "outrage" as conduct "beyond all possible bounds
of decency . . . atrocious and utterly intolerable in civilized society." After
just five and a half hours of deliberation, the jury decided that Monsanto
had knowingly poisoned Anniston residents and then had hidden the danger from public knowledge.[1]

PCBs—polychlorinated biphenyls—once prized as heat-resistant fluids,
are associated with serious health problems, from liver disease to immune
disorders to neurobehavioral deficits in children. Both the U.S. Environmental Protection Agency (EPA) and the International Agency for Research
on Cancer (IARC) have labeled the chemicals probable human carcinogens.
PCBs lodge in nearly every person around the globe, but the trial had revealed exceptionally high concentrations of these compounds in residents
of Anniston, where Monsanto produced the chemicals for nearly forty
years.[2]

Marketed under the brand name Aroclors, PCBs were first fabricated
commercially in the United States in 1929 by the Swann Chemical Company
in West Anniston. From 1935 on, the Monsanto Chemical Company held a
monopoly on the U.S. manufacture of these profitable chemicals.[3]

PCBs are a large and diverse family of chemicals—209 in all. Largely
odorless, often colorless, and tasteless, these heavy, oily, waxy substances,
some viscous liquids, some solids, were put to multiple industrial uses,
mainly as insulating fluids to prevent fires in transformers and other electrical equipment. Many of the chemicals Monsanto produced, including

Aroclors, were sold not directly to the consumer but to industrial customers, who used PCBs to make a variety of consumer goods, including plastics, paint, pesticides, adhesives, caulk, carbonless duplicating paper, and dishwasher detergent. Monsanto was, in effect, industry's industry, a role that buffered the company from consumer concern about the toxicity of its chemicals and displaced some pollution costs onto industrial purchasers of Monsanto's products. Shipped all over the world, PCBs became ubiquitous but largely invisible. Once revealed, PCBs rivaled DDT as emblematic of the chemical consequences of global dominance by corporate power.[4]

Not easily broken down in the environment, PCBs gather in dust, soil, air, water, tree bark, and in the blood and tissues of living beings. PCBs can be ingested in food, through the skin, or by inhalation. The chemicals bioaccumulate in living organisms and also undergo biomagnification, increasing in concentration at successive levels in the food chain. The chemicals' effects are intergenerational. A gestating fetus can be exposed to PCBs through the placenta; PCBs can also pass to infants via breastfeeding. Research found the chemicals so hazardous that Congress banned them in 1976, requiring Monsanto to phase out manufacture, distribution, and sale of PCBs, with limited exceptions, by 1979.[5]

One version of the PCB narrative was told in much the same way Monsanto presented its case in court, as a story of corporate responsiveness and regulatory success. Once a young chemist working in Sweden, Søren Jensen, "discovered" the chemicals to be persistent, pervasive, and toxic in 1966, the Monsanto Chemical Company discontinued producing them in Anniston. Soon thereafter, Congress banned the chemicals. Even before the congressional ban took effect in 1979, Monsanto stopped making the chemicals at its only other U.S. production site in Sauget, Illinois. A few "hot spots" remained, but the PCB problem was not a cause for general concern. Indeed, average human exposure levels were declining by the 1990s.[6]

The Anniston PCB cases unearthed decades of internal documents that suggest a different narrative. Evidence presented at trial revealed that renowned Harvard physiologist Cecil K. Drinker had alerted Monsanto to possible "systemic" toxic effects of PCBs as early as 1937. Monsanto obtained further documentation of the chemicals' hazards, boasting "the world's best reference file" on PCBs in 1971, information that the jury found had been actively suppressed. Monsanto's successor company, Solutia, continued to dispute the disease claims, maintaining in 2002 that "studies of industrial workers have shown no illnesses attributable to PCB exposure, other than an acne-like skin rash and a temporary elevation of some liver enzymes."[7]

Map 1.1. Key sites in the history of PCBs. The St. Louis–based Monsanto Chemical Company, which held a monopoly on polychlorinated biphenyls (PCBs) in the United States, manufactured the chemicals in Anniston, Alabama, from 1935 to 1972. Sauget, Illinois, was the only other U.S. site at which Monsanto produced PCBs. Map by Charles Jones.

PCBs continue to pose an ecological and public health problem, not only in Anniston but also globally. On the national level, the 1976 ban and subsequent EPA exemptions left 750 million pounds of PCBs in use in the United States alone, mostly in aging electrical transformers that not only are vulnerable to fires and leaks but also pose a disposal problem that is coming due.[8]

Nor did the halt to production end the problem of PCB pollution in Anniston. More than forty miles of waterway remain lined with contaminated

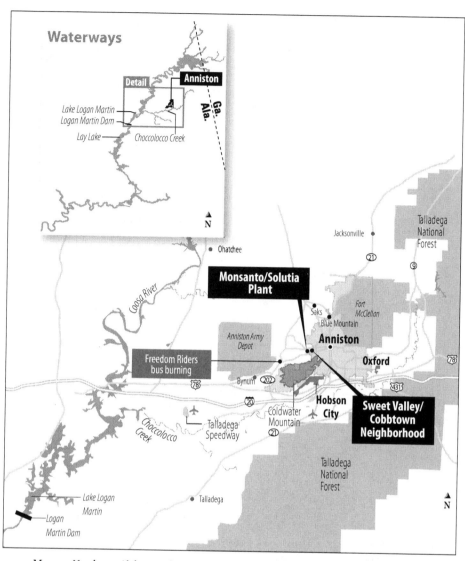

Map 1.2. Northeast Alabama, showing waterways impacted by PCBs. According to the EPA, PCBs line more than forty miles of waterways south of the Monsanto plant (now the Solutia facility, owned by Eastman Chemicals) in West Anniston, stretching as far as Lake Logan Martin and Lay Lake. Map by Charles Jones.

sediment. The exposure pathway leads through "creeks, rivers, flood plains and lakes," through Snow Creek to Choccolocco Creek, then through the Coosa River to Lake Logan Martin and Lay Lake, stretching toward the Gulf of Mexico. The "no-consumption" fish advisory Alabama health officials issued for a stretch of this waterway in 1993 remains in place.[9]

Bark from oaks and magnolias in the "Town among the Trees" also yielded evidence of the spread of PCBs. The historical record was inscribed on human bodies as well. "This is by far the most contaminated community that I have ever encountered," one scientist had testified, "in the United States or anywhere else." Anniston residents bear a toxic burden of PCBs in their blood four times greater than the average U.S. adult. Yet not until 1993, when a contractor pulled a badly deformed bass out of Choccolocco Creek near Anniston, did anyone seriously begin to address the impact of the chemicals at their point of origin. Before 1995, no meaningful action was taken to address the health of individuals who lived near Monsanto's Alabama plant—not until West Anniston residents themselves demanded redress.[10]

THE EXTENSIVE PCB POLLUTION alone had been enough to provoke the national press to label Anniston "Toxic Town, USA." However, as the penalty phase of the PCB trial ground on in early August 2003, the U.S. Army fired up a billion-dollar chemical weapons incinerator ten miles west of town. Declining Cold War antagonisms had earlier led U.S. and Soviet officials to negotiate reductions in their respective chemical arsenals; subsequently, the multilateral Chemical Weapons Convention had set a deadline of 2007 for the world's nations to destroy many of their chemical weapons. Only when residents found out that the Army planned to burn the weapons did most people learn that the toxic nerve agents—designed to kill—were stored nearby. Militarization had defined Anniston's environmental fortunes more than most people knew.[11]

On August 9, cutting off more than a decade of contentious public debate over the Army's plan for disposing of the weapons, operatives began incinerating more than 2,000 tons of chemical weapons that had been stored at the Anniston Army Depot since 1963. With upward of 112,000 residents in 2000, Calhoun County sits amid one of the most populous of the U.S. stockpile sites at which the Army has incinerated chemical agents. Located just north of Interstate 20, Anniston also lies close to major population centers in Birmingham, sixty miles west, and Atlanta, ninety miles east. Residents feared an explosion at the incinerator would cause a chemical disaster or that by-products from burning would endanger their health.[12]

Following close on the commencement of weapons burning in 2003, enterprising Army officials launched a public relations campaign, posting a billboard on Interstate 20 leading into Anniston dubbing the civilian workforce "'The Pit Crew' of the American Warfighter." Celebrating the depot's role in supplying U.S. troops in Iraq by invoking auto racing's Talladega Superspeedway fifteen miles to the west, the slogan accurately described the key role the depot workforce played for the U.S. military—indeed, for the nation—including the hard, often chemically dangerous work of refurbishing America's tanks. For decades, soldiers and civilian workers in this city tucked away in the southern Appalachian foothills had been loyal, hardworking, behind-the-scenes mechanics, preparing equipment for military extensions of American empire abroad.

"Talla-Damn-Dega!" hollered a drive-time commentator into his Atlanta WSB talk radio microphone on the Monday morning after the September 28, 2003, NASCAR race. Eighty thousand people attended this thirty-fourth anniversary race. The Superspeedway, which opened in 1969, generates huge amounts of cash for northeast Alabama; *SportsBusiness Journal* estimated in 2001 that each NASCAR race has a roughly $42.4 million financial impact on the surrounding area. The largest display at the 2003 Talladega race was the U.S. Army recruiting station. "AN ARMY OF ONE" screamed the recruiters' banner. The Army was mining productive terrain. The sport became so popular that a 2004 Democratic presidential hopeful sponsored one driver's Ford Craftsman pickup truck, plastering it with "Bob Graham for President" signs. President George W. Bush professed his NASCAR fandom that same year.[13]

The racetrack culture evokes a broader ethos celebrating whiteness, masculinity, and militarism. RVs, campers, and mobile entertainment centers encircled the track, nestled on 2,000 acres in the scenic Coosa Valley basin, where many fans had camped out for the weeklong buildup to the race. Assorted banners waved proudly: flags of a fan's favorite driver, the checkerboard finish line marker, the stars and stripes, and, frequently, the Confederate stars and bars. There were very few black attendees. *Time* magazine in 1999 compared the Talladega infield to "a Klan picnic." At the semiannual race in 2004, fans at the starting line yelled racial slurs at newly crowned Miss America Ericka Dunlap, an African American, as she officially began the race with the classic opening line, "Gentlemen, start your engines." Protests by the Association of Minority Racing Fans broke out at the track that year.[14]

Considerable distance—more than the actual fifteen miles—separates the Talladega Superspeedway from Anniston's stately eastside homes and tree-lined boulevards and its working-class neighborhoods, but the city's economy remains similarly entwined with the U.S. military. Today, with a $260 million operating budget at the Anniston Army Depot, which has an estimated $1.1 billion annual economic impact on the area, Anniston typifies the South's heavy economic reliance on military facilities.[15]

In Anniston, as in the nation, chemical contamination has been inextricably linked with the machinery of war. As a result of World War I, the chemical industry had gained a near monopoly on patented knowledge of synthetic organic chemicals, concentrating power over their use in the hands of select experts in relatively few companies. The American chemical industry nurtured the symbolic association of chemicals with national pride to ensure continued government support and public acceptance. Tying chemicals to the national interest long protected the industry from oversight. Few knew, for example, of Monsanto's secret work in Anniston for the Chemical Corps in the 1950s.[16]

The chemical industry and the military, deeply intertwined at the national level, also grew in tandem in Anniston. Monsanto's predecessor in Anniston, the Swann Chemical Company, got its start as a munitions company during World War I and sought to produce chemical weapons. A fledgling Spanish-American War supply depot in the city's heart made way for a major World War I army training center, Camp McClellan, that by 1951 was the home of the Chemical Corps Training School.

Environmental degradation thrived in a culture that valorized militarism. As Anniston's experience shows, war exacts a profound toll on human health and the geophysical environment, even in places untouched by physical combat. The South as a whole hosts a disproportionate share of the U.S. military's hazardous environmental legacy. Cleanup is estimated at $4 billion. Boom-bust cycles driven by fluctuating military expenditures created economic insecurity that may have increased tolerance for polluting industries. The U.S. Army at times has claimed to be exempt from the nation's environmental laws.[17]

SEVERAL TIMES IN 2002 AND 2003, Anniston reached the top of the national news pyramid. CBS television's *60 Minutes* featured Anniston and Monsanto's PCBs. A four-page spread in *People* magazine highlighted the opposition to PCBs by the local Sweet Valley/Cobbtown Environmental Justice Taskforce. A Bill Moyers special, "Toxic Communities," examined health concerns related to the PCB exposures. PBS producers included the depot incinerator in the television miniseries *Avoiding Armageddon*.

Calhoun County native and *New York Times* reporter Rick Bragg wrote several articles on the disputes over the incinerator, including one titled "Burning of Chemical Arms Puts Fear in Wind." Bragg has described northeast Alabama as "the most beautiful place on earth." Bragg loved the land where he grew up, "where the gray mists hid the tops of low, deep-green mountains," but he also considered that life in this upland South locale could be "mean as a damn snake."[18]

How did Anniston, "The Model City of the South," once heralded as a promising exemplar of diversified "New South" development, come to be labeled by *Forbes* magazine "the worst city in America"?[19]

Understanding how this east Alabama city of 24,000 became an iconic site of toxic contamination requires tracing its history in the context of national and global developments: the southward expansion of a multinational chemical industry, the growing economic dependence of a community on military installations built to project U.S. power abroad, and the global migration of persistent organic pollutants. A 1992 article Bragg wrote for the *St. Petersburg Times* had starkly outlined the choices left by Anniston's economic dependence on polluting military installations, headlined "Poison or Poverty?"[20] The military and industrial economic development model that had promised to end poverty had driven the city deeply into toxic debt. Industrial growth strategies that cast the options as poison or poverty were problematic, not least because, for the residents of West Anniston, the result has been "both." Those who have borne the brunt of industry's burdens have received the fewest of its benefits.

Other cities once identified as models—Love Canal, New York, for one—became toxic towns. Anniston had always planned to be different. The city's creation was viewed as a unique experiment in the reconstructing South, in which northern and southern business interests partnered even as Civil War hatreds still flared to build a model industrial town. This was the city that would escape the toxic burdens of southern history, the dual legacies of slavery and defeat.[21] Now, the city was overlaid with a disproportionate dose of pollution.

In some ways, Anniston's toxic history reflects a regionwide approach to economic growth that privileged industrial prerogatives over environmental and public health. The concentration of hazardous chemical and military sites in key southern states deepened with the South's integration into the national and international political economy. As James Cobb argued in his 1982 survey, *The Selling of the South*, southern states, from roughly the 1930s into the 1980s, pursued a desperate quest for industrial growth. The South's promoters sustained a favorable business climate by promising corporations low wages, lax regulation, and the "freedom to exploit the region's resources and contaminate its air and water."[22] In Anniston, which industrialized much earlier than most of the South, it is tempting to push that argument back in time. Some elements of that model were clearly established at the time of the town's founding, in an instrumental conception of nature and labor wherein both were resources to be mined; in rampant boosterism that represented industrial growth as an uncomplicated path to progress and prosperity; and in a marketing plan that highlighted extractive riches.

By the time Swann Chemical began manufacturing chemicals in Anniston, the city was already industrialized, a major center for iron manufacturing, "the soil pipe capital of the world." The early wave of industrialization contributed to the toxic burden Anniston bears today, most notably in deposits of heavy metals such as lead. An approach to economic development that mined the South's human labor and ecological riches but did little to protect its people or the land was already well established. Though they built schools and churches and underwrote theaters and parks, the paternalistic industrialists who established the model iron manufacturing center delineated the distribution of industrial pollution as they laid out the city's residential and industrial streets.[23]

The environmental degradation that accompanied Anniston's first wave of industrialization was mostly immediate and visible—smoke-filled skies, clear-cut forests—and, except for municipal wastes, not understood as particularly hazardous to human health. The advent of a science-based chemical industry brought hazards of a different type on a different scale. As "embodiments of a new knowledge of nature," synthetic chemicals could alter nature and human bodies in unanticipated ways.[24]

The accumulation of chemical pollution was gradual, unspectacular, and often imperceptible, its health impact latent.[25] Chemical pollution moves by intimate invasion, at a minute scale often apprehended only by chemical tests or biological assays, illegible without specialized equipment and training.

When made aware of the hazards of industrial production, people locally were not quiescent. Within Swann Chemical's first decade of operation, residents of East Anniston had complained of emissions that peeled the paint from cars; plant workers in the 1930s sued for ill health resulting from occupational exposure.[26]

The interwar period during which PCBs were first manufactured commercially at Anniston saw a significant increase in the application of new chemical knowledge in industry and greater recognition of the hazards chemicals posed to industrial workers. Industry leaders conceived key elements of their standard approach to environmental hazards during the interwar years, underwriting academic occupational health research, vehemently opposing government regulation, and locating the primary responsibility for protection against industrial hazards with workers themselves. By World War II, the chemical industry was already celebrating its "unobtrusive penetration" into the U.S. political economy and modern life.[27]

In Alabama, as elsewhere, it was apparent from the early stages of the chemical industry's development that chemicals posed serious hazards to factory workers, whose exposures were sustained and sometimes acute. With the dirtiest jobs reserved for black workers, evidence suggests their exposure may have been particularly severe. Recognizing that chemical manufacturers were privy to toxic knowledge inaccessible to the layperson, the Alabama Supreme Court mandated in 1937 that employers had a "duty to warn," that "an obligation rests upon the employer to acquaint his employee with *the danger which can be ascertained by knowledge of scientific principle governing substance and processes* used in the employment."[28]

Race and class biases shaped both the disposition of environmental hazards and the response to them. Early approaches to occupational poisoning included firing sick workers and replacing them with "new men." Gauging the impact of toxic chemicals on workers' health required technical expertise, often in the hands of experts employed by or otherwise financially beholden to industry. The nation's class and race politics permitted a crude (but profitable) experiment on workers. One company official noted in the 1930s that "there has been quite a little human experimentation" at Monsanto's Aroclors plants. Through at least the 1950s, some experts responsible for evaluating the health of occupationally exposed workers ascribed adverse reactions to chemical exposure to presumed racial or character traits among the exposed themselves.[29]

ACTIVISTS AND SCHOLARS BEGAN IDENTIFYING environmental racism— or environmental injustice, incorporating class as well as race—in the 1980s to describe unequal concentrations of noxious facilities and other undesirable land uses in low-income areas and neighborhoods where people of color reside. Environmental injustice is also reflected in uneven regulatory enforcement and the disparate distribution on the landscape of environmental benefits as well as costs.[30]

Within Anniston, as in many locales, researchers have mapped pollution geographically, correlating residential proximity to environmental hazards with race and income. The majority of residents in the neighborhoods north and east of Monsanto's chemical division spinoff in West Anniston—the Solutia facility—are African American; whites live south and west of the plant. People living in the working-class neighborhoods nearest the plant were found to be the most exposed to the toxic chemicals. African American adults in Anniston have an average body burden of PCBs three times greater than do whites in Anniston.[31] West Anniston was also located in the incinerator's Pink Zone, the area emergency planners identified as most vulnerable to an adverse event at the incinerator.

The unequal allocation of environmental hazards extends over space, but it also occurs over time. The production of environmental injustice is not just a matter of the disparate siting of noxious facilities; it also results from a complex layering of race and class, political economy and geography. "Racialization," writes urban sociologist Kevin Fox Gotham, "refers to the way in which racial categories sort people, society distributes resources along racial lines, and state policy shapes and is shaped by the contours of society."[32]

Pollution is related to other forms of inequality. For African Americans, the racialization of pollution may have antecedents in the Redeemer bargains and white racial anxieties of the post-Reconstruction South, but it was forged in the rigid social spaces established under Jim Crow. In language linking racial purity and the vote, durable fictions associating blackness and pollution were codified in the 1901 Alabama state constitution, bolstering white resistance to equality and the integration of public space. Naturalizing African Americans and the poor as casualties of pollution is related to other patterns of discrimination. Unequal access to sanitation, health care, substandard public facilities—toilets, drinking fountains—imposed under Jim Crow produced inequality on both practical and ideological planes. "Pollution beliefs shore up social systems of political exclusion," writes literary scholar Patricia Yaeger, "they provide the rhetorical basis for acts of human disposal, for converting those who are described as dirty into rubbish, the disappeared, throwaways."[33]

Medical assessments of chemical exposure were mediated by racial and class ideologies, blunting the recognition of chemical injuries. In the 1920s and 1930s, industry leaders and military commanders racialized susceptibility—and immunity—to industrial chemicals and chemical weapons. Scientific racism—fixing perceived racial difference in assumed biological attributes—regarding health and contagion was transposed onto chemical exposures.[34]

Over time, "racially identified space," as Richard Thompson Ford has argued, "both creates and perpetuates racial segregation," even in the absence of active racism. In much the same way, concentrations of toxics and waste both create and perpetuate environmental injustice. Once space is identified as toxic, the already stigmatized space becomes more undesirable, more stigmatized, devalued. Once in place, pollution not only reinforces but also exaggerates existing disparities as, for example, the value of land and homes drops, bringing a further decline in funding for schools, parks, and so on. Meanwhile, physical distance, like other forms of difference, invites people to deny their responsibilities to those they perceive as distant. Environmental injustice becomes naturalized, part of the landscape.[35]

Granting agency to geographical space should not obscure the role of the individual decision makers whose actions channel resources and hazards—of corporate decision makers, government environmental regulators, and policymakers. Key decisions that impacted Anniston residents—for better and for worse—were made in boardrooms in St. Louis, civilian and military government offices in Washington, D.C., research labs in Sweden, executive suites as far away as Brussels, and courtrooms from Birmingham to New York.

At various junctures in Anniston's history, pollution was quite clearly deemed, to use Cobb's phrase, "the price of progress." An immense distance, physical and social, separated decision makers who deemed pollution a price worth paying and the people who paid the highest price. But to truly calculate the cost of pollution requires knowledge of its scope and risks, knowledge that most residents of Anniston lacked. So long as the consequences of pollution remained concealed in corporate archives and behind boardroom doors, no one outside of Monsanto could assess the hazards and benefits of PCB production. In the absence of regulation, the responsibility for deploying toxic knowledge safely was left largely to the manufacturers themselves. That is not to say that the state did not fail the public once PCBs came under regulatory scrutiny in the 1960s. Alabama's agencies responsible for regulating pollution failed Anniston miserably and repeatedly. The Alabama water quality department was so inadequate that the state legislature voted to disband it in 1971 in order to retain state control over implementing new federal clean air and water standards. The successor state environmental agency, the Alabama Department of Environmental Management (ADEM), did such a mediocre job that in 1998 a state court judge said he would rather turn remediation over to Monsanto than to ADEM.[36]

A METAPHORICAL LINK BETWEEN POISON AND KNOWLEDGE dates to the Garden of Eden. *Toxic knowledge*, as used here, has multiple meanings. In the most straightforward sense, "knowledge of toxicity" or "knowledge of toxic substances" is awareness of chemical compounds, their properties and effects. The chemical industry gained its power in part from "chemical know-how," deriving profitable commercial applications from novel chemical research.[37] The failure to warn, the refusal to share crucial toxic knowledge, became a deciding element in the mass tort trials over PCBs.

However, the term *toxic knowledge* also enjoys a rich interdisciplinary provenance that enlarges its meaning. Beyond official silences and the corporate withholding of knowledge, those who wish to know and address toxic exposures confront multiple unknowns and uncertainties. Geneticists and bioethicists deploy *toxic knowledge* to describe knowledge that results from learning that one carries a disease that has no cure. Learning of the PCB contamination brought fear and uncertainty, as people attempted to understand what having PCBs stored in their bodies might mean for their own and their children's health. Sociologist Stephen Couch and colleagues use *toxic knowledge* to denote the ongoing stress from catastrophic experiences. Some Anniston residents confronted the knowledge that they carry a body burden of toxic chemicals for which there is no known antidote, the physical and emotional consequences of what these scholars term a "slow motion technological disaster."[38]

Offering insights from an altogether different disciplinary vantage point, Patricia Yaeger probes the unspoken awareness of social hierarchies revealed in southern literature as "a toxic knowledge of race and place." In this sense, to uncover "toxic knowledge" is to bare the unseen but intuitively understood toxicity of deeply rooted unequal social relationships as marked on particular landscapes.[39]

The transnational movement of scientific knowledge regarding PCBs can be traced through the lens of Anniston. Yet, as political scientist Frank Fischer asks, "How can citizens participate in an age dominated by complex technologies and expert decisions?" Corollary questions arise: What is our evolving understanding of toxic hazards, the interaction between chemicals and nature, over time? How do people in affected neighborhoods access the complex scientific information necessary to unearth toxic problems? Who owns toxic knowledge and by what authority are they remaking nature

and human bodies? Validating the authority derived from experience becomes difficult, limiting who can "testify" as to the nature of environmental
harms. In establishing claims for environmental justice, the knowledge that
is valued and who owns it become central, because knowledge undergirds
a claim to justice.[40]

That highly exposed people are at higher risk of numerous serious health
effects of PCBs is well established. However, industry uses its scientific authority to generate uncertainty, to shroud toxic knowledge. Further, framing the response to environmental hazards in terms of scientific certainty
demands a standard of proof that positivist science often cannot provide.
It is extremely difficult to predict what a high body burden of PCBs will
mean for any one individual's health; a wide range of factors contribute to
the presence or absence of health or disease. Not all of the assaults on West
Anniston residents chemical in origin. Proximity to environmental hazards
reinforces other structural inequalities. Pollution, which can interfere with
human growth, brain function, and overall health, compounds the effects
of inadequate schools, physically demanding jobs, and absence of adequate
health care, factors that likewise intensify the consequences of pollution.[41]

BOTH THE MOVEMENT TO HOLD MONSANTO ACCOUNTABLE for PCB contamination and the parallel campaign for safe disposal of chemical weapons owed much to an earlier generation of civil rights activism in the city.
Among a wider public, the burning of the Freedom Riders bus on Mother's
Day, 1961, has defined Anniston's civil rights history. While the national
spotlight came and went after this episode, Anniston has a long indigenous
tradition of resistance against the constraints of Jim Crow. Anniston was
also known as a city in which moderate white elites would respond when
racial violence threatened, allying with black leaders to support biracial
efforts, promote calm, and, when pressed, allow gradual racial change,
maintaining a hospitable environment for business.

As the incremental advances, regressions, and resistance in civil rights in
the decades before and after the 1960s suggest, the black freedom struggle
is now often viewed as a protracted period reshaping American racial policies, what scholars have called "the long civil rights movement," led by local
as well as national African American leaders. Taking a broad view of what
is classified as environmental, as the environmental justice movement has
done, suggests a "long environmental justice movement" as well. Despite
popular thinking to the contrary, environmental concerns—writ broadly—
were not new to the late twentieth-century black freedom struggle. Social

injustice has long been inscribed on working landscapes—sharecropped fields, iron-rich mines, and chemical dumps. And African Americans were *never not* concerned with the justice of human relationships to those physical landscapes. At various moments, if not continuously—as newly mobile freedpersons chose Calhoun County for its clear waters, as Depression-era Negro Health Extension Service officials surveyed industrial workers' health, or as early 1970s civil rights coalitions protested the sewage ditches flowing through the west end of town—African Americans in Anniston were directly engaged with what are now considered environmental concerns.[42]

The reframing of environmental causes as social justice issues in the 1980s marked a more explicit linkage of race, class, and environment and an upswing in activism, in ways that influenced both the challenge to PCB pollution and the anti-incinerator fight.[43] Anniston activists garnered support from and contributed to that larger movement, which is multiracial, decentralized, locally based, and global in scope.

Anniston's PCB and anti-incinerator campaigns revealed fault lines both within and between the environmental and civil rights movements. In its early stages, the anti-incinerator fight mainly attracted white middle-class and professional people, some of whom collaborated with PCB activists; the PCB struggle was primarily rooted in the African American community, which was divided over the incinerator. Activists in the two campaigns joined forces, at times uneasily. The environmental struggle against Monsanto linked the fates of the families and friends of whites who had been among the 1960s instigators of racist violence with African American neighbors near the Monsanto plant in West Anniston, who had sometimes been the targets of that violence.

"Slow violence," literary scholar Rob Nixon's term, offers a useful way for thinking about how pollution was sustained in Anniston. Nixon emphasizes not only the spatial distribution of pollution but also its slow accretion over time. Nixon distinguishes the "slow violence" of pollution from "personal violence," that is, the direct physical assault, and structural violence, which is systemic, institutional, and indirect. Slow violence is also systemic, but is, by contrast, "violence that occurs gradually and out of sight, a violence of delayed destruction that is dispersed across time and space, an attritional violence that is typically not viewed as violence at all."[44]

As the nonviolent black freedom struggle made the personal violence that sustained segregation visible, so, too, have opponents of pollution used creative tactics to make the impact of slow violence visible—using coffins to block Monsanto's bulldozers, staging die-ins to protest chemical weapons burning, donning Tyvek cleanup suits at rallies, and publishing soil test results and thousands of pages of internal company documents on the Internet—in addition to more traditional forms of civil rights protest: marches, litigation, and written exposés.

Like the larger national movements of which they were a part, activists in Anniston also had to contend with well-honed industry strategies for managing environmental protest, a context that makes their achievements even more remarkable. Activists confronted corporate public relations techniques including "manufacturing doubt," a strategy borrowed from the tobacco industry. This technique fosters the illusion of a lack of scientific consensus about the impact of toxic chemicals on human health, even in areas where significant agreement among researchers has been reached. Industrial "risk management" approaches were aimed not at the sources of outrage but at "outrage reduction."[45] By 2003, these strategies had made their way into the George W. Bush–era EPA in the form of the "Enlibra" approach, a new-age creation that twisted popular demands for greater community involvement in environmental decision making into corporate attempts to manage not only the environment but also the environmentalists.

AFTER THE JURY'S 2002 DECISION, the penalty phase of the PCB litigation dragged on for another year and a half, becoming the longest jury trial in Alabama history. Then, abruptly, on August 20, 2003, attorneys for Monsanto and those representing more than 21,000 plaintiffs surprised nearly everyone by agreeing to settle the Anniston PCB cases. The global settlement, as it was called, contained the largest such award for industrial pollution at a single site in the United States: $600 million. It was an enormous victory. Formerly disfranchised local people overcame powerful odds to force a global agrochemical giant to make good on a long overdue environmental debt. The agreement also committed Monsanto and its partner companies to spending $100 million on cleanup and to funding a health clinic in Anniston.

Anniston's story has been told as a classic redemption tale. A baptism—in water or by fire—out of which the city is reborn. Anniston is given to narratives of renewal and rebirth. The legal victory was a signature achievement by any account, won at considerable cost. "The system worked," Anniston's mayor declared, as Monsanto would be called to account and held liable under existing legal standards. "This is about as good as it gets," one person said when the large PCB award was announced.[46] At the same time, much would remain unsettled. For activists, the struggle against pollution did not end when the news cameras left Anniston in August 2003.

The rest of the nation has often measured itself by how far away it is, geographically and politically, from Alabama. But centered as it is in this Deep South state, this story is not just about Alabama or the South. Local spaces are sites at which global processes take place. This southern locale may have borne "the price of progress," but the industrial project it represented was thoroughly national in origin and international in impact. As PCB supplier and America's "Pit Crew," the north Alabama region's entrepreneurs and laborers were doing work for the nation as a whole. The convergence of the PCB cases with the launch of the chemical weapons incinerator illuminates an American story and a global one. As Judge Joel Laird said during one of the major PCB trials, "This war is bigger than this little piece of ground in here in this courtroom."[47]

CHAPTER ONE

The Model City *A Romance of the New South*

There is no other place in the Southern states so healthy,
so beautifully situated, none where the air is purer, the water clearer, and
where there are so many pleasant inducements to the full enjoyment
of these luxuries of life.—Atlanta Constitution, 1883

An 1883 display ad in Henry Grady's *Atlanta Constitution* proclaimed Anniston the healthiest place in the southern states. The "Best, Healthiest, and Most Invigorating Climate in the World" claimed the city's founders and publicists. In Anniston could be found the "Three Essentials of a Good Home: Pure Air, Good Water, and a Salubrious Climate." Nature itself invited industry, the city's promoters implied. "Nature favors them marvelously," wrote the *New York Times*. The Baltimore-based *Manufacturers Record*, an industrial journal, boasted in 1889 that Anniston's "mountain air and pure water . . . insure the health and comfort of the workman and his family; . . . stimulate and lighten labor" and not only "enabled Anniston's citizens to create her past and present prosperity" but also would "secure her future."[1]

The story that leads from this nineteenth-century portrayal of Anniston as a healthful Eden past its twenty-first-century designation as "Toxic Town, USA" is neither uncomplicated narrative of adversity overcome nor simple chronicle of environmental decline. Not a few of the conditions that permitted the Monsanto Chemical Company to keep discharging toxic chemicals in West Anniston for so long were embedded in a set of natural resource regimes, economic structures, and attitudes toward race and the health of the laboring classes that had been in formation since the town's founding in 1872. When in 1935 the Monsanto Chemical Company in St. Louis absorbed one of its largest competitors in the South—the enterprising north Alabama chemical firm named for its flamboyant owner, Theodore Swann—the company profited from more than a half century of southern industrialization and militarization. Theodore Swann's biographers concluded that Anniston was "an unlikely setting for the events that occurred," but, for its purposes, Monsanto had chosen well. Beyond the obvious benefit of consolidating its hold on a competing chemical producer in a resource-rich region of the South, the company-town origins of Anniston must have appealed to Monsanto. In its various expansions, Monsanto often eponymously named (or renamed) the entire surrounding town—as in Monsanto, Illinois; Monsanto, Idaho; and Monsanto, Tennessee. Significantly, Anniston kept its own identity.[2]

WHEN IRON AND MUNITIONS MANUFACTURER Samuel Noble visited north Alabama in 1869 via steamer down the Coosa River from Rome, Georgia, he found "a literal mountain of brown hematite ore, with heavily wooded foothills, guarding the entrance to a valley of surpassing beauty." A few years later, Noble brought former Union general Daniel H. Tyler to explore the terrain on horseback. General Tyler had experience in iron manufacturing and, as important, had amassed considerable wealth investing in railroads. (The Tylers were also well connected; General Tyler's granddaughter married Theodore Roosevelt in 1886 and served as first lady from McKinley's death until 1909.) Roaming the Alabama hillsides piqued his interest in Noble's proposal for a new proprietary town.[3]

For three days in the spring of 1872, the pair surveyed the iron-rich outcroppings amid the longleaf pines. Each night, the men rode two miles south to a hotel in Oxford and, sipping the aging general's favorite Chinese green tea, discussed their plans. In a vast, shallow bowl of Alabama clay between the verdant, low mountains, they would build a model city. The primary industry—iron manufacturing—would tap the unexploited mineral resources that lay barely beneath the surface of the soil. Nature would be the instrument for realizing their dreams.[4]

Geologic forces had deposited Alabama's iron riches during the Silurian Period, more than 400 million years earlier. A vast underwater manufacturing process took place in these swamps during the Paleozoic Era, producing high-quality coal. As the master continent, Pangaea, formed during the Pennsylvanian Period, "Alabama was at center stage in this geologic spectacular," one Alabama geologist explained. The ecological assets that launched north Alabama's industrial experiment with iron manufacturing would profit the chemical industry as well; coal tar, a coal by-product, would form the basis of many synthetic chemicals.[5]

One of the southernmost counties in the Appalachian range, Calhoun County lies close to the border of the Piedmont plateau, in the ridge and valley region of this Deep South state. The Coosa River, which forms the county's western border, winds its way from north of Rome, Georgia, to the

Alabama River and the Gulf of Mexico. Like New England and the western territories, the land was often described in gendered metaphors, as "part a barren field, and part a virgin forest," inviting man's intervention, but this had long been a working landscape. From the earliest "Flush Times" in 1830s Alabama, a devil-may-care approach to resource use prevailed. The area had "every natural advantage," Noble recognized, though "it had long been gashed and starved by man."[6]

Virtually all of the Creek Indians had been driven out in the 1830s. Sally Ladiga, widow of Creek Chief Ladiga, sued all the way to the U.S. Supreme Court to win recognition of her right to remain. By 1840, however, the erasure of Native Americans from this territory was all but complete. Their legacy lingered in place names such as Choccolocco Creek, translated as "Big Shoals," for the wide, flat, stony sections of the waterway.[7]

Alabama's state geologists not only mapped Alabama's resources but also aggressively marketed them to outside investors. The state's underground wealth held "deposits tempting in their abundance and unique in their combination." The geological riches seemed inexhaustible. "A century of labor would not begin to impoverish this mighty depository," early boosters believed.[8]

The north Alabama hill country had both coal and iron "in unexampled proximity." The 110 acres Samuel Noble purchased in 1869 for the hefty price of $6,000 contained prime woodlands and ores. Within easy distance of Noble's tract were all the necessary products for making iron: rich ore outcrops, limestone, and the coal fields and dense pine forests that provided the fuel for industrial development. At the time, Alabama was already first among southern states in iron production and fourth among iron-producing states nationally.[9]

Anniston's founding families came to Calhoun County in 1872 to construct a profitable Eden. The founders envisioned a unique experiment, an exceptional city in a distinctive region. Anniston would be a willing partner to modernization within the reluctantly reconstructing South. The Nobles and the Tylers first established the Woodstock Iron Company in 1872 as a private town. (Another Alabama town was called Woodstock, so they named the city for Anne Scott Tyler, wife of the general's son, Alfred Leigh Tyler, in recognition of her key role in securing additional capital through family ties with a New York financier.) At the town's official opening to the public in 1883, Atlanta newspaperman Henry Grady, the most prominent spokesman for an urban and industrialized New South, declared the vision realized, dubbing Anniston "the Model City of the Southern States."[10]

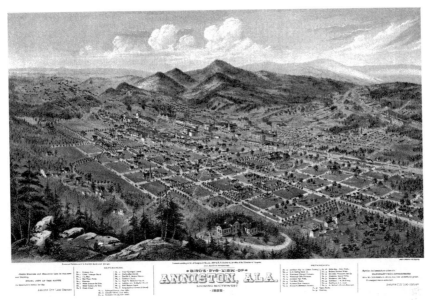

"A Bird's Eye View of Anniston, Ala." (1888). Artist's rendering of the industrial town of Anniston, "the Model City of the South." Looking southwest, the smokestacks of the industrial
district and Coldwater Mountain are in the distance. The founders' residences occupy the
left foreground; the "Colored" Congregational Church lies at right, within a few blocks of
the Woodstock Coke Furnaces and the Anniston Pipe Works. Drawn and published by E. S.
Glover; printed by Shober & Carqueville Litho. Co., Chicago.

THE NORTHERNMOST COUNTY in Alabama to have voted in favor of secession, Calhoun County's name revealed its strong sectional loyalties.
Originally known as Benton County, the Alabama legislature renamed
the county in 1858 for a foremost proslavery secessionist, Senator John C.
Calhoun of South Carolina. Built after the Civil War, Anniston was put forward as a place that would escape what C. Vann Woodward termed "the
burden of southern history," marked by slavery and defeat. The new city's
leaders aimed to set the town apart not only from the slums of the industrialized Northeast but also from the inhumanity of southern plantation slavery.[11]

The relationship between Anniston's founding families has often been
portrayed as a symbol of sectional reconciliation between a Confederate
arms manufacturer (Noble) and a Union general (Tyler), "a Connecticut
Yankee with capital." Typical in this regard is the Federal Writers' Program
volume on Alabama, published in 1941, which said of Anniston: "Not the
least unusual part of the story of the founding of the town is the fact that
men of such widely divergent backgrounds, with Northern and Southern

affiliations, were able to unite in the enterprise so shortly after the War between the States."[12]

The North-South reconciliation narrative made a good story: an unlikely economic partnership overcoming wartime differences and yielding mutually beneficial industrial development. In fact, neither man was a southerner. Noble was an Englishman by birth; his sectional loyalties derived mainly from a desire "to associate with the region from which he derived most of his trade." (Noble's journey south from Pennsylvania in the mid-1850s included one notable misadventure. On the way to Rome, Georgia, he shared a car with Jefferson Davis and, not recognizing the then secretary of war, had him arrested—mistakenly it turned out—for the theft of a carpetbag containing $4,000.)[13]

Anniston stood at the center of a battle waged by competing railroad magnates for political and economic control of Alabama. The white supremacy candidate for governor in 1874, Democrat George S. Houston, won the fight by a substantial margin. Setting a pattern that would remain durable and leave state coffers impoverished, Governor Houston imposed generous tax exemptions for railroads and other corporate interests.[14]

Railroads made possible the intense exploitation of the forest resources that powered the commercial production of iron in north Alabama. (The few local laws governing conservation in this period were passed for industry's benefit. Anniston regulated tree cutting to preserve fuel for the city's herbivorous furnaces.) The two enterprises were mutually dependent—railroads required iron, and iron manufacturers needed dependable transportation. Iron riches and reliable rail transport eventually made Anniston "the soil pipe capital of the world," connecting the city's sewer pipe factories to distant markets around the globe.[15]

Over time, the railroad itself defined racial spheres. Rail travel contributed to newfound black mobility, spurring white fears of "racial pollution," of breaching racial hierarchies.[16] Train tracks also often separated the wealthy white residential sections of town from the ones that housed poor whites, African Americans, and polluting industries. On railcars and at railroad stations, barriers to racial interaction would not be broken until black and white civil rights protesters took direct action, at Anniston and elsewhere, almost a century later.

Violence both maintained racial inequality and retarded industrial development. Not long before Anniston's founding, one of the largest mass lynchings in Alabama occurred in northern Calhoun County, where in July 1870, Klan marauders murdered seven men. The lynchings revealed the fragile limits of former slaves' newfound freedom, targeting black mobility, Reconstruction hiring policies, and black education. The events, which Anniston newspaperman Harry Mell Ayers later described as a "lynching bee," led New York financier John Jacob Astor to cancel plans to build a new industrial town near Cross Plains, now Piedmont.[17]

In contrast to the violence at Cross Plains, the Nobles and the Tylers built Anniston "according to the doctrine of the Episcopal Church and the platform of the Republican Party." In Anniston, the new order would be healthy, orderly, and civil. The founders invested in the social, educational, and cultural infrastructure of the town, priding themselves on its theater, shops, and schools. Publicists' rhetoric emphasized that concern for factory workers' health distinguished Anniston from the urban, industrialized North, contrasting the company town's "pretty cottages" and "vine-covered porches" with northern tenements rife with "discomfort and disease." One promotional brochure declared, "The pale, pathetic faces, with their weary, timid look, so often seen in great manufactories, are unknown in this place, where air and exercise, clean houses, pure water and wholesome food are afforded to all."[18]

The Colored Congregational Church in Anniston housed the school for children of the formerly enslaved, which was "second probably to no other of that class in the state of Alabama," wrote General Tyler. "We have done all we could," said Tyler, "to invite into our company the best class of labor, white or black, that we could obtain, and to give to their children such an education as would elevate them, if possible, in their future careers."[19]

The Model City rhetoric masked the contrast between a spoken reverence for human and natural resources and industrial practices that exploited both. In the model town, the rights of both African Americans and the white laboring population were carefully circumscribed. Anniston's founding families would later be described not only as "visionaries" but also as "oligarchs." Town governance left little room for dissent. Southern historian Woodward later singled out the city as "the very [arche]type of industrial paternalism." The town's founders promised pay and amenities slightly higher than the state average; in exchange they expected from workers loyalty and strict adherence to discipline. "We made up our minds that, in order to get good labor, it must be paid for liberally," General Tyler explained, "believing that it was our duty to give them the means of making a comfortable living, in order to exact from [laborers] a rigid obedience of the laws."[20]

Paternalistic industrialism reinforced racial hierarchy. One vignette in an early industrial history portrayed Samuel Noble as the benevolent

The iron manufacturing industry employed black and white laborers in factories such as the Kilby Car and Foundry Company, the Anniston Foundry, and the Alabama Pipe Company. By the time this image was taken, circa the 1920s, the city had become "the soil pipe capital of the world." Photo from glass negative by Russell Brothers. Courtesy of the Public Library of Anniston/Calhoun County, Alabama Room.

master overseeing the work of the dutiful servant. "The ironmaster beckoned, as a Napoleon, from astride his horse, to a black worker who trotted obediently behind carrying the young trees in his arms. Among the young plants were included the species of elm, maple, and water oak." Remaking nature, the town's founders were also reinforcing the terms of white control over black workers. The pastoral scene additionally showed the important role of black workers in reconstructing nature in a company town heavily dependent on black labor.[21]

The prospect of employment and newly gained postwar mobility brought an influx of freedpersons to Anniston. By 1900, African Americans comprised 40 percent of the population. Migrating from the Carolinas, Dock Bigsby, who was of Geechee descent, chose Anniston not only because of opportunities for work but also for its clear-flowing creeks. "It was said that he stopped here because he was thirsty," said his granddaughter Barbara

Bigsby Boyd, "and the water—a stream of water was flowing down and so cool and refreshing [that] he thought this would be a good place to live."[22]

The completion of the Anniston Inn in 1885 made this interior city a resort locale, known for its therapeutic waters—not only healthy but curative. But if health was the promise offered by "attractive Anniston's" advertisers, another reality became almost immediately apparent. The foundry workforce employed roughly equal numbers of Anglo and African Americans, as was the pattern in iron foundries throughout southern Appalachia. Work in the blazing hot iron smelters was dirty, dangerous, and demanding. Laborers put in twelve-hour days in the incessant heat of the blast furnaces. Black workers tended to be assigned the dirtiest and most dangerous jobs. There were obvious physical dangers—the hazards of handling molten iron and exposure to toxic by-products. Ironworkers suffered high rates of injury and were sometimes killed. In the early twentieth century, recalled dentist Gordon Rodgers Jr., son of one of the first African Americans to open a general medical practice in Anniston, "every two or three years, a worker would fall into the vats."[23]

Anniston was not a pre–Civil War market center built around a town square. As historian Lewis Mumford has noted about cities elsewhere, "the factory became the nucleus of the new urban organism; every other detail of life was subordinate to it." Initially, the company town admitted only the families of ironworkers, skilled craftsmen, and laborers needed to operate the mill. The unemployed were invited to leave. Decisions about where the new town's citizens would live, considered part of enlightened urban planning of the period, established class- and race-based housing patterns. Exercising power through the allocation of space, town planners delineated residential, commercial, and industrial zones, reserving purely residential areas for upper- and middle-class whites. Housing for workers white and black, including a handful of integrated boardinghouses, was laid out in the industrial section. Noble Street was the city's major dividing line. Except for a few black families who lived east of Noble for the convenience of the white families in whose homes they worked, most African Americans and working-class whites lived in various pockets on the west side of town. The places "where the work folk live[d]" were within sight, smell, and walking distance of the giant iron mill, amid the dust and fumes of polluting factories, next to the din and odors of the smoking furnaces.[24]

Polluted air gave its name to the streets, "Smokey Row," where the black workers made their homes, just west of the No. 1 furnace, and "Cinder Row," in the West Tenth Street area, which became majority white by the late 1890s. African Americans lived in Liberia, where the Colored Congregational Church and school were located, and near Fifteenth Street; white laborers lived in Factory Town and Glen Addie. Over time, Anniston saw even greater racialization of space, as white workers moved out of the factory district.[25]

AN INSTRUMENTAL VIEW OF NATURE and the increasing deployment of segregation as a way of making and defining power were intertwined with changing notions about pollution and disease. The term *pollution* has long referred to waste. For much of the nineteenth century, the word more commonly invoked immorality: to be polluted was to be profane. Places identified as polluted and dirty, and often the people in them, were viewed as morally impure. Pristine places, by contrast, were projected as healthy and virtuous.[26]

At the same time, "contagionist" and "anticontagionist" views dominated the discourse on the spread of disease. Contagionists believed that disease was spread by contact with an infected person, while "miasma" theories held that "filth," inanimate particles spread via foul or contaminated air, caused disease. Concerns about pollution during this period focused not on industrial chemical discards—which were sometimes regarded as germicidal and protective of health—but on bodily wastes. Misplaced fear of contagion drove whites to implement public health measures for black neighborhoods.[27] Industrial pollution was not contagious, so it did not require such measures.

A statistical survey made in the early 1890s revealed that differential mortality rates were markedly lower for blacks in Anniston than in other southern cities, and lower than death rates for whites in the larger tidewater and coastal cities of Richmond, New Orleans, and Savannah, confirming the appraisal by black Annistonians that the city was a relatively better place to live than other parts of the urbanizing South. Within Anniston, however, death rates for blacks (20.50 per 1,000) were 75 percent higher than death rates for whites (11.75).[28]

Drives to improve public health were motivated in part by the desire to create better workers by promoting attendance and acting as a "civilizing" influence among workers. The paternalism of the town's founders was embodied in the medical authority of the company doctor, hired to "take charge of the health" of the workers and their families. (No evidence exists that the town doctor connected the particularly high rates of pneumonia he observed among black residents of Anniston with the industrial smoke of Anniston; pollution was still largely viewed as a product of nature, not a consequence of technology).[29]

Access to medical treatment and public sanitation differed sharply by race. Henry Givahn observed that when his family moved from the Alabama Black Belt to Anniston in the early 1900s, "there were a few white doctors that would treat Negroes, if they knew them." Gordon Rodgers Jr., whose father was among the first black doctors in the city, recalled among his earliest memories the slop wagon that hauled away human waste. Black residents suffered a double indignity. Black neighborhoods lacked sewer lines well into the 1920s because the town that became known as "the Soil Pipe Capital of the World" failed to install sewers for all of its citizens. When indoor plumbing was installed in white neighborhoods, Rodgers explained, some of the town's best families nonetheless kept their outhouses for use by their black domestic servants. Local quarantine ordinances passed during this period may have had as much to do with social dislocation as with public health, spurred by increased passenger rail travel and reflecting white concern about racial interaction.[30]

AS THE UNITED STATES entered the Spanish-American War, Anniston enjoyed economic power on three fronts—agricultural, manufacturing, and military—exporting iron pipe and cotton to buyers as far away as China and launching a military supply and training depot to service the Caribbean. Located in view of the cotton fields, Camp Shipp increased the market for other farm products, and the prosperity it brought to farmers made city leaders eager for the Army's return.[31]

Northern acquiescence to the increasing segregation in the South made way for the global projection of American power abroad. As historian Grace Hale has noted, accompanying that sectional bargain was the adoption of a "common white male martial ideal," an ideological linking of race, body, and nation that defined who was fit to fight and to enjoy the rights of citizenship. Black soldiers stationed at Camp Shipp saw more fighting in the city's streets than they did outside the state. In the fall of 1898, white soldiers stationed in Anniston and local civilians repeatedly taunted and attacked the soldiers of the 1,200-strong all-black Third Alabama Regiment. In one incident, three black soldiers, a white soldier, and a civilian died in racial fighting that spread from Tenth Street to Fifteenth Street downtown. A few days later, after another attack by whites on the Third Alabama soldiers, the local newspaper reported eleven unconfirmed deaths among the combatants. The white press labeled the events the "Battle of Anniston."

"Camp Shipp in the Land of Cotton." During the Spanish-American War, the U.S. Army located a training camp and supply depot amid the cotton fields that surrounded Anniston. In 1898, in what became known as the Battle of Anniston, white soldiers and local civilians attacked soldiers of the 1,200-strong all-black Third Alabama Regiment stationed at the camp. Courtesy of the Alabama Department of Archives and History, Montgomery, Alabama.

The black troops were never deployed, but were sent home, quietly, in the spring of 1899.[32]

Increasing residential segregation in Anniston was reinforced by actions just to the south in Oxford. In 1896, the city of Oxford approached the state legislature to redraw the city's boundaries to exclude a black neighborhood then known as Mooree Quarters to keep black voters from becoming a "controlling factor" in future Oxford city elections. Black residents of Oxford had reasons to want their own municipality. They were, for example, forced to pay school taxes but excluded from the city's schools. The residents of Mooree Quarters turned Oxford's political maneuvering to advantage. On August 15, 1899, fifty-seven voters unanimously approved the incorporation of Hobson City, making it one of a few black-run towns in the country.[33]

Just over a square mile in land area, with only a few hundred inhabitants, Hobson City became for African Americans a cultural hub as well as a political refuge. The town was a destination for black Annistonians on weekend outings to its seventeen-and-a-half acre recreational park. Named for Booker T. Washington, the park featured a swimming pool, tennis court, baseball diamond, bowling alley, and "a huge pavilion for roller skating and dancing." Even more significant, the tiny town housed C. E. Hanna Elementary School, founded in 1905 by Principal Charles Edgar Hanna, and the Calhoun County Training School, built in 1923. "County," as the training school was familiarly called, produced generations of African American leaders, many of whom became significant figures in civil rights and public health.[34]

In Anniston, the Republican Party and the Afro-American Patriotic League "held out the promise of racial agency" to a small rising class of black professionals. In the early 1890s, African-American investors tried to launch an independently owned mill to be named the Afro-Alabama Cotton Mill Company. Among them was Charles E. Thomas, one of the first practicing black physicians in Alabama. By 1893, his pharmacy was the "largest drugstore in the U.S. owned and operated by a Negro." Thomas and other African American medical professionals were financially independent of white patronage and played leading roles in black civic life. Dr. Gordon Rodgers Sr. would become the first president of the Anniston-Hobson City branch of the NAACP, founded in 1919.[35]

A thriving community developed on Anniston's west side. An African American–owned Penny Savings Bank served residents. "There were twenty businesses owned and operated by Negroes" in downtown Anniston between Ninth and Twelfth on Noble Street, explained Henry Givahn. West Fifteenth Street was a center of black life. "It was not as harsh and as bitter as it was in some other sections of the South, but we lived under strict segregation," said Givahn. "We had the old chain gang system. Men worked in chains on the streets of Anniston. And of course there was [a] majority of Negro prisoners on the gang. You had no voice against a white man."[36]

ALABAMA'S CONSTITUTION OF 1901 CODIFIED deepening segregation and black disfranchisement. Anniston's boosters, like other New South business leaders across the southern states, adopted the discourse and alliances of the Old South even as they sought to advance industrial development and hasten reintegration into the national political economy. John B. Knox, a railroad corporation lawyer from Anniston, was president of the 1901 Constitutional Convention. For Knox, discrimination, including disfranchisement, could be justified as long as it was based not on "race" per se but instead on moral and intellectual capacity. "If we would have white supremacy," Knox urged the delegates, "we must establish it by law—not by force or fraud. These provisions are justified in law and in morals," Knox stated, "because the negro [sic] is not discriminated against on account of his race, but on account of his intellectual and moral condition."[37]

Of course, white supremacy was entirely defined by race and backed by both force *and* fraud. Sixteen mob murders of blacks took place in Alabama during the year of the Constitutional Convention alone. For Knox and the other delegates, allowing black citizens to vote polluted the electoral process. "Our aim should be for a correction of all evils which threaten the purity of the ballot and the morals of the people," Knox claimed. Making an ideological link between race, the franchise, and "purity," the 1901 Constitution cemented white supremacy's political hold. After "an uncomfortably hot and contentious summer of parliamentary maneuvering," Knox and his allies at the state Constitutional Convention of 1901 sealed Alabama's legal approach to race for the coming century, disfranchising African Americans and many poor whites as well.[38]

Anniston's founding phase ended as the twentieth century began. The utopian experiment that seemed an open possibility in 1872 was foreclosed by 1901. General Tyler died in 1882, Samuel Noble in 1888. Paternalism's perquisites declined, while its negatives remained. The Woodstock Iron Company's fortunes sputtered in 1887 and "control of the company itself gradually slipped from local hands" into absentee ownership as waning timber and ore supplies forced a reorganization of the business. The iron trade revived, and business boomed off and on for another decade. But in 1899, after twenty-seven years of production, the Woodstock Iron Company was dead. The town the Nobles and the Tylers envisioned was not.[39]

Paternalistic industrialism would continue to shape the city's labor relations, map the geography of health, and reinforce the racial subjugation that underlay southern industrial development. Within a generation, the blazing iron furnaces had devoured much of the valley's once plentiful forests of longleaf pine, undermining the resource base for the model town's industry. As Calhoun County's forests declined, the locus of production had long since shifted from Anniston, the model town, to Birmingham, the Magic City, where deeper coal reserves promised more sustained fuel for industry.[40]

The West Fifteenth Street neighborhood would continue to endure forced insularity, building a vibrant cultural life within circumscribed political options. With their tiny enclave standing as evidence of both racial repression and political resistance, leading citizens of Hobson City set about establishing an educational system that would train generations of African American leaders. Within this political, economic, ecological, and social context, a new generation of entrepreneurs would develop the electrical and chemical industries in Anniston and link their fortunes to the U.S. military. Elsewhere in 1901, events unfolded that would shape the city's future. In St. Louis, an ambitious young drug salesman, John Francis Queeny, wooed skilled chemists from Europe, imported the latest chemical formulas, and founded the Monsanto Chemical Company.

CHAPTER TWO

The War for Chemical Supremacy

Both the physical form and the institutional life of the city . . . , were shaped in no small measure by the irrational and magical purposes of war. . . . Even more, war fostered practices of regimentation, militarization, compulsive conformity. War brought concentration of social leadership and political power in the hands of a weapons-bearing minority, abetted by a priesthood exercising sacred powers and possessing secret but valuable scientific and magical knowledge.
—Lewis Mumford, *The City in History* (1961)

John Francis Queeny opened the Monsanto Chemical Works next to the Diamond Match factory on the south side of St. Louis in 1901 at the dawn of "the Chemical Century." Ambitious to take its place in an expansive vision for turn-of-the-century America, the new company used rapidly developing knowledge of chemical processes to create and fill an expanding market for synthetic organic chemicals.[1]

A son of Irish immigrants who lost their modest real estate holdings in the Great Chicago Fire of 1871, Queeny went to work at age twelve as an office and delivery boy for a drug company. He moved up the ranks of the pharmaceutical business, eventually taking a sales job with I. L. Lyons in New Orleans, where he quickly became a leader among the up-and-coming Crescent City business elite. By 1894, Queeny had left New Orleans to become a sales manager for the New York drug firm Merck. There he met and married Olga Mendez Monsanto, whose wealth and aristocratic Spanish background contrasted with John F.'s rough beginnings. In 1897, he took a job as a purchasing agent for the Meyer Brothers Drug Company, then "the most important wholesale drug house west of the Mississippi," and settled in St. Louis, at the time the nation's fourth-largest city. By 1901, Queeny had begun moonlighting to establish his own chemical operation.[2]

Queeny named the endeavor for his wife, whose family name meant "sacred mountain." Known for his signature Maredona Coronas Cuban cigars and his bloodstone ring, Queeny's tightfistedness was legendary. "John F. Queeny would walk down the aisle of stenographers to see if they were using both sides of the shorthand notebook," said an employee. One Monsanto

A son of Irish immigrants who settled in Chicago, John Francis Queeny (pictured here in 1924) founded the Monsanto Chemical Company in St. Louis in 1901. For nearly thirty years, he served as president of the firm named for his wife, Olga Monsanto Queeny. Queeny fought with the German chemical industry, other competitors, and U.S. government regulators to establish Monsanto as a leading chemical firm. Photo courtesy of the Monsanto Chemical Company.

manager described Queeny as a "benevolent tyrant." After three tough years in the red, the company began to make money and expanded rapidly. By the time of the 1904 World's Fair in St. Louis, Queeny was able to devote all his considerable energy to his chemical firm. He took as its slogan the Monsanto family's motto, *in bello quies*, meaning "steadfast in strife" or "calm in war."[3]

Before World War I, U.S. synthetic chemical manufacturing was a "fledgling industry." Monsanto was "the only American-owned-and-operated producing unit in the field of coal-tar medicinals," synthetic compounds used to make drugs from the chemical by-products of manufacturing coke from coal. Initially regarded as waste, coal tar was a "black evil-smelling liquid." At a time when the public viewed coal tar as nothing more than black roofing pitch, Monsanto called the substance "nature's storehouse." Monsanto produced not only ingredients for medicines but also saccharin, vanillin, and additional small-volume, high-priced compounds used primarily in the manufacture of other products.[4]

Using first coal-tar derivatives and later petroleum, chemists not only replicated compounds scarce in nature to meet industrial demand but also invented new compounds not found in nature. Synthetic organic chemicals are, by definition, carbon-based human creations. The element carbon bonds easily with other carbon atoms and with hydrogen and other elements to form the basic building blocks of all life. The products of the growing field of applied chemistry, synthetic organic chemicals embodied "a new knowledge of nature," new understandings about how basic physical processes work.[5]

The new chemical knowledge conferred extraordinary power over the human and natural world, a power bordering on the divine. Writing in the 1950s, journalist Hubert Kay captured the sense of power that the early synthetic organic chemists must have felt. Chemists were cast as "modern magicians," possessors of an occult knowledge largely unknown and inaccessible to the layperson. In creating "new materials for a new age" chemists were intervening, as Kay put it, in "the Grand Design." The hydrocarbon bond is "the heart of the mystery" of organic chemistry, wrote Kay, "the key to the chemist's ability to duplicate or, for human purposes, to improve on the products of Nature." The research chemist envisaged a "fruitful Creation," an "orderly, logical, world in which to proceed from the known to the unknown." Orderly creation was not always apparent at the point of production, however. The first attempt to produce biphenyl at the Swann Chemical Company's Anniston Works produced an explosion that rocked the plant.[6]

Although the new chemical science bestowed the power to create catastrophic damage, whether by accident or by design, aggressive commercialization of the latest chemical knowledge led to the rapid entrance into the market of new synthetic chemicals. Both the chemical industry and those industries that benefited from its development forcefully promoted the power of new compounds to bring progress and prosperity by "improving" on the products of nature. Despite efforts to regulate additives to food and medicines, new industrial compounds were developed, manufactured, and marketed with little testing and without seriously questioning the consequences of their use. "The chemical industry was born of the union of scientific knowledge and the needs of industry," explained one Monsanto pamphlet. "The young science was drafted to the service of the new order."[7]

MONSANTO'S FIRST MAJOR CORPORATE BATTLE, "The Great Saccharin War," started almost immediately after the business began operating, with the company's attempt to initiate U.S. production of the artificial sweetener. Queeny undertook a pitched legal challenge to wrest control of the patent for the sweetener from Germany, where competitors undercut his prices in a nearly successful attempt to kill his business before it began. He also clashed with the sugar industry, which feared losses for its lucrative imports. In addition, Queeny fought off government restraints and attempts to regulate his product.[8]

From the very beginning, Monsanto's coal-tar products encountered controversy. Saccharin was fiercely opposed by Harvey Washington Wiley, who headed the Bureau of Chemistry in the Department of Agriculture (forerunner to the Food and Drug Administration [FDA]). Wiley objected to marketing a substance he regarded as a potentially harmful food additive with no nutritional value and pushed for state-by-state bans on saccharin production and sale. Despite a determined campaign waged by Wiley and his "Poison Squad"—a team of healthy volunteers who consumed synthetic compounds like saccharin to gauge their adverse impact on health— Monsanto continued to market the sweetener.[9]

Initially, Queeny opposed government attempts to regulate chemicals in food and medicine. In 1904, Queeny testified before Congress, resisting Wiley's efforts to pass a tough law that would grant the Bureau of Chemistry broad authority to monitor chemicals in food and medicine. Plans to require chemical manufacturers to follow a government formulary for making chemicals were too restrictive in a rapidly changing marketplace, Queeny argued, and the proposed law concentrated power in the hands of a few. Queeny eventually broke with his peers in the chemical industry to endorse regulating chemicals in food and drugs, wrote Monsanto public relations director Dan Forrestal in his 1977 corporate history, hinting that the endorsement may have helped win approval for saccharin. Or, perhaps, Queeny was simply in luck; Theodore Roosevelt's physician had prescribed the president saccharin for weight loss. In either case, though Queeny would continue to undermine Wiley's efforts, an ad hoc task force appointed by the president eventually, according to Forrestal, "gave saccharin a clean bill of health."[10]

These early days presaged a pattern: a litigious company driving hard to generate profitable new products based on scientific applications using synthetic chemicals, and engaging aggressively with government regulators.

In 1910, with profits from selling caffeine to Coca-Cola, Queeny purchased the old match factory site next door, which became home to the Queeny plant. Across the river, south of East St. Louis, he located the Krummrich plant (which later joined Anniston's plant as the only other U.S. site producing chlorinated biphenyls). For Monsanto factory workers in those years, "the work was hard, messy," according to the plant's personnel manager, Jules Kernen. "The equipment wasn't very good and was always breaking down," and "the night shift worked thirteen hours a day, seven days a week." Kernen said. "Pay was low compared to other industries; pay comparable with other industries only came with Edgar [Queeny in 1928]."[11]

The abrupt cessation of trade following the outbreak of World War I exposed how deeply American manufacturers depended on Europe, especially Germany, for both raw materials and "intermediates," partially processed chemicals. Intermediates are indispensable tools—"the chemical equivalent of hammer, screwdriver, and paint brush." And, with the exception of vanillin, every substance produced by the Monsanto Chemical Works required the importation of intermediates. There were men who saw promise in the advent of war—for the chemical industry and for the South. World War I would not be a setback for the American synthetic organic chemicals industry but its awakening. "1914 is considered the date of creation" of the U.S. synthetic chemicals industry, Queeny's son Edgar wrote in hindsight.[12]

NEARLY A GENERATION would pass before Monsanto acquired its factory in Anniston and began manufacturing PCBs. Monsanto's predecessor in producing the chemicals was a flamboyant Birmingham mogul and New South industrialist named Theodore Swann. Amid depressed wartime economic conditions, Swann and his employer—the Alabama Power Company—launched Anniston's electrochemical industry, joining a new wave of industrial development in the South.

Industrialization, especially attracting science-based industry, the South's boosters argued, held out the promise of modernization and prosperity. In general, industrialization—and its environmental impact—lagged in the southern states. Agriculture continued to dominate the southern economy, and the population would remain predominately rural until 1960. "With few exceptions," environmental historian Albert Cowdrey has noted, "industrial impacts on the environment remained of small account, as did southern production: in 1890 the South's entire output was worth less than half of that of the state of New York." With its early industrialization and foundry discharges, Anniston may have been one of the exceptions. In the southern states, poverty and underdevelopment contributed to the impulse to attract industries of whatever kind, regardless of long-term pollution, which was often viewed as a sign of progress.[13]

The chemical and other science-based industries helped usher in what historian Frank Fischer has termed the "Age of Expertise." Emerging not out

Birmingham-based entrepreneur Theodore Swann's chemical company in West Anniston first began producing chlorinated diphenyls, as PCBs were then known, for commercial sale in 1929. Swann parlayed interests in the electrical industry, chemical manufacturing, and military production into the South's leading chemical company. Photo courtesy of Carolyn Green Satterfield.

of a craft or trade but directly out of scientific discoveries, the chemical industry and its close ally, the electrical industry, as historian David F. Noble has argued, redefined the relationship of knowledge to commodity production. These fields, Noble explained, "produced the people—industry-minded physicists and chemists and, especially, the electrical and chemical engineers, who would carry the scientific revolution into the older and the new industries." As Noble noted, these commercial enterprises controlled not only the "*products* of scientific technology" but also the "*process* of scientific production itself."[14]

Scientific authority in these industries and the field of medicine undergirded "social, state, and corporate power," historian of science Ronald G. Walters has argued. Knowledge of chemistry became as much a source of corporate capital as the raw materials from which the chemicals were derived. At the same time, the choices and biases of industry decision makers channeled scientific inquiry. Science is a product of research, Walters noted, but it is also "a product of choices, of exclusions, of interpretation."[15]

As salesmen above all else, chemical industrialists understood the value of expertise and the power conferred by scientific authority. Increasingly, in this "Age of Expertise," political as well as commercial decision making rested in the hands of those with technocratic knowledge. Over time, the ascendance of knowledge derived from expertise over knowledge borne of experience would have resounding consequences for democratic participation in deciding the disposition of toxics.[16]

The foremost promoter of chemistry as the South's economic salvation was a southerner, Charles Holmes Herty, a forester, inventor, and chemist from Georgia. In 1915, Herty left a position at the University of North Carolina to take the helm of the American Chemical Society (ACS), the national professional organization, based in New York City, that represented the industry's commercial interests. Promoting the industry as a clean, efficient, and scientific way to meet growing consumer needs and wants, Herty was also a staunch and lifelong advocate of chemical manufacturing as the ideal path to southern industrialization. "It will be through chemistry," he later declared, "that the South will receive its most lasting stimulation and its most permanent reward." Herty was attuned to the opportunities created by World War I for chemical commerce in general and for the southern chemical industry in particular. According to his biographer, Germaine Reed, Herty believed "that the South would always remain primarily agricultural but that the European war would stimulate industries in the region 'undreamed of at present' and that the resulting accumulation of wealth would relieve the 'hardship and privation' suffered by the southern masses ever since the Civil War."[17]

Herty was joined in linking war to regional economic growth by publisher Richard H. Edmonds, another highly influential advocate of southern industrialization, whose *Manufacturers Record* had tracked Anniston's industrial experiment since the city's opening to the public in 1883. Edmonds seized on the state of war to argue that further militarization of the southern states was essential not only to the regional economy but also to the national defense. Without heavy investment in the South, munitions production would remain concentrated in the North Atlantic, and, Edmonds declared, "this country would be hopelessly unable to defend itself in time of war."[18]

At the state level, the Alabama Power Company both underwrote and promoted increased industrialization and militarization as a means to broaden the commercial market for electrical power. Toward that end, the new Birmingham-based power company invested heavily in Anniston, which in 1882 had been the first Alabama town to use electricity commercially.[19]

IN 1915, ALONG "ATTRACTIVE ANNISTON'S WHITE WAY," incandescent bulbs illuminated the way to the movie theaters on Noble Street. Charlie Chaplin, billed as "the Funniest Man in the World," was slated to open at the Alamo theater in late October. The *Star* advertised that the Noble Theatre had reserved an "Entire Gallery for Colored" for its showing of *Mutt & Jeff in College*. The most prominent film to show in Anniston that year was *Birth of a Nation*, which opened at the Noble Theatre on April 24. The *Star* noted that the film "exhibits the negro [*sic*] in an unfortunate light" and "is calculated to engender racial animosity," but it also lavished praise on D. W. Griffith's cinematic portrayal of the Lost Cause.[20]

The benefits of modernization would not be shared equally. When photographer Lewis Hine visited the city twice earlier in the decade, he found white laborers' lives desperate, especially among those working in Anniston's textile industry. The Anniston mill village was "run down and greatly in need of sanitary improvement." Children as young as ten labored in the mills. Unlike the public school for white, middle-class students, the mill school was "miserably equipped" and provided only eight weeks of schooling.[21]

As for black workers, Henry Givahn, who left Anniston around 1915, recalled that "the living conditions weren't too good, low pay, long hours. It was these conditions that caused so many of our people to seek a better living in northern cities." In departing for Tuskegee and then New York, Givahn joined a broader migration of blacks out of the South.[22]

Bald proclamations of racial intellectual superiority from white supremacists such as John Knox were coupled with barriers to African American education designed to fulfill the false claim and perpetuate subordination. Givahn said, "I don't believe they had anything [for Negro citizens] in public school above fifth grade." African American families in Anniston went to great lengths to secure decent educations for their children. Anniston dentist Gordon Rodgers Jr. explained that his mother started a small concession in Talladega, twenty-five miles distant, selling food to Talladega College students, to enable her children to live in that town and go to the historically black college's secondary school.[23]

Despite having undergone early industrialization and electrification, on the eve of U.S. entry into World War I, Anniston and Calhoun County reeled from a number of economic reversals. The boll weevil officially arrived in 1915. Local farmers and merchants had expected to have another year before the "dreaded pest" reached them. Repeated calls for crop diversification had gone largely unheeded. Wide infestation by the cattle tick had already made area farms inhospitable to beef production. With its forests depleted, Anniston's ability to compete in pig iron production had declined. In addition, Anniston's eight pipe foundries were struggling against heavy competition over the South American market. So, amid news of the boll weevil's advance and more illicit distilling cases than the term of court could handle, local residents welcomed the news that the city would become home to an arms factory.[24]

The Alabama Power Company was the driving force behind securing for Anniston the million-dollar arms factory to which the Monsanto Chemical Company traces its roots in the city. In 1915, having negotiated a contract with the British "to manufacture war munitions and electrical steel," Alabama Power president James Mitchell and general counsel Thomas G. Martin committed $150,000 (about $3.5 million in 2013) toward the munitions factory and persuaded Anniston businessmen to put up additional funds. Meeting in mid-November at the Calhoun County Courthouse, local businessmen raised $66,000 ($1.5 million) in just thirty-five minutes to have the plant sited in their city. Anniston Ordnance Company was to house the state's first industrial furnace to run on electricity, a six-ton Héroult furnace costing $20,000. Electrical power overcame the deficits of nature, and the significant outlay of capital virtually guaranteed the plant would be converted to peacetime use once the demand for weaponry declined. Mitchell named as vice president of the Anniston Ordnance Company his rising young star salesman, Theodore Swann.[25]

The son of a Confederate soldier, Swann was born in Dandridge, Tennessee, in 1886, to a town and a family divided by the Civil War. In 1913, when Alabama Power recruited him to organize its new commercial sales department, the ambitious young sales executive and his auburn-haired wife, Catherine Dunwoody, moved to Birmingham. Swann represented the power company on the "state munitions board," set up to advise the Wilson administration on industrial capacity. The position gave him an excellent vantage from which to survey business opportunities and may have sparked his interest in chemicals. Following the munitions venture, Swann would parlay his sales position at Alabama Power into a range of enterprises that made him an "international industrial giant" in his own right. Swann's principal business interests spanned three interdependent spheres—the expanding electrical power industry, the munitions business, and the newly emerging field of synthetic organic chemicals.[26]

When the munitions deal was arranged, Swann telephoned the *Star* from Alabama Power headquarters to make the news official: a vacant railcar works would be taken over by the Southern Munitions Corporation (later the Anniston Ordnance Company). The company would employ 300 skilled workers and complete its first order of 50,000 shells by the summer of 1916. As Anniston's new patron, the Alabama Power Company not only launched Anniston Ordnance but also Anniston Steel. The company also owned the city's gas line and streetcar railway. "Anniston has found a new friend at the court of capital," gushed the *Star* in gratitude to "James Mitchell and his associates on the board of the Alabama Power Company."[27]

Richard Edmonds was elated; he wrote a piece both congratulating Anniston for landing the British munitions contract and urging further government investment in southern militarization. Federal defense plans coincided; President Wilson focused military investment in the interior South, his home region. (In 1917, the U.S. Army began building a training camp in Anniston on 18,000 acres of former farmland northwest of the city. Camp McClellan opened the following year.)[28]

A year and a half after helping establish the Anniston Ordnance Works, Swann launched the Southern Manganese Company, Anniston's first chemical company and his first independent venture. (Swann continued to live in Birmingham, but he located an office on Tenth Street in Anniston.) In anticipation of sustained wartime demand, the factory was to produce ferromanganese, a chemical used to manufacture high-grade steel. Swann built Southern Manganese with Alabama Power's blessing; the two industries were interdependent. The availability of relatively cheap power fueled the high-temperature ovens used to combine chemicals. And, because the ovens demanded a great deal of electricity, the power company could count on a ready customer. Swann built the new factory on farmland just outside the city limits, west of town. Alongside the facility he built houses—as the Woodstock Iron Company had done—unpainted, shingle-roofed cottages to accommodate workers.[29] The war in Europe had been under way for three years when Theodore Swann founded Southern Manganese. Two weeks later, the United States declared war on Germany.

For Swann and other industrialists, war held economic promise. For African Americans in Anniston, war engendered hope of racial change. Shortly after the United States entered World War I in 1917, Rev. Harry E. Jones, pastor of one of the most influential black churches in Anniston, delivered a remarkable speech at a mass meeting on the Calhoun County Courthouse steps. The *Star* published the speech in full—perhaps the first time the paper had done so for an African American speaker. A Fisk graduate described by a contemporary as "a liberated theologian," Jones urged African Americans to fully participate in the war effort, partly in expectation of "readjustment" after the war. "Self preservation demands that the Negro be patriotic," he preached. "The question arises, 'Shall the Negro be loyal to the country in which he is proscribed and oppressed?' 'Shall he be loyal to a country that has allowed the practical disfranchisement of a race of ten million?'" Even to pose such questions publicly was an act of bravery. For beneath the question was a manifesto: African American men's wartime loyalty and military service should be rewarded with the full rights of citizenship, including the vote.[30]

ON APRIL 22, 1915, a German attack on Ypres, Belgium, rained gas weapons on Allied soldiers. A British chaplain described the effects of the yellow-green chlorine gas as "the most fiendish, wicked thing I have ever seen." Chemical weaponry had been used since antiquity, but never in a modern war on so grand a scale. The Hague Declaration of 1899, signed by England, Germany, France, and other European powers (but not by the United States), had pledged signatory nations "to abstain from the use of projectiles the object of which is the diffusion of asphyxiating or deleterious gases." The Hague Congress of 1907 had again expressly rejected the use of "poisons or poisonous weapons." With these international agreements in place, the suddenness and scope of the Germans' use of gas weaponry at Ypres brought widespread shock and revulsion. Allied forces took but a few weeks to respond in kind.[31]

The United States was still neutral in the conflict and, if the Wilson administration had seemed slow to respond to the German use of gas, the American chemical industry was not. Just six months after the gas attack at Ypres, the American Chemical Society held its national convention at Grand Central Palace in New York. With Charles Herty at the helm, the ACS centered its attention on the importance of chemistry to national defense. The society would use the exigencies of war to push through protective tariffs on chemical products and soon became deeply involved in the creation in 1918 of the Chemical Warfare Service (CWS), a division of the U.S. Army expressly devoted to chemical warfare. The two organizations even bore the same symbolic colors: cobalt blue and gold.[32]

Sometimes called "the chemical war," World War I created a market for chemicals to be used as weapons. Chemical industry historian Fred Aftalion calculated that more than a quarter of the munitions used in World War I contained chemical agents. General William Sibert, first chief of the CWS, boasted that by war's end, the United States was "actually manufacturing more gas than all three of the Allies put together."[33]

At the urging of the War Department, Theodore Swann agreed to produce chemical munitions—elemental phosphorus used in smoke bombs, incendiary shells, and tracer bullets—although the war ended before a contract could be issued. To do so, he incorporated a second chemical firm in 1918, the Federal Phosphorus Company, which obtained procurement status as a supplier to the CWS. Courting U.S. government contracts, Swann now frequently included not "Anniston" or "Southern" but "Federal" in the names of his new enterprises: Federal Abrasives, the Federal Electro-Chemical Company, and Federal Fertilizer.[34]

World War I launched a period of extraordinary growth for the U.S. chemical industry, particularly in the field of synthetic organic chemicals. During the war, rapid expansion of the chemical industry was facilitated by U.S. government subsidies and tariff protection, as well as by increased wartime demand for synthetic organic chemicals used in war industries, including those used as weapons. World War I benefited the chemical industry in both practical and symbolic ways. "The war did give Monsanto muscle," company historian Dan Forrestal wrote, adding that "the Federal Government became a prime customer for the first time."[35]

After the war, both the U.S. Army and the American chemical industry nurtured the symbolic association of chemicals with national pride in order to ensure that chemical manufacturing continued to receive government support and public acceptance. Linking chemicals for commerce and chemistry for war not only yielded government contracts; tying chemicals to the national interest enabled the growth of the industry.

The postwar era proved even more significant for chemical firms, which acquired new knowledge as part of the spoils of conflict. Soon after war's end, the U.S. government used its position among the victors to seize ownership of German patents for synthetic chemicals. Congress established an "Alien Property Custodian" to manage the patents, naming A. Mitchell Palmer (later attorney general) to the post. Palmer auctioned the first round of patents at a deep discount directly to chemical manufacturers. After protests of unfairness from smaller companies, the United States created the Chemical Foundation, a private, not-for-profit institution, to manage the patents. The foundation instituted a leasing system, issuing nonexclusive licenses to manufacture patented chemicals to multiple companies. By 1921, the foundation possessed 4,764 patents, for which it had paid less than $300,000. By this means, the chemical industry gained a near monopoly on patented knowledge of synthetic organic chemicals. The proceeds of the patent leases went to the foundation, which used the bulk of them, in turn, not only to promote the study of chemistry but also to lobby on behalf of the industry. Among the foundation's early promotional efforts was a high school essay contest on "The Relation of Chemistry to the National Defense."[36]

The remarkable growth of the U.S. synthetic organic chemical industry during wartime had been unrestrained, heavily subsidized, and cloaked in strong nationalism. Seeking to extend the benefits of war to peacetime, the businessmen who helped establish the Chemical Warfare Service continued to nurture the identification of chemicals with not only war but patriotism. Evidence of how crucial World War I was to the industry was evident even twenty years later, when one Monsanto official proclaimed "1917 as the date of the declaration of American Chemical Independence." If World War I marked the commercial rise of synthetic chemical production in the United States, the period immediately after the war heralded a "war for chemical supremacy," declared Lloyd F. Nickell, a St. Louis chemist who went to work for Monsanto in 1917. Competition from the resurgent German chemical industry was used as one patriotic rationale for continued government subsidization of the young U.S. industry.[37]

As industrialist Lammot du Pont put it, the synthetic organic chemicals industry was "almost unique in being the only peacetime industry to be deliberately developed as part of the scheme of national defense." The chemical industry sought to extend the link between chemicals for commerce and chemicals for weapons, partly on the grounds that commercial production could be easily converted to military production. As one CWS general put it, the nation should "keep such perfect plans that we can turn all the wheels of peace into the wings of war on a moment's notice."[38] Linking the nation's capacity for defense to its strength in chemical production proved a durable and rewarding strategy for the industry. The military possessed a privileged status that often required secrecy. Chemical manufacturers invoked patriotism and the national defense, claiming a privileged status as well.

The Ypres attack forever altered the nature of warfare. Chemical warfare expanded the control of nature, as historian Edmund Russell has argued, and new ways of controlling nature expanded the scale of war, bringing "profound changes in civilian life, science, and war." During the course of World War I, roughly 1.3 million men were wounded by chemical weapons; an estimated 91,000 died. Countless others suffered exposures whose long-term consequences were unknown. Mustard gas, an exceedingly painful and disfiguring blister-causing agent, was responsible for 400,000 injuries. Chlorine was among the most common gases used; in concentrations of one part per thousand or greater it is lethal. As one gas specialist observed in his war diary, some chemical weapons "eat out the cells of your lungs." Chemical weapons used molecules as projectiles and often went undetected until their targets sickened or died. Health effects were not limited to the battlefield. Responding to reports of ongoing health problems among veterans who had been exposed to chemical weapons, the CWS's postwar director said, "We do not claim there may not be some who are suffering permanent injuries from gas." However, he emphatically declared, "permanent after-effects are very rare."[39]

Seeking to institutionalize the chemical warfare program, the political coalition that nurtured its founding mounted a defense of chemical weaponry. Both the ACS and the CWS suggested that chemical warfare was "the most scientific" form of warfare and that chemical weapons were more "humane" than conventional arms. One defense of chemical warfare posed the matter as a choice between "Swords or Science." Some even claimed that chemical weapons were beneficial to health, suggesting that gas weapons destroyed germs and that gas wounds, unlike other injuries, were "completely sterile." Divorcing the impact of toxic chemicals on the human body from its moral context, the first CWS director, General William Sibert, openly lamented that the service had not completed "the newest creations of our Research Division" in time to test them in war. Chemists with the CWS, he said, had developed new "gases that we have all regretted that we could not try out on a human subject."[40]

It would be decades before the U.S. Army's Chemical Corps would locate its headquarters in Anniston, but the groundwork was laid during and immediately after World War I. In the month following the war's end, the CWS honored its director with a dinner at the Maison Rauscher in Washington, D.C. General Sibert was from Gadsden, Alabama, and "Sibert's Boys" in the CWS included not only his five sons but also Captain Harry Mell Ayers, a sharp young newsman from Anniston, who, in the midst of World War I, temporarily left his editorship of the *Anniston Evening Star and Daily Hot Blast* for military service at CWS headquarters in Washington. Ayers, who had hoped to see action in Europe, wrote that he was "greatly disappointed that I had to miss the Big Show in 1918," but his brief stint at the CWS nurtured a lifelong commitment to making the military a linchpin of Anniston's economy.[41]

At such galas, dining together on squab and sea bass meunière, were chemical industrialists, military brass, and congressmen on whom the Army chemical division's fate depended. At the third annual dinner in 1921, Chemical Foundation president Francis P. Garvan and chemical manufacturers such as A. H. Hooker of Hooker Chemical (later known for its waste site at Love Canal) joined regulars like Charles Herty. Anniston once again had a seat at the table, represented by Assistant Surgeon General Robert

E. Noble, nephew of founder Samuel Noble. Also present were Harvey W. Wiley, former chief of both the USDA Bureau of Chemistry and the ACS, and a little-known official in the Justice Department, the young J. E. Hoover.[42]

At stake was not just continued congressional funding for the CWS but support for the industry in general. "Feats of chemists in C.W.S should give capitalists confidence in American chemists," Herty scribbled on one dinner program, "Congress should protect Am. industries begun during war period until they can stand alone." After considerable debate, in 1920 Congress would make the CWS a permanent section of the U.S. Army. Sealing the CWS-industry union, Herty, already the most prominent civilian advocate of the Chemical Warfare Service, became president of the CWS advisory board.[43]

DASHED HOPES FOR WHAT SERVICE IN WAR would bring to Anniston's black citizens were immediately apparent after the war as black soldiers returned from fighting for democracy abroad to face the American failure to extend democracy's entitlements to black citizens, especially, though not exclusively, in the South. In December 1918, Sergeant Edgar Caldwell, a black officer and war veteran, boarded the Alabama Power Company's Constantine line streetcar in Anniston. It is not clear whether Sergeant Caldwell defiantly asserted his right to a place in the section reserved for whites or became embroiled in a dispute over the fare, but the uniformed black serviceman met with violence at the hands of the white conductor. Beaten, evicted from the streetcar, and kicked in the stomach while he lay in the dirt, Caldwell fired his army pistol, killing the conductor and injuring the motorman.[44]

Sergeant Caldwell's supporters argued that "as a soldier, Caldwell was entitled to a trial by a military court, where he had a chance for clemency, rather than a state court, in which execution was certain." African American church leaders and businessmen in the city "rallied to the support of this soldier," his contemporary Henry Givahn explained, pooling donations to hire a Birmingham criminal lawyer to assist the local attorney handling Caldwell's case. Anniston preacher Rev. R. R. Williams made contact with the national office of the NAACP. Despite the fact that the shooting was unpremeditated and in self-defense, an Alabama jury speedily returned a guilty verdict of first-degree murder. The NAACP appealed the case to the U.S. Supreme Court, which let the conviction stand. The NAACP continued to seek clemency, approaching both U.S. attorney general A. Mitchell Palmer and President Woodrow Wilson. Wilson urged Alabama governor Thomas Kilby, who was from Anniston, to commute Caldwell's sentence, but the efforts failed. "Southern governors simply did not spare black men convicted of killing whites," wrote historian Mark Schneider about the case. On the date of his execution, July 30, 1920, Caldwell addressed several thousand people outside the Calhoun County jail: "I am but one of the many victims among my people who are paying the price of America's mockery of law and dishonesty in the profession of world democracy."[45]

The Caldwell case mobilized black citizens, prompting the founding in 1919 of the Anniston–Hobson City NAACP. W. E. B. Du Bois called Caldwell's execution "a legal lynching." In the immediate aftermath of the execution, fearing a more militant response, a biracial coalition of Anniston's clergy and businessmen appealed for calm. White and black clergy, joined by local industrialists, published a joint statement in the *Anniston Evening Star*. (Swann was not among them, though one of his prime backers, W. H. Weatherly, of the First National Bank of Anniston, signed.) "There is no issue between the white and colored races," read the statement. "There is no ground for hatred or revenge on the part of those who are honest and right thinking," the statement continued. "Let all cooperate to uphold the majesty of the law." The focus on maintaining order in the interests of business was explicit: "[Unrest] interferes with business, brings on unreasoning fear to the heart of the timid and uninformed and leads to a point where trouble might follow."[46]

In this context, some members of black Anniston's middle and professional classes still managed to prosper, so much so that in 1924 successful druggist Charles E. Thomas could call Anniston the "best city for Negro development in the United States." However, the intensified assertion of white supremacy in Alabama in the decade that followed the Caldwell hanging severely impeded the activities of the NAACP in Anniston, as in the state. Reverend Jones's expressed belief that service in wartime conferred democratic rights went unfulfilled. It would be another generation, after another stint of wartime service, before black Americans would begin to see anything like the profound change that Reverend Jones imagined in his speech on the courthouse steps.[47]

IN GENERAL, U.S. CHEMICAL SOLDIERS were received as heroes. Dubbed the "Hell's Fire" troops, they "caught the fancy of America" in the popular press. And, despite systematic exclusion in Jim Crow America, black soldiers had served bravely in World War I, including in at least two all-black chemical warfare battalions. However, General Sibert's successor as CWS chief, General Amos A. Fries, reinforced the ideology of racial exclusion among its officer corps.[48]

Lecturing his officers on questions regarding troop training in 1921, Fries encapsulated "the white male martial ideal," envisioning white soldiers as "more highly developed" on the battlefield. Reinforcing essentialist notions of whiteness and blackness, Fries suggested that the wartime performance of all-black battalions had not met an image of idealized manhood. The CWS commander viewed black soldiers as both unfit for the new modes of warfare *and* uniquely suited to serve as shock troops on the front lines. Characterizing persons of African descent as "semi-savages" compared to the "highly sensitive white man," Fries drew on deeply embedded racist tropes. "In some cases," Fries said, acknowledging obliquely the courageous role of black troops on the front lines, "dark-skinned troops were kept only as shock troops to be replaced by the more highly developed Caucasian."[49]

Fries's speech illustrated the circular illogic sustaining the idea of race, a persistent kind of "race-thinking" at the heart of American notions about knowledge. "The safety of a modern Nation," said Fries, is "dependent on its trained manhood." Purported racial differences in "intelligence" and "control of the body" displayed in wartime, General Fries argued, justified racial inequality not only during wartime but in the fields of "science" and "manufacturing" afterward. "The same training that makes for advancement in science," he said, "and success in manufacture in peace gives the control of the body that holds the white man to the firing line no matter what its terrors." Expressing little respect for the black soldiers under his command, Fries said, "A great deal of this comes, because the white man has had trained out of him all superstition."[50]

Race alone did not define the fit gas soldier. Documents from 1921 submit that "the majority of casualties" from gas were "among the careless, the reckless, the dullards and the panic-stricken," suggesting that gas casualties could be avoided by exercising greater self-control. The headline "GAS FAVORS MOST INTELLIGENT" suggested that soldiers themselves were somehow responsible for their own injuries.[51]

(Black soldiers would make up a disproportionate number of the enlisted troops in the Chemical War Service during World War II—more than 17 percent in mid-1943—though they did not see combat until late in the war. According to Army historians, these troops demonstrated "very good combat records." Except for the smoke generator units, the chemical companies were considered to be service troops, and relatively few African Americans served as CWS officers.)[52]

Medical justifications in the 1920s echoed Fries's rationalization of disparate exposure, transposing a long history of white imaginings about differential racial susceptibility to disease to ideas about racial vulnerability to chemical exposures. Medical writers claimed that black soldiers were uniquely impervious to the weapons' effects. "It has been stated that 78 percent of negroes [sic] are resistant" to mustard gas, wrote Edward Vedder and Duncan Walton in *The Medical Aspects of Chemical Warfare* in 1925.[53]

Opposition to chemical warfare grew dramatically after World War I. On June 17, 1925, the major European powers signed the Geneva Protocol outlawing gas warfare. The political coalition of chemical industrialists and military leaders that had succeeded in creating a permanent section of the Army devoted to chemical warfare now argued forcefully against U.S. ratification of the Geneva agreement. Most prominent among them were General Fries and Charles Herty. Fries linked opposition to the chemical warfare treaty to American nationalism, in language that anticipated Cold War rhetoric. In a 1925 speech titled "Making America Safe for the Reds," Fries equated members of the Women's International League for Peace and Freedom, who supported the Geneva Protocol, with proponents of communism, saying, "No matter in what other ways they may differ, the Pacifist, and the Communist, the misguided optimist and the Red Soviet of Russia have one thing in common; they are all trying to disarm America." Amid the Red Scare, Chemical Warfare Service advocates again rationalized chemical warfare—and the production of chemical weapons—as patriotic, necessary to American world power. The U.S. Senate declined to ratify the Geneva Gas Protocol (and would not do so until fifty years later).[54]

AFTER THE WAR, the Monsanto Chemical Company began enlarging its product base and sales by incorporating other chemical firms into a growing global empire. John F. Queeny had made at least seven trips across the Atlantic between 1905 and 1921. His son Edgar—who at age twenty-two became Monsanto's new advertising manager—accompanied him on three annual voyages between 1919 and 1921. In the postwar period, the company sought not just overseas markets but operating plants. Seeking access to British and other European markets while avoiding British tariff restrictions, in 1919 Queeny partnered to form what would become the first overseas acquisition, the Graesser-Monsanto Chemical Works Ltd., in Ruabon, North Wales, which later became a PCB manufacturing site.[55]

Meanwhile, the American Chemical Society increased its focus on the South, where both necessary resources and markets were located, and Richard Edmonds, Charles Herty, and Theodore Swann redoubled their efforts to attract capital (both human and finance) for southern chemical industrialization. Swann and Herty were among a select group of regional boosters who envisioned solving the South's economic problems through a partnership of science, industry, and military production. Chemistry, including a southern-based chemical research capacity, they believed, would usher in a new postwar South.[56]

Agriculture remained the South's economic mainstay, generating business opportunities for chemical suppliers. "Inasmuch as the largest consumption of fertilizers is in the South where the necessary raw materials, phosphate rock, coke, ammonia, and electric power, are all available," Swann argued in 1922, "plants for the manufacture of concentrated fertilizer should be located here and such products economically utilized for southern agriculture."[57]

Expanding his chemical operations in Anniston, Swann launched a new wave of development in the city. Not content for the South's economic role to be solely as exporter of raw materials, Swann built a scientific research laboratory at his plant. Using phosphate rock from east Tennessee, coke from Birmingham, and local sand, Swann Research devised new industrial and agricultural applications for chemicals. Building on his thwarted wartime foray into manufacturing phosphorus-based compounds for the military, Swann began manufacturing ferrophosphorus, a hardening agent for steel. The operation later became the core of Monsanto's extensive Phosphate Division, which would also oversee the production of PCBs.[58]

The American Chemical Society, with its national membership swelled to 15,000, held its 1922 annual meeting in Birmingham. Swann was among the speakers. Referring to the visiting chemists as "delvers into Nature's hidden secrets," a *Birmingham News* editorial suggested that "the chemist wrestles with giants bigger and deadlier and stronger and more potent either for destruction or salvation of the human race than any other." Advancing the idea that knowledge was increasingly—and necessarily—ceded to chemical experts, the editors wrote, "*The Birmingham News* welcomes these quiet supermen, these modest titans, these unassuming captains of industry, in fact, without whose guidance in this new world we would be as children groping and stumbling in the darkness."[59]

For their part, Herty and Edmonds redoubled their efforts to attract capital, helping to mount a series of "Southern Expositions" in northern cities that aimed to showcase, as well as propel, southern development. (In 1924, while planning the first Southern Exposition in New York, Herty met with one Mr. Queeny, surely John F. or Edgar of Monsanto, before meeting with New York's governor that afternoon.) Herty was especially keen to further the South's role in industrial research. Edmonds's *Manufacturers Record* awarded a $5,000 prize to the best state exhibit; Alabama won in 1924. Swann's Federal Phosphorus Company was among the exhibitors at the second Southern Exposition in 1925, as were Alabama Power, the Anniston Junior Chamber of Commerce, and Tuskegee Institute. Exposition organizers sought to prove, in the words of one journalist, that "the new South is keeping step with the most modern movements in agriculture, industry, education, highways, sanitation, and other lines."[60]

Just as in the military, racist defenses for exclusion pervaded the industry. J. E. Mills, writing in 1930 for the nation's leading scientific organization, the National Research Council, in a report titled *Chemical Progress in the South*, lauded the region's natural surroundings, but he was much less complimentary of a significant sector of its workforce. "The negro [sic]," wrote Mills, "plays at the present time almost no part in the industrial development of the South. This is not due," Mills contended, "as many outside of the South suppose, to the wishes of the southerner, but to the negro himself." Mills deployed false tropes developed in defense of slavery to justify persistent exclusion, writing, "The negro does not object to hard work, but every fiber of his being seems finally to resist regular work."[61]

The emergence of a research-based chemical industry in the South paralleled the hardening of Jim Crow segregation. Notwithstanding George Washington Carver's research in agricultural chemistry and Tuskegee Institute's inclusion in the Southern Exposition, African Americans were largely locked out of the new field of chemical knowledge and professional roles in the new industry; as potential chemists or inventors they were barred from most postsecondary educational institutions and denied capital investment and access to laboratories. Rarely were black workers—North or South—hired in skilled positions in the industry; the few opportunities available were as laborers, janitors, and laundrymen. Significant change in industry hiring practices would not begin until the 1960s.[62]

The wartime expansion of the synthetic chemicals industry created extraordinary prospects for the chemical field. These conditions provided the context in which Swann's research chemists developed chlorinated diphenyls, as PCBs were first called, for commercial sale in the late 1920s, at the Anniston Works of the firm that became the Swann Chemical Company. As Anniston's Woodstock Iron Company had done earlier, Swann Chemical embodied the South's great hopes for industrial development. Out of Swann's industrial research came the commercial production of PCBs, synthetic chemicals that the electrical industry came to regard as indispensable.[63]

CHAPTER THREE

Monsanto's Move "Down South"

It is sad to know what Monsanto did to us and [had] not told anybody.
I don't believe that a lot of the people would be in the shape we are in today if it had
been told where you could have done something about it then. My opinion is that they
were just looking at dollar marks and not at what it would do to human lives.
—Opal Scruggs, West Anniston resident, 2003

Opal Scruggs was born in 1935, the year the Monsanto Chemical Company acquired Swann's holdings and took over producing PCBs. Scruggs was born Opal Ferguson in a little white clapboard house in West Anniston, near where a Huddle House later stood. The Fergusons lived in the Mitchell Hill area, two miles west of downtown. Birmingham Highway was little more than a wagon road then, the Old Coldwater Road. The population of Anniston was about 22,000. By the time Opal was born, the chemical factory had been producing chlorinated biphenyls for half a dozen years. Two generations of Fergusons had worked at the plant and lived in the white, working-class neighborhood west and south of the sprawling 640-acre site. Scruggs's grandfather, Jefferson A. Ferguson, went to work for the company when it was still Swann Chemical. She remembers going to greet her grandfather when he got off work: "For years I would walk down the railroad track and meet him at the back part of the gate and walk home in the afternoon with him," holding his hand. She wonders if that simple act had anything to do with high levels of PCBs in her body now. In her living room on Parker Street in West Anniston rests a photograph taken June 21, 1936, just before her first birthday. The panoramic view shows dozens of family members at a gathering at Wesleyan Methodist Church nearby. She wonders as well whether living near the plant contributed to the high rates of cancer among them.[1]

Monsanto legend has it that Theodore Swann began looking for ways to make diphenyl after returning from the 1920 Kentucky Derby with a contract to produce two railcar loads of the "new magic fluid," even though he did not know what it was. Eastman Kodak was selling the chemical at forty dollars a pound; Swann challenged his research chemists to find a way to replicate diphenyl at lower cost. According to one account, the first attempt to produce diphenyl at Swann's Anniston Works sent "fire, glass, lead, iron, benzol, and water blast[ing] the walls of the room." The diphenyl experiments more likely were carried out in 1927. In any case, once Swann's chemists had successfully processed diphenyl, they began experimenting with chlorinating the compounds.[2]

The array of twisting pipes and smokestacks resembled a giant still, not unlike those used to make moonshine. Because of the open architecture of the chemical factory, production often took place uncontained. Few prohibitions governed the chemical distillery; covert, mysterious, poisonous, and potentially lethal, the financially promising new chemicals went unregulated.[3]

Figuratively at least, Swann's chemists turned coal by-products into gold. Processing the ecological bounty of north Alabama yielded coal wastes, a source of benzene used to make diphenyl. Benzene was first isolated from coal tar in 1845. Chemist August Kekulé described the structure of benzene in 1866 as a ring of six carbon atoms, a vision that he reported came to him in a dream. Coal-tar residue yielded three families of chemicals. The product family depended on the grade of oil derived from the coal: light tar oil yielded benzene and its relatives toluene and xylene; medium oil produced phenol, naphthalene, and lubricating oils; and heavy tar oil provided anthracenes, the products most often associated with coal by-products, such as roofing tar.[4]

The chemistry behind synthesizing chlorinated diphenyls from benzene was known as early as 1881, but no company in the United States produced the compounds commercially before Swann did so in 1929. When two benzene rings are combined at high temperatures under the proper conditions, diphenyl is produced. The chemical bond between the two benzene molecules leaves ten possible positions for chlorine to be added. Chlorination yielded 209 potential different substances, or congeners, representing all possible combinations of chlorine and benzene molecules.

Swann's chemists manufactured chlorinated diphenyls using a three-step procedure. Chlorine was gradually pumped into a mixture of melted diphenyl and iron filings and agitated. In about two hours, the mixture formed "a blue-black paste." Using iron filings as catalyst for the reaction was a novel and successful approach, but the filings had to be filtered out and the remaining mixture washed with hydrochloric acid, leaving a product that was "yellow to light brown in color." Then, that product was distilled, sometimes more than once, resulting in clear or milky colored

Hexachlorobiphenyl (PCB-153)

PCBs are chlorinated hydrocarbons, synthetic carbon-based chemicals that combine two benzene rings with chlorine atoms attached in different combinations, making 209 possible related chemicals, or congeners. The chemicals were widely used, primarily in insulating fluids. PCB-153, with six chlorines, is particularly persistent in the human body and was a component of a number of the Aroclors compounds Monsanto made in Anniston. Illustration by Charles Jones.

liquids—later termed polychlorinated biphenyls or PCBs. Swann chemist Russell Jenkins and co-authors Rogers McCullough and C. F. Booth submitted a description of their method for synthesizing chlorinated diphenyl to the *Journal of Industrial and Engineering Chemistry* on September 27, 1929, a day before Jenkins filed for a patent on the procedure. The work had been under way for a year.[5]

Writing in 1930, Swann chemist Chester H. Penning extolled the "commercial possibilities" of the new chlorinated diphenyls; their extraordinary heat resistance suggested a wide range of applications. He imagined "multitudinous" potential uses, including protective coatings, water- and flameproofing, electrical insulation, adhesives, "printing inks, artificial leather, leather finishing, [and] textile finishing." (The chemicals were a boon to the electrical industry because they made it possible to build more compact transformers.) Penning's account of the early fabrication of PCBs conspicuously avoided mentioning the explosion, opting instead to say that "the first plant had been completely dismantled." The chemist's perfunctory observations on toxicity suggest that the lab directed only the most rudimentary attention to the issue. Most chlorinated diphenyls were "practically odorless, and tasteless," and, he claimed, had "no appreciable action upon the skin." Penning acknowledged that "the concentrated vapors are irritating to the nasal passages, and cause violent headaches to some persons." Otherwise, he wrote, "no toxic effects have been noted."[6]

Marketed under the brand name Aroclors, chlorinated diphenyls were immediately profitable and in high demand. By 1930, the Anniston Works was producing approximately 3,000 pounds of the chemical a day; the company shipped nearly 350,000 pounds of Aroclors to customers that year. According to Swann company ledgers, the price per pound in May 1930 was $17.72, with a profit margin of 6 percent; a year later, profits increased eightfold while per-unit production costs declined slightly. The May 1931 per pound sales price was $26.46, 47 percent profit.[7]

The revolutionary potential of these extraordinary new chemicals seemed unlimited. Swann took great personal pride in the new discovery and received numerous accolades. Charles Herty made one of several visits to the Anniston Works of Swann's Federal Phosphorus Company shortly after chemists at the plant succeeded in producing chlorinated diphenyl. Afterward, company officials arranged to send him samples of the new product.[8]

SWANN CHEMICAL WAS BILLED as the leading chemical operation in the South in 1930 and featured in a National Research Council special report on *Chemical Progress in the South*. The Wall Street crash had little immediate adverse impact on the Anniston plant; payroll rose by nearly 18 percent from $933,970 in 1928 to $1.1 million in 1929, and continued to increase, leveling off slightly in 1930. Salaried employees endured the onset of the Depression better than plant workers paid weekly, however.[9]

Heralding the "Chemical Possibilities of the Southeast" as "major sources of new wealth," the American Chemical Society held its professional meeting in Atlanta in 1930. The gathering of 1,000 chemists featured an address by chemist (and CWS advisory committee member) Harrison Howe titled "Chemistry Comes South." A United Press staff correspondent reported that the convention "graphically reveal[ed] a new industrial South to itself."[10]

Swann's skill in recruiting investors was, by now, fabled. Once during his early years, he is said to have rented a Packard limousine to drive a group of New York, Philadelphia, and Baltimore bankers from Birmingham to Anniston, supplying the passengers with plenty of sour mash whiskey for the ride. The group toured three different iron furnaces at the Anniston Works, evidence of the grand scale of Swann's Anniston operations. Stops for more "refreshments" between each demonstration permitted Swann's only crew of ironmongers sufficient time to sneak to the next furnace before the molten ore exploded, sending the "the very essence of hell all over everything." The display made his workforce and furnace operations seem far more extensive and worthy of capital investment than they were; the intoxicated investors appeared to have been none the wiser. As the entourage left Anniston's West End to return to Birmingham, Swann had an agreement for the capital needed to expand.[11]

At the height of his success, Swann personified the prosperous New South entrepreneur. He traveled widely, in the United States and internationally, and joined country clubs in Alabama, Florida, and Long Island. He served on the boards at the First National Banks of Birmingham and Anniston and associated with the economic and political elites of Birmingham known by their political rivals as the "Big Mules," such as one might see tied to the back of a farm wagon laden with corn, munching the contents as a smaller mule labored to pull the load. (The Swanns' daughter Virginia later married into the most prominent Big Mule family, the DeBardelebens, founders of DeBardeleben Coal Company and the industrial town of Bessemer.)[12]

In 1930, Swann consolidated most of his ventures into a holding company called Swann Chemical. His home, "Swann Castle," a grand replica of a Norman chateau, was located in a fashionable suburb of Birmingham, and a family retreat, "Black Swann Lake," on the Cahaba River. With the Depression under way, he invited employees and family members on an all-expense-paid trip to Pasadena to accompany the University of Alabama football team on its third trip to the Rose Bowl.[13]

Soon thereafter, however, Swann's fortunes began to decline. He had splurged extravagantly and was also hit by high transportation costs and dwindling supplies of phosphate rock. Then, in 1933, Swann's New York financiers called in an outstanding loan. Swann left for St. Louis to seek help from his friends Edgar Monsanto Queeny of Monsanto Chemical Company and Edward Mallinkrodt Jr. of Mallinkrodt Chemical Works. He returned to Alabama with a $700,000 loan, two-thirds of it from Monsanto, secured by Swann Chemical stock. The stopgap financial arrangement prevented northeastern bankers from taking charge of the company.[14]

A short time later, Monsanto, ever alert to new acquisitions, turned its controlling interest in the Swann Chemical Company's debt into a takeover of the foremost chemical enterprise in the South. Swann Company stockholders approved the "merger" in April 1935. Monsanto issued 113,082 new shares of stock, retaining 15 percent of them because of its controlling interest, and fully acquired the plant in Anniston. Monsanto kept Swann on as president of the Federal Phosphorus Company, and he continued to run Swann Research in Birmingham, but Swann never regained control of his Anniston-based business. Through most of the 1930s, Swann continued to advocate for industrial development in Alabama and the South, serving with Governor Bibb Graves on a committee to survey the state's industrial resources. A bankruptcy judge assessed his holdings at more than $2 million in 1944 (about $26 million in 2012 dollars).[15] Swann's fortunes rose and fell. The plant that in 1929 had begun producing PCBs was now wholly owned by the Monsanto Chemical Company.

Monsanto Chemical, now rapidly expanding, took over its most prominent potential competitor in the South under the regime of a new corporate president. When John F. Queeny learned that he had cancer of the tongue, he promoted his son Edgar from general sales manager to president. Edgar was just over thirty when he took leadership of Monsanto in 1928. Like both his father and Theodore Swann, Edgar Queeny was primarily an entrepreneur and salesman, not a scientist. The senior Queeny was "no chemist," according to a Swiss chemist who was one of the many European scientists John F. Queeny had hired. Similarly, although Edgar held a degree in chemistry, he was, according to chemical industry historian Fred Aftalion, "not a brilliant student."[16]

Edgar had served in the Navy during World War I and had graduated from Cornell in 1919. As a young man, Edgar Queeny was lanky and aloof. "Enigmatic" and "personally unapproachable" were the words one Monsanto executive used to describe the young Edgar. John Francis Queeny worried that his son might lack the drive and focus to run the company. But, having assumed Monsanto's helm just a year before the Wall Street crash, Edgar would successfully direct the company's operations for thirty years, overseeing a major expansion of the Monsanto empire.[17]

During Edgar Queeny's early years as president of Monsanto, he threw himself into building and diversifying the business. Depression-era conditions held back the recruitment of many new industries to the southern states. However, even during the lean years, the chemical industry continued expanding southward. As company historian Dan Forrestal noted, "The new jump was 'down South'—to Birmingham and Anniston, Alabama." In a 1933 *Manufacturers Record* essay, "The Chemical Industry Turns to the South," Edgar Queeny quoted an unnamed observer as saying that "during the next ten years the South probably is destined for greater chemical progress than any other section of the country."[18]

Edgar Monsanto Queeny took over from his father as president of Monsanto in 1928 and expanded the chemical firm's reach in the U.S. South and internationally. During Edgar Queeny's thirty-year tenure, corporate net worth grew from $12 million to $805 million. Photo courtesy of AP/Wide World Photo.

Describing the chemical industry as "virile," "ambitious," and "creative," Edgar Queeny saw several advantages in pushing south: "the abundance of raw materials," "adequate transportation facilities by land and water," "reasonably cheap power," "the proximity of markets," and "proper climatic and labor conditions." Monsanto reported in 1938 that "during the so-called depression years Monsanto made the greatest advances in its history." A strong antiregulation business climate in the South paved the way for hugely profitable new divisions of the company to operate with little oversight.[19]

By absorbing Swann Chemical in the mid-1930s, Monsanto expanded into one of the most modern, industrialized results of New South development. Ranked sixth in size among Alabama cities at the end of the decade, Anniston was disproportionately significant in its industrial capacity. A postcard image from the time situates the Monsanto factory's barnlike structures in a field of green pastures surrounded by trees, highlighting the marriage of industry and agriculture. In a *Nation* magazine article at the end of the decade, Southern newsman Jonathan Daniels observed that Calhoun County was still "old time cotton country." Cotton *was* still a major

In 1935, the Monsanto Chemical Company acquired the Swann Chemical Company, "one of the largest chemical plants in Anniston, [with] approximately 1,000 employees," just west of Anniston. Postcard by E. C. Kropp Company, Milwaukee, Wisconsin, ca. 1940.

crop. But, noted Daniels, Anniston's industrialization stood out in the region, in part because of the city's absentee-owned "big Monsanto chemical works."[20]

Edgar Queeny paid an extended visit to Anniston on the eve of taking over the Swann plant in 1935, renaming the Swann holdings the Monsanto Chemical Company of Alabama. The Anniston plant played a key role in positioning Monsanto for further growth. Swann's Chemical Warfare Service procurement status made the South's largest chemical company a further asset. According to Forrestal, the Swann acquisition brought to Monsanto "new products, new technology, new customers and new people, many of whom would in the years ahead take over positions of commanding importance—up to and including chairman of the board." Most of Swann's senior managers and chemists took jobs with the new owner. In many ways, the spirit of Swann Chemical became the corporate culture of Monsanto. "Monsanto did not really take over the Swann enterprise," Swann's biographers contend, "in the end Swann's men took over Monsanto."[21]

CHEMICAL MANUFACTURING CREATED workplace hazards of a different order than other industries, a distinction noted as early as 1916 by chemical industrialists, government investigators, and medical researchers alike. "In spite of the undoubted enormous industrial menace to the health and lives of the workers, there is no industry, so far as I know, in which the human element is so woefully neglected as in the chemical," wrote New York state factory investigator George M. Price in 1916. Between that time and the start of World War II, the industry worked out a set of strategies for responding to the complaints that inevitably followed. Medical researchers developed laboratory techniques for assessing the impact of the "dangerous trades" on the body.[22] New techniques in toxicology and the rise of industrial hygiene enabled researchers to document some of the dangers workers faced in handling toxic chemicals. However, the information appeared in industry and medical journals, which workers, nearby residents, and even their doctors would have been unlikely to read.

Attention to the dangers chemical workers faced had first emerged in Europe, where synthetic organic chemicals were first produced. In the United States, physician David Edsall published "Diseases Due to Chemical Agents" in William Osler and Thomas McCrae's classic medical textbook *Modern Medicine* in 1907. (Edsall became dean of Harvard Medical School and a champion of the field of industrial medicine. He helped develop the Division of Industrial Hygiene at Harvard, where studies of chlorinated hydrocarbon chemicals were conducted in the 1930s.)[23]

By 1912, following close on two national conferences on occupational disease, the New York Section of the American Chemical Society had established a Committee on Occupational Diseases in the Chemical Trades. Chemist Charles Baskerville persuaded the ACS to host a two-hour session on the subject at its national conference in 1916. Among the presenters at the 1916 Symposium on Occupational Diseases in the Chemical Industry were Dr. Alice Hamilton and Dr. Joseph W. Schereschewsky, both pioneers in the field of "industrial hygiene." By 1916, Dr. Hamilton, an investigator with the U.S. Bureau of Labor, had been researching industrial exposures for more than a decade. Her methodology involved direct observation of workplace conditions, an approach that put her at odds with factory owners. Dr. Schereschewsky directed research on industrial hygiene for the U.S. Public Health Service, including conducting physical examinations of large groups of workers in particular trades.[24]

At the 1916 Symposium, Dr. Schereschewsky noted that "the specific hazards provided by the nature of chemical substances add to the complications of the chemical industries." Other participants emphasized the need for employers to closely monitor the health of chemical workers. However, realizing that chemical company owners were apt to closely guard damaging information about their processes and products, one participant suggested that factory physicians be required "to report to the state the details of occupational poisonings." A doctor from the New Jersey Department of Labor, "plead[ed] for frankness between the manufacturer and employees and stated that many manufacturers did not explain the dangers of their industries to employees because they were afraid to do so." One doctor noted the tendency among employers to shift the responsibility for protection against hazards to the workers themselves, a practice that would prove enduring. Dr. Lester L. Roos, of the New York State Industrial Commission, critiqued "the fallacy of the statement by capitalists that labor is unwilling to use hygienic safety devices."[25]

Attendees gave particular attention to the toxicity of coal-tar products, including the necessity of handling them with "unusual precaution since the poison is absorbed through the skin, through open sores and from fumes; even leather shoes permit infection." Dr. Hamilton explicitly warned of the poisonous effects of "benzene and toluene and their many derivatives" on munitions workers, emphasizing that that these "materials are dangerous from the poisonous side as well as the explosive."[26]

Participants recognized that the long latency period between the time of exposure and the appearance of symptoms made causation difficult to ascertain.[27] Chemical manufacturers were in the best position to observe the impact of long-term exposure to their products (though they were least likely to wish to broadcast the information).

John F. Queeny was made dramatically aware of the workplace hazards of chemical exposure in 1916, when Monsanto workers manufacturing phenacetin, a component of fever-reducing drugs, began dying. As Queeny recounted: "In my plant, the men engaged in this work suddenly began to sicken with a mysterious disease. Three died and twenty-five were in almost a dying condition. Doctors examined them, but could not discover the cause of the illness. The sick men had no symptoms of any known disease. But in the men who died it was noted that the blood corpuscles had broken down into a sort of watery serum. They had literally bled to death without a wound."[28] Comparing the factory floor to a battlefield, Queeny continued, "For a time we were completely baffled. Men who would have faced bullets without flinching recoiled from the mysterious terror of the chemical laboratory. It began to look as if we were going to be beaten. Then it was discovered that the poison was entering through the skin. Chemicals would slop over containers and get on the men's shoes and clothing. At a certain stage in the manufacture of phenacetin, we found that the product was intensely poisonous if allowed to remain on the skin. It penetrated and destroyed the blood."[29]

Chemists recognized that small scale lab experiments could not predict the impact of hazards posed by the more sustained exposures to high volumes of chemicals experienced by factory workers. "Chemists in their laboratories have worked for years with benzol, and none have dreamed of the danger that lurks in its use in large quantities," wrote chemist Lloyd Nickell in 1916. Nickell specifically warned of dangers of extended exposure to benzol, a primary product of coal tar, from which PCBs were derived. "When subjected to the fumes of benzol for a long period of time with his clothing frequently wet by the liquid, the workman, if his habits of cleanliness are not the best, often suffers serious and *insidious systemic derangements*."[30]

"Overcoming such dangers often means an enormous expenditure of time and money," Nickell cautioned, "and even then many of them cannot be overcome." For this reason, Nickell acknowledged that government regulation might prove necessary. Nickell was among those optimists who had faith, however, in chemical producers: "We may rest assured that American manufacturers will do all in their power and knowledge to minimize these hidden dangers; and should accidents occur, as they are bound to do, we may be sure that the fault does not lie within the present knowledge of the manufacturer." (Monsanto hired Nickell in 1917 to direct its Krummrich plant in Illinois, in the town now known as Sauget. By 1930, he was head of Monsanto Chemicals, Ltd., in Britain.)[31]

CONCERN ABOUT THE HEALTH HAZARDS posed by chemicals grew alongside the industry. But the field of industrial hygiene located the problems of chemical exposure almost entirely within the workplace; industrial hygienists gave little consideration to effluent and air pollution leaving factories. The production of synthetic chemicals affected not only workers but also people living near chemical factories.

The noxious by-products of Swann's early operations had generated local protest when brown dust and white smoke from producing ferrophosphorus began "eating paint from automobiles, houses, lawn furniture, and other metal items" on the more affluent east side of town. Of course, dust and smoke had never been far away from the workers who lived adjacent to the polluting factories, but eastside residents "did not intend to endure the abuse." Swann responded by installing pollution control devices, electrostatic precipitators, also known as scrubbers, that, incidentally, recovered phosphoric acid of "high strength and exceptional purity." Within a decade, Swann Chemical was using this acid to produce 30 million pounds annually of trisodium phosphate (TSP), which would, like Aroclors, bring high profits and health complaints from workers. TSP was later banned in fifteen states.[32]

Having lived in segregated neighborhoods west of Noble Street since the city's founding, by the late 1920s, African Americans had moved further into West Anniston. Like the Ferguson family who lived just west of the plant, African Americans closest to the plant on the east recognized the fact of pollution, even if they had not been informed of its dangers. Gordon Rodgers Jr.'s family, whose father's medical practice served the African American community, had long lived in segregated West Anniston not far from the plant when the chemical assaults that would make the location so especially dangerous emerged in the late 1920s and 1930s. (The plant would have been under Swann ownership when Gordon Jr. was in his teens.) "My momma would say, let's go into the house, they're shaking those furnaces out at Monsanto Chemical," Rodgers recalled in 2005. "They are shaking out those furnaces and they are poison," he continued. "So all my life, I've heard about the poison in the air. In this place where we used to go swimming, they claimed that they had some bad chemicals in it and said that you shouldn't swim in that place or you'll get sick."[33]

While no records log the chemical wastes leaving the West Anniston Monsanto plant in effluent or by air in the 1930s, one can only assume that, except for differences due to the scale of production, conditions were no better than during the later periods for which some measurements exist. However, clean streams were understood to be essential to public health. "The importance of controlling stream pollution was widely understood in the early 1900s," one plaintiffs' expert told a court considering the Anniston PCB situation in 2001. (Charles Holmes Herty attended a meeting in New York to discuss stream pollution as early as November 1922.)[34]

Prior to World War I, municipal sanitation efforts tended to focus on sewage, not industrial wastes, which were sometimes even regarded as "germicidal." However, as the chemical industry arose in the United States, pollution was coming to be understood in a different way, not only as bodily wastes but also as industrial discards. By the end of World War I, urban historian Martin Melosi has noted, industrial wastes were already "viewed as a major problem that affected water purity and complicated the process of sewage treatment." Alabama had been among the earliest states to pass a law against dumping in streams, with legislation governing the highly industrialized Birmingham area adopted in 1907.[35]

IN THE 1930S, concern about workplace health hazards was rising in Alabama, though the state allocated few resources to the problem. By 1936, the Alabama State Board of Health had begun to include a section on industrial hygiene in its annual report. That year, the report noted that as "industrial activities develop and multiply there will be real need for adequate health supervision for certain industries carrying health hazards for their employees. In truth, such need already exists; but has not been met because of financial straits."[36]

African Americans living in Anniston were clearly concerned about both neighborhood and occupational health, as evidenced by the work of C. Jacob Jones, who directed the first local office of the Negro Health Extension Service. Jones opened his office in Anniston in November 1930, the same year that National Negro Health Week came under the wing of the U.S. Public Health Service. Building on the work of Booker T. Washington, who had initiated National Negro Health Week fifteen years earlier, the local effort was supported financially by black churches and white business leaders.[37]

Jones used the position to advocate broadly for the physical and economic health of the black population, including that of black veterans. Together with the "colored Woman's Welfare club of West Anniston" and local "colored women's missionary circles," Jones initiated health and sanitation projects that today would be classed as "environmental"—community cleanup campaigns, gardening and raising small livestock in vacant lots, and canning and preserving homegrown vegetables. In demand as an orator and preacher, Jones took particular pains to distinguish his efforts from Communist labor organizing campaigns in the state. The stress of the job was great; Jones was hospitalized with a nervous breakdown within a little over a year. Still, working from his office at 1831 Mulberry in West Anniston, Jones managed in 1931 to conduct a health survey of industrial workers. Though Jones's findings are apparently lost, newspaper accounts suggest his work linked the public and occupational health of Anniston's black population with social issues such as poverty and unemployment with which public health was inextricably bound.[38]

By 1932, the state had created a Division of Industrial Hygiene, which announced having hired "a physician especially trained in occupational diseases and their control," who would "render a valuable and appreciated service to many of the industries in this state." The same year, the Medical Association of the State of Alabama, which was responsible for protecting public health in the state, noted, "It becomes the duty of this department to appraise the nature and extent of exposures to industrial dusts, gases, fumes, skin irritants and poisons." Monsanto had its own half-time physician, Dr. R. Emmet Kelly, based in St. Louis, who oversaw industrial hygiene at all the company's plants.[39]

BY THE TIME MONSANTO TOOK OVER the production of Aroclors in Anniston, virtually every person working with chlorinated diphenyls had complained of "a severe type of dermatitis." All of "the men were exposed to dust and fume from the hot Aroclors," noted a June 1935 Monsanto report. The company claimed, however, that "several of the men had been subject to the same exposure for three years previous to this and had suffered no ill effects." The company attributed the skin ailments to impurities in the benzol used to make diphenyl, resulting in the release of hydrochloric acid, causing a vapor that irritated the skin. Toxic effects were persistent and, the report continued, "the cure of the disease was found to be slow and difficult." As a result, at least four of the workers, including one or more African Americans, sued. (The company eventually paid up to $5,000 in damages to each claimant.)[40]

Roughly two dozen workers were involved in processing Aroclors at the Anniston plant, Monsanto's only production facility for the chemicals at the time. The organizational chart for the unit identifies four operators (or distillers) per shift. During the day shift, they were joined by a maintenance man who operated the boiler, two assistants, and four "Negro" laborers, including a shipper/janitor, a laundryman, and "two Negro helpers." Predictably, the black workers were employed in particularly hazardous jobs, drumming the chemicals, and in cleanup and in the laundry.[41]

In a study carried out in "full cooperation with the manufacturers," two Atlanta physicians working in segregated clinics at Emory University examined twenty-four men who had worked in the manufacture of chlorinated diphenyl from summer 1932 to October 1933. Jack W. Jones and Herbert S. Alden reported their findings in the *Archives of Dermatology and Syphilology* in 1936. Twenty-three of the workers had developed "an acneform eruption on the face and body."[42]

The researchers reported in detail on one particular case: "O. D., a Negro aged 26, [who] began work in the distillation of chlorinated diphenyl in

April 1930." By May 1933, the patient had severe chloracne: "Blackheads began to appear on the chest, back and lower part of the abdomen, around the navel and on the scrotum and penis." The blackheads, they reported, "became infected, discharging thick pus." Jones and Alden cited a number of studies reporting similar skin abscesses among workmen exposed to chlorobenzenes. But O. D. had other disturbing symptoms. In December 1933, "the patient complained of lassitude, loss of appetite and loss of libido," though in the doctors' opinion, O. D. "seemed in good general health." When Jones and Alden reported the case to their peers at the May 1935 annual meeting of the American Dermatological Association (ADA), they rejected O. D.'s "complaint of lassitude," claiming it "was not borne out by anything more than the usual temperament of the Negro toward work."[43]

Other doctors in attendance were not so quick to dismiss the possibility of effects that were less visible than the sores from chloracne. In the discussion following Jones and Alden's presentation, Marion B. Sulzberger raised the issue of hormonal consequences, anticipating by several decades findings that chlorinated hydrocarbons can disrupt the endocrine system. "It is interesting that many derivatives of tar are closely allied with the estrogenic hormone," said Sulzberger, "and that the estrogenic hormone must perhaps be incriminated in the production of acne vulgaris."[44]

In 1934, Frederick B. Flinn and N. E. Jarvik of the School of Public Health at Columbia University conducted further research on chlorinated diphenyls. Using chemicals supplied by Swann Research, Flinn and Jarvik conducted patch tests on rabbits to determine the impact of Aroclors on the skin. These researchers concluded that impurities in the chlorinated diphenyls were causing the skin irritations. The researchers also suggested that the liver, which is one of the body's organs for filtering toxics, was a possible site of injury. If leaks, spills, or skin contact occurred, "immediate bathing . . . should be insisted on," Flinn recommended in May 1934.[45]

The corrective steps Monsanto took as a result of the chlorinated diphenyl injuries focused less on mitigating the source of exposure than on eliminating the persons exposed. "All affected men were removed from the operation and new men substituted as rapidly as they could be trained," read the guidelines for manufacturing diphenyl derivatives. The decision to remove ailing workers, simply replacing them with "new men," had been used at the worst workplace environmental exposure of the 1930s, the Hawks Nest Incident at Gauley Bridge, West Virginia, in 1933. In that episode, crews hired by Union Carbide to build a railroad tunnel contracted the disabling lung disease, silicosis. Many of the workers were migrant laborers; African Americans comprised 75 percent of the workforce. Before the practice of sending in new teams to work under known hazards at Gauley Bridge was ended, an estimated 764 miners had died. As of June 1935, Monsanto's guidelines for the diphenyl department stated, "No man who shows a tendency to dermatitis is employed in the department."[46]

REPORTS BEGAN TO SURFACE that workers were falling ill at other factories using chlorinated hydrocarbon chemicals, including Aroclors. In the spring of 1936, three fatal instances of jaundice occurred among workers using chlorinated diphenyls and other halogenated compounds at the Halowax Corporation, headquartered in New York. Halowax was one of Monsanto's Aroclors customers and a user of related chemicals, chlorinated naphthalenes. That company enlisted prominent industrial hygienist Dr. Cecil Kent Drinker, of the Harvard School of Public Health, in the search for causes and cures.[47]

Drinker had come to Harvard Medical School in 1916. The son of wealthy Philadelphia Quakers (his father had been president of Lehigh University in Pennsylvania's industrial belt), Drinker was a brilliant student. He rose quickly through the ranks at Harvard, becoming dean of the School of Public Health. Together with his wife, Dr. Katherine Rotan Drinker, he specialized in the analysis of the impact on workers of dust and fumes; the Drinkers also co-edited the leading journal in the field, the *Journal of Industrial Hygiene*. Cecil Drinker had been one of a very few physiologists to question the use of tetra-ethyl lead in gasoline in 1925. His new laboratory techniques made him sought after by industry as a consultant on industrial poisoning.[48]

Drinker's methodology moved the study of occupational medicine out of the factory and into the laboratory. Whereas pioneers in the field like Hamilton and Schereschewsky had directly examined workplaces and workers, Drinker's researchers relied on controlled tests of chemical exposure using animals, dissecting and examining organ tissues. Though Drinker and his peers sometimes visited workplaces, the new industrial hygiene was for the most part quite removed from the bodies and experiences of individual workers.[49]

At the same time, Drinker was part of new trend in public health that, beginning in the 1930s, led to a reconsideration of the environment's importance. By 1934, Drinker was corresponding with conservationist Gifford Pinchot and was lecturing his introductory physiology students about ecology. Industrial hygienists like the Drinkers filled their labs with dust and chemical fumes, attempting to replicate factory conditions.[50]

Physiologist and industrial hygiene researcher Cecil Kent Drinker explored the health effects of chlorinated hydrocarbon chemicals in his laboratory at the Harvard School of Public Health, concluding in 1937 that "these experiments leave no doubt as to the possibility of systemic effects from the chlorinated naphthalenes and chlorinated diphenyl," as PCBs were then called. Photo courtesy of the Boston Medical Library in the Francis A. Countway Library of Medicine, Boston, Massachusetts.

By the time Cecil Drinker began studying the Halowax deaths, corporate funding of research in industrial hygiene was the norm. Drinker's mentor, Walter B. Cannon, the eminent Harvard physiologist, traced the rise of industrial hygiene as a field to World War I, with "the establishment of relations between the problems of industry and the research activities of the large medical institutions." In the immediate postwar period, Harvard had set about establishing the country's foremost program in industrial hygiene research, but it had trouble finding funding to study worker health. The Rockefeller Institute, the major foundation supporting health research at the time, did not want to become embroiled in "controversial questions concerning fatigue, length of labor day and wages in relation to standards of living and of health." Harvard then sought and obtained direct business investment in the school's public health research programs.[51]

Halowax funded the Drinkers' studies through gifts to the Departments of Industrial Hygiene and Physiology in the Harvard School of Public Health. Harvard administrators, and Cecil Drinker personally, were clearly troubled about the conflict of interest posed by corporate funding of research on occupational health and the constraints this might place on researchers. According to Hamilton, who was a colleague at Harvard, Drinker had at one time believed that studies commissioned by industry should not be published without the sponsor's approval, a posture that shifted after one company explicitly contradicted his findings in reports to the press.[52]

Drinker and his colleagues worked on the Halowax cases for at least three years, reviewing prior studies and experimenting with various compounds in the lab. On June 30, 1937, the researchers explained their findings to industry representatives and state and federal government health officials at a one-day "Symposium on Certain Chlorinated Hydrocarbons" at the Harvard School of Public Health. The meeting convened Sandford Brown and John A. Hookey of the Halowax Corporation, F. R. Kaimer from General Electric, R. Emmet Kelly from the Monsanto Chemical Company, R. R. Sayers and Louis Schwartz of the U.S. Public Health Service, and others to hear reports on the investigations.[53]

In Drinker's assessment, the persistent skin rashes resulted from exposure to Aroclors. The other companies represented at the meeting had been using Aroclors, alone and in combination with other chemicals, as insulating fluids in various processes and electrical equipment. Drinker and his colleagues had run animal tests, exposing rats to Aroclors mixtures, reviewing the possible routes of absorption of the chlorinated compounds—through the skin, by ingestion, and through breathing, which Drinker concluded was especially harmful. Many of the effects were subclinical, that is, they did not yet manifest as obvious symptoms of disease.[54]

Particularly significant was the researchers' finding that even very small amounts of the chemicals were harmful. The chlorinated compounds "are capable of causing liver injury when inhaled steadily in quite low concentrations," the researchers noted, concluding that, of various compounds tested, "chlorinated diphenyl is certainly capable of doing harm in very low concentrations and is probably the most dangerous."[55]

Drinker and his colleagues recognized that distinct Aroclors compounds behaved differently in the body. Because chlorination and toxicity were believed to be linked, Drinker was surprised to note in his 1938 report to the Monsanto Company that Aroclor 1268, "the highest chlorine figure of any compound tested by us during the past three years," was "of low toxicity," and "if handled with ordinary precautions as to ventilation should be entirely harmless to workmen. While it cannot be given an absolutely clean bill as to health, it is preferable to #4465 and #5460." Drinker's findings hinted at a problem that would trouble PCB researchers in later decades: that lower-chlorinated Aroclors might sometimes be *more* toxic than higher chlorinated compounds.[56]

Mixtures of chlorinated diphenyl and highly chlorinated naphthalenes appeared to increase toxicity over exposure to either substance alone. Drinker and his colleagues were explicit, "These experiments leave no doubt as to the possibility of systemic effects from the chlorinated naphthalenes and chlorinated diphenyl." Harvard researchers told industry representatives that the compounds could probably be manufactured without causing further serious harm, but only in very low concentrations, and with other precautionary measures in place. If, as Drinker concluded, inhalation, not skin contact, was the primary route of exposure, then individual hygiene measures such as changing clothes, washing hands, and applying cold cream were insufficient to prevent exposure. Preventing inhalation would require the company to install "precautions as to ventilation," including tanks, hoods, and other safeguards for workers, that is, engineering controls.[57]

The discussion at the Harvard meeting foreshadowed a number of industry stratagems that would forestall limitations on the sale and use of toxic chemicals. Those present observed the "conventions of confidentiality," which, as historian Christopher Sellers has noted, governed discussions of adverse chemical impact on worker health at the time of the Drinker studies. "Corporations that paid for these inquiries," wrote Sellers, "gained not just preventive knowledge about the hazards of their workplaces but significant control over their appearance in print." At the Harvard meeting, Halowax, for example, was concerned about the public relations impact on their trade name "halowaxes" and requested that the compounds be referred to only by their chemical names in order to "avoid condemnations which are both troublesome and misleading," a request that for the most part was honored. The silence was targeted, not total. Drinker and his colleagues published their findings on "certain chlorinated hydrocarbons" and a synopsis of the discussion at the 1937 meeting in the *Journal of Industrial Hygiene and Toxicology*. The studies were referenced by other scientists. (Rachel Carson cited the Drinker studies on chlorinated hydrocarbons twenty-five years later in *Silent Spring*.)[58]

At the close of the meeting, Sandford Brown of the Halowax Corporation thanked state authorities and fellow industrialists for their cooperation in the investigation. "In collaboration with the Monsanto Chemical Company we have a much more comprehensive program in view to carry on," said Brown. "Therefore we want to continue the same kind of cooperation." Brown urged discretion in sharing the toxic knowledge revealed at Harvard that day, warning that government safety inspectors sent to factories using chlorinated diphenyls and naphthalenes must be persuaded of the "necessity of not creating mob hysteria on the part of workmen in the plants." Brown also predicted, "This thing may continue, probably will continue for years."[59]

As Monsanto's medical representative at the Harvard meeting, R. Emmet Kelly, a part-time factory physician for the Queeny Plant who would come to direct Monsanto's medical department throughout much of the PCB era, was dismissive. He acknowledged that a crude experiment was under way in Monsanto's plant. "I can't contribute anything to the laboratory studies but there has been quite a little human experimentation in the last several years," said Kelly, "especially at our plants where we have been manufacturing this chlorinated diphenyl."[60]

Still, Kelly refused to admit the possibility that Aroclors could cause systemic harm to workers. "It has been our observation," he continued, "that although on one occasion we did have a more or less extensive series of skin eruptions which we were never able to attribute as to cause, whether it was an impurity in the benzene we were using or to the chlorinated diphenyl, we have never had any systemic reactions at all in our men." Kelly reasoned that if the skin eruptions could be attributed to impurities in a product's ingredients, the product itself was safe. (Industry used this strained logic repeatedly in the years ahead.) Kelly rejected the relevance and validity of animal studies, suggesting that the studies to date were inconclusive. "I don't believe that we can transpose the laboratory results into the actual humans," he said, "without paying considerable attention to the volatility of different substances and the way they are being used." (Kelly himself suggested to a colleague in 1950 that Aroclor 1268 was more toxic than even Drinker had allowed.)[61]

Given the Halowax deaths and a range of studies demonstrating "the chronic toxicity of chlorinated hydrocarbons," some of the corporate leaders meeting in Boston that day in 1937 considered, but rejected, abandoning Aroclors. "We had 50 other men in very bad condition as far as the acne was concerned," General Electric representative F. R. Kaimer said at the Harvard meeting. "The first reaction that several of our executives had was to throw [the product] out—get it out of our plant," said Kaimer, "but that was easily said but not so easily done." The electrical industry in particular had come to consider Aroclors indispensable and would continue to play a major role in keeping chlorinated diphenyls in use. Kaimer continued, "We might just as well have thrown our business to the four winds and said, 'We'll close up,' because there was no substitute and there is none today in spite of all the efforts we have made through our own research laboratories to find one."[62]

After the meeting, a Monsanto official, L. A. Watt, prepared a short synopsis of the findings for use by Aroclors salesmen. The brief report warned that "prolonged exposure to Aroclor vapors evolved at high temperatures or by repeated oral ingestion will lead to *systemic toxic effects*" and "an acneform skin eruption." Watt concluded with the researchers' recommendation that "suitable draft ventilation to control the vapors . . . , as well as protection by suitable garments from extensive bodily contact with the liquid Aroclors, should prevent any untoward effect."[63]

Monsanto officials were clearly apprised of their duty to warn workers of chemical hazards. In fact, an Alabama Supreme Court ruling on employers' duty to inform had come just two months *prior* to the Harvard meeting in a case that directly involved Monsanto. In that case, J. W. Gentry, who "was engaged in the business of making, preparing, mixing, and refining" a different chemical, TSP, had filed suit against Swann Chemical in 1934, charging that he was required to perform the duties in an unventilated room, with the windows closed or welded shut. Gentry alleged that the workroom was filled with "fumes, dust, and small particles and that the same would settle on or stick to his skin and body" and that he *"was ignorant* of the qualities of said 'Tri-Sodium Phosphate' or its effect on the human system." Gentry charged that the exposures caused him "to suffer severe sinus trouble, rheumatic pains, his nervous system broken down and disordered, his lungs impaired, caused to suffer great physical pain and mental anguish, to lose sleep, weight; and he lost his vigor and vitality and became less able to work and earn money and is permanently injured." Gentry contended that the company "knew of its effect upon the human system and knew that to inhale the same would inflame and destroy the lining of the nose and nasal cavities and throat and would cause great sores to appear upon the surface of the skin."[64]

In deciding that case in 1937—after Monsanto had taken over the company—the Alabama Supreme Court noted that "an obligation rests upon the employer to acquaint his employee with *the danger which can be ascertained by knowledge of scientific principle governing substance and processes* used in the employment, and to which in his ignorance the employee will otherwise be subject."[65]

IN MAY 1939, two years after the Harvard meeting, Cecil Drinker published a table of "Permissible Limits for the Air in Workrooms," a precautionary measure against inhaling chlorinated diphenyls and other chemicals. Drinker's recommended exposure limit of 0.5mg/m^3 provided a basis for setting maximum allowable concentrations (MACs) of certain chemicals in the workplace, though internal memos suggest that the limits on Aroclors recommended by Drinker were not enforced and expert testimony later questioned how evenly these measures were applied.[66]

In the years following the Drinker studies, Monsanto's internal communiqués with sales staff acknowledged some of the dangers of working with Aroclors. The 1944 *Monsanto Salesmen's Manual* carried a muted warning about the toxicity of Aroclors products that read: "All chlorinated hydrocarbons have measurable degrees of toxicity to the animal organism, Aroclors are no exception." The manual suggested "permissible" limits to Aroclors exposure and included detailed information about the chlorine content of various Aroclors. In its manual, Monsanto listed the following symptoms of Aroclors poisoning:

1. Pore-acne (chlor-acne) modular eruptions of the hair follicles or sebaceous glands as a result of insufficient cleansing of the skin.
2. Acute yellow atrophy of the liver in which the liver cells show swelling, hypergranulation, hyaline inclusions and vacuolation as a result of extensive exposure over long periods of time.[67]

The manual recommended that employers using Aroclors provide employees with separate lockers for work and street clothes, regularly launder employees' work clothes, enforce the removal of work clothing and washing of face and hands, and supervise showers at the end of each shift. The manual urged that "engineering controls of plant operations cannot be overemphasized," but it failed to offer specific recommendations. "It would be wise for a plant using this class of materials [i.e., Aroclors] to check their control measures with the state industrial hygiene agency," it stated. The manual advised purchasers to obtain an "insurance carrier and some competent consultant before occupational disease occur[s]."[68]

Monsanto treated Aroclors exposure as a matter of individual hygiene. Workers were to be provided daily changes of clothes, right down to a pair of "combination underwear." A 1935 Monsanto report stated that among Aroclors workers, "each man is required to rub his face, neck and areas with ['theatrical quality'] cold cream before going to work and to take a thorough bath and rub himself with alcohol after work." The report concluded that, "As a result of these precautions there has been no reoccurrence of dermatitis among the operators."[69]

The Aroclors production building at the Monsanto, Illinois, factory, was rated "a toxic department," which suggests that workers there were made aware that the chemicals were especially hazardous. Despite the understanding that hot humid temperatures exacerbated the effects of exposure to Aroclors, Monsanto abandoned issuing clean clothing for Anniston workers prior to World War II, according to Monsanto's A. C. W. Pennington. "At Anniston," reported Pennington in 1950, "no special protective clothing is provided for the Diphenyl and Aroclors operators," although leather gloves and face shields were made available. "A daily change of clothing was provided in the past," Pennington continued, "but this practice ceased before the war."[70]

AS MONSANTO OFFICIALS learned in the late 1930s how injurious Aroclors compounds could be, the company took additional steps to shape how the general public viewed chemicals. Edgar Queeny, who had begun his work in the family business in advertising, created the company's public relations department in 1939. The company's early advertising had read simply, "Fine Chemicals of Quality." In the late 1930s, the company adopted a new slogan, "Serving Industry Which Serves Mankind."[71]

Queeny himself charted the public relations department's policy, stating that "no faulty policy or product could be 'saved' by communication techniques." As Queeny outlined it, company advertising sought "to identify Monsanto with that which in an individual would be good morals and good manners. So-called good public and employe [sic] relations will be determined by the way we treat our employes [sic], by the way we treat our shareowners, by the way in which all our business and community contacts are handled."[72]

Shortly after Queeny established the new department, Monsanto embarked on its first major national ad campaign, with a series of full-page brand advertisements in *Fortune* magazine. The inaugural ad, promoting Monsanto's Massachusetts-based Plastics Division, appeared in September 1939. Titled "It's Plastics Picking Time down South," the ad depicts a field of black men, women, and children picking cotton. A smiling man shouldering a basket of cotton wears overalls, one shoulder hanging unbuttoned. A woman, foregrounded, wears a bright rag head wrap. Beaming children cavort barefoot on piles of freshly picked bolls. "Below the Mason and Dixon's line, there's a drift of white across the map," the ad copy begins, as if iconography alone would not suffice to conjure the Old South in service of the New.[73]

Advertisers deployed racial images for a variety of products in this *Gone with the Wind* era, but this ad, taken out within a few years of Monsanto's acquisition of its first plant in the Deep South, stands out for the way it links labor, synthetic chemicals, nature, and race. In choosing the starkly racist

"It's Plastics Picking Time down South." The Monsanto Chemical Company advertised its brand in *Fortune* magazine using this image in September 1939. Artwork by Felix Schmidt.

imagery of the "Plastics Picking" ad to sell chemicals, Monsanto executives clearly did not fear alienating the businessmen, North or South, who were likely to read *Fortune*.

At this time, Monsanto sought to move beyond intermediates and heavy industrial chemicals into consumer-oriented goods. The ad appears designed to appeal to the broader white public and to counter public perceptions of synthetic chemicals as inferior—and potentially hazardous—imitations. "That vegetable products are always harmless while mineral products are always harmful is the general belief of the non-scientific public," a draft of a Monsanto Chemical Works promotional piece had complained in 1930. "'Artificial' and 'synthetic' [had become] synonymous with cheap, nasty, harmful, false," Monsanto historian Hubert Kay later wrote. The 1939 ad suggests that chemistry would make affordable a "well-nigh endless" stream of possibilities for plastic consumer goods, from "steering wheels" and "colorful radio cabinets,"—"manmade materials undreamed of a generation ago . . . new articles of universal usefulness."[74]

"Plastics from *cotton*?" the advertisement queried, "Yes—from cotton, from wood pulp and from chemicals that have their genesis deep in the earth as coal and limestone, on the earth as corn, above the earth as elements of the very air itself." To position coal-tar and other chemicals as products of nature by associating them with what they were made from attempted to erase the natural-artificial divide. The ad also familiarizes synthetic chemicals by associating them with what they are made *into*: common everyday items, a fountain pen, a typewriter, glasses. Tying synthetic chemicals to the purity of "Nature," specifically "snowy cotton," again invoked race, but also rhetorically downplayed chemical harms.[75]

If Monsanto executives considered stopping Aroclors production at this time because of workers' experiences in Aroclor operations or the Drinker studies, they rejected that option. Federal regulations had begun requiring "nonflammable cooling compounds in transformers used inside buildings," so the insulating fluids were in demand. The company had expanded production of the chemicals to the Krummrich plant at Sauget soon after purchasing the Anniston plant, though the bulk of Aroclors production remained at Anniston until the late 1960s. At a meeting in St. Louis of Monsanto research directors in 1940, Executive Vice President Charles Belknap "stated that it is the intention of the Executive Committee *not* to shut down Anniston but to build up this plant as Monsanto's southern plant." Monsanto would expand production at Anniston in anticipation of the "current war boom."[76]

CHAPTER FOUR

A Technological High Command

There is need, therefore, to give a warning. —Robert M. Brown, chief,
Industrial Hygiene Section of the St. Louis Division of Health, 1947

In July 1943, James W. Irwin, assistant to the president of the Monsanto
Chemical Company, spoke at the Anniston Rotary Club Tuesday luncheon.
"In every industrial field you will find the infiltration of this ever growing
octopus—the chemical industry," Irwin said. "Now the searchlight of war
has brought out in bold relief the chemical meshes which support and reinforce all our modern industrial effort. How fortunate we are that this
unobtrusive penetration took place over the past twenty years so that today
it is strong enough to support the enormous pressure of war-time production!" Expressing a kind of chemical xenophobia, he spoke of work on "new
weapons of war" in bitter competition with "the Japanazi scientists." As
Irwin boasted of chemical firms' "unobtrusive penetration" into every field,
he unconsciously underscored masculine bravado while urging increased
national reliance on chemical expertise. Irwin called for the formation of a
national "Technological High Command," not only as a temporary force to
boost the war effort but also as one that would be maintained in peacetime.[1]

Between World War I and World War II, Anniston's economic dependence on military markets and installations deepened. After languishing
for a decade following World War I, the military camp at Anniston was
upgraded to a fort in 1929. When General Charles P. Summerall read the
order promoting the Army camp to Fort McClellan that year, Governor Bibb
Graves, former governor Kilby, Senator Hugo Black, and Congressman
Lister Hill were all invited guests. Colonel Harry Mell Ayers (who earned
his lifelong title of colonel from his appointment by Kilby to the Alabama
National Guard, not his CWS rank) and the young Edward A. O'Neal (who
had gone to work washing beakers for Swann Chemical Company in 1926
and would eventually become Monsanto's chairman of the board) served
on the committee that planned the official dedication.[2]

Anniston remained at a crossroads in the South's economic development. The city and the fort continued to grow. The Bankhead Highway and

the Florida Short Route intersected in town, and automobile traffic between Birmingham and Atlanta and between the Midwest and the Florida shore steadily increased. The Works Progress Administration (WPA) operated a camp at the fort in the 1930s; Civilian Conservation Corps (CCC) laborers built officers' quarters and the Remington Hall officers' club, all in a grand Mediterranean tile-roofed style. Georgia Calhoun, whose father was one of a number of African Americans who worked at the CCC camp, remembers playing outdoors in Choccolocco Valley as a child, racing home across the hillsides east of the fort to avoid the mock maneuvers of soldiers in training. With the outbreak of World War II, Fort McClellan became "a vast military city," training as many as 500,000 troops. In 1942, the Alabama Department of Public Health noted that because of this influx of soldiers, the sewage in Choccolocco Creek needed to be addressed.[3]

The War Department had prohibited peacetime manufacture of chemical weapons since 1922, but by 1936, as war loomed, the Army was already considering locating a "wartime white phosphorus shell-loading plant on or near the site of Swann properties" in Monsanto (Columbia), Tennessee. In 1937, the U.S. Congress accorded the American Chemical Society a special status, further strengthening the political power of the chemical industry. As military historians have noted, "The society became one of the few organizations, which include the American Red Cross, to be chartered by Congress[, taking on] a semi-official character in presenting information to government agencies."[4]

In public perception, the fortunes of the chemical industry were so linked with war production that in 1939 Monsanto president Edgar Queeny felt obliged to disavow the connection. In an Associated Press article headlined, "Says War Will Hurt Chemical Industry Here: Monsanto Head Declares Contrary Public Belief Is Erroneous," Queeny took note of an "unfortunate association in the public mind of chemicals and war." That association, Queeny indicated, "probably resulted from rapid growth and temporary large profits of the American industry in the World War, when this country was cut off from its former sources of supply in Germany and chemical prices soared." Seeking to counter accusations of price-gouging, he said, "The American market now is supplied from American sources with all necessary chemicals and at prices that in most instances are far below those prevailing in pre–World War days."[5]

Queeny's protestations notwithstanding, Monsanto had recently faced charges of price-fixing over the sale price of chlorine, a case settled by consent order in 1938. In July 1945, Monsanto pleaded no contest to two wartime indictments under the Sherman Antitrust Act for conspiring to fix prices on sulfuric acid and muriatic acid, paying fines totaling $9,000.[6]

The Monsanto Chemical Company would profit from generous contractual relationships with the federal government in World War II, much as it had in World War I. Monsanto's extensive involvement in World War II and Cold War military projects intensified an already close relationship with the U.S. Army. Chemical production and sales became a military operation.

On December 8, 1941, the day after Pearl Harbor, Monsanto's executive vice president, Charles Belknap, cabled Secretary of War Henry L. Stimson, offering the company's full services. By the end of the month, the company already "had four major war plants under construction or on the drawing boards," according to a company historian, "two for the Chemical Warfare Service, one for the Army Ordnance Department, and one for the Rubber Reserve Company, a government agency." Within a year, Monsanto reported that the company was "more than 90 per cent converted to war materials."[7]

By December 31, 1945, Monsanto had garnered nearly 2 percent of the government investment in World War II production facilities. In East St. Louis, the U.S. Chemical Warfare Service invested $5,758,613 in building, equipment, and production machinery at the "Government-Owned Contractor-Operated Plant" Monsanto ran.[8]

In addition, Monsanto personnel took on key wartime positions in government. Executive Vice President Belknap, a former Navy commander, served on the national Chemical Warfare Advisory Board. The company loaned at least four "dollar-a-year-men" to the government, paying their salaries while they worked for the War Production Board. Under strict instructions from Belknap not to use their positions for undue influence in securing procurement contracts, the loaned executives divided their time between the government and Monsanto, traveling back and forth between the nation's capital and St. Louis.[9]

Military spending subsidized the research and development of new products. Monsanto's contract work with the government involved secret projects at several locales, including Anniston. Not until after World War II, of course, did Monsanto unveil the company's role in researching and producing the atom bomb: Charles A. Thomas, of Monsanto's Dayton, Ohio, research division (formally Thomas and Hochwalt), coordinated the Manhattan Project work on refining plutonium. At its Duck River plant across Alabama's northern border in Tennessee, Monsanto produced both offensive and defensive chemicals for the armed forces, including antidotes to gas weapons. At this plant, "the Monsanto Co., under CWS contract, set up two pilot plants for the development of a large-scale method of purifying carbon monoxide [a by-product of phosphate production] and manufacturing phosgene." The Columbia Monsanto plant supplied white phosphorus to the CWS between April 1943 and April 1946.[10]

New technologies and innovative uses for existing products developed during the war would become enormously profitable for industry in the postwar period. "We had some very good technology that came out of our own work that originally began, you know, at Anniston, as part of the government contract work on chemical agents," Monsanto executive Howard K. Nason explained in 1981.[11]

Monsanto also continued to supply the government with the fine chemicals and pharmaceuticals on which the company had built its initial business and reputation. Along with other medicinals, including acetylsalicylic acid (aspirin) and the new sulfa drugs, Monsanto produced dichloroamine-T, an ingredient in triacetin, an ointment used as an antidote to mustard burns. Monsanto contributed in other ways to the war effort, providing intelligence drawn from its global operations. A Monsanto corporate sales representative, for example, passed along information about the location of sulfuric acid plants in Japan.[12]

Demand grew for products made in Anniston—calcium carbide, diphenyl, and Aroclors. New uses for Aroclors were "even more directly tied to the war effort," explained a Monsanto report on the company's contributions to the cause. "The Aroclors are used in all degaussing [demagnetizing] cables with which all merchant and fighting ships are equipped for protection against magnetic mines." This report, released after war's end, also alluded to confidential work carried out in Anniston for the U.S. Army, saying only that "an important research activity of the Company has been carried on under a secret contract with the Chemical Warfare Service."[13]

Anniston workers carried out top secret production for which workers and management received "the Navy's highest token of commendation." In 1942, the Navy presented Edgar Queeny and Charles Belknap with the Bureau of Ordnance flag and conferred Navy "E" pennants on the company's Anniston and Columbia, Tennessee, plants. Monsanto would receive numerous such awards before the close of the war.[14]

Although the Navy commended Monsanto publicly for its work at the Anniston plant, the nature of the chemicals produced for the military was not revealed. The awards simply acknowledged "the production of naval ordnance materiel vital to national defense." Monsanto cooperated with the CWS on "Silent Shrapnel" but was understandably circumspect about the work on gas weaponry. "For the Chemical Warfare Service," noted one account in February 1943, "we have carried out a confidential contract for research on poison gas." Monsanto officials in Illinois emphatically denied producing chemical weapons, though they expressed a willingness to do so. "While none of Monsanto's chlorine production is now going into such products [poison gases] and we are not manufacturing poisonous gases of any description," said one official, "as much as necessary of our chlorine capacity can be diverted to such a use should the order come."[15]

The few protective measures for Aroclors workers instituted at Anniston before the war were apparently set aside, even as production expanded. Chloracne was "a common affliction" among workers handling chlorinated hydrocarbons at other wartime facilities. The Navy experienced several deaths and a "relatively large number of acne or dermatitis cases arising during the war, in connection with fabricators of Navy cable coating materials using a mixture of Aroclor 4465 and Halowax." Memos about a postwar agreement between chemical manufacturers and the U.S. Public Health Service regarding labeling of chlorinated diphenyls and other compounds emphasized two points: "One is that this combination of chlorinated hydrocarbons is more toxic than the chlorinated biphenyl or terphenyls alone; and secondly, in this program of operations, proper working facilities and cleanliness were overlooked." Alarmingly, the afflictions went beyond the Navy shipyards to the workers' homes. "In fact," noted the memo, "the workers' wives at home even acquired acne dermatitis which was traced back to the halogenated hydrocarbon compounds."[16]

The war both increased the nation's reliance on Aroclors and disrupted research on their health effects. Among the few researchers who continued to investigate the human health effects of chlorinated compounds was Leonard Greenburg, who worked for the Division of Industrial Hygiene in the New York State Department of Labor. In 1943, Greenburg reported a large number of cases of dermatitis and "several deaths due to liver damage among workers" handling chlorinated naphthalenes and diphenyls. In general, the industrial hygiene research agenda was sharply curtailed as researchers shifted their focus to war-related fields. Cecil Drinker, for example, began designing gas masks that better protected soldiers from chemical exposures on the battlefield. Drinker's personal life also intervened. As his sister recounts, he lost a debilitating fight with alcoholism that cost him his leadership position at Harvard in 1942.[17]

By the time Monsanto president Charles Belknap resigned from the CWS Advisory Board on July 22, 1946, Monsanto's chemical contributions to the war effort had brought substantial gains: profits, positioning, and new products. Monsanto emerged from World War II ranked fifth among U.S. chemical manufacturers.[18]

The industry as a whole fared well. "Since 1925 the rate of growth of the chemical industry has been from two to three times the average of all manufactures," reported a June 1953 article in *Chemical and Engineering News*. Not only did the chemical industry experience a greater rate of increase than other industrial production, but the expansion proceeded more evenly, including during the Depression. Production and sale of industrial and agricultural chemicals expanded more rapidly than other branches of the chemical industry.[19]

As in World War I, war multiplied industry's allies and intensified reliance on expertise. "The most important legacy of the war effort for the chlorine industry," noted biologist Joe Thornton in his 2000 book on organochlorine pollution, "was the new and permanent alliance of government, industry, and academic scientists." Thornton's assessment held true for not only the chlorine industry but the chemical industry as a whole.[20]

THE TWO PRIMARY TRAINING SITES during World War II for the Chemical Warfare Service were located at Edgewood Arsenal in Maryland, and at Camp Sibert, near Gadsden, Alabama, thirty miles north of Anniston. At Camp Sibert, the Army conducted live agent training, using mustard gas, flame throwers, white phosphorus mortar shells, and other conventional weapons. The government terminated its leases for the Gadsden site on December 13, 1946. After limited cleanup by the Army, the land reverted to local government and was used as an airstrip for the municipal airport and for private homes and farms. (The site remains hazardous today.)[21]

After the end of World War II, *Anniston Star* editor Harry Ayers redoubled his efforts to retain and expand local military installations. Alabama senators Lister Hill and John Sparkman could rally little federal interest in continuing, and certainly not in expanding, operations at Fort McClellan. But with the intensification of the Cold War and on the eve of the Korean conflict, the CWS had to decide where to relocate its Chemical Corps Training School. In 1950, Ayers wrote to Senator Sparkman that "we would much prefer having the Chemical Warfare Service here to the National Guard"; the Chemical Corps, he explained, was more likely to be "permanent."[22]

The live agent training that military leaders thought necessary for training chemical soldiers was difficult to conduct near highly populated areas. The primary CWS training facility at Edgewood Arsenal was located on limited space in a densely populated area near the port of Baltimore. The Army rejected two active sites in Georgia because, according to a now-declassified report, "it is felt that the peculiar requirement of the Chemical Corps for using toxic gases, radiological and biological agents in instruction and training, makes locating this school at a station shared with other units or activities dangerous and extremely undesirable."[23]

Colonel Ayers succeeded. Military officials chose Anniston for the Army's chemical warfare training mission for some of the same reasons the site originally had attracted industry and lured military installations during earlier conflicts. The scenic area, favorable climate, and a multiyear construction campaign at McClellan during the 1930s provided the Anniston site with exceptional amenities, including fine housing for officer personnel. Cheap labor and cheap power were elements in the decision, as Army officials argued for the commercialization of gas weapons manufacture during peacetime. The Chemical Corps Training Center opened at McClellan in 1951.[24]

Monsanto, which had a representative on Colonel Ayers's Chamber of Commerce "Military Affairs Committee," continued its working relationship with the Chemical Corps. In 1951, the company constructed a special analytical laboratory for the new training school. Under a subcontract with the Universal Oil Products Company, a research consortium created by a group of oil companies twenty years earlier, Monsanto carried out "investigations and research" for the Chemical Corps and purchased construction materials, glass instruments, stopcocks, and chemicals. Some evidence suggests that Monsanto may have produced small quantities of intermediates used to make chemical warfare agents, including ingredients of the nerve agent GB, also known as sarin; a chemical engineer who worked for Monsanto in the late 1960s gave sworn deposition testimony in the Anniston PCB cases that "precursors for chemical warfare agents were produced at Monsanto in Anniston."[25]

Chemists who had played key roles in wartime research on atomic weapons took on significant postwar roles for Monsanto. Charles Allen Thomas, who had coordinated the Manhattan Project work on purifying plutonium, became president of Monsanto in 1951. Another veteran of the Manhattan Project, the renowned Harvard chemist George B. Kistiakowsky, corresponded with Phosphate Division research director Russell Jenkins about the company's biphenyl and Chemical Corps work and consulted with Monsanto chemists in Anniston in the early 1950s.[26]

ON NOVEMBER 27, 1952, a blazing wall of chemical fire officially opened the U.S. Army Chemical Corps and Training School. A *Birmingham News* reporter described the ribbon-cutting spectacular: military personnel fired "evil-looking flame-throwers," shooting "a roaring tongue of flame" at the ribbon, enveloping the entire area in a "sea of flame." An entire hillside exploded, a quite literal "ground-breaking." The initial display of fiery force was followed by a dense smoke screen. "Six 'land-mines' of deadly napalm which had been ignited, sent a half-acre wall of flame skyward. A huge column of oily-black smoke then mushroomed upward forming a double umbrella pattern associated with the 'A-bomb' blasts."[27]

Although the Army had highlighted the need to isolate chemical and biological training from other missions and dense populations, shortly after opening the school in Anniston, the Army based another mission at the site. The Women's Army Corps (WAC) School was founded in 1952, and two years later, 3,000 WAC officers and enlistees were stationed at Fort McClellan. In 1953, the two facilities—Fort McClellan and the Anniston Ordnance Depot—employed close to 12,000 people and had a $20 million payroll.[28]

Fort McClellan trainees were not strictly "chemical soldiers" but dealt with biological and radiological weapons as well. The facility supplied officers with teaching materials ranging from mimeos on "Nerve Poisons" to lesson plans on Biological Warfare and the nature and use of Chemical Agents (including "New Agents and Agents of the G Series"), the "Psychological and Public Health Aspects of Atomic Weapons," and "Decontamination." Course materials on the "Use of Chemical Agents in Riot Control" suggest that trainees were being prepared to encounter domestic as well as foreign enemies.[29]

The use of "live agents," battlefield chemicals or rough equivalents, sought to toughen the soldiers, teach self-control in response to chemical attack, and instill confidence in the effectiveness of protective gear. In an endurance test of soldiers' fitness and adherence to a masculine martial ideal, a "mustard spot," a dot of live mustard agent placed on the skin, branded each soldier with the symbol that he had endured the test of live exposure. Testing in open air was routine. (Despite protests that briefly interrupted the practice in 1970, open air testing continued in Anniston until the Chemical Corps Training School at Fort McClellan shut down in 1973.)

The laboratory at Fort McClellan was one of two sites in the country (the other was Edgewood Arsenal) authorized to make small amounts of chemicals for use in live agent testing, according to present-day Department of Homeland Security Center for Domestic Preparedness staffer John Lawry.[30]

By the U.S. Army's own account, health and safety conditions at the Fort McClellan training facility were less than ideal. Reviewing the site in 1953, Colonel Richard R. Danek, Deputy Commander of the Chemical Corps, reported that "the Decontamination Area and the new Flame Thrower Area were totally unsatisfactory." Besides scores of minor, routine infractions, such as the latrine in the Decontamination Area being "filthy and unfit," a crate in the Lab B classroom "contain[ed] liquid-chemical poison [that] should be in [a] storeroom." Danek noted that the "chemical service truck has been on deadline for months—not known when it will be operative." In the colonel's opinion, "The entire Area gave the appearance of an unregulated dumping ground."[31]

Army photos taken in the 1950s reveal that decontamination practices at McClellan consisted of dumping bags of bleach slurry and DANC (a decontaminating agent) on the live agent from a helicopter onto open terrain. The process of decontamination was itself "a definite health hazard," wrote Chemical Corps secretary Major Thomas A. Mitchell to his commanding officer in 1953.[32]

For Annistonians and Army personnel stationed at McClellan, the dangers were not only chemical but biological. In a 1952 incident that was not revealed until 1976, when *Newsday* broke the story, the U.S. Army simulated attacks using live biological agents, releasing the bacterium *Serratia marcescens* in major cities, including in the New York City Subway system, and at military installations in Key West and Panama City, Florida; three California sites; and Anniston. The release at the military installation in Anniston reportedly led to twice the normal occurrence of pneumonia in Calhoun County that year.[33]

MONSANTO EXPERIENCED TWO MAJOR ENVIRONMENTAL DISASTERS during the post–World War II period, both unrelated to its Anniston plant. On April 16, 1947, explosions immediately adjacent to the Monsanto Chemical Company in Texas City, Texas, killed 567 people, including 227 Monsanto employees. The series of explosions near the port in Galveston Bay had started with a fire in the hold of the *Grandcamp*, a ship carrying ammonium nitrate fertilizer from U.S. government ordnance plants to South America. The *Grandcamp* was docked next to the styrene plant Monsanto had purchased from the U.S. Army in 1946. The blast blew up the docks, two other ships, and nearly destroyed the Monsanto Chemical plant. Afterward, Edgar Queeny drove in from an American Airlines board meeting in New York City. R. Emmet Kelly raced to the scene from his work in Oak Ridge, Tennessee, to survey the damage and relief efforts.[34]

Legal action that followed the Texas City explosion raised ethical questions about withholding knowledge from the public of the hazards associated with the mass production of chemicals and called for greater foresight, or precaution, in the use of new chemical technologies. A civil lawsuit brought by Elizabeth Dalehite, whose husband was killed in the Texas City explosion, sought damages from the U.S. government, which were awarded by a lower court. The U.S. Supreme Court, however, upheld an appeals court's reversal of the damages. Dissenting from the high court's majority decision, Supreme Court justice Robert H. Jackson outlined a precautionary approach. Writing for two other justices, Felix Frankfurter and Alabamian Hugo Black, Justice Jackson wrote:

> We who would hold the Government liable here cannot avoid consideration of the basic criteria by which courts determine liability in the conditions of modern life. This is a day of synthetic living, when to an ever-increasing extent our population is dependent upon mass producers for its food and drink, its cures and complexions, its apparel and gadgets. These no longer are natural or simple products but complex ones whose composition and qualities are often secret. Such a dependent society must exact greater care than in more simple days and must require from manufacturers or producers increased integrity and caution as the only protection of its safety and well-being.[35]

In an early formulation of precautionary language, judges on the nation's highest court acknowledged the potential for insidious harm from new chemical technologies. Noting the particular challenge posed by new and obscure technical knowledge, Justice Jackson specifically emphasized that the public be advised of "latent harms": "Where experiment or research is necessary to determine the presence or the degree of danger, the product must not be tried out on the public, nor must the public be expected to possess the facilities or the technical knowledge to learn for itself of inherent but latent dangers. The claim that a hazard was not foreseen is not available to one who did not use foresight appropriate to his enterprise."[36] The dissenting justices' assessment that manufacturers had a duty to foresee and notify the public of such hazards acknowledged a mounting problem in the Chemical Age.

Two years later, in March 1949, Monsanto experienced another major chemical disaster, this time inside its plant at Nitro, West Virginia. Two hundred and twenty-eight workers were exposed to a chemical used in the manufacture of the agricultural herbicide 2,4,5-T, a synthetic plant hormone that contains dioxin. (2,4,5-T would later be used to make Agent Orange, the most widely used defoliant in the Vietnam War.) Health effects from the dioxin exposures later became the subject of extensive litigation.[37]

Two months after the Nitro exposures, Edgar Queeny appeared on the cover of *Forbes* magazine as one of the nation's top fifty business leaders. "Queeny Is King," read the headline.[38]

EVIDENCE OF THE EXTREME TOXICITY of Aroclors was available, but the public was not, as Judge Jackson might have wished, advised of "latent harm." Anniston's Monsanto plant was one and a half miles from the city center, considered the "outskirts" of the city. But African Americans and working-class whites had lived in neighborhoods surrounding the site since before Monsanto arrived, before Swann began producing PCBs. The most noticeable menace in the 1950s was odor emerging from the facility, probably sulfur (PCBs are largely odorless), oppressive on a hot summer day as far as ten miles away, where Georgia Calhoun lived in the Choccolocco Valley. Mothers in West Anniston brought their children indoors to escape the stench at its worst.[39]

In September 1947, Robert M. Brown, chief of the Industrial Hygiene Section of the St. Louis Division of Health, responded to an article in *The Chemist Analyst*, whose author had suggested that Aroclors be substituted for sulfuric acid as an insulating fluid in manufacturing processes. The health chief wrote plainly: "There is need, therefore, to give a warning. For the toxicity of these compounds has been repeatedly demonstrated, both from the standpoints of their absorption from the inspired air, as well as from their effects in producing a serious and disfiguring dermatitis when allowed to remain in contact with the skin." While Brown did not oppose outright the use of Aroclors, he advised caution and clear labeling about the chemicals' toxic effects. "In recommending the use of a material with which is associated a potential hazard from the health standpoint," wrote Brown, "it is very important that the possible consequences be presented together with recommendations for correct handling."[40]

Shortly after Brown's comments appeared in print, Clarence Barbre, of the Krummrich plant, Monsanto's only other production site for Aroclors, forwarded them to Russell Jenkins, director of Phosphate Division research at the Anniston plant. Jenkins was already clearly concerned about the dangers associated with inhaling Aroclors fumes. He had consulted other chemists about Aroclors off-gassing but the worries gained little traction. In the plant newsletter, the Monsanto *Record Buster*, Monsanto commended the biphenyl workers for their safety record in May 1953.[41]

In a 1955 report on polychlorinated biphenyl production at Anniston and Sauget, company official E. Mather noted that "since the Aroclors are such effective solvents, they damage, and are damaged by, ordinary paints, lacquers, [and] insulating varnishes." By now, Monsanto officials were aware that chlorinated diphenyl compounds were capable of causing serious harm to workers, even death. Pursuant to an agreement with the U.S. Public Health Service, apparently prompted by the Navy deaths during World War II, Monsanto had begun to label Aroclors products as having "possible toxic effects."[42]

Labeling the products may have been implemented initially only at Sauget, however, not Anniston. As Mather put it, "Packages of Aroclors leaving the Krummrich plant bear a label calling attention to possible toxic effects."[43]

At the same time, despite having questioned the validity of animal testing to establish the hazards of human exposure, Monsanto commissioned its own animal studies of Aroclors to establish "safe limits" of human exposure. Conducted by the Medical Department at the Kettering Laboratories in Cincinnati, Ohio, at a cost of $15,000 to $20,000, these were short-term studies—not the kind of long-term toxicological studies that would have been necessary to gauge the impact of chronic exposure, or "latent harms." Alert to the prospect that setting exposure limits would have little persuasive value if the company were sued for bodily injuries, Emmet Kelly wrote in 1955 to a colleague in London: "MCC's [Monsanto Chemical Company's] position can be summarized in this fashion. We know Aroclors are toxic but the actual limit has not been precisely defined. It does not make too much difference, it seems to me, because our main worry is what will happen if an individual developes [sic] any type of liver disease and gives a history of Aroclor exposure. I am sure the juries would not pay a great deal of attention to MACs [maximum allowable concentrations]."[44]

In the 1950s, Monsanto expanded significantly its production capacity at Anniston, adding two more chemical products. A chlorine plant, established in part in anticipation of military demand for the chemical, was pleted in 1952. On April 16, 1957, another disaster occurred at Nitro, time at Monsanto's parathion plant. The explosion at Nitro—a city ʟnat began as a wartime "boom town"—killed eight people and destroyed the production area. The insecticide parathion interferes with nerve and brain function. Even short exposures can "cause death, loss of consciousness, dizziness, confusion, headaches, difficult breathing, chest tightness, wheezing, vomiting, diarrhea, cramps, tremors, blurred vision, and sweating." Effects can last for months. Rather than discontinuing manufacture of parathion, Monsanto constructed a new processing facility at Anniston, moving the operation closer to the chlorine supply and to agricultural markets. (Until the mid-1980s, Monsanto produced the pesticide in Anniston, earning the city the title of the "continent's parathion capital" in 1983.)[45]

In 1958, Monsanto Anniston discontinued one highly toxic chemical, Compound 1080, because it was not profitable. A powerful rodenticide, Compound 1080 causes convulsive, painful deaths in animals within hours, and sometimes within minutes, of exposure to even small amounts. Though touted as one of the company's "firsts," "it wasn't making much money and was a terrible nuisance," said one Monsanto sales executive. "It just was not paying off for the company at all." In 1958, Monsanto spun off the production of Compound 1080 to Tull Chemical Company, which still produces the chemical in Anniston, largely for sale outside the United States; U.S. use of the chemical was banned (with rare exceptions) in 1972.[46]

IN THE POST–WORLD WAR II PERIOD, Monsanto began repositioning its chemical products, until then largely little known industrial intermediates, as helpful companions in the home. Monsanto's public relations arm directly appealed to its growing consumer market. Among the opening day attractions at Disneyland in 1955 was the Monsanto "Hall of Chemistry." Two years later, Monsanto unveiled an all-plastic model "Home of the Future" at Disneyland. A mobile display called the "Plastics Fair" familiarized shoppers with the Monsanto brand at department stores around the nation. Through these skillful advertising campaigns designed to allay consumer skepticism about and resistance to synthetic chemicals, such products were transformed from dirty coal-tar derivatives to disinfectants safe enough to clean the modern home.[47]

During this phase, Monsanto continued to enlist the support of individuals with powerful political connections. The trustees elected Herbert Clark

Hoover Jr., son of former president Herbert Hoover and himself a former undersecretary of state, to the Monsanto board in 1958. Daniel Forrestal, son of James V. Forrestal, undersecretary of the Navy during World War II and the nation's first secretary of defense under President Harry S. Truman, joined Monsanto that year and was director of public relations until 1974. They joined a team of men who exemplified the corporate culture of Monsanto. Many of them came from the Anniston plant.[48]

The men from Monsanto's Phosphate Division, based in Anniston, assumed a disproportionate number of leadership positions in the postwar period and in many ways set the tone at the corporate level. Whether "the sand and gravel boys" were so named because they dealt in high-volume heavy chemicals, including the department's extensive work with Aroclors and other organochlorines, or because many of their other products were made from phosphate rock, the nickname stuck. Many had been managers under Swann, including Chairman of the Board Edward A. O'Neal, Executive Vice President Robert R. "Rush" Cole (who left a stylish Victorian home on Tyler Hill for a position in St. Louis), Senior Vice President John L. Christian, President Edward J. Bock, and Vice President Felix Noble Williams.[49]

At a time in the 1950s when corporate aviation signaled a company's wealth, prestige, and capacity for innovation, Monsanto began buying jets and hired Ralph C. Piper, a World War II pilot and a "pioneer in executive aviation," to fly them. Piper's recollections of the hard-drinking, hard-selling corporate sales culture of the era were recorded as part of a Monsanto oral history project in 1981, in conversation with fellow employee James McKee. Piper recalled one time that Edgar Queeny had so many martinis he could not remember on which of two Monsanto corporate planes he had left his change of clothes. McKee and Piper reminisced fondly about Felix Noble Williams, who in 1923 reportedly came to his interview for a job at the Swann Chemical plant in Anniston driving a red Stutz Bearcat and wearing a white flannel suit. Williams rose to head the Plastics Division in 1944 and served on the Monsanto Board of Directors from 1947 to 1964.[50]

"Remember the night we were in New Orleans with Felix and the Directors of the Society of the Plastics Industry," McKee asked, "and there were no hotels to be had and we set up beds in the old airport upstairs on the top floor?"[51]

"Yes, I do," said Piper.

"And then half the crowd never got into bed and we were ready to leave for St. Louis when three or four taxis pulled up and they all got out," McKee continued. "Felix was leading the singing of 'Onward Christian Soldiers' and they had a whole bunch of hookers with them."

"I remember that," said Piper. "Nobody got any sleep."

Another incident, in California, illustrated the masculine swagger and bravado that characterized the 1950s corporate élan. In an excursion reminiscent of Theodore Swann's cross-country rail expedition to the Rose Bowl in 1931, Felix Williams organized a "gate crashing of the highest degree" at the Hollywood Bowl. On Easter Sunday, with Piper at the helm, Williams flew a group of Monsanto execs from a plastics convention in Santa Barbara to Los Angeles for the sunrise service at the stadium. Everyone wondered why Williams had twelve boxes of long-stemmed Easter lilies delivered to the plane.[52]

"We didn't have tickets" to the Easter Sunday event, Piper recalled, but Williams marched the group and their cargo of Easter lilies past the security barriers, through the gate at the Hollywood Bowl and straight to the front row. "People would come in and have tickets and say, 'These are our seats,'" Piper continued. "All he said was, 'We have the Easter lilies,' and that did it," said Piper. "Hollywood celebrities were everywhere. And just like Hollywood, on cue rises up the sun, right past the Hollywood big cross that is out there, you know, and it was the most beautiful production, you'd think it was some director who had timed all this and it was working out. And here we sat with the Easter lilies. And that's how we got into the Hollywood Bowl—crashed it—first class."[53]

Under Edgar Queeny's leadership, Monsanto's corporate net worth grew from $12 million in 1928 to $805 million thirty years later. The workforce was small when Edgar took over, roughly 2,000 employees at all plants combined. By 1960, Monsanto employed 35,000 workers worldwide.[54]

For the thirty-plus years he remained at the helm, Edgar Queeny was the personality of Monsanto, said Piper. Queeny was "a Fourth of July American," according to Monsanto vice president Frank Curtis. He also was an outspoken critic of attempts to strengthen government regulation. In 1943, he published an anti–New Deal manifesto, *The Spirit of Enterprise*, which had a brief run as a national nonfiction bestseller. Queeny's wartime condemnation framed government involvement in monetary policy, and any aspect of private enterprise, as "an alien, malignant collectivism," managing in one phrase to skewer government regulation as foreign, disease-like, and communistic. Ironically, the critique appeared as Monsanto was, by its own account, directly benefiting from government procurement and tariff protection.[55]

When not managing Monsanto's growing holdings, Queeny cultivated his reputation as a filmmaker and naturalist. Some of the films celebrated salmon bounding upstream and prairie birds taking flight, species and habitats that would be among those most threatened by his company's products. Queeny also produced a series on central West Africa in collaboration with the American Museum of Natural History. The safari "documentaries," which opened to large crowds at first-run theaters across the nation, earned him the company nickname of "The Big White Father."[56] The "natural history" films give insight into both his conceptions of nature and the racial imaginary of many whites at midcentury.

In one of the most prominent and commercially successful of the films, *Latuko* (1951), Queeny depicted the Sudanese as "a picturesque and primitive congregation." The film's narrator described Queeny's vision of the scene: "There was much of the primeval here, something sinister and shadowed. These were the faces of equatorial Africa, the somber, savage look of a people who since time forgotten had lived by the instinctive law of their own untamed wilderness." Queeny cast his African "actors" as both closer to "Nature" and in opposition to "Science." In these films, "nature is both close and harsh"; Africans are "stark, savage and pagan." West African students living in the United States and Sudanese government officials condemned the films, which, as historian Amy Jane Staples has noted, portrayed Africans as "incapable of full participation in civilization and ultimately, of self-government."[57]

Queeny had given only a glimpse of his personal views about racial equality in the United States in his 1943 book *The Spirit of Enterprise*. "The Negro race in America has been denied social equality," Queeny acknowledged, though he criticized those who were overly "impatient for results."[58] Edgar Queeny's films reflected a colonial outlook just as action to overturn racial discrimination was stepping up in the United States.

BY THE LATE 1950S, despite the absence of imminent war, proponents of chemical warfare as an element of U.S. military strategy seized on a new argument. With rhetoric that took advantage of the rising antipathy to nuclear weapons in the aftermath of Hiroshima and Nagasaki, Chemical Corps leaders wrote, "In the time of a nuclear stalemate, the military planners are forced to turn to another weapon." A small but vocal antinuclear lobby that emerged in the late 1950s had been pushing political leaders to reject atomic weapons testing. Public sentiment was influenced by news that Strontium 90, a radioactive artifact of nuclear testing, had made its way into American children's baby teeth. The Soviet Union had a chemical arsenal. Military planners urged political leaders to reassess their strategies for the use of chemical weapons—including the newly available nerve agents—in the event of war.[59]

To counter public concern over the use of toxic agents on the battlefield, the Army's chief of research and development launched a public relations effort designed, as one reporter summed it up, "to make chemical weapons more respectable." The new classes of nerve weapons were promoted with much the same rhetoric used to promote their predecessors. Chemical weapons were not "barbarous" but "humane." Chemical weapons, Pentagon consultants argued, aimed to "eliminate death from war."[60]

As the Cold War escalated, U.S. production of chemical weapons increased. Between 1961 and 1964, during the Kennedy and Johnson administrations, the annual U.S. military budget for chemical and biological warfare tripled.[61]

On April 9, 1960, Alabama governor John Patterson joined Colonel Harry M. Ayers, civic leaders, and military brass in Anniston on the ninth anniversary of the opening of the Chemical Corps Training School to celebrate a major new development: the Army would transfer the U.S. Chemical Corps Command to Anniston, making Fort McClellan "the free world's largest training center for chemical, biological, and radiological warfare." On Fort McClellan's "Dixie Day" celebration three months later, Governor Patterson returned with Governor Ross Barnett of Mississippi. The two segregationist governors watched proudly as the Thirty-first Infantry, "the Dixie Division," marched in an "impressive parade of 8,000 men, with division aircraft flying overhead."[62]

Within two years, the Army had moved the entire Chemical-Biological-Radiological (CBR) Corps Command to Anniston. Around that same time, the Army also chose Anniston as an ideal site for chemical weapons storage. According to Michael Abrams, public affairs officer with the Anniston Chemical Agent Disposal Facility (ANCDF), military decision makers chose Anniston as a storage site for chemical weapons in the 1960s because it offered access to seaports via rail but lacked the vulnerability of coastal towns. "There was a good workforce here," continued Abrams. "There was already a military installation here. The military was already welcomed in 1942, the Depot was opened and the initial mission was to store weapons."[63]

The "influx of new soldiers" to Fort McClellan in late 1961 brought complaints about inadequate lab facilities but "no racial trouble," remarked the *Birmingham News*. Soon thereafter and unbeknownst to all but a select cadre of Anniston residents, the Anniston Army Depot became home to a sizeable tonnage of deadly nerve agents, as one of eight sites quietly selected to warehouse the nation's growing chemical weapons stockpile. Secrecy surrounded the depot's new mission; people were at risk, but they did not know it. By the time President Dwight Eisenhower warned the nation in 1961 of the dangers of overdependence on the military-industrial complex, Anniston's technological high command was already in place.[64]

CHAPTER FIVE

War in a Time of Peace

Place is never simply "place" in southern writing, but always a site where trauma has been absorbed into the landscape. —Patricia Yaeger, *Dirt and Desire* (2000)

Imogene and Grover Baker were already on a solemn mission on Mother's Day, 1961. Returning from a funeral in Birmingham, the Bakers were driving down picturesque Highway 202 when they noticed smoke and flames up ahead, just outside Anniston. Coming closer, Imogene Baker could make out the silhouettes of passengers stumbling out of a vehicle, nearly blinded by the haze and fumes. "By the time we stopped, some of them were laying outside the bus and the bus was burning," she said. She got out of the car to help. "My husband went up the road further and parked the car," she said with obvious emotion more than forty years later. "He was coming back. I started to come across the road. They tried to run over me and he jerked me out of the way," Imogene recounted. Sturdy and indomitable, dressed in her Sunday best, Mrs. Baker would not be deterred. As the highway patrolmen approached, she heard local whites taunting the Freedom Riders and shouting, "Let 'em burn!"[1]

The bus was one of two traveling through the South challenging Jim Crow segregation in public transportation facilities. Sponsored by the Congress of Racial Equality (CORE), the carefully selected group of nonviolent activists was testing the U.S. Supreme Court's 1960 decision in *Boynton v. Virginia*, which extended the Court's 1946 ruling banning segregation on interstate buses and trains to include station waiting rooms, restrooms, and restaurants. The Greyhound bus, which left Washington, D.C., on May 4, 1961, carrying nine Freedom Riders and three journalists, had already met with violence. In Rock Hill, South Carolina, attackers beat two passengers, one black and one white—seminary student John Lewis from Troy, Alabama, and Albert Bigelow, from Cos Cob, Connecticut—and police arrested a third person for using the restroom labeled "white" in the Greyhound station. Riders James Peck, who was white, was beaten, and Henry "Hank" Thomas, a nineteen-year-old African American student from Howard, was hauled into jail for attempting to order hamburgers at the station

One of the most violent attacks on nonviolent civil rights protesters occurred just four miles west of Anniston on Mother's Day, 1961, when a white mob firebombed a Freedom Riders bus near Forsyth's Grocery. Freedom Rider Hank Thomas, foreground center, described the assault during the groundbreaking for the Freedom Riders Park in October 2012, saying: "The Klan attempted to burn us alive, and they brought their wives and their children to watch." Photo by Joseph Postiglione. Courtesy of the Birmingham Civil Rights Institute.

in Winnsboro, South Carolina. But these assaults, terrifying as they were, turned out to be skirmishes compared to what was to come. On Sunday morning, May 14, the Riders departed Atlanta heading west to Birmingham. A second bus, a Trailways, left Atlanta just behind the Greyhound, carrying more Freedom Riders headed for Alabama.[2]

In the hot glare of that Sunday afternoon, the first bus pulled up beside the yellow-beige brick Greyhound station on Gurnee Avenue between Tenth and Eleventh in downtown Anniston, and was immediately surrounded by an armed mob of about fifty whites. Anticipating Klan violence, the FBI had notified the Anniston police chief well before the Freedom Riders' arrival, but no police presence was visible. The white throng battered the bus with pipes and chains as it sat trapped at the Greyhound depot.[3]

After police finally arrived, the driver was able to depart. Many members of the mob pursued in cars. With its tires damaged in the station assault, the Greyhound bus was struggling as it rounded the Monsanto curve, passing the chemical plant. The chase continued along the Birmingham Highway,

Highway 202, until pursuers forced the bus to a halt in front of Forsyth and Son's Grocery just short of Bynum, near the Anniston Army Depot, about five miles west of Anniston. There, a crowd had already gathered and the mob descended again, smashing more windows and lobbing a fire bomb into the bus. Again, police appeared belatedly. Ell Cowling, a plainclothes Alabama trooper stationed on the bus, blocked the attackers from entering, but billowing smoke soon forced all of the passengers from the flaming vehicle. "The Klan attempted to burn us alive," Hank Thomas said later. "They brought their wives and their children to watch."[4]

As the first black residents of Anniston to appear at the scene, Grover and Imogene Baker set to work, offering aid to the smoke-incapacitated Riders. "One lady lying outside the bus said, 'Give me some water,'" Mrs. Baker recounted. The white woman Baker asked for water at a nearby house refused. "I knocked on the next door," Baker explained, and there the woman just pointed to a nearby hydrant. "There was a jar sitting out there so I filled it up and I started washing the lady's face," Baker recalled. "Someone ran up and said, 'Don't wash their faces, let them die.'"[5]

Also aiding the Riders was twelve-year-old Janie Forsyth, daughter of the white family who ran the grocery, who brought cups of water to the victims of the mob. "I knew what I did wasn't the popular thing among my neighbors," Janie Forsyth McKinney said, "because they were the ones doing this." Some of the Riders were seriously injured; they were taken to Anniston Memorial Hospital, where they were met by more Klansmen and where, as one rider described to historian Ray Arsenault, they "found the medical care in Anniston almost as frightening as the burning bus."[6]

Meanwhile, the second bus had arrived at the Trailways station at Ninth and Noble and was ready to depart with seven Freedom Riders (four black passengers, seated at the front of the bus, and three whites) as well as twenty-three other white passengers, several of whom were Alabama Klansmen who had boarded in Atlanta. Forewarned of the violence ahead, the driver refused to leave the station unless the black passengers moved to the back. The Klansmen took this opportunity to begin punching and beating the Freedom Riders, throwing them over the seats, and kicking one older white Rider, Walter Bergman, repeatedly. Again, Anniston police failed to intervene.[7]

Police made no arrests at either scene. Freedom Riders faced further beatings in Birmingham, Montgomery, and in Jackson, Mississippi, where they were arrested for entering the "whites only" waiting room. Meanwhile, scores of additional Freedom Riders mobilized. In late May, representatives of CORE were served, without reprisals, at both the Greyhound and Trail-ways stations in Anniston. And on May 29, President John F. Kennedy issued an executive order banning segregation in interstate transportation facilities.[8]

The Freedom Riders' actions were part of a coordinated national campaign, deploying nonviolent tactics to speed the pace of racial reform. Their presence made the violence of segregation visible to the nation, catalyzing change in the South. Many of the Riders came from northern cities and campuses, but they found supporters like Imogene and Grover Baker in southern black communities such as Anniston with long-standing indigenous movements for racial change. The bus burning cast in sharp relief Anniston's constituencies: a sizeable black population straining against segregation, a sector of whites willing to meet any renegotiation of racial hierarchies with violence, and white civic leaders who sought to maintain a favorable business climate (characterized by low wages and labor peace) and control racial advancement. Alabama courts had blocked a moderate path to change, enjoining the NAACP from operating in the state in 1956.[9]

By the time of the bus burning in Anniston, nonviolent student civil rights protests had spread across the South. Students had been sitting in at lunch counters, beginning in Greensboro, North Carolina, in February 1960. Similar actions in Richmond, Nashville, and Atlanta spawned the Student Nonviolent Coordinating Committee (SNCC) later that spring. Students had been in the forefront in Anniston, too. On January 5, 1961, 400 black students from nearby Talladega College marched from the Carver Center to Gurnee Avenue in downtown Anniston protesting two separate Klan beatings, one of a black cab driver and another of a black student and custodian from the college. The bus burning only reinforced the resolve of Anniston's black leaders, who crafted a strategy to bring about change in their city, one that moved beyond the unrecorded resistances of daily life and into the public arena of electoral campaigns and segregated facilities. They worked under the constant threat of violence.[10]

Since the 1954 *Brown v. Board of Education* decision, an active white terrorist network had been based in Anniston, recruiting members and exporting racial violence to other Alabama cities. "Anniston was a violent place," said Rev. Nimrod Quintus Reynolds, who in 1960 became pastor of Seventeenth Street Baptist Church, one of the oldest African American churches in Anniston. "Anniston was the hotbed of the Klansmen," said Reynolds, "a feeder for Birmingham and the other areas." There was also a White Citizens' Council in the city. To Rev. J. Phillips Noble, the white minister who pastored the First Presbyterian Church from 1956 to 1971, it was clear that "Anniston had the capacity for racial violence that was equal to any other community in the South."[11]

The Bakers' courage in stopping to aid the Freedom Riders on that day in 1961 had been shaped by early experiences of hardship and resistance in rural counties of Georgia and Alabama. Moving from Heard County, Georgia—where she had been born in 1919—to Randolph County, Alabama, Imogene left school at the eighth grade to work for whites who ran a local dairy. "The pay was to give me milk," she explained. "Miz Alice would pour my gallon thing half full of milk and pour the rest to the cats in the yard. She knew mama had five kids. Yet she would give it to the cat in place of filling my container up—and after I'd worked all the morning for her."[12]

For the Bakers, embracing protest was not new. Their experience showed that much of the daily resistance to Jim Crow happened between individuals—outside the written record or media spotlight. Early in their married life, they had stood up against the southern sharecropping system. When the farmer who owned the land they worked demanded half of their corn harvest, they challenged the terms usually offered to sharecroppers. "I said, 'Now Grover can stay here and work with you, but I'm not working on half,'" recounted Imogene Baker. After that, "Grover worked for him, so he paid Grover by the day," she explained. "I cooked in the house for them. It was some lovely times and it was some bad times."[13]

After moving to Anniston, Grover Baker worked briefly for Monsanto. His wages were paid in cash, in an envelope of two-dollar bills, evidence to local merchants of the source of their customers' pay. Grover Baker left that work for the Union Foundry, first stacking iron pipes, then working at the tar pit. By the 1960s, he had moved to another foundry, M & H Valve, and was active in the segregated local of the International Molders and Foundry Workers Union, Local 414.[14]

After the Riders had come and gone, the Bakers began receiving threats. "After the bus burning and all," said Imogene Baker, "when we returned home, there was a telephone call. And they said, 'Imogene Baker, we are going to bomb your house.'" She did not recognize the caller's voice. "It has been a puzzle to me," she said. The phone rang again. "My husband answered and they repeated the same thing again." The Bakers' son answered the phone the next morning. David Baker later recalled the threat, "'Nigger, we gone bomb your house tonight at ten o'clock.'" David remembered, "It had come out that my father and mother were the first ones to the Freedom Riders' bus."[15] His parents' steadfastness in the face of threatened retaliation would inspire David's early civil rights activism and undergird his later involvement in the environmental justice fight.

The day after the bus burning, Mrs. Baker "went on to work," reflected her son David, "and we had to go on to school." That evening, to be safe, the children were sent to their grandmother's house. West Anniston neighbors organized to provide protection for the Baker family "and guarded our house for about three days," said David. (Armed self-defense played a greater role in the nonviolent southern civil rights movement than often is acknowledged.) "That was a stand I always appreciated—and marked myself after," he said.[16]

When Imogene Baker told her boss, Dr. Tom King, about the calls threatening her family, he picked up the phone and dialed. "I don't know who he was talking to," she recalled. But she overheard him saying, "'You leave Imogene alone. She don't know a thing in the world about this.' I wondered and wondered who was he talking to," said Imogene. "I don't know if he was talking to the policeman or the Ku Klux Klan." The phone calls stopped.[17]

THE BRUTALITY UNLEASHED ON MOTHER'S DAY, 1961, was part of a long history of violent defense of Jim Crow. Segregation perpetuated exclusion from public spaces and blocked access to knowledge, health care, and political power, and it confined blacks to less desirable, often polluted neighborhoods, as it had done for decades. The movement that arose to resist segregation reshaped Anniston's political landscape and produced local African American activists who would later tackle environmental injustice.

Racial violence had long plagued north Alabama. In Reconstruction-era Cross Plains, on the post–World War I streetcars, violence exploded at times in places to compel the segregation of public space, to keep the color line from being crossed, to enforce political power and control. In 1931, north of Anniston, near the Tennessee line, the arrests of nine young men on false charges of rape in what became known as the Scottsboro Boys cases inflamed the region. In 1936, the near lynching in Anniston of Roosevelt Collins, who faced attempted rape charges, was blocked only by the intervention of the Alabama National Guard.[18]

Racial violence—and the resistance to it—had often been intertwined with the presence of the U.S. military. Some of Anniston's most violent racial incidents had involved military personnel or had occurred on or around the city's military installations, including the 1898 "Battle of Anniston" at Camp Shipp and the 1920 hanging of Sergeant Edgar Caldwell. The military presence in the South had both reinforced and undermined Jim Crow. After

President Truman's 1948 order desegregating the armed forces, the U.S. Army provided an avenue for advancement for black soldiers. The Army implemented racial changes before many local institutions did so. The base school at Fort McClellan was desegregated in 1963, a few years prior to desegregation of the public schools in Anniston and Calhoun County. But periodic racial unrest continued at area military installations. After a November 1971 incident, more than 100 black WACs and GIs had been placed under arrest for various charges, including failure to work, resisting arrest, and threatening an officer. Employment discrimination by the Army and its civilian contractors at the Anniston Army Depot would remain a focus of civil rights protest up into the late 1980s.[19]

Black protest had a long local history, dating at least to Caldwell's hanging and the formation of the Anniston–Hobson City branch of the NAACP in 1919. When Aaron Henry, who would go on to lead the Mississippi NAACP, came from Coahoma County, Mississippi, to Anniston for basic training with the 381st Infantry Division at McClellan in 1943, he found an active NAACP branch in town.[20]

After World War II, formal activism in Anniston grew, as black soldiers demanded the rights of citizenship. African American soldiers returning to Anniston, like black veterans elsewhere, sought to spread democracy at home. Yet German prisoners of war stationed at Fort McClellan had experienced better treatment than returning black veterans. Gordon A. Rodgers Jr. practiced dentistry after World War II just a block down Cooper Street from Seventeenth Street Baptist Church. He followed in the footsteps of his father, who had helped establish the local NAACP branch after World War I. Both father and son used their relative independence as professionals serving the segregated community to work for expanding African American rights. Gordon Rodgers Jr. and others organized a black American Legion post and later formed the Calhoun County Negro Veterans Organization to press for GI benefits. "The idea of segregation wasn't quite so strong here in Anniston as in Birmingham or Tuskegee," Rodgers said. However, in the Anniston of the 1940s, Rodgers explained to historian Catherine Fosl, "black people were reluctant to identify openly with any movement."[21]

Even before the 1960s, civil rights activism was beginning to have an impact on national policy. The passage of the Civil Rights Acts of 1957 and 1960 signaled a federal willingness to ease restrictions on voting, though the laws had limited practical effect. At the same time, the Cold War would be an important factor in loosening segregation's grip. The international pressure that resulted from press coverage of the scenes in Anniston,

Birmingham, and elsewhere provided added impetus for federal action, if only to improve the nation's image abroad.[22]

NINE WHITE MEN WERE INDICTED in the assault on the Freedom Riders. Among them was Kenneth Adams, a service station owner and member of the KKK. Adams, the most active local perpetrator of racially motivated physical assaults, carried out violent acts largely unpunished for nearly two decades. (Adams Oil Company's main station was located on Eulaton Road just a mile west of the Monsanto plant.) In 1956, Adams was one of three men who assaulted singer Nat "King" Cole at a concert at Municipal Auditorium in Birmingham, but he was never charged for the attack. In 1960, Adams was listed as the agent in Alabama for Dixie Klans Inc., Knights of the Ku Klux Klan, based in Chattanooga, Tennessee.[23]

In the fall of 1961, Judge Hobart Grooms acquitted Adams on a directed verdict of "not guilty" for lack of evidence, one of two acquittals, before declaring a mistrial in the seven remaining cases. Georgia attorney J. B. Stoner, also a segregationist, had represented Adams at trial. Five of the men pleaded "no contest" to lesser charges the following year. Eventually, in 1970, Adams was convicted of assault with intent to murder eighteen-year-old Albert Lee Satcher. At the corner of Twelfth and Clydesdale, Adams had shot the black teenager at close range, in the arm and the abdomen, after Albert asked him for jumper cables to restart his stalled car. Adams had replied that he had no jumper cables but that he "had something to kill niggers with." Albert Satcher survived the assault. An all-white jury sentenced Adams to just two years in prison.[24]

Kenneth Adams may have been the most publicly identified and physically violent Klan activist in Anniston, but he was not alone. When Adams ran for Calhoun County sheriff shortly after the bus burning, he garnered 13 percent of the vote. Supremacist pamphleteer Charlie Keyes published racist tracts, including The Keyes Report, throughout the 1950s, and Asa Earl Carter headed the North Alabama Citizens Council. Carter, who hailed from Oxford, Alabama, has been described as "one of the most rabid and dangerous racists in the post–World War II South." Identified by historian Dan Carter (not a relative) as "one of Alabama's two most prominent Klansmen," Asa Carter often left direct participation in physical violence to subordinates. He and Robert Shelton are believed to have orchestrated Adams's assault on Cole. As one of the foremost ideologues of the white supremacist movement in Alabama, Asa Carter found a much more powerful niche at the state level, as advisor and speechwriter for George Wallace's 1962 gubernatorial campaign.[25]

The profane rhetoric of race cannot be ascribed to a fringe few. Even when led by relatively moderate whites, Anniston was a place in which the existing racial order was backed up by the threat of physical violence. White civil rights activist Anne Gambrell McCarty Braden grew up in a privileged family and spent her teens in Anniston. In her 1958 memoir, *The Wall Between*, Braden recounted a conversation she had in the late 1930s with a "Southern white man a generation older than mine. He was one of the kindest men I had ever known. He was a leader in his church and in the community, and no man in need—friend or stranger, black or white—who ever went to him for help was turned away." But he believed in segregation "with a violence that squared with nothing else in his personality," Braden wrote. The two argued over a proposed antilynching law. "Suddenly," wrote Braden, "in the heat of the argument, he said, 'We have to have a good lynching every once in a while to keep the nigger in his place.'"[26]

The persistence of violence and the lack of effective prosecution against violent acts into the 1960s suggest that a cohort of whites still shared a similar view: they would not dream of committing such an act but nonetheless countenanced violence to maintain segregation. Not until many years later did Braden reveal the identity of that white southern gentleman; he was her father. "I thought to myself then and have often wondered since," she wrote, "*What could segregation do to the Negro as terrible as the thing it had done to this white man?*"[27]

By the time Braden wrote these lines in the mid-1950s, *Anniston Star* publisher Harry Mell Ayers had been running his hometown newspaper for more than forty years. As a New Dealer, Ayers considered Klan members like Adams to be extremists; by contrast, Ayers was a moderate. In April 1956, the American Society of Newspaper Editors (ASNE) invited Ayers to its annual meeting in the nation's capital to speak on a panel addressing the "problems of integration" from the vantage point of the press. His speech jolted the other journalists in attendance. Giving public voice to opinions that were held privately by many of his white contemporaries, Ayers began by defending Jim Crow. Since the Civil War, "We have had to lift ourselves up by our bootstraps," he claimed on behalf of white southerners, "and also carry on our back at the same time an illiterate and sometimes vicious people." Articulating a standard defense of school segregation, he said, "We do not want integration in the schools of Alabama, because we have a hard enough time trying to lift ourselves educationally up to the average of the United States." Ayers then launched into a diatribe purporting to explain the Negro race to the northern press corps. "Negroes are dirty, are unreliable, are liars," he flatly declared, rationalizing segregation through perverse and long-standing claims about dirt and disease. Citing a Calhoun County health officer, he claimed that among those treated for venereal disease in the county, "ninety percent of them are Negroes." Ayers continued, "We do not want to subject our children to that sort of thing." When he went on to say that the "consuming desire of every Negro is to possess a white woman," the moderator mercifully ended the rant. Though most journalists at the convention were shocked, Ayers faced little censure when he returned home to Anniston. His son Brandy later emphasized that the ASNE talk reflected the early stages of Alzheimer's.[28]

Ayers continued to speak out in his newspaper and elsewhere, decrying Klan violence but defending segregation. The fact that a few local supporters wrote to congratulate him on speeches filled with similar racist vitriol made plain that in the minds of some whites, disease, pollution, and segregation were linked, that at the psychological root of Jim Crow lay the view that apartheid must be maintained to avoid "polluting" or "infecting" whites. As his biographer, Kevin Stoker, wrote, Ayers refused to acknowledge "that the blame also rested on the shoulders of those of higher rank, those who molded a New South society based on the racial and caste system of the old one."[29]

As civil rights activism emerged in more locales and desegregation inched forward, the choice for white moderates was sharply drawn. In the immediate aftermath of the bus bombing, the president of the Citizens and Southern National Bank of Atlanta, Mills Lane, urged moderation, suggesting that Anniston's white civic leaders accept gradual racial change. With first John Patterson and then George Wallace deploying racial hatred to mobilize their political bases and sustain their reigns as governor, few places in Alabama followed a moderate course. Anniston was the most prominent among them. Speaking to the Anniston Rooster Coffee Club's monthly coffee and doughnuts breakfast session at the Anniston National Bank, Lane advised Anniston businessmen that "desegregation is coming and the city ought to be prepared to meet the problems." If not, he suggested, "the South will be set back 10 or 15 years in industrial progress." Incremental change was the price paid to avoid mass demonstrations and SNCC sit-ins. The alternative to interracial cooperation was radicalism. Lane conjured images of "'irresponsible, hot-headed' Negro students," of a "new Negro, directly opposite of the old, conservative one [who] is easily led." Following a pattern historian Joseph Crespino has called "strategic accommodation," the moderate biracial formations that emerged in Anniston and other southern cities coexisted with white racial violence and black resistance.[30]

AFRICAN AMERICAN LEADERS in Anniston charted their own path forward, even as they sought biracial cooperation. A new generation of black leaders in Anniston confronted not only racial terror but also the limitations of moderate liberalism. As a challenge to "the new black sense of self," historian Timothy Tyson suggests, white paternalism was "nearly as toxic as white backlash."[31]

In 1962, local black ministers and other community leaders formed the Calhoun County Improvement Association (CCIA). The CCIA modeled itself on the Montgomery Improvement Association, which had steered the successful campaign to integrate buses in the state's capital in 1955 and 1956. The Anniston group launched local civil rights campaigns based on the philosophy of nonviolent confrontation and affiliated with the Southern Christian Leadership Conference (SCLC), headed by Rev. Martin Luther King Jr.[32]

In the summer of 1962, just one year after the attack on the bus, civil rights activist Gordon Rodgers Jr. took a very bold step: he ran for Anniston police commissioner. He was the first African American to seek public office in the city during this period. Rodgers had been president of Alabama State Conference of Branches of the NAACP in the 1950s, braving the banning of the organization initiated by state Attorney General John Patterson in 1956. From this position, Rodgers mentored and encouraged a generation of young leaders, including future Calhoun County state representative Barbara Bigsby Boyd, elected in 1994, whose legislative post would involve her in the antipollution fight.[33]

Rodgers made the formation of a biracial commission to address racial barriers the central plank in his platform. Although he was backed by a number of individuals and organizations in West Anniston, including laborers in the Molders Union (the local to which Grover Baker belonged), Rodgers did not win the post of police commissioner. But his idea of forming a biracial commission gained traction and the support of Claude Dear, who was running for mayor. In a runoff election that year, voters elected Dear. Mayor Dear did not immediately follow through on the promise.[34]

That same year, two young African American ministers, Rev. Nimrod Quintus Reynolds and Rev. William B. McClain, enlisted white Presbyterian minister Rev. Phil Noble in their efforts to mobilize acceptance of racial change among Anniston's white establishment. Their first joint effort was an interracial ministerial alliance, which joined in the call for a biracial commission on integration. It would take another year, and another outbreak of violence, to finally push Mayor Dear into naming such a commission.

Perversely, each year, the Klan marked Mother's Day—the anniversary of the bus bombing—with more violence targeting African Americans. On Mother's Day, 1963, marauding whites fired shots into the homes of two black families and into a nearby church. Days later, Mayor Dear made good on his promise, announcing the formation of the biracial Human Relations Council. Reverend Noble was named the council's first president, heading the majority-white body, with five white and four African American members. Although Rodgers had placed the biracial commission on the city's agenda, he was not selected to serve. For safety, the group met in secret, announcing meetings just before they were to be held. (On the day he announced the appointments to the council, Mayor Dear made a point of going to Kenneth Adams's service station, walking in, and buying a soda, just to show he would not be cowed.) Although the act of naming the council was a cautious step toward change, it won national attention. President John F. Kennedy sent a letter commending the City of Anniston for exemplary action and suggesting that similar steps be taken by other communities.[35]

In appointing the biracial commission, Anniston's leaders rejected the reactionary stance—adopted, most notoriously, by public officials in Birmingham—of meeting demands for civil rights with "massive resistance." Pursuing "negotiated settlement" leaned more toward the path taken by white and black leaders in Atlanta. Anniston's power brokers had chosen to chart a moderate course, a choice rooted in the tradition of paternalistic industrialism. They aimed to make the city better for business, while sustaining existing power relations as much as possible. "In truth the elite did just enough to avoid federal intervention and prevent large-scale demonstrations," wrote historian Gary Sprayberry in his assessment of the period.[36]

Anniston's biracial initiatives received positive, if tempered, reviews among black leaders. "The human rights commission was appointed to try to help," explained Reverend Reynolds. "And maybe it did help," he said. The Human Relations Council braved intimidation and threats just to conduct its meetings, which provided a forum for identifying instances of racial discrimination, such as the refusal of treatment to a black patient at Anniston Memorial Hospital, and for discussing plans to desegregate public places, such as the library. Many moderate whites, however, deplored

African Americans' expressions of impatience with the pace of change as much as they disapproved of white violence. As Reverend Noble noted, city leaders were often motivated by concern that adverse publicity would affect the business climate. Enthusiastic about the modest progress that the Human Relations Council made, Reverend Noble nevertheless noted its limits. "How little can we give and still keep demonstrations and boycotts from happening might best summarize the attitude of the white members of the Council," he wrote.[37]

The establishment of the Calhoun County Improvement Association in 1962 and the appointment of the biracial commission in 1963 were soon accompanied by a changing of the guard at the *Anniston Star*. After serving as editor and publisher for fifty years, Colonel Ayers retired. His son, Harry Brandt "Brandy" Ayers, came home from his job as Washington, D.C., correspondent for the *Raleigh News and Observer* to assist in leading the family newspaper. The younger Ayers coaxed his brother-in-law, Philip Sanguinetti, who had worked for Monsanto for twenty years, both in Anniston and overseas, to join the paper's staff. Sanguinetti would assume various roles: editor, treasurer, and, by 1969, vice president and general manager. Brandy and his wife, Josephine, the vivacious granddaughter of North Carolina governor J. C. B. Erlinghaus, brought home with them more liberal ideas about race than his father had and pushed the paper into supporting moderate change toward integration.[38]

IN 1963, AFRICAN AMERICANS in Anniston turned to direct action as a means to achieve more rapid reform. Significantly, they opted to desegregate first those institutions that provided access to knowledge: the public library and the public schools. On September 15, 1963, four months after the formation of Anniston's Human Relations Council and two and a half years after the firebombing of the bus, the two ministers who had initiated the ministerial alliance attempted to desegregate Anniston's public library. That Sunday, Reverend Reynolds and Reverend McClain had planned to enter the Carnegie library on Tenth Street downtown. They had hoped to do so discreetly, just the two of them, without publicity. That day, many Annistonians joined the rest of the world in horror at the murder of four young girls attending Sunday school at the Sixteenth Street Baptist Church in Birmingham. "I always wondered why I couldn't remember the Birmingham bombing, though I was seven years old," said Anniston attorney Cleophus Thomas. "That's because the Anniston library was desegregated the same day, and Reverend Reynolds and Reverend McClain were beaten in the attempt." (Thomas himself broke racial barriers. Now a University of Alabama trustee emeritus, in 1976 Thomas was the first and, as of 2013, only African American president of the school's Student Government Association.)[39]

Lofty in stature if not in height and comfortable in all kinds of settings, Reverend Reynolds had been born in Chambers County, 100 miles south of Anniston, and trained at Atlanta's Clark College and at the Interdenominational Theological Center, a leading black seminary in the South. In 1960, he came to lead Seventeenth Street Baptist Church, one of the largest African American churches in Anniston, and made it a hub of civil rights activity in the city. Reverend Reynolds brought a brand of activism he had learned while pastoring a small church not far from Montgomery, where he had become increasingly involved in civil rights and formed a friendship with Rev. Martin Luther King Jr.[40]

Rev. William B. McClain was twenty-four and the newly named pastor of Haven Chapel United Methodist Church. Originally from Gadsden, he had arrived in Anniston in 1962, almost immediately after graduating from the Boston University School of Theology. (He managed to squeeze in his honeymoon before taking up the pastorate.) Reverend McClain refused to accept that the "human arrangements" of segregation "were either final or creditable."[41]

"We had everything segregated when I came here," said Reverend Reynolds, "black and white water fountains, colored and white restrooms, you got a sandwich out of the back of a restaurant, couldn't go to the library, just totally a segregated situation here in town. Of course, we started working on that. We decided to try to do the library first." So, two weeks after he marched on Washington with Martin Luther King in late August 1963, Reverend Reynolds, along with Reverend McClain, started up the sidewalk to Anniston's public library. Although they had not publicized their intent, between 60 and 100 thugs were milling around the Carnegie Library Building when the clergymen arrived.[42]

"Somebody told those rabble-rousers, and so they got prepared for us," said Reynolds. "It might have been the police department [that leaked their plan]. We were on our way there, talking about Sixteenth Street [Baptist Church in Birmingham], how awful it was for those little girls to be killed, that same day. That's when they began converging on us." Members of the mob forced Reynolds to the ground. "I stumbled to my hands," said Reynolds, "and that's when I got stabbed several times in the buttocks." The mob beat both men with chains and, when the two sought refuge in

Reverend Reynolds's car, fired shots into the vehicle. Finally the ministers managed to escape, fleeing the mob on foot. They were picked up by passing African American motorist Dolly Hughes and taken to Anniston Memorial Hospital.[43]

In 2003, on the fortieth anniversary of the library assault, Reverend Reynolds was asked if he felt set up. "Perhaps," he replied. (A lone officer had been stationed in the basement of the library to "protect" the two ministers.) "But God is good, and I guess we broke away on time."[44]

That night, while Reverend Reynolds lay in bed recovering, more than 300 black Annistonians gathered at his church to hear Reverend McClain preach calm in the face of anger. President Kennedy called that evening to lend encouragement and reassurance; federal troops were already standing by at Fort McClellan in response to the Birmingham bombing.[45]

The following afternoon, Reverend McClain and Rev. George Smitherman, pastor of Mt. Cavalry Baptist, the largest African American congregation in town, entered the library. Joining them was a group of prominent white Annistonians: Reverend Noble, City Commissioner Miller Sproull, library board chair Charles Doster, and a Jewish woman member of the library board, Carleton Stern Lentz. Accompanied this time by a sizeable police escort, the two black clergymen were able to check out books without further violence.[46]

On September 13, 1964, on the first anniversary of the attack on Reynolds and McClain, the Calhoun County Improvement Association published in the *Anniston Star* "The Anniston Manifesto." Countering the "Southern Manifesto," the segregationist tract signed in 1956 by 100 southern congressmen, including every member of the Alabama delegation, "The Anniston Manifesto" articulated the demands of Anniston's black residents, calling for equality in hiring, houses of worship, accommodations, training programs, and health care. Invoking not only the U.S. Constitution but also the town's long-standing rhetorical claim to being a model city, the manifesto challenged the terms of industrial paternalism. "Anniston, our 'Model City,'" the CCIA declared, "for a hundred years has mistreated part of her children." Justice and tranquility, the manifesto argued, called for a more equitable distribution of the fruits of industry.[47]

DESPITE THE BEST EFFORTS of the biracial commission, violent white supremacists continued their assaults. Anniston schools were slated to be desegregated in the fall of 1965; the Klan responded by stepping up attacks. In May, again on the anniversary of the bus burning, roughly 500 people paraded in a Klan rally down Noble Street. Afterward, 1,000 whites gathered at the city auditorium to listen to invective against school desegregation. Less than a week later, just before dawn on May 13, a bomb ripped apart Pine Grove Christian Methodist Church in the black town of Hobson City. No one was injured. Army demolition experts from Fort McClellan confirmed that the splintered pews and shattered windows resulted from homemade bombs; plastic containers filled with sticks of dynamite had been placed five feet inside the church door.[48]

That summer, the random murder of a black foundry worker on his way home from work focused Anniston leaders' attention on the need to stop the violence in a way that earlier assaults had not. During three nights in mid-July, white supremacist preacher Rev. Conrad "Connie" Lynch held a series of "white man's rallies," using the white marble steps of the Calhoun County Courthouse in Anniston as his platform. Lynch spoke night after night, whipping up a frenzy over maintaining white supremacy. On Thursday, July 15, Reverend Lynch applauded the recent killing of white civil rights activist Viola Liuzzo, who had been shot at point-blank range while driving with a black civil rights worker after completing the Selma to Montgomery voting rights march. "If it takes killing to get the Negroes out of the white man's streets and to protect our constitutional rights, then I say yes, kill them," Lynch urged. As the night's rally came to an end, the second shift at the Alabama Pipe Company had just let out. Willie Brewster and three other black foundry workers were headed home, carpooling to Munford and Talladega, some twenty miles away. Brewster's pregnant wife, Lestine, and their two children waited at home.[49]

After making a quick stop for gas at the Tenneco Service Station on West Tenth Street, Brewster took over the wheel for his friend whose feet were aching. Brewster pulled the black 1957 Pontiac onto Highway 202. Four miles west of Monsanto, not far from the site of the bus bombing, gunfire rang out from a two-tone Chevrolet that had been tailing the men. A bullet through the shattered back windshield lodged in Willie Brewster's spine. He died three days later in the segregated ward at Anniston Memorial Hospital.[50]

Local white civic and business leaders and African American leaders like Reverend Reynolds and Reverend McClain responded to the killing overnight, signaling a new urgency. Willie Brewster was shot late on a Thursday night. By the time of his death on Sunday, white and black civic leaders had raised more than $21,000 as a reward for reliable information about the murder. Brandy Ayers devoted extensive space in the *Star* to encouraging informants to come forward. The coverage was instrumental in flushing out a confidant of the shooter whose testimony would prove crucial.[51]

Charged in the shooting were three white men: twenty-three-year-old Hubert Damon Strange, who worked for Kenneth Adams at Adams Oil Company; Johnny Ira DeFries; and Lewis Blevins. (Adams was arrested on a separate charge of receiving stolen ordnance from the Army base.) Representing Strange at the trial was a National States Rights Party attorney named J. B. Stoner who had not only attended the rally at the courthouse but would later himself be convicted of bombing a black church in Birmingham. In the end, an all-white jury in Anniston found Strange guilty of second-degree murder. The verdict marked a milestone—the first conviction in Alabama history of a white person for killing a black person. And, as *Life* magazine reported at the time, of the thirty-four race killings in the South during the previous five years, this was only the second to end in conviction. No one ever served a prison term for Brewster's murder, however. DeFries was acquitted, Blevins was never tried, and Strange was killed in a fight while out on bond and awaiting appeal.[52]

Civil rights historian Gary Sprayberry, who grew up just west of Anniston, suggests that the murder of Willie Brewster had an even greater impact on local attitudes toward race than the bus bombing. After the Brewster murder, white acceptance of the level of personal violence that had been used to sustain racial hierarchy diminished. Adams was increasingly ostracized. His wife had left him, one FBI investigator noted, at least in part because "he is completely crazy on the Negro subject." The offer of reward money and the very real threat of facing murder charges seemed to have distanced some of Adams's coterie of young hoodlums from his schemes.[53]

Perhaps Brewster roused particular sympathy among moderate whites because he was not a civil rights protestor but an exemplary foundry worker on his way home to his young family at the end of a long shift. Certainly, the cumulative impact of repeated white brutality—the calculated attack on the Freedom Riders in 1961, the stabbing at the library in 1963, the ambush that killed Brewster, and countless lesser assaults—combined with increased local African American demands for fair treatment, forced a change. Perhaps a reservoir of shame and anger from the bus bombing could no longer be displaced onto ostensibly anonymous outside agitators—white or black. While the random nature of the violence terrorized Anniston's black residents, the response to Brewster's murder set the CCIA even more firmly on its course, activating its regional network with the SCLC and helping to identify white allies in town.

Many of the tumultuous events of the early sixties swirled around the Monsanto plant in West Anniston. (McClain's parishioners at Haven Chapel, he later wrote, included "laborers and workers at that deadly Monsanto Plant that I can still smell after forty years.") However, plant managers were conspicuously absent from local racial politics. None could be identified among the signers of the ad offering the reward for information about Willie Brewster's murder or among the members of the Human Relations Council. Some Monsanto managers attended Rev. Phil Noble's church. "I do not recall that they took any active part in anything," he said, "except I am sure that they would have been quiet supporters . . . sort of a balance to some [members of the congregation] who would have been more extreme the other way. But so far as I know they never really did anything."[54]

African American civil rights leaders responded to Brewster's shooting by escalating their demands. Less than a month after the Brewster shooting, the CCIA and the local NAACP chapter marched downtown from Seventeenth Street Baptist Church under police protection, undeterred by the prospect of violence. Days earlier, President Lyndon Baines Johnson had signed the Voting Rights Act of 1965 into law. On August 11—the same day the Watts riots broke out in Los Angeles—marchers walked silently and solemnly to the courthouse steps where Reverend Lynch had applauded racial murder. Laying claim to the courthouse site, Reverend Reynolds and Reverend McClain demanded immediate implementation of the provisions of Voting Rights Act. Black residents began picketing regularly outside the courthouse, carrying signs reading, "We Want Federal Registrars Now."[55]

Neither the specter of Watts nor the prospect of accountability to a sizeable African American electorate were lost on Calhoun County leaders. Gordon Rodgers Jr. had won nearly 16 percent of the vote in his bid for local public office in 1962, and under the provisions of the Voting Rights Act, more voters would be able to register.[56]

As African Americans began to succeed in desegregating public places and white acceptance of overt racial violence declined, racial inequality would be increasingly upheld by quieter means. Whites withdrew to all-white enclaves, including private academies, and segregation itself, the marking of places by racial boundaries, took on more of the work of physical violence. As local civil rights leaders turned to address structural and institutional racism, educational opportunity—access to knowledge—remained a top priority. However, on the very same day as the first attempt to desegregate the library, white civic leaders celebrated the opening of a new private school, the all-white Anniston Academy, forerunner to the present-day Donoho School. Children of well-off white families would have an alternative to desegregated schooling, and the dual educational system would continue to reinforce and replicate age-old disparities—sustaining segregation through different means.[57]

Some black parents began exercising their right to send their children to formerly all-white schools under the newly instituted "Freedom-of-Choice" plans. "Freedom-of-Choice," which had been put in place in southern states to forestall desegregation after the passage of the 1964 Civil Rights Act, led only to limited admittance for black students at the Calhoun County school that served West Anniston, Walter Wellborn High.[58]

The Bakers' oldest daughter, Janice, helped to desegregate Wellborn, which was attended by whites who lived south and east of Monsanto, including Kenneth Adams's sons. Although Janice ended up graduating from Wellborn, her mother worried about Janice's safety every day. "The whole time she went there," recalled Imogene, "I had to get a cab or escort for her." In 1967, the second year that a few black students were allowed to attend Wellborn, the Bakers' son, David, attempted to attend the school. "He went to Wellborn," explained his mother, "but they didn't let him integrate out there. Some white boys jumped on him" as he tried to attend classes. "It was September 1967," David explained. "I went to Walter Wellborn High School, right after integration had begun in 1966 in Alabama. My mother made me go." David described the scene at Wellborn High as he and six or seven friends arrived: "We got to the school that morning, [and] the principal lined us up like we were in the Army. He said, 'You are at a white folks school, you're going to have to stop talking like a nigger.' He said, 'If anybody says anything to you, don't say nothing back. Because, if you drop dead in the hallway, we won't never know who did it because it will be so crowded.' I went on to class."[59]

The morning proceeded without incident. "Just before lunch time," David explained, "this guy kicked me in my butt with his steel-toed boots, cowboy boots, and we got to fighting. We fought for about ten minutes." David and his friends sought protection on what he hoped would be neutral territory. "We finally found the principal's office." But, said David, the principal said, "'I told you niggers not to go down the back stairs.' I said, 'Who you calling a nigger?' and I cursed him out. He said, 'Come here, boy,' and I ran."[60]

Before the principal could catch him, Baker headed out the front door of the high school and began sprinting the three miles toward home. "I ran every step of the way. I passed a corn patch. I passed an all-white neighborhood. I ran by the Adams Service Station which Kenneth Adams owned, which I was really afraid of because Adams really religiously hated black folks and he had no conscience in what he did. His sons and some of his nephews were the ones we had gotten into the fight with." When he arrived home, sweating and hot, his father and a neighbor were sitting on the front porch. As he told his father about the fight, his mother came home from work. "It was by the grace of God," Baker said, "[that] Daddy had his shotgun." Grover and a neighbor were headed to the school. "She took the [car] keys," David said, and "wouldn't let them go."[61]

"That was my experience at integrating school," Baker said. "I went at eight o'clock and I got out at twelve." He opted to attend Calhoun County Training School in Hobson City rather than return to Wellborn.[62] Grover and Imogene Baker's children would follow in their parents' footsteps, becoming involved in union activism and, eventually, the environmental justice campaign.

"Freedom-of-Choice" plans placed all the burden of integration on individual African American students and their parents—another form of structural violence—and achieved minimal results. As black families reached for greater access to knowledge and opportunity, whites who resisted desegregation saw a threat to white supremacy. Consequently, Wellborn High remained a focal point of racial unrest into the 1970s. Surrounded in his office at Seventeenth Street Church by memorabilia from more than four decades of activism, Reverend Reynolds reflected on the 1971 effort to achieve more than nominal desegregation and to end institutionalized discrimination inside the school. "Violence really erupted" then, said Reynolds. On Friday night of the week that parents presented their demands to the principal to open up access to the best classes, sports, and extracurricular activities for black students attending Wellborn, assailants "fired into [Rev. John] Nettles house, shot twenty-one bullets into his house, almost killing his wife, as she sat just right by the window."[63]

What followed was "a very serious racial crisis," noted a report from the Committee of Unified Leadership (COUL), a new biracial group that emerged in response to the "fire bombings, shootings in homes, division among our people, utter chaos to the point where local law enforcement agencies could not cope with the situation in a peaceful manner." The idea of creating a broad-based citizens group had actually surfaced some months earlier, in the spring, motivated by white civic leaders' desire to "make Anniston eligible for an 'All American City' Award." The goal was to create "a constructive new thrust that could identify, analyze and focus public attention upon root causes of community problems and deficiencies . . . and remove barriers." But the effort was limping along, explained a COUL report, until violence had surfaced in late October with the shooting into the Nettles' home, after which black youth erupted in anger.[64]

COUL grew to become an inclusive group of 300 citizens from different occupations, civilian and military. COUL leaders attributed part of the organization's success to keeping the news media out of its meetings, which minimized posturing and kept participants' names out of the news. COUL had the benefit of a decade of collective experience. The CCIA was now ten years old and an anchor chapter for the SCLC in Alabama. The CCIA set the agenda for COUL in a way that the black members of the Human Relations Council had been unable to do.[65]

In addition to negotiating changes at Wellborn, COUL deployed a selective buying campaign to tackle African American concerns about employment. Two years earlier, in early spring 1969, the CCIA had picketed downtown retail businesses, in an effort to force storeowners to hire black clerks in visible sales positions. When business owners refused to act, Reverend Reynolds told them, "We'll just stay out here and march against you." That campaign had achieved some hiring gains, but now, COUL systematically sent black and white teams to visit Calhoun County employers, particularly retail operations, to inquire about the racial makeup of their workforce, and offered to refer black candidates recommended by the CCIA for open positions. Businesses that refused to budge landed on a boycott list.[66]

By the early 1970s, the collective impact of the long history of civil rights activity in the South and in Anniston was evident. Henry Givahn commented on the change: "I left here I believe in 1915; you would hardly believe that you were in the same place on returning to Anniston in 1969." Certain hiring barriers gave way, if slowly. Gordon Rodgers Jr. was elected to the Anniston City Council that year, becoming the first African American ever to serve in city government.[67]

As New York Times reporter and author Rick Bragg framed it, life in Anniston settled into "an uneasy and imperfect peace." Reverend Reynolds continued to provide local civil rights leadership in Anniston, as the CCIA became a formal chapter of the SCLC in 1973 and hosted the organization's national convention in 1975. Reverend McClain left Anniston to pursue his ministry, which eventually took him to Wesley Theological Seminary in Washington, D.C. Reverend Nettles continued to lead civil rights and labor protests from his base at Mount Olive Baptist Church, remaining active until his death in 1999.[68]

The Calhoun County Improvement Association formed in 1962 and became a formal chapter of the Southern Christian Leadership Conference in 1973. Marchers repeatedly challenged discrimination in hiring by retail stores, at the Anniston Army Depot, and by other local employers, as in this protest around 1971. *Front row, from left*: Frederick Moore, Rev. John Nettles, Rev. Nimrod Q. Reynolds, and Rev. R. B. Cottonreader Jr. Photo by Stephen Gross, *Anniston Star.*

COUL signaled a turning point in local action to address discrimination in employment and education, even if did not encompass all of the demands of a more militant younger generation. During the violence that sparked the growth of COUL, Johnny Ford, later mayor of Tuskegee, was serving as a representative of the U.S. Justice Department. Sent to Anniston to quell the reaction to desegregation at Wellborn, Ford told young black men like David Baker—who were less willing to meet violence with nonviolence—that their best alternative was to get out of town. Baker took Ford's advice and left that evening for New York, where he worked for more than two decades in the city's public hospitals and the hospital workers union.[69]

David Baker looks back on that time with sadness, because that is when he lost his younger brother. Terry was just seventeen. Born just two years apart, the two had always been close. Terry had been in and out of the local hospital, with severe asthma and migraines, since entering high school. Doctors had found a large tumor on his brain; an autopsy revealed an enlarged heart. Family members had always been puzzled about Terry's death at so young an age. Only much later would David come to wonder if Terry's fatal ailments were associated with exposure to PCBs.[70]

By taking on segregated institutions, African American leaders had begun dismantling the pillars that supported structural violence. The shift from de jure segregation to more covert forms of racial discrimination was carried out in part through the reliance on a hierarchy of experts. An expert culture holds power by withholding knowledge. Withholding knowledge sustained segregation and perpetuated inequality. "Slow violence," as Rob Nixon has characterized environmental assaults on the poor, existed alongside some of the more easily recognized personal and structural forms of violence.[71] Racial oppression never had spared black citizens' private worlds; chemical pollution invaded intimate spaces, too.

Though targeted personal violence initially fueled the growth of COUL, the organization's work on structural discrimination in education and employment proved crucial, opening a path for leaders who would go on to challenge environmental injustice. Slow violence—including the many longer-term problems associated with pollution—remained submerged, but not indefinitely. The civil rights activists of the 1960s and 1970s in Anniston gained access to a measure of political power. They nurtured—and in some cases literally raised—the next generation of activists, who continued the effort to gain access to knowledge and the tools to tackle other forms of injustice. Activists engaged in the long struggle for political rights and access to public space would explicitly raise environmental concerns by the end of the 1960s. One of COUL's main agenda items was a polluted ditch than ran through the West End.

CHAPTER SIX

The Nature of the Poison

We don't want pollution, of course, but we don't want to kill the goose that lays the golden egg. —Anniston Chamber of Commerce official, 1971

In late May 1961, while Anniston's attention was riveted on the aftermath of the bus attack out on Birmingham Highway, thick sludge from Monsanto's Anniston plant overwhelmed the local water department's treatment station downstream in Oxford and, for three or four days, heavy concentrations of untreated industrial waste poured directly into Choccolocco Creek. When approached by a local reporter, Monsanto's representative attributed the discharge to a temporary malfunction in the plant's waste treatment center—implying it was an isolated incident, not an inherent aspect of production. At the same time, the company pled ignorance of hazards associated with its chemical waste. "We thought it was harmless, and we have no evidence to change that opinion at this stage," claimed plant production manager Carl Edelblut soon after the incident.[1]

Within days, the Alabama Water Improvement Commission (AWIC), the State Department of Conservation, and the U.S. Public Health Service opened a joint investigation into "an apparently extensive fish kill in the lower reaches of Choccolocco Creek." This investigation, however ineffectual, marked the first regulatory attention to stream pollution flowing from the Anniston plant. Upon completion of its investigation, AWIC, the agency charged with enforcing regulations against stream pollution in the state, offered a brief exculpatory statement. "We do not have any criticism to offer in any way concerning the manner in which the problem was handled," Joe L. Crockett, of AWIC, told the *Anniston Star*.[2] Crockett would prove a valuable ally of Monsanto in coming years.

Even after the massive fish kill in 1961, toxic discharges received little notice in the local press. In general, the *Star* reported accidents but did not treat pollution as an ongoing threat. Offensive odors and periodic small explosions at the plant were regarded as nuisances, the necessary consequence of having a leading division of one of the world's most successful chemical corporations next door. In the early 1960s, with local unemployment pegged at 8 percent, city leaders were loath to criticize the pillars of the region's industrial base. Despite the expansion of the chemical, biological, and radiological warfare training center at Fort McClellan in 1960, the local economy sagged. Seeking federal designation as a "depressed area" in hopes of improving opportunities for local businesses to bid competitively for federal contracts, city leaders featured the Monsanto plant prominently. Even with the sluggish economy, Monsanto had increased production in Anniston by 50 percent in 1960, prompting an *Anniston Star* editorial that called the plant "one of our best industrial advertisements."[3]

Monsanto's statement to the press that its chemical wastes were "harmless" is directly contradicted by internal records that document long-standing corporate knowledge of PCBs' toxicity. In communications to industrial clients, Monsanto revealed that, in fact, waste that contained PCBs posed serious danger, especially to aquatic life. Nearly a year *prior* to the massive fish kill in Choccolocco Creek, an industrial hygienist in Monsanto's medical department warned of precisely this danger in relation to the company's Pydraul fluids, which contained Aroclors. In a memo to a Pennsylvania tool manufacturer and Monsanto customer, the hygienist warned, "If the material [Pydraul] is discharged in large concentrations it will adversely effect [*sic*] the organisms in the bottom of the receiving stream which will effect [*sic*] the aquatic life in the stream."[4] Monsanto officials shared with industrial customers (at least those who made inquiries) precisely the same knowledge that they pointedly denied in statements to the local news media.

Scattered protests predated awareness of PCBs. Residents of West Anniston had long complained of "obnoxious gases, smoke and vapors" from the plant. A meeting in the spring of 1958 for "organizing a committee in regards to the unpleasant odors and smoke created by Monsanto Chemical Company which is plaguing our community" aimed to speed installation of pollution control equipment. Joe Fincher and other residents who lived near the plant had filed suit against Monsanto after the plant launched its parathion insecticide operation in January, citing a stench from the plant "so severe that on many occasions complainants or their families have vomited, have been unable to eat, and have been made seriously sick." In ruling that Fincher could proceed with his lawsuit, the Alabama Supreme Court declared it likely that Monsanto, "unless restrained, will continue the operation of the plant so as to cause the nuisance complained of."[5]

In time, knowledge about PCB contamination and its effects on wildlife and human health would no longer be confined to confidential corporate

An aerial view of the Monsanto Chemical Company plant in West Anniston and the "Monsanto curve" prior to the rerouting of Highway 202 in the 1970s. Photo courtesy of the *Anniston Star*.

memos, arcane scientific journals, or closed-door meetings. For the moment, however, through paternalistic reassurances that its operations were safe and aggressive management of public relations and the press, Monsanto officials effectively deflected deeper inquiry. Waterway contamination in West Anniston occasionally prompted government intervention. But carefully cultivated allies in state and federal agencies repeatedly protected the company's economic interests and often echoed company denials of harm. After concluding the investigation of the 1961 fish kill, Alabama water commission field director Crockett assured the public, "If any mistake was made, we are satisfied that it was not intentional and was due primarily to a lack of information on the part of everyone concerned."[6]

SITUATED AT A BEND IN THE ROAD toward Birmingham about two miles west of downtown, Monsanto's chemical factory dominated the landscape of West Anniston, marking the divide between neighborhoods segregated by race. Until Interstate 20 was mostly completed in the 1970s, the road curving past the Monsanto gate, the Birmingham Highway, was the main route west. It was the route traveled by the Freedom Riders' Greyhound bus and wound through neighborhoods whose residents held opposing views of the Freedom Riders' crusade. Whites lived along the highway near where the bus had careened to a stop and burst into flame. Black residents were concentrated in the neighborhoods that bordered the east side of the plant. Ranged along Clydesdale Avenue north of the railroad tracks and the plant were a few white-owned businesses, Anniston Quality Meats and McCord's Grocery, which became a gathering place. African American and white customers—people from the pipe shops, from Anchor Metals, and from the textile plant—would come in, buy groceries, and chat. Later, the Choo-Choo Burger Inn and a branch of the Southtrust Bank opened, too. Other businesses—like the ice plant, Swift's Motor Car Company, and the Lucky Seven Club—shared the south side of the tracks with Monsanto.[7]

The plant site was a rambling jumble of smokestacks, buildings, loading and staging areas, and waste pits. An extensive network of outdoor industrial piping completed the chemical distillery, which in the 1960s employed more than 200 union laborers and another 100 chemists, managers, and supervisory personnel. A railroad spur brought tank cars in and out of the plant loading docks. Indicative of its importance in Monsanto's product line, the combined biphenyl/Aroclors operation occupied one of the largest of the barnlike structures at the plant. Beside the production areas lay a half-acre plot where workers stacked drums filled with PCB and other chemical wastes. Forty years later that plot would be identified as the hottest spot on the plant site, containing "principal threat waste," still measuring an estimated 16,620 mg/kg (16,620 parts per million) PCBs. (Concentrations of chemical contaminants are reported in different ways. In technical documents, they are expressed in metric measures. In the popular press, they are written in parts per million [ppm] or parts per billion [ppb]. Today, the EPA considers 1 ppm to be the threshold above which contaminated soil must be removed from residential areas at this site.)[8]

PCBs were produced in a two-story structure with catwalks running indoors and out. One operator ran the chlorinators; another helped with the chlorinators and ran the acid department; a third ran the Aroclors stills. Bill Hughes, who worked in the Aroclors department during most of the 1960s, explained, "You'd put certain amounts of this [biphenyl] material into the chlorinator, then you'd add chlorine to it." Operators would periodically sample the mixture. "You had to keep check on temperatures," Hughes explained. The product remained in the chlorinator for one to twelve hours, depending on the final percentage of chlorine sought. Then it was pumped to blowing tanks, where the by-product, hydrochloric acid (HCl), also quite toxic, was segregated. "You had air in there to drive off the HCl, the gas, off

TOP Workers at Monsanto's Anniston plant, ca. 1951. Aroclors, as PCBs were known, were produced in West Anniston from 1929 until the early 1970s. BOTTOM Monsanto laborers routinely handled toxic chemicals at the plant in West Anniston in the early 1950s. Photos courtesy of the *Anniston Star*.

the product." Then the HCl off gas was transferred to a "scrubber" and on to a "drowning tower," yielding hydrochloric acid, also called muriatic acid. Some of the Aroclors that remained in the acid was trapped in a big, covered iron pot. Some of that reclaimed material was reprocessed, put back through the cycle to make more Aroclors. After the HCl gas was removed, the dense liquid went on to stills where it was heated under vacuum pressure, then sent through a filter to a storage tank.[9]

The waste compounds in the bottom of the Aroclors distillery reached 380 degrees Celsius (716 degrees Fahrenheit) and were kept heated so they would not solidify before reaching the waste pit. High temperatures made certain PCB compounds easily transported via air. Nearly thirty years after production of PCBs was halted at Anniston, researchers were still finding evidence of their presence in tree bark around the town.[10]

Though the production team was small, a sizeable number of people beyond those distilling Aroclors came into frequent contact with the chemicals. Night-time photos taken at mid-century show particulate matter and fumes kept in constant motion during the production process. Laborers in the filtering and drumming operations faced "the most severe exposure," according to plant records. They stood directly under the Aroclors distillery, drumming liquids, bagging solids, and weighing compounds. They also stood over open pits containing hot Aroclors wastes, which were quite volatile and therefore easily inhaled. Monsanto warned workers not to eat near the Aroclors building; the company had understood the danger of ingesting PCBs since at least the mid-1950s.[11]

Until 1966, when the Anniston plant hired its first white laborer, all of Monsanto's laborers in Anniston were black and virtually all black employees were laborers. "The plant was not integrated," explained former laborer Charles Chatman, "so we had a separate laborers' and operators' bathhouse." Prior to the late 1960s, the chemical industry as a whole employed few black workers other than unskilled laborers and semiskilled operatives, especially in the South, where many new chemical plants were located. (Monsanto hired its first black chemist, Dr. John Daniel Cotman, after World War II to work in the Springfield, Massachusetts, office. He was one of the few African Americans to hold a professional or technical position at the company at the time.)[12]

Periodically, new evidence of the "known toxicity of these substances" [Aroclors] appeared in medical and industry journals. A 1954 study in the *Journal of the American Medical Association* noted that "in nearly every worker exposed sufficiently to these chlorinated compounds for a few months these lesions will develop." The researchers examined workers using Aroclors at an organic acid manufacturing plant in Connecticut. Seven of the fourteen workers exposed to very low concentrations of airborne PCBs, measuring one-tenth of the recommended maximum allowable concentration at the time, developed chloracne after an average of just over fourteen months of exposure. *Chemical and Engineering News*, reporting on the Yale study, stated, "The fact that tests of the air, even in the presence of vapors, showed only negligible amounts of chlorinated hydrocarbons indicates that this type of intermittent but fairly long continued mild exposure is *not innocuous.*"[13]

The Yale researchers, led by J. Wister Meigs, an associate professor of occupational medicine, found that in addition to the seven exposed workers in the Connecticut factory who developed dermatitis, one had borderline impaired liver function. The cases were discovered at the end of the warm summer months, suggesting that heat exacerbated the exposure. At the same time, the Yale study surmised that vulnerability to Aroclors-induced dermatitis might differ by race. "Skin pigmentation may be a factor," wrote the researchers; of the workers they had examined, "three of the workers were Negroes, and none of them had chloracne."[14]

Before a limestone neutralization pit was installed in the late 1960s, Monsanto pumped wastes directly into the ditch that flowed under Clydesdale Avenue, past nearby homes, and into Snow Creek. When filters in the four ten-by-thirty-foot acid tanks were flushed each day, the runoff was "backwashed into the ditch." Sometimes as much as one-third of the acid output, laced with PCBs, was simply pumped into the ditch that led to Snow Creek.[15]

Why would Monsanto discharge—daily—large quantities of Aroclors and the acid that was a by-product of its manufacture, when both were significant sources of revenue? The answer lies in the intertwined process of manufacturing Aroclors and hydrochloric acid (HCl). In order to produce high-quality HCl, chemical operators had to strip out the organic components, that is, purge the PCBs. The purged PCBs that were not reprocessed were simply dumped. And, since the company produced significantly more hydrochloric acid than it could sell, this too was dumped. The plant's manager, William Papageorge, was later asked whether the sewering of up to 30,000 pounds per day of hydrochloric acid had been "intentional because the operation is trying to purge organic material" [i.e., Aroclors]. Papageorge replied simply, "Yes." The chemicals were so inexpensive to manufacture—and so profitable—that Monsanto could afford to waste them.[16]

Monsanto deposited other waste PCBs into an unlined dump just south of the plant, uphill from Sweet Valley on the slope of Coldwater Mountain. Among the most hazardous of these wastes were the Montars or "still bottoms," the heavy, highly chlorinated PCB compounds left in the bottom of the scrubber after Aroclors distillation. Monsanto attempted to sell some of this distillation residue, but it was not marketable; Monsanto workers trucked the remainder to the dump. Some of the dumped Montars adhered to soil particles, which leached down the hillside as a result of erosion during rainy periods. Carl Smith, a maintenance laborer in the Aroclors department in the sixties, recalled hauling drums of Aroclors bottoms in an old flatbed Chevrolet truck to the Coldwater Mountain waste pit. "There was a huge hole in the ground," explained Smith, "and we backed up to a certain stop where the truck wouldn't go in, and our job was to get up on the truck and roll these particular drums into this hole." Monsanto's PCBs were reaching West Anniston residents and their food chain in at least three ways, via direct stream discharges, air dispersal, and as leachate from the South Landfill.[17]

BY THE MID-1960S, waterway contamination severely threatened the health of the once abundant game fish in Choccolocco Creek. A 1966 episode killed an estimated 56,200 fish. Dairy farmers' livelihood was put at risk; they and other landowners along the river in Talladega County had to bury or burn the "stinking fish carcasses," water moccasins, and turtles that littered the banks of their farms and lake lots. The fish kill disrupted farming and recreational opportunities for nearly a year and prompted property owners downstream from Monsanto's plant to demand that the state of Alabama take the company to court. The state did so, in one of few such cases filed by AWIC at the time, seeking $225,000 in damages. The state only enforced existing laws against dumping refuse into public waterways when under pressure.[18]

In the course of the lawsuit, Monsanto hired Denzel Ferguson, of the Zoology Department at Mississippi State University, to test the health of Snow Creek near the plant. Ferguson and his student Mack Finley found the stream to be "devoid of life." The researchers found problems in other nearby creeks, describing Coldwater Creek as "highly polluted" and noting fish kills in Dry Creek. In his capacity as Monsanto's expert in pending litigation, Ferguson deemed the company's waste treatment plant "effective," but he warned Monsanto that "Snow Creek is a potential source of future legal problems."[19]

Describing later the fish that he and Ferguson examined, Mack Finley said, "Their skin would literally slough off, like a blood blister on the bottom of your foot." While denying there was yet "evidence that these [synthetic chemical] materials are harmful to fish," the consultants' report recognized that "their presence constitutes *damaging evidence of pollution*." For this reason, the company's consultant recommended, "Monsanto needs to monitor the biological effects of its effluents" to protect itself against "future accusations."[20]

In one test, Ferguson and Finley submerged cloth cages filled with bluegills in samples of water drawn from a tributary of Snow Creek. In the effluent from the chemical factory, "the fish lost equilibrium in the full strength water in 10 seconds and all died in less than 5 minutes," the researchers reported to Monsanto. "Choccolocco Creek fish populations are subject to continued low-level mortality and periodic massive die-offs," the researchers concluded. They expressed particular concern that the dying fish displayed "reversed pectoral fins," an indicator of pesticide poisoning. Ferguson and Finley identified a number of "lethal agents" in the factory's waste, including parathion, phosphoric acid, hydrochloric acid, and mercury.[21]

The legal scrutiny that resulted from the 1966 fish kill did not reveal the extent of Aroclors pollution in local waterways. It appears that Monsanto made no mention, even to its own researchers, that Aroclors might be present. Although Ferguson and Finley did not test for polychlorinated biphenyls, they were puzzled by the peaks appearing in the results of the chemicals analyses that suggested the presence of an as yet unidentified chemical.[22]

Monsanto requested, and won, a change of venue in the case, which was transferred from Talladega County, where the pollution's impact was most evident, to Calhoun County, where Monsanto's factory was based. Both the Anniston Industrial Development Board and the Anniston Chamber of Commerce sided with Monsanto, pledging "full and wholehearted support to the Monsanto Co. in any way possible toward the company's continued success in the community, as well as support in its pending court case pertaining to the alleged fish kill in local streams." One Chamber official testified at a water quality hearing, "We don't want pollution, of course, but we don't want to kill the goose that lays the golden egg." A year later, the suit was "quietly dismissed." Afterward, "Monsanto generously donated $20,000 to the State Conservation Department to be used to build recreation facilities along Logan Martin Lake."[23]

In closest proximity to the east drainage ditch that collected runoff from Monsanto's dump in the side of Coldwater Mountain were black residents in the Sweet Valley and Cobbtown neighborhoods just downhill from the dump. Residential segregation by race and class intensified during the 1960s and 1970s. As Alabama schools integrated, more and more whites moved out of the neighborhoods surrounding the plant. White-occupied homes were closest to the West Landfill. These were upstream if not always upwind of plant emissions.

In Sweet Valley, severe flooding was a regular occurrence. Floods deposited PCBs and other chemical waste on backyards along Tenth Street, between Boynton and Montrose, and down Eighth Street from Crawford to Boynton. PCBs do not dissolve appreciably in water but adhere to organic matter in soils and sediments, collecting in a stream's silt. In 1970, silt from above a sump pump leading to the drainage ditch contained extreme concentrations of PCBs. Murky floodwaters often rose into people's homes, leaving behind PCB-loaded silt. "Snow Creek ran right behind there," anti-PCB activist Cassandra Roberts later explained, pointing to an abandoned stretch of Sweet Valley where homes once stood. "Once those ditches and gutters got stopped up, all the houses used to flood every time there was a hard rain," she said. "There was easily two inches of mud in people's houses."[24]

Unaware of the toxicity in the mud and local creeks, Monsanto's neighbors caught and ate the fish that managed to survive in nearby streams. Neighborhood children explored the unfenced areas of Coldwater Mountain beyond the Monsanto dump where "there were barrels with skeletons and crossbones on it, sitting in the woods, and we rode them like horses," remembered West Anniston resident Opal Scruggs. Arthur Bowie described slipping off to "the skinner," as he called his favorite swimming hole, a pond downhill from the dump. Pregnant women, continuing age-old practices, baked and ate local clay. None were made aware of the presence of PCBs, much less the health hazards PCBs posed by their daily routines.[25]

BETWEEN 1930 AND 1969, Monsanto transformed from a company employing slightly more than 2,000 people, mostly in the United States, to a global conglomerate with more than 60,000 employees worldwide. With increasing internationalization and expansion into fields other than chemistry, the Monsanto Chemical Company renamed itself the Monsanto Company in 1964.[26]

The early 1960s marked a big forward push in international acquisitions and marketing, as Monsanto consolidated its status as a multinational corporation. In 1959, Monsanto garnered 20 percent of its total sales revenue from overseas sales. By the end of the decade, Monsanto's total corporate sales registered $1.97 billion. Of that total, overseas sales made up $467 million, a "brisk" 3.5 percent increase over the previous year. That figure would grow an additional 5 percent in 1970. Monsanto remained the only company in the United States manufacturing PCBs and one of a handful of producers in the world.[27]

The entire family of PCBs figured prominently in Monsanto's research and development efforts. Since World War II, PCBs had found their way into a greater and greater variety of products destined for homes and offices. While the bulk of Monsanto's PCBs continued to be produced for insulating fluids, Monsanto marketed PCBs to manufacturers who used them in an expanding number of consumer goods. As the plastics industry grew, PCBs were increasingly developed as "plasticizers" used for softening brittle plastics and rubber. Toxicologists Ian Nisbet and Adam Sarofim later determined that prior to 1970 "approximately 60% of [Aroclors] sales were for closed-system electrical and heat transfer uses, 25% for plasticizer applications, 10% for hydraulic fluids and lubricants, and less than 5% for miscellaneous application such as surface coating, adhesives, printing inks, and pesticide extenders." For a time, PCBs were used in the dishwasher detergent Electrasol at the level of 5 ppm.[28]

As corporate investment in Aroclors production increased, profitability rose. In 1958, with sales of $3.9 million, the Aroclors had brought Monsanto's Organic Chemicals Division a 35.6 percent return on investment, making it the company's fourth most profitable product line. By 1970, Monsanto estimated its worldwide sales of Aroclors at $22 million, with nearly half of that amount, $10 million, being profit.[29]

IN THE EARLY 1960s, chemical manufacturers held far more scientific knowledge of the chemicals they produced than university researchers or anyone in the general public; few outside the electrochemical industry knew about PCBs or their toxicity. With the exception of industrial hygienists and some government health officials, the circle of people privy to such knowledge was comprised almost entirely of Monsanto personnel—executives, managers, scientists, and company doctors—and corporate PCB customers, the electrical, paper, and other companies who used their products in manufacturing. The U.S. Navy had discontinued using PCBs on its submarines in the mid-1950s following several deaths and widespread problems with chloracne among Navy cable fabricators using Aroclors mixtures, but, observing long-standing conventions of confidentiality, the Navy had also promised to be "commercially discreet."[30]

Aroclors and other synthetic organic chemicals were subject to virtually no federal regulatory oversight. To the extent that federal rules existed, regulation of synthetic chemicals largely focused on drugs and food products. Studies of chemical exposure in occupational settings had resulted in recommended workplace air concentration levels, but little attention was paid to global dispersion or to exposures of communities in the vicinity of factories. Monsanto's internal memos expressed concern over the threat of regulation. But as of 1960, Monsanto reported having had no prior regulatory experience regarding discharge of PCBs.[31]

A private memo circulated in 1958 neatly encapsulated the company's stance regarding regulation: "It is our desire to comply with the necessary regulations: but to comply with the minimum and not to give any unnecessary information which could very well damage our sales position in the synthetic hydraulic fluid field," in which PCBs were widely used.[32]

Legal rationales for regulating water pollution derived from several sources. Downstream users had a common law riparian right to water with "quality unimpaired and quantity undiminished." State-based statutory authority to regulate stream pollution had long been in place. The 1899 Federal Refuse Act, also known as the Rivers and Harbors Act, prohibited industrial dumping of solid wastes in navigable waterways without a permit. (The primary impetus for that law was to prevent interference with navigation, not to prevent pollution, but the statute had been used effectively against polluters.) Federal water pollution control legislation, first passed in 1948 and frequently amended, provided federal statutory authority for regulating water quality, but it left primary implementation authority with the states.[33]

Federal authority over pollution was diffused among several agencies. The U.S. Public Health Service focused primarily on waterborne bacteria, not toxic chemicals. U.S. Department of Agriculture policies were intertwined with pesticide and agricultural business interests. What impetus existed within government to investigate stream pollution came from the Department of the Interior's Fish and Wildlife Service, the agency that conducted key studies on dichloro-diphenyl-trichloroethane (DDT) that informed Rachel Carson's work.[34]

Congress had updated the federal Food and Drug Act in 1938, requiring manufacturers to submit new drugs and food additives for review and approval before they could be marketed. The act, however, did not regulate nonfood and nondrug chemicals. The FDA's authority to regulate chemicals in food products and packaging expanded in 1958 under the Delaney

Clause, which authorized limits on cancer-causing chemical residues in food.[35]

Until midcentury, pollution control was largely left to states and localities. The Alabama Department of Conservation, consolidated in 1919, is one of the oldest state conservation departments in the South. The Alabama Water Improvement Commission had existed since the late 1940s. But Alabama's state water pollution control law had explicitly exempted from regulation industrial discharges in existence when the law was enacted in 1949. State enforcement was spotty, uncoordinated, and limited to the more egregious, visible, and well-publicized "accidents," such as large fish kills, not ongoing daily exposures.[36]

In addition, Monsanto had powerful friends in state politics. In mid-1965, a bill in the Alabama House called for immediate water cleanup and "equal wildlife and industry say so" on the water pollution board. State senator C. A. Shelton of Calhoun County, chair of the Senate Health Committee, argued for *less* regulation, including "'one or more' two year periods of grace for industries dumping their wastes in public waters." One proponent of stronger regulation declared that "Shelton backed the industry measure because Monsanto Chemical Company has a plant in his home county."[37]

The chemical industry had grown accustomed to the absence of oversight and had become quite protective of its prerogative to develop new synthetic chemicals with few parameters limiting toxicity, production, sale, or use. Then, after the publication in 1962 of Rachel Carson's *Silent Spring*, public concern about pollution intensified, galvanizing efforts to establish limits to the "unobtrusive penetration" of the chemical industry into modern life.[38]

BY THE EARLY 1960S, scientists investigating precipitous population declines among a number of animal species had begun examining the impact of pesticides and other known toxic chemicals on animal life and human health. Media attention held up industry practices to public scrutiny. Industrial chemistry was called to task both from within the field, by independent chemists analyzing the presence and precise impact of synthetic organic chemicals on animals, and without, by biologists and ecologists trying to identify causes of threatened species extinctions.

Despite its own growing archive pointing to similar evidence, the chemical industry responded with an all-out attack on the scientists themselves. Such strategies ultimately undermined the industry's claim that it put science at the heart of its work. Questions posed by scientists independent of the industry were met with strong proprietary objections to sharing knowledge. Even more striking were the abuse and misuse of science.

Silent Spring outlined in clear and poignant detail the dangers that the pesticide DDT posed to songbirds, as well as to humans and other mammals. Unrestricted pesticide use, Carson argued, threatened to eliminate some species entirely. Her book showed links between toxic chemicals and environmental health, spurring international research on DDT. Carson shaped public understanding of the damage wrought by pesticides, launching a new phase of environmentalism. *Silent Spring* emerged at a time when the public was ready to hear ecological ideas. A series of well-publicized incidents in the late 1950s had ignited concern about ecological routes of human exposure to toxic chemicals. Troubling magazine articles had reported on the evidence that, because of atomic tests, nuclear fallout in the form of Strontium 90 was widespread. Pesticide contamination of cranberry bogs virtually eliminated holiday season consumption in 1959. Then, in 1961, FDA officials seriously considered licensing the sleep drug thalidomide, which had been banned in Europe after being linked to deformities in newborns. The thalidomide scandal raised doubts about the government's willingness to challenge industry in order to protect the public from harmful products.[39]

As part of the broader family of chlorinated hydrocarbons, or organochlorines, PCBs share a number of chemical properties with DDT, which was also manufactured by Monsanto. Both sets of chemicals combine the element chlorine with life's building blocks, carbon and hydrogen. Strong chemical bonds make the compounds durable and resistant to degradation when subjected to heat; the chlorine contributes to toxicity to living organisms. Although Carson did not mention Aroclors by name in her best-selling book, she did cite Cecil Drinker's 1930s studies on the health effects of chlorinated chemical compounds, noting that liver disease and deaths had resulted from their use. Carson focused primarily on pesticides, and although PCBs were sometimes used in pesticides as extenders, that is, as the medium to deliver an insect-killing compound, Aroclors were not primarily marketed to kill pests. Monsanto did advertise Aroclors in 1946 as suitable "for control of termites in soil," but, in the wake of *Silent Spring*, Monsanto sought to distance PCBs from these uses.[40]

Carson's indictment of DDT called into question the freedom from oversight long enjoyed by the chemical industry. Particularly threatening to industry was the cautionary approach Carson urged toward synthetic chemicals, that chemicals should not be produced and marketed without considering the consequences. "It is all of a piece," Carson told a press gathering in New York, "thalidomide and pesticides—they represent our willingness to rush ahead and use something without knowing what the results are going to be." Industry leaders responded with a well-financed public relations assault that historians John Stauber and Sheldon Rampton called "the PR equivalent of a prolonged carpet-bombing campaign." Industry associations portrayed Carson as overly emotional, claiming—inaccurately—that she was not a scientist and therefore not authoritative. For its part, *Monsanto Magazine* carried a lengthy rejoinder to Carson's opening chapter, "Fable for Tomorrow," in which she had envisioned a world bereft of wildlife as a result of pesticide overuse. Monsanto officials circulated a parody, "The Desolate Year" to newspapers around the nation, decrying instead a world *without* pesticides, a world overrun by bugs, rodents, and disease. Perhaps more effective than the all-out assault on Carson's ideas was a subtler dismissiveness. Gendered portrayals of Carson as a gentle nature writer concerned primarily about songbirds tended to shift attention from her well-researched and provocative data about human health and chemical carcinogens. The industry attack may well have served to spread her message rather than undermine it.[41]

Carson's book aroused national and international concern about pesticide use and chemical contamination, leading to a U.S. ban on DDT within ten years and becoming a catalyst for increased government regulation of toxic chemicals in the United States.[42] Then, with national attention newly focused on ecological poisons, a resourceful young scientist at Stockholm University, half a world away from northeast Alabama, awakened public awareness of PCBs.

AN ENERGETIC AND ENGAGING young Danish agronomist, Søren Jensen, had moved to Sweden to study chemistry in 1957. He was impressed with the "miraculous" agricultural potential of DDT. After Carson's book exposed DDT's ecological impact, Jensen and his mentor, Swedish chemist Gunnar Widmark, began investigating the role of chlorinated hydrocarbons in declining populations of fish and other wildlife in the Stockholm archipelago. Employing recent scientific advances in gas chromatography, Jensen detected peaks characteristic of DDT and its by-products in fish. Jensen was puzzled, however, to find fourteen additional peaks—one researcher later called them "DDT ghost peaks"—in the chemical footprint. Testing the feathers of eagles archived by the Swedish Museum of Natural History, Jensen found more evidence of chemical contamination—these same fourteen "ghost peaks"—in a bird killed in 1944, that is, *before* DDT came into commercial use. After two years of chemical sleuthing, Jensen linked the peaks to a family of chemicals that German chemists had first described in the 1880s and that Monsanto had been manufacturing for almost forty years. Jensen identified the mystery peaks as biphenyls, polychlorinated biphenyls, on June 4, 1966. The discovery coincided with his thirty-ninth birthday. Not only had Jensen correctly identified the compounds; he coined the acronym "PCB."[43]

Jensen was extremely thorough. Through his research at the Institute for Analytical Chemistry in Stockholm, he began working out the pathways by which PCBs traveled. In addition to finding PCBs in dead white-tailed eagles and pike from the Swedish marine ecosystem, he detected PCBs in seals from the Stockholm archipelago, even in his wife's and his five-month-old daughter's hair. Jensen suggested that the route of human exposure was likely via PCBs carried in industrial smoke, deposited in waterways, then consumed by fish that were in turn consumed by humans. The infant's exposure, Jensen reasoned, came through her mother's breast milk.[44]

To understand how the chemicals interfered with species survival, Jensen studied small mammals. Marine biologists had noticed a sharp decline in seal populations in the Baltic, Jensen explained, with only 20 percent of female seals bearing pups. In the past, 100 percent had reproduced each year. Through controlled studies with minks, which had a reproduction cycle similar to that of seals, Jensen documented reproductive effects of PCBs in mammals. Giving pregnant minks a variety of feed mixtures, Jensen and his colleagues found that a control group fed neither PCBs nor DDT bred the normal six pups per year. PCBs appeared to interfere with implantation. "The DDT [group] was also quite normal," said Jensen, but, "the one with pure PCB and the one with PCB plus DDT didn't get any pups at all."[45]

No PCB production facilities existed in Sweden; the nearest manufacturer was in Germany, across the Baltic Sea. However, Swedish paper mills processed paper coated with PCBs, and Monsanto's Scandinavian customers, including the Swedish "one million new apartments program," were using PCBs in caulk and other building materials. The shipping industry also spread PCBs. "Most boats were painted with bottom paint that contained large quantities of PCB (mainly [Aroclor] 1254) to protect it against algae and higher organisms," explained Jensen. "We analysed cod from the Archipelago of Gotheburg, with a big ship-building industry. The level of PCB in their liver was about 10 ppm and therefore banned for consumption."[46]

Jensen, who went on to lead the Swedish Environment Protection Board's Special Analytical Laboratory at its founding in 1969, suggested that the chemicals entered the environment through the "back door," that is, through industrial emissions and sewage disposal. Engineered for stability, precisely the quality that made them useful to the electrical industry, PCBs were remarkably persistent. As one early report summarized, Jensen found that "PCB is much harder to break down than DDT, and there is every reason to suppose that it is much more difficult to get it out of the system." Like DDT, PCBs bioaccumulated, growing in concentration as they moved up the food chain. Jensen's research corroborated what had been known about PCB health effects since the 1930s: PCBs are "particularly harmful to the liver, and also the skin."[47]

Jensen's research finally made public that PCBs were harmful, persistent, and pervasive. A concise report in the London journal *New Scientist* in December 1966 publicized Jensen's conclusion that PCBs were "related to and as poisonous as DDT."[48]

Jensen's findings set off global concern. Because PCBs could be identified in diverse locales far from production sources, the *New Scientist* reported, the compounds "can therefore be presumed to be widespread throughout the world." The recognition that PCBs were harmful, enduring, and distributed globally attracted international attention after Jensen outlined his findings at Stockholm's renowned Wenner-Gren Center for Scientific Research in the late fall of 1966. Jensen was "surprised," he said in a 2010 interview, by the outpouring of scientific interest all over Europe. When other researchers had come across the mystery compound, they had "just called it 'avian compound 1-2-3,' if it came from a bird," said Jensen, "but now suddenly they could see it was PCB." Clearly, people engaged in manufacturing PCBs and consumers in direct contact with Aroclors products were not the only ones who could be exposed. Routes of exposure for humans and wildlife included air, water, soil, and food. Sweden took immediate steps toward a nationwide ban on the chemicals. In January 1972, Swedish law prohibited the "use, manufacture, importation and sale of PCB without permission of the authorities."[49]

Jensen's results appeared just as Monsanto was launching a five-year plan to expand its Aroclors market in Sweden. A letter from Monsanto's sales representatives in Sweden to the company's European headquarters in Brussels informed Monsanto of Jensen's research as reported in the Swedish press.[50]

Public attacks on scientists risked backfiring, as they had in the campaign against Rachel Carson. In any case, Monsanto generally preferred to mute criticism quietly, sometimes by involving critics in corporate projects

Chemist Søren Jensen receives the Great Prize of 1975 given by the Royal Swedish Academy of Sciences from King Carl XVI Gustaf for "his contribution to the identification of organic substances potentially harmful to the environment." In 1966, after two years of chemical sleuthing, Jensen identified PCBs as persistent, pervasive, and "as poisonous as DDT." Photo courtesy of Scanpix Sweden AB, successor to "Svenska Presstjänst."

or enticing them with research funding. For example, Monsanto contracted with one environmental chemist from the University of Wisconsin who had identified low levels of PCBs in dishwasher compounds, with one company official arguing in a memo, "If we do agree to some arrangement we could tend to neutralize any tendency on his part to criticize Monsanto."[51] If efforts to co-opt did not succeed, Monsanto found ways to publicly discredit the scientists' work.

Monsanto's first line of defense was to question Jensen's methodology. The company sent a representative, David Wood, from Brussels to Stockholm to learn more about the methods used by Jensen and his colleagues. Jensen did not attend the meeting. But Gunnar Widmark, Jensen's advisor and research partner, met with Wood and also accepted an invitation to visit Monsanto headquarters in St. Louis. With Widmark's assistance, using gas chromatography and mass spectrometry in their own labs, Monsanto chemists replicated the Swedish scholars' identification of PCBs. The new measurement techniques improved detection capabilities by orders of magnitude, making possible independent verification of the presence and extent of synthetic chemicals. Monsanto could no longer refute the technical methods by which researchers identified the presence of PCBs. To avert disruption of its Aroclors profit stream, the company would have to act quickly; the next big PCB news was just about to break.[52]

Soon after Jensen's revelatory breakthrough, Monsanto officials began following closely the work of University of California marine researcher Robert W. Risebrough, who was also studying PCBs. While investigating the precipitous decline of California's peregrine falcons, Risebrough found a direct link between exposure to PCBs and the species' failure to reproduce offspring. Risebrough and his co-authors wrote that PCBs were among "the most abundant of the chlorinated hydrocarbon pollutants in the global ecosystem." The team studied birds from Panama to the Farallon Islands off the California coast. They noted especially poor reproductive success among black petrels, which had high levels of both DDT and PCBs. Pairs in this peregrine group failed to hatch or fledge more than a single offspring in a season, where previously two to four young had been typical. (Industrial health researchers had suggested as early as 1934 that ingestion of halogenated compounds could influence reproduction in humans by causing changes in endocrine function, affecting the bodily systems that regulate hormones, growth, and metabolism. Carson had also reported that chlorinated hydrocarbons disturbed reproductive systems.) Risebrough's work proposed one mechanism by which PCBs affected reproduction in avian species. Risebrough described "a widespread change in the chemical environment which affected the calcium physiology of these species," a change that had occurred since World War II. Specifically, the chemicals reduced the calcium content of eggshells, making the shells fragile. The consequence was a reduction in hatchability for the young birds, a failure to reproduce. PCBs appeared to degrade estrogen hormones, which are essential to reproduction in humans as well as birds. Risebrough and his colleagues found PCBs to have approximately five times the estrogen-degrading potential of DDT and noted effects that did not kill the birds but reduced their numbers in succeeding generations. Risebrough made clear the intergenerational impact of toxic chemical exposures. "It is unlikely," he wrote, "that any species has the genetic capacity to meet the selection pressures resulting from the abrupt environmental change which had produced the thin eggshells."[53]

In December 1968, Risebrough and his colleagues at the Institute of Marine Resources at Berkeley reported these findings in the British journal

Nature. Here was evidence, not from a seemingly distant Baltic region but in the San Francisco Bay, of reproductive failure due to PCB exposure, over a remarkably brief period. Reporting on Risebrough's research, the *San Francisco Chronicle* labeled polychlorinated biphenyls "a menacing new pollutant."[54]

The increasing knowledge about the global transport of pollutants through air and oceans made the world seem smaller, Risebrough said later.[55] The findings enhanced the understanding of ecological connectedness across geographic space and scale, contributing to the very notion of a globalized world.

At Monsanto, a spate of internal memos followed publication of Risebrough's results. On December 30, Bill Richard at Monsanto's Research Center wrote to Bill Kuhn and others at headquarters about the "legal-political problems facing Aroclor." Richard noted, "We are taking 3 steps to protect ourselves." These steps included repeating the analytical identification tests conducted by independent researchers in hopes of obtaining different results, conducting "feeding tests done on animals to establish a 'safe' level," and restricting "Aroclor to uses which can be controlled." Wrote Richard, "That is the only way I see to survive."[56]

Monsanto staff scrambled to assemble information on "public relations, legal and scientific findings on Aroclor and its products." In February, Monsanto chemist Scott Tucker wrote to his superiors about the West Anniston site: "If the PCB accusation turns out to be true, and the government people become more active, we should plan on an extensive evaluation of the extent of contamination in this area." Tucker recognized the potential for extensive waterway contamination in Calhoun County and beyond, even as he proposed to act on PCB pollution only if the government pressured Monsanto to do so. If this occurred, wrote Tucker, "samples should be taken further down Snow Creek, down Choccolocco Creek and even from the Coosa River if necessary."[57]

The implications of Risebrough's research for ecosystems and for human health were deeply alarming. In March 1970, after the findings were made public, Monsanto dispatched a high-powered delegation to California to meet with Risebrough. Leading the team was William B. Papageorge, who had joined Monsanto in 1951 as assistant chemical engineer at the Queeny plant in St. Louis. Papageorge had taken charge of the Anniston plant at a pivotal point, just before Jensen's research became known. (He would eventually be promoted to the new position of environmental manager for Monsanto's Organic Chemicals Division, a position that earned him the moniker of "Monsanto's PCB czar.") Accompanying Papageorge to the meeting were Manager of Applied Sciences Robert E. Keller and Elmer P. Wheeler of the Medical Department.[58]

From his home in the Berkeley hills in 2010, Risebrough described the tenor of those early meetings as "cordial but tough." The line between scientific inquiry and outright intimidation was noticeably thin. Papageorge visited not only Risebrough but also his superiors. Despite attending closely to the work of independent scientists investigating PCBs, Monsanto officials resisted sharing even basic information on PCB products. At a meeting at Monsanto headquarters in early 1972, Risebrough requested PCB production figures. "We said to them," Risebrough explained later, 'To really predict the impact, we need to know how much.'" The company continued to withhold the information, claiming proprietary and competitive concerns. After nearly a year of stalling, Monsanto finally released numbers showing PCB production figures for the previous decade. The company had sold 353,093 tons, or 706 million pounds, of PCB compounds between 1960 and 1971.[59]

Sales had grown despite the fact that, in the mid-1960s, Monsanto had begun warning some industrial customers to exercise caution when handling PCBs. In a September 1965 internal memo, Wheeler reported on his communications with the Reliance Electric and Engineering Company of Cleveland. Reliance Electric used Aroclors as a coolant in electric motors, some of which were deployed in mines. Responding to complaints from miners working near the electric motors in close quarters, a Reliance official reported to Monsanto "that in his own plant hot Aroclors spills on the floor were common and that his own employees had complained of discomfort." Wheeler's reply leaves no doubt that Monsanto officials knew in 1965 that they were dealing with a potentially deadly substance: "I was brutally frank and told him that this had to stop *before he killed somebody* with liver or kidney damage—not because of a single exposure necessarily but only to emphasize that 8-hour daily exposures of this type would be completely unsafe." Monsanto knew about these dangers in the mid-1960s, but neither Wheeler's memo nor the dangers of which it warned were made public until decades later.[60]

In 1968, the most significant—and immediately fatal—suspected PCB contamination in food confirmed that acute exposure to PCBs posed serious hazards to human health. That February, about 1,600 people became ill in Japan after consuming PCB-contaminated rice-bran oil, called *yusho*. Five people died. Others suffered severe disfigurement. Most of the individuals exposed to Kanechlor 400, a PCB compound produced in Japan, developed severe chloracne. (Follow-up studies in the 1970s revealed birth defects in babies born to mothers who had been exposed to contaminated rice oil.) This prominent case of mass ingestion of the chemicals, in quantities sufficient to cause immediate illness, and in some cases death, suggested the need for prompt corporate response and regulatory action. Another year and a half would pass before Monsanto executives would initiate work on a "PCB Pollution Abatement Plan."[61]

In the face of mounting evidence of the extreme toxicity of one of its most profitable families of chemicals, Monsanto's Board of Directors voted in May 1969 to *increase* production at "the solid Aroclor® facilities at the Anniston, Alabama plant." With the $1.1 million expansion, board members envisioned maintaining the "supply into the mid-1970s," perhaps anticipating restrictions or a government ban.[62]

The year 1969 was critical for the company's efforts to manage the growing accumulation of toxic knowledge regarding PCBs. That year, Monsanto established an "Ad Hoc Committee" on PCB pollution to contain the growing concern over PCBs, if not the chemicals themselves. Convened in early September 1969 and chaired by Wheeler, the committee included a representative from Monsanto Research, W. R. "Bill" Richard, and another from the PR department, E. V. John. Paul B. Hodges was the most familiar with conditions at the Anniston plant and served as the committee's secretary. While their final report was titled *PCB Environmental Pollution Abatement Plan*, the committee's name better revealed its purpose. The group called itself "The 'Ad Hoc' Committee in Defense of Aroclors." It had two central aims—to protect Monsanto's profits, sales, and image and to avoid legal liability for PCB pollution. The confidential minutes of the first meeting laid out the committee's priorities and objectives:

1. Permit continued sales and profits of Aroclors and Terphenyls.
2. Permit continued development of uses and sales.
3. Protect image of Organic Division and of the Corporation.[63]

Monsanto clearly understood the threat: PCBs posed a global ecological problem and the Anniston plant environs were at particular risk. "I believe Anniston is vulnerable and that off-gas HCl and Aroclor should be 100% controlled," wrote Richard. The "Krummrich [plant] may also need help." Internal communications from the committee indicate an abiding preoccupation with defending Aroclors and give little or no attention to environmental public health.[64]

The threat of imminent government regulation, perhaps even a ban on PCB production, was clearly driving corporate strategy. The growing environmental movement was flexing its political muscle, demanding a centralized federal agency to address ecological issues, seeking strict regulation of toxic chemicals, and pushing for a ban on DDT. "We probably have 6 months to 1 year," Richard continued, "while [the wildlife people] fight out the DDT case." One Ad Hoc Committee exchange noted that "the Dept. of Interior and/or State authorities could monitor plant outfall and find ppm of chlorinated biphenyls at Krummrich or Anniston anytime they choose to do so. This would shut us down depending on what plants or animals they choose to find harmed."[65]

One committee report noted that "the most critical problem at present is water contamination." Nonetheless, in a discussion of discharge from the Anniston plant, where "gross losses" of PCBs were acknowledged, the committee concluded that, "until the problems of gross environmental contamination by our customers have been alleviated, there is little object in going to expensive extremes in limiting discharges from the plants." That is, since contamination was already widespread and other firms had contributed to it, Monsanto need not address PCB pollution within and around its factories.[66]

PCBs had been found in fish, oysters, shrimp, and birds in industrialized and coastal areas around the globe: Great Britain, Sweden, the Rhine River, Lake Michigan, the Pensacola Bay, and the American West. Ad Hoc Committee members understood both the pervasiveness of PCBs and their persistence, stating that the "rate of natural (bio-degradation) is *very low*." The science of PCBs had made Monsanto's first instinct untenable; the committee reluctantly concluded that "it will be impossible to deny the presence and persistence of Aroclors 1254 and 1260 at least."[67]

In 1969, the Anniston plant was dumping at least 250 pounds of PCBs per day into the drainage ditch that led to Snow Creek, according to Monsanto's records. In Monsanto's own tests, fat from a blacktail shiner collected from Choccolocco Creek contained 37,800 ppm of PCBs. "That's the most contaminated fish I have ever heard of anywhere in the wild," Massachusetts toxicologist Ian C. T. Nisbet testified much later in state court. "Usually under experimental conditions, by the time a fish has that amount of PCBs, it's dead."[68]

By now, Monsanto officials knew they faced "a worldwide ecological problem." Absent from the minutes of Ad Hoc Committee meetings, however, is any discussion of means to address the potential health consequences PCBs posed for wildlife or humans. The company had long couched its work as a scientific mission, but the committee's overriding concerns were maintaining profits and limiting liability and bad press. The men strategized about how to "maximize the corporate image." Of particular concern was "gain[ing] precious time needed to develop new products" to prevent competitors from supplying the market with safer substitutes.[69]

While the Ad Hoc Committee was preparing its report, the Anniston plant was idled by what the company called a strike and the workers termed a lockout. Monsanto had long had a contentious relationship with organized labor. Chemical workers nationally were represented by a variety of unions. Some joined the Oil, Chemical, and Atomic Workers Union; workers at the Anniston plant were members of the International Chemical Workers Union (ICWU), Local 125, which was chartered on December 4, 1944, the same year the ICWU formed. A four-month strike of 4,000 ICWU members had idled Monsanto plants in 1946 and again in the summer of 1953. ICWU president H. A. Bradley was bitter about the union's relationship with Monsanto, according to notes for the company history that journalist Hubert Kay began writing in 1951. "Ninety-eight per cent of the companies we deal with in the chemical business are good fellows, we get along with them," Bradley told his interviewer; "Monsanto leads the other two per cent."[70]

In 1969, with Monsanto Anniston still posting record sales, an overwhelming strike vote at the Anniston plant targeted Monsanto's policy of paying its southern workers less than their counterparts, a 94.5-cent hourly wage differential between Anniston and St. Louis. "It is time," International Chemical Workers Union Local 125 president William Cambron told the *Star*, "that the low-wage days of the South disappear and these giant, multi-plant companies pay the same rates and offer the same conditions of employment as they do in other sections of the country." Health and safety issues were noted only obliquely, in the demand that southern workers enjoy "the same conditions" as employees in the company's northern plants.[71]

Monsanto's Ad Hoc Committee in Defense of Aroclors issued its major report in October 1969. The Committee's *PCB Environmental Pollution Abatement Plan* proposed three potential courses of action: (1) do nothing, (2) stop manufacturing PCBs, or (3) stop manufacturing some PCBs but continue manufacturing others. The wisdom of each approach was measured by two factors: estimated profits and potential liability. The first, the "Do Nothing option," the committee projected, would yield rising profits through 1971, then fall off dramatically—to zero—in less than two years, anticipating a likely ban on PCB manufacture. Liabilities, on the other hand, would rise. The second option—to halt manufacture—would put an immediate end to profits, while liabilities would climb. "We would be admitting guilt by our actions," the Ad Hoc Committee concluded. The handful of men gathered around the table instead recommended restricting sales of PCBs to those intended for "closed uses," an approach that would preserve profits and, perhaps, limit liability. Production of PCBs for electrical fluids would continue at full speed, preserving 75 percent of the $8–11 million in annual PCB sales. In a chart appended to the report, profits and liability were the only two variables considered, suggesting a strategy to continue production as long as regulators and the threat of further litigation would allow. "We can't afford to lose one dollar of business," a manager at headquarters wrote to various Monsanto branch offices a few months later.[72]

More than a decade passed between scientists' identification in 1966 of PCBs as particularly widespread global pollutants and the enactment of the congressional ban on their production. During that time, Monsanto's Ad Hoc Committee acknowledged that PCBs "may be a global contaminant." The committee even considered halting production. Significantly, however, Monsanto's Board of Directors had responded to the news about PCB hazards by increasing production. The preferred strategy for the present, as one official scribbled in his marginal notes, was to "sell the hell out of them."[73]

BY 1970, MONSANTO was no longer able to forestall national press attention. The work of independent scientists had moved PCBs beyond academic journals and specialized industrial publications and into public view. In the popular press, PCBs now rivaled DDT as evidence of the toxic chemical consequences of global economic integration. In late October, *Sports Illustrated* featured an article by Robert H. Boyle on PCBs and pesticide residues in U.S. game fish. A study by the University of Wisconsin Alumni Research Foundation (the WARF Institute) had examined mercury, DDT, and PCB residues in U.S. coastal waters. "PCBs are present in the flesh and eggs of all samples," the WARF researchers found. Boyle's article in *Sports Illustrated*, a widely accessible national publication, implicated chemical industry sales culture in the spread of dangerous pesticides and heavy metals. Quoting Robert van den Bosch of University of California at Berkeley, Boyle noted that chemical salesmen required no special training, "yet this person deals with extremely complex ecological problems and utilizes some of the most deadly and ecologically disruptive chemicals devised by science." In

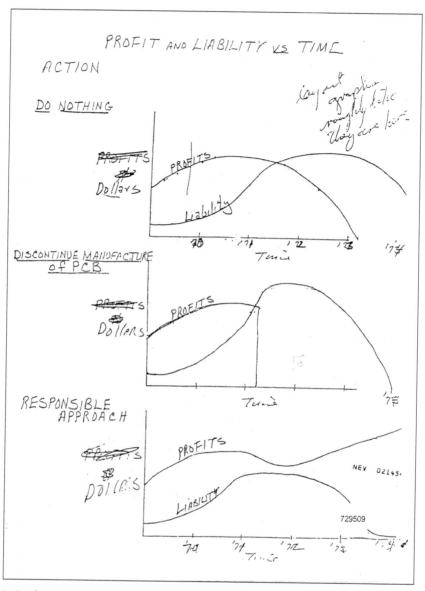

In October 1969, faced with mounting public awareness that PCBs were persistent, pervasive, and toxic, Monsanto's Ad Hoc Committee for the Defense of Aroclors projected three "profit and liability" options for addressing its PCB problem: do nothing; stop manufacturing PCBs; or stop manufacturing some PCBs but continue manufacturing others. Between then and the time PCBs were banned by Congress and Monsanto stopped manufacturing them in 1977, millions more pounds of PCBs were produced and distributed worldwide. From *Abernathy* documents.

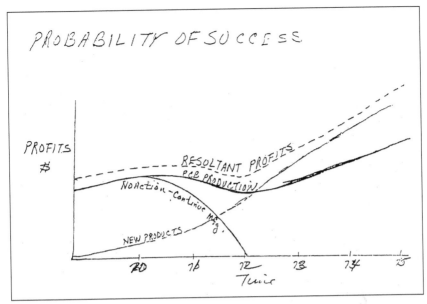

Monsanto's Ad Hoc Committee for the Defense of Aroclors charted the consequences for profits of its three options for addressing its PCB problem against a time frame for developing substitute products. In contrast to halting production immediately in response to reports of the chemicals' toxicity, a gradual phase-out of PCBs would realize an additional $6.1 million dollars in sales. From *Abernathy* documents.

a passage that must have been profoundly disconcerting to the industry, Boyle proposed suing chemical companies under the Federal Refuse Act.[74]

"If You Think DDT's a Problem, Meet PCB," wrote the *New York Times* in September 1971. Being invisible in the consumer marketplace may have helped shield PCBs from criticism in the past, but as news of PCBs in food, animal feed, and common household objects began to appear in major U.S. print media, the company was no longer protected by invisibility. The use of PCBs in carbonless duplicating paper routinely handled by office workers and many business executives became a focus of news stories that year as well. In addition, the carbonless copy paper containing PCBs had been recycled into various paper products that also contained PCBs, including cardboard used in food packaging. In 1971, the FDA found PCBs in the average American nineteen-year-old's diet via cardboard cereal boxes.[75]

Multiple PCB contaminations of food between 1969 and 1971 underscored the urgency of addressing the PCB problem. Farm animals destined for human consumption, including 88,000 chickens in North Carolina, had to be destroyed after consuming feed that had absorbed PCB fluids from a leaking heating system. Farmers found PCBs in Minnesota turkeys bound for dinner tables. Regulators identified PCBs in milk sold by dairies near Columbus, Ohio, that Monsanto believed could be traced "to deteriorating coating applied to silos in 1967" and in fish meal sold to five companies in Alabama and dozens of companies in other, mostly southern, states. Shrimpers scooped PCB-infused seafood from Florida's Escambia Bay.[76]

A few days after the *Sports Illustrated* article hit the newsstands, Anniston pollution control engineer Eugene "Bunky" Wright reported that Aroclors 1242 had reached exceedingly high levels (64,800 ppb) in tests at a new sump pump located below the Anniston plant landfill. The overall tone of the pollution abatement plan notwithstanding, Monsanto had set a target of 50 ppb for PCB levels in plant waste. Once the pump was installed, levels fluctuated from 2,800 to 35,000 ppb. By that summer Monsanto knew about the problem in Anniston and knew that state regulators would have no choice but to act were PCB contamination in Anniston to attract media attention. The company sought to keep the damaging information out of the news. Monsanto's Jack T. Garrett wrote to J. C. Landwehr at the Anniston plant, "If this issue hits the Alabama press AWIC would be forced to close Choccolocco Creek. The state of Alabama has no choice but to follow the guidelines of the FDA which calls for no more than 5 ppm PCB in fish." Globules of Aroclors were visible in the ditch. Rainy periods aggravated the problem. In subsequent tests, taken over several days, Aroclors levels dropped substantially but remained extraordinarily high. Nonetheless, Wright did not plan to continue testing for PCBs unless the pump was overflowing into Snow Creek.[77]

As Monsanto managers devised a global strategy for sustaining sales of Aroclors in the face of the national and international news describing their dangers, the PCB pollution in Anniston remained a nagging problem for the company. In a major spill on November 6, 1,500 gallons of PCB-containing wastes flowed directly into Snow Creek from a busted pipe. Two smaller spills followed the next year, 400 gallons one time, 200 gallons another. Still, no word was shared with Monsanto's neighbors about the dangers posed by PCBs or the contamination in the creek.[78]

CHAPTER SEVEN

The Death of Aroclors

Chemicals alter human relationships.
—Environmental historian Gregg Mitman, 2010

Shortly before Christmas, 1970, a representative from the Monsanto plant approached West Anniston resident Jeremiah Smith with an unusual request. Monsanto wanted to buy all fifty of his hogs—at ten dollars a head. Smith raised pigs for a little fresh meat and an occasional bit of supplementary income, as did several of the chemical factory's other African American neighbors. The animals were free to root around in the streams and often foraged on the plant's unfenced land without objection from Monsanto. Factory officials never explained to Smith why they bought his entire herd. The company had bought the herds of other hog owners as well. More than twenty-five years would pass before any of them learned the significance of the purchases.[1]

Monsanto quietly conducted tests for PCBs on the animals they rounded up. Before the month was out, the "Hog Analysis Results" were circulating within the company. The animal fat registered extremely high levels of PCBs—19,000 parts per million (ppm), at a time when the Federal Water Quality Administration recommended against consuming fish measuring above 5 ppm PCBs. The tests focused only on PCBs and confirmed what company officials must have suspected: seriously high levels of polychlorinated biphenyls in animals regularly consumed by the people who lived just beyond the plant gates. Of the three major pathways to PCB contamination of adult bodies—breathing, eating, absorption through the skin—ingesting PCBs in contaminated livestock, fish, and other foods is particularly dangerous, because the PCB congeners that tend to bioconcentrate in fish and other animals are also considered the most likely to cause cancer. With foreknowledge, this pathway to contamination is also easily avoided. But Monsanto personnel told none of their neighbors in West Anniston about the health hazards of consuming locally grown pork that company officials now knew could be riddled with PCBs. As the chemicals garnered ominous headlines in Stockholm, San Francisco, and Japan, PCBs and acid wastes continued

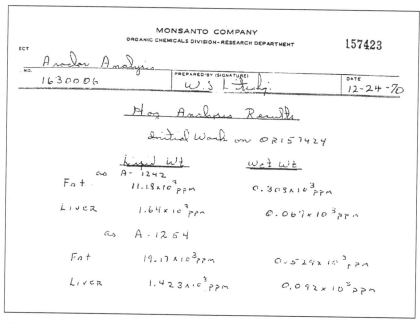

MONSANTO COMPANY
ORGANIC CHEMICALS DIVISION - RESEARCH DEPARTMENT   157423

ECT
NO. *Aroclor Analysis*
1630006   PREPARED BY (SIGNATURE) W. S. *[illegible]*   DATE 12-24-70

Hog Analysis Results

initial Work on OR157424

	Lipid Wt	Wet Wt
as A-1242		
Fat	11.18×10^3 ppm	0.308×10^3 ppm
Liver	1.64×10^3 ppm	0.067×10^3 ppm
as A-1254		
Fat	19.17×10^3 ppm	0.529×10^3 ppm
Liver	1.423×10^3 ppm	0.092×10^3 ppm

"Hog Analysis Results." In December 1970, Monsanto conducted tests on hogs purchased from West Anniston residents and found very high levels of PCBs in the hog fat, 19,000 parts per million (ppm), at a time when the Federal Water Quality Administration recommended against consuming fish measuring above 5 ppm PCBs. From *Abernathy* documents.

pouring into Snow Creek with little fanfare, snaking unnoticed past the West Anniston neighborhoods of Sweet Valley and Cobbtown.[2]

Monsanto faced several setbacks in the early 1970s. After record sales in 1968, and despite growth in overseas sales, Monsanto reported a nearly 30 percent drop in earnings in 1970 after strikes at tire, auto, and appliance manufacturers interrupted demand. Prices of the raw materials extracted from petroleum were rising. And environmentalists, aided by progressive labor leaders concerned about worker health and safety, found an advocate in Congress to press for a nationwide toxic chemicals policy.[3]

In 1970, prompted by constituent concerns about DDT on Long Island and press reports about PCBs in the Hudson River, Representative William Fitts Ryan (D-N.Y.) announced plans to introduce legislation tightening regulation of these and other toxic chemicals. Ryan initiated discussion about banning the production and use of PCBs in the United States.[4]

Already, the broad threat posed by PCBs and other chemical pollutants had contributed to the push to consolidate responsibility for environmental oversight scattered among several cabinet departments. President Richard

The Monsanto Chemical Company plant dominated the West Anniston landscape as seen from this view from the South Landfill looking northeast across Highway 202, probably taken in the late 1970s. Photo courtesy of the *Anniston Star*.

M. Nixon created the Environmental Protection Agency by executive order in the summer of 1970, and the new agency opened its doors in early December.[5] It was the same month that Monsanto purchased Jeremiah Smith's hogs. Among the EPA's early targets were PCBs.

By 1971, Nixon's Council on Environmental Quality (CEQ) was focusing high-level executive branch attention on PCBs. As EPA administrator Russell Train later recounted, the CEQ warned that, though the chemicals had commercial advantages, they "could have serious adverse effects on human health." Edward D. Goldberg, of the prestigious Scripps Oceanographic Institute, declared PCBs to be "first order threats" to the world's oceans. After the first U.N. Conference on Environment and Development (UNCED) met in Stockholm in 1972, the member countries of the Organization for Economic Cooperation and Development (OECD) announced their decision to prohibit most uncontained industrial and commercial uses of PCBs.[6]

The launch of the EPA, in particular, appears to have pushed Monsanto to make some effort toward cleaning up their Anniston operations. A flurry of activity at Monsanto in late 1970, including the Hog Analysis tests and tentative discussions of discontinuing Aroclors production at the Anniston plant, suggests the company was expecting greater federal scrutiny of the site.[7]

Pollution-control equipment installed in 1969 had slowed the hemorrhaging of PCBs from the Clydesdale Avenue plant. FDA and EPA inquiries in 1970 and 1971 contributed to reducing the amount of chemical wastes pouring into Calhoun County's streams. Still, high levels of pollution persisted in West Anniston. None of Monsanto's plants in the United States and Britain met the company's discharge goals of 50 ppb (later 10 ppb), much less the EPA target of "no detectable amount." The reported average PCB levels in effluent from the Anniston plant remained the highest (321 ppb) of any Monsanto facility, and almost double those at Sauget (177 ppb).[8]

By now, federal regulatory staffers were aware of PCB pollution in Anniston's aquatic food chain. Just one month before Monsanto's hog purchase, the FDA had released results of their tests on local fish. Catfish from Choccolocco Creek measured "PCBs at more than 50 times [the] acceptable level" for human consumption. FDA testing had identified contamination in carp at eight times the standard more than forty miles downstream. A fisheries expert from a nearby hatchery, speaking at a meeting of the Calhoun County Clean Up the Environment (CUE) group in mid-1971, labeled Choccolocco Creek south of Oxford "a dead creek."[9]

Members of the Committee of Unified Leadership (COUL) were deeply troubled about air and water pollution in West Anniston. COUL's Priority No. 2 in 1972, second only to improving medical services at Anniston Memorial Hospital, was "Air, Water, and Noise Pollution." Of particular concern was the open ditch running through West Anniston. "One of the tremendously sore spots with the black community on the West side of Anniston is the condition of an open ditch. This ditch runs some eight to nine blocks through the black community and affects everyone on the West side of town in some way; flooding, insects, offensive odors, rodents, and unsafe for children." The issue of the ditch had been "on the agenda almost from the inception of COUL" in 1971. Emphasizing that the "storm drainage system near Monsanto and West Anniston [was] inadequate," COUL recognized that the ditch was part of "a problem of greater magnitude," the "inadequacy of the entire drainage system for the City." These explicit complaints about pollution were put to rest by Monsanto's assurances that its processes were safe and by the belief that the federal government was taking action to limit pollution. Confident "that these problems are being solved by the federal government," the organization moved on to other priorities. Even as they expressed concern about pollution in West Anniston, members of COUL were not made aware of the extent of PCB pollution or the potential for harm.[10]

At national headquarters, one Monsanto official privately fretted over the growing national concern over PCBs, complaining, in gendered terms, that "the pollution *hysteria* continues to grow." The company possessed "the world's best reference file on PCBs," a trove of health studies, worker experiences, and industry information going back to the 1930s. In news releases, however, Monsanto continued to maintain that "PCB is not a highly toxic material." At the same time, the company redoubled efforts to thwart a U.S. ban on PCBs. Monsanto's internal records reveal the company's calculated response to increased scrutiny and the prospect of government regulation—deflection, denial, and minimum compliance—all the while exhibiting a veneer of cooperation in service of public interest.[11]

Plant officials anticipated that when Alabama laws requiring improved measures at landfills went into effect at the beginning of the 1970s, "it is highly probable that the Monsanto (P.C.B.) dump area could be classified as a serious water pollution source." With eighty pounds of PCBs spewing from the plant on a single day in September 1970, Monsanto officials were already guarding against being held liable for their toxic legacy, carefully choosing which information to share with state and federal regulators: "From the Legal standpoint, there is extreme reluctance to report *even the relatively low emission figures* because the information could be subpoenaed and used against us in legal action." The company began taking more decisive steps toward shifting liability to its Aroclors customers, requiring them, for example, to sign indemnity agreements holding the company harmless for "any contamination of or adverse effect on humans, marine and wildlife, food, animal feed or the environment by reason of such PCB's." William Papageorge, the former Anniston plant manager now overseeing Monsanto's PCB problem, wrote, "We must ensure that these warnings are fully documented so that they will support the action we have taken in this area should we become involved in legal actions." At the same time, the Monsanto Company devolved responsibility for the manufacture of PCBs—and, potentially, pollution liability—to a subsidiary, the Monsanto Industrial Chemicals Company (MICC).[12]

On the Sunday before Thanksgiving 1970, the *Anniston Star* ran a front-page story summarizing the FDA's findings of PCB contamination in local fish. Responding to the FDA report, the company denied the existence of scientific evidence on the adverse health impact of PCBs. "We can't find any documented evidence at this point" of harmful effects of PCBs on living organisms, one Monsanto official told *Star* readers at their breakfast tables that Sunday morning. "In any case," plant manager Gene Jessee assured the public, "I don't see cause for worry from the public health standpoint."[13]

At Monsanto headquarters in St. Louis, the public relations office was pleased with the tone of the *Star* coverage. "The feature emphasized the PCB problem was relatively new, was being solved by Monsanto, and, at this point, was no cause for alarm," E. V. John wrote. He applauded local plant management for realizing "the value of cooperation with news media planning PCB stories." Skillful handling of the press deflected further inquiry.[14]

Efforts to reduce the toxicity of effluent from the Anniston plant had no effect in reducing the PCB levels in the fish in Choccolocco Creek. Monsanto's biological consultants, Royal D. Suttkus and Gerald E. Gunning, continued to find "deformed" and "sick or listless fishes." In 1971, the biologists noted that Aroclors "residues have not decreased as we had hoped they would." Acknowledging the awkward timing of their findings, which coincided with a negative congressional subcommittee report, Suttkus and Gunning concluded their report by saying, "We are very sorry that we can't paint a brighter picture at the present time." Crossing the normal bounds of scientific objectivity to suggest ways to spin the unfavorable results, the researchers advised that the company might "derive some favorable publicity" by highlighting the reduction in discharges rather than the persistence of contamination. However, Monsanto's consultants cautioned against reporting the actual discharges: "Certainly you would not want to give the figures in a news release."[15]

By the time of the hog purchase, Monsanto's internal strategy for aggressively managing their PCB problem was beginning to shift, even as the company prepared to expand Aroclors production and mount a forceful public defense of the products. Earlier that year, in July 1970, as eventual restrictions on PCB production and use appeared likely, Monsanto abruptly had announced that the company would voluntarily limit sales of PCBs to those used in "closed systems." These liquid compounds, which were used in sealed transformers and other electrical equipment that purportedly contained the product, could be justified as enclosed or "controlled." Using that rationale, Monsanto stood to protect much of its Aroclors business, which was concentrated in electrical fluids sales. "We are discontinuing sales into 'open systems'—adhesives, sealants, chlorinated rubber, specialty paints, etc.," company spokesperson Howard L. Minkler said.[16]

One of the foundations of the closed-uses strategy was the widely held notion that the most highly chlorinated PCBs, the ones that had more chlorine atoms attached to their benzene rings, were also the most hazardous.

These Aroclors were mainly used in plastics, paints, carbonless duplication paper and other open uses, the ones that would seem most threatening to the general public. Highly chlorinated PCBs are comprised of heavier molecules than low-chlorinated PCBs, so are generally *less* volatile, that is, less easily transported via air, but *more* persistent, both in soil and in body fluids and tissues. In fact, as Cecil Drinker had suggested as early as 1937, the relationship between toxicity and chlorination is complex. Scientists now understand that toxic effects depend on multiple factors, including the position of chlorine atoms in the PCB molecule, temperature, and other factors, as well as the level of chlorination.[17]

Although the company projected the shift to "closed uses" as a unilateral step toward pollution abatement and a quick phase-out of PCBs that could not be "strictly controlled," the decision was strategic, a step that anticipated new regulatory standards and might avoid an imposed ban. If the new plan succeeded, Monsanto could continue producing the majority of its PCB products indefinitely—or at least until the research and development staff could devise acceptable substitutes.[18]

Industrial purchasers were becoming wary of the highly chlorinated Aroclors. To counter concern, the company introduced a new product, Aroclor 1016. In the standard nomenclature of the Aroclor line, the last two digits represented the percentage of chlorine the mixture contained. "The *lower* the grade number, the less chlorinated and more biodegradable is the product," claimed a Monsanto sales publication in 1972. The designation "1016" implied that the compound was less persistent than existing Aroclors. In fact, 1016 contained not 16 but 41 percent chlorine, only 1 percent lower than Aroclor 1242.[19]

Monsanto ceased open-use PCB production as much because of market dynamics as because of environmental pressure or the threat of litigation. Company officials were careful to emphasize that "Monsanto had not been pressured into action by any legislation or organized group." Monsanto's monopoly on PCB production in the United States, Canada, and Britain gave the company relative stability in PCB sales. The market for PCBs destined for transformers and capacitors was concentrated among a relatively few purchasers of large lots—another advantage—whereas the sales of withdrawn products were scattered among many smaller customers. Nor was the sale of all discontinued PCBs to end immediately. The company had calculated that while phasing out PCBs gradually over the next year and a half, it would realize an additional $6.1 million in sales. The closed-uses decision was a strategic sacrifice disguised as good faith.[20]

The very idea of "closed systems" was problematic. At the time, ecologists were questioning whether any system on earth remained closed or separated from the rest of nature. Transformers and capacitors can be, and often are, breached, from either routine aging of equipment or accidents. Even before Monsanto announced this strategy, reporter David Perlman had quoted Robert Risebrough as saying that the idea that PCBs were safe in localized uses was "misleading, irrelevant, and wrong." PCB-filled equipment is subject to explosions and fires, as a series of high-profile incidents in the 1980s and 1990s has since demonstrated. Monsanto's PCB chief William Papageorge himself later acknowledged that closed systems "tend to malfunction and leak and what have you."[21]

Producing PCBs in any form exposed workers and made the factory surroundings vulnerable to the hazards of production. Restricting PCB use to closed applications, Environmental Defense Fund scientist Ellen Silbergeld noted in 1983, "did not lead to a clear and ongoing downward trend of environmental levels" of PCBs.[22]

Once the closed-uses strategy was in place, the company was faced with excess production capacity. In December 1970, the month of the unexplained hog purchase, Monsanto's Ad Hoc Committee had discussed "mothballing" the Aroclors operations in Anniston. A year and a half later, Monsanto shifted all Aroclors production to its Krummrich plant in Sauget, Illinois. The Monsanto team debating the future of the Anniston plant felt that though "PCB control at [the Sauget facility] could become politically 'hot'" in Illinois, "the legal threats are more imminent and the problems more visible" at Anniston. PCB contamination at Monsanto's Anniston plant had been briefly mentioned in a congressional hearing in late July 1971. Closing the Aroclors production operations at Anniston also obviated the need to install what was variously estimated at between "$280M and $1000M" in EPA-mandated pollution control equipment. "PCB pollution capital [investment] at Anniston should be held to minimum," advised one internal memo. After the decision to shut down PCB production in Anniston was made, Papageorge declared cleanup "economically impractical." Although some industrial customers were increasingly skittish about buying Aroclors, Monsanto continued to produce PCBs in Sauget until 1977. Left only with the closed-uses market, domestic production dropped from 85 million pounds in 1970 to about 40 million pounds annually by 1974.[23]

IN THE COMPETING ETHICS of science and the marketplace, commercial interests dominated. As a company whose products were the result of aggressive commercialization of new knowledge based in scientific re-search, Monsanto continued to reject new scientific evidence implicating PCBs. Monsanto repeatedly summoned the authority of science to delay regulation of PCBs and justify their continued use.[24]

In order to delay outside action against PCBs, Monsanto's Ad Hoc Com-mittee had set an explicit goal to "Make the Govt, States and Universities prove their case." Donning the mantle of scientific authority to buttress its defense of Aroclors, Monsanto raised doubts about the toxicity of PCBs. Company representatives proposed that PCBs themselves were not toxic unless "adulterated" or destabilized by other chemicals. This claim invoked "an industrial idea of contamination," suggesting that a component of the chemical was "taking away from the purity of the product." Indicting a for-eign ingredient or particular combination of chemicals as the hazardous agent—not the chemical itself—deflected responsibility for toxicity to those who supplied raw materials. Alternatively, the problems associated with PCBs could be attributed to purchasers' improper handling by suggesting that somehow the compounds became adulterated after being shipped.[25]

Nonetheless, Monsanto acknowledged internally the potential for syner-gistic effects, that is, for PCBs to compound the toxicity of other chemicals. In private correspondence, the Ad Hoc Committee suggested that "PCB[s] may be contributing to or exaggerating the effects of other chlorinated aromatics."[26]

In addition to making government and other scientists "prove their case" that PCBs were toxic, Monsanto aimed to "prove bioharmless" the Aroclors products and to establish "safe" levels of exposure for people, mammals, and fish. Toxicological tests of workers had become routine in industrial hy-giene, undergirded by the faith that scientists could determine "safe levels" at which exposure caused no harm. Although the Ad Hoc Committee had acknowledged that some species, at least, were harmed at very low levels of exposure, Monsanto continued to insist that at some concentration PCBs were safe.[27]

For help in proving safe levels of exposure to various Aroclors com-pounds, Monsanto contracted with Industrial Bio-Test Laboratories (IBT Labs), based in Northbrook, Illinois. At the time, IBT Labs conducted an estimated one-third of the industry-wide toxicology studies submitted to federal regulators, that is, they did so until the firm's principal partners were found to be manipulating and falsifying study results.[28]

Monsanto arranged with Joe Calandra of IBT Labs to conduct more than forty tests on its Aroclors products. The studies began in 1963, increased in the early 1970s, and were designed "to establish FDA type limits" for exposure to PCBs.[29]

Eventually, key personnel at IBT Labs were indicted in what reporter Eric Francis later called "one of the most far-reaching scandals in modern science." IBT researchers, while purportedly using scientific techniques, carried out work riddled with bias and, in at least one instance—not involving PCBs—outright fraud. Three defendants were convicted of "concealing unfavorable test results, lying about the scope of the tests and cutting short one study of the capacity of a chemical to cause cancer in mice," the *New York Times* reported. Monsanto's PCB studies were not investigated in the IBT cases and Monsanto was not charged, but the inquiry did bring to light an exchange of memos between Monsanto and the lab's research staff regarding IBT's Aroclors studies.[30]

At least one of the IBT Aroclors studies appears to have been conducted in direct response to Risebrough's work on avian reproduction. The initial results were "not as favorable as we had anticipated," Scott Tucker at Monsanto's Research and Development lab informed Eugene Wright in Anniston in January 1970. "Particularly alarming," Tucker wrote, "is evidence of effect of hatchability and production of thin egg shells regards white leghorn chickens." Not to be deterred by the adverse findings, Tucker assured Wright, "Some of these studies will be repeated to arrive at better conclusions."[31]

The memos reveal intervention by Monsanto personnel in the IBT studies to suggest altering research findings. One IBT analyst worried that data from studies conducted for Monsanto were "either fudged or collected with carelessness or incompetence," according to a handwritten internal communication. The researcher, who identified himself only as "Otis," flatly stated, "I am ashamed to publish the work done in these studies." Otis continued, "This is perhaps the most significant of the Aroclor studies and some of my conclusions are not in agreement with those of the reports (which I signed without detailed analysis) or with statements that have been made by Kip and by Monsanto in discussion with FDA and environmental groups." Still, Monsanto personnel continued to request changes to IBT Labs reports that would cast its controversial chemicals in a more favorable light. A letter to Joe Calandra from Monsanto's manager for environmental assessment and toxicology, George J. Levinskas, about revisions to reports on Aroclors studies reads as follows: "In 2 instances, the previous conclusion of 'slightly tumorigenic' was changed to 'does not appear to be carcinogenic.' The latter phrase is preferable. May we request that the AROCLOR 1254 report be amended to say 'does not appear to be carcinogenic.'"[32]

Especially suspect is Monsanto toxicologist Paul Wright's transfer to IBT Labs to supervise tests on Monsanto products and subsequent return to his position managing toxicology for Monsanto's Department of Medicine and Environmental Health after they were completed. Wright and two other IBT researchers were convicted on multiple counts of falsifying chemical tests for other firms. Wright was fired from Monsanto after being convicted. The scandal was an embarrassment to multiple federal agencies that had relied on IBT data as the basis for setting maximum allowable concentrations of countless chemicals in food, detergents, pesticides, and other products.[33]

IN THE FACE OF MONSANTO'S continued defenses of its Aroclors products, the regulatory handling of PCBs illustrated both the impact and the limitations of what environmental movement historian Robert Gottlieb has labeled the new "eco-bureaucracy" of the 1970s. Chemical manufacturers aimed to influence not only the federal standards but also the regulatory timeline. In 1970, Monsanto learned from a contact at the Ohio State Health Department that the FDA would soon impose limits on PCB content in all foodstuffs. Monsanto appealed to scientific uncertainty, arguing that establishing limits would require further study. Agencies heeded Monsanto's appeal as a rationale for delaying regulation. The company expressed concern that the agency would take "precipitous action before adequate information could be gathered," a process the company estimated would take "at least one year" before studies would be complete. After reviewing a report on PCBs from Monsanto's director of medical research, the FDA hesitated to recommend comprehensive guideline levels for PCB contamination in food. Basing his decision on Monsanto's summary of research on PCBs, FDA toxicologist H. Blumenthal cited a "lack of complete toxicologic data," and when coupled with an "essential lack of information about background levels of contamination in foodstuffs in general," resisted setting guidelines except on a case-by-case basis. The FDA opposed an outright ban on PCBs in 1971. On the basis of Monsanto's research, an FDA spokesperson told the *Wall Street Journal* that the evidence against PCB contamination in foods "doesn't warrant scare headlines."[34]

As memos from the Ad Hoc Committee showed, and as a jury would later rule, Monsanto suppressed knowledge that could have alerted the public to the serious PCB contamination in West Anniston, but other factors contributed to the company's success in downplaying the potential dangers of PCBs. Inadequate enforcement at the federal level and the complicity of state regulators obscured the extent of the threat PCBs posed.

For the most part, regulators conformed to long-standing "conventions of confidentiality."[35]

Monsanto continued to cultivate government allies, not just regulators but also influential members of the executive branch and the military. For example, soon after he retired as chairman of the Joint Chiefs in 1970, General Earl G. Wheeler joined Monsanto's board, a position he held until 1975.[36]

Monsanto moved swiftly to take an active role in shaping the terms of environmental regulation. Acting to secure favorable conditions for continued production, Monsanto advised on the PCB standards to be used by the electrical industry as set by the American National Standards Institute (ANSI), the business association that sets voluntary norms and guidelines for commercial products, which held weight with federal regulators.[37]

The EPA was sufficiently alarmed about PCB levels in Anniston streams to press Monsanto to reduce discharges, but the agency did so quietly. On November 11, 1971, while violence flared in West Anniston over racial discrimination at Wellborn High, EPA officials summoned Monsanto representatives to their southern regional office in Atlanta to consider a report labeled "Company Confidential." At the time, Monsanto was under threat of a lawsuit by the Justice Department for PCB pollution in Anniston. Under discussion were "PCB Effluents from Anniston Plant to Snow Creek, Choccolocco Creek." According to a Monsanto memo summarizing the meeting, EPA director of enforcement John White would take the company's side. Monsanto's representative reported, "We received strong indications that the Southeastern Regional EPA Office will recommend strongly against a [Federal] Refuse Act suit by the Federal Department of Justice on PCB pollution." In response to Monsanto's request for a disposal permit to continue dumping PCBs, White was less forgiving, reiterating that the agency standard for the level of PCBs in discharge was "no detectable amount." Monsanto gauged that the EPA might be swayed by the corporation's state contact, Joe Crockett at AWIC, who argued that limits this low represented "an undesirable approach."[38]

Crockett had frequently stepped in on Monsanto's behalf. Earlier, when the company was under investigation by the FDA, for example, representatives of Monsanto traveled to the state capitol in Montgomery to talk with longtime ally Crockett. On that occasion, an internal Monsanto memo labeled "Confidential—F.Y.I. and Destroy" reported that Crockett "will try to handle the problem quietly without release of the information to the public at this time." Crockett shared Monsanto's views regarding informing the public about PCBs. In fact, Crockett recommended that Monsanto "give no statements or publications which would bring the situation [PCB contamination] to the public's attention."[39] Crockett also promised to be discreet.

Monsanto officials left the Atlanta meeting with the impression that the agency would rely on company data, as they had hoped. Monsanto was selective about which data to share with the feds; the Hog Analysis Results, for example, they kept to themselves.[40] The EPA's willingness to meet privately with Monsanto, to consider relaxing its own proposed standards, and to advocate against litigation not only aided Monsanto but undermined the agency's own power. The EPA's actions kept the conversation about PCBs at the Anniston plant behind closed doors. Ultimately, at that time, the agency's efforts at Anniston focused more on the health of waterways and fish than on the impact of PCBs on the people who lived along and fished in the rivers and streams.

State and federal agencies were not only aware of the serious PCB contamination in Anniston, but they also had the tools to act more vigorously to reduce pollution, tools that went unused. In October 1972, Congress augmented the Clean Water Act, making it national policy that "the discharge of toxic pollutants in toxic amounts be prohibited." The law also called for prompt action. Under congressional mandate, the EPA was to identify key toxic chemicals within ninety days and establish "toxic amounts" of exposure within six months. But the EPA was excruciatingly slow to act. Only after lawsuits by the National Resources Defense Council and other environmental groups did the EPA submit its list of toxic pollutants, PCBs among them. Nine months had passed. It would be July 1976, another four years, with federal legislation to ban PCBs pending, before the agency formally promulgated a standard for PCB discharges. "The history of EPA's PCBs proceedings is a history of frustration of a congressional mandate for action," wrote a Washington, D.C. appeals court in 1978. The court cited the "lack of toxicological and biological data for many chemicals and scientific disputes over what amount of a 'toxic' pollutant can be considered safe" as the reason for the delay. It was the rationale industry had orchestrated.[41]

The EPA had joined with industry in a paradoxical posture: scientific uncertainty did not preclude industry from selling toxic chemicals, but scientific uncertainty did prevent *blocking* toxic chemicals from being sold. Congress's precautionary mandate for the "EPA to protect against incompletely understood dangers," the federal appeals court ruled, "could not be carried out if we were to adopt the proof requirements advocated by industry"—that is, that a substance be proved definitively harmful.[42]

Yet proof was available. PCBs were placed on the list of the nine most toxic pollutants in 1973 "because of their high order of toxicity to man and aquatic organisms and because of their bioaccumulative potential." The EPA's proposed rules as finally promulgated in July 1976 clearly noted the harmful health effects: "PCBs have been conclusively proven to produce lethal and sublethal toxic effects at low dose levels upon a wide range of fish, mammals, and other wildlife, and have also demonstrated adverse health effects to humans." The agency's toxicity data suggested that because "chronic toxic effects may occur at extremely low concentrations, it becomes virtually impossible to state with confidence that any number above zero provides an ample margin of safety for man."[43]

Monsanto officials counted on contacts in various agencies as they mounted a defense of PCBs. Upon learning that the National Air Pollution Control Administration (NAPCA) in Cincinnati was seeking data on the hazards of incinerating PCBs, Monsanto personnel took comfort in the fact that NAPCA had designated Bob Day, a Monsanto employee from Pensacola on temporary assignment to NAPCA in order to fulfill his military commitment, to handle the request. Wheeler was satisfied that Day was not a "Knight on a White Horse" but would "try to present Monsanto's views to wit: 'We cannot conceive how the PCBs can be getting into the environment in a widespread fashion and that the company is actively involved in research to try to shed some light on the situation.'"[44]

Contacts in government also gave company officials advance notice of upcoming investigations. Elmer Wheeler received one such heads-up regarding PCB pollution from the "boys" at the Federal Water Pollution Control Authority. The "FWPCA boys," wrote Wheeler, let it be known that "we can anticipate that the Feds will be looking at creek, river, or lake water below Anniston for PCBs."[45]

THE PROPERTIES OF PCBS themselves compounded the difficulties in uncovering their presence. Even though they were deployed in hundreds of uses, PCBs remained virtually invisible to the public. Many forms of PCBs were colorless and odorless. Others were bright orange waxy solids but disappeared once mixed with other materials to produce finished goods. "PCB is not a household product," Monsanto declared publicly in 1970, when PCBs were common components of many consumer goods. "To our knowledge it is not used in plastic food wrap, house paint, cellophane, asphalt, or tires." While it was technically true that, as chemical intermediates, PCBs were not sold over-the-counter by name to individual buyers, manufacturers used them in familiar consumer products ranging from building caulk to printer's inks. A company survey reported in April 1970 that Aroclors were used in a number of "questionable applications," including shoe polish, fabric coatings, perfumes, and "Xmas Tree Flameproofing and Sealing." DDT was an insecticide sold directly to the public and quite noticeably sprayed along neighborhood roadsides everywhere, but farmers were unlikely to know that they were applying PCBs used as pesticide extenders to their fields because they had not bought them directly. PCBs flowed mostly unseen in the riverways and streams around Calhoun County, although, at times, Monsanto was dumping quantities sufficient that "'free' globules of aroclors can be seen in Snow Creek." Even then, there was a "point of last visible evidence" downstream, beyond which water sampling with scientific equipment was the only means of detecting the presence of PCBs.[46]

No matter how central Monsanto was to the local economy, when the pollutants were apparent and obviously noxious, people near the plant protested. Monsanto frequently got calls from neighbors "raising cane" about the factory's smell, said Bill Cambron, who worked at Monsanto beginning in the 1960s. When complaints came in from various sites, Cambron was sent to see if he could detect any odor, but says he rarely talked with residents. According to the *Star*, residents living near the plant complained of dying vegetation and "dizziness, coughing spells and respiratory ailments from a cloud they believed originated at the plant." In addition to the concerns advanced by residents and through COUL, groups such as Calhoun County Clean Up the Environment (CUE) and GASP, of Birmingham, held forums and raised questions about pollution to reporters.[47]

In response, the Alabama Air Pollution Control Commission considered legal action against Monsanto in 1973. The company's reaction to residents' complaints about offensive odors was dismissive. According to one state air pollution control official, "They have been reluctant to wholeheartedly find a solution to the problem." At the same time, representatives of the Alabama Attorney General's Office placed Monsanto "under surveillance" for sulfur dioxide pollution.[48]

During the window between 1971 and 1978, under the state's youngest attorney general, Bill Baxley, Alabama enjoyed its first—and really only—period of "aggressive enforcement of environmental laws," explained Henry "Hank" Caddell, who came out of law school to head the environmental unit in the attorney general's office. In response to the federal Clean Air Act and pending water pollution control legislation, Alabama revised its corresponding state statutes, if for no other reason than to avoid ceding control of state environmental regulation to the feds. Alabama passed in 1971 one of the toughest environmental statutes in the South, setting penalties for water pollution violations of up to $10,000 a day, higher than any other southern state. "The new statute was much of an improvement," said Caddell. The law revamped AWIC, so that industry no longer appointed half of the board members, provided for repayment of cleanup costs, and authorized civil suits to recover from damage to fish and wildlife. The passage of the Alabama law coincided with Monsanto's decision to halt Aroclors production in West Anniston, driven by the decline in production due to the withdrawal from open uses and the high costs of pollution control equipment.[49]

Sports fisherman concerned with preserving popular fishing spots had earlier voiced opposition to pollution of streams. In 1970, the Bass Anglers Sportsman Society (BASS), a national organization based in Montgomery, brought suit against nearly 200 Alabama firms, including Monsanto, as well as several local jurisdictions that were dumping wastes into the state's streams. Filing under the Federal Refuse Act, the anglers sought to enforce by private legal action rules the state government had not. However, nearly all of the firms, including Monsanto, were dismissed from the lawsuit.[50]

In the face of growing opposition, Monsanto's public posture regarding the impact of PCBs on human health often directly contradicted its internal memos. As the debate over U.S. chemical policy unfolded, Monsanto's PCB chief, William Papageorge, wrote to Westinghouse Electric, "The polychlorinated biphenyls in Inerteen [a Westinghouse product made with Aroclors] can have permanent effects on the human body." Accordingly, Papageorge wrote, "I cannot overemphasize the need to properly control the use and handling of Inerteens to prevent their escape into the environment." Yet Papageorge proposed a message to workers that did not match the health information he shared with managers he regarded as peers. "In discussing this information with your employees," he wrote, "I strongly recommend that the perspective gained from over 40 years of experience in which no human harm has resulted, be emphasized."[51]

In March 1998, William Papageorge continued to insist that he and other Monsanto officials had seen no reason to inform workers or residents about PCBs at the Anniston plant in the early 1970s. Though Monsanto explicitly warned industrial customers about contact with PCBs, Papageorge persisted in the belief that "there was no reason to give anybody such warning."

In his words, "There was no rational reason for talking to anybody, so they didn't do it."[52]

MULTIPLE FACTORS DROVE CHEMICAL POLICY REFORM in the early 1970s: new measuring techniques and more accessible scientific information about the presence of pollutants in ecological systems, international restrictions targeting specific toxic chemicals, rising public concern about environmental health, and an ecology movement that was gaining sophistication and effectiveness in the Washington legislative arena. Environmentalists sought to renegotiate power over the control of toxic chemicals, urging a new paradigm of premarket scrutiny of chemicals. Industry broadly resisted change.

The Toxic Substances Control Act (TSCA, pronounced "tosca") identified PCBs as a particular menace and proposed outlawing domestic production. A promising initiative, TSCA was severely weakened by heavy industry lobbying during six years of legislative debate.[53]

Proponents of TSCA strove to fill gaps in the emerging federal regulatory system. The body of environmental law that Congress had passed in the decade after *Silent Spring* was far-reaching but largely governed the receiving medium—air, water, soil—not the polluting substances. The vast majority of chemicals on the commercial market were not subject to regulatory oversight. The FDA was authorized to regulate chemicals in food; pesticides and rodenticides were subject to regulation under a separate law.[54]

A broad coalition of environmental, health, and labor groups united behind Congressman Ryan's push for legislation controlling toxic chemicals in the United States. Supporters of TSCA included organized labor, consumer and health advocacy groups, and the new environmental lobby, which was beginning to flex its policy muscle. Members of the environmental coalition backing the bill included the Center for Science in the Public Interest, Environmental Action, the Environmental Defense Fund, the Environmental Lobby, the Environmental Policy Center, Friends of the Earth, the National Audubon Society, the Natural Resources Defense Council, the National Wildlife Federation, the Sierra Club, and the Urban Environmental Conference. Also pushing for passage were large health lobby associations, including the Blue Cross Association, the American Lung Association, and the National Foundation of the March of Dimes. Consumer and good government groups such as Consumer Action Now, the Consumer Federation of America, and the League of Women Voters were major supporters as well. In Senate hearings on the bill, Ralph Nader's Center for the Study of Responsive Law charged both the FDA and the USDA with failure to "adequately protect the consumer from PCBs and other contaminants" and failure to notify the public about its findings of PCBs in food and food packaging. Also prominent in the coalition were the AFL-CIO and individual labor unions, most notably the largest union in the chemical industry, the Oil, Chemical, and Atomic Workers (OCAW). Given the divide often apparent between labor and environmental groups, OCAW's involvement was especially significant. Organized labor had just waged a successful drive to pass the Occupational Safety and Health Act (OSHA) in 1970; OCAW legislative director Tony Mazzocchi had led his union's central role in that fight and brought valuable experience to the TSCA campaign. The International Chemical Workers Union (ICWU), the union representing Monsanto's Anniston plant workers, was less visible in both legislative efforts.[55]

Given the long latency period between exposure to toxic substances and the onset of illnesses they caused, coalition members sought a precautionary approach that required chemicals be tested and approved *before* they appeared on the market, rather than after the fact. Some, like Mazzocchi of OCAW, insisted "that there should be no exemptions . . . from the testing or premarket notification provisions of the legislation." The provision was so important that Mazzocchi said he "would rather see no law than a weak one offering only an illusion of protection."[56]

The unions in particular emphasized the need for premarket scrutiny of synthetic chemicals, because, as John J. Sheehan, legislative director for the United Steelworkers of America, remarked, "Our primary method of identifying hazardous substances is counting the bodies that they leave behind." Sheehan was particularly concerned about long-term health impact of prolonged contact with chemicals in the workplace, saying, "The manifestation of cancer is coming of age with regard to the chemical barrage we have subjected ourselves to in the past several decades."[57]

The campaign to regulate toxic substances spanned three legislative sessions and encountered heavy opposition from the chemical industry. The effort suffered a serious setback during the Ninety-second Congress when the bill's primary champion, Representative Ryan, died in September 1972. Congress adjourned that year without acting on the legislation. Beset by the Watergate hearings the following session and divided over whether to require premarket scrutiny, Congress once again was unable to agree on a bill. "A protracted conference failed to reach agreement," Representative John Murphy (D-N.Y.) told the *New York Times*, "because a weak House bill failed to provide premarket screening safeguards that the Senate deemed essential, and the House conferees refused to yield." The protracted debate over the legislation also centered on whether to single out *any* specific chemical, including whether to ban PCBs, and how soon to do so.[58]

The EPA convened a major national conference on the health and environmental consequences of exposure to polychlorinated biphenyls in November 1975 during the third round of congressional debate. In his opening remarks, EPA administrator Russell Train noted that in the three years since both the FDA and the EPA had promised to reduce PCB pollution, "we find that, although PCB levels in food have steadily declined, PCB's are present in our environment to a far greater degree and at higher levels than we have previously thought."[59]

Particular concern about the possible carcinogenic effects of PCBs had recently been heightened by the work of Renate Kimbrough, a young researcher working at the EPA (and later at the Toxicology Lab at the Centers for Disease Control). Kimbrough conducted a series of studies on liver carcinoma in female rats exposed to PCBs. In one study, 26 of the 184 rats fed Aroclor 1260 developed liver tumors. The "tumors showed severe disruption of the normal liver architecture," Kimbrough and her colleagues reported.[60]

Researchers at the 1975 conference presented new and striking evidence of the serious health consequences of human exposure to PCBs and associated compounds. Masanori Kuratsune of Japan reported that seven years after consuming PCB-contaminated rice oil, *yusho* patients were still manifesting various clinical symptoms, indicating lesions of the skin, damage to the liver, and changes in reproductive systems. Japanese doctors also noted that a high percentage of female patients who had ingested the PCB-contaminated oil reported disruptions in their menstrual cycles. The chlorinated dibenzofurans that are sometimes associated with PCBs were especially persistent in the livers of *yusho* patients who had died. (Nine years after the *yusho* incident, researchers were finding six times as many liver-cancer deaths among exposed men and three times as many among exposed women as among unexposed people.)[61]

Various animal studies also indicated that PCBs were probable carcinogens. One showed that exposure to PCBs "disturbed reproduction in monkeys." Those findings, said J. G. Vos from the Netherlands, "greatly increase our concern of PCB as a health hazard."[62] As hoped, the EPA meeting helped to convince Congress of the urgent health threat posed by PCBs just as legislators were considering a ban.

Chemical industry opposition to TSCA was vigorous and well financed. The Synthetic Organic Chemical Manufacturers Association (SOCMA) played a lead role. Monsanto's people were also heavily involved. The company assigned one of its vice presidents, Monte C. Throdahl, the task of building a business coalition against the bill to negotiate the best possible terms for industry. During congressional debate, Monsanto sent its "director of regulatory management," Winthrop R. "Wink" Corey, to Washington three or four times a month to coordinate industry opposition. A letter-writing campaign insisted that tighter regulation would hamper the industry economically. R. T. Phelps, plant manager at Monsanto Textiles Company of Greenwood, South Carolina, wrote to Senator Strom Thurmond, decrying the legislation's "overly burdensome" and "all-encompassing nature." Opposing "costly and unnecessary testing requirements" and "uncertainty in enforcement," Phelps raised the specter of plant shutdowns and job losses in that state.[63]

General Electric joined Monsanto in lobbying against TSCA. The electrical industry had been the major purchaser of PCBs since Theodore Swann began selling them in 1929. On the issue of banning PCBs, Monsanto and electrical industry allies argued that the fire retardant qualities of the chemicals made them sufficiently indispensable to electrical products as to outweigh the risk of exposure. While some companies supplied by Monsanto were cutting back on their Aroclors purchases, General Electric urged Monsanto to continue producing Aroclor 1254 and 1260 "on the basis that information available was not adequate to incriminate these Aroclors."[64]

"I have never seen such an effective lobbying effort as was done against this legislation," said the primary Senate sponsor of the legislation, John V. Tunney of California, during hearings on the bill. As debate raged between a tougher Senate bill and a House version more acceptable to industry, Senator Tunney said, "the chemical industry had marshaled its forces and was going to do everything it could to sabotage the legislation in a way that was considered unacceptable not only to the Environmental Protection Agency, but to the Senate conferees as well."[65]

Ultimately, only six senators voted against the legislation. A whistle-blower provision, protecting workers who revealed industrial hazards, survived a challenge led by Senator Jesse Helms (R-N.C.) and remained in the final bill. Senator James Browning Allen, a Democrat from Gadsden, not far from Anniston, proposed an amendment to restrict the definition of covered chemicals to those that posed an "imminent hazard." This definition targeted acute exposures and minimized the dangers of chronic long-term contact; the amendment was accepted without objection. (Senator Allen, who later died in office, would be replaced in a special election by a young state senator from Anniston, Donald Stewart, who would later become the lead attorney in cases suing Monsanto for PCB contamination in his hometown.)[66]

Not until a third congressional session did the bill finally succeed, and only after proponents had made significant concessions to the chemical and electrical industries. Congress enacted TSCA on October 11, 1976, though many of the act's provisions would not take effect until 1979. In 1977, pursuant to water pollution control legislation, not TSCA, the EPA set a prohibition on dumping wastes that exceeded 1 ppb of PCBs, with limited exceptions. The 1 ppb limit forced Monsanto's electrical industry customers to stop using PCBs, because they could not meet the standard. Without the electrical industry, Monsanto's customer base was gone. The company shut down the Aroclors production operation in Sauget in 1977, in advance of the 1979 TSCA deadline.[67]

PCBs were so pervasive and so clearly hazardous that TSCA singled them out. It was the first federal law to expressly ban an entire family of chemicals. Section 6 of TSCA forbade any person to "manufacture, process, or distribute in commerce or use polychlorinated biphenyls." The ban was not total, however. At the urging of Monsanto and General Electric, among others, the law codified the "closed uses" approach, allowing for continued PCB use in a "totally enclosed manner." The EPA was authorized to make other exemptions on a case-by-case basis. Companies were to provide clear warnings and instructions for care in processing, handling, and disposing of these toxics. The law did not require the removal of PCBs already in use, whether in transformers, capacitors, or fluorescent light ballasts, leaving in circulation 750 million pounds of PCBs in the United States alone. The law also failed to anticipate future disposal problems, a debt that would come due in the 1990s, as aging electrical equipment reached the end of its usable life. Nor did TSCA adequately address existing PCB pollution.[68]

Given the vigor of industry opposition and the normally glacial pace of legislative reform, the length of time from TSCA's introduction to its passage was not unusual. However, during the six years that TSCA was under debate, Monsanto distributed millions more pounds of PCBs worldwide.[69]

TSCA was both a remarkable achievement and a spectacular disappointment. The law outlawed PCBs and authorized the EPA to regulate chemicals, but it grandfathered in more than 60,000 chemicals already in use. TSCA gave the EPA the authority to review new chemicals. But the law was "markedly deficient," as historians Samuel and Barbara Hays have noted. Because the agency put more emphasis on acute exposures than on evaluating "long-term cumulative impact," they argued, if TSCA had not banned

PCBs, the law would not, in all likelihood, have prevented them from being introduced as a new chemical. Although the law required companies to submit new chemicals for EPA review prior to introducing them commercially, the EPA had only ninety days to conduct its evaluations. In addition, the law helped sustain the conventions of confidentiality. It neither required companies to share toxicological data, which could be considered "confidential business information," with the EPA nor gave the EPA sufficient resources to conduct its own research. By failing to facilitate robust testing of chemicals prior to their circulation and leaving the burden on the EPA to prove a chemical harmful, the law basically set up what one observer called an automatic "conveyor belt" for the introduction of new chemicals. Even the implementation of TSCA was hampered by long delays at the EPA in rule-making, the process by which a federal agency drafts regulations to implement a new law.[70]

Just three years after TSCA's passage, the *yusho* experience seemed to repeat itself in Taiwan, China. More than 2,000 people became ill after consuming PCB-contaminated cooking oil. *Yucheng*, or "oil disease," caused skin pigmentation changes, acne, peripheral neuropathy (characterized by tingling, numbing, even loss of muscle control), and other symptoms. Long-term follow-up studies revealed neurocognitive deficits in children born to mothers afflicted with PCB poisoning, even among those conceived *after* their mothers had been exposed.[71] This 1979 incident served as a reminder that PCBs used as heat transfer fluids could breach "semi-closed" systems. However, once the "ban" on PCBs was in place, the kind of public attention necessary to win more thorough-going reform waned.

NATIONAL CONCERN AND CONGRESSIONAL ACTION had forced an end to PCB production, clearly a major advance. Stopping PCB manufacture is considered a real success story, one of the tangible successes of the environmental movement. However, PCBs remained a global problem and went unaddressed at the local level in Anniston. The passage of TSCA had little direct impact on pollution in West Anniston. By the time the final vote on TSCA was held, PCBs had not been manufactured at the West Anniston site for more than four years. The fish contamination in Alabama that figured in 1971 hearings on the bill was not mentioned in later phases of the congressional debate.[72] Monsanto had withdrawn its Anniston facility from Aroclors production in the middle of TSCA negotiations, shifting attention away from the serious contamination at Anniston at precisely the time that PCBs were becoming a national legislative policy issue. By halting production at Anniston in 1972, the company decreased the likelihood of further government investigation at its most polluted and problematic site, while deriving what public relations benefit could be gained.

PCB production had come to a formal end in Anniston in May 1972, but PCB discharges did not. PCBs continued to enter the plant environs, in part because chlorinated biphenyls continued to be mixed with other polyphenyls the factory produced. Monsanto made limited effort to address the burden of existing contamination in Anniston streams or the leachate and airborne PCB emissions from its landfills. Plant manager Gene Jessee hoped to reduce the toxic discharges, telling his superiors that "equipment would be installed to vastly improve [PCB] separation by July 1, 1972, and . . . a further reduction in PCB in effluents would be effected."[73]

In the wake of TSCA's passage, Monsanto launched a major pro-chemicals television ad campaign in 1977. The company was aiming to "replace purely emotional approaches with the best science we can muster," declared Monsanto's booklet on the effort, casting concern about chemicals as uninformed sentiment, though the campaign explicitly targeted television because of its "emotional impact."[74]

At that time, no one looked back at PCBs' point of origin. Anniston was named an All-America City by the National Municipal League in 1977–78. COUL's existence and its work were major factors in the league's choice of Anniston as one of a dozen cities nationwide to be so designated.[75]

A 1980 EPA hazardous waste site report, prepared by Alabama Department of Public Health Division of Solid Waste officials, estimated 10 million pounds of PCB wastes in Monsanto's landfill. Debris from the decommissioned PCB production area and Montar residues had been added to the landfills, which were unlined and until 1995 capped only with soil and vegetation.[76]

Ironically, as the Ad Hoc Committee had begun meeting in 1969, Monsanto entered the potentially lucrative environmental cleanup business, creating Monsanto Enviro-Chem Systems Inc. (MECSI). MECSI anticipated a $70 billion market for anti-pollution technology and services. Monsanto also planned to reap public relations benefits from offering these services. MECSI was "our white hat," President Edward J. Bock said later.[77] A reputation as an environmentally sensitive company would be an asset in this burgeoning field.

By the late 1970s, Monsanto had grown self-conscious about the racial composition of the company's all-white, nearly all-male board. Monsanto responded in part by electing St. Louis attorney Margaret Bush Wilson, an

Monsanto's South Landfill during the reconstruction of Highway 202 in West Anniston. The Monsanto dumps, unlined and mostly uncapped until the 1990s, contain an estimated 5.5 to 10 million pounds of PCB-contaminated waste. Photo courtesy of the *Anniston Star*.

African American woman and chair of the National Board of Directors of the NAACP, to the Monsanto board in 1977.[78]

Around the same time, a not-yet-thirty-year-old lawyer in Monsanto's agriculture and pesticides division submitted a complaint to the African American manager of affirmative action compliance at the company. "Monsanto employed a number of talented blacks who should have been moving up the corporate ladder far more quickly," wrote the young lawyer, Clarence Thomas, who worked in Monsanto's legal department from 1977 to 1979. Even as he was reversing his own views about affirmative action programs, Thomas was concerned about Monsanto's failure to advance black employees. "In time I figured out," Thomas continued, that the affirmative action officer "saw Monsanto's black managers as nothing more than fungible percentage points on a government form."[79]

Thomas's work for Monsanto subsidiary Monsanto Industrial Chemicals Company included assessing Monsanto's waste disposal contracts. In that context, Thomas also began reading about "the physiological effects of human exposure to toxic waste." After poring over company documents, "I felt sure that the company had a hugely serious problem on its hands," wrote Thomas. "I grew ever more concerned as I came to better understand the dangers of some of the highly toxic substances created as by-products of our operations, especially after I started reading the animal studies that were being performed for Monsanto in order to establish the safety of its new products." Thomas's language reflected the corporate slant, casting only the by-products and not the products themselves as dangerous and portraying the animal studies as designed to demonstrate safety, not to identify potential sources of harm. But his reading of Monsanto documents made him remember a neighbor in Savannah, paralyzed after years of working with creosote, a compound that can cause neurological injury: "How many other hard-working people, I wondered, had been robbed of their livelihoods because of the toxic chemicals manufactured by companies like Monsanto?"[80]

IMMEDIATELY AFTER THE AROCLORS SHUTDOWN, biological consultants Suttkus and Gunning reported the results of a new round of tests on Calhoun County waterways: "We continue to find deformed, sick and lethargic fishes in our collections." Nonetheless, after an unseasonably dry period in early fall showed low releases, Monsanto sought to be released from monthly monitoring of its chemical wastes. In 1972, the state of Alabama, with the EPA's concurrence, granted Monsanto's request.[81]

During the decade between Jensen's identification of PCBs as global contaminants and the passage of TSCA, the U.S. environmental regulatory paradigm had shifted, from one that left most handling of environmental pollution up to localities and states to one that rested significantly at the federal level. The civil rights and environmental movements were still quite distinct, but in looking to the national state to enforce clean air and clean water laws, environmental advocates were following a pattern modeled on the nation's recent civil rights legislation. The executive branch had established a sizeable federal eco-bureaucracy, but one that remained underfunded and understaffed, inadequate to the task of monitoring and testing all the new toxic chemicals that would come on the market each year.

Nationally, environmentalists had effectively deployed coalition politics and developments in ecological science to achieve new regulatory requirements for monitoring hazardous chemicals. Altering medical research findings to their own ends and selectively withholding damaging results had become a way of doing business for corporations professing to meet new federal environmental standards. The threat that stringent limits on waste effluent would be set under the Clean Water Act, perhaps even more than the TSCA ban, had staunched the heaviest flows of PCBs and acid into Snow Creek. But the legacy of forty years of PCB production remained inscribed on the landscape of West Anniston. In a 1985 memo, Henry Hudson, who was investigating PCB contamination in Snow Creek on behalf of the Alabama Attorney General's Office, explained what remained unknown to West Anniston residents: "We have an environmental/food chain threat."[82]

Monsanto medical director Emmet Kelly's job expanded in the 1970s to include a new product assessment program in which the medical department was to screen new products for their impact on "waste disposal, environment and toxicology." Yet comments he made in 1981 raise questions about how seriously he took the new responsibilities. Kelly complained about the "125 Ph.D.s who had grants from the government to work on PCBs." As to why such research would be needed, he told a colleague, "God knows what or just to see whether it caused snakes to get cancer or birth defects or something!"[83]

Looking back on the TSCA debates, Monsanto executives congratulated themselves. "Wink" Corey, Monsanto's negotiator on TSCA, said, "I think Monsanto handled itself admirably." In another interview, James E. McKee, the company's public relations officer, concurred: "I think we handled it all very well."[84]

Monsanto continued to maintain that the company's waste disposal practices were above industry standards. The plant's "wastewater treatment facility was a 'model for the industry,'" plant manager Ed Jurevic boasted to an *Anniston Star* reporter in 1983. "'If we sound a little arrogant you'll have to excuse us,' [said] Jurevic. 'We feel we are the best around.'"[85]

State sampling in 1983 found evidence of significant PCB contamination in Choccolocco Creek. State Game and Fish Division director C. E. White called attention to bass drawn from Choccolocco Creek that measured more than eighteen times the amount permissible in food, prompting the Alabama Attorney General's Office to intervene. Confronted with the findings, company officials reacted in disbelief. "Monsanto's Chief Counsel said he didn't believe the state's data," the attorney general's office reported, "so Monsanto resampled, not at exactly the same locations, but close. Monsanto's data were even higher than the state's with the highest result being about 1250 ppms." The attorney general's office also took note of "highly contaminated soils in Snow Creek." In 1985, Alabama attorney general Charlie Graddick wrote directly to Monsanto president Richard J. Mahoney in St. Louis demanding to meet with company representatives "as soon as possible." Monsanto conducted a superficial cleanup that addressed roughly 100 feet of Snow Creek.[86]

In the aftermath of TSCA, the company began a radical departure toward biotechnology and away from its longtime mainstay, the production of industrial chemicals. An effort to sell the Anniston plant in the mid-1980s was unsuccessful. The factory remained a key operation in Monsanto's chemical division.[87]

The end of PCB production in 1972 had left as the Anniston plant's leading product parathion, a widely used pesticide. A brown liquid organophosphate chemical that acted on the nervous system even in very small quantities, parathion had never been patented and was inexpensive to make. As Monsanto's environmental spokesperson, Glynn Young, explained, parathion was "very effective in killing the boll weevil and just about anything else if you misuse it." Prompted by two major chemical disasters at other companies in the mid-1980s, the methyl isocyanate explosions in Bhopal, India, and Nitro, West Virginia, Young said, Monsanto dropped parathion from its list of chemicals produced at the Anniston plant in 1986.[88]

The same year that Monsanto closed its parathion operation, white residents of West Anniston, Lillar and Arthur Skinner and others, confronted Monsanto plant manager Ed Jurevic at an environmental impact hearing with petitions signed by more than 1,200 people. The group was opposing Monsanto's planned expansion of its South Landfill on Coldwater Mountain. Monsanto had applied for a hazardous waste landfill permit, in advance of tougher Resource Conservation and Recovery Act (RCRA) rules that were soon scheduled to go into effect. Willis T. Motes of Oxford told a reporter, "What I want to know of these people," referring to Monsanto representatives, "is how they think it they can dig a hole and it won't get into the water." Despite local protest, the Alabama Department of Environmental Management (ADEM) issued the landfill permit, and Monsanto consigned additional chemical wastes to the PCB-contaminated landfill near the neighborhoods of West Anniston.[89]

At that time, no one living in the vicinity of the plant knew about the danger posed by PCBs amassed just uphill. Monsanto's PCB contamination was upstaged by news about the Army's extensive stockpile of chemical weaponry stored nearby.

CHAPTER EIGHT

Challenging the Green Dragon

*History proves that an effective implement of war has never been discarded
until it becomes obsolete.*—Brigadier General Amos A. Fries, 1921

Awareness of the town's toxic legacy first came to Anniston residents not because of PCBs, but through revelations in the late 1980s that the U.S. Army
had amassed a substantial arsenal of outdated Cold War–era chemical weapons at the Anniston Army Depot. News about the weapons stockpile came
as a double shock, revealing not only that highly poisonous and potentially
explosive munitions were stored just west of the city but also that the Army
intended to burn the weapons on-site. The Army's plan to build a hazardous waste incinerator raised fears of chemical contamination, both from the
nerve agents themselves and from the by-products of incineration, including
trace amounts of dioxins and PCBs. After an initial wave of fear, this toxic
knowledge motivated a segment of people locally to question the secrecy surrounding chemical weapons disposal and to confront the U.S. Army. Subsequent events generated profound mistrust among people who had previously
defended Calhoun County's largest employer uncritically. The ensuing struggle highlighted the region's global significance to the American war-fighting
machine and the environmental impact of war far from the battlefield.

In response, a locally based, cross-class, and ultimately biracial grassroots movement developed, demanding safe destruction of the weapons by
means that would not put residents at risk. This bipartisan group took on
the seemingly omnipotent U.S. Army, protesting incineration by both pressuring Congress and marching in the streets. Their stand put them at odds
with many of their neighbors, who saw opposing incineration as blocking
speedy destruction of the weapons and endangering the region's economic
lifeblood. The battle over the best means to dispose of the waste of the Cold
War and the military-industrial-chemical age was "the most difficult issue
to strike our community since racial desegregation," editorialized the *Anniston Star* in 1992.[1]

By the early 1980s, military and political leaders had recognized that
chemical weapons storage and disposal posed a significant problem

globally. Within the United States, according to the Army Corps of Engineers, more than 1,700 sites contained chemical weapons, including three in the vicinity of Anniston: the Army Depot, Fort McClellan, and Camp Sibert, a World War II testing ground and training center near Gadsden, thirty miles north. The weapons stockpiles at the depot and other large Army storage facilities posed the most serious threat. For strategic reasons, these facilities were geographically scattered; in addition to Anniston, the sites included one on Johnston Atoll in the Pacific and seven other locations in the continental United States: Madison County, Kentucky; Pueblo, Colorado; Tooele, Utah; Newport, Indiana; Aberdeen, Maryland; Pine Bluff, Arkansas; and Umatilla, Oregon.[2]

More than 7 percent of the nation's chemical weapons stockpile was housed in neat rows in dozens of domed igloos at the Anniston Army Depot. The grid of igloos covered a 764-acre territory at the northeast corner of the 18,000-acre depot site, less than ten miles west of Anniston, upwind of town. Angular concrete facades marked the entry to each of the 155 earth-covered bunkers that housed the nerve agents—2,254 tons in all. The stockpile comprised missiles containing neurotoxic agents—sarin (GB) and VX—and the blister agent, mustard gas. (Though they are commonly referred to as "gases," these chemicals can be stored as liquids or solids and therefore are more properly termed "agents.") Sarin canisters were stacked three pallets high inside some of the bunkers. Other igloos contained loaded projectiles, missiles such as M55 rockets filled with nerve agent, nearly ready to be fired.[3]

The idea of inhaling fumes from the incineration of chemicals *designed* to kill people made the prospect of incineration especially terrifying. More than half the weapons in the Anniston cache belonged to a deadly class of neurotoxic substances. Chemically similar to organophosphate pesticides, nerve agents work by inhibiting cholinesterase, a chemical the body uses to prevent overstimulation of the glands and muscles, and thereby interfering with breathing. Sarin, a clear, odorless, and rapidly acting nerve agent, made up 19 percent (437 tons) of the Anniston stockpile. Thirty-seven percent of the Anniston stockpile (829 tons) was VX, the most powerful of the nerve agents. Amber in color, odorless, and tasteless, VX evaporates very slowly and, therefore, is also the most persistent. "It is possible," according to the Centers for Disease Control, "that any visible VX liquid contact on the skin, unless washed off immediately, would be lethal." Larger still was the cache of mustard agent (44 percent, 988 tons), which attacks the body differently, causing severe blistering of the skin, as well as damage to the eyes, mucous

Map 8.1. U.S. chemical weapons sites. From the early 1960s until incineration was completed in 2011, the Anniston Army Depot was one of eight chemical weapons storage sites in the continental United States, storing roughly 7 percent of the U.S. stockpile: 2,254 tons of nerve agents—sarin and VX—and mustard, a blister agent, outdated and dangerous weapons of the Cold War. Map by Charles Jones.

membranes, and respiratory tract.[4] None of these compounds occur naturally in the environment. All were stockpiled for use in warfare, for incapacitating or killing enemy soldiers.

Of immediate concern to people in Anniston and the other stockpile sites, the stored unitary weapons were aging and feared to be either leaking or in imminent danger of doing so. Calhoun County, with a population of 116,000 in 1990, and with two much larger cities within 100 miles, was one of the more heavily populated stockpile sites. Downwind of the depot were poultry growers, a catfish pond, a dairy farmer, pockets of low- and middle-income whites and African Americans, and a number of wealthy landowners, all of whom were concerned about the risks posed to people and livestock by chemical contaminants that might be released by burning the weapons.[5]

The need to destroy existing chemical stockpiles was driven by a combination of technological innovation, concern for public health, and geopolitical changes. By 1987, updated chemical weapons technologies had made the stored unitary weapons militarily unnecessary. "History proves that an effective implement of war has never been discarded until it becomes obsolete," Brigadier General Amos A. Fries, commander of the U.S. Chemical Warfare Service, had said in 1921. The new binary weapons available by the 1980s required two compounds to be combined to create a toxic effect; these could be stored and transported separately, posing less risk of accidental deployment.[6]

As the Cold War wound down, the United States and the Soviet Union had negotiated bilateral agreements in 1989 and 1990 to dispose of their respective unitary chemical arsenals. Officials in several countries were concerned about "toxic terror," that extremists might access stockpiled weaponry for use in terrorist attacks. Finally, in January 1993, the multilateral Chemical Weapons Convention, which had been under negotiation for twenty years, was signed by the United States and other nations, and submitted to the U.N. member states for official ratification. Toward an eventual aim of eliminating chemical weapons, the convention prohibited "the development, production, acquisition, stockpiling, retention, transfer and use" of an entire class of unitary chemical weapons. Though the convention would not take effect formally until 1997, when it would be ratified by the U.S. Senate and by other nations, the United States and other signatories had already begun making plans to destroy their chemical stockpiles.[7]

The Army had committed to incineration as the "centerpiece of its chemical weapons demilitarization program" by 1988, if not earlier, constructing a massive incinerator at the Johnston Atoll southwest of Hawaii. Despite protests and multiple uncertainties about the hazards of burning chemical weapons, the Army remained firm in its resolve to construct incinerators at all eight of the continental sites. At the request of the undersecretary of the Army, the National Research Council (NRC), a leading independent scientific body, established in 1987 the Committee on Review and Evaluation of the Army Chemical Stockpile Disposal Program, known as "the Stockpile Committee," to advise on disposal plans.[8]

ANNISTON TRANSPLANT BRENDA LINDELL began noticing newspaper articles about the plan to construct a chemical weapons incinerator in Calhoun County in the fall of 1991, when her children were five, six, and eleven years old. The Lindells lived in a ranch-style home in East Anniston. Brenda Lindell and her husband, Alan, a minister who specialized in pastoral counseling, had moved to town in the early 1980s, seeking a quiet, safe, hospitable place to raise their family. One day, their backyard neighbors Donna and Jim

Harmon invited Brenda to meet a group they had formed with a handful of others. "We called it Families Concerned about Nerve Gas Incineration, because not everybody at that time was against it," Lindell explained. As she learned more about hazardous waste incinerators, her first impulse was to leave Anniston. Deep religious faith prevented her from turning away. "I have never felt such an inner drive to do something," said Lindell. "It was almost like I didn't have a choice." A homemaker and antitax Republican who considered herself an unlikely activist, Lindell surprised herself by becoming a leader in the movement against burning chemical weapons.[9]

People like Lindell were transformed by this struggle. Jim Harmon, likewise a "reluctant" activist, was motivated by the "perceived threat to our dreams and desire to enjoy the quality of life offered in Calhoun County." Their small group, Families Concerned, took on the demanding project of informing themselves about the technical aspects of chemical weapons and the available technologies for destroying the arsenal, and mobilized to challenge the military's claim to scientific authority. Together with their counterparts at other chemical weapons stockpile sites, these activists ensured that environmental public health figured prominently in the national policy debate over disposal options. What they learned underscored the need for precaution, even, or perhaps especially, when national security was involved.[10]

Anniston activists joined a movement that helped to pierce the hegemony of the Cold War military–chemical industry alliance. Waning Cold War tensions permitted the negotiation of the agreement to destroy chemical weapons; the decline in Cold War hostilities also made it possible—not easy, but possible—to question the military in a place where livelihoods were deeply entangled with war production.

THE REGION'S ECONOMIC DEPENDENCE on the military hung over the entire debate. Throughout the 1990s, military cutbacks and federal Base Realignment and Closure (BRAC) commissions closed numerous Army facilities. Many people locally felt it unwise to antagonize the military or congressional armed services committee members by resisting incineration when the future of Fort McClellan and the Anniston Army Depot was at stake.[11]

Calhoun County's investment in its military installations was considerable. Reporter Rick Bragg reminded readers in 1992 that local citizens had "scraped up $130,000 of their own money to buy land for a military base, what became Fort McClellan," when the Army installation opened in World

War I. The thickly forested tract that became the bomb storage depot during World War II was not contiguous with the fort, but it came to house Army maintenance and production facilities as well as weapons stockpiles. During the intervening decades, the combined civilian workforce at the two facilities rose and fell, but at the end of 1992 it numbered about 3,500.[12]

Fluctuations in military spending made the local economy more vulnerable. Though many people held well-paying jobs at the depot, Calhoun County's poverty level in 1990 was 24.4 percent, almost twice the national average of 13.2 percent. "Our local economy's over-dependence on military spending—in hindsight—too narrowly defined our growth," *Anniston Star* executive editor Chris Waddle said later. "We were lulled by patriotism into delay of diversification." Economic dependence left the region more likely to tolerate environmental abuses. Now, like the seven other communities across the continental United States hosting Army chemical weapons stockpiles, Anniston discovered itself saddled with the toxic waste of the Cold War era.[13]

The significant role of Anniston's primary employer in chemical warfare was never a complete secret. The flashy pyrotechnic displays that accompanied the opening of the Chemical Corps Training School in the early 1950s and the pomp that heralded the transfer of the CBR Command to the fort in 1961 celebrated the fact. Chemical Corps training had been going on at the fort for decades. During the Vietnam War, the CBR trained thousands of soldiers in the use of chemical defoliants. The fort became known as "the bug farm" because of the weaponized insecticides handled there.[14]

Public health alarms had been raised previously. In 1969, national "rising concern over the Army's handling of poisonous chemical munitions" prompted a brief halt to the fort's open air, live agent training. Army spokespeople repeatedly assured the public that the chemicals used in training at Fort McClellan were not hazardous to people living nearby. "Nerve gas is being used at the fort," one top officer told the *Birmingham News*, but "it poses no threat to any form of life." Army personnel were unequivocal. "We are 100-per-cent safe," said one. "I can look any resident in the eye," another spokesman said, "and tell him that we are not dangerous." Training resumed that October.[15]

Top Army brass knew early on, however, that disposing of obsolete chemical weapons would pose massive problems. In 1970, as Fort McClellan prepared to celebrate the fiftieth anniversary of the Army Chemical Center and School, a national furor developed over the Army's plans "to ship train loads of nerve gas filled M-55 rockets from Anniston, Ala. and Bluegrass, Ky. Depots to Sunny Point, N.C." for offshore disposal. In what

med Operation CHASE (for "Cut Holes and Sink 'Em"), the
e loaded onto an old ship, which was sunk 300 miles off Cape
ain, Army officials had assured Americans that transporting
as safe.[16]

...ston had mostly embraced the presence of the Chemical Corps,
though this mission, too, was subject to boom and bust cycles. As the Vietnam War was winding down in 1973, the Chemical Corps School closed,
resulting in the loss of nearly 700 military and civilian jobs at the base.
The chemical weapons training center remained shuttered until 1980. At
the time the loss seemed permanent: the school's mascot, a statue of the
Chemical Corps emblem—the Green Dragon—was shipped to a museum
at the Edgewood Arsenal.[17]

When the Chemical Corps returned in 1980, the *Birmingham News* projected that Anniston would realize a "growth in personal income of $6.1
million per year, an increase in business volume of $9.5 million per year
and 900 new jobs created indirectly by the action." The Army's planned
"smoke generating exercises may have an adverse impact on the environment," the *News* reported. As for the resumption of use of live agent, Army
officials said, "the rest of the training—using chemicals, simulated biological agents and radiological materials—should cause almost no harm to the
environment."[18]

Calhoun County received $49,489,000 in prime military contracts
in 1981 and ranked sixth among Alabama counties in receipt of military
spending. Contributing to the boom brought by the return of the Chemical
Corps to Fort McClellan was an increase in tank production and refurbishing at the depot. Adopting the decidedly Cold War label of "Tank Capital of
the Free World," Anniston then housed the only U.S. government site refurbishing such equipment. Depot personnel repaired tanks nicknamed
"Mother's Helper," "Septic Tank," and "Mortician's Dream."[19]

Military discipline, if not necessity, required discretion, and like industrial paternalism, encouraged compliance and constrained resistance. The
military's dominance over the local economy engendered a culture that
made asking questions difficult, if not unpatriotic. According to Charles
Sherrer, whose father was a civil service pharmacist at Fort McClellan in
the 1970s, "People would end up having to turn a blind eye, or not report
certain things they were seeing to authorities, because, you could lose your
job, or be ostracized."[20]

The military's presence both nurtured and benefited from a climate of
secrecy, a history that hindered it in providing the transparency the public

demanded regarding the incineration plan. Up through the Reagan years, residents of Anniston had little information about the size of stockpile that had been their silent neighbor for more than thirty years. The exact amounts of mustard gas, sarin, and VX agents at each locale were classified. *Star* editor Chris Waddle figured out, however, that the United States must have revealed to Soviet negotiators the number of weapons under treaty consideration. So he put the question to the visiting assistant secretary of defense. "Mr. Secretary, you have told the Russians," Waddle said; "if you can tell the Cold War enemy, you can sure as hell tell us." A week later the newsman had an answer. Roughly "50 million pounds of aging chemical weapons" were scattered around the country; Anniston's stockpile was the fifth largest by weight.[21]

Brenda Lindell's experience underscored the difficulty of getting information from the Army. When she complained to Army public affairs officer Mike Abrams that an official had not been forthcoming at a Senate subcommittee hearing, according to Lindell, Abrams replied, "Well, maybe he didn't have permission to give that information." Lindell was furious. "'What you're telling me is that anything that you tell me, I have to look at it from the perspective of, I don't know if you have permission to tell me the truth or not, and, you know, that blows your credibility all to pieces.' And he said, 'Yeah, that is a problem.'"[22]

According to Army leaders, classified status was a reason the nation's environmental laws should not apply to military installations. In the 1970s, the Anniston Army Depot sought to be exempted from Clean Air Act standards. The environmental protection division of the Alabama Attorney General's Office successfully sued the Army (and the Tennessee Valley Authority), leading to a 1974 landmark decision requiring domestic military sites to abide by U.S. environmental laws and EPA regulations. The decision was undermined by subsequent rulings, and the Army often continued to behave as if environmental standards did not apply to military bases.[23]

Both military installations in Anniston housed a host of environmental hazards. Fort McClellan received multiple notices of violation from ADEM and the EPA for its hazardous waste management practices. In 1989, the EPA designated the depot's Southeast Industrial Area a Superfund site, in response not to stored weapons but to the accumulated chemical waste in the form of PCBs, lead, solvents, pesticides, and herbicides. Trichloroethylene (TCE) from the depot site threatened to contaminate Coldwater Spring, which supplied drinking water for 72,000 people, approximately 60 percent of the population of Calhoun County. (As recently as 2010, in its five-year review, the Army Corps of Engineers reported to the EPA that "high contaminant levels remain onsite and low levels of contaminants continue to migrate offsite.")[24]

DESPITE THE SOUTH'S HEAVY ECONOMIC RELIANCE on military facilities, southern grassroots protests of hazardous military wastes in the 1980s and 1990s were widespread, including demonstrations against disposal of low-level nuclear waste at Barnwell, South Carolina, attempts to block renewed plutonium enrichment at the Savannah River nuclear weapons facility, standing opposition from the Oak Ridge Environmental Peace Alliance (OREPA) to waste practices at Tennessee's uranium enrichment plant, and resistance to docking nuclear subs along the south Georgia coast. A loose alliance blended opposition to militarism with environmental advocacy, linking veterans of national peace and environmental campaigns with local citizens whose farms and homes were threatened by proximity to military installations.

But the grassroots anti-incinerator movement marked the first sustained, collective challenge to chemical contamination in Anniston. In Families Concerned, the majority of members were white, middle-class professionals. In addition to Lindell and the Harmons, the group included Suzanne Marshall and Rufus Kinney, both professors at Jacksonville State University (JSU), thirteen miles north of Anniston. Independent business owners like David Christian, whose architectural firm had recently redesigned the Calhoun County Courthouse, and Vicky Tolbert, a graphic designer, also joined Families Concerned. Edward Wood, a congregant at Rev. Nimrod Reynolds's Seventeenth Street Baptist Church, served on the founding board, and Jeannette Champion came from the working-class neighborhood just south and west of the Monsanto plant. Helping fund the campaign was Alice Donald, daughter of James Inzer, the ultraconservative former lieutenant governor who had served with populist governor Big Jim Folsom from 1947 to 1951. Donald's late husband, dentist T. C. Donald, had helped raise the reward to snare Willie Brewster's killer in 1965. Others whispered their support for the Families Concerned group and passed along donations behind the scenes.[25]

Families Concerned members found their most significant ally in the Chemical Weapons Working Group (CWWG), based in Berea, Kentucky. The CWWG formed in 1991 as an arm of the Kentucky Environmental Foundation to carry out full-time work on the safe disposal of chemical weapons. Kentuckians had been concerned about chemical weapons storage since

1979, when chemical smoke from the Army's Blue Grass Depot wafted across Interstate 75 near Lexington, sending forty people to the hospital. The CWWG brought together citizen groups from all eight chemical weapons storage facilities. It also drew in representatives of Greenpeace, the Military Toxics Project of the National Toxics Campaign, and the Sierra Club, as well as safe disposal advocates from Russia and Asian Pacific Islanders troubled by problems at the Johnston Atoll incinerator. Through a complex network of whistleblowers, leaks, and public information, CWWG founder and director Craig Williams led the network in piecing together the details of the Army's overall incineration plan and its potential consequences for human health and safety.[26]

The Army and environmental activists both favored the treaty mandating safe weapons disposal, but a lengthy fight ensued over the best means of destroying chemical weapons at the depot. Activists advocated chemically reprocessing nerve agents to neutralize their harmful effects. Army personnel argued that incineration would be far better than neutralization. Either method improved on continued storage, which put the population at risk from leaking munitions, but the parties differed on how close technicians were to developing effective neutralization technologies and how long the stockpile would remain safe from leaks. Opponents of burning charged that neutralizing the chemicals posed fewer immediate and long-term risks to human health. Stack emissions raised particular concern. "Incineration is an inherently toxic technology," Craig Williams said.[27]

The logistical and technical problems of disposal were daunting. The sheer variety of materials posed a challenge. At least four types of materials needed to be destroyed: "agent, energetic materials [propellants], metal parts, and dunnage (packing and other miscellaneous materials)." Much of the chemical agent was stored in metal casings that were not easily disassembled. Some of the chemicals were stored by the ton in large containers, but most were packed in cartridges, projectiles, rockets, and mines. The Army had concluded that "high temperature [incineration] is the only proven way to decontaminate metal and solid waste."[28]

A vigorous debate centered on how imminent the danger posed by leaking munitions was. While the CWWG and the Anniston activists did not advocate continued storage, Williams and others argued that safer methods of detoxifying chemical agents already existed or could be quickly developed.[29] Families Concerned members were especially alarmed about potential threats to human health—the long-term impact of incineration by-products or the hazards of an accidental release. What plans were being made for oversight and monitoring of the disposal process? Would people have time to evacuate if an explosion occurred? Would this hazardous waste incinerator, once built, become a permanent fixture, attracting additional wastes?

SUCH WERE THE QUESTIONS on Brenda Lindell's mind in mid-June 1992, when she packed her kids into the car and drove the 90 minutes to the Atlanta airport to pick up Craig Williams. A decorated Vietnam veteran, the tall, indefatigable Williams had been campaigning for safe chemical weapons disposal for five years. Families Concerned had invited Williams to speak to their small group at the Anniston City Meeting Center. To their surprise, 450 people showed up. "That was essentially the occasion that blew the lid off the issue," Lindell said. "Until that time very few people knew about it."[30]

After the 1992 meeting, opposition to the Anniston incinerator broadened; the organization gained new members, new supporters, and new donors. Having shifted from simply being "concerned" to being outright opposed to burning, and in support of neutralization, Families Concerned members helped form two new local groups to fight incineration, explained Suzanne Marshall, who studied environmental activism as part of her research at JSU. At Jim Harmon's urging, Marshall became recording secretary and a leader in Families Concerned. In an organizing strategy designed to draw in different constituencies that would play complementary roles, activists created Serving Alabama's Future Environment (SAFE), a nonprofit arm, and "Burn Busters," which played on the title of the popular film *Ghostbusters* to appeal to students at JSU. "Families [Concerned]," said Burn Busters president Mike Marvinny, "doesn't want to offend anybody." Burn Busters took a more oppositional approach, intentionally becoming the movement's "radical fringe."[31]

Burn Busters organized protests in Jacksonville, Anniston, and Montgomery. One demonstration at the state capitol was particularly creative. "We got mouse heads from the theater and put lab coats on them," said Marshall. "The message was, 'We were being used as lab rats here in Anniston,'" she said. Members appeared on talk radio and, taking advantage of an election-season hiatus in Alabama's ban on roadway signage, posted "No Incineration" signs along Interstate 20. The creative tactics brought Burn Busters so much attention that the group sometimes had to scale back its activities to get the press to focus on other important events. Even then, said Marshall, "the press would call up [and ask,] 'When [is] Burn Busters going to be around again?'"[32]

Despite the growing support for their efforts, questioning the Army's incineration plan was not easy. "We were called 'un-American,'" Marshall explained. "We went through all of that, communist, outside agitators, stupid, emotional, hysterical women—that's what they called Brenda. We weren't a popular movement, so we had developed ties to each other." Regional and national ties were especially important to sustaining activists' resolve. Marshall attended a Stop the Pollution (STP) workshop at the Highlander Research and Education Center in east Tennessee. At Highlander, she met others engaged in antitoxics struggles, including several opponents of proposed civilian incineration sites, who were having some success in blocking the siting of hazardous waste incinerators, winning a limited EPA moratorium on their construction. Such connections were important, said Marshall, if for no other reason than to remind the group that "you are not alone down there, even though it feels like it."[33]

In September 1992, the *New York Times* covered the prospect of incineration in Anniston, describing the issue as "polarizing." An Anniston-area pro-incineration contingent with about forty members—Friends of SPRING (Supporters of Proven Reliable Incineration of Nerve Gas)—was registering support for the incinerator in letters to the *Star*. Supporters of the Army's plan to burn the weapons accused anti-incineration groups of causing "needless delay," prolonging the threat posed by stored chemical weaponry. "We are for the treaty," Marshall and the others repeatedly had to explain. "We want to get rid of the weapons, too. We just want to do it in the safest manner possible." Jim Harmon, of Families Concerned, called for common ground, noting that opponents of incineration represent "a true cross section of the community and include a large number of both active and retired military and AAD [Anniston Army Depot] employees."[34]

People who did not align with pro- or anti-incineration groups were concerned, too, about what the Army's controversial project would mean for the city. Real estate agents were beginning to get nervous about the impact an incinerator would have on land and housing sales countywide. A copy of journalist Rick Bragg's *St. Petersburg Times* article on the planned incinerator, "Poison or Poverty?," turned up in a fax between realty companies with a note appended: "Every thing [*sic*] surrounding economic welfare of this county dictates that 'Speed is of essence,'" in sealing a pending real estate deal.[35]

With their constituencies demanding information and action, state and congressional leaders became involved. Southerners in Congress had long held important seats on military affairs committees, positions from which they had often successfully advocated for increased spending. Now, Alabama's Third District congressman, Glen Browder, a Democrat from Jacksonville who held key assignments on both the House Committee on Armed Services and the Committee on the Budget, began to raise questions about the Army's plans.[36]

Pressuring Congress to require the Army to consider safer alternatives to incineration was a major goal of the CWWG organizing efforts at each of the sites. In 1992, activists succeeded in temporarily killing federal funding for chemical weapons incineration, winning an eighteen-month moratorium. The NRC's Stockpile Committee recommended that the Army more thoroughly study alternatives to incineration. That year Congress withheld funds for incineration, directing "the Army to evaluate alternative disposal approaches that might be 'significantly safer.'"[37]

A number of Alabama newspapers editorialized against the incinerator, citing the heavy waste burden already borne by a state that already housed the nation's largest hazardous waste dump. "Anniston could be to chemical weapons disposal what the Emelle toxic waste landfill has become to hazardous waste disposal," wrote the *Montgomery Advertiser*. The *Advertiser* applauded Congressman Browder for raising questions during hearings in Washington. The *Anniston Star* urged further investigation of alternatives as well.[38]

One of the Army's arguments for incineration backfired badly: the economic advantage of having a hazardous waste incinerator in the Model City's backyard. Army staff argued that once the incinerator completed its military mission, the facility could be converted to long-term use burning outside hazardous waste, providing opportunities for employment. The proposition handed incinerator opponents one of their most effective counterarguments. Even many people who were willing to accept that incineration was necessary feared that, once built, the incinerator would be used to process not only the onsite weapons and waste but also those shipped in from other sites. Rather than ridding itself of chemical hazards, the county would become a magnet for additional toxic wastes. Even Friends of SPRING, the pro-incineration voice, decried any effort to make the depot "a regional disposal site, because we *all* vigorously oppose any such effort."[39]

Such concerns were not unfounded. Congress had already approved funding to study the possibility of continuing to use the chemical weapons incinerators for other purposes once the stockpiles had been destroyed. And in 1990, as the incinerator at Johnston Atoll, 700 nautical miles south of Hawaii, was undertaking the destruction of its local stockpile, the Army shipped more than 100,000 U.S.-owned GB- and VX-containing projectiles from Germany to the island for disposal, despite protests.[40]

Establishing the incinerator as a military necessity, those concerned about safe disposal feared, might provide civilian waste contractors a way in the back door. There was money to be made in waste, waste contractors had argued, and some southern governors had agreed.[41] Because the hazardous waste industry was having difficulty winning public approval for the construction of new incinerators, such facilities were in short supply. Almost no one wanted Anniston to become a permanent site for burning hazardous waste.

Building an incinerator in Anniston would end up costing $1 billion. Even if the Army agreed in advance not to "repurpose" the incinerator—either to destroy weapons from other sites or to import other kinds of hazardous waste—residents were skeptical that the military would follow through on promises to tear down such an expensive facility. As a hedge against repurposing, Representative Browder offered an amendment to the Defense Authorization bill that would delay construction until another site was authorized, to reduce the likelihood that Anniston would be targeted for burning weapons from other sites.[42]

Several Families Concerned members were appointed to citizen advisory committees that had been mandated by Congress in the National Defense Authorization Act of 1986 to permit public involvement at each of the chemical stockpile sites. Jim Harmon and Dr. Doris Gertler were appointed by Governor Jim Folsom Jr. in December 1993 to the Alabama Chemical Demilitarization Citizens Advisory Commission (CDCAC), which Gertler chaired.[43] The CDCAC provided another forum to press the case for alternatives.

THE EARLY YEARS of the Clinton administration were crucial for the incinerator fight. Multiple problems at the existing incinerators at Johnston Atoll and Tooele, Utah, kept everyone on edge. The Johnston Atoll incinerator, which would be the model for the furnaces at other sites, including Anniston, had suffered a series of alarming accidents since it began test burns in 1990. News that a fire had broken out in the containment area at Johnston Island while weapons containing mustard agent were being dismantled spurred the campaign for safer alternatives. Concern heightened again when a sarin leak at the island incinerator in March 1994 forced site personnel to don masks and evacuate all nonessential workers. No nerve agent was detected at the perimeter of the facility, but the fact that several downrange personnel did not hear the alarm was special cause for worry in Anniston, a far more populous site.[44]

In early 1993, the CWWG and the local citizen groups achieved another victory when the National Research Council formally recommended that the Army conduct site-specific analyses at each of the continental depots. Buoyed by the NRC's recommendation, which would also buy time to explore neutralization, the CWWG met that April in Annapolis, Maryland. The first face-to-face meeting since 1991 convened about fifty activists from the eight sites, as well as a Russian representative from Chapayevsk, a town that had successfully forced the closure of its chemical weapons neutralization facility. The meeting coincided with lobbying plans; Brenda Lindell spoke in favor of neutralization at a May 3 press conference on Capitol Hill. In 1995, Lindell visited the former Soviet Union. "This is not just Anniston," she told the *Star*. "This is an international issue."[45] The international exchanges placed their work in a global context, heightening the sense of mission felt by activists in both countries.

Activists focused especially on the potential for an explosion or accident. The U.S. General Accounting Office (GAO) testified in 1993 that "although $176 million has been spent over the last five years on the Chemical Stockpile Emergency Preparedness Program, local communities are not prepared to deal with a chemical accident." Representative Browder sought guarantees that Calhoun County citizens would not be harmed by the disposal of chemical weapons and that the Defense Department would provide "maximum protection."[46]

A major turning point in the national debate over incineration came in February 1994, when the NRC's Stockpile Committee issued its major recommendations. Despite acknowledging "considerable uncertainty" about the risk of leaks during continued storage and about the safety of various means of disposal, the committee reported that "today's evidence suggests that any reduction in disposal risk afforded by an alternative technology will be more than offset by the larger cumulative risk from extended storage." The Stockpile Committee therefore concluded that, "given this evidence, the disposal program should not be delayed pending development of detailed information on alternative technologies." The NRC could identify "no feasible alternatives to incineration for energetics [propellants] or for high-temperature detoxification of metal parts." The GAO released a parallel report in March, *Chemical Weapons Destruction: Advantages and Disadvantages of Alternatives to Incineration*. While the GAO favored continued exploration of alternative methods to destroy agents stored in bulk form, this report repeated the claim that most alternative technologies for assembled weapons remained a decade away from full implementation.[47]

Regarding the controversy over the danger of leaks during storage, the Stockpile Committee's report included a recommendation that the Army update its assessment of "the relative risk of storage, handling, and disposal activities . . . as soon as possible," but the committee did not find the differing assessments a reason not to proceed. As for concerns about stack emissions, the NRC scientists suggested that scrubbers would remove "trace organics such as dioxins" and "chlorinated compounds." Reiterating that the Army was not exempt from environmental laws, the NRC noted that the Resource Conservation and Recovery Act (RCRA), the Toxic Substances Control Act (TSCA), and the Clean Air, Clean Water, and Hazardous Materials Transportation Acts would all apply to the incineration of chemical weapons.[48]

Yet activists remained wary. "I still believe that incineration is liked by corporations and the Army, because once it's burned, it's out [of] the stack," said SAFE founder Suzanne Marshall. "And you can't pin a label on a molecule and blame anybody, so there are no lawsuits. Yet it's not gone; it's just transformed and it's everywhere, dispersed."[49]

Especially troubling was the fact that the NRC had come to its conclusions without assessing "the latent health hazards associated with storage, handling and disposal activities," even though it acknowledged that "these latent risks represent one of the major concerns voiced by the public." Admitting that "chronic health risks from disposal operations are not well understood," the NRC specifically noted the risks of even low levels of exposure to nerve agents and established a committee to deal with the "nature and probability of health effects associated with incineration." Further site-specific analyses, the NRC stated, could "be conducted concurrently with other activities." The NRC specifically remarked on the need for "improved communication and greater community involvement" because, public comment notwithstanding, "the Army is not as well informed of public sentiment as desirable."[50]

Greenpeace promptly released a report on the proposed Anniston incinerator that was critical of the NRC findings. Based on the Army's reports of emissions from the Johnston Atoll incinerator, Greenpeace chemist Pat Costner wrote, furnace operations could lead to incomplete combustion and the potential release of trace amounts of dioxins, in violation of EPA standards. The NRC had made no attempt to quantify other products of incomplete combustion (PICs) or unidentified chemicals generated during prolonged storage. Furthermore, incineration generated waste, 1 million pounds at the incinerator in the South Pacific, roughly 600,000 pounds of which had been shipped to continental U.S. landfills. In sum, Greenpeace claimed that the NRC had not thoroughly assessed the risks posed by incineration.[51]

In a conversation with Craig Williams, two members of the NRC Stockpile Committee also expressed concerns about the committee report's assessment of the risks of continued storage. These committee members were also critical of the NRC's failure to conduct an independent analysis, relying only on data supplied by the Army, and the fact that little consideration had been given to comparing the risk of incineration to the risk of alternative technologies.[52]

Reaction to the NRC report showed the power of scientific authority in channeling political debate. However contested by activists and some committee members, the NRC report proved definitive in winning over both the *Anniston Star* and Alabama's members of Congress. After the report's release in 1994, the *Anniston Star* endorsed incineration, becoming a pivotal ally of the Army's incineration plan. Executive editor Chris Waddle (who had visited Johnston Atoll and Tooele) now felt persuaded that while incineration had drawbacks, it was the preferred strategy given the condition of the stored weapons and official projections about the time needed to develop alternatives.[53] Families Concerned members remained unconvinced.

Even as the NRC and others endorsed incineration, opposition mounted. Three hundred marchers held a demonstration in Anniston to highlight claims that neutralization technologies were closer to practical application than recognized by the GAO and the NRC. The march was timed to coincide with the visit to Anniston of a neutralization expert invited by the Alabama Citizens Advisory Commission. Joe Bunnett, chairman of the International Union of Pure and Applied Chemistry Task Force on Scientific Aspects of the Destruction of Chemical Warfare Agents, explained that a pilot test of neutralization of sarin could be run within four months, not the one to seven years Army engineers had projected.[54]

The functioning incinerator at Johnston Atoll suffered precisely the problems that concerned CWWG activists at the other sites. After the March 23 sarin release at Johnston Atoll incinerator, all of the local CWWG member groups renewed their demands for a safer means of disposal. They had gained additional allies. In early 1994, Scott C. Mohr of Physicians for Social Responsibility of Boston called the Army's plan to construct eight incinerators similar to the one used at Johnston Atoll "a serious mistake."[55] Based on a review of the test reports from the Southern Research Institute, the military engineering consulting firm Mitre, and Greenpeace, Mohr projected that the incinerators would themselves create "300,000 tons of hazardous waste." Environmental factors such as "weather, altitude, [and] seismic activity" had not been taken into account in the Army's planning. Fifty years of storage of the nerve agents might have created by-products that would "unpredictably influence the course of incineration—and hence the pattern of emissions." Mohr made clear that Physicians for Social Responsibility supported the treaty commitment to destroy the stockpile, and that he did not think continued storage was free of danger. But chemical deactivation was greatly preferable to incineration, since the former would "provide maximum protection of the public health and minimum threat to the environment." He emphasized that "the great virtue of a chemical deactivation protocol lies in its ability to maintain the toxic agents in an isolated system until destroyed."[56]

In June 1994, shortly after the NRC issued its report, the Alabama CDCAC submitted its own carefully crafted recommendations to the Senate Armed Services Committee, expressing opposition to destroying chemical weapons via incineration. CDCAC cochair Jim Harmon emphasized in his letter to Chairman Sam Nunn (D-Ga.) that 96 percent of the enclosed "hundreds of letters, position papers, and petition signatures are opposed to incineration."[57] Governor Folsom also forwarded the Alabama committee's sixteen recommendations to Congressman Ron Dellums (D-Calif.), chair of the House Armed Services Committee.

The CDCAC urged that research on neutralization be "fast-tracked" and emphasized the need to "minimize risk." The CDCAC members also expressed the need for oversight and monitoring of the disposal process, whatever method was to be used. If an incinerator were to be built in Anniston, the committee recommended that there be no transportation of weapons from other sites, no use of the facility other than destroying the local stockpile, and that the incinerator be completely dismantled after this limited purpose was complete.[58]

Representative Browder misread the CDCAC's stance, replying, "I interpret your carefully worded report as acceptance, with some serious concerns and recommendations, of the national program for the destruction of these weapons." Harmon minced no words in clarifying Browder's mistaken impression, writing, "The CAC did not endorse incineration."[59]

Pointing to several sources that showed that safety improvements at the stockpile sites had reduced storage risks, the CWWG charged that the Army had delayed correcting reports that inflated the risk of stockpile leaks until after the Joint Conference Committee on the 1995 Defense Authorization and Appropriations Act had approved the $9.5 billion sought for the incineration program, a charge the Army flatly denied. Nonetheless, Army officials later acknowledged that chemical weapons propellants may have a longer storage life than they had previously reported.[60]

Senate Armed Services Committee chairman Sam Nunn wrote to Jim Harmon, pointing out that in addition to funding the incineration program, the 1995 Defense Authorization bill dedicated $25 million to the study of alternative technologies. Of the alternative technologies funds, $2 million was dedicated to "health effects research and other chemical abatement technologies" and $500,000 to public outreach.[61]

The Army's risk assessment for the Anniston incinerator projected that stack emissions would contain trace amounts of heavy metals and other chemicals, including PCBs and dioxins—substances the EPA had concluded in 1994 were harmful to human immune systems and reproductive organs at very low levels—but the Army had determined that the slightly elevated risks posed no environmental or human health concern. One analyst critiqued the Army's studies for underestimating the potential noncancer risks from dioxin exposure and for failing to evaluate cumulative risk, that is, the prospect of adding even minute quantities of incineration by-products—including PCBs—to an environment already burdened by multiple chemicals.[62]

Families Concerned member Rufus Kinney wrote to the *Birmingham News* in late May emphasizing the potential health consequences of emissions for the highly populated area and the concern that the incinerator would bring additional hazardous waste to Alabama: "If the incinerator is built, Alabama will have a one-two knockout combination at Emelle and Anniston, which will ensure our being the regional dumping ground for toxic wastes in the Eastern U.S." Kinney highlighted the lack of plans for evacuating 50,000 people from the surrounding area; emergency preparations concerned incinerator supporters as well.[63]

A Families Concerned press release in early August 1994 noted that "the Army's prototype incinerator in the Pacific has been constantly plagued with careless operation and problems that have resulted in the release of nerve agent." Jim Harmon wrote to the *Anniston Star* critiquing the Army's risk analyses for failing to consider the long-term health effects of such releases.[64]

The Chemical Weapons Working Group kept up grassroots pressure, coordinating an International Day of Action for Safe Disposal of Chemical Weapons on September 25, 1994. Activists at each site held a "Positive

Demonstration in Support of Neutralization of Chemical Weapons." Three hundred people marched in Anniston, where supporters included not only Families Concerned, Burn Busters, and SAFE but also representatives of the Aniyuniwiya Indian Nation, POP (People Opposing Pollution), and the Anniston Chapter of the Alabama Conservancy.[65]

Less than two weeks earlier, a prime military contractor had fired the chief safety inspector at Tooele, Utah, where the Army was building the first chemical weapons incinerator located within the continental United States, for revealing thousands of problems with the incinerator's design and operation. (Army contractors would be basing the design for the Anniston facility on modifications made at Tooele of the Johnston Atoll model.) In August 1994, during tests at Tooele in anticipation of startup the following year, Steve Jones, safety manager for EG&G Defense Materials, lead contractor at the site, reported multiple safety deficiencies. Jones, a former Navy safety manager, had come to Tooele with twenty years' experience, including service in the Army Inspector General's Office and with Army Materiel Command at the Pentagon. He identified violations of standard operating procedures, including problems with accident reporting, hazard analysis and abatement, safety training, industrial hygiene, and monitoring. In short, Jones found inadequacies in nearly every aspect of the Tooele operation.[66]

On September 14, Jones was fired after refusing to state that the problems he identified at Tooele constituted "acceptable risks." In an interview with Craig Williams that week, Jones said that the president of EG&G Defense Materials, Henry Silvestri, had told him, "Don't *ever* put anything in writing negative about this plant," a claim Silvestri has since denied. Particularly troublesome was Jones's revelation about chemical agent releases from the Tooele plant. Small quantities of diluted "GB agent [are] being released into the atmosphere every day," Jones reported to Williams and the press. "In my professional opinion they should shut the plant down now," Jones told the *Tooele Transcript-Bulletin*. Senator Orrin Hatch (R-Utah) quickly expressed concern over the reported safety violations, noting that Jones had a "solid reputation" and was not a "frivolous whistleblower."[67]

Under sustained pressure from activists who mobilized press attention and from legislators around the country to consider alternate means of disposal, the Army convened in early 1997 a national body on Assembled Chemical Weapons Assessment (ACWA, pronounced "aqua") to reconsider the feasibility of alternatives to incineration, including neutralization.[68]

The Army had already awarded in February 1996 a $575 million contract to Westinghouse to construct and operate an Anniston incinerator, but incineration opponents did not stop pressing for an alternative method of disposal. Some indicators argued in their favor. As late as March 1997, the Army's ACWA liaison, Mike Parker, told the House National Security Committee that existing designs for an Anniston incinerator could be retrofitted for an alternative technology. However, on June 19, 1997, ADEM issued the air, water, and hazardous waste permits necessary to begin construction at Anniston. Even as legislators in other states continued to press for alternatives, by mid-1998, Senator Richard Shelby (R-Ala.), though expressing continued support for ACWA funding, had endorsed incinerator construction under way. Families Concerned member David Christian participated in the ACWA process. The depot incinerator was already in the "throes of construction when the ACWA process came down," Christian said later; for Anniston, he said, ACWA may have been "just a side show."[69]

Despite the sustained opposition to incineration in Anniston and the other sites, despite obvious problems with existing incinerator design, despite scientists' projections that safer technologies could be available sooner than projected, and despite evidence that the Army had overstated the immediate hazards posed by continued storage, the Army's Chemical Demilitarization Unit was plunging ahead with plans for destroying the Anniston stockpile weapons by incineration.

Local opposition to incineration only grew. In Rome, Georgia, downwind and only sixty miles east of Anniston, Carrie Baker, a young parent and leader of the grassroots Coosa River Basin Initiative (CRBI), wrote to Georgia governor Zell Miller, Senator Max Cleland (D-Ga.), and Georgia Department of Natural Resources director Harold Reheis concerning "the health risks of emissions of hormone disruptors to breast-feeding infants." In responding to Baker's inquiries, EPA regional administrator John Hankinson stated that while "combustion of chemical weapons and agents was *not* expected to pose an *unacceptable risk* to the general population," guidance for handling endocrine disruptors was not yet available.[70]

Activists also made extensive use of the courts in attempt to halt incineration at the stockpile sites; in December 2000, nine separate legal actions were under way. In a suit brought by the CRBI, a Montgomery Circuit Court judge ruled that ADEM had failed to follow the proper rule-making procedures for assessing cancer risk before issuing a hazardous waste permit for the incinerator.[71]

In the mid-1990s, white activists in the anti-incinerator campaign re-framed their message to embrace social justice concerns. Marshall was among those who reached out to key African American leaders in West Anniston, and the groups began to make common cause. Marshall made the connection explicit in her 1996 report, *Chemical Weapons Disposal and Environmental Justice*, noting that African Americans made up 44 percent of the population in Anniston (in a state with a black population of 25 percent) and that a number of the other weapons storage sites were located near minority and low-income areas. Marshall linked up with black activists John McCown, southeast regional director of the Sierra Club, and Aaron Head, who had been working on landfill issues, giving talks about the incinerator around the state.[72]

Perhaps the boldest action the anti-incinerator activists took was on June 8, 2001, marching from the Shady Acres Trailer Park on Morrisville Road right up to the incinerator gate. Timed to coincide with the ribbon-cutting at the incinerator, the "ribbon burning" march marked a breakthrough in establishing ties with the local SCLC chapter, according to Rufus Kinney, the JSU English professor who had been regularly penning letters to the *Star*. Kinney invited Reverend Reynolds to the June march, and Reynolds reciprocated by inviting Kinney to attend the August 2001 SCLC convention in Montgomery, where Kinney spoke on PCBs and chemical weapons before the SCLC Board of Directors. The alliance led to collaboration on a major protest the following year.[73]

African American activist Antoinette Hudson first got involved the incinerator campaign in 2000 and, as a member of the Calhoun County Chapter of the SCLC, helped to organize the September 2002 march. The CWWG and the Anniston groups partnered with the SCLC; Rev. Fred Shuttlesworth, who had led the Birmingham civil rights campaign, and Rev. Martin Luther King III joined in the march and rally through Anniston's downtown. "Pollution knows no color and is no respecter of persons," said Reverend Shuttlesworth at the rally in Zinn Park, and "if more white people worked with their black sisters and brothers, we'd soon get over most of the problems in this country." Craig Williams also spoke at the event, saying, "Pollution is a violent crime, threatening our health and our children." Hudson stressed the mutual respect she felt working with the white academics in the incinerator fight.[74]

As incinerator startup approached, activists took on the inadequacy of the Army's proposed "shelter-in-place" equipment, sheets of plastic and rolls of duct tape and gas masks designed for one-time use, which provided only a four-hour window of protection. Emergency trainers counseling on evacuation routes told residents that in case of "an agent exposure, 'Do not go to school and pick up your children. Just immediately leave town,'" Brenda Lindell recalled. "Excuse me," she said. "I may die trying, but I'm not leaving town without first going to school and picking up my children."[75]

The fight for safe disposal of chemical weapons was a post–Cold War protest movement; with the decline in U.S.-U.S.S.R. hostilities, it had become more possible to challenge the military in a place the Cold War had sustained. The movement did not represent an oppositional culture as it began, but as people gained more knowledge about the Army's plan, activists lobbied Congress, created street theater, and held protest demonstrations. Families Concerned, SAFE, Burn Busters, and their allies in the CWWG and elsewhere altered the course of the weapons disposal program. The CWWG's work and the ACWA process resulted in the most important victory of the safe weapons disposal fight: a decision by the Army not to employ incineration at four of the eight facilities in the continental United States.

Even with this significant success, concerns about environmental injustice remained. As Rufus Kinney pointed out, "All of those locations represent the four most affluent." Incineration, he said, was slated for those locations "where you have high percentages of minorities and working-class whites." The decision did not halt plans to burn weapons in Anniston; construction plans were well under way and Alabama had not mustered the level of sustained political opposition by elected officials in other states where incineration had become "politically untenable." The opponents of incineration often felt isolated and beleaguered. Although they were unable to prevent the construction of an incinerator in Anniston, their exertions contributed to blocking incineration at half of the chemical weapons stockpile sites. "That's pretty good when you think about it," said Marshall. "Maryland, Indiana, Colorado, Kentucky will not have incinerators."[76]

In the early years of the anti-incinerator movement, the activist groups were comprised almost entirely of middle-class whites. When the Army first decided on incineration in the late 1980s, African Americans were still fighting their way into the depot workforce. Rev. John Nettles was leading protests at the Anniston Army Depot to end discrimination in employment. Racial discrimination and racial attacks persisted in the Army and among the private contractors who serviced the military production and maintenance operations that were prospering at the depot. (As late as October 2, 2007, a noose hung on a utility pole at the depot terrorized

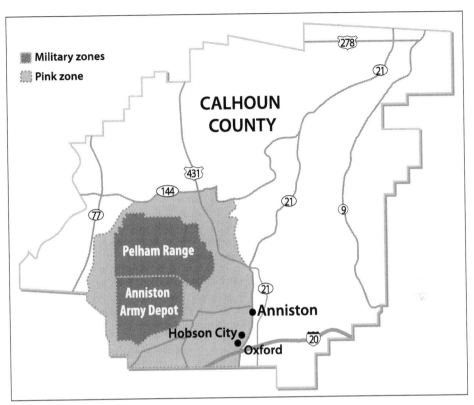

Map 8.2. Anniston Pink Zone Emergency Management areas. The Pink Zone designated civilian sites of highest concern in case of an accident at the Anniston Army Depot incinerator and included the African American and low-income white neighborhoods of West Anniston. Map by Charles Jones.

African American employees.) Jobs at the depot now provided livelihoods to some residents of West Anniston and their relatives. Despite being part of a unionized workforce, few residents, white or black, who held well-paying, sometimes hard-won jobs at the depot joined Families Concerned. Even if troubled by the plan, they were understandably reluctant to speak out.[77]

SAFE, the CWWG, the Sierra Club, and individual residents had challenged the discriminatory impact of the incinerator in 1998, after ADEM had issued permits for the facility. The discrimination complaint filed with the EPA relied on a provision of Title VI of the Civil Rights Act of 1964, which environmental advocates had begun using to challenge disparate siting of toxic facilities, with very limited success. The EPA dismissed the request to review ADEM's decision for disparate impact without evaluating

"Know Your Zones." The African American and working-class white neighborhoods of West Anniston were located in the Pink Zone, the ring around the Anniston Army Depot most at risk in case of accident during chemical weapons incineration. Photo by author.

the claim, saying that it had been filed two days after the 180-day deadline for lodging complaints.[78]

As it became increasingly clear that the Pink Zone—the ring around the incinerator site most vulnerable in case of an accident at the incinerator—included many African American neighborhoods, Southern Christian Leadership Conference leaders, including Reverend Reynolds, Rev. Fred Shuttlesworth, and Rev. Martin Luther King III, joined in protesting incineration plans.

In the mid-1990s, incineration and the fate of the fort continued to dominate the news cycle in Anniston, even as awareness of PCB contamination came to light. Despite the fact that incinerator construction was moving forward, Fort McClellan was closed by the Army. Having escaped the BRAC axe several times, the fort was decommissioned in 1999.[79]

In 2002, Families Concerned, aiming to prevent incineration and still seeking to win an alternative method of disposal at the site, filed suit against the Army based on the Army's failure to evaluate the environmental and human health effects of incineration, but their claim was eventually denied. Governor Donald Seigelman had taken legal action against the

Southern Christian Leadership Conference leaders join Families Concerned about Nerve Gas Incineration and the Chemical Weapons Working Group in protesting the U.S. Army's proposed chemical weapons incinerator on September 8, 2002. *Front row, from left*: Charles Steele (partially obscured), Rufus Kinney, Rev. Nimrod Q. Reynolds, Rev. Pamela Chaney, Rev. Raleigh Trammell, Elizabeth Crowe, Rev. Fred Shuttlesworth, unidentified woman, Rev. Martin Luther King III, and CWWG director Craig Williams. Photo by Charles Nesbitt, *Birmingham News*/Landov.

planned burning as well, charging that the Army had reneged on promises to provide gas masks and other protective measures for residents of the Pink Zone.[80]

The major march in Anniston with Reverend Reynolds, Reverend Shuttlesworth, and Rev. Martin Luther King III in partnership with the CWWG and the local groups in September 2002 did much to raise the profile of the anti-incinerator fight, but it did not stop the inexorable march toward burning. By 2003, as incinerator startup loomed, the Sierra Club hired SCLC activist Rev. Henry Sterling to work on the anti-incinerator campaign. Sterling was especially stung by the fact that the incinerator was slated for startup before depot contractors had completed protective measures such as pressurization of church and school buildings in West Anniston, which

On August 16, 2003, one week after startup, activists protested the Anniston Army Depot chemical weapons incinerator, demanding safety monitoring of potential releases at the facility. Photo by author.

had been agreed to under emergency management plans for the county, in case of leaks or explosions. "This is a fight I never dreamed of fighting," said Reverend Sterling, "with a Sierra Club, earth folks?" But he signed on. "If you are going to start burning before the place is ready," he said, as "my grandmamma used to say, something in this milk's not clear."[81]

"Uncle Sam's Pyrotechnics," read a sign on the side of the once bright yellow and red trailer, now pockmarked and faded. By 2003, the portable fireworks stand was shuttered like much of the decommissioned fort. The base closure brought a decline in Anniston's population. Local purchasing power dropped and commerce declined. The closure magnified the local economy's dependence on the depot, which had long been the largest driver of the region's economy. More than one observer has speculated that the threat of a similar fate for the depot prodded local acceptance of the incinerator.

For most of the more than a decade the anti-incineration activists spent challenging "Uncle Sam's Pyrotechnics" out at the depot, they remained fiercely at odds with the *Anniston Star*. But as vexed as the relationship was, the *Star* acknowledged in an editorial, "In Praise of Protest," that because of the activists' work, "the Army isn't going to get away with casually dismantling and discarding its weaponry in flames or any other manner without due care." With grudging respect, *Star* executive editor Chris Waddle remarked later, "If they had not existed, we would have had to create them."[82]

In Anniston, the process of incineration would be safer as a result of activists' persistence. An emergency management infrastructure, developed as a result of demands from activists and state and local government officials, led to the pressurization of buildings and training for emergency personnel and residents. Having made themselves knowledgeable on the highly technical issues involved and engaged in the national—indeed, international—arena of chemical weapons disposal, activists made it clear that even the powerful and secretive Army could be challenged. They would continue fighting incineration even as incinerator construction moved forward. They had extracted a promise that the Anniston incinerator would be dismantled and not be used for any purpose other than burning chemical weapons.

CHAPTER NINE

Contaminated Bodies, Contaminated Soil

Taking action can itself be a powerful means of increasing knowledge.
—Ellen K. Silbergeld, Environmental Defense Fund

Like many of the people who mobilized for safe disposal of chemical weapons, Cassandra Roberts had not planned on becoming an environmental activist. Nevertheless, Roberts would become a principal leader in the fight over PCB contamination that pitted West Anniston residents against one of the world's most powerful agrochemical conglomerates. The tough, compassionate probation officer for Calhoun County from West Anniston and her husband, Jerry, lived in a comfortable home in Bynum, about seven miles from the Monsanto plant, near Jerry's job at the Anniston Army Depot. Upon learning that persistent, toxic PCBs permeated her old neighborhood, Roberts, along with several West Anniston neighbors, founded the Sweet Valley/Cobbtown Environmental Justice Taskforce. With their mission of "making the link between health and environmental justice," this women-led taskforce stepped up to challenge the noxious chemical presence just outside their back doors. They joined in a lawsuit on behalf of 1,600 residents to hold Monsanto to account for PCB pollution in West Anniston, to win a measure of justice and redress where state and federal regulators had failed. Like those protesting the Army's incinerator, they drew on the power and expertise of outside allies. But the emergence of this vigorous and sustained local movement was key in challenging the conventions of confidentiality that had kept PCB pollution from public view.[1]

Cassandra Roberts had grown up in Sweet Valley, and although she now lived a few miles away, she remained deeply involved in her former neighborhood. She continued to serve as clerk at the church where she had been baptized; Mars Hill Missionary Baptist stood two blocks east of the Monsanto plant and up the hill from her childhood home. She had not given much thought to pollution until the news about PCBs broke.

"It was the fishes that squawked on them," exclaimed Sylvester Harris, director of the Model City Funeral Home just across Clydesdale Avenue from the plant. In 1993, people in the neighborhoods adjacent to the

The Alabama Department of Public Health issued a "no consumption advisory" for all species of fish from Choccolocco Creek in 1993; the prohibition remains in effect in 2013. Photo by author.

Monsanto plant began hearing about a deformed catfish that a contractor had pulled out of Choccolocco Creek. Testing revealed the fish to be full of PCBs, prompting an advisory against eating the local catch and a string of lawsuits by lakefront property owners downstream. Every catfish tested registered above the FDA's "action level" of 2 ppm; one showed levels nineteen times that amount. The initial advisory against fish consumption covered the length of the waterway between Snow Creek at Oxford and Lake Logan Martin. Ritta and Gordon Sewell, owners of Sewell's Fish Market, had to halt their Choccolocco Creek fishing operation due to contamination in the creek. Authorities ultimately found PCBs in sediment lining more than forty miles of waterway winding south from Snow Creek in West Anniston all the way to Lay Lake. Twenty years later, the "no consumption" advisory remains in effect.[2]

Concerns over massive PCB content in local fish were compounded by the nearly simultaneous discovery of PCBs in land near the Monsanto plant. In April 1993, the Alabama Power Company alerted the EPA and ADEM that it had found a "hardened tar-like material" that "could contain as much as three percent PCBs" on landfill property purchased from Monsanto in 1961. Alabama Power paid Monsanto $775,000 to take the land back. The

Star warned that the PCB contamination at the Alabama Power substation threatened public health; the power company assured the public that there was no "reason to believe that there is any danger to anybody."[3]

Follow-up tests by state and federal health agencies in early 1995 showed very high PCB concentrations in the ditch that flowed from Monsanto's South Landfill straight through the Sweet Valley and Cobbtown neighborhoods. "I'm worried to death," said Margaret Williams, whose house directly abutted the ditch. Soil tests also revealed Mars Hill Missionary Baptist Church to be an exceptionally contaminated site. The modest red brick church stood two blocks east of Monsanto and downhill from its south dump. "One heavily wooded area near Mars Hill Baptist Church registered a whopping 200,000 ppm" of PCBs, the *Star* reported. Federal guidelines at the time mandated removal and high-temperature incineration of soils exceeding 500 ppm of PCBs.[4]

As we stood in the church's tar-and-gravel parking lot in 2003, Cassandra Roberts described how a PCB-laden tributary of Snow Creek once fed the cement block baptismal pool at Mars Hill. "I was baptized in it," said Roberts. She pointed to a depression in the soil where the pastor once performed the sacred rites. "See that sinkhole right there," she said. It was "right down here, where Snow Creek used to run." The baptismal pool is now gone. Crews "covered that all up," she said, "instead of cleaning it up."[5]

The back-to-back reports of PCB contamination in West Anniston finally pushed state and federal agencies to assess the extent and impact of PCB pollution in the vicinity of Monsanto's plant. In January 1995, the Alabama Department of Public Health (ADPH) and the federal Agency for Toxic Substances and Disease Registry (ATSDR) began sampling for PCBs in the "surface soil, surface water, groundwater, and in-house dust" of West Anniston. In a study conducted over the next year and a half, the agencies also tested for PCBs in the blood of area residents.[6]

A year later, in January 1996, ADPH convened a meeting at Bethel Baptist Church in the heart of Sweet Valley and Cobbtown to report the preliminary test results. The proceedings were contentious from the start. As public health advisors warned residents to avoid eating homegrown vegetables and local meat and fish, to close their windows on windy days, and to cover their faces to avoid breathing in dust, one woman protested, "They're telling us to live in isolation; we can't do that." Anniston attorney Donald Stewart, who represented 200 people in a potential lawsuit against Monsanto, repeatedly interrupted the state toxicologist conducting the meeting, demanding answers to his clients' queries. "How did y'all decide who

Leader of the Sweet Valley/Cobbtown Environmental Justice Taskforce Cassandra Roberts surveys the site where her neighborhood once stood, 2003. Photo by author.

would get tested?" a woman shouted from the back. People left the session more troubled and uncertain than when they had arrived.[7]

Awareness of PCB pollution and shared concern for home, family, and basic justice propelled residents into activism over the next several years. Multiple local groups emerged. A number of West Anniston residents formed a second organization—Community Against Pollution (CAP). A third group, Citizens for Environmental Justice (CEJ), comprised of residents of the mostly white West End community next to Monsanto's South Landfill, formed later. The PCB contamination was a clear case of environmental injustice, members of each group argued. Given the array of organizations already protesting incineration, the city became an epicenter of environmental justice activism in Alabama and the Southeast. The local groups established relationships with regional and national environmental organizations, outside technical experts and PCB researchers, attorneys, supportive staffers within the EPA and ATSDR, and a few sympathetic legislators, locating themselves within what scholar-activist Phil Brown describes as a "field-of-movements" to challenge Monsanto's legacy.[8]

If civil rights activism arose as multiple local movements, as civil rights historians have argued, this was even more the case in the environmental

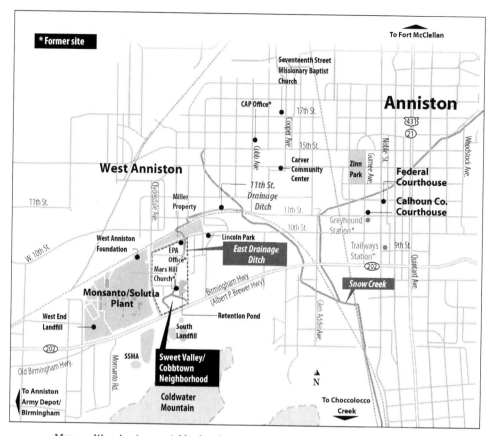

Map 9.1. West Anniston neighborhoods near the Monsanto/Solutia plant. PCB contamination required the relocation of residents from the Sweet Valley and Cobbtown neighborhoods just east of the Monsanto plant and the removal of PCB- and lead-contaminated soil from the yards of an additional 600 homes in West Anniston. Map by Charles Jones.

justice movement. There was no single national center; instead, there were numerous nodes around which organizing coalesced. Regional or state-wide coalitions and periodic national conferences linked local individuals and organizations. Part of the power of this movement derived from the linkage of identity-based organizations with struggles grounded in place. The Sweet Valley/Cobbtown Environmental Justice Taskforce joined the African American Environmental Justice Action Network, which linked groups, most of them from small communities in Alabama, who gathered to share strategies, political analysis, and organizing techniques. Research and advocacy centers, often based at historically black colleges and universities, lent a hand.[9]

IN A SENSE, like Cassandra Roberts, the U.S. environmental justice movement was baptized in PCBs. The chemicals lay at the center of the Warren County, North Carolina, dispute that ignited the mass movement linking environmental concerns to civil rights. On September 15, 1982, an interracial alliance of Warren County residents and their allies attempted to block with their bodies the landfilling of 60,000 tons of PCB-contaminated dirt in a low-income, predominantly African American neighborhood. Deploying the direct action tactics of the black freedom movement, protesters squared off against state authorities and government regulators, impeding trucks loaded with soil from North Carolina roadsides that had been sprayed with PCBs. Among those arrested in the protests were thirty-nine youth whose participation and choice of name—Students Concerned about the Future— underscored the potential long-term impact of PCBs.[10]

The Warren County cause attracted significant regional and national support, including direct action by members of the Congressional Black Caucus and the SCLC. SCLC president Rev. Joseph Lowery called the PCB dumping "an assault on the life and dignity of the citizens of Warren County." Arrested at the site, he and his wife, Evelyn, each spent a night in jail. Also prominent was Rev. Benjamin Chavis, the freedom struggle activist (and former chemistry teacher) from nearby Oxford, North Carolina, who coined the term *environmental racism*—shorthand for the power dynamics that produce and sustain the unequal allocation of environmental hazards by race and class. Although unable to stop the landfill from accepting the PCB-laden soil, the Warren County protests ushered in a new phase of the long civil rights movement, reframing environmentalism as a matter of social justice.[11]

After Warren County, a series of studies documented a discriminatory pattern in the siting of hazardous waste dumps. In 1987, Reverend Chavis, with his colleague Charles Lee at the Racial Justice Commission of the United Church of Christ, published *Toxic Wastes and Race*. The landmark report showed that African Americans, Hispanic Americans, Asian Americans, Pacific Islanders, and Native Americans were far more likely than whites to live near hazardous waste sites, a pattern especially prevalent in the South and Southwest. Robert Bullard's 1990 book *Dumping in Dixie* also documented the concentration of toxic waste facilities in low-income and African American communities across the U.S. South and highlighted the emerging movement for environmental justice.[12]

In 1991, activists convened the first National People of Color Environmental Leadership Summit, reconceptualizing environmentalism. This new vision of the environment, they argued, encompassed not only the endangered wild species and places that had often been the focus of main-stream conservation groups but also the people and urban spaces where most people "live, work, play," where they worship and go to school. Summit participants understood pollution as a silent and often invisible form of violence against racialized bodies, compromising public health in marginalized communities. To achieve environmental justice, they demanded greater representation of persons of color in national environmental organizations and called on the federal government to address environmental discrimination. As political scientist Dorceta Taylor put it, this reframing represented "a revolution within the history of U.S. environmentalism."[13]

Environmental justice struggles had emerged as, on the one hand, legal barriers to racial equality were being dismantled, and on the other, the gains of both the civil rights revolution and landmark environmental legislation came under siege. Retrenchment took place even as new toxic assaults were recognized. Hazardous waste siting decisions, redevelopment projects, and environmental "cleanup" intensified unequal exposures to pollution, often with direct or potential long-term consequences for public health. For virtually all of the environmental justice movement's short thirty-year history, then, advocates have navigated the search for remedies amid retrenchment on many of the nation's civil rights and environmental laws.

Like their predecessors in the civil rights movement, environmental justice activists insisted that the federal government fulfill a meaningful role as guarantor of rights. The movement of the earlier generation had the benefit of the new federal laws they had demanded to aid in dismantling segregation. Environmental justice activists had no such legislation. In 1992, civil rights veteran Representative John Lewis (D-Ga.) and Senator Al Gore (D-Tenn.) had introduced a proposed Environmental Justice Act, which would have required federal agencies to assess environmental health hazards in highly impacted areas and restrict further dumping in those locales. But the political climate toward race-based remedies to discrimination of any kind was unreceptive, and over the next twenty years, the bill would be reintroduced in subsequent sessions, only to remain buried in committee.[14]

Though Congress failed to act, the executive branch instituted limited measures toward environmental justice. Reverend Chavis and Bob Bullard served on President Bill Clinton's natural resources transition team and pushed his administration to aggressively tackle environmental injustice. In 1993, the EPA responded to movement pressure by forming the National Environmental Justice Advisory Council (NEJAC, pronounced "knee-jack") to advise the agency on addressing environmental disparities.

At the insistent urging of NEJAC, the EPA's Office of Environmental Equity, created in 1992, became the Office of Environmental Justice in 1994. That year, Clinton issued an executive order mandating that all federal agencies evaluate their actions for evidence of "disproportionately high and adverse human health or environmental effects on minority populations and low-income populations." Because they were federal in scope, these modest but significant steps brought greater attention to environmental dispari-ties. Still, pursuing particular occurrences of environmental injustice was largely left to local initiative.[15]

By the time West Anniston residents began protesting PCBs, the envi-ronmental justice movement had grown into a multiracial, decentralized, nationwide crusade with links to global activism. Reframing environmen-tal concerns as civil rights issues had reenergized environmentalism and broadened that movement's base. As sustained, collective renegotiations of power, social movements depend not only on resources, such as money and education, but also on a sense of meaning, identity, and agency. Giv-ing new meaning to environmentalism also reframed the meaning of civil rights. "To be honest with you," long-time civil rights and labor activist David Baker admitted, "I really did not know [or] care about environmen-tal [issues] before the PCB fight." A number of veterans of the civil rights years joined in protesting Monsanto. Reverend Reynolds, as head of the local SCLC, brought nearly forty years of experience as a civil rights leader to the struggle for environmental justice in Anniston; CAP sometimes met at his church.[16]

Several participants in the Anniston PCB fight were part of a much broader reverse migration of African Americans, people who had returned south from Chicago, Buffalo, Rochester, or New York City to escape deterio-rating cities, to care for aging parents, to launch second careers, or to retire near the grandchildren. The reverse migrants returned with perspectives influenced by their roles as educators and other professionals in urban con-texts; through the PCB dispute, they put their experience to work in Annis-ton. In addition to Baker, with his trade union experience, these individuals included PCB plaintiff-activist Kay Beard, HAZMAT (hazardous materials) educator James Hall, and community health advocate Bessie Jones.[17]

Local activists, Monsanto officials, scientists, and government represen-tatives moved in a complex choreography as the PCB fight unfolded. Ac-tivists encountered increasingly sophisticated company efforts to manage environmental opposition. Affected residents had to contend not only with corporate efforts to counter regulators' findings and apparent stonewalling by Monsanto but also with what scholars have called "toxic uncertainty"—the limitations of science and medicine in predicting the health impact of the PCB burden in their bodies. For example, after fish consumption advisories had been issued in 1993 by the Alabama Department of Public Health, plant manager Jack Mayausky told the *Star*, "By the time storm water reached Snow Creek, any PCB content would be so small as not to be measurable." A Monsanto attorney similarly "discounted the possibility" of continued problems, telling the *Star* in 1995, that "storm-water samples have shown PCB levels too low to account for the concentrations found in Choccolocco fish," attributing the problem instead "to dredging and snagging operations in the creek that were halted when the fish warnings were posted." Given these company statements, even to document the extent of PCB exposures in their soil, air, water, and bodies required enormous effort. Once these exposures were known, residents needed perseverance to pressure government agencies to use their power and mandate to address pollution. To effectively challenge an agrochemical colossus like Monsanto would require significant resources.[18]

COMING MORE THAN A DECADE after the environmental justice movement had emerged, the movement against PCB pollution in Anniston confronted a corporate entity that had grown adept at responding to environmental protest. Richard J. Mahoney, as Monsanto CEO from 1984 through 1995, headed the company as it moved to hire corporate communications strategists and cultivate relationships with key figures in the environmental movement. Mahoney choreographed the corporation's approach to environmentalism and environmentalists, instituting policies that were in place in the mid-1990s, when Anniston's anti-PCB activism arose.[19]

Mahoney had come to Monsanto in 1962 with a degree in chemistry from the University of Massachusetts, Amherst (where his graduating class of 1955 included other future highly successful industrialists, Jack Welch, CEO of General Electric, and General Motors chief Jack Smith). Mahoney joined Monsanto at age twenty-eight and rose in the ranks in marketing and sales, then the agricultural pesticides division, then plastics. Becoming CEO in 1984, Mahoney carried out a dramatic revamping of the corporation and its subsidiaries. One of his main missions was to polish the corporation's environmental image.[20]

To Mahoney, Monsanto had grown "stodgy." By the 1980s, significant changes buffeted even the largest and longest-standing chemical firms. The OPEC oil embargo of 1973–74 initially boosted chemical industry profits, as their products were in short supply. At the same time, many major petro-chemical companies, which had once simply sold off oil by-products as raw materials to chemical firms, had begun processing their own intermediates, competing with their former customers in the chemical industry. As a result, the chemical industry faced flagging sales and an identity crisis. Eighty years after John F. Queeny and his son Edgar built the Monsanto empire on coal-tar chemicals, company leaders concluded chemistry was no longer the most cutting-edge, lucrative field. As Mahoney explained it in 1988, "No major new chemical families of products have come along in the fields of interest to Monsanto." By moving into biotechnology, the company would still garner its profits from remaking nature, but in technologically new ways. As Monsanto CEO Hendrik Verfaille put it in 2001, "We can do anything through biology that can be done through chemistry."[21]

Although the major public revelations in Alabama came in 1993, two years before he left the company's helm, Mahoney largely succeeded in disassociating himself from Monsanto's PCB problem. While he was CEO, however, Mahoney was keenly aware of environmental critics and pursued a novel set of strategies to counter them. Throughout the company's history, consumer and environmental advocates had targeted Monsanto products: saccharin, tampons, off-gassing carpets, parathion, and PCBs. Former vice president of research and development Ted Hochwalt was once cited as saying that "everything he'd ever worked with now has turned out to be illegal or immoral."[22]

By the late 1980s, the chemical industry as a whole felt the need to bolster its image. In 1988, the Chemical Manufacturers Association introduced the Responsible Care™ initiative, a public relations campaign designed to demonstrate the industry's concern for the environment. Still, a 1990 industry survey showed that, at a time when three-fourths of the American public identified as "environmentally concerned," "mostly to very favorable" opinions of the chemical industry had dropped from 55 percent in 1965 to 4 percent in 1990. "Unfavorable" views of the industry had increased from 4 percent to 39 percent over the same period.[23]

Under Mahoney's leadership, Monsanto deployed its own diversified strategy against environmental detractors, using tactics more sophisticated than the blunt-edged personal assault his 1960s predecessors had inflicted on Rachel Carson. In Anniston, for instance, the company maintained the profile of good corporate citizen, operating the Monsanto Fund, awarding scholarships, and donating to local charities. The plant hosted picnics to which West Anniston's residents were invited and held Easter egg hunts on

Monsanto land for neighborhood kids. "Over the years it's been as if that plant were the home of a trusted and benevolent wizard," Jonathan Sapers of the *Anniston Star* wrote in 1985.[24]

In addition to employing an in-house director of environmental communications, in 1988 Monsanto turned to the same public relations consultant who helped devise Responsible Care, industrial psychologist Peter Sandman. Using an approach he called "outrage reduction," Sandman aimed to change public perceptions of environmental hazards and the risks they posed. In this schema, angry people, not pollutants, were the problem. Using the formula *Outrage = Hazard + Risk*, Sandman got the Monsanto executives thinking about how people perceived risk. "People saw chemical plants as much more inherently risky than smoking cigarettes, for example," explained Monsanto's environmental communications director, Glynn Young, "because people see themselves as [having] a personal choice, some personal control over that activity as opposed to a chemical plant where they did not have control." Sandman reasoned that people accept risks and hazards as long as they believe themselves to be making the choice to take them. "He would ask these real basic questions like, 'Do you feel safer driving a car or riding in the passenger seat?' Or, 'if there's a big hunk of ham that you have to slice, would you rather hold the knife or hold the ham?' What he was talking about of course," Young explained, "was the whole idea of control." Using Sandman's approach, Monsanto, like many other companies, developed means to give their critics a sense of control. "That's how we got into advisory panels," Young explained. (This approach would be put to use by Monsanto in Anniston as major trials against Monsanto wound to a close.) Though instituted in response to activists' demands for greater participation in environmental decision making, these advisory panels often became a variant of industrial paternalism, projecting the illusion but not the reality of shared control.[25]

Under Mahoney as CEO, Monsanto was especially attuned to the power of science in framing regulatory policy. "Almost all of the public policy issues in which Mahoney was involved while at Monsanto," noted the journal *Reputation Management*, "centered around scientific advances, scientific methodologies, and debates over valid vs. 'junk' science and the vast gray area between the two." Such tactics were coupled with efforts to roll back laws targeting pollution. For example, "Project 88," an initiative undertaken by Monsanto along with Chevron, ARCO, and other corporations, aimed to replace "polluter pays" regulatory policies with market-based strategies.[26]

On a broader scale, Monsanto began to trumpet its commitment to the environment, publicizing voluntary efforts to implement environmental controls, such as the Monsanto Pledge. By 1988, it was clear that the first federally mandated Toxic Release Inventory (TRI) database of industrial emissions would soon be made public. The TRI would reveal that, based on the company's 1987 reports, Monsanto had discharged 20 million pounds of toxics nationwide. The TRI "had exactly the effect that environmental groups hoped it would have," Young said later. "There is nothing like a good dose of embarrassment to make change happen." Pre-empting the TRI announcement, Mahoney pledged "to reduce all toxic and hazardous releases and emissions, working toward an ultimate goal of zero effect" and to "manage all corporate real estate, including plant sites, to benefit nature." The company would "search worldwide for technology to reduce and eliminate waste from our operations, with the top priority being not making it in the first place," and would keep the door open to communities near its sites. In a dramatic move, Monsanto pledged to cut air emissions by 90 percent worldwide by 1992. Mahoney acknowledged that the steps were aimed, in part, at "mitigating the possibility of more draconian rules."[27]

A decade and a half after the ban on PCBs, average PCB levels had begun declining in the environment but remained a serious problem in various "hot spots" nationwide. New York's Saint Regis Mohawk Tribe was demanding that General Motors clean up the PCBs dumped in the tribe's Hudson River fishing grounds, a fight that would take decades to resolve. A state office building in New Paltz, New York, was declared uninhabitable after being contaminated with PCBs released by a fire on the premises. On the Fox River in Wisconsin, residents were challenging NCR paper mills for discharging PCBs just seven miles upstream from Green Bay. The Transwestern Pipeline Company had filed suit against Monsanto in Los Angeles for PCB contamination of gas pipelines destined for California homeowners' kitchens. The EPA established a Superfund site at Commencement Bay, Washington, at the south end of Puget Sound, where PCB pollution was devastating the salmon population.[28]

To shore up the company's image, Mahoney took the unexpected step of engaging directly with national environmental organizations. Since the early 1980s, the National Wildlife Federation (NWF) had been working across the deep divide between environmentalists and business, convening an annual conference, dubbed Synergy, where "select industry, government, and environmental leaders" discussed environmental concerns. Environmental activists were split over the strategy. While notable examples of corporate environmentalism exist, avoiding disingenuous participation by industry executives proved challenging. One environmental leader called Synergy "the pinnacle of Washington environmentalists' accommodation to the ways of corporate America."[29]

At Synergy '94, Monsanto's Mahoney chaired the roundtable discussion on "Community Responsibilities of Sustainable Development." Attendees came by invitation only. All remarks were "'off the record' to encourage candid and constructive discussion," according to Monsanto's Synergy training manual. Also in attendance were some of the most important and influential advocates for environmental justice; Rev. Benjamin Chavis gave the keynote address.[30]

As its CEO convened with top environmental justice advocates in Washington, D.C., the company's 1994 *Environmental Equity Vulnerability Analysis* acknowledged "potential vulnerability in several sites" to environmental justice claims. "The Anniston, Alabama; Delaware River, New Jersey; and August[a], Georgia plants appear to have some limited vulnerability based on the surrounding population," the commissioned report stated. The "vulnerability analysis" focused *not* on the public's vulnerability to chemical hazards but on Monsanto's vulnerability to public protest. "There is no indication that the issue is active at these locations," Monsanto's consultants concluded. In the case of West Anniston, that assessment soon proved faulty.[31]

IN 1995, AFTER RETURNING to Anniston from New York City, David Baker landed a job as an environmental cleanup technician at Monsanto. After publicized discoveries of PCBs in West Anniston, federal and (eventually) state agencies had finally begun to press the company to make some effort to clean up the area surrounding the plant site, but technicians like Baker were not told what chemicals they were handling. Baker worked on a crew decontaminating an area just west of the Monsanto plant "where the kids were out there playing at the Christian school," he explained. The work paid relatively well but was clearly hazardous. "We had to wear level A [Tyvek protective] suits," Baker said. "We had to put on two pair of gloves." At a trailer the company stationed nearby, "we had to decontaminate ourselves," said Baker. "We had to go and wash our hands three or four times [before we could] use the bathroom or smoke a cigarette. We could not smoke or eat or anything out there on the site." Baker worked on the cleanup project for seven or eight months.[32]

No one who lived in the community yet understood how toxic their environs were. "I would say to Sylvester Harris, the guy that owned the funeral home," said Baker, "I would say, 'Hey man, look, y'all contaminated,' and we would be joking about it, not understanding how serious it was." As to the Monsanto Pledge to "keep our plants open to our communities" and to "ensure no Monsanto operation poses any undue risk to our employees and our communities," Baker recalled no such transparency. Not long into the job, he recounted, a neighbor walked over to the cleanup site: "This white guy came out to the fence one day and asked, 'Why are y'all wearing this equipment?'" One crew member responded, "'Because this stuff is contaminated.'" That was it, a brief exchange, but "the very next day," Baker said, "the lady [from Monsanto] from Birmingham came in. And she said, 'Anybody out here ask you from now on out, what's going on, y'all direct them to the office.'" Baker said, "It was somewhat like, hey, they weren't going to tell everybody."[33]

Baker said that Monsanto plant management told cleanup crews not to talk to anyone about the project, and not long after, "one of the engineers said to me one day that there were high levels of PCBs and the stuff was contagious and that probably every place around the plant was contaminated." (Because PCBs can be passed from one individual to another—physically on clothing from worker to family, or from mother to infant via the placenta or breastfeeding—they are transmissible, if not "contagious" in the way that medical professionals use the term.) What Baker learned, in passing, on the job that day, the rest of the neighborhood would learn when Monsanto declared its intent to purchase much of Sweet Valley and Cobbtown and relocate residents. "From that point on, the very next day," Baker said, Monsanto "put up a trailer out there in the parking lot. And that's when they had people coming and buying their homes and stuff, selling their property."[34]

In the fall of 1995, Monsanto moved quickly and quietly to buy out properties downhill from the South Landfill. In fact, even as they were attempting to purchase the most severely contaminated properties, Monsanto officials maintained that the area was safe. Plant manager Jack Mayausky was quoted by the *Star* as saying, "The health officials that surveyed the area said that there was no route for uptake (of the PCBs) and there was no health concern."[35]

Buyout offers were the means by which many residents came to learn that a significant portion of West Anniston was too toxic for human habitation—and had been so for a very long time. Although Monsanto acknowledged that the relocation was prompted by the presence of PCBs, the company divulged little information about the nature or extent of the public health risk. As Cassandra Roberts explained at an EPA regional meeting on relocation the following spring, residents were not given enough information about the extent and potential consequences of the PCB contamination to make an informed decision about the buyout offers.[36]

The buyout plan, prepared for Monsanto by Prudential Residential Services, covered roughly eight square blocks of West Anniston. It knocked out the heart of Sweet Valley and Cobbtown, thirty-five homes centered around two neighborhood churches, Mars Hill and Bethel. Plan boundaries abutted the Clydesdale Avenue plant to the west, Tenth Street to the north, and Highway 202 to the south but excluded Montrose Avenue and Lincoln Park. As an inducement to sell, owner-occupied homes would be purchased at 75 percent above appraised value; homeowners were to receive a $4,000 moving allowance. Renters were offered $1,000 to relocate. Expecting to negotiate purchase agreements quickly and with little fuss, the company set up a temporary information center to be open daily for the next two weeks and one day a week thereafter. Anyone who planned to sell was to act within four months, by early February 1996. To intensify the pressure to sell quickly, Monsanto promised bonuses of $3,500 to those who accepted their offer before Christmas. The negotiations did not go as smoothly as Monsanto planned.[37]

Among the properties Monsanto planned to purchase was the home of Cassandra Roberts's grandmother, Eloise Mealing, whom Cassandra had grown up calling mother after her own mother died. In addition to the family home of forty years, Mealing owned two other lots, each with a house that her husband, Frank, had built during his hours off work at the Anniston Foundry. One housed Mealing's Beauty Shop; another lodged a renter and had provided her income since Frank's death. By 1995, Mealing had retired from the beauty shop but, like her granddaughter, remained active in neighborhood affairs. After learning that PCB contamination put Mrs. Mealing in danger of losing all three houses, including the home in which she had been raised, Cassandra Roberts became an environmental activist. "That's when I went to fighting," she said.[38]

More than one in five people in the census tract surrounding the PCB-contaminated neighborhoods had an income below poverty level. Nearly one in seven was, like Eloise Mealing, elderly and living on a fixed income. Michael Lythcott, an independent consultant who assessed the relocation process on behalf the PCB plaintiffs' attorneys in 1997, stated that, given the socioeconomic status of the neighborhood, the relocation plan "may constitute undue pressure on them to sell." Home ownership, often a hard-won asset, had been one means of accumulating a modest nest egg to pass to the next generation. Many had owned their homes for several decades. Like the lakefront landowners downstream who had already filed suit, people living near the plant were confronted with plummeting land and home values and received offers insufficient to cover a new home mortgage. Reportedly, appraisers hired by Monsanto were told not to factor in the condition of a property or the extent of contamination. Nonetheless, the standard practice of basing appraisals on comparable properties ensured low valuations, as Lythcott also noted.[39]

If the PCB relocation plan was intended to defuse outrage, it backfired. The buyout plan had done one thing Monsanto officials did not anticipate: it confirmed to local residents the seriousness of the city's PCB threat. The Sweet Valley/Cobbtown Environmental Justice Taskforce formed in the fall of 1995 and spent much of the next year working for more just relocation provisions. For residents of the relocation area, there seemed to be no good option. They could accept Monsanto's terms, sell their homes, sacrifice their businesses, and leave the community they had built. They could stay in a place they now knew to be toxic. Or they could wage a long, drawn-out fight against a very rich and powerful corporation in hopes of leaving on terms they considered fair.

Roberts joined with Eloise Mealing, Ruth Mims, Jacqueline Brown, Dennis Gibson, and others to create the taskforce. The group applied for and received a $20,000 grant from the EPA for their educational work toward environmental justice. *The Justice Track*, the group's newsletter, described the taskforce as "an organized assembly dedicated to communication and education, and combatting the premeditated cruel indignities placed on people of color and poor whites in the community as well." Taskforce members picketed outside the Monsanto gate. Cassandra Roberts's sign at one rally in early February 1996 spoke to the aggravation felt among West Anniston residents: "Monsanto Corp., you have made our life so complicated."[40] Residents were angry that Monsanto had pressed them to decide very quickly—within two to four months—about whether and where to move. People particularly resented the December timing of the $3,500 signing bonus, which seemed to be calculated on the presumption of a desperate need for holiday cash; it was a pressure tactic many considered paternalistic and racially insensitive.[41]

Because Monsanto made relocation offers in only a portion of the contaminated area, the relocation plan seemed arbitrary and divisive. The relocation plan excluded both African American residents of Lincoln Park and white residents of the West End, both neighborhoods within a mile of the

Cassandra Roberts of the Sweet Valley/Cobbtown Environmental Justice Taskforce and Sherrill Marcus of the Southern Organizing Committee for Social and Economic Justice protest Monsanto's PCB Relocation Plan, 1996. Photo by Bill Wilson, *Anniston Star*.

plant. Residents of these areas had to choose whether to relocate on their own or to stay in polluted neighborhoods. Concerns about their family's health led Arthur and Bettye Bowie to deplete their retirement savings to move from their Lincoln Park home. "We didn't plan to ever leave the park," said Arthur. Bettye reminisced about the "lovely park there where my kids grew up. We had a vegetable garden there and I had lovely flowers." They received no offer of relocation but watched while Monsanto relocated many of their neighbors. Monsanto "bought the whole of western Anniston to Tenth Street," said Bettye, "from the Lucky-7 Club back—where the ice plant was and the service station going back that way—all of those businesses." For several years, they stayed on, but in 2001, they fled.[42]

Residents were angry that Monsanto withheld news about PCB poisoning for so long. "There we are still planting vegetables, still sweeping our yards, still sweeping the indoor-outdoor carpet on the porch. Just think of inhaling all that dust," said Bettye Bowie. "The bad thing is that I really didn't learn about it," said Arthur. "Here I am retired—retired early and now here I got to buy somewhere else to live, because I'm scared to live there."[43]

Relocation cleared inhabitants from the neighborhood, adding forty acres of land to the plant site. To Monsanto, the buyout was damage control, the neighborhood now a buffer zone for PCB wastes that would continue

PCB activist Herman Frazier protests Monsanto's Sweet Valley/Cobbtown relocation plan at Monsanto's Anniston plant, 1996. Photo by Bill Wilson, *Anniston Star*.

to leach down Coldwater Mountain from the South Landfill. Consultant Michael Lythcott noted that corporate-managed relocations commonly thwart the emergence of collective protest. Ultimately, Anniston plaintiffs alleged, the PCB relocation plan was a blatant attempt by Monsanto to reduce the number of people who might sue. (The purchase agreements Monsanto drafted did not protect sellers' rights to sue until their attorneys pushed for a clause that would do so.)[44]

Perhaps even worse than the economic loss was the decline in neighborhood cohesion and the profound disruption of being uprooted. Chemical contamination alters human lives, as those who chose to remain in West Anniston attest. Arthur Bowie's sister, Sallie Bowie Franklin, was one of the few people who decided to stay in Lincoln Park, remaining at her home on Montrose Street until her death, at age sixty-eight, in 2005. Her gray frame home sat adjacent to the chain link fence cordoning off Mars Hill Church and right next to Monsanto's new retention pond. She remembered gathering plums and muscadines in that area as a child. Franklin explained how PCB pollution changed her life irrevocably. "My brother used to live next door and my friend used to live on the right of me," she said. "I did have neighbors I could run out and talk to. We would sit in the yard and sit on the porch, now I'm just down here by myself." Alone amid vacant houses and abandoned lots, Franklin said in court, "I feel terrified." Her five children and thirteen grandchildren used to come home for a family reunion every two years. "They don't come any more," she said, "because of the soil being contaminated with PCB and also my house."[45]

Monsanto's dumping in these neighborhoods was exacerbated by a history of segregation and poverty, while segregation and poverty were made worse by proximity to pollution. Segregation had kept African Americans out of city pools, so they swam in (polluted) local swimming holes. Poverty kept supermarkets from locating in the neighborhood, while home gardens exposed residents to contaminated dirt. Relying on small livestock and locally caught fish, promoted decades earlier as a progressive reform, part of Negro Health Week campaigns for nutritional self-sufficiency, ironically had made them vulnerable to Monsanto's pollution as well. In circular fashion, being home to a polluting plant depressed neighborhood home values and repelled business development, thereby increasing poverty.

Contamination of the soil had particular class and race implications because of the cultural practice of eating clay. "When I was pregnant, I would eat it," Bettye Bowie explained. "I craved it," she continued. "We would bake it in the oven. Sometimes, it was so good." Geophagia, or pica, as medical specialists term the practice, was once common among both whites and blacks in poorer areas in the South. As a traditional or folk remedy, certain clays may have provided needed dietary minerals, Alabama historian Wayne Flynt has noted, and were consumed to "fight nausea, indigestion, and diarrhea, and even counter ingested poisons." Pregnant women often consumed clay to reduce nausea. "I used to see ladies walk for miles to get that soil when they were pregnant," Arthur Bowie said. "It was poison," said Bettye, "but we didn't know then about PCBs."[46]

In Sweet Valley, the outrage at Monsanto's silence about PCBs was palpable. "I was very angry," said Jacqueline Brown, a taskforce member who grew up in Cobbtown and was one of the first African Americans to teach in the Gadsden schools. "When I look back," she said, "and think about the many times that we were afraid because of the sounds that we would hear in the night or during the day as if something was going to explode." Brown explained that as a child, "I was afraid that it would take my family away. We would hear the fire trucks as they would come in, then it was gone. Something happened, but we didn't know what, because it was never publicized." Brown's family had been forced to move once before, to make way for an extension of Highway 202 that required Monsanto to relocate its PCB dump. ADEM officials now believe that Monsanto's "earth-moving activities" at that time had further dispersed PCBs and "may have contributed to fish contamination in Snow and Choccolocco Creek."[47]

All the more unsettling, the new toxic knowledge redefined the past, reordered personal histories, reconceptualized relationships between people and place. For the activists across town who had mobilized to fight the chemical weapons incinerator, the fear was of the future—of "accidents," of procedural failures, of the unknown health impact from the potential by-products of incineration. For those mobilizing against PCBs, fears of the past emerged as well. Baptisms (undergoing ritual purification in contaminated water), childhood haunts, and wild muscadines took on new, deeply disturbing meanings. The revelations of pollution renegotiated residents' perceptions of places important to them, undermining any sense of control, one of the effects of "slow violence." The impact was the same as with any other trauma, a term sociologist Kai Erikson defines as "confusion, despair, and hopelessness . . . a deep sense of loss."[48]

Like Arthur and Bettye Bowie, Opal Scruggs received no offer of relocation in the initial plan and decided to remain in her mainly white West End neighborhood, which despite its proximity to the plant was outside the relocation area. Her well-kept home sits on a double lot alongside Highway 202. The plot could have been prime commercial property, but now, she explained, "You can't even give it away." Scruggs's family's whole existence—living and working, celebrating and dying—lay close to the plant. Except for some time in Texas, "We've been within four blocks of Monsanto for all of our lives," she said. "When you go back out here to the railroad track and go to the right," she explained, "it dead-ends at Monsanto's landfill—one of their landfills." Scruggs felt especially betrayed by the PCB contamination because her grandfather had worked for Monsanto. Learning about PCB pollution changed the meaning of her childhood memories of meeting him at the plant gate and walking home from work holding his hand.[49]

The Confederate rose bush beside Opal Scruggs's front porch grew in dirt that registered 1.3 ppm, slightly above the standard at which the EPA requires soil to be removed. Lab tests revealed that Scruggs had 65.4 ppb of Monsanto's PCBs in her blood—more than forty times the average level found in the general U.S. population. Many PCB scientists believe *no* level of exposure is safe.[50]

People worried about the link between PCBs and disease, knowing that a connection or lack thereof in any one individual would be hard to determine. Many of Scruggs's family members died of cancer. "I would say that probably 90 percent of these people," she says, gazing at a family photograph, "the

Opal Scruggs lived within four blocks of Monsanto for most of her life. Scruggs is pictured here with a 1936 photo that includes several family members who worked at the Monsanto plant. Photo by author.

elderly people, have died from some form of cancer, including my brother, the oldest one." Scruggs had been his donor for a blood stem cell transplant. "I didn't know that I had PCBs in my body," she explained. She worries now that she may have contributed unwittingly to his death.[51]

Scruggs was also angry that the news of PCB contamination perpetuated disparaging attitudes about West Anniston. "Another thing that sticks in my craw, is West End, West End, West End," she said. Scruggs sounded a theme common in environmental justice settings, one that emerged repeatedly in interviews and at community meetings in Anniston: "They just think that we're nothing but stupid, illiterate people out here, just because we live in West End," she said. "But they forgot one thing, we are human beings and we don't need to be treated like some people are being treated, we're humans." The neighborhood had changed dramatically by the time Scruggs and I first talked in 2003. "A lot of good people . . . have left our neighborhood and made good of themselves," she said, "but you look at it today, and what do we have? Contaminated houses, contaminated soil, and contaminated bodies, with no cure."[52]

FEDERAL AND STATE AGENCIES released the results of tests for PCBs in the neighborhoods of West Anniston in June 1996. The report declared Sweet Valley/Cobbtown "a public health hazard." Individuals living there were at risk of "adverse health effects from exposure to PCBs in soil, sediment, dust, and surface water." Surface water overflowing the East Drainage Ditch that ran past Mars Hill and Bethel churches, the ATSDR and ADPH reported, was "the main pathway for contaminants to reach the area." PCBs had found their way indoors, permeating dust, carpet, and furniture. Because PCBs now pervade soil and human blood and tissues around the world, researchers assume an average or "background level" of PCBs against which to weigh results. The thirty-one samples of soil from Sweet Valley and Cobbtown were all above the background level at the time of 0.18 ppm; PCB concentrations ranged from 0.51 to 496 ppm.[53]

In Anniston as elsewhere, the environmental justice movement repositioned human health to the center of environmental concerns. Like their counterparts across the country, members of the Sweet Valley/Cobbtown Environmental Justice Taskforce both gathered and disseminated knowledge about the effects of the pollutants that for decades had been seeping into neighbors' homes and bodies. Residents were suddenly confronted with the fact that they had endured long-term exposures to toxic chemicals in sufficient quantities to cause serious health effects. Uncertainties arose about the impact on their bodies of a lifetime of exposure to PCBs. Might the chemical contamination explain all the miscarriages and migraines? Was it safe to garden? Should new mothers breastfeed? What precautions should residents take? The taskforce tried to find answers to those questions.

Fear of illness was widespread. "We feel that it did at that time affect our bodies," remembered Jacqueline Brown, who grew up in Cobbtown. "I think about the times that my dad was ill, about the times that I was diagnosed with terrible allergies. I suffered severe headaches to the point that my mother would put me in the room, in the bedroom, and cut the lights off. I was angry because we were not informed of it. If we had been informed of it, my parents probably would have moved."[54]

Residents were especially worried about the children, because PCB research had shown particular effects on developing bodies. Once it was understood that chemicals transmitted via the placenta from the mother to the gestating fetus could cause learning deficits, special concern focused on women's bodies and the intergenerational effects of PCBs. Apprehension about the health of their seven grandchildren was one of the main reasons that Arthur and Bettye Bowie left West Anniston. "We learned that it was especially devastating on kids six and under," said Arthur. "You couldn't walk out there for the kids ten years ago. Now, there's no more kids in that area." Arthur and Bettye Bowie were both treated for cancer. Sometimes it seemed like everyone they knew was sick. Like other residents, the Bowies were aware of how difficult it is to know whether the cancers were linked to PCBs. The not knowing was especially painful. Speaking of the PCBs in her body, Bettye said, "You try not to dwell on it, but you know it's there."[55]

The initial round of blood samples drawn from 103 residents of West Anniston found PCBs ranging from undetectable to 303 ppb. Twenty-seven percent (28 people) had greater than 20 ppb, exceeding levels "found in 95% of the general population." Of this group, five had extremely high levels, greater than 100 ppb of PCBs in their blood. The study found that PCB blood levels were higher in older residents and depended on how long people had lived in the neighborhood. "Excretion of PCBs is slow," the report noted, "so accumulation occurs even at low exposure levels."[56]

Soil and blood levels were correlated, especially among persons under twenty, suggesting that ongoing exposure came in part through contact with dirt. Among the findings of greatest concern was that among children between the ages of one and eleven, PCB blood and dust levels in the home were also strongly correlated, indicating that household dust was a route for contamination as well. This small study found no correlation between reported consumption of local game and fish and elevated PCBs in the blood, though a subsequent, much larger study of more than 750 people in and around West Anniston found that people who reported eating locally raised meat and fish were more likely to have elevated PCBs. People who consumed locally grown vegetables were more than six times more likely to have elevated PCB blood levels than people who did not. (People may have been at "even greater risk from *working* in [the] garden than eating the produce," one EPA official concluded.)[57]

"Cease and mitigate exposures" was the foremost conclusion of the 1996 ADPH/ATSDR report. Based on preliminary findings, ADEM had already signed a consent order requiring Monsanto to "enlarge the offer of relocation to include all residences" within the investigated area, including several households originally excluded from Monsanto's property purchase program. The order mandated immediate relocation of the residents of twenty-four of the homes that had been sampled for PCBs in dust. Relocation of these households was to begin within seven days and be completed within twenty-one days. ADPH/ATSDR recommended sampling an even wider geographic area, monitoring the groundwater for PCBs, and establishing a community public health education program.[58]

Monsanto contractors destroy homes contaminated by PCBs in West Anniston, 1996. Photo by Bill Wilson, *Anniston Star*.

Little more than a year after Monsanto announced the relocation plan, the Sweet Valley and Cobbtown neighborhoods were gone. A few residents held out until October 1996, when Mrs. Mealing and most of the remaining residents left their homes. As instructed, they left behind carpets and cloth furniture that may have been permeated with PCBs. They took with them the PCBs in their bodies. Mealing was seventy; tests measured 240 parts per billion of PCBs in her blood.[59]

FAR FROM FORESTALLING PROTEST, the mandated relocation had spurred the work of the Sweet Valley/Cobbtown Environmental Justice Taskforce. Not long after she learned of the proposed church buyout, Cassandra Roberts and her neighbors held their first meeting at Sylvester Harris's Model City Funeral Home in Sweet Valley and met leaders of the Southern Organizing Committee for Social and Economic Justice (SOC, pronounced "sock") for the first time. The taskforce found ready allies in SOC, whose cochair, Anne Braden, had lived in Anniston as a teen. Cofounded by Rev. Benjamin Chavis, SOC had deep roots in Alabama, tracing its long history in the southern civil rights and labor movements to the Southern Conference on Human Welfare (SCHW), founded in the late 1930s. The multi-issue social justice group was now deeply engaged in environmental justice activities, having sponsored a major conference on the subject in New Orleans in 1992. Braden's cochair was Birmingham freedom struggle veteran Rev. Fred Shuttlesworth, who also joined Anniston activists protesting the incinerator. Working out of Atlanta was SOC executive director Connie Tucker, who led that organization's environmental justice campaign. SOC had embraced the rising movement as a vehicle for extending a radical critique of U.S. society and for encouraging mass mobilization against systemic racism. Anniston was particularly important to SOC not only because of the seriousness of the PCB pollution and the chemical weapons fight but also because of the city's significance in the long movement for civil rights.[60]

After that first meeting at the funeral home, residents organized a protest of Monsanto's tearing down people's homes. "Mr. Harris let us use one of his coffins," Roberts explained, which they placed in front of the bulldozers. "We were prepared to go to jail." Eloise Mealing had called Reverend Reynolds, asking him "if we had to go to jail to come and get us out." In order to stop Monsanto from digging in the neighborhood while people were still present, "one of the guys laid down right down in front of the bulldozer." *USA Today* and CNN were there, and the digging was halted. "That was our first protest," said Roberts, "and I was so proud of it, because we ran Monsanto off that day."[61]

SOC aided the taskforce in making regional connections with other activists, in getting grants, and in trying to make the EPA and ATSDR investigate. It introduced the taskforce to independent health experts and environmental lawyers. Taskforce activists picketed the Monsanto plant. With EPA support, activists from Anniston traveled to Baton Rouge, Louisiana; Washington, D.C.; Memphis, Tennessee; Brunswick, Georgia; and other cities, where they met people engaged in similar fights against industrial pollution in residential neighborhoods. "Those conferences showed us the poison that was going all over," Roberts said.[62]

In early May 1996, at the urging of SOC, Cassandra Roberts traveled to Florida to attend the EPA's Superfund Relocation Roundtable Meeting. Monsanto also sent a representative to the EPA meeting in Pensacola, where the company had another chemical factory. Michael Pierle, Monsanto vice president for environment, safety, and health, represented the company at the Pensacola meeting and had garnered a slot as a business representative to NEJAC, the body set up to advise the EPA on environmental justice.[63]

Through SOC, Roberts also met anti-incinerator activist Suzanne Marshall, the JSU history professor who was one of the white activists who moved easily between the anti-incinerator and anti-PCB movements. The two collaborated to host a workshop about the Superfund site at the

Anniston Army Depot. Robert Bullard and the Environmental Justice Resource Center held the workshop at the Carver Center in West Anniston in mid-November 1996. Roberts and Marshall worked together again when Roberts brought Love Canal veteran and Citizens' Clearinghouse on Hazardous Wastes (CCHW) director Lois Gibbs to town.[64]

Dissatisfied with the lack of information on the health effects of PCBs they were receiving through official channels, local people sought other sources of knowledge. Residents engaged in "popular epidemiology," a practice laypersons in other contaminated locales had used to identify toxic sites and disease patterns. In West Anniston, activists collected and recorded family histories of childhood illnesses, rashes, and headaches and relatives who had died young. They wondered if a connection could be traced between these ailments and PCBs.[65]

With this interest in more fully characterizing the diseases present in the community, the taskforce and CAP each conducted neighborhood health surveys. That process itself was a form of empowerment. Canvassing for the health studies served as an organizing tool and helped to identify people who wanted to join the lawsuits. Among the efforts to identify patterns of disease was an inventory kept by West Anniston convenience store owner Shirley McCord. On a roster next to the store's register, McCord collected seventeen pages of names, and a litany of diseases including cancers of various organs—liver, lung, stomach, bladder, pancreas, and throat; cancers of the reproductive tract in women and men—ovarian, breast, and prostate; brain cancer, bone cancer, and leukemia. Two brothers—one lived in Sweet Valley, one on Duncan Street—both died with liver cancer. The majority of cancers noted were unspecified. Occasionally noted also were diabetes, heart disease, and stroke.[66]

However, like their counterparts in other locales, residents had to contend not only with "the intentional production of ignorance, uncertainty, and blatant misinformation," as one scholar has put it, but also with the fact that "it may not even be possible to predict the staggeringly vast number of chemical interactions that may occur." The seriousness of the exposures was confirmed when the EPA published in 1996 its long-awaited PCB reassessment, based on a comprehensive overview of the significant studies of the effects of PCBs on animal populations and on human health. Of particular concern was the report's conclusion about possible synergistic effects of the chemicals on human bodies. "The different health effects of PCBs may be interrelated," the EPA noted, "as alterations in one system may have significant implications for the other regulatory systems of the body."[67]

NEITHER THE PUBLIC HEALTH HAZARD nor Monsanto's knowledge of it was new. However, as with the shutdown of PCB production twenty-five years earlier, company officials presented the relocation of Eloise Mealing and her neighbors as a prompt, responsible corporate reaction to newly identified threats. Moreover, Monsanto's decision on which homes to include in the relocation area divided neighborhood residents who were contesting their pollution legacy. The relocation process deeply damaged relationships among West Anniston neighbors, creating rifts that still remain.[68]

Cassandra Roberts explained the politics of space in West Anniston. "Do you see that hill over there?" she asked during a 2003 visit to what remained of the devastated Sweet Valley and Cobbtown neighborhoods. She was pointing toward Lincoln Park. "If you go over that hill a little bit, that's where we used to play at every day. And it's contaminated also, but Monsanto when they came in, they didn't go over the hill and the people became angry, you see, causing a split in the community." The consent decree signed between Monsanto and ADEM in March 1996 expanded the relocation area but still excluded people like the Bowies and Opal Scruggs. Defining the "exposed" community narrowly limited Monsanto's relocation costs and wrought havoc among residents of West Anniston. Relocating the Sweet Valley and Cobbtown neighbors but not the residents of Lincoln Park split the African American community. Refusing to offer buyouts to the people living close to the plant on its west side angered whites in the West End.[69]

Even more contentious were Monsanto's closed-door negotiations with the Mars Hill pastor and deacons. As the residential property purchase program was proceeding, Monsanto had moved forward quietly to buy out the two prominent churches in Sweet Valley: Bethel Baptist Church and Mars Hill Missionary Baptist Church. These negotiations set neighbor against neighbor and Roberts against the pastor and deacon board of her church.

The holiday turkey was already in the oven on Thanksgiving morning, 1995, when local attorney Donald Stewart went to meet with Andrew Bowie, Pastor Morris Weatherly, and other members of the deacon board at Mars Hill to discuss Monsanto's offer to buy the church. Bethel Church had accepted Monsanto's offer, and the pastor and deacons of Mars Hill were inclined to do the same. Reviewing the terms offered to Mars Hill, Stewart advised the church deacons they could demand more. Years later, the attorney recalled being surprised at Monsanto's desire to purchase the church. After all, Stewart said, "they're not in the religion business."[70]

Cassandra Roberts and most of the congregation learned about the offer to buy out Mars Hill when they read about it in the newspaper. Some members were angry that the pastor and deacons had "turned down a $1 million offer to relocate their sanctuary." Others thought the church leaders should hold out for more. In any case, the congregation, including Cassandra Roberts, the elected clerk of the church, had not been consulted. Fighting the marginalization of women in the decision-making process, an insurgent group at Mars Hill, led largely by women members of the congregation, attempted to block the church's settlement with Monsanto. Angered both by Monsanto's perceived secretiveness and the deacon board's failure to alert church members to the proposal, the majority of church members voted that August to fire Pastor Weatherly. He refused to leave his post. Two weeks later, Mars Hill Church members filed suit to effect the termination. Judge Joel Laird ruled that Weatherly could keep his job. In a state where the separation between church and state is honored more in the breach than in the observance, Laird issued an order citing Scripture and urging that a prayer session be held to settle the dispute.[71]

Donald Stewart sued Monsanto on behalf of Mars Hill Church, resulting in a settlement of $2.5 million. The deacon board used the funds to build a new church, while for many years, Cassandra Roberts and other taskforce members continued to worship at the old Mars Hill chapel, which stood gated and surrounded on three sides by land Monsanto now owned.[72]

Movements are rarely homogenous; organizing is often disrupted by internal disputes. So it is not surprising that differences arose over strategy. But the gender dynamics and internal divisions in West Anniston became particularly acrimonious after Monsanto pursued the relocation plan. During the Mars Hill relocation lawsuit against Monsanto, Stewart, attorney for the pastor and deacons, some of whom were members of CAP, questioned Roberts closely about the work of the Sweet Valley/Cobbtown Environmental Justice Taskforce. Stewart grilled Roberts about funds awarded to the taskforce (the organization had purchased a computer, file cabinet, and office supplies for the group's office, which was in her home, legitimate expenses not at issue in the case). Stewart dropped the matter, but the bitterness remained, with Monsanto's buyout plan having sundered the potential for effective collaboration between the taskforce and CAP.[73]

AS THE MARS HILL CONTROVERSY played out, David Baker emerged as the leader of CAP. After leaving Anniston in 1971, Baker had found work in a New York City hospital and become deeply involved in the robust, militant unionism of the American Federation of State, County, and Municipal Employees. Baker was personable and outgoing, with a ready smile and generally affable demeanor. At the same time, working under white labor leader Jerry Wurf, Baker learned a brash, top-down approach to leadership and a hardball brand of labor activism quite different from the grassroots organizing tradition of the black freedom movement in the South.[74]

Until Baker took the helm, CAP had floundered. It had first formed in 1996 as Citizens Against Pollution, led by Andrew Bowie, chairman of the deacon board at Mars Hill and Arthur's brother. "It died because we couldn't get it off the ground," Bowie explained later, "couldn't get it funded." A reorganizational meeting of the group, now called Community Against Pollution, convened at Reverend Reynolds's Seventeenth Street Baptist Church two years later, with David Baker as a leader with the audacity to help them take on the chemical giant. In addition to Andrew Bowie and Reverend Reynolds, the group included funeral home director Sylvester Harris and David's family friend Sarge Stroud, both African American residents of West Anniston. The owner of the old Clydesdale Bank building offered the group office space rent free, and volunteers collected enough money from supporters to pay the utilities. Eventually CAP raised sufficient funds to move to a more comfortable office, a house on Cobb Avenue, several blocks north of the Monsanto plant, near Fifteenth Street.[75]

Though racial solidarity fueled the group's work against environmental discrimination, in reflecting on the politics of fighting PCB pollution, Baker often emphasized black-white unity, a strategic choice. He had lifelong friends—black and white—in the neighborhoods on either side of the plant: "Even though I was run out of Wellborn High School, I had a lot of friends over there," said Baker, referring to the white, working-class area southeast of the Monsanto plant. "I just loved the people anyway. I still feel that the people that lived on the other side [of the plant, where whites resided] were left out [of the buyout plan] intentionally and it was wrong."[76]

Shortly after he began working with CAP, Baker's wife, Betty, died in a car accident. Despondent, he had all but decided to leave Anniston again, dropping his part in the PCB fight, when he met Shirley Williams, a licensed practical nurse working with Mothers and Daughters Protecting Children's Health, which grew out of an ATSDR childhood lead-screening project that began in 2000. The two married and worked closely together in CAP's Cobb Avenue office. Shirley folded her own work on PCBs and maternal and child health into CAP's mission. David handled much of the public speaking and Shirley interviewed residents and collected data on PCBs

Anniston native and long-time labor organizer David Baker returned to his hometown in the 1990s and became president of Community Against Pollution, one of the main environmental justice groups to take on Monsanto in the PCB fight. Photo by Jacob M. Langston.

and environmental health. She became expert at deciphering the reams of highly technical documents from the EPA, ATSDR, and plaintiffs' lawyers.[77]

CAP allied itself with the Environmental Working Group (EWG), a Washington, D.C., think tank. Like SOC, the EWG recommended organizing strategies and provided research and technical assistance to selected grassroots groups. Unlike SOC, the EWG concentrated on policy, lobbying Congress rather than coordinating direct-action protest. CAP also drew on Baker's union ties and gained the support of the Coalition of Black Trade Unionists (CBTU). Under the leadership of Bill Lucy, the CBTU sponsored training for "environmental technicians," who would obtain jobs cleaning up hazardous waste.

On December 31, 1998, Baker wrote to Carol Browner, the Clinton appointee who headed the EPA. The letter, composed with the assistance of attorney Donald Stewart and accompanied by a petition signed by more than 250 "Citizens of Calhoun County," was sent in the name of the "West Anniston Environmental Justice Task Force," seeking more direct EPA involvement in Anniston.[78]

Prior to this time, federal and state authorities often had evaded responsibility for ensuring that Monsanto cleaned up PCB contamination in Anniston. Both the EPA and ADEM had a history of failures in environmental enforcement in Anniston, a major contributing factor to Monsanto's being able to avoid cleaning up or notifying its neighbors for so long. ADEM and its predecessor, the Alabama Water Improvement Commission (AWIC), had repeatedly been called to Anniston and had repeatedly failed to act: in 1961, 1966, and 1971, Joe Crockett had helped keep PCB pollution from becoming public knowledge. Efforts toward remediation conducted in the 1980s by Monsanto under ADEM's watch (and without oversight from the EPA) may have actually made the situation worse. "It is likely that past cleanup efforts spread contamination in Area A," health researchers wrote in 1996. The EPA's first records of finding PCBs in Anniston dated to 1979. The agency made a preliminary assessment of PCB contamination in Anniston in 1985 but failed to act and did not issue a notice letter officially notifying Monsanto of violations until August 2000, two years after Baker's appeal for help.[79]

Once Monsanto's PCB contamination became public knowledge in the 1990s, ADEM asserted its authority over the company's onsite cleanup and the EPA deferred. But in 1996, when the Alabama Department of Public Health requested that ADEM undertake offsite PCB soil sampling, ADEM refused. Doubting ADEM's willingness and ability to handle the job properly, staff of the federal ATSDR went so far as to consider submitting the site for federal Superfund status but decided not to, as that move would leave the federal government, not Monsanto, financially responsible for the cleanup. However, given the state health department data and federal insistence, in February 1996 ADEM ordered Monsanto "to relocate the affected residents and conduct additional sampling" of the soil in the areas surrounding the plant. An ADEM official wrote to the EPA regional waste management director, welcoming the agency's "input" and "presence" but rejecting direct federal involvement. Once again, the EPA agreed to leave operational oversight to ADEM.[80]

Foot-dragging by state regulators in holding Monsanto and other industrial polluters to account had been obvious since Joe Crockett's days at AWIC. Alabama environmental activists had little expectation that ADEM would be any more responsive to their concerns. The department had limited credibility even with more neutral parties, including the judge in a class action lawsuit against Monsanto in the late 1990s. "I have very little confidence in ADEM," Circuit Court judge Bob Austin said from the bench. "If ADEM is doing the supervising, I'd just as soon turn this over to Monsanto. It's just not real comforting to know that if I'm blind, that ADEM's going to show me the way." If any real attention was going to be paid to PCBs in West Anniston, it would have to come from the federal level. Finally, in 1999, after residents had petitioned the EPA to get involved, ADEM acceded, asking the EPA to take the lead in "offsite" remediation.[81]

West Anniston residents' New Year's Eve 1998 petition for EPA assistance was well-timed. Coming during Clinton's second term and on the heels of the federal ATSDR's alarming report on PCB blood levels in West Anniston, Baker's letter prompted EPA administrator Carol Browner to send an EPA team to investigate the following year. "I think it was seven EPA people showed up at my door," David Baker said. In 1999, CAP won a $20,000 grant from the EPA's Environmental Justice Small Grants Program to support community outreach and education regarding PCBs. In early 2000, the EPA opened its own community outreach office in downtown Anniston and, although the companies remained responsible for financing and conducting the cleanup, the EPA's Emergency Response and Removal Branch began assessing soil contamination in West Anniston, as it would have at a Superfund site. The EPA would, by mid-2003, set up a second office in West Anniston, in the old pawn shop on West Tenth Street, a few blocks from Monsanto's plant. NEJAC, along with a group from South Africa, made a "toxic tour" of the city in the spring of 2000. Demonstrations against Monsanto continued. Jeannette Champion, founder of CEJ, led a protest that November peppered with signs, "Kids and PCBs Don't Mix!" "STOP: The Cover-up Is Killing Us," "EPA's Going to Let Solutia Study Our Town to Death," and "Monsanto's Motto: Without Chemicals Life Would Be Impossible. Our Motto: With Their Chemicals Our Lives Are Impossible!"[82]

Five antipollution groups—Annistonians for a Clean Environment, Community Against Pollution, Families Concerned about Nerve Gas Incineration, Serving Alabama's Future Environment, and the Alabama chapter of the Sierra Club—came together in January 2001 to discuss ways to link concerns about PCBs and opposition to incineration. Unity faltered, though, when CAP—having concluded that fighting the incinerator was futile—opted instead to push for protective equipment for West Anniston residents. The rift rippled through the environmental movement, even beyond Anniston.[83]

By this time, the local groups, in collaboration with regional and national partners, had altered the dynamics regarding PCB contamination in West Anniston, pressing the EPA to get involved, thereby wresting oversight from ADEM. For its part, Monsanto responded forcefully, contesting claims about health concerns raised by activists and regulators. In early April

2000, for example, ATSDR scientists presented a poster session at a biennial PCB workshop in Lexington, Kentucky. Titled "Move the Mountain or Move the People? PCB Contamination in Anniston, Alabama," and based on the agency's health research in Anniston, the session itself came under fire from the company for even raising the possibility of moving the PCB waste rather than relocating the residents. Calling the session's title "inflammatory and emotionally charged," Solutia (Monsanto's successor company) enclosed a twenty-three-page rebuttal to the agency's draft public health assessment. Even with a strong local movement pressing federal regulators to act, the dispute between West Anniston residents and Monsanto would only be addressed after the conflicting parties had their competing medical and scientific claims weighed, this time before a jury, in federal and state court.[84]

CHAPTER TEN

Witnessing the Explosion in Toxic Torts

You have to fight, you have to cover the ground you stand on, as my grandmama used to say.—Shirley Baker, Community Against Pollution (2006)

In early 1996, as Monsanto's relocation plan uprooted families living nearest the chemical factory, residents of West Anniston saw no alternative but to take Monsanto to court. After learning of the contamination, individual property and business owners in Anniston and along the waterways filed multiple lawsuits against Monsanto seeking compensation for damages caused by the pollution and an injunction against further dumping of PCBs. The litigation became a mechanism for uncovering both what Monsanto had known for decades, as well as for expanding knowledge about the residents' levels of exposure and the health effects of PCBs. The Sweet Valley/Cobbtown Environmental Justice Taskforce and CAP continued to push government agencies to protect public health in West Anniston, as the dispute between industry, government, and residents over corporate responsibility and PCB science moved into state and federal court.

Attention centered on three major lawsuits. Many residents of Sweet Valley and Cobbtown joined in the first, *Walter Owens v. Monsanto* (*Owens*), which was initially filed on behalf of Coosa River property owners. In the second case, several members of the Bowie family, Opal Scruggs, and David Baker of CAP, were among the 3,500 people who signed up with Anniston lawyer Donald Stewart and his co-counsel in *Sabrina Abernathy v. Monsanto* (*Abernathy*). A third large suit, *Tolbert v. Monsanto* (*Tolbert*), was an amalgam of several lawsuits filed beginning in 2001 and ultimately involved more than 18,000 plaintiffs.[1]

Prior to these three large legal actions, downstream landowners along Choccolocco Creek and vacation homeowners on Lay Lake and Lake Logan Martin lodged two multi-plaintiff lawsuits for "conscious and deliberate" pollution in Jefferson, Talladega, and St. Clair counties. Complainants in these suits included long-time residents as well as recent transplants and retirees (attracted by the recreational opportunities), who were concerned about their health and about property values and water quality of popular lakes. These litigants were on the whole wealthier and more likely to be white than plaintiffs in the subsequent lawsuits who had lived, worked, and gone to school in and around West Anniston.[2]

The lawsuits that drew plaintiffs from West Anniston highlighted the health effects of PCBs, pitting experts aligned with Monsanto, on the one hand, against experts representing residents and the overwhelming weight of scientific opinion, on the other. Monsanto "challenged the science, they influenced or attempted to influence the regulators," said Donald Stewart in the courtroom. "They pretended to be acting responsibly when, in fact, they attempted to avoid responsibility." Robert Kaley, environmental affairs officer for both Monsanto and its spinoff, Solutia, testified in 2002, "Solutia and Monsanto have acted fairly and responsibly in dealing with the community and regulators about PCBs in Anniston."[3]

The Anniston PCB lawsuits were part of a legal trend that Alabama attorney Rhon Jones, who represented one group of plaintiffs, called an "explosion in toxic torts." Descending from medieval common law, tort suits allow injured parties to claim damages from the person or entity deemed to have caused an injury to their property or person. A "toxic tort," then, is a "civil wrong arising from exposure to a toxic substance," explained Jones. Nuisance suits, as they were sometimes called, had long been used to challenge pollution issues, but not until the late 1970s were toxic torts formally recognized as a distinct legal field.[4]

Toxic tort litigation yielded vigorous debate over PCB science and public health. To prevail in a toxic tort case, plaintiffs "must identify the harmful substance, trace the pathway of exposure, demonstrate that exposure occurred at levels at which harm can result, establish that the identified agent can cause injuries of the kind complained of, and rule out other possible causes." In the Anniston PCB cases, plaintiffs' attorneys had to prove that Monsanto's PCBs were "more likely than not" to have caused an injury.[5]

By 1996, mass tort suits against environmental polluters were making major news. Citizens of Woburn, Massachusetts, who identified a leukemia cluster among children sued W. R. Grace and Co. for contamination of the water supply in a case that became widely known through the bestselling 1995 book by Jonathan Harr, A Civil Action, and later the John Travolta film. In California, in a case also later made into a feature film, paralegal Erin Brockovich pushed attorney Ed Masry into bringing a challenge that recouped what was at that time the largest settlement in a toxic tort lawsuit for chemical pollution at a single site: $333 million for the roughly 600 plaintiffs who had been exposed to toxic hexavalent chromium that

Pacific Gas and Electric dumped in the water supply in the community of Hinkley.[6]

Increased awareness of toxic pollution was only one cause of the upswing in cases. Mass tort litigation had become more common, in part simply because computers made managing the large and potentially huge caseloads easier. But more important, as toxic tort litigation enjoyed increasing success, more attorneys were willing to take on large and powerful firms such as Monsanto. The prospect of redressing egregious environmental harms while reaping significant financial settlements motivated attorneys to tackle these complex, lengthy, and expensive lawsuits.[7]

While these factors fueled an increase in toxic tort cases, a recent change in the federal rules of evidence had made toxic tort lawsuits harder to try. A 1993 Supreme Court ruling in *Daubert v. Merrell Dow Pharmaceuticals* gave trial judges more control over the admissibility of expert testimony, directing that judges "determine whether expert testimony is scientifically reliable and 'fits' the facts of the case before it can be presented to a jury."[8] The *Daubert* standards brought directly into question whose knowledge is valued and, equally important, who decides. As Supreme Court justice Stephen Breyer put it, "*Daubert* assigned the trial judge a 'gatekeeping responsibility,'" the power to decide whether an expert's methodology was applicable and appropriate. The new *Daubert* rules acted as an impediment to bringing science-based claims. Judges, who might not have any scientific training, made key decisions about qualifying and excluding expert witnesses. Though the new rules could be deployed by either party and were used by both sides in the Anniston lawsuits, the new rules disadvantaged plaintiffs, making it more costly to bring such cases. Relying on *Daubert*, Monsanto repeatedly attempted to block PCB health experts from testifying.[9]

The Anniston cases would vividly demonstrate that the toxic tort lawsuit is as an essential but imperfect means of redress for environmental injustice. Claims of injury are, by definition, complaint-driven; while the threat of suit may have some deterrent effect, torts can be brought only *after* the damage has been done. The burden of proof rests with the injured party. Plaintiffs or their attorneys must bear the costs—which can run into millions—of filing a suit, hiring experts, and documenting injuries. Plaintiffs' attorneys recover those costs only if their clients prevail. In addition, some environmental lawyers have noted that the toxic tort process is apt to *dis*empower people in polluted neighborhoods. The trials can take years; the legal and scientific jargon can be impenetrable; and plaintiffs often relinquish control to attorneys and experts. Luke Cole, former director of California's Center for Race, Poverty, and the Environment and a veteran of dozens of legal battles against polluters, warned against overreliance on toxic torts, because they have "disempowered and disillusioned many low-income communities and communities of color." Such lawsuits do little to fundamentally alter the long-term balance of power between polluters and the people who are subject to pollution. As crucial as the PCB lawsuits were in achieving a measure of justice, Anniston's experience would bear out these observations.[10]

People turned to toxic torts partly because the existing legal framework offers few other tools to prevent discriminatory exposure to environmental hazards. The nation's environmental laws do little to prohibit disparate exposures, while civil rights laws only obliquely address toxic hazards. The legislative remedies for racial discrimination enacted in the 1960s and 1970s were largely premised on the liberal notion that racial inequalities were "residual" vestiges of a distant past, and these remedies were poorly suited to recognizing environmental justice claims. Constitutional challenges under the Equal Protection Clause had proven ineffective in tackling environmental disparities; at the time the Anniston cases began, such suits had "a 100 percent unbroken losing streak," as Cole pointed out.[11]

Toxic torts do offer power to gain knowledge, and they can yield significant compensation. As a result of the litigation, residents gained access to scientific experts, amassed health data, and pried loose tightly held company information, bringing internal corporate documents into public view. As the string of memos going back to the 1950s indicating Monsanto's preoccupation with avoiding litigation illustrates, without the threat of lawsuits, corporations might act with even greater impunity.[12]

West Anniston residents were aware of the drawbacks of toxic tort litigation, but relocation was imminent. "We had to hire attorneys" to sue Monsanto, said Cassandra Roberts, "because they wouldn't treat us fair." Finding effective representation was not easy. "We fired three attorneys," said Roberts, before finding the right team. Grover Hankins, a SOC contact and former NAACP organizer, had filed numerous suits on behalf of environmental groups. Hankins introduced the group to Ralph Knowles and Bob Shields, Atlanta-based personal injury lawyers. Slight in physical stature but a legal powerhouse, Knowles knew Alabama politics intimately. Born in Huntsville and a 1969 graduate of the University of Alabama Law School, Knowles had civil rights credentials that included a stint with the Selma Interreligious Project, working for racial justice in the aftermath of the Bloody Sunday attack on voting rights marchers. His partner, Bob Shields, was also an experienced toxic tort litigator; their firm had successfully sued Dow Corning over silicone breast implants in the mid-1990s. They partnered with Tommy Jacks, of the Texas firm Mithoff and Jacks, to take on Monsanto.[13]

Aware that they could be marginalized during litigation, members of the Sweet Valley/Cobbtown Environmental Justice Taskforce insisted on direct community involvement in decisions. In the years their suit was in process, "the lawyers never made a decision without confronting the taskforce," said Jacqueline Brown. "And the taskforce always contacted the other people who were on the lawsuit to get their opinions—whether we would continue, whether we would drop it, whatever happened—to get their feelings about what they thought should happen."[14]

The *Owens* and *Abernathy* lawsuits were filed within a month of each other in early 1996. It would be five years before either case went to trial.[15]

ON SEPTEMBER 1, 1997, in a move widely read as an attempt to devolve responsibility for chemical pollution, Monsanto spun off its beleaguered chemical division, branding the new firm "Solutia Inc." Monsanto's shares rose 10 percent afterward. The "creative use of subsidiaries," as Anniston attorney Cleo Thomas, who was not a party to the litigation, had termed it, had long characterized Monsanto's business approach. A penchant for reinvention had been a hallmark of the company, dating back to the Swann Chemical era. Various mergers, acquisitions, and devolutions sought to exploit new business ventures, divest problematic enterprises, and even take advantage of opportunities created by rising environmental concern. Known internally as "the spin," Monsanto's move to create a distinct chemical company flowed in part from the shift toward biotechnology. Divesting their chemical holdings might also distance the Monsanto name and corporate coffers from the PCB lawsuits, shielding the company from litigation and cleanup costs.[16]

In an interview, Monsanto environmental communications specialist Glynn Young claimed that liability for toxics was not at issue in the decision to divest. According to Young, "It wasn't the environmental issues at all" that concerned Monsanto managers at the time of the spin. "The liability that got the most attention internally and externally," he explained, "was the debt. Executives talked about it, people on the outside talked about it, employees talked about it." (The debt Monsanto shifted to Solutia included pensions for chemical workers and managers, in addition to the potential "legacy liabilities" for chemical pollution.) "Monsanto had loaded itself with a billion dollars' worth of debt," Young continued. Young made an intriguing linguistic choice here, using "itself" to mean Solutia. The extent of separation between Solutia and the parent company remains unclear. For its first two years, Solutia headquarters remained on Monsanto's "campus" in Creve Coeur, Missouri, and many employees kept their offices. Personnel shifted back and forth between the two companies, and Monsanto stockholders retained shares of Solutia stock. The two companies have different corporate cultures, though, according to Young, who has worked for both. "Solutia is still very much a manufacturing culture," said Young, who had "spun with Solutia" but was back on the Monsanto payroll. In contrast, he said, "Monsanto is very much a marketing culture." In any case, Young had pinpointed a problem—Solutia's debt—that would have further repercussions in Anniston.[17]

A series of corporate mergers resulted in a second spin. In March 2000, the Monsanto Company merged with the Swedish pharmaceutical company Pharmacia and drug giant Upjohn, calling the new company Pharmacia, which was later purchased by Pfizer. Then, in August 2002, with agricultural division profit expectations dampened slightly by public resistance to genetically modified foods, Pharmacia spun off its wholly owned subsidiary, Monsanto Ag Company (the "new Monsanto"). The double spin did not ultimately release the Monsanto Company (the new Monsanto) or Pharmacia (the old Monsanto) from toxic liabilities. The companies agreed that if Solutia was held liable for chemical pollution and unable to pay, both Monsanto and Pharmacia would remain financially accountable. Although these complex restructurings and spins had multiple objectives (and generated considerable confusion), the moves protected the valuation of Monsanto stock. Wall Street was "certainly aware of the difference" between the two companies, wrote Associated Press reporter David Scott. "In the days following the start of the [Abernathy] trial in Alabama," wrote Scott in 2002, "stock in Solutia fell about 35 percent[,] . . . while Monsanto's stock remained largely unaffected."[18]

The "new" Monsanto took the contradictory posture of declaring itself a new company while also laying claim to the "old" Monsanto's more than 100-year history. At the same time, in a Web posting that strained credulity, Monsanto officials attempted to deny responsibility for the PCB suits: "Monsanto recognizes that there has been confusion because we took the historic name of Monsanto when our company was formed in 2000. However, *today's Monsanto is not a party to the litigation in Anniston*. The

Monsanto Company references with respect to PCBs and Anniston are to Pharmacia Corporation—which was incorporated from the former Monsanto Company. Indeed Pharmacia Corporation (formerly known as 'Monsanto Company') is a defendant in the Anniston, Alabama case." As extraordinary measures to distance the Monsanto name and assets from PCB contamination in Anniston, the reorganizations did not succeed. Every major news story about the cases focused on Monsanto's legacy, including a segment on Bill Moyers's *Toxic Communities* in mid-2002 and a CBS News documentary on *60 Minutes* in the spring of 2003.[19]

AFTER LENGTHY PREPARATION, the *Owens* plaintiffs were the first of the three major groups to have their cases heard in court. Monsanto could have avoided a trial in the *Owens* case. The parties were negotiating a pretrial settlement but ultimately could not agree. As a result, the case opened in federal court in Birmingham on April 2, 2001. Some details about past practices at the plant had trickled out in the *Anniston Star*, but the testimony in the *Owens* lawsuit would mark the first time a comprehensive history of Monsanto's PCB pollution in West Anniston was laid out to the public.[20]

Attorneys for the Sweet Valley/Cobbtown Environmental Justice Taskforce had set up a "war room" at their hotel near the Hugo Black Federal Court Building. Selected to serve were nine federal jurors—six women and three men, six whites and three African Americans—almost all from rural northeast Alabama. Clinton appointee Judge Inge Johnson presided. Of Finnish origin, Judge Johnson had earned a reputation as a "bright" and "assiduous" judge who set demanding standards.[21]

Nearly four inches of rain greeted Anniston residents who traveled sixty miles by van or car to attend the second day of trial. In opening arguments on April 4, Bob Shields spoke for the plaintiffs. He quoted damaging internal memos, including the one by a Monsanto staffer who had written "sell the hell out of them" in the margins of the 1969 strategy document on PCB pollution. Shields noted the impact on residents' property—that home values in West Anniston were "down 60 or more percent"—and outlined plaintiffs' health concerns including "internal organ[,] biochemical and cellular injuries that they have as a result of their exposure to PCB's." Shields emphasized that "most of the information I am providing you today is not controversial, it is information that has long been known from the scientific studies."[22]

In his opening statement, Birmingham-based veteran corporate defense attorney Jere White took aim at the scientific consensus on PCBs, maintaining, "There is no clear and convincing evidence that PCB exposures are causally associated with adverse health effects in humans." Exposure to PCBs was unavoidable, White suggested, simply "a result of living in a commercial industrial society." Implying that the toxic burden was equally shared, White said, "It's an unfortunate reality that all of us do have a lot of foreign material in us." Acknowledging PCB releases from the Anniston plant, he said, "Environmental factors are a concern. But it's also family history, diet, lifestyle, exercise, things like that which determine whether most of us are going to get sick."[23]

As the trial opened, corporate officials took other opportunities to question the scientific findings documenting the human health effects of PCBs. (The tobacco industry had long pursued a similar strategy—of "manufacturing doubt"—regarding the link between cigarette smoking and lung cancer.) In a special section in the *Anniston Star* titled "PCBs: Just How Dangerous?," Solutia environmental affairs director Robert Kaley argued that the evidence of health effects from PCBs was unconvincing. In an op-ed titled "Chemical Studies Are Flawed and Inconclusive," Kaley wrote, "The lack of consistent findings with respect to occupational PCB exposure and mortality in studies conducted to date would suggest a lack of association." Ecologist John Peterson Myers, who had written about the hazards of organochlorine chemicals, countered, "When significant statistical associations are identified between people and contaminants, when laboratory experiments with animals show the same patterns, and when basic science gives insights about the biological mechanisms that are consistent with the effects, then reasonable scientists unfettered by economic interests are going to give credence to the weight of the evidence and conclude that PCBs cause human health problems."[24]

Taking Monsanto to court gave people far more knowledge about the scope and severity of the PCB exposures. Plaintiffs' experts described internal memo after internal memo revealing Monsanto's long-standing knowledge of both the extent of PCB exposure and its detrimental impact on health. Explaining his organization's decision to post thousands of pages of these documents online, Ken Cook of the Environmental Working Group said, "These companies have too much power over information, and too much control over science."[25]

THE *OWENS* ATTORNEYS had capped participation at 1,600 clients, whose cases went before the court in groups. The first group of ten was comprised of people with especially compelling stories, including three children.

Observers agree that the outcome was clinched at this stage of the trial, when Ruth Mims, a lifelong resident of West Anniston, was called to testify. Mims was born on August 16, 1931, and grew up on Rural Route 4, a dirt road in an African American neighborhood people then called Henderson Hill. Her mother worked at home, raising thirteen children; her father, a Holiness minister, farmed the bottomland near Monsanto's east drainage ditch.[26]

She grew up in the shadow of Coldwater Mountain and Monsanto. As a child, she played barefoot in the dirt and swam and caught tadpoles in the drainage ditch, where her family's cattle also got their water. Thinking back, she remembered all the dead minnows in the ditch. There was no public school for black children; she attended the one-room Cobbtown School at Mars Hill Church. For years, she had worked as a sewing machine operator. Now nearly seventy, she had PCBs in her blood at levels expert witness David Carpenter would characterize as "outrageously high," unusual even among the occupationally exposed. The PCB soil levels in her yard were 13.7 ppm, "above what the government will consider safe for human habitation," Shields explained. Six of her thirteen siblings had died in childhood. "The way I feel about PCB, it's a death sentence," said Mims.[27]

With Mrs. Mims on the stand, plaintiffs' attorney Ralph Knowles read aloud from Monsanto's 1967 reports from biologist Denzel Ferguson. Ferguson had warned that Monsanto's outflow contained "extremely toxic materials" that, even when diluted, killed fish in less than twenty-four hours and "may represent a potential source of danger to children, domestic animals, et cetera."[28]

Cross-examined sharply by Monsanto attorney Harlan Prater about a minor inconsistency in her deposition, Mims replied, clearly angry, "You was pressing on me so hard." During questioning, Prater attempted to shift responsibility to other industrial polluters—asking Mims about the iron foundries and businesses like Reformation Paint—that might have contributed toxic substances to the creek. Unlike Monsanto, Mims explained, those businesses were located *downstream* from her family's land.[29]

Like her neighbors, Mims had been approached by Monsanto agents about her hogs. Just before Christmas, 1970, the Monsanto representative knocked on her door. He said, "We'll give y'all twenty-four hours to move those hogs," Mims recalled. Then the agent left. Puzzled, Mims closed the door. A few moments later, the Monsanto agent knocked again. This time, he offered $25.00 a head for the animals—plus a pint of white corn liquor. Mims did not partake, but she acquiesced. In the intervening thirty plus years, Monsanto personnel never told Mims about the high concentrations of PCBs found in the hog tissues. Mims's evidence was pivotal. "Her testimony was just dynamite," Ralph Knowles said. "The evidence was strong in our favor scientifically and emotionally. There was a lot of fire in the case."[30]

After Mims testified, the plaintiffs' attorneys called a series of expert witnesses, who laid out Monsanto's history of PCB production and the health effects of PCBs. People in the courtroom listened intently; the details were instructive, if excruciating, to hear. Chemical engineer Jack Matson testified that Monsanto failed to take reasonable steps to protect nearby neighborhood residents. A wiry, animated professor of environmental engineering at Penn State, Matson was especially credible as an objective witness for the plaintiffs because he had once partnered with Monsanto to commercialize a new biocide that attacked microorganisms in wastewater. Matson anticipated one of Monsanto's key claims, that the chemical exposures were entirely legal, an artifact of the past, when few understood the folly of dumping in streams. While cross-examining Matson, Jere White invoked precisely this benefit of hindsight. "My point is simply this," White said. "When our grandchildren all look back from the year 2075, the way we are doing a lot of things in our life, including environmental things, they are probably going to scratch their head and laugh and say, I can't believe those folks taught [sic] that was the way to do it."[31]

However, Matson explained, measures for controlling the outflow of pollution, such as filtration systems, catch basins, and sump pumps, had been in standard use since the 1920s. Unlike other companies, he noted, Monsanto failed to take these simple steps toward reducing pollution until the late 1960s. These steps came only after independent scientists called public attention to PCBs. For this reason, he said, Monsanto had not met the "standard of care."[32]

After he and his associates had combed through thousands of pages of company documents, Matson testified that Monsanto had significantly underreported PCB releases, misleading AWIC regulators. The underreporting was not only significant but also acknowledged internally. Samples of PCB discharges from Anniston retested in St. Louis "were 2 to 4 times greater than those reported by Anniston," Monsanto's analytical chemist had told his superiors in 1971. Immediately after Monsanto was released from reporting to the state on its PCB releases in 1972, the levels of PCBs in waste streams "jumped back up again," Matson later said.[33]

Ian Nisbet, who specialized in reconstructing historical levels of discharges, testified that PCB exposure levels for West Anniston residents must have been significantly elevated in the past, as the oldest people were the most exposed. Nisbet noted that the 209 distinct PCBs have different decay rates. The more highly chlorinated congeners, he explained, "stay in the body virtually forever." For the people most exposed, he said, "their exposure over their lifetimes has been between 100 and 200 times the average of the general population." Moreover—and particularly distressing for those present in the courtroom—the plaintiffs in this group, he explained, "have had *recent* exposure which is roughly two or three times higher than that is typical for the United States population in the 1980s."[34]

The *Owens* attorneys also called to the stand David Carpenter, a public health research physician and former dean of the School of Public Health at SUNY Albany. Of all the plaintiffs' PCB health experts, Carpenter was possibly the most reviled by Monsanto. Ruddy-faced, white-haired, and straight-talking, Carpenter had conducted public health research at Love Canal, where PCBs were among the major contaminants, and had studied PCBs in the Mohawk population in New York State. He would become outspoken in the press about the extreme exposures in Anniston. In spite of his credentials, Monsanto lawyers tried more than once to get Judge Johnson to block Carpenter from testifying.[35]

In his first day on the witness stand, Carpenter summarized several widely recognized PCB health studies, outlining the familiar symptoms known since the 1930s, chloracne and liver ailments. He also described more recent research implicating PCB exposure in various forms of cancer, as well as cardiovascular, immune system, and hormonal disorders. Carpenter reviewed for the jury major ways that adults can be exposed to toxic substances: ingestion, breathing, and through the skin. He explained that PCBs could also be transmitted via exposure in the womb or through breastfeeding. "When a woman becomes pregnant, her baby is drawing on the fat from her body," said Carpenter. "A breast fed baby is going to be sampling the PCB level the mother has had for a long time."[36]

As for links between PCBs and cancer, a key 1981 study, conducted by David P. Brown and Mark Jones for the National Institutes of Occupational Safety and Health, showed statistically significant elevation "of cancers of the liver and the gallbladder and biliary tract" among former capacitor workers using PCBs. Brown's follow-up study in 1987 showed a "statistically significant excess of deaths" among workers studied who had those types of cancers. A 1986 Swedish study again showed elevated cancer risk in humans and also suggested PCB exposure was associated with greater risk of cardiovascular disease. PCBs cling to fat molecules (lipids) in the blood,

Carpenter explained, and PCBs both increase lipids in the blood—"a major risk factor for cardiovascular disease, heart attacks, [and] stroke"—and cause "direct damage to the lining of the blood vessel."[37]

Carpenter noted a 1997 study by Dana Loomis and colleagues, which found that utility workers, whose jobs often put them near PCB-filled transformers, had statistically significant higher levels of malignant melanoma. Especially noteworthy was a major nonoccupational study of 25,000 people in Maryland, by Nathaniel Rothman and colleagues, which found a statistically significant trend linking PCB exposure and the form of cancer known as non-Hodgkins lymphoma.[38]

Carpenter cautioned that the data in these studies could neither prove nor disprove that PCBs caused cancer in a given individual. Even if a causal connection could be established, a complex relationship exists between chemical exposures, other environmental exposures, and nonenvironmental factors. Studies of breast cancer indicate just how complicated the burden of scientific proof can be. Researchers had determined that some PCBs—the more highly chlorinated ones—tend to break down estrogen, while the lower chlorinated congeners enhance estrogenic effects. So, there are "some PCBs that you would expect to promote breast cancer, some that you would expect to reduce it," Carpenter said. Some breast cancer studies illuminate the interaction between environmental factors and genetics, he explained. One study of Great Lakes area women who consumed high amounts of fish containing PCBs showed higher rates of breast cancer among women who had a genetic mutation affecting enzyme production, a condition shared by 15 percent of the population. Another large North Carolina study showed that while Caucasian women with high PCB levels were not at increased breast cancer risk, "if you looked exclusively at African American women, then there was a statistically significant elevated risk" of breast cancer.[39]

Turning to other systemic health effects of PCBs, Carpenter reviewed a 1996 study published in the *New England Journal of Medicine* that showed small but significant IQ deficits in eleven-year-olds whose mothers had been exposed to PCBs, as evidenced by the levels of PCBs in the children's stored umbilical-cord blood. Recent research, still in press at the time, linked increased PCB blood levels to diabetes.[40]

Carpenter noted as well that PCBs altered thyroid and sex hormones, affecting brain development and reproduction. Researchers had suggested as early as the 1930s that chlorinated synthetic chemicals disturbed hormone function. However, these effects garnered more significant attention after Theo Colborn and colleagues published *Our Stolen Future* in 1996, linking organochlorine chemicals with endocrine disruption in both males and females in a range of species, including humans. (Endocrine disruption refers to interference with the body's hormone signaling system, the system that regulates human growth and development.) Developing fetuses and infants are especially vulnerable. Hormone-disrupting chemicals can have an impact on human bodies even in very, very small amounts, down to parts per trillion. As a result, Carpenter testified, "In my opinion, there is no level of exposure where you don't have effects on the organ systems."[41]

Carpenter described only one study that showed no ill effects on human health; that study was conducted by Renate Kimbrough, who would become a key witness for Monsanto in the upcoming state court case. Having examined the records of serum PCB levels for 3,000 Anniston residents, Carpenter testified, "I can say without any question that this is the highest exposed population that I have ever seen in the United States that was not exposed occupationally." Furthermore, he concurred with Nisbet that present reported levels "grossly underestimate" exposures in the past.[42]

During cross-examination, Monsanto attorneys tried to paint Carpenter as a "fringe scientist," pointing to research he had conducted on the health effects of electromagnetic fields. Carpenter had based his opinion that PCBs caused ill effects among the Anniston claimants on the plaintiffs' serum blood levels of PCBs. The toxicological profile on PCBs recently released by the Agency for Toxic Substances and Disease Registry (ATSDR)—which Carpenter himself had acknowledged was an authoritative source—held that "blood levels of PCBs alone do not predict whether harmful or health effects will occur." Because of this, attorney Warren Lightfoot argued for the defense, Carpenter's statements "do not rise to the level of proof required for scientific opinion." Lightfoot highlighted methodological limitations in the studies Carpenter had cited—small sample sizes in some cases, tentative conclusions pending replication in others, and the role of confounding factors. When asked if he had evaluated the plaintiffs' blood for evidence of lead or mercury exposure, Carpenter replied, "No, I have not." According to Lightfoot, Carpenter had "by his own admission failed to exclude or consider other possible causes for the plaintiffs' conditions." Furthermore, said Lightfoot, "He cannot say that a single plaintiffs' injury was caused by PCBs."[43]

Sensing the rising tension in the courtroom two and a half weeks into the trial, Judge Johnson called the attorneys together and urged them to come to agreement. Settlement talks were held over the Easter weekend.

Cassandra Roberts, Jacqueline Brown, Ruth Mims, and the others went home to Anniston, attended church at Mars Hill that Sunday, and waited anxiously while the attorneys wrangled. After intense negotiations, the parties agreed: $40 million in damages. Knowles estimated that the minimum recovery for each plaintiff would be about $5,000 with the average payment about $12,000. The settlement also included what is known as a "most favored nation clause": if participants in another multiplaintiff case involving PCBs from the Anniston plant were awarded higher damages, then the *Owens* plaintiffs' award would be raised to an equal amount. Monsanto would not be required to acknowledge legal liability or actual wrongdoing.[44]

The settlement was a clear triumph; after a series of small meetings held by the Sweet Valley/Cobbtown Environmental Justice Taskforce and their attorneys to review the terms, plaintiffs readily accepted. The outcome confirmed that people remote from power could take on a formidable corporate opponent and win. Lay testimony, backed by expert witnesses, could be a powerful tool for winning justice, even when the scientific findings were fiercely disputed. The resulting agreement required direct payments to the injured parties and provided resources to establish a foundation, to be run by the plaintiffs. Almost immediately, the taskforce took on new form as many of its key members joined the board of the new settlement-funded West Anniston Foundation (WAF). The foundation's missions: to carry out community health research and education and to monitor environmental cleanup.[45]

After five long years, the *Owens* case had resolved abruptly. "It is my belief that the new owners wanted to get this behind them," said Ralph Knowles in retrospect. "The change in ownership was a change in strategy. When Pharmacia and Pfizer took over," their strategy was, "'Bad things happened in Anniston; get it behind us and move on.'" But *Owens* was only the first of the major Anniston PCB cases to go to trial. *Abernathy* and *Tolbert* were yet to come.[46]

WHY HAD MONSANTO settled with the *Owens* plaintiffs but continued to aggressively fight the *Abernathy* lawsuit? Since *Abernathy* had more than twice the number of plaintiffs, the potential price tag may have been a factor. Perhaps Monsanto hoped that by settling the claims of those living closest to the plant, arguably the most aggrieved, and incidentally, the smallest of the plaintiff groups, the company could declare its obligation to West Anniston paid. Company strategists may have felt they had a better shot at winning in state court, where *Abernathy* was unfolding, especially after the Alabama Supreme Court ruled in the *Hinton* case.

Nona Hinton, who lived near the factory, had filed suit against Monsanto on behalf of her son Travis and others exposed to PCBs. As Birmingham attorney Bob Roden, who represented the Hintons, explained, the family was "asking for what is called medical monitoring, for the company to pay to monitor these people, to pay to test them" for the health effects associated with PCB exposure. CAP, the Environmental Working Group, and the *Abernathy* plaintiffs signed on in support with amicus briefs. Roden had anticipated a win, but, he said, "the Supreme Court of Alabama, out of eighteen states that have decided that issue, [allowing plaintiffs to pursue claims for medical monitoring,] they're the only ones that said no."[47]

The ruling in *Hinton* was based on a 1979 Alabama decision that placed injured parties in a double bind. Plaintiffs must file suit within two years of a toxic exposure but cannot sue if they have no apparent illness or injury. In cases where illnesses develop after years of latency, this legal standard is impossible to meet. The problem is compounded when, as with exposure to PCBs, the plaintiff was not made aware of having been exposed. "We do not deny that they have suffered a wrong at the hands of a negligent manufacturer, assuming the plaintiffs' allegations can be proven," the Alabama Supreme Court continued. But the court ultimately declined to require "redress for a plaintiff who has no present injury or illness." The *Hinton* case pointed to a primary problem for lawyers seeking damages for PCB-exposed clients: How could people win tort claims when they had demonstrably elevated PCB levels in their blood but no manifest illness?[48]

If Monsanto's lawyers were relying heavily on *Hinton* in their decision to go to trial, they underestimated bulldog local attorney Donald Stewart and his cocounsel, the Manhattan firm of Kasowitz, Benson, Torres, and Friedman. The *Abernathy* plaintiffs held other advantages as well—familiar terrain, a known judge, and a jury pool drawn from the surrounding area. From the first call that Andrew Bowie made to Donald Stewart, many West Anniston residents wanted the tough, well-known local attorney, a former state legislator and one-time U.S. senator, as their advocate in the PCB case.

The *Abernathy* case—the only one of the three major cases in which Monsanto's liability was decided by a jury—also followed the most circuitous path, with several trips to the Alabama Supreme Court to resolve trial-related disputes. In preparation for trial, the *Abernathy* attorneys hired health researchers to evaluate the levels of PCBs in the bodies of their clients, many of whom lived beyond the immediate relocation area.

Describing the results of blood tests for a subset of ninety-four plaintiffs, Carpenter again noted "a very, very extremely exposed population." Among a larger group of 2,075, Carpenter found that "16.7 percent or 347 people had serum PCBs in excess of 20 ppb." Assuming background levels of 3 to 5 ppb, "twenty is outrageously elevated," he said. Anniston is "the most contaminated site in the U.S," Carpenter told CBS's *60 Minutes*.[49]

Judge Joel Laird, appointed to the Calhoun County Circuit in 1990, presided over the *Abernathy* case. Born and raised in Calhoun County, Judge Laird cultivated a Mayberry image, complete with an Andy Griffith–style 1964 police cruiser. He owned the restaurant next door to the Anniston Courthouse, which served Barney's Breakfast Special every morning. Laird's sense of humor was evident in his lunch menu, which offered "Remediation Soup—Alphabet Soup with the PCBs removed." In the courtroom, however, Judge Laird took his judicial charge seriously, deploying the homegrown stereotype to both conceal and complement his legal savvy and negotiating skill, even when his own role in the case became a matter of dispute.

With the *Abernathy* case set to open in March 1999, Judge Laird had begun jury selection and Donald Stewart was prepared to argue the case when attorneys for Monsanto sought to move the trial from Anniston and to sever the case into 3,500 individual trials. The pretrial disputes delayed trial for another three years. With the change of venue to Gadsden and the decision made to try the cases in groups, Judge Laird held court at the Etowah County Courthouse, thirty miles northwest of Anniston. As the *Abernathy* opening arguments got under way in January 2002, Anniston garnered headlines nationwide. The *Washington Post* ran a major story on New Year's Day titled "Monsanto Hid Decades of Pollution."[50]

Before testimony even began, Judge Laird dismissed the personal injury claims of all healthy plaintiffs, in keeping with the *Hinton* ruling. The move was not unexpected, but it further underscored the tough burden of proof that lay ahead. Over the next seven weeks, Stewart laid out an even fuller and more damaging picture than time had permitted in the *Owens* case. He posted scores of Monsanto's internal memos on a large screen in the courtroom. Chemist Jack Matson took the stand again, referring to excerpts from Monsanto's internal communications that reported the dumping of up to 10 million pounds of hazardous PCB waste in West Anniston landfills and visible globules of Aroclors in Snow Creek. These internal communications acknowledged the health hazards associated with exposure to PCBs while the corporation was publicly minimizing them. Matson pointed out

particularly egregious contradictions between Monsanto's internal documents and their statements to regulators, congressional leaders, and the
press. For example, in 1969, shortly after the *yusho* exposures in Japan and
a similar instance of PCB-contaminated peanut oil in Holland, Monsanto's
manager of divisional public relations, Tom Ford, had written the publish-
ers of the *Wall Street Journal* saying, "To date nobody has even reported
finding PCB in food."[51]

Between testimony from health researchers, Monsanto officials, real
estate appraisers, and other expert witnesses, Stewart called West Anniston residents to the stand: Arthur and Bettye Bowie, who had fled their
home on Brockman Avenue; Arthur's sister Sallie Bowie Franklin, feeling
scared and alone in an empty neighborhood; Opal Scruggs, on the other
side of the plant; Jimmie Curvin and Gene Tomlin, co-owners of Anniston
Quality Meats; seamstresses; warehouse managers; domestic workers;
and welders—all testified to the trauma of learning that they carried in
their bodies chemicals that could cause serious harm.

Sallie Bowie Franklin, who had chosen to stay in the house on Montrose
Street where she had raised five children, had received letters from the Alabama Department of Public Health around Christmas, 1995. One letter said
that the PCB levels in the soil around her house were high and another
stated that she had 80.6 ppb of PCBs in her blood. "I didn't know anything
about PCB and what it might cause," Franklin said. "So it made me very,
very nervous to know I had that much in my blood." A third letter reporting
PCB levels in dust at the threshold to her home "made me very angry, not
knowing what to do." It was all so confusing, she said, "telling me to wash
my hands but yet I'm breathing it twenty-four hours a day in my home."
Monsanto attorney Prater replied, "She cannot recover under Alabama law
for a perceived risk of future illness. That law is as clear as it can be."[52]

THE *ABERNATHY* LAWYERS would need a sophisticated rationale to avoid
the catch-22 in Alabama law that had doomed the *Hinton* case.[53]

At the end of the second week of trial, Judge Laird, in conference, spelled
out the distinction that was beginning to emerge between the *Hinton* ruling, which prohibited any recovery for fear of future onset of disease, and
the present case. In *Abernathy*, fear of future disease was not at issue; *Hinton* made that claim untenable. But if plaintiffs' fears of PCB contamination
due to their *current* body burden could be proven to be causing emotional
distress, then a claim of outrage could be submitted to the jury for consideration. The plaintiffs would not be allowed to recover damages, Laird

said, "for something that they don't have, but if they are currently scared to death about what effects these levels of PCBs are having in their blood, they're going to be able to testify to it and recover for it if the jury determines they should." As *Owens* attorney Ralph Knowles put it: "The exposure is the injury." In essence "toxic knowledge," the emotional distress of knowing that they carried PCBs in their blood, was injury enough.[54]

Another expert, Mark Hermanson, an environmental chemist from the University of Pennsylvania, and his colleagues had sampled PCB air emissions in Anniston from May 1997 to June 1998, using air monitors that resembled large birdhouses, one of which was perched on the roof of Mars Hill Missionary Baptist Church. All of the Anniston values exceeded EPA guidelines. The PCB values in air samples at Mars Hill Church, he reported, were forty times greater than the highest values found in another highly impacted polluted area in Michigan. Not only did Hermanson's studies illuminate the history of exposures, but the air samples also ominously suggested that "there is a sustained source of PCBs in the atmosphere." Monsanto had tried to prevent Hermanson from testifying, arguing that his information about ongoing exposures was "likely to confuse the jury."[55]

Hermanson also sampled tree bark, which absorbs from the air and stores in its fatty tissues PCBs, especially the higher chlorinated ones. Testing the bark of oak, ash, sweet gum, and magnolia trees at twenty-four sites, including one each in Gadsden and Birmingham, Hermanson found that the samples from Anniston, and "particularly from Mars Hill Baptist Church, had the highest concentrations I have ever measured in tree bark." As distance from the plant increased, concentrations of PCBs in tree bark declined.[56]

As the focus shifted from the presence of PCBs in the West Anniston environment to their impact on public health, Monsanto attorneys struggled hard to keep Harvard-trained epidemiologist Richard W. Clapp from testifying. Among other grounds for denying Clapp's testimony, Monsanto attorneys argued, without irony, that hearing Clapp's testimony about the diseases associated with PCBs might cause emotional distress to the plaintiffs present in the courtroom.[57]

Surviving the challenge, Clapp gave the court a basic lesson in epidemiology, describing in lay terms what are known as the Hill Principles, after British epidemiologist Austin Bradford Hill, for evaluating the relationship between exposure and disease. These principles spoke directly to providing the proof of causation that lay at the heart of most toxic tort cases. The first two factors were the strength and consistency of the relationship between exposure and disease across different studies. The third factor is specificity, that is, whether a specific exposure causes a specific disease. (PCBs present a complicated case here, since different congeners affect various body organs in distinct ways.) Chronology is important, too, Clapp explained: "If the exposure happened after the disease, then it couldn't have caused that disease." Clapp referred to the recent work on PCBs and non-Hodgkin's lymphoma to illustrate the fifth Hill criterion, best known as the dose-response relationship. In that study, Clapp pointed out, "as the dose goes up the risk of non-Hodgkin's lymphoma goes up." (The study Clapp referenced noted greater risk of the disease at even at relatively low exposures of 6.7 ppbs in the blood; in the Anniston population tested, average blood levels were 47 ppbs. Of the potential for developing the disease among PCB-exposed plaintiffs in Anniston, he said, "I would expect their risk to be higher than the highest category on this table.") Other Hill factors include whether a plausible biological mechanism explains how the substance might cause disease, whether the scientific findings match existing knowledge about the etiology of disease, if the symptoms subside if the substance is removed, or, by analogy, if current findings parallel another result that follows a similar pattern. Clapp noted that none of the nine criteria were by themselves determinative, and none were absolutely required to show cause and effect.[58]

Stewart then called Robert Kaley, Solutia's director of environmental affairs, who had worked for Monsanto from 1973 until the 1997 spin. Stewart had Kaley read aloud from a letter William Papageorge had written to a hospital administrator in 1970: "Monsanto has manufactured Aroclors for about 40 years and throughout the period we have not observed any harmful effects on our employees or our customers['] employees." Asked if the statement had been accurate at the time, Kaley said, "I believe it was, yes."[59]

Former plant manager William Papageorge testified during the plaintiffs' case via video deposition. "Mr. PCB," as plaintiffs' attorney Charlie Fell nicknamed him, was as familiar as anyone with Monsanto's PCB problem. "I was first exposed to Snow Creek in 1965," said Papageorge, "and from that point on, my personal observation and discussions with plant people, we were all under the definite impression that it was lifeless." Asked if "part of the strategy that Monsanto devised to defend PCBs was to question the evidence that PCBs were harmful to the environment and to fish," Papageorge replied, "That's correct." Having aged thirty years since his time as Monsanto's PCB chief, Papageorge reflected that, "at a minimum, it is just not prudent to discharge knowingly any kind of industrial chemical, whether it be PCBs or any other material. . . . It just wasn't a practice that was considered to be responsible. That's all."[60]

Since none of the plaintiffs in this first group of sixteen alleged that they had health problems due to Monsanto's PCBs, their claims to injury were based on lost property value and emotional distress. A real estate expert from Birmingham, Richard Allen Maloy spoke from extensive experience measuring property values with the Appraisal Institute for the Southeast. By the most conservative estimates, he testified, the homes and land in West Anniston were valued at 50 percent below the appropriate figure.[61]

"We can't afford to lose one dollar of business," one Monsanto official had written in 1970. The decline of Anniston Quality Meats, a wholesale and retail meat processing plant on Clydesdale Avenue just north of the plant, testified to the losses experienced by local businesses as a result of the PCB contamination and the resulting relocation. Jimmy Curvin and his partners had formed the business in 1969 and built a thriving enterprise, including significant state and federal contracts. According to Birmingham accounting expert J. Wray Pearce, total sales at the meat processing plant were down by approximately 40 percent from the store's 1990s peak. The losses were more than six times greater than those of the partnership's comparable facility north of Anniston in Saks. Competition from the new WalMart, losses in state school contracts, and the closing of Fort McClellan had hurt both facilities. "The only difference you can identify," said Pearce, "is that the neighborhood that this store is in, that the business district has basically gone."[62]

IN CONTRAST TO THE *OWENS* CASE, in which the parties reached a settlement before Monsanto and Solutia attorneys presented defense witnesses, the *Abernathy* trial laid out the companies' case. PCBs were not as harmful as the plaintiffs' attorneys would have everyone believe, Monsanto experts argued. The reams of scientific studies documenting problems with PCBs were "flawed and inconclusive," Kaley suggested. To amplify the claim, Monsanto called Renate Kimbrough, a research physician who had focused on PCBs for most of her thirty-three-year career. Her résumé included twenty-five years at the CDC, with stints at the FDA and EPA, where she had been a special assistant during the terms of presidents Ronald Reagan and George H. W. Bush. Through her work with the industry-funded Institute for Evaluating Health Risks, she had consulted with the American Chemistry Council, General Electric, Bayer, Monsanto, and Solutia. Kimbrough testified that she now considered her own findings from the mid-1970s linking PCBs and liver cancer in lab rats both methodologically flawed and limited in their applicability to human subjects.[63]

Kimbrough summarized her conclusions about the health effects of PCBs from a review essay she had published in the late 1980s: "Based on the reports of workers in the general population, no clear and convincing evidence that PCB exposures were causally associated with the adverse health effects was advanced." Kimbrough continued, "This included cancer for a wide range of body burdens and exposures" to PCBs as measured in blood and adipose tissue. Referring to the *yusho* and *yucheng* poisonings, where highly toxic furans had been present with the PCBs, Kimbrough reiterated her earlier conclusion that "in humans, acute poisoning outbreaks have only occurred following exposure to a combination of PCBs and PCDFs [polychlorinated dibenzofurans]." In other words, she said, they were exposed to "this other chemical that is much more toxic."[64]

Not only did Monsanto offer witnesses who directly contradicted the plaintiffs' experts, in some cases, the opposing sides read the exact same evidence very differently. Stewart had pointed to a Monsanto document, "Recommendations from the Legal Standpoint," and said, "This is dealing with the field of manufacturer's liability. It's talking about PCBs. It says, 'Provide adequate warnings to customers and users, including advice as to disposal methods.'" What Stewart read as a narrow focus on liability rather than human lives, Monsanto interpreted as having demonstrated concern. In another instance, William Papageorge had written, "Please do let me know if there is anything I can do or any way I can help in getting these actions started and getting our information together so that we can make sure our Aroclor business is not affected by this evil publicity."[65] Stewart focused on the attempt to avoid "evil publicity"; Monsanto focused on the offer of assistance.

In closing arguments for Monsanto, Gadsden attorney George P. Ford spun a narrative that he must have thought would appeal to a north Alabama jury. PCBs had helped electrify and industrialize the South. Companies like Monsanto had saved the South from financial ruin. "We could have been devastated and destroyed and left with nothing after the Civil War and Reconstruction," Ford said, appealing, somewhat unexpectedly, to southern nationalism. As if to forestall the image of a carpetbagging northern company opportunistically exploiting southern workers, Ford said, "Northern industries and others wanted to come here . . . for several reasons. We have a great climate. Back then weather was a big problem with manufacturing. We had good people to work, and we had lots of natural resources. And one of the natural resources we had was water. Back then the environment wasn't much of a concern. . . . Companies disposed of their wastes by placing them into streams. That is the way it was done. There wasn't any EPA. There wasn't any emphasis on the environment because we had better things to do." Counterposing safe production to wartime patriotism and nation-building, Ford said, "We were worrying about World War I and World War II and the Korean War, producing products that would allow America to become what it is."[66]

Once PCBs were discovered in Europe, Monsanto took pre-emptive steps to address the alleged problems with PCBs, the defense argued. As soon as scientists in Sweden had identified PCBs in the environment, Monsanto met with researchers to understand their methods. "From the earliest emergence of environmental concerns about PCBs," Kaley had testified, "Monsanto worked with the government and academic scientists and researchers, to help learn as much as possible about PCBs, their environmental levels and behavior, and their potential health effects."[67]

Company officials were as perplexed as anyone about how these compounds could be getting into the environment. "We had family picnics on the grounds," said Jerry Brown, a Monsanto research chemist for thirty-two years who now consulted for the company. Managers brought their wives and children to Easter egg hunts at the plant, he explained; that's how safe it was.[68]

By 1970, William Papageorge had testified, with the discovery of PCBs "in places that we never suspected was perceived to be unacceptable and we were trying to reduce the opportunity for PCBs to get there in the future." Protections had been in place to ensure the safety of workers, Ford argued.[69] Out of an abundance of caution, the company voluntarily withdrew from manufacturing the product for open uses, maintaining only those applications that were essential. PCBs were indeed durable, made to be that way, for fireproofing. No substitutes were as effective. As for the waste problem, why would Monsanto dump into streams a product the company was producing for sale? The company voluntarily reduced emissions, then shut down production at Anniston.

Why did the company get out of the business in the 1970s? "I think Monsanto was of the opinion that there were safe systems in which Aroclor could be handled where you controlled the way Aroclor was being handled," said Ishmael Ransaw, whom Monsanto had assigned to research its PCB wastes in the 1970s, "but there was a lot of publicity, and I think, rather than labor under the publicity, I think Monsanto stopped."[70]

Later, after finding PCBs in local streams in the 1980s, technicians cleaned up Snow Creek, Monsanto witnesses had noted. As soon as Alabama Power notified Monsanto in 1993, an excavation was conducted. Once problems became known, managers informed AWIC, ADEM, and the EPA. In the 1990s, when PCBs were found in particular spots in West Anniston, Monsanto promptly offered to relocate residents, one of few companies to take such a step voluntarily. Its successor company, Solutia, had already committed close to $40 million to cleanup. If Donald Stewart would only let his clients grant Solutia and EPA access to impacted properties, any lingering residues would be addressed.[71]

"Did we do some things we wouldn't do today? Of course," Kaley had told the press before the trial. "But that's a little piece of a big story. If you put it all in context, I think we've got nothing to be ashamed of."[72] The company undertook philanthropic initiatives to benefit people in Anniston, including the West Anniston neighborhoods.

"What you need to consider," Monsanto's attorney Ford said to the jury in closing, "in determining these horrendous things Mr. Stewart has told you they sued Monsanto for involves the consciousness and knowledge." Monsanto, Ford maintained, did not know the extent of the contamination in West Anniston neighborhoods. By now, the presence of PCBs in West Anniston, he said, was "not a liability issue anymore because it happened so long ago."[73]

In his closing argument on February 20, Donald Stewart urged jurors to base their verdict not only on Monsanto's corporate knowledge and practices regarding PCBs in the past but also on how the company reacted to public knowledge of PCBs in the present. "You have heard a great deal of evidence about Monsanto's sordid history," said Stewart. "That history tells you what these defendants knew and when they knew it. . . . They have known about the dangers of PCBs since 1935." However, what Monsanto did to West Anniston residents in the 1990s troubled Stewart as much or more. "But what makes it even worse is *what they knew* when they did it to them in the nineties."[74]

Once news of PCB contamination spread through the neighborhoods in West Anniston, people "feared the very air they breathed," Stewart said, but once again Monsanto and Solutia "went to their public relations people, their lobbyists and their lawyers, and they did everything they could to contain the media issues, to cover up the PCB problem, to avoid cleaning up the mess that they had made in this community. The damages that these folks have suffered and are suffering [are] as a result of those actions even today."[75]

"Monsanto's PCB dump is a continuing source of contamination of these properties because they haven't put in an effective remediation and control plan *in the nineties*," Stewart said, pointing out that Solutia's projected 2006–10 budget dedicated no funds to residential cleanup. Monsanto planned to pursue a "multiple-bang" public relations strategy in response to the current litigation, Stewart pointed out, "issuing press releases, even into this trial, of trying to bolster their fading image and falling stock prices, while our folks were still suffering from severe emotional distress."[76]

A telling moment during the trial had been calculated to underscore Stewart's claim about the ongoing contamination. After Monsanto had presented its case but before the closing arguments, Stewart called Solutia plant manager David Cain as a rebuttal witness. Cain had been working for Monsanto since 1985, had spun with Solutia in 1997, and was promoted to plant manager in Anniston in September 2000, in the midst of the PCB fight. He was the first African American to hold the post. His reserved geniality and devout faith had carved a place for him and his family in Calhoun County, even among some West Anniston residents who were at odds with the company. Cain stressed the company's local philanthropic record: the land on Coldwater Mountain donated to Forever Wild, a wildlife conservation group; the Nehemiah Center for community-based nonprofits next door to the plant. Cain had attended every day of the trial. As Cain was about to leave the stand, Stewart asked him one last question: "Do you live in Jacksonville?" All the jurors knew Jacksonville was more than a dozen miles from the plant. "Yes," Cain replied. His answer said it all: no plant manager would locate his own family near this polluted site.[77]

Judge Laird had repeatedly urged the attorneys to settle *Abernathy*, sometimes expressing irritation at their unwillingness to do so. "Utterly ridiculous," he termed the weak attempts—on both sides—to come to terms.[78] A lengthy session the day before closing arguments failed again to produce results. So, during the seventh week of the trial, the case went to the jury. Each side was hopeful; despite the weight of the evidence, it was by no means clear which way the decision would go.

THE JURY'S DECISION was stunning and swifter than anyone had predicted. After deliberating for five and a half hours, the jury unanimously found Monsanto and its corporate partners liable on six of the possible counts: "suppression of the truth, negligence, trespass, nuisance," "wantonness," and "outrage." Reaction erupted all over town. "They found Monsanto guilty!" one of Bettye Bowie's coworkers shouted. (In legal terminology, guilt or innocence suggests a criminal trial. Monsanto and partners were tried civilly for the PCB contamination in Anniston and held "liable" for damages. But the popular perception elided the difference.)[79]

"I just screamed," Bettye Bowie recounted. "Here I am here at work. And I was thinking, 'An organization like Monsanto with all that money, they are going to pay the judge and the jury to lie for them.' But when I was told it was different, I thought, 'Oh my God, you know, we've come a long way, but we've got a long way to go.'"[80]

The case had turned on toxic knowledge, on Monsanto's long-standing, closely held "consciousness and knowledge" of the toxic effects of its product. "Ultimately, Monsanto's own words did them in," said Brendan De-Melle, an analyst for the Environmental Working Group. For the plaintiffs, the verdict acknowledged toxic knowledge of a different sort: not fear of future disease but real and present emotional distress caused by knowing about the toxic burden carried in their bodies.[81]

However much it signaled victory for people in West Anniston, the longest phase of the trial still lay ahead. The jury's verdict would apply to all of the plaintiffs, but still to be decided by the jury was how much the corporate partners would pay each of the 3,500 plaintiffs. Also, the judge had yet to rule whether to grant plaintiffs' demand that Monsanto pay for cleanup and health monitoring.

At this point, Monsanto attorneys once again tried to dislodge Judge Laird, mainly on the grounds that he had depicted Monsanto's attorneys as "less than honest" in discussions aimed at resolving the case. The Alabama Supreme Court deemed Laird's comment appropriate to the defendants' conduct during the trial and left him in charge.[82]

In the meantime, Monsanto officials were pursuing another tack that might permit an end run around Laird's authority to set the terms of remediation and health monitoring, one that once again involved the EPA. Since January 2001, early in the George W. Bush administration, Pharmacia and Solutia had been negotiating with the EPA over plans to mitigate the PCB contamination in West Anniston neighborhoods. ("The litigation and the regulatory activities have been uneasy neighbors," Anniston Star reporter Elizabeth Bluemink had written early in the Abernathy trial.) On March 6, 2002, less than two weeks after the Abernathy jury found Monsanto liable, Bush administration EPA chief Christine Todd Whitman held a closed meeting with a dozen staffers to discuss the situation in Anniston. Whitman had requested a briefing because, she said, "interest in the situation has been heightened by extensive media coverage." Shortly thereafter, on March 25, the EPA lodged a proposed consent decree in federal court in the EPA's separate enforcement action against Pharmacia (including Monsanto, Solutia, and new parent company, Pfizer). This consent decree governing remediation in West Anniston was considerably weaker than a draft version the EPA had proposed one year earlier. Coming just a month after the *Abernathy* verdict, but *before* Judge Laird had ruled on the plaintiffs' requests for cleanup and health monitoring, the weakened consent decree was criticized as an attempt to pre-empt the state court's decision, a "sweetheart deal" that would save the companies millions in cleanup costs.[83]

Having watched over the entire process, CAP was determined not to let the consent decree stand. Given broad local concern over the EPA's handling of the cleanup to date, Alabama's senior senator, Richard Shelby, and Representative Bob Riley (R-Ala.) had already called for an investigation. With Shelby's intervention and the assistance of the Washington-based Environmental Working Group, CAP succeeded in gaining an audience on the subject with a subcommittee of the Senate Committee on Appropriations. David and Shirley Baker and CAP vice president James Hall flew to Washington to testify, requesting effective cleanup, medical monitoring, and health studies.[84]

Senator Barbara Mikulski (D-Md.), who chaired the subcommittee, was a feisty former community organizer herself and sympathetic to the West Anniston concerns. Bill Lucy, president of the Coalition of Black Trade Unionists (CBTU), whom Baker knew from his years in the New York City labor movement, came to support the Anniston activists, and Mikulski welcomed Lucy as a longtime friend and ally. As to the sweetheart deal, Baker explained, the much stronger consent decree drafted a year earlier would have required a more extensive remediation plan for West Anniston, with EPA oversight, and would have demanded that Monsanto reimburse all costs that the EPA and ATSDR incurred in evaluating the site. The weakened decree would allow Monsanto to conduct its own assessment of risk to human health, a departure from EPA policy. Reimbursement to the agencies would be capped at $6 million. A plan for Monsanto to pay for a comprehensive health study and medical monitoring had been dropped; a $10 million independently administered education fund had been reduced to a $3.2 million fund administered by Monsanto. "The Federal Government has failed the people of Anniston," Baker declared. The real purpose of the oddly timed agreement, Baker suggested, was "to disrupt the court process" in *Abernathy*, circumventing a more robust remedy being considered by Judge Laird. "EPA's consent decree with Monsanto is a blatant attempt to snatch defeat from the jaws of victory," Baker said.[85]

Questioning by Mikulski and Shelby exposed the repeated failures of both the EPA and ADEM regarding PCB contamination in Anniston. "These agencies were, at the very least," said Shelby, "complacent in their dealings with Monsanto. If you are just going to look where PCBs have been discovered thus far, that sounds like a sham cleanup," one that would do little to engender trust. Mikulski was also clearly upset that it appeared that both the EPA and Solutia had attempted to circumvent the February 2002 decision in *Abernathy*. "EPA says the timing was coincidental," Mikulski continued. "I find it surprising."[86]

Mikulski was also taken aback that potential conflicts of interest had forced two key EPA officials to recuse themselves from negotiations of the consent decree, "leaving a leadership void on the Anniston issue." Whitman's deputy administrator, Linda Fisher, had worked for Monsanto in the 1990s. Region 4 administrator Jimmy Palmer also had to step aside, because he formerly represented several Anniston foundries involved in a dispute with Monsanto over which entities should pay for cleaning up PCB and lead contamination in West Anniston. (Donald Stewart later accused Whitman herself of limiting cleanup expenditures because she and her husband had financial ties to Citigroup, which did business with Solutia.)[87]

At the close of the Senate hearing, an emotional exchange took place between Senator Mikulski and David Baker. "What do citizens need to do when they are the Davids," asked Mikulski, "and all they have is this slingshot, and they do not even know what rocks they have?" Baker acknowledged the support that CAP had received from the EPA and ATSDR in the form of grants and health information. Mikulski lauded CAP's efforts, thanking "all those people who cooked, and baked, and sang, and rallied, and so on, and put in their own tremendous sweat equity. I know that you put in three shifts. You put [in] one in the marketplace, earning a living; you put in another shift with the family to make sure the living is worthwhile; and now you put in a third shift, both as a union leader and as a community activist."[88]

Echoing Baker's appeal for medical monitoring and health studies was the ATSDR's assistant administrator, Henry Falk, who told the committee that his agency had found PCB exposures in Anniston to constitute an ongoing "public health hazard." As a direct result of CAP's testimony at the Senate subcommittee hearing, the ATSDR later awarded a three-year $3.2 million grant for PCB health research in Anniston. Vehement public opposition to the sweetheart decree forced its withdrawal, and the EPA eventually made revisions that met several of the activists' demands before the decree was ordered into effect the following year.[89]

THE *ABERNATHY* JURY had ruled against Monsanto in early 2002. The penalty phase of the trial dragged on for another year and a half, making this the longest jury trial in Alabama history. By July 2003, the jury was still working its way through the 3,500 plaintiffs, twenty people at a time, routinely returning substantial financial awards for almost everyone. In the first fifty-one cases, the jury had returned property damage verdicts totaling $11.8 million, making Solutia's potential exposure as much as $3 billion. Public interest had not waned; people from Anniston continued to make the thirty-mile trek to pack the courtroom each day. As is not infrequent in such cases, Solutia was threatening bankruptcy because of the liabilities with which Monsanto had encumbered the company at the time of the spin. Judge Laird had grown exasperated. Several of Monsanto's lawyers had stopped showing up in court on a regular basis. One day, in the midsummer heat, Laird scolded all the attorneys present, out of the jury's hearing, "Can't you show a bit more sympathy? Daily for months, you stand up and make the same arguments. I want this jury to get back to their lives. There is no reason that either side" cannot come to an agreement.[90]

As the *Abernathy* case ground on in state court, thousands of additional plaintiffs had come forward. At least four firms filed lawsuits for an eventual 18,000 plaintiffs, a number equal to roughly one-fifth of the county's population, including many former residents who had moved away. Known as the *Tolbert* litigation, many of these lawsuits had been filed in federal court in Birmingham on January 23, 2002, during the initial phase of the *Abernathy* trial. These plaintiffs' high-profile roster of attorneys from Birmingham and Montgomery included Bob Roden, who had argued the unsuccessful *Hinton* medical monitoring suit, and former lieutenant governor Jere Beasley, a founding partner of the highest profile personal injury firm in Alabama, whose long history in state politics included standing in as governor after the assassination attempt against George Wallace in the summer of 1972. CAP leaders had also approached internationally renowned criminal defense lawyer Johnnie Cochran about taking on PCB cases. The Los Angeles–based Cochran, whose astounding win in the O. J. Simpson murder case in 1995 had jolted a transfixed nation, came to Anniston to meet with potential clients in August 2001. Five thousand residents from Anniston and beyond streamed to greet Cochran at the Anniston Entertainment

Complex, and many signed up as plaintiffs with his firm. It was like "a tent revival," Roden said.[91]

As Laird grew ever more impatient with the slow pace of the proceedings in his courtroom, the *Tolbert* litigation loomed. *Tolbert*, which now included Cochran's clients, was projected to get under way in federal court in Birmingham, assigned to Judge U. W. Clemon. Named to the court during a window of progressive judicial appointments by President Jimmy Carter, Clemon was the first—and, at the time, the only—African American federal judge appointed in the Northern District of Alabama. Clemon was familiar with Calhoun County. In 1971, as an attorney in Birmingham, he had initiated lawsuits on behalf of the NAACP, the Calhoun County Voters League, and the Calhoun County Improvement Association concerning complaints by parents of black students at Wellborn High School. Judge Clemon had set a mid-October date for the *Tolbert* trial to begin.[92]

In the waning days of July and early August, the mounting total payments in *Abernathy*, Solutia's threats of bankruptcy, and the impending *Tolbert* case shifted momentum in favor of settlement. Still, on August 20, 2003, nearly everyone was surprised when attorneys for Monsanto and those representing the now more than 21,000 plaintiffs agreed to settle the Anniston PCB cases. The global settlement—totaling $700 million, including the cleanup costs—was not only the largest award to remedy industrial pollution at a single site in U.S. history. The agreement also contained innovative features, including a key demand of local activists: funding a health clinic in Anniston.[93]

The two judges had proved instrumental in bringing both sets of cases—state and federal—to a simultaneous conclusion. "Ordinarily, federal and state courts don't interact," Judge Clemon said later. But the companies were not going to settle unless the parties could resolve all of the cases pending in federal and state court. After several negotiating sessions, some in his offices in Birmingham, Judge Clemon had gone to Anniston to talk with Judge Laird about a joint settlement. Overhanging the state cases was the prospect that the conservative Alabama Supreme Court might overturn all the verdicts hammered out in Laird's court. When the landmark accord was announced in Judge Clemon's Birmingham courtroom, all of the lawyers rose to acknowledge the judges, with a standing ovation.[94]

CHAPTER ELEVEN

Aftershocks

How just is justice? —Calhoun County Improvement
Association, "The Anniston Manifesto," 1964

Optimism prevailed in Anniston as State Circuit Court Judge Laird and Federal District Court Judge Clemon stood on the sweltering south-facing steps of Anniston's restored brick judicial building on August 21, 2003, and told the growing crowd of the record settlement in damages and cleanup costs against Monsanto. People flooded in from Atlanta, Mobile, and the surrounding counties to hear the announcement firsthand. Though the *Abernathy* trial had taken place in Gadsden, and the settlement accord was first announced in federal court in Birmingham, the judges came to Anniston to share the news on the Calhoun County Courthouse steps.

The site evoked the city's long, complex history. Inside this courthouse, Alabama Power officials had raised the money in 1915 to launch the Anniston Munitions Company, Theodore Swann's first undertaking in the city and the forerunner to the Monsanto plant. On these same steps, on the eve of U.S. entry into World War I, Rev. Harry Jones had urged black soldiers to fight for their country in anticipation of being rewarded with the rights of full citizenship. A half century later, on a hot July night in 1965, the vitriolic segregationist preacher Rev. Conrad "Connie" Lynch had issued a speech so incendiary that the night ended in the murder of Willie Brewster, an Alabama Pipe foundry worker on his way home from work. And it was to this place that just a few weeks after Brewster's murder and days after President Johnson signed the 1965 Voting Rights Act, Anniston's African American community had silently marched to claim their right to register to vote.

The unprecedented PCB settlement capped a momentous few weeks in Alabama. The Anniston Army Depot had begun burning chemical weapons just two weeks earlier, an event PBS producers had highlighted in its television miniseries *Avoiding Armageddon*. Now that depot personnel had begun destroying the chemical weapons arsenal and the largest Monsanto lawsuits were settled, the city's business elite hoped they might begin to put the "Toxic Town" label to rest.[1]

In other news, Alabama Supreme Court chief justice Roy Moore was waging a fight to keep a Ten Commandments monument in the courthouse at the state capitol. Republican governor Bob Riley had launched a campaign to raise the state's historically low tax rate in order to fund education reform; the vote was slated for early September.

On this day, however, TV cameras, satellite trucks, and reporters from Birmingham, Atlanta, and Washington, D.C., were focused on documenting what had become an international story. People leaned against the windowsills of the building across the street; others had pushed up close to see and hear the various celebrities. At the appointed hour, from behind the locked white doors of what was once the grand front entrance of the courthouse, the principal participants emerged: the courageous, if beleaguered, judges; the jurors, relieved to be returning to their normal lives; the victorious plaintiffs' lawyers; the corporate officers and their legal team, ready to put their best spin on the outcome. Also arrayed on the marble courthouse steps were jubilant activists and the smiling mayor.

The trial judges descended the white steps to the podium. Judge Laird personally acknowledged each of the *Abernathy* jurors, men and women who had endured twenty months of trial, listened to lengthy and painful testimony, and returned verdict after verdict against Monsanto. "As you may have heard, there will be some money flowing around," said Judge Clemon in his understated manner, prompting "amens" and applause. The award totaled $600 million in damages, with another $100 million for cleanup.[2]

The global agreement included the concurrent approval of a revised EPA consent decree—one made stronger by pressure from activists and the U.S. Senate committee. The consent decree promised "clean-up, including the residential sites," Judge Clemon explained, and also "established a foundation to provide some educational assistance for those children who have been victimized by the process." And as part of the *Tolbert* settlement, Clemon said, "there will be a clinic." The promise of a health clinic spoke to specific demands of West Anniston residents, and was especially gratifying for David and Shirley Baker. Having made their demands in Washington and helped thousands of new litigants join the federal suit, the Bakers relished seeing their labors bear such sweet fruit. These leaders of a small locally based environmental group, so underfunded that the CAP office phones had been cut off that week, had triumphed. Cassandra Roberts took a short break from her work inside the courthouse to celebrate, too.[3]

Standing beside the judges on the gleaming courthouse steps, leading the swarm of plaintiffs' attorneys, twenty-seven in all, stood Donald

Donald Stewart, the lead attorney for PCB plaintiffs in *Abernathy v. Monsanto*, speaks at the press conference on the Calhoun County courthouse steps in downtown Anniston announcing the $700 million PCB settlement as Judge Joel Laird, David Baker, Johnnie Cochran, and jurors look on, August 21, 2003. Photo by author.

Stewart, rightfully beaming. Reflecting on the seven and a half years he had invested in suing Monsanto, Stewart credited the people of West Anniston. "When everybody said that nothing could be done," said Stewart, "you are the ones that stood tall, had patience, and stood in the breach."[4] Johnnie Cochran, whose presence on the legal team could only have added to the pressure to settle the *Tolbert* cases, was in attendance as well.

Plaintiffs' attorney Jere Beasley emphasized how determinedly the chemical companies' lawyers had fought Anniston residents' claims. "If anybody believes that we would be here voluntarily today without a federal court, without a state court, without these judges, you are badly mistaken," Beasley said to the crowd. "Never in my life have I been involved in tougher negotiations."[5]

Solutia CEO John Hunter, pale but composed, and plant manager David Cain represented the corporate partners: Solutia, Monsanto, and Monsanto's parent companies, Pharmacia and Pfizer. Chastised, if not penitent, the corporate team had reasons to be glad these lawsuits were ending as well.

From left: David Baker, Mayor Hoyt "Chip" Howell Jr., Johnnie Cochran, and Shirley Baker Carter at the press conference announcing the major PCB settlement on August 21, 2003. Photo by author.

Hunter would be retiring soon as head of the six-year-old spinoff corporation. "We never produced PCBs," Hunter stated, oddly, "but we are proud and pleased to be a part of this resolution and the longtime continuing memory of this community." David Cain would be out of the hot seat in Anniston, on to head a larger Solutia plant in Alvin, Texas, on the Gulf Coast. And, despite threats of impending bankruptcy during settlement talks, Solutia's stock price, which had declined sharply, jumped nearly 344 percent after the settlement.[6]

Anniston mayor Hoyt "Chip" Howell Jr. delivered the benediction. In keeping with local custom, Howell thanked the Lord for the glorious day, the settlement, the judges, and even the heat. "This is a great, great day for Anniston, our state, and our nation, because our system works," he said. Whether the system worked for West Anniston residents remained to be seen. However, city officials, corporate spokesmen, and activists alike heralded the moment as one of hope that the deeply riven town might unify.[7]

Thousands of Anniston residents savored the enormous legal victory; it was vindication, a triumph. But the decade of discord over PCB contamination had generated deep mistrust that did not easily dissipate. The 2003 agreement ended the largest suits against Monsanto, but new groups of plaintiffs launched additional PCB litigation. Residents still faced persistent health problems and concerns about continued reexposure, as well as disputes over the speed and effectiveness of the cleanup. Though the victory over Monsanto was an unparalleled success, the global agreement left much unsettled.

Absent details, Rev. George Bates, the new pastor at Mars Hill, spoke for some others when he said, "We'll have to wait and see." When the *Owens* settlement had been signed more than two years earlier, Jacqueline Brown remembered, "people were saying, 'We're going to be rich.' 'No, no, no,' I tell them. 'That will be just enough to get us into a nursing home when that poison starts taking advantage of our bodies. You've got to look at the truth. You can't replace your health with money.'" Andrew Bowie agreed. "Some things a settlement can't bring back," said Bowie, who worked at the Anniston Army Depot until his death in 2005. Bowie wanted an apology from Monsanto. "In my opinion," he said, "some persons need to come forth and speak out and tell the community, 'We wronged you.'"[8]

The large and innovative PCB settlement was transformative for people in Anniston. But the difficulty of reckoning with the displacement Monsanto's pollution had caused—along with unsettling fears that accompanied the incinerator startup and news of other toxics—suggested, perhaps just as important, why it was not more so.

ANNISTONIANS HAD GREETED the nearly simultaneous startup of the chemical weapons burning alternately with fear and relief, anger and resignation. Anti-incinerator activism had continued as the PCB cases unfolded, even as incinerator construction neared completion. On August 16, local activists and the CWWG, Rev. Fred Shuttlesworth, and the SCLC chapter reprised the major anti-incineration march of the year before, protesting startup and demanding heightened attention to safety in depot incinerator operations. But incineration had moved inexorably forward. Whether they had opposed incineration or not, burning chemical weapons at such close range scared people. In anticipation of an accident, some had their route out of town planned and their escape bags packed and waiting by the door. Opposition activism surged briefly again in 2004, when depot staff reported problems that forced a shutdown of incinerator operations.[9]

A moment of particular ire came when Talladega Speedway officials requested—and incinerator facility officials agreed—that munitions not be transported to the incinerator during race week, though burning operations would be allowed to continue. Evacuation routes were already a nightmare at race time, depot officials explained. However, the decision left some local residents angry that their safety appeared to be of less concern than that of race attendees.[10]

While PCBs and the incinerator remained the central concerns, worrisome news about multiple other contaminants, including lead deposits all over town, had only reinforced the "Toxic Town" label. The *Anniston Star* had earlier reported that, in the course of producing the raw materials to make PCBs in the 1950s and 1960s, Monsanto had dumped roughly ten truckloads "as many as 40–50 tons of liquid mercury into its waste stream." Even small amounts of methyl mercury compounds can cause nerve disorders and physical disabilities. Solutia environmental consultants issued a twenty-six-page letter of denial to ADEM. Scientists were working on ways to model the health impact of multiple pollutants, but had yet to calculate the danger of synergistic exposure.[11]

For a time during the summer and fall of 2003, each week seemed to bring fresh toxic news. In early July, brownfields cleanup at the defunct Chalk Line textile plant resulted in refuse fires that filled Anniston skies with smoke. On and near the depot Superfund site, levels of some contaminants remain high.[12]

In August 2003, at a Carver Community Center meeting in West Anniston, a civilian contractor for the Army reported finding the highly toxic solvent trichloroethylene (TCE). Depot officials acknowledged that TCE, which may be linked with cancer, had leached into the soil in quantities that exceed standards in the Federal Safe Drinking Water Act. Seepage of the colorless or pale blue chloroform-smelling liquid threatened the county water supply. In early November, several fifty-five-gallon drums labeled "Poison" were found in Choccolocco Creek. On at least two occasions in 2004, ADEM officials traced drums containing hazardous materials back to the depot.[13]

At the city's southern edge in Oxford, Tull Chemical Company continued to produce Compound 1080, the potent rodenticide, within shouting distance of residents' homes. The same month, an EPA study identified dangerous levels of arsenic, mercury, and selenium in soil and groundwater samples in the neighboring African American town of Hobson City.[14]

In the course of their PCB investigation, the EPA and ATSDR also identified elevated levels of lead in soil in and around West Anniston. Lead has long been known to affect neurological functioning, especially in growing children. After finding lead at levels of concern in the yards and driveways of West Anniston and Hobson City, the EPA targeted the iron foundries. Anniston's foundries had used PCBs as electrical insulating fluids and in sand molds for molten iron. That sand, likely containing both PCBs and lead, was distributed all over Anniston as fill dirt to augment landscapes and level parking areas.[15]

The end of the PCB litigation launched a new stage in environmental health activism in Anniston, one that revealed further tensions between corporate practices, on the one hand, and the needs of residents of contaminated sites, on the other. Of the five mechanisms of redress promised by the global settlement and concurrent agreements, the promise of the health clinic, the health study, and the educational foundation were innovative, a direct result of environmental justice activists' demands.[16]

IN REACTING TO THE GLOBAL SETTLEMENT, everyone focused first on the financial details—the proverbial bottom line. Ultimately, Monsanto had to absorb more than half of the settlement costs arising from its PCB dumping. "Monsanto Struggles Even as It Dominates," the *New York Times* had characterized the company's status in May 2003. Monsanto reported a loss of $188 million in its fourth-quarter earnings for 2003, attributing a ninety-six-cents-per-share loss to the Anniston PCB settlement.[17]

In accordance with the terms agreed to in the Anniston PCB lawsuits, Monsanto would pay $550 million of the settlement costs, of which $390 million came from company funds and $160 million from insurance. Solutia Inc. was to pay $50 million in ten equal installments beginning in August 2004. Given the number of claimants and the settlement's complexity, Judge Clemon had appointed Alabama attorney Ed Gentle to guide the dispersal of the *Tolbert* funds and the establishment of the health clinic agreed to in the settlement. The *Abernathy-Tolbert* settlement was "financially challenged" from the start, said Gentle at the CAP annual dinner at the Anniston City Meeting Center in October 2004, a year after the agreement had been signed. His assessment was shared by most dinner attendees.[18] Growing awareness that the *Tolbert* clinic was underfunded and that the plaintiff groups were compensated differently also fueled discontent.

Views about the settlement terms ranged from elation to deep distrust. There was no doubt that the money was welcome, a sort of reparation for the injustice done. For many participants, however, the damages awards proved meager when compared with their losses. Even if a settlement check covered the down payment for a house across town, elderly people displaced from their homes were ill-equipped to take on a new mortgage.

Dissatisfaction with the amount of money, how it was divided, the pace at which it arrived, and how much of it went to the lawyers infuriated people for more than a decade afterward. Even had the money been adequate, dollars alone could not restore health.

On reflection, some observers—both locally and nationally—felt that the corporate players had paid less dearly than they deserved. Rumors flew that the corporate partners had budgeted $1 billion or more to resolve the PCB litigation in Anniston; projections based on the early *Abernathy* damage awards were three times that amount. "Monsanto got away with it," remarked *Rachel's Health and Environment Weekly* publisher Peter Montague, who had endured his own running legal battle with Monsanto over libel charges in the 1990s. The news that Solutia's stock prices nearly quadrupled the day after the settlement fueled speculation that the companies had expected even steeper penalties.[19]

Relations between Solutia and local environmental organizations changed markedly in the years following the various settlements, however. Company personnel were as surprised as anyone. "If you had told me a year ago that I would be sitting here about to get an award from CAP, I would have said you were crazy," said Craig Branchfield, Solutia remedial projects manager in Anniston, just before he accepted an environmental justice award from the organization at its 2004 annual fundraiser.[20]

Many of the *Owens* plaintiffs had been happy with their individual settlement awards, even as they remained concerned about equity among the different lawsuits. "I think my mother's very satisfied at what she's got," said Cassandra Roberts. "She's got another house. It's not a new house, it's on the west side, but she's really enjoying it." Members of the Sweet Valley/Cobbtown Environmental Justice Taskforce had made a certain peace with Monsanto after their settlement in 2001; their newly established West Anniston Foundation (WAF), funded by the *Owens* settlement, had moved into a building Monsanto owned. (At the time, these developments had further aggravated the relationships among former neighbors, who were still litigating against Monsanto.) But now, plaintiffs in the *Owens* case sued to enforce the "most favored nations" clause of their settlement, since the average payouts to the *Abernathy* plaintiffs were greater than the *Owens* participants had received. Monsanto opposed reevaluating the *Owens* payments, and Judge Inge Johnson refused to enforce the clause, a decision that was upheld on appeal.[21]

Meanwhile, among *Abernathy* and *Tolbert* plaintiffs, the mistrust once focused on Monsanto was displaced, with no small irony, onto the very attorneys who had won the settlement. Because the lawyers who brought both the *Abernathy* and *Tolbert* suits had taken the cases "on contingency," their financial stake in the outcome was significant. In such cases, costs of expert witnesses, depositions, transcriptions, as well as attorneys' fees are paid from the amount recovered; attorney's fees can range from one-third to as much as one-half. In the two largest Anniston PCB cases, attorneys' fees were set at about 40 percent. In a settlement worth $600 million, the attorneys collectively stood to receive $234 million. Some people believed that their lawyers, especially Donald Stewart, deserved to be well paid. Stewart had worked long and hard since filing the cases in 1996; he and his co-counsel had shouldered huge costs in ferreting out Monsanto's internal documents, gathering PCB health data, hiring experts, and shepherding the case against Monsanto through three trips to the Alabama Supreme Court. The legal team should be credited, many felt at the time, with producing results in *Abernathy* that led also to the speedy settlement of the *Tolbert* claims.[22]

But, by any standard, the fee amounts were exceptionally large, "almost unconscionable," retired Judge Clemon reflected ten years later. Individual plaintiffs in the *Tolbert* cases, for example, received, on average, $7,725. Many claimants received more; most received less. By contrast, the attorneys stood to receive millions. When the figures hit the *Anniston Star* that fall, plaintiffs went ballistic. The attorney-client contracts regarding fees were legally binding, but the uproar was uncontainable. Picketers marched outside Donald Stewart's office on Leighton Street. Angry former plaintiffs filed suit demanding an accounting and questioning the distribution of settlement funds. In Los Angeles, Johnnie Cochran and his firm attracted particular rage from people who were dispirited beyond belief that a man many regarded as a hero would receive so much of the resource pool (an estimated $29 million to his firm), when he had come late to a case that had not even gone to trial. After an explosive hearing on the issue that November, *Abernathy* Judge Joel Laird blocked the filing of further lawsuits challenging the dispersal of funds. At a heated March 2004 community meeting of participants from both suits, Beverly Carmichael, a *Tolbert* plaintiff who had been chosen for a community advisory group on the implementation of the settlement, demanded from the podium that Johnnie Cochran and the other attorneys in *Tolbert* give back half of their fees. People remained furious. Eventually, the four Alabama law firms involved in *Tolbert* contributed a combined $1 million to the Montgomery-based Alabama Civil Justice Foundation for educational projects in Anniston, but none entertained a renegotiation of their fees. The dispute over how the *Abernathy* funds were spent remained active ten years later. Stewart won a round in the Alabama Supreme Court in 2012, though street demonstrations continued.[23]

The terms of the global settlement also fueled antagonisms among the plaintiff groups. The agreement gave equal portions to each: $300 million for the 3,500 *Abernathy* plaintiffs and $300 million for the more than 18,000 *Tolbert* plaintiffs. Simple math made clear that the average amounts distributed to plaintiffs in the *Abernathy* lawsuit would be far greater, regardless of the merits of individual health or real property claims. "The federal [*Tolbert* plaintiffs] feel that they've been victimized again," said Shirley Baker, "and that they cannot be compensated enough for any of the suffering and pain that they have endured." *Abernathy* participants, in contrast, were angry that only *Tolbert* plaintiffs would have access to the *Tolbert*-supported health clinic, a feature their agreement lacked.[24]

Some African Americans in West Anniston believed that race played a role in determining the size of the payments. Multiple factors influenced the allocation of funds. Stewart had been litigating *Abernathy* for nearly seven years; the court had already ruled the company liable in that case; and the jury had begun assigning hefty damage awards for personal pain and suffering and property damage to many of the plaintiffs. On average, the *Abernathy* plaintiffs may have lived closer to the plant. The *Tolbert* suit, which had more than five times as many plaintiffs, had barely begun.[25] Still, although attorneys have not made available demographic data on their clients, for many people the perception stuck that Stewart's plaintiffs fared better because more of them were white.

The anger against Monsanto was also displaced inward against activist groups, much as some veteran environmental advocates had warned it might be. Resentment was directed toward CAP, specifically at David and Shirley Baker. After Shirley Baker broke down the math on average payouts to plaintiffs at a CAP-sponsored community meeting, the rage increased. Though she was only the messenger of this disheartening news, a few people leveled charges that CAP had profited directly or that the Bakers had somehow benefited disproportionately from the settlement arrangements. Some people whose names had been accidently omitted from the attorneys' master plaintiff list blamed CAP. David received phone calls threatening his life. At a special meeting at the Carver Center in March 2004, David gave an impassioned speech. "We continue to work for you," he said. A physically imposing presence even in the large community meeting hall, David outlined what he had done with the $22,000 he had received in settlement in the *Abernathy* lawsuit. He had paid CAP staff and then, like everybody else, paid down his car note and mortgage. As to the death threats to himself and his family, he said, "Do not threaten my wife."[26]

Welcome as the settlement checks were, a host of new problems cropped up to complicate life: ambiguity about their impact on government benefits like Supplemental Security Income and on child support obligations or receipts, and questions about how the settlement monies would be taxed. Even the tax professionals were stumped. At every stage, fresh perceptions of unfairness kept the wounds raw and open. A year after the global settlement was announced, plaintiff Myrtle Joshua had not received a payment; she anticipated a disruption in government benefits resulting from the settlement. (As we spoke, a bulldozer rumbled across her backyard, replacing PCB-contaminated dirt with new fill.) "Whatever you get, Medicaid is going to have their 10 percent," she said. Retired from the Alabama Cooperative Extension Service and her own business, Myrtle's Sweet Shop, Joshua received a Social Security check each month for $385. Her Medicaid card "would pay the doctor bills that Medicare didn't pay," she said. "So, whenever I do make my settlement, I have to let the card people know and they will see if I'm eligible or not eligible to stay on there." If not, she explained, "then they are going to take all that help away."[27]

A complex matrix of factors was used to determine individual claims. Disparities in how the payments were determined appeared arbitrary. Some diagnosed diseases were factored in; others were not. Payments for *Tolbert* were calculated according to "(i) proximity and duration of residence in the West Anniston or Oxford area; (ii) PCB blood levels; (iii) long-term diseases with criteria to be developed by medical experts; (iv) property damage; or (v) other factors."[28]

Rancor rose and fell as payments were rumored, then delayed, fueling an atmosphere of mistrust. When the individual payouts did begin to come about four months after the settlement, the result was an influx of cash into the city. People fixed up their homes, bought cars, set money aside for health care, a college fund, or retirement. Businesses took advantage of the infusion—"Monsanto Money Welcome!" read the sign at Billy Bailey Auto Sales in Oxford.[29]

Compensation for emotional pain and suffering amounted to less than payments for property damage. As a result, people who had more property received substantially higher payments regardless of the status of their health, reinforcing class inequalities. Sometimes people living in the same household received widely varying treatment. "They left off everybody in my family except me," said one person at a 2004 neighborhood meeting.[30]

Nor was litigation completely ended. Since the Anniston PCB lawsuits were not class actions that might apply to everyone similarly affected but an amalgamation of more than 23,000 individual toxic tort cases, attorneys continued to file additional PCB lawsuits on behalf of Anniston residents. One new suit sought compensation for exposed residents who had developed diabetes and cardiovascular disease. Despite the growing number of studies demonstrating a correlation, including one Anniston-based study linking PCB exposure to diabetes risk, a Jefferson County jury ruled in favor of Monsanto.[31]

THE LOCAL FUROR WAS KEPT IN MOTION when Solutia made good on its threat to declare bankruptcy on December 17, 2003. Though strategically timed to avoid jeopardizing the payout of the bulk of the settlement funds, the bankruptcy nonetheless slowed cleanup and delayed payments to the education fund. The bankruptcy may also have limited further litigation; declaring bankruptcy has served as a convenient strategy to avoid liability in other tort cases. Once a bankruptcy is declared, potential creditors are required to submit their claims within a specified timeframe or be barred from bringing suit for past actions by the bankrupt party.[32]

The bankruptcy also exposed rifts between the corporate entities. "Solutia has been a distraction" for Monsanto, one business analyst told Reuters in early June 2005. The corporate entities eventually agreed that Solutia would pay for costs of cleaning up the plant site and for monitoring and maintaining the landfills. Monsanto would pay costs of residential cleanup. Despite their dispute, the two corporations remained tightly bound. The bankruptcy agreement, presented in Judge Prudence Carter Beatty's courtroom in New York Bankruptcy Court in 2005, returned a 30 percent equity interest in Solutia to Monsanto.[33]

Documentation submitted during the bankruptcy proceedings revealed that Anniston was not the only site operated by Monsanto and Solutia that left a dangerous—and expensive—PCB inheritance. At Sauget, Illinois, Monsanto had continued producing PCBs until 1977. Though the Toxic Substances Control Act (TSCA) forbade their manufacture in 1976, the ban did not formally take effect until 1979. Twenty years later, the EPA filed suit to require Monsanto and its successor corporations to pay for cleanup of hazardous wastes dumped from the company's Krummrich plant at Sauget. EPA investigators found the area "littered with corroded drums, metal waste and demolition debris." The Dead Creek site at Sauget was "a continuous source of fire." The EPA reported "waste streams generated by the Queeny and Krummich plants" containing multiple chemicals, in addition to PCBs. Subsequent EPA investigations showed the Monsanto operators had dumped wastes not only into Dead Creek but also into the Mississippi River. Remediation is ongoing and the lawsuits over who will pay remain incompletely resolved in 2013.[34]

In addition to Sauget, Monsanto's environmental legacy included "more than 50 sites with active remediation projects and approximately 200 additional known sites and offsite disposal facilities, as well as sites that have not yet been identified."[35]

Even before the landmark settlement, Solutia had taken another step to spread the cost of PCB cleanup to customers, suing nineteen Anniston iron foundries for also dispersing PCBs. The foundry lawsuit, filed in June 2003 *before* the global settlement was reached, included four companies that still operated in Anniston—McWane (a pipe and valve manufacturer), Huron Valley Steel, Tull Chemical Company, and United Defense—as well as Halliburton and others no longer in operation. Because the foundry sand distributed around town as fill dirt also contained PCBs, Solutia sought to include the foundries as potentially responsible parties.[36]

Both the bankruptcy and the lead lawsuits hindered residential cleanup in West Anniston. For a few months in early 2004, "there was a standstill which should not have been allowed to be," said Shirley Baker, "because EPA should have come and said, 'Now that Solutia has filed bankruptcy, Monsanto, you must pay.'" Despite the pressing need for lead abatement, Solutia's lawsuit against the foundries would take two years to resolve, slowing the progress of residential cleanup while the companies debated liability.[37]

Activists continued to cajole and push local, state, and federal government agencies to provide robust enforcement regarding cleanup. Both CAP and the Environmental Working Group were concerned that the "EPA is trying to go easy on Monsanto." The EPA had been reluctant to designate a Superfund site if the responsible party had been found liable and agreed to clean it up. As EPA national community involvement coordinator Leslie Leahy explained, the agency realized that it was not "doing towns any favors" from a public relations standpoint by putting them on the Superfund National Priorities List. However, the Solutia bankruptcy had reopened the prospect that the EPA might have to assume the cleanup under a weakened federal Superfund program. Left to languish under the George W. Bush administration, Superfund resources were badly depleted. So the Anniston

PCB and lead remediation sites were handled through the Superfund Alternatives Approach. Nonetheless, the potential that Solutia might default inhibited EPA onsite coordinators in setting more stringent cleanup standards. If Solutia were to default, the agency personnel could be left with EPA-imposed cleanup requirements more stringent than the EPA could afford to implement, given the dwindling Superfund dollars.[38]

"Cleanup" is often a euphemistic misnomer in toxics disputes; even containment would be a challenge in this locale. The engineering problems of the PCB cleanup were daunting: a large and complex site with two landfills and four "operable units"—two residential areas, the plant site itself, and the contaminated waterways downstream from the plant. During the first phase of the cleanup, Solutia tore down virtually all the homes in the heart of Sweet Valley and Cobbtown. The houses on Boynton Avenue that Frank Mealing built were gone, leaving behind vacant land. No evidence remained that Bethel Missionary Baptist Church once stood across the street. Small vestiges of neighborhood life were still visible, remnants of a foundation, an odd angle of fence. Nearby, two decaying houses were gradually being swallowed by kudzu vines. In 2003, the Mars Hill Church still stood, up a short lane from the Monsanto plant gate, behind a chain link fence. By 2013, the church itself would be gone, unceremoniously demolished.

If the cleanup operations were to have any transformative effect on the environmental health and economic landscape of West Anniston, activists would have to fight as hard as they had during the litigation. The consent order signed by the EPA and Pharmacia (acting for Monsanto and Solutia) defined the terms of environmental cleanup, which included establishing a community advisory group (CAG) to monitor the process. An outgrowth of demands by the environmental movement, community advisory groups were intended to institutionalize meaningful public participation in environmental decision-making. Demands for greater public involvement had made their way into environmental law with the National Environmental Policy Act, signed by President Nixon in 1970. The Federal Advisory Community Act, an "openness in government" law passed in 1972, also called for community advisory groups. In the 1990s, the National Environmental Justice Advisory Council (NEJAC) renewed the call for meaningful community input into decisions about toxic sites. NEJAC's formulation emphasized the value of lay knowledge and cross-cultural exchange of perspectives. The EPA published guidelines encouraging public participation in Superfund project decisions in 1995 but stressed that these formations were advisory and not intended to wield decision-making power.[39]

Under EPA guidelines for choosing members of a community advisory group to monitor cleanup, there is no formal vote in the affected neighborhood; the EPA selects the board members. Once chosen, the board may hire consultants or facilitators to help mediate their process, if desired. But Solutia pre-empted that process, engaging a New Jersey firm, the Ross Public Affairs Group, whose work included setting up and managing community advisory groups. By July 2003, weeks *before* the settlement announcement, the consultants were already in place. At the quarterly meeting held by the EPA in West Anniston that month, they stood along the back wall of the large Carver Center auditorium at West Fourteenth and Cooper, scoping out the crowd. From this vantage point, it would be easy to identify the more forceful, militant activists and the more middle-of-the-road potential allies. David Baker's reaction was immediate. "We don't need facilitators," he said. Picket signs in the audience echoed this sentiment. In the coming months, Solutia's consultants aggressively campaigned to shape the composition of the EPA's West Anniston Monsanto PCB Site Community Advisory Group, known in the neighborhood simply as "the CAG."[40]

Billing itself as "one of the nation's leading environmental communications firms," the Ross Public Affairs Group followed in the tradition of "outrage reduction" strategies Peter Sandman introduced to Monsanto executives in the 1980s. Schooled in "risk communications," the group's founder, Stephen Ross, had thirty years of experience in working with community advisory groups. (His first involvement with a southern site had been in assisting in siting a low-level radioactive waste dump in Barnwell, South Carolina, twenty-five years earlier.) Part of a growth industry in public relations, these consultants marketed themselves as experts in "Dealing with Angry People"; Ross had co-taught a Harvard seminar on the subject. Ross's "risk communications" techniques were, he said, modeled on those used by law enforcement personnel in dealing with hostage-takers.[41]

Ross would not disclose the amount of his yearly contract with Solutia, only that it was a six-figure contract for a few days of work each month. "We had been assigned the responsibility of developing a plan for establishing a community advisory group. The chemical industry adopted the model as part of their Responsible Care initiative," Ross said, referring to the public relations plan put forward by the chemical industry during the 1980s. All of the members of the American Chemistry Council were expected to follow the guidelines, he explained. Acknowledging that environmental awareness and activism "has forced companies to incorporate environmental issues into many of their critical business decisions," the public relations firm markets its services by advising companies that "failure to take environmental issues into account can have a real impact on a company's bottom line."[42]

Outrage reduction strategists disrupt the work of building solidarity and framing issues, classic functions of movement building. Even the sheer time involved to participate effectively in such formations takes time away from neighborhood organizing. The corporate public relations consultants' work in environmental disputes promises companies to identify and "work with those stakeholders toward an outcome that meets your goals. . . . during controversial and potentially controversial situations." Consultants focus their pitch on managing environmental opposition.[43]

"How to convert opposition into support for something" is what we do, said Ross. "Managed correctly," the company's promotional material explains, a community advisory panel or CAP, as the Ross site termed it, can result "in improved environmental performance, better public perception and better operating results for a project or facility. We've been involved in cases where a group, including former opponents, became active advocates for the company when dealing with elected officials and regulators." However, Ross's site warns, "Managed incorrectly, a CAP can become a credible and powerful opponent to a company's best interest. We're aware of cases in which the CAP used company funding to attack its critical business interests." Citing an "unblemished record" in organizing and managing CAPs, the site concludes, "The Ross Public Affairs Group is expert in ensuring that CAPs work with a company and not against it."[44]

Who is in and who is out in defining a community is a matter of power, a fact understood by all of the players who contested the composition of the advisory group that would monitor the Anniston PCB cleanup. For the first several months following the settlement, the focus of the CAG was not on cleanup at all but on who would be on the board. Solutia's consultants proposed a board comprised of two people from each of five affected neighborhoods, by which they meant West Anniston and Hobson City (which would have African American representation) and Oxford, Lake Logan Martin, and Lay Lake (which would most likely send white representatives). The brunt of the PCB contamination was borne by people in West Anniston, where the most visible and outspoken protest groups were based. Lakefront and other downstream neighborhoods were not subject to residential dirt removal but would be affected by creek dredging upstream. To many people in West Anniston, Solutia's schema for selecting CAG members not only misrepresented the racial geography of pollution but would dilute the voting strength of African Americans, who were the most outspoken activists on the CAG board.[45]

The EPA criteria for community advisory group membership are ill-defined but generally loosely geographic. Stephanie Brown, the EPA's community involvement coordinator in West Anniston, assigned to help establish the CAG, revealed the extent of Solutia's efforts to influence CAG membership, including who would represent West Anniston. "They sent me names of people who they thought should be on the CAG," she recalled, referring to the Ross Public Affairs Group. "'I can't accept this,' [she told them.] 'I have to select and I can't explain you giving me a list of names who are being paid by the company. Do you not see the conflict?' It was kind of rocky at the start because they really wanted to have their hands in it."[46]

At the CAG's organizational meeting in November 2003, fireworks blazed over who would represent West Anniston. Brown said later, "I don't think—and this is my personal opinion—I don't think that anybody who the company handpicked and who the company is paying is neutral." Ultimately, downstream areas garnered two representatives each, and six representatives came from West Anniston, though over time attendance at CAG meetings by downstream constituencies has declined.[47]

During the approximately one year they worked for Solutia in Anniston, Ross and his associates accomplished some of Monsanto's and Solutia's aims: influencing the composition of the CAG and shaping the basic structure and content of its meetings, which stifled input and questions, particularly from concerned residents who were not members of the CAG board. (This structure accentuated divisions in the community.) In the monthly meetings, paternalism toward the working-class black and white residents of West Anniston continued to surface in forms that were both bald and subtle. Residents had to fight not only to be heard but also to be informed. "They think they are talking to dummies," said Shirley Baker, in reference to Solutia and their consultants' attitudes toward neighborhood residents. "If you'll notice," she said, "they don't think that community folks have the capability of understanding technical issues. We're always having to remind them, 'Well, we aren't so dumb about this, you know.'" Women, she said, faced particular challenges in this regard: "You have to always fight for your space among the men. They always seem to think that we don't have the understanding[,] . . . that women don't have the expertise."[48]

Though Solutia facilitators tried to "correctly manage" the community advisory group on many decisions, the Anniston CAG board members would not be bullied. By the end of the following year, Solutia terminated Ross's contract. "We won that one, too," David Baker said.[49]

Still, the protracted debate over representation and process had kept the CAG from focusing on key decisions about the cleanup that was already under way. As the composition of the advisory group was being debated, the corporate partners continued to reshape the landscape of West Anniston. Of most immediate concern were the contaminated residential yards in the neighborhoods surrounding Sweet Valley and Cobbtown—roughly 600 homes, most of which remained inhabited. Remediation plans required contractors to remove the soil around these homes until tests showed that less than 1 ppm of PCBs remained.[50]

This was a massive dirt-moving operation. Federal regulations required PCB-contaminated soil containing more than 10 ppm to be landfilled at a licensed hazardous waste dump. That meant that the most toxic of the PCB wastes removed from Anniston were shipped to Emelle, the huge hazardous waste facility in majority-black Sumter County, deep in Alabama's Black Belt, which had long been a focus of environmental justice advocates.[51]

The EPA authorized Solutia to truck some low-level contaminated waste soil (with less than 10 ppm of PCBs) to the Miller property, a small tract near the heart of what was once Sweet Valley. Activists intervened to question the wisdom of siting contaminated soil back in West Anniston, on property situated alongside the Eleventh Street ditch, where flooding had long been a problem. A review by independent consultants judged the plan "acceptable." (But by spring 2006, Solutia contractors had dumped soil on the Miller property well in excess of what the EPA had approved.)[52]

A particular challenge for activists during this phase was the fact that they remained reliant on corporate entities—in whose actions they had little trust—and the EPA—whose record was uneven—for technical information about the progress of the cleanup. To address this problem, West Anniston activists applied to the EPA's Technical Assistance Grant (TAG) program, which offered grants of up to $50,000 that permitted neighborhood residents to hire knowledgeable independent monitors who reported directly to them. The TAG program—instituted after demands from environmental activists—was a modest recognition that the technical decisions governing environmental cleanup often remain in dispute and are not divorced from political context and corporate economic interests. As further evidence of this fact, Solutia worked to unseat the West Anniston Foundation's first choice of technical advisor.[53]

While community advisory groups have provided a forum for dispensing information to the public and for interjecting community knowledge and concerns into the regulatory process, they have also had a number of "'chilling effects' on public participation in decision-making," as some environmental policy analysts have noted. Aware of the limitations of community advisory groups as a vehicle for empowerment and despite continuing mistrust, neighborhood leaders worked hard within the community advisory process to glean information and provide oversight of the cleanup.[54]

Over time, despite the difficulties, the CAG meetings provided one forum to raise questions about how cleanup was proceeding. For residents such as Rev. Thomas Long, the cleanup operations represented a further invasion. Reverend Long reported that Solutia's cleanup contractors surprised him at his front door one morning prepared to relocate his family to a hotel for two weeks while bulldozers scraped and replaced the dirt in his neighbor's yard. "They didn't come out there to remove me and my family until the day they were out there digging," said Reverend Long.[55]

Residents remained concerned about the old Monsanto dumps, fearing ongoing exposures from the buried cache of PCB-contaminated wastes. As the ATSDR had announced, PCB exposures were ongoing, quite possibly "at high levels." Max McCombs, Solutia vice president for environment and health, acknowledged that, in 2004, thirty-two years after Monsanto reported halting production at the plant, air monitors measuring PCB levels still registered higher than background levels in some low-lying areas near the facility. Solutia remedial projects manager Craig Branchfield offered no explanation for the continuing emissions from the site.[56]

Community Against Pollution members considered demanding removal of these landfills' toxic contents, but they were persuaded that earth moving put the neighborhood at even greater risk than leaving the landfills intact. Furthermore, they did not wish to add to the toxic burden at Emelle, another disadvantaged community. Solutia sought and the EPA granted a permit to expand the existing South Landfill in 2006 to handle additional low-level wastes. The expansion compounded concerns about ongoing exposure, especially for the dozen or so white families who lived closest, on the other side of Monsanto Road, which bordered the dump. Lurking always was the worry that the measures being taken—the Miller property dump and the new South Landfill—might be making the situation worse.[57]

People wanted the dirt in the crawl spaces beneath their houses tested for PCBs and removed if contaminated. Solutia refused. Residents wanted to know whether flooding would recontaminate their yards. What if their property had been decontaminated but their neighbor's had not? If it rained, should their property be retested?

By early 2004, the sense of urgency felt by industry brought on by pending lawsuits seemed to have dissipated and the pace of cleanup grew sluggish. The EPA and the companies each contended that the other was responsible for months-long delays. Monsanto and Solutia charged the EPA with being slow to supply requisite documents and specific work plans, while the EPA threatened fines for Solutia's inaction. By now, all realized that containing the PCB and lead exposures in West Anniston would take more than a decade.[58]

Civil rights activists of an earlier generation faced all kinds of challenges, including physical threats, intimidation, and economic retaliation. But with the "slow violence" that characterizes the post-1960s era, the system of racial and class controls maintains itself in part through the reliance on a hierarchy of experts. This industry of experts who manage dissent pose a different kind of threat, one that has developed over the thirty years that outrage reduction consultants have been in business. These risk communications specialists appropriate elements—and in some cases the personnel—of movement organizing, together with information they glean about community dynamics, in an attempt to shape a response that meets corporate needs. Their emergence is both a testament to the movement's power and a distortion of its demand for participatory democracy.

IN OCTOBER 2003, as the debate over managing PCB cleanup unfolded in Anniston, the U.S. Senate confirmed President George W. Bush's new appointee to head the EPA, Utah's Republican governor Michael O. Leavitt. Christine Todd Whitman had resigned, unable to press forward even a limited environmental agenda under a hostile administration. Given the apparent close ties between Whitman's aides and Monsanto, activists in Anniston were not sorry to see her go, but they had no indication that the EPA under Leavitt would be any more responsive to their concerns. President Bush's selection of Leavitt, known as a pragmatic states' rights governor, to head the EPA was part of a broader market-driven approach toward environmental management.[59] Leavitt stayed only a short time at the agency, but it was long enough to institutionalize a strategy toward environmental dissent that had been crafted during more than a decade of environmental contests over land use in the American West: the Enlibra strategy.

The Enlibra Era marked a new phase in environmental regulation, as the agency more fully embraced the discourse and practices of risk communications. The Enlibra strategy was couched in carefully crafted language of balance and collaboration and often implemented through community advisory groups. Enlibra had been honed in battles between environmentalists and logging and mining interests in the Northwest. "It's Darwinism at its best," says *The Enlibra Toolkit*, a 2003 promotional handbook, "a kind of environmental 'getting to yes.'"[60]

The approach Leavitt brought with him to Washington had emerged from the Western Governors' Conference in the winter of 1997 with the debut of *Enlibra*, a term that Leavitt and former Oregon governor John Kitzhaber, a Democrat, are credited with coining. Invoking the seventh sign of the zodiac, the term combines the elements *en* ("move toward") and *libra* ("balance").[61] Like Sandman's rhetoric about community advisory groups, Enlibra sounded innocuous, even reasonable. However, the New Age neologism masked an approach to environmental management that often undermined public participation in addressing environmental hazards. Aimed primarily at managing environmental dissent, Enlibra was designed to leave environmental management in industry hands and local power relations essentially unchanged. It was "outrage reduction" under another name.

One of Enlibra's eight principles, "Science for Facts, Process for Priorities," separated subjective choices from objective data gathering, directly addressing the ongoing debate about the neutrality of scientific knowledge. This principle failed to recognize how deeply in dispute the "facts" remain, viewing scientific data as divorced from political and cultural context. Environmental debates had centered on the term *sound science*, which became a catch phrase wielded by industry and critiqued by environmentalists. The actual proceedings of any cleanup process rely a great deal on political choices as well as technical expertise, including which facts are considered relevant and how they are conveyed.[62]

Leavitt and Kitzhaber were quite explicit about their reasons for adopting Enlibra as "A New Shared Doctrine for Environmental Management Policy." The governors sought to circumvent environmental regulation, which they viewed as federal "heavy-handedness" in environmental policy, and to implement "risk-based, cost-effective decisionmaking." Throughout the George W. Bush years, Enlibra remained official EPA policy.[63]

The fundamental outlines of this "environmental management" approach were not new. Some would root the outlook in the utilitarian and instrumental views of nature propounded by the conservationists of the early twentieth century. The Enlibra approach, however, went beyond the idea of managing the environment to managing the environmentalists. Environmental activism was treated as one more obstacle to the corporate business plan.[64]

THE GLOBAL SETTLEMENT and related actions created several novel mechanisms for redressing the grievances resulting from long-standing PCB exposure in Anniston. As a result of citizen demands, new institutions put in place through PCB litigation and federal agency intervention—the West Anniston Foundation (WAF), the Anniston Community Education Foundation (ACEF), the *Tolbert*-related health clinics, and the planned health research—offered hope, a way forward, a chance for renewal. While none was unique in such cases, the combination of interventions offered arenas through which activists could further their hopes of transforming the city. These mechanisms went beyond compensation to individuals to address collective needs. A major challenge for each of these initiatives is the finite nature of their funding, at the most ten or twelve years, which have passed quickly.

Women have assumed major leadership roles in implementing these settlement gains. Funded by the *Owens* lawsuit, the West Anniston Foundation continues its work monitoring the technical assistance grant and doing health education, including for a time a weekly radio show. Former resident Kay Beard has staffed the foundation since its inception; Cassandra Roberts succeeded Jacqueline Brown as the group's president.

The Anniston Community Education Foundation was funded by $3.2 million over a twelve-year period, a condition of the consent decree between the EPA and Pharmacia. Based in part on the rationale that PCBs are associated with neurocognitive deficits in children that contribute to learning disabilities, the consent decree required Monsanto, Solutia, and their corporate partners to provide support for educational efforts.[65] The ACEF operates as an independent foundation, granting scholarships to young people annually and funding organizations that support the Anniston public schools and provide afterschool enrichment programs for students. Just as with the community advisory group, African Americans in West Anniston who had highlighted the need for the foundation had to fight for a role in its leadership. One seat was reserved for Solutia public relations staff. Again, however, neighborhood activists largely won the day, and women play leadership roles. Shirley Baker and Alabama state representative Barbara Boyd, who had campaigned for civil rights since she was a teenager in the 1950s, were key in launching the new foundation; Boyd became the foundation's first president.[66]

The legal settlement in *Owens v. Monsanto* included the formation of the West Anniston Foundation, a community-led group that promotes "the health and education of economically and socially disadvantaged residents and former residents of West Anniston." The 2013 Board of Directors includes, *from left*, Jerry Glover, Judy Washington, Dennis Gibson, Alma Turner, Cassandra Roberts, and Jacqueline Brown. Not pictured are Bud Turner and Derek Conrad Brown. Photo by author.

Attention to education was particularly needed, as the Anniston City Schools had been in decline for years. The city of Anniston in 2013 is 51.5 percent African American. Black students make up 97 percent of the population at Anniston High, while Wellborn High's students are 22 percent African American and 77 percent white. Many blacks and whites regarded the dismal state of Anniston's educational infrastructure as both cause and evidence of deep and continuing inequalities.[67]

In addition to addressing educational needs, the *Tolbert* settlement set aside $25 million (to be paid out in equal portions over a period of ten years) to establish a health clinic for claimants in that suit. The clinic also represented a way to provide not simply individual benefits but also social goods. While it quickly became clear that the allotment for the clinic was insufficient to establish a freestanding facility within walking distance for West Anniston residents, as activists had hoped, the existing Quality-of-Life Clinic on Noble Street opened its doors to the *Tolbert* plaintiffs in June 2005. In another example of women's leadership, physician Angela Martin operates the separate pediatric clinic that resulted from the *Tolbert* settlement. The services offered to *Tolbert* clients were also not without controversy. Pfizer, one of the Monsanto parent companies at the time of the global settlement, had promised free prescription drugs to those eligible for the clinic, but then Pfizer began charging copays.[68]

THE TRIALS HAD BROUGHT to the surface mountains of data, both individual health status and family histories, as well as thousands of tests documenting PCB blood levels. But a comprehensive portrait of the real magnitude of the health problems in Anniston remained elusive. Based on 2009 data, Calhoun County shows substantially elevated measures of death from coronary heart disease, lung cancer, and stroke when compared with the national average; deaths from breast and colon cancer occur at rates slightly above the national average. Without further data and evaluation, however, it would be difficult to correlate PCB exposure levels and reported county-level figures.[69]

A $3.2 million ATSDR grant—an outcome of the 2002 Senate hearing—was awarded in 2003 to a group of PCB researchers to study the health impact of the chemicals on this highly exposed population. The proposed studies offered the best hope for characterizing the health consequences of PCB exposure in Anniston. Even beyond the usefulness of the data to the broader public for gaining a better understanding of PCBs and health, the health screenings of blood pressure and blood glucose levels might aid in identifying individuals with undiagnosed conditions; patients could then be referred for treatment and ongoing care.

Howard Frumkin, then chair of environmental and occupational health at Emory University's Rollins School of Public Health, had cajoled several of the nation's top PCB research specialists to collaborate. The result was the Anniston Environmental Health Research Consortium, based at Jacksonville State University, in the School of Nursing, where Dean Martha Lavender and nursing professor Jane Cash (a veteran of the Triana, Alabama, DDT-exposure investigation) launched the project.[70]

The consortium brought together PCB researchers from thirteen academic institutions. Though the effort largely tried to distance itself from the contentious aftermath of the lawsuits, some of the researchers had testified as experts in the PCB litigation against Monsanto, including David Carpenter of SUNY Albany, Jim Olson of SUNY Buffalo, and Allen Silverstone of Syracuse University. Several Alabama-based academics with no connection to the litigation were also involved, including Max Michael, dean of the School of Public Health at the University of Alabama at Birmingham (UAB); Alan Percy and Rusty Foushee, also at UAB; and Rhoda Johnson, director of women's studies at the University of Alabama, who had conducted health-related studies in the Alabama Black Belt. John Stone, who directed the Center for Bioethics at Tuskegee University, served as ethics ombudsman. Shirley Baker represented CAP.[71]

Roughly 20,000 people had taken tests to determine the levels of PCBs in their blood as part of the *Tolbert* litigation, almost assuredly the world's largest pool of data on PCB blood levels in a highly exposed population, but that data was not available to the consortium. The consortium established an office on Noble Street managed by JSU nursing instructor and co–principal investigator Christie Shelton, and began recruiting Anniston residents who would participate in the health studies. Overcoming the inevitable association with the sour aftermath of litigation and the routine problems of retaining recruiters, survey takers, and study participants absorbed much of the energies of consortium health study staff. Despite these obstacles, between 2005 and 2007 the researchers collected blood samples from 765 volunteers from a randomly selected group of 1,110 of Anniston residents. Forty-six percent were African American and 70 percent were women. The median age was fifty-five. The CDC's National Center for Environmental Health evaluated each of the blood samples for thirty-five PCB congeners.[72]

The consortium made a determined effort to invite genuine participation in its Community Advisory Committee (CAC). Many residents welcomed the new knowledge that the PCB health research might bring, but others hesitated to participate, given the ignoble history of medical research on African American populations in Alabama. Divisions that had split the community over the lawsuits and settlements spilled over into the health arena. For the CAC itself, the unequal reward structure common to community-based research was a limitation, as the academic researchers were receiving significant grant funding, while community representatives on the CAC received, at most, a modest stipend for their participation. Some community members left the committee over the imbalance.[73]

However, the consortium's decision to make a major health survey the centerpiece of its work came largely at the urging of its neighborhood representatives. The survey was designed to characterize the routes of exposure and the prevalence of cardiovascular disease, diabetes, and other health conditions and to help understand whether the high PCB exposures found in present and former Anniston residents were associated with higher rates of disease than in other study populations. Given neighborhood concern about the impact on children, the consortium also conducted a neurobehavioral study, examining learning deficits among middle schoolers.[74]

The Anniston Environmental Health Research Consortium confirmed in 2009 that Anniston residents studied bear a toxic burden of PCBs four times greater than the average U.S. adult. Within Anniston, the PCB exposure is unequally allocated not only by geography but also by race, class, gender, and age. The consortium study also documented what many people in the neighborhood suspected: the PCB contamination disproportionately affected African American residents. Across all age levels, African American residents who were tested had higher mean PCB exposure levels than local whites who were tested. African American adults in Anniston have an average body burden of PCBs three times greater than their white neighbors. The study identified three factors associated with high serum blood levels of PCBs in the body: age; proximity to the plant, a consequence of residential segregation by race; and a diet that included local livestock, fish, and clay—the last a consequence of class and culture.[75]

Both age and gender, researchers found, were related to health effects associated with exposure to PCBs. As expected, people over age sixty had the highest levels. Highly exposed women, especially those under age fifty-five, were at greater risk of diabetes. Results confirmed findings by other researchers that mild learning difficulties in children correlated with their mothers' PCB levels. Researchers also found that concentrations of certain PCB congeners in the blood were associated with high blood pressure—a risk factor for death from cardiovascular disease and stroke—among adults in the study who were not being treated for hypertension. In 2013, the ATSDR and the National Institutes of Health are proposing a follow-up study to monitor changes in PCB levels, measure other chemicals, and provide "a more complete profile of human exposures and health in Anniston."[76]

A series of focus groups designed by University of Alabama professor Rhoda Johnson and conducted for the consortium by Johnson and Anniston native Judy Dothard Simmons documented, not surprisingly, deep feelings of "betrayal, anger, and confusion" that persisted well beyond the conclusion of the trials. Reporting informally at a public meeting at the Greater Thankful Baptist Church Family Life Center in April 2008, the researchers identified several major themes. "I feel some resentment, betrayal because way back in the early 1970s," one person explained to the researchers; "the officials knew it and they hid it." Loss of confidence in government was evident. "The running joke is that it should be PCBB because it stands for 'politicians can be bought,'" one respondent said. As for the settlement, "Money has divided the community," another observed.[77]

Many focused on death and dying. "PCB has ruined so many people in our lives," said one participant. Deploring "that stuff getting in our system, in your yards, everywhere," others said, "if we [are] on *60 Minutes*, we got to be bad." A "sense of loss of connection to community" was pervasive. "It broke up a whole neighborhood," one respondent said. "Our community has been robbed." Another lamented the loss of connection to nature for future generations: "I mean as simple as it seems and as trivial as it is, the next generation won't enjoy the pleasures of being able to pick a plum or grow things in the garden . . . so they're deprived of the simple pleasures."[78]

Remodeling the Model City

Genuine healing requires a candid confrontation with our past.
—Timothy B. Tyson, *Blood Done Sign My Name* (2003)

"You don't go around and do things like this to people and get away with it," says Opal Scruggs. Scruggs believes that Monsanto officials, those who knew about the hazards associated with PCB exposure and did not act to protect Anniston residents, will get justice, eventually. "I'd like to be at the Pearly Gates when some of them goes up there and listen to their excuses. It's just money, but they have profited off of all of us out here. And yet, they think they've done nothing wrong."[1]

Despite the inadequacies of the PCB settlement and its messy fallout, the legal victory over Monsanto is evidence of what grassroots groups can achieve. Activists succeeded by raising their own democratic voices, through standard routes of political protest, and by making full use of the legal tools (both limited and limiting) at their disposal. They persevered in overcoming silences by opening up structures of knowledge to mobilize alternate scientific voices and incorporate powerful lay testimony.

Anti-incinerator activists succeeded, too, forging a national campaign with global linkages, forcing the Army to provide residents with protective equipment, requiring greater precision and some degree of transparency in the incinerator operations, and preventing the facility's reuse. Though ADEM had fined the Army and its contractor Westinghouse several times for improper handling of waste and other violations, community skepticism waned as each class of weapons was destroyed. As to health consequences of stack emissions, given what is known now, "by and large it has not been a long-term disaster," said Families Concerned member David Christian, but "the environmental questions are unanswered."[2]

Just as activists had warned, as the destruction of the local stockpile neared completion, the Army considered repurposing the facility. The Calhoun County Chamber of Commerce requested a congressional study of the matter. From its startup in August 2003 to September 2011, when the last weapons were burned, the economic impact of the incinerator had been substantial, providing major funding for depot contractors. The incinerator had provided close to 1,000 well-paying jobs for government and contract workers during its operation. Activist Rufus Kinney published another letter in the *Star* congratulating depot staff on destroying the weapons but protesting the U.S. Army's possible breaking of its vow to Calhoun County residents to shut down the incinerator after eliminating the stockpile. Activists' vigilance and intervention ensured that the facility was dismantled rather than preserved as a permanent magnet for outside hazardous wastes. On September 22, 2011, representatives of the Organisation for the Prohibition of Chemical Weapons, which oversees treaty implementation, were on hand to witness the destruction of the last mustard canisters. In 2012, incinerator staff began dismantling the facility piece-by-piece, concluding this aspect of Anniston's Cold War work for the nation.[3]

Despite these significant advances, Anniston faces an ambiguous redemption. Most people believed the conclusion of the trials and the cessation of the burning would bring an end to Anniston's troubled period, but the road to rebuilding has been steep. Social injustice continues to be mapped on the north Alabama landscape. Toxic knowledge does not go away. People live with the awareness that chemicals embedded in the landscape may still find their way into human bodies, that PCBs in blood and tissues may continue to yield systemic, intergenerational toxic effects. Slow violence from the cumulative toxic legacy overshadows economic revitalization, especially on the west side of town.

Ten years after the 2003 events made national headlines, residents of West Anniston are left with losses that cannot be compensated: broken neighborhood ties, deep anger and mistrust, insufficient resources to address housing and new or persistent health problems, and fear of continuing exposures. Between 5.5 and 10 million pounds of PCB-containing wastes remain buried near the plant in the side of Coldwater Mountain, prompting continued concern.[4]

People continue to reckon with displacement. A massive reorganization of space in Anniston has resulted from the PCB contamination and the closure of Fort McClellan. The buyout and relocation program added substantially to Solutia's landholdings, increasing the size of its footprint in West Anniston. Dislocation of people from West Anniston led to dispersal to Anniston's east side and to other sections of Calhoun County—Golden Springs, Jacksonville, Alexandria, and Saks. Anniston experienced a nearly one-third decline in population during the three decades prior to 2010; one section of West Anniston dropped by 23.5 percent. The number of city residents—23,106 in

2010—was barely higher than its population in the mid-1930s, whereas Calhoun County's population has more than doubled during that time.[5]

Collateral damage continues. Vandals broke into the Bowie's vacant home on Brockman Avenue, stripped its copper tubing, and left the house open to the elements. Former neighbors have described similar break-ins, Bettye Bowie said. After Arthur died in 2007, she finally managed to sell the house, with full disclosure. She feels unsettled in her new neighborhood in East Anniston, apprehensive about her safety working in the yard. Opal Scruggs has stayed in the family home on Parker Street, though her children keep urging her to move. She worries more for her neighbors who live across Highway 202 on Monsanto Road, even nearer to the new South Landfill.[6]

By the time the EPA closed its West Anniston outreach office in 2012, contractors working for Monsanto had removed contaminated soil and replaced the yards of close to 600 homes. People in these homes continue to worry about PCB recontamination, runoff, and flooding.

Even after more than ten years of cleanup, PCB air emissions remain elevated in the area surrounding the plant. EPA Region 4 site coordinator Pamela Scully announced at a CAG meeting in early 2013 that air monitors continued to record above-background levels of PCBs, levels below those the EPA considers of concern but higher than those in other cities. The highest level was recorded on Parker Street, in Opal Scruggs's yard. "Does Anniston have a higher concentration of PCBs than anywhere in the country?" the EPA's Region 4 Superfund director Franklin Hill asked at the meeting. "I won't deny that. The accountability rests with Solutia and the EPA." In addition, Hill warned that climate warming may exacerbate the impact of pollution over the long term.[7]

"If this hits the paper tomorrow," said David Baker at the meeting, "the people that are not here tonight are gonna want to know, 'How do you still have PCBs in Anniston, Alabama, higher than anywhere else, and they stopped making it in 1972 or '71?'"[8]

Activists continue to press for a more thorough cleanup. "You are putting a Band-Aid on a problem," Representative Barbara Boyd pressed Solutia and the EPA representatives. "We are just sitting on a hotbed" of concern.[9]

Almost no scrutiny has been directed toward the environmental impact of Solutia's current operations—a subject corporate personnel were chary to discuss. Solutia decided to expand its Anniston operations in 2005, the same year the J. F. Queeny plant in St. Louis closed, citing "uneconomic capacity." In Anniston, the company now produces Skydrol, a hydraulic fluid used in aviation, as well as SkyKleen, a "noncombustible aviation cleaning solvent." Solutia has remained profitable; Eastman Chemicals purchased the company for $3.38 billion in January 2012.[10]

The decade of remediation deprived West Anniston of commercial re-development, businesses that would anchor rebuilding. Few stores remain active along Clydesdale Avenue. Shirley McCord closed her struggling convenience store, which had been an informal neighborhood hub for forty years. She sold the property in 2005 and died in 2007. The building that housed Anniston Quality Meats sits empty and decaying. As West Anniston's remaining residents continue to wrestle with the uncertainties associated with PCB contamination in their bodies and from Monsanto's landfills, few resources have come to West Anniston, though there has been a rush to develop other parts of town.

Evidence of a racial divide persists. The now majority African American population could achieve significant black empowerment, but the population shift could also lead to further abandonment by white elites. Anniston has yet to elect a mayor from its black majority. Anniston mayor Chip Howell was unseated in 2008 by Gene Robinson. Robinson doomed his mayoralty on the day after the election when he said to the *Star*, speaking of the voters who helped put him into office, "I bought into the black corruption in Anniston" to get elected, referring to a Get Out the Vote effort he had underwritten. "And it worked," he said. After an administration marked by bickering, Robinson was defeated in 2012 by consensus candidate Vaughn Stewart, who bested a field of ten without a runoff, promising to bring civility and economic development.[11]

IF ANNISTON STANDS AS EVIDENCE that southern locales frequently paid too great a price for progress, what does the city do now to reckon with dislocation and ongoing exposures? How does it balance the continued dependence on a fluctuating military with stable economic development? What can be done not just to erase the "Toxic Town" label but also to truly overturn the paternalistic industrial model, to overcome the persistent class and racial divides that left the toxics in place?

As their predecessors had often done, local civic leaders responded to the "Toxic Town" label with proposals to remold the Model City's image. Plans aimed at remaking the landscape in post-settlement Anniston spoke loudly about the priorities of decision-makers at the local, state, and federal level. One project, Streetscape, the cosmetic revamping of Noble Street, contrasted with the "nuisance abatement" program to tear down untended houses on city's southwest side.

Incredibly, Anniston briefly flirted with producing biological weapons. In 2006, the city submitted a bid to host the National Bio and Agro-Defense Facility (NBAF), a $23 million research project planned by the Department of Homeland Security. The *Star* editorialized in favor of the facility. In registering its support, the Anniston Chamber of Commerce invoked the Model City rhetoric yet again. "Image is everything," said the organization's president, Sherri Sumners, in 2003. "It will be incumbent on us to go from toxic town to techno town," she told the *Star*, with no hint of irony. The NBAF was sited instead in Manhattan, Kansas.[12]

Alabama's economy remains heavily dependent on the U.S. military. In 2010, federal defense spending comprised 7 percent of Alabama's state gross domestic product (twice the national average). Depot operations still drive Anniston's financial well-being. In 2012, more than 4,000 civilian workers depended on the Anniston Army Depot for their paychecks, an estimated $120 million payroll. The Anniston Army Depot actually gained missions and workforce during a mid-decade round of BRAC closures. With wars in Iraq and Afghanistan, funding for tank repairs remained strong, but as of 2012, the Army no longer plans to make tanks. Though depot officials expected no immediate loss of jobs—there might be increased need for repairing old tanks—the prospect raises familiar economic uncertainties.[13]

In 2003, the Army transferred to the City of Anniston the last 4,692 acres of Fort McClellan, effectively doubling the city's size. The Anniston–Calhoun County Joint Powers Authority, a quasi-public governing board, earmarked the land for a new industrial park and an anchor for the development of ecotourism. One of the biggest boosters of the project is Consolidated Publishing Company, publisher of the *Anniston Star*, which built the first new commercial building on the site to house the newspaper offices.

After the World Trade Center bombing on September 11, 2001, the Department of Homeland Security pumped millions—$57 million in 2005 alone—into the Center for Domestic Preparedness (CDP) already established at the old fort. With the post-9/11 militarization of civilian life, the CDP maintains a live agent training mission for first responders from across the country, complete with a room-size replica of a "Model City." Still, site redevelopment has been slow to take hold. Federal funding provided an initial $48.5 million in funds for cleanup and conversion of the scarred Army land. Cleanup of the site was daunting, plagued with difficulties, and sometimes quite hazardous. In the summer of 2004, Army contractors found a dozen unexploded 81 mm rounds but moved the ammunition to another

Anniston City Limit. Highway 431 entering Anniston at the bridge over the railroad tracks just north of Oxford. Photo by author.

part of the site and covered it with leaves, reportedly in order to be able to certify having cleaned a certain contaminated area.[14]

The economic development strategy attracting the most attention is counterintuitive. A study commissioned by the Calhoun County Chamber of Commerce in 2003 recommended reimagining Anniston as a hub for ecotourism. Make the city "a beacon for our environment," Mayor Chip Howell urged.[15]

Ten years later, in 2013, Calhoun County's latest rebranding campaign—"A Natural Attraction"—aims to bring more ecotourists. According to Sumners, Calhoun County boasts the densest concentration of federally protected lands in the Southeast, all four types of wilderness designation—wilderness, refuge, forest, and park. In an ironic twist, one of the nation's oldest stands of longleaf pine flourished at Fort McClellan. Frequent small fires from years of exploding practice rounds of ammunition limited the growth of competing understory trees, enhancing longleaf survival. The U.S. Fish and Wildlife Service now manages the Mountain Longleaf Wildlife Refuge on part of the old McClellan property. Attracting ecotourism is being pursued in other locales badly damaged by military toxics. But with a price tag of up to $30,000 an acre, clearing McClellan of hazardous materials is a slow process.[16]

Pete Conroy, director of the Environmental Policy and Information Center at JSU, who worked with others to raise federal dollars for preservation of wildlife habitat, envisions a natural resources center at the McClellan site. Curving around the tract is the Ladiga Trail, named for Creek Chief Ladiga, whose wife, Sally, resisted forced removal in the 1830s. The route is attracting bicycle enthusiasts who ride the 100 miles between Anniston and Atlanta.[17]

The wildlife refuge seems a world away from West Anniston. Conroy believes that few of the changes at the old fort will directly benefit the people who live to the south and the west of Anniston. Black leaders have complained about the lack of significant involvement of African American entrepreneurs in contracting or land ownership at the former fort. "Of all the resources left out at that place," said Reverend Reynolds in 2003, "there isn't a single black person that has any access" to business opportunities. The hotel, the Burger King, the bowling alley, the officers' quarters, and the apartments all went to other investors, he said. "I guess what we should have done is to start protesting and marching and raising hell."[18]

The city's penchant for image building in the face of catastrophe has again left environmental disparities incompletely addressed, especially when it comes to new amenities. The power of capital is profoundly geographic. The extensive plans for the old Fort McClellan site, the remodeling of Noble Street, a new Eastern Parkway leading from Interstate 20 to the McClellan industrial park and wildlife refuge, and a bustling new mall in Oxford contributed little directly to rebuilding the city's west side. The move toward ecotourism has raised particular ironies in the face of the persistent environmental problems on the west side of town. In 2012, Solutia donated land on the edge of Coldwater Mountain for a bike path trailhead, which brought more outrage at the March 2013 CAG meeting when activists raised questions about potential hazards facing recreation seekers.[19]

Recruiting new industry has been particularly difficult in West Anniston. When the French-owned Lafarge cement company arrived in April 2003, the company's shiny white silos became West Anniston's first new enterprise in several years. Before he left Anniston, Solutia plant manager David Cain offered the idea of developing a farmers' market on a strip of land directly across from the Solutia plant, where a car repair shop currently sits. On the wall inside the West Anniston Business Center are artist's renderings of Cain's vision for "Sunshine Village."[20] But neighbors have shown little interest in buying organic vegetables across the street from the chemical plant, and by 2013, Solutia's plans for the mini-mall lay forgotten.

Despite the limitations of the community advisory group process, activists from the West Anniston Foundation and Community Against Pollution have continued to engage with this mechanism for monitoring the cleanup process. Cassandra Roberts leads the West Anniston Foundation, raising funds to sustain the organization's work beyond Monsanto/Solutia's required twelve years of annual payments. David Baker gets called on to share his organizing experiences at environmental justice and labor gatherings across the country. David and Shirley divorced in 2004. In 2013, they still serve together on the CAG board, where they trade affable barbs over David's freewheeling style as chair, both still working to hold the corporate entities and the EPA accountable for cleaning up West Anniston.

Questions about whose knowledge is valued remain at the center of the environmental justice debate. In 2004, the Alabama African American Environmental Justice Action Network, supported by Representative Artur Davis (D-Ala.), who represented Alabama's Black Belt region, called for the formation of an Environmental Justice Unit at the state environmental agency. But support within ADEM for the unit had been slim. A single staffer ran the unit; his retirement in the spring of 2006 left the position vacant. In June 2006, ADEM director Otis "Trey" Glenn III described the unit's aim as being to "provide sound, unbiased, scientific information to those groups of people possibly *lacking the intellectual sophistication* to discern that information offered for baser, manipulative reasons." Glenn also openly questioned the need for the unit, prompting demands for change from the ADEM Reform Coalition, a broad alliance of environmental groups that sought to expand the unit's mission beyond outreach and education to include "reviewing and approving permits with protection of environmental justice communities in mind."[21]

In 2012, fresh challenges confronted north Alabama environmentalists. Natural gas mining companies targeted the surrounding Talladega National Forest for hydraulic fracturing, or "fracking." Large turnouts at community meetings in nearby Heflin suggest overwhelming opposition to this latest environmental threat.[22]

ANNISTON MAKES A PARADIGMATIC CASE for the need for precaution, for addressing toxic chemical exposures not after the fact but before damage is done. Activists remain concerned that uncertainties about the degree of harm are used as a wedge against restricting dangerous chemicals rather than a reason for caution in marketing them. A reinvigorated conception of justice would shift the burden of proof to manufacturers to demonstrate a reasonable certainty of no harm. Decisions regarding toxic chemical safety would value multiple sources of knowledge, require greater corporate transparency, and invite inclusive, meaningful public participation in decision-making. By the 1990s, as the Anniston lawsuits got under way, environmental advocates worldwide were proposing a new "precautionary" standard for regulating hazardous chemicals. Perhaps best summarized in the Wingspread Statement of 1998, the precautionary principle holds that "when an activity raises threats of harm to human health or the environment, precautionary measures should be taken even if some cause-and-effect relationships are not established scientifically." Such an early warning approach might have forestalled some of the worst PCB exposures.[23]

The United States once led the world in policies regulating toxic chemicals, but it now has fallen far behind other industrial nations. Implemented in 2007, the European Union's Regulation, Evaluation, and Authorisation of Chemicals (REACH) protocol incorporates a precautionary paradigm and is clearly impelling U.S. reform. Even the American Chemistry Council, a staunch opponent of restricting toxic chemicals, has recognized the need to "modernize" toxic chemical control policy, if only out of concern for retaining global markets. A few months before REACH went into effect, DuPont's Linda Fisher, the senior Bush administration EPA official who also once worked for Monsanto, told Fortune magazine that if the European Union bans a chemical, "it's going to be hard to explain to our markets and our public in the United States or in Asia why the Europeans don't think it's safe for them, but we're going to continue to expose you."[24]

Chemical control policy in the United States is badly in need of reform. Despite wide agreement that tighter regulation is needed, Congress has yet to update the Toxic Substances Control Act (TSCA), the 1976 law that continues to regulate toxic chemicals. A reform proposal first offered in 2010 by Senator Frank Lautenberg (D-N.J.) included a central demand of reformers: requiring chemical manufacturers to demonstrate that their chemicals are safe before marketing them. Whereas under TSCA, the EPA must demonstrate that a chemical poses an "unreasonable risk of injury" to health and the environment before imposing restrictions, Lautenberg's legislation as first proposed would shift the burden of proof from the EPA to industry and require proof of "reasonable certainty of no harm" before chemicals could be marketed. Without greater authority and resources, the EPA cannot enforce premarket testing of chemicals. The legislation aims to ensure that corporations can no longer hide unfavorable health data by citing "confidential business information." Further provisions in the bill would address aggregate and cumulative exposures to chemicals and increase protection for "vulnerable populations," particularly children. As for industry's role, "green chemistry" initiatives offer hope of change, though a broader corporate reconception of responsibilities to various publics is necessary. The industry lobby against TSCA reform rehashes arguments from the 1970s—the proposed reforms represent an overly broad delegation of authority to the EPA, stymie innovation, are costly, and have a negative impact on jobs—all of which minimize the human and environmental costs of not acting. An industry-favored measure introduced in 2013 also aims to pre-empt states from enacting tougher restrictions on toxic chemicals.[25]

The Obama-era EPA has sought broader regulatory authority and more resources to control toxic chemicals. The president's 2010 report, *Reducing Environmental Cancer Risk: What We Can Do Now*, recognizes the link between cancer and chemicals, specifically noting polyhalogenated biphenyls, the broad category that includes PCBs. Environmental justice legislation, long stuck in congressional committee, could give clear authority to consider disparate treatment, as did the Clinton executive order. Absent legislative action to help it improve monitoring, the EPA in 2010 began reassessing how it regulates PCBs. The PCB reassessment offers an opportunity to strengthen regulation consistent with the EPA's findings that "any exposure of human beings [to PCBs] . . . may be significant." Just as the scientific findings regarding PCBs in the 1960s influenced global understanding of the interconnectedness of ecological processes, continued research has contributed to the globalization of environmental regulation. International pressure for better control of toxic chemicals, including the implementation of the REACH protocol, has since 2007 added impetus to global chemical reform. International organizations, including the PCBs Elimination Network, seek to phase out PCBs and other persistent organic pollutants by 2028.[26]

REFLECTING ON ANNISTON'S BAPTISM in toxic chemicals brings forth strong religious symbolism: the endurance of suffering, the ritual purification washing away the old. Baptism suggests a regenerative act, redemption. *Redemption* is a complicated term in American history. It is familiar to historians of the U.S. South as applied to the "Redeemers," white leaders who, depending on differing interpretations, at the close of Reconstruction either returned the South to its former owners or set up a new class that drove the nation toward Jim Crow. "Redemption turns out to be a false idol," writes southern historian Edward Ball.[27]

Without more forceful government action to hold industry to a higher standard, the weight of poverty and political economy continues to sustain environmental injustice. "We vastly underestimated the legacy of apartheid," South African Truth and Reconciliation Commission (TRC) co-chair Alex Boraine once noted. Recognizing that losses such as have been experienced in Anniston cannot be fully addressed by money or even by medical treatment, several efforts have emerged to promote spiritual healing. When the Anniston Environmental Health Research Consortium brought her to visit in 2005, health researcher Mindy Thompson Fullilove suggested resilience-building strategies from her work with other neighborhoods that have undergone the "root shock" of relocation. Karen Green opened the Blessed and Renewed Beauty Salon on Highway 21 just south of Fort McClellan's gates, with an aim to link physical renewal and spiritual healing in a successful business. She created a space where women, dispersed by relocation, gather to recreate community.[28]

In 2007, a local effort modeled on South Africa's TRC was led by Rev. Alberta McCrory, who later became mayor of Hobson City. Reverend McCrory convened "Anniston Reconnecting: A Catalyst for Healing (ARCH)" at Haven United Methodist Church, also borrowing from the approach used in Greensboro, North Carolina, after the 1979 Klan shootings that killed five protestors. The Truth and Reconciliation paradigm may prove hard to implement in a case of slow violence. "Unlike Greensboro," wrote *Star* reporter Dan Whisenhunt, "Anniston has no one singular event, no point of demarcation to crystallize what happened—PCB pollution happened over decades and the effects are still being felt today." The occasion marked a recognition, Mayor Chip Howell said, that "everyone was impacted, whether they were touched by contaminants or not."[29]

Still, the impacts persist unevenly. "As far as healing the community, I don't think you can heal a wound when you keep stabbing it in the same place," said Sallie Bowie Franklin.[30] For West Anniston residents, Monsanto's PCBs erased home places, sites of cultural significance, including Mars Hill and its baptismal pool. Corporate decisions severed connections to the land—livestock, vegetable gardens, and fish from the creek. Beyond the implications for physical health, these connections were emblems of economic independence and links to history.

NEGATIVE PUBLICITY HAS LONG WORN ON everyone. "Write something good about Anniston," Lula Palmore, wife of Anniston City councilman Herbert Palmore, greeted me as she welcomed attendees to a public meeting

University students from around the nation visit the historic site of the Greyhound Bus Station in Anniston, where murals commemorate the Freedom Riders who were assaulted in the firebombing of the bus on Mother's Day, 1961. Photo by author.

on revitalizing the city's declining public schools. Ironically, not only justice but Anniston's economic revival may depend on acknowledging the turmoil provoked by pollution and by Anniston's racially violent past. As Betsy Bean, executive director of the Spirit of Anniston, a downtown revitalization program, said about the city's efforts to memorialize the Freedom Riders, "If Anniston is ever going to come back, we must acknowledge its past."[31]

Resistance to memorializing Anniston's complex history extends beyond the city. The Alabama Historical Commission denied in 2003 a request from educator Georgia Calhoun to place an official marker at the site of the Freedom Riders bus burning, arguing that "the place was not preserved properly to qualify for historical markers." However, by the time of the fiftieth anniversary of the Freedom Rides, a coalition, including Calhoun, state representative Barbara Boyd, and the Spirit of Anniston had succeeded in placing large plaques near both the old Greyhound terminal and the former Trailways stop. A new generation of young people learns about the African American freedom movement through annual college tours. Freedom Rider

On October 18, 2012, Anniston elementary school students unveiled a sign announcing the creation of Freedom Riders Park at the location of the bus burning. Signs at the site were twice burned and twice replaced. Photo by author.

Hank Thomas, a successful businessman in Atlanta, returned to Anniston for the fiftieth anniversary commemoration. "I'm sorry for what happened," forty-seven-year-old white Anniston resident Richard Couch told Thomas tearfully. "Anniston is not the same town that you found fifty years ago. We don't have the same hearts. *Welcome* to my town." In the fall of 2012, a broad coalition of Anniston and Calhoun County residents broke ground on Freedom Riders Park. Within two weeks, however, the sign publicizing the planned memorial was vandalized by fire. Destroyed a second time, the sign was again restored.[32]

The strongest antidotes to the toxic poisoning of a town are openness and democracy. Justice requires genuine transparency, not the apparent transparency of orchestrated consultancies. Democracy requires messy, prolonged, polarizing, vigorous debate, not the ersatz democracy of corporate risk communications. Healing may come in unheralded ways. Several times on the anniversary of the *Abernathy-Tolbert* settlement, residents displaced by PCBs have reunited in Lincoln Park, occupying the ground and reclaiming a sense of community. "It was a magnificent struggle," says David Baker, "and we are not at the end."[33]

NOTES

Abbreviations

Abernathy documents	Records and other documents from *Abernathy v. Monsanto*, Etowah County Courthouse, Gadsden, Ala.
Abernathy transcript	*Abernathy v. Monsanto*
Ayers Papers	Harry Mell Ayers Papers, W. S. Hoole Special Collections Library, University Libraries Division of Special Collections, The University of Alabama, Tuscaloosa, Ala.
CHEMEWG	Chemical Industry Archives, Environmental Working Group, www.chemicalindustryarchives.org
COUL Papers	Committee of Unified Leadership Papers, private collection, Anniston, Ala.
Herty Collection	Charles Holmes Herty Collection, Manuscript, Archives and Rare Book Library, Emory University, Atlanta, Ga.
Hill Papers	Lister Hill Papers, W. S. Hoole Special Collections Library, University Libraries Division of Special Collections, The University of Alabama, Tuscaloosa, Ala.
HML	Harvard Medical Library in the Francis A. Countway Library of Medicine, Harvard University, Boston, Mass.
Incineration Archive	Incineration Archive, Alice Donald Papers, private collection, Anniston, Ala.
Monsanto Records	Monsanto Company Records, University Archives, Department of Special Collections, Washington University Libraries, St. Louis, Mo.
NARA-CP	National Archives and Records Administration, College Park, Md.
NARA-DC	National Archives and Records Administration, Washington, D.C.
NARA-Morrow	National Archives and Records Administration, Morrow, Ga.
Owens transcript	*Owens v. Monsanto* (2001)
PLACC	Alabama Room, Public Library of Anniston–Calhoun County, Anniston, Ala.
RG	Record Group
Risebrough Papers	Robert W. Risebrough Papers, private collection, Berkeley, Calif.
SCLC Papers	Southern Christian Leadership Conference Papers, Manuscript, Archives and Rare Book Library, Emory University, Atlanta, Ga.
Silbergeld Papers	Ellen K. Silbergeld Papers, Schlesinger Library, Radcliffe Institute, Harvard University, Cambridge, Mass.

SLA   International Molders and Allied Workers Union of North
       America, Local 324 (Anniston, Ala.), Southern Labor Archives,
       Georgia State University Special Collections, Atlanta, Ga.

Preface

1. Rachel Carson, "A Fable for Tomorrow," in Carson, *Silent Spring*, 1–3.

2. Ferguson, *Final Report*, 6; Dr. David O. Carpenter, in Kroft, "Toxic Town"; Dr. Ian C. Nisbet, *Abernathy* transcript, January 24, 2002; Anniston Army Depot, Region IV: Superfund, Site Summary Profile, http://epa.gov/region4/superfund/sites/fedfacs/anarmydptal.html (August 24, 2012); ATSDR, "Potential Exposure Pathways."

3. *Anniston Hot Blast*, August 18, 1883, 2; H. Brandt Ayers, *In Love with Defeat*, 23.

4. Sullivan, "'To Make America Safe for Democracy,'" 83.

5. ADEM did cite and fine the Army and its contractors for various waste handling and reporting violations. CMA, "ADEM Reviews ANCDF Self-Reported Concerns, Issues Notice," press release, September 19, 2012. Cameron Steele, "Anniston Chemical Demil Facility Cited for Environmental Violations," *Anniston Star*, September 20, 2012; LaHaye and Jenkins, *Armageddon*; interviews with Timothy and Kama Cherry, July 16, 2003.

6. Marcel Pagnol, cited in Washington, *Medical Apartheid*, 12; Drinker, Warren, and Bennett, "Problem of Possible Systemic Effects"; W. R. Richard, Research Center, to W. A. Kuhn, December 30, 1968, *Abernathy* documents; W. R. Richard to E. Wheeler, "Defense of Aroclor—F. [Functional] Fluids," September 9, 1969, 6; Jack Matson, *Owens* transcript, April 6, 2001, 726; William B. Papageorge, deposition in *Mars Hill Missionary Baptist Church v. Monsanto*, March 31, 1998, 45; *Ex parte Monsanto and Solutia* (*Abernathy v. Monsanto*), February 26, 2003, 4; interview with Chris Waddle, November 19, 2003.

7. Michael Grunwald, "Monsanto Hid Decades of Pollution," *Washington Post*, January 1, 2002; interview with Shirley McCord, August 26, 2004.

8. Pavuk et al., "Assessment of Human Exposure to PCBs in Anniston"; interviews with Arthur and Bettye Bowie, September 29, 2003; "Living on Poisoned Ground," *People*, March 25, 2002, 60–65; interview with Opal Scruggs, September 25, 2003. West and East Anniston are not separate jurisdictions but parts of the city.

9. Interview with Chris Waddle, November 19, 2003.

Introduction

1. *Ex parte Monsanto and Solutia* (*Abernathy v. Monsanto*), February 26, 2003, 4; Restatement of the Law, Second, Torts, §46, The American Law Institute, 1965; Vicki McClure, "Monsanto, Solutia Liable, Verdict Means Companies Face Hundreds of Millions in PCB Claims," *Birmingham News/Birmingham Post-Herald*, February 23, 2002.

2. ATSDR, *Toxicological Profile for Polychlorinated Biphenyls*, 16; Birnbaum, "Third Biannual International PCB Workshop," 3; EPA, *Drinking Water Criteria*

Document for PCBs," I-12; WHO/IARC, *IARC Monographs, Carcinogenic Risks to Humans,* 371.

3. Technically, Swann's Federal Phosphorus Company first manufactured PCBs. Swann consolidated multiple ventures into the Swann Chemical Company, a holding company, in 1930. Federal Phosphorus Company vice president B. G. Klugh to Dr. Charles H. Herty, February 21, 1929, box 94, folder 13, Herty Collection; Penning, "Swann Corporation," 151.

4. For an overview of global organochlorine pollution, see Thornton, *Pandora's Poison.*

5. "Report of a New Chemical Hazard," 612; "PCB Problem Unfolded as Environment Hazard," *Anniston Star,* November 22, 1970; ATSDR, *Toxicological Profile for Polychlorinated Biphenyls,* 7. Monsanto reported shutting down Aroclors operations in Anniston in August 1971. D. B. Hosmer, "PCB Effluents from Anniston Plant to Snow Creek, Choccolocco Creek, etc.," meeting at Southwest [Southeast] Regional Office of EPA, November 12, 1971, 2, *Abernathy* documents. Formal shutdown came on May 1, 1972. Daniel E. Cooper to Gene L. Jessee, November 13, 1972, CHEMEWG. Toxic Substances Control Act of 1976, 15 U.S.C. 53 §§2601–92; the section banning PCBs is 15 U.S.C. §2605, sect. 6(e).

6. "Since the 1970s, researchers have noticed a decrease in PCB concentrations in human blood serum. In a study of 1,631 individuals from 1978 to 1979 living in the United States, the mean PCB concentration in human blood serum was 6.4 ng/g (Kreiss et al. 1982). In 2000, mean serum PCB levels range from 0.9 to 1.5 ng/mL in individuals who do not have a diet high in fish, especially fish from the Great Lakes." ATSDR, *Toxicological Profile for Polychlorinated Biphenyls,* 557–60.

7. Drinker, Warren, and Bennett, "Problem of Possible Systemic Effects"; Elmer P. Wheeler to Don Otto, "PCB Literature Search," August 6, 1971, CHEMEWG; *Ex parte Monsanto and Solutia (Abernathy v. Monsanto),* February 26, 2003, 4; "Solutia Fires First Shot in War of Words with *Post* over PCB Article," *EHS Today: The Magazine for Environment, Health and Safety Leaders,* January 4, 2002, http://ehstoday.com/news/ehs_imp_35056/ (September 29, 2009).

8. Monsanto concluded in 1969 that PCBs posed "a worldwide ecological problem." "PCB Environmental Pollution Abatement Plan," October 15, 1969, 3, *Abernathy* documents. EPA, "Polychlorinated Biphenyls (PCBs): Reassessment of Use Authorizations," 40 CFR 761 (EPA-HQ-OPPT-2009-0757; FRL-8811-7), *Federal Register* 75, no. 66 (April 7, 2010), Proposed Rules, 17645–66, at 17648.

9. EPA Region 4 deputy regional administrator Stanley Meiburg, in U.S. Senate, Committee on Appropriations, *PCB Contamination in Anniston,* 6; Alabama Department of Public Health Fish Consumption Guidelines, September 2012, http://www.adph.org/tox/assets/2012_Advisory_Table.pdf (September 16, 2013).

10. Hermanson and Johnson, "Polychlorinated Biphenyls in Tree Bark"; Dr. Ian C. Nisbet, *Abernathy* transcript, January 24, 2002. Nisbet based his conclusion on blood serum PCB levels. Beginning in 1999, the *National Report on Human Exposure to Environmental Chemicals,* based on data from the National Health and Nutrition Examination Survey (NHANES) conducted biennially by the Centers for Disease Control and Prevention, provides national averages for numerous

common PCBs that can be used for comparison. For example, the sum of PCB congeners 138, 153, and 180 blood serum was 1.66 ppb (ng/ml, wet weight) for the people surveyed by NHANES in 2003–4 compared to 7.21 ppb for the 764 adults tested in Anniston. Pavuk et al., "Assessment of Human Exposure to PCBs in Anniston." Care must be taken in comparing data across studies. Variations in exposure by age, for example, make it necessary to have figures from similarly aged people for appropriate comparison. Toxic Substances Control Act, 15 U.S.C. §2605, sect. 6(e); "Officials Doing Little about Choccolocco Creek Pollution," *Anniston Star*, July 10, 1994.

11. Kroft, "Toxic Town"; Organisation for the Prohibition of Chemical Weapons, "Status of Participation in the Chemical Weapons Convention," http://www.opcw. org/index.html (June 1, 2006).

12. Brandon Tubbs, "Protestors March against the Incinerator," *Anniston Star*, August 17, 2003; U.S. Bureau of the Census, *Profile of General Demographic Characteristics*.

13. "From Soybean Field to NASCAR's Most Competitive Track," n.d., http:// www.talladegasuperSpeedway.com (March 16, 2005); Norm Froscher, "Old Airport Took Off as SuperSpeedway," official souvenir program, EA Sports 500, Talladega, Ala., September 28, 2003, 60; Jim Szymanski, "Joliet's Jury Still Out on Track's Economic Effects: Town Sought Track as Solution to Image and Financial Issues," *Joliet (Ill.) Olympian*, July 19, 2004, http://www.theolympian.com/home/ news/20040719/topstories/100313_ARC.shtml (August 29, 2004); Jonathan Miles, "NASCAR Nation," *New York Times*, May 22, 2005; Tim Appelo, "The NASCARing of the Northwest," *Seattle Weekly*, June 30–July 6, 2004, http://www.seattle-weekly.com/features/0426/040630_news_nascar.php (April 25, 2005).

14. Steve Lopez, "Babes, Bordeaux & Billy Bobs: How I Learned to Love NASCAR and Not to Hate Superstar Jeff Gordon," *Time*, May 31, 1999, http://www.time. com/time/archive/preview/0,10987,991083,00.html (April 27, 2005); author's notes on the race, September 28, 2003.

15. Anniston Army Depot, http://www.anad.army.mil/about.htm (July 26, 2006); ANCDF, "Disposal Operations to Continue after 'Ivan,'" press release, September 17, 2004; Matthew Korade, "Top Guns: Save the Depot!," *Anniston Star*, January 8, 2004; Barry Yeoman, "Deadly Dependence: The South's Economic Reliance on Military Bases Has Left a Toxic Legacy throughout the Region," *Creative Loafing*, August 25, 2004, 38.

16. Monsanto Chemical Company, Detail Listing of All Charges, Letter Contract DA-18-108-CML-1879, General Correspondence, Commercial Series, 1955–58, folder 161, Monsanto Chemical Company, Records of the Chemical School, Fort McClellan, Ala., Records of the Chemical Warfare Service, 1917–63, RG 175, NARA-CP.

17. Seager, *Earth Follies*, 14; Melosi, *Sanitary City*, 14; Russell, *War and Nature*; Coates et al., "Defending Nation, Defending Nature?"; *Alabama v. Seeber* (1974); Anniston Army Depot, Region IV: Superfund, http://epa.gov/region4/ superfund/sites/fedfacs/anarmydptal.html (August 24, 2012); Brophy, Miles, and Cochrane, *Chemical Warfare Service: From Laboratory to Field*, 254–55, 328–29,

451; Barry Yeoman, "Deadly Dependence: The South's Economic Reliance on Military Bases Has Left a Toxic Legacy throughout the Region," *Creative Loafing*, August 25, 2004, 38; phone communications with Henry Caddell, September 12, 2003, May 21, 2013.

18. Kroft, "Toxic Town"; Bill Hewitt, with Linda Trischetta and Siobhan Morrissey, "Living on Poisoned Ground," *People*, March 25, 2002, 60; Moyers, "Toxic Communities"; Sesno and Guarino, *Avoiding Armageddon*; Rick Bragg, with Glynn Wilson, "Burning of Chemical Arms Puts Fear in Wind," *New York Times*, September 15, 2002; Bragg, *All Over but the Shoutin'*, 3, 4.

19. "Five Worst Smaller Places," *Forbes*, May 9, 2002, http://www.forbes.com/2002/05/09/bestplaces.html (September 27, 2005).

20. Rick Bragg, "Poison or Poverty?," *St. Petersburg Times*, September 13, 1992.

21. Gibbs, *Love Canal*; Woodward, *Origins of the New South*, 136.

22. Cobb, *Selling of the South*, 229.

23. Gates, *The Model City*, 111.

24. Tarr, *Search for the Ultimate Sink*, 344, 345; Melosi, *Sanitary City*, 162; Price, "Health Problems in the Chemical Industries," 1159; Richard Rhodes, "Nuclear Options," *New York Times Book Review*, May 15, 2005, 7–8.

25. Nixon, *Slow Violence*, 2.

26. Griffith and Satterfield, *Triumphs and Troubles*, 43; R. Williams to B. O. Severson, January 20, 1971, Plaintiff's Exhibit 4A12, *Abernathy* documents.

27. Sellers, *Hazards of the Job*; "Chemicals Just Coming into Own, Says Monsanto Official," *Anniston Star*, July 25, 1943.

28. *Gentry v. Swann* (1937), 318 (my emphasis).

29. Drinker, Warren, and Bennett, "Problem of Possible Systemic Effects," 307; Meigs, Albom, and Kartin, "Chloracne from an Unusual Exposure to Arochlor."

30. U.S. General Accounting Office, *Siting of Hazardous Waste Landfills*; Commission for Racial Justice, *Toxic Wastes and Race*; EPA, "Environmental Justice"; Robert Bullard, *Dumping in Dixie*.

31. African Americans in the study lived closer to the plant (median distance of 2.19 km) than whites (3.83 km). Pavuk et al., "Assessment of Human Exposure to PCBs in Anniston," 1084.

32. Gotham, *Race, Real Estate*, 12–13. Also see Radway, "What's in a Name?," 11; and Lipsitz, "Racialization of Space."

33. C. Vann Woodward identified the Redeemers as post–Civil War southern business and political leaders who sought "not the return of the old system" but a new economic order that "laid the lasting foundations in matters of race, politics, economics, and law for the modern South." Woodward, *Origins of the New South*, 21–22. Yaeger, *Dirt and Desire*, 277.

34. For discussions of differential susceptibility and immunity, see, for example, Nash, *Inescapable Ecologies*, 39–40; Washington, *Medical Apartheid*, 37–42; and Valenčius, *Health of the Country*, 237–38.

35. Ford, "Boundaries of Race," 1845; Yaeger, *Dirt and Desire*, 227, 132; Theo Van Goldberg, "Lingering Legacies," talk presented at Emory University, December 2004; Young, "Harvey's Complaint," 41; Robert Bullard, *Black Metropolis*.

36. Laura Nation, "Class Action Suit against Monsanto Proceeds," *Anniston Star*, September 29, 1998.

37. Marchand and Smith, "Corporate Science," 150; Walters, *Scientific Authority*, 51.

38. Wexler, *Mapping Fate*, 266; Stephen R. Couch and Anne Mercuri, "Toxic Water, Toxic Knowledge, and A Subculture of Distress," talk at the Eastern Sociological Association noted in *BSED in Touch* 3, no. 1 (Fall 2001): 3; Couch and Kroll-Smith, "Patterns of Victimization and the Chronic Technological Disaster."

39. Yaeger, *Dirt and Desire*, 258; communication with Allen Tullos, January 2004.

40. Anonymous reader; Fischer, *Citizens, Experts, and Environment*, 6; Egan, "Toxic Knowledge: A Mercurial Fugue"; Harding, "Who Knows?"; Haraway, "Situated Knowledges."

41. EPA, "Health Effects of PCBs," http://www.epa.gov/osw/hazard/tsd/pcbs/pubs/effects.htm (June 15, 2013); Walters, *Scientific Authority*, 51; Harvey, *Justice, Nature*, 374–75.

42. Kimberly Smith, *African American Environmental Thought*, esp. 2–6; Alaimo, *Bodily Natures*, 29; Jacquelyn Dowd Hall, "Long Civil Rights Movement," 1235. In "The 'Long Movement' as Vampire," Sundiata Keita Cha-Jua and Clarence Lang critique the long civil rights movement thesis for overstating continuities. Interview with Representative Barbara Bigsby Boyd, February 25, 2005; "Negro Health Service Leader Moves Office," *Anniston Star*, February 26, 1931; COUL Annual Report, November 1972 to October 1973, 42–45.

43. Dorceta E. Taylor has outlined the significance of that reframing in "The Rise of the Environmental Justice Paradigm." A substantial literature on the environmental justice movement includes Robert Bullard, *Confronting Environmental Racism*; Robert Bullard, *Unequal Protection*; Pulido, *Environmentalism and Economic Justice*; Cuesta Camacho, *Environmental Injustices*; and McGurty, *Transforming Environmentalism*.

44. Nixon, *Slow Violence*, 2. For discussion of pollution as violence, see also Murdocca, "'There Is Something in That Water.'"

45. Oreskes and Conway, *Merchants of Doubt*; Littlemore, "Manufacturing Doubt," 41; Case, "Manufacturing Doubt"; Jere White, *Owens* transcript, April 4, 2001, 453; Bob Burton, "Advice on Making Nice: Peter Sandman Plots to Make You a Winner," Center on Media and Democracy, *PR Watch: Public Interest Reporting on the PR/Public Affairs Industry* 6, no. 1 (First Quarter 1999): 1–6, Center on Media and Democracy, http://www.prwatch.org/files/pdfs/prwatch/prwv6n1.pdf (December 12, 2005).

46. Author's notes on the Anniston PCB Settlement press conference, held by judges R. Joel Laird and U. W. Clemon, Anniston, Alabama, August 21, 2013.

47. Judge R. Joel Laird, *Abernathy* transcript, February 5, 2002.

Chapter One

1. William D. Kelley, "Anniston: A Romance of the New South," in Kelley, *Old South and the New*, 47–67; Henry Grady, "The Model City of the Southern States," *Atlanta Constitution*, July 8, 1883; H. A., "The City for a Monument: The Gift of

a Yankee Hero to the South," *New York Times*, February 5, 1887; "Anniston: 'The Model City of the South,'" *Manufacturers Record*, April 27, 1889, 20.

2. Griffith and Satterfield, *Triumphs and Troubles*, 115.

3. Henry Grady, "A Man and a Town," *Atlanta Constitution*, June 10, 1883.

4. Ibid.; Samuel Noble to Alfred L. Tyler, February 1, 1883, in William D. Kelley, *Old South and the New*, 51–52; Morris, *Edith Kermit Roosevelt*, chap. 5.

5. Lacefield, *Lost Worlds in Alabama's Rocks*, 42, 60, 56.

6. Kolodny, *Lay of the Land*; H. A., "The City for a Monument," *New York Times*, February 5, 1887; Baldwin and Justus, *Flush Times*; Henry Grady, "A Man and a Town," *Atlanta Constitution*, June 10, 1883.

7. Sally Ladiga won her U.S. Supreme Court case, but she never regained the land; *Ladiga v. Roland* (1844). Also see Rogers et al., *Alabama: History of a Deep South State*, 90–91; and Calvin Wingo, "A History of Choccolocco Valley in Calhoun County, Alabama," 6, ca. 1988, PLACC.

8. Brett Buckner, "Unearthing a Legacy: State Geologist Honored with Photo Exhibition," *Anniston Star*, January 31, 2004; *Anniston in North Alabama*, 1.

9. Bond, "Social and Economic Forces in Alabama Reconstruction," 376; Grace Hooten Gates, *Model City*, 26; William D. Kelley, *Old South and the New*, 93, 100.

10. The trope of "a problematic Eden" runs throughout contemporary environmental history. Cronon, *Uncommon Ground*, 37. Grace Hooten Gates, *Model City*, 39–40. Anniston was frequently compared to the model town of Pullman, Illinois, though Anniston was founded first. See Grace Hooten Gates, *Model City*, 53–54; and Henry Grady, "The Model City of the Southern States," *Atlanta Constitution*, July 8, 1883.

11. Moore, *Calhoun County, Alabama, Boy*, 12; Flynt, *Poor but Proud*, 36–38; Brewer, *Alabama: Her History, Resources, War Record, and Public Men*, 151; Woodward, *Burden of Southern History*, 27. The Calhoun County population in 1860 included 17,169 whites, 28 free blacks, and 4,343 slaves; Flynt, *Poor but Proud*, 15.

12. Grace Hooten Gates, *Model City*, 11; Federal Writers' Program (Alabama), *Alabama: A Guide to the Deep South*, 161.

13. Grace Hooten Gates, *Model City*, 13, 17, 18; "A Gold-Laden Gripsack: The Story of a Theft for Which Jeff Davis Was Arrested," *New York Times*, August 15, 1888.

14. Bond, "Social and Economic Forces in Alabama Reconstruction," 381; Woodward, *Origins of the New South*, 9–10; Hackney, *Populism to Progressivism in Alabama*, 12; Grace Hooten Gates, *Model City*, 148.

15. Grace Hooten Gates, *Model City*, 34, 111; Federal Writers' Program (Alabama), *Alabama: A Guide to the Deep South*, 66.

16. Hale, *Making Whiteness*, 128.

17. Howard, *Death at Cross Plains*. One of those lynched, a white Canadian clergyman who had come south on a mission to educate the formerly enslaved, wrote to his wife on the day he died. That letter and other documents about the lynchings are available online through the Alabama Room, Public Library of Anniston/Calhoun County, http://publiclibrary.cc/archive/SpecialCollections/hangingofluke/hangingofluke.htm (May 28, 2013); Harry Mell Ayers, "City Subverted by a Lynching," *Birmingham Age-Herald*, October 2, 1910.

18. Gertrude Williams, "Origin and Early Development of Anniston," preface; "Anniston, as Seen by Judge Kelley," *Manufacturers Record*, December 1886, reprinted in Howard, *1887–88 Anniston City Directory*; *Anniston in North Alabama*, 20.

19. General Daniel Tyler to Hon. J. Little Smith, January 18, 1879, in William D. Kelley, *Old South and the New*, 48–49.

20. Interview with Chris Waddle, November 13, 2003; Grace Hooten Gates, *Model City*, 11, 40–41; Woodward, *Origins of the New South*, 136; General Daniel Tyler to Hon. J. Little Smith, January 18, 1879, in William D. Kelley, *Old South and the New*, 49.

21. Industrial paternalism was tied to racial subjugation; see, for example, Kelly, *Race, Class, and Power in the Alabama Coalfields*. Grace Hooten Gates, *Model City*, 41; "Early History of the Industrial City of Anniston, 1872–1889," 73, vertical files, PLACC, citing *Anniston Weekly Watchman*, June 18, 1887, and *Anniston Weekly Hot Blast*, February 2, 1888; Edith Alston, "Trees Growing Part of Town History," *Anniston Star*, September 10, 1978.

22. Grace Hooten Gates, *Model City*, 151; interview with Representative Barbara Bigsby Boyd, February 25, 2005.

23. "Facts about Anniston," Anniston City Land Company, 1889, vertical files, PLACC; Donald Davis, *Where There Are Mountains*, 152; interview with Gordon Rodgers Jr., February 5, 2005.

24. Mumford, *City in History*, 458; Grace Hooten Gates, *Model City*, 125, 162, 154; H. A., "The City for a Monument," *New York Times*, February 5, 1887.

25. Grace Hooten Gates, *Model City*, 164, 170; General Robert E. Noble, "Anniston History," 2, n.d., vertical files, PLACC; William D. Kelley, *Old South and the New*, 66–67. Early maps called the district "Libera," but that designation disappeared by 1889. Grace Hooten Gates, *Model City*, 171. Interview with Henry Givahn by Grace Hooten Gates, February 29, 1980, PLACC. Also see Grant Martin, "Vibrant West 15th Street Past Is a Fading Memory," *Anniston Star*, February 17, 2002.

26. "Pollution," in *Oxford English Dictionary*, 1081; Douglas, *Purity and Danger*, 9; Thorsheim, *Inventing Pollution*, 194; Tarr, *Search for the Ultimate Sink*, 344.

27. Porter, *Health, Civilization, and the State*, 81–82; Melosi, *Sanitary City*, 162; Tarr, *Search for the Ultimate Sink*, 344–45; Karen Kruse Thomas, *Deluxe Jim Crow*, 11.

28. Insurance company representatives cited differential mortality statistics in those southern states where racial breakdowns were available to justify charging higher rates to black clients: "Richmond—White, 22.34; colored 29.50. Savannah—White, 20.75, colored 38.75; Mobile—White 17.97; colored 24.25; Anniston—White, 11.75; colored 20.50. Birmingham—White 14.85; colored 26.34. New Orleans—White, 23.97; colored, 35.01." "Colored Persons Poor Risks," *New York Times*, April 24, 1893.

29. See, for example, Tullos, "Great Hookworm Crusade"; and Thorsheim, *Inventing Pollution*, 195.

30. Interview with Henry Givahn by Grace Hooten Gates, February 29, 1980, PLACC; interview with Gordon Rodgers Jr., September 5, 2005; Markel, *Quarantine!*, 185; Hale, *Making Whiteness*, 128.

31. "Thousands of Men Train . . . : Army Camp Is One of Finest in the Nation," *Anniston Star*, Club and Industrial Edition, March 6, 1924, 4.

32. Hale, *Making Whiteness*, 75, 252; Rogers et al., *Alabama: History of a Deep South State*, 338–42; Grace Hooten Gates, *Model City*, 182; "Soldier Riots at Anniston," *New York Times*, November 26, 1898.

33. Grace Hooten Gates, *Model City*, 182; Charlotte Tubbs, "Separated, but Equal?," *Anniston Star*, February 22, 2004; "Hobson City Centennial Celebration: 1899–2000," 1, reprinted from *People's Journal*, Jacksonville, Ala., July 27, 1899, 1–2, in author's possession.

34. Charlotte Tubbs, "Separated, but Equal?," *Anniston Star*, February 22, 2004; Blackmon, *Story of the Progress of the Negro Race*, 30; interview with Henry Givhan by Grace Hooten Gates, February 29, 1980, PLACC. The best-known graduate of the Calhoun County Training School may be David Satcher, U.S. surgeon general during the Clinton administration; other graduates include Anniston educator Georgia Calhoun, environmental justice activist David Baker, and state representative Barbara Bigsby Boyd.

35. Hale, *Making Whiteness*, 35; Grace Hooten Gates, *Model City*, 183–85; Flynt, *Alabama in the Twentieth Century*, 167; Grant Martin, "Vibrant West 15th Street Past Is a Fading Memory," *Anniston Star*, February 17, 2002.

36. Fifteenth Street Historic District Application, National Register of Historic Places, 4, PLACC; interview with Henry Givhan by Grace Hooten Gates, February 29, 1980, PLACC.

37. Flynt, *Alabama in the Twentieth Century*, 7, 16. Knox based his legal argument on *Van Valkenberg v. Brown* (1872). *Official Proceedings of the Constitutional Convention*, Day 2: May 22, 1901, 13, http://www.legislature.state.al.us/misc/history/constitutions/1901/proceedings/1901_proceedings_vol1/1901.html (May 28, 2013) (my emphasis).

38. Hackney, *Populism to Progressivism in Alabama*, 184; *Official Proceedings of the Constitutional Convention*, 13; Hackney, *Populism to Progressivism in Alabama*, 191–92. The intent of framers and the exact consequences of the 1901 constitution for poor whites are debated among southern historians. See Kousser, *Shaping of Southern Politics*; and Feldman, *Disfranchisement Myth*.

39. Grace Hooten Gates, *Model City*, 234, 102–4.

40. Edith Alston, "Trees Growing Part of Town History," *Anniston Star*, September 10, 1978.

Chapter Two

1. "The Chemical Century," *Fortune*, May 1950, 76; Hubert Kay, "Monsanto and the American Idea," June 1958, F-66, series 6, box 1, Hubert Kay (first draft), Monsanto Records. Several copies of Kay's first draft exist, including one with a few handwritten notes by Monsanto president Edgar M. Queeny. All references to the manuscript are to Kay's copy.

2. Forrestal, *Faith, Hope, and $5,000*, 12–13; Hubert Kay, "Monsanto and the American Idea," June 1958, F-9–10, F-73, series 6, box 1, Hubert Kay (first draft),

Monsanto Records; Hodding Carter, *Lower Mississippi*, 311; Forrestal, *Faith, Hope, and $5,000*, 12–14; Francis J. Curtis, "Early Days of Monsanto," December 9, 1950, 2–3, series 10, box 3, folder: Monsanto Company History (Historical Accounts, Gaston DuBois), Monsanto Records.

3. Charlotte J. Kuhn, "From the Archive: The Monsanto Name," March 13, 1997, 1, series 10, box 3, Early Days, Pioneers Period (1928–42), Monsanto Records; Hubert Kay, "Monsanto and the American Idea," June 1958, F-58, F-60, series 6, box 1, Hubert Kay (first draft), Monsanto Records; interview with Ralph C. Piper by James E. McKee, September 11, 1981, 2, series 10, box 3, Monsanto Co. History (Oral History Project), Monsanto Records; Forrestal, *Faith, Hope, and $5,000*, 21, 28.

4. Aftalion, *History of the International Chemical Industry*, 115; Haynes, *Chemical Pioneers*, 239. Dr. Lloyd F. Nickell, "Coal-Tar," 1916, 1, series 3, box 1, Products (Coal Tar), Monsanto Records; Monsanto Chemical Company, "How Monsanto Serves: The Story of the Monsanto Chemical Company" (St. Louis, 1938): 8, Anniston—Monsanto, PLACC; Forrestal, *Faith, Hope, and $5,000*, 259.

5. Richard Rhodes describes nuclear weapons as embodying "a new knowledge of nature," but this was also true of chemistry ("Nuclear Options," *New York Times Book Review*, May 15, 2005, 7–8).

6. Hubert Kay, "Monsanto and the American Idea," June 1958, C-39, C-56, series 6, box 1, Hubert Kay (first draft), Monsanto Records; Griffith and Satterfield, *Triumphs and Troubles*, 54.

7. Monsanto Chemical Company, "How Monsanto Serves: The Story of the Monsanto Chemical Company" (St. Louis, 1938), 4–5, Anniston—Monsanto, PLACC.

8. Francis J. Curtis, "Early Days," April 1, 1951, 1–2, 7, series 10, 3 (Historical Accounts, Louis Veillon, Gaston DuBois, Jules Bebie), Monsanto Records; Forrestal, *Faith, Hope, and $5,000*, 17–24.

9. Forrestal, *Faith, Hope, and $5,000*, 21–24; Oser, "Highlights," 535–36; Hubert Kay, "Monsanto and the American Idea," June 1958, F-25–26, series 6, box 1, Hubert Kay (first draft), Monsanto Records.

10. Statement of John F. Queeny, U.S. Congress, Senate Report no. 1209, 58th Congress, 2nd session, February 24, 1904, 100; Coppin and High, *Politics of Purity*, 61, 147–48; Forrestal, *Faith, Hope, and $5,000*, 21–22. In fact, a decades-long contest over the safety of saccharin in food ensued; see Oser, "Highlights."

11. Francis J. Curtis, "Early Days," April 1, 1951, 16, series 10, box 3, Monsanto Company History (Historical Accounts), Monsanto Records; Monsanto Chemical Company, "How Monsanto Serves: The Story of the Monsanto Chemical Company" (St. Louis, 1938), 9, Anniston—Monsanto, PLACC; Jules Kernen, quoted in Francis J. Curtis, "Early Days," February 19, 1951, 5, series 10, box 3, Monsanto Company History (Historical Accounts), Monsanto Records.

12. Hubert Kay, "Monsanto and the American Idea," June 1958, F-14, series 6, box 1, Hubert Kay (first draft), Monsanto Records; Edgar M. Queeny, "Our Chemical Industry Comes of Age," *Journal of Business*, November 1935, 18.

13. Cowdrey, *This Land, This South*, 103; Kirby, *Rural Worlds Lost*, 275; Cobb, "Price of Progress"; David Noble, *America by Design*, 5–6.

14. Fischer, *Citizens, Experts and the Environment*, 5; David Noble, *America by Design*, 5–6 (emphasis in original).

15. Walters, *Scientific Authority*, 51.

16. Haynes, *Men, Money, and Molecules*, 6. Educational philosopher John Dewey recognized at the time the challenge that increased reliance on expertise posed to democratic participation. Fischer, *Citizens, Experts, and the Environment*, 6–7.

17. Dr. Charles H. Herty, "An Urgent Message to the South," address to the Association of Southern Agricultural Workers, January 31, 1935, 1, box 144, folder 10, Herty Collection; Reed, *Crusading for Chemistry*, 88.

18. Richard H. Edmonds, "Anniston Is Congratulated," *Anniston Sunday Star and Daily Hot Blast*, November 21, 1915.

19. T. D. Johnson, "The New Industries Division of Alabama Power Company: Its Purpose and Functions," ca. 1940 (accession no. 5.1.1.98.237): 42, courtesy of Alabama Power Company Corporate Archives; Martin, *Story of Electricity in Alabama*, 11.

20. "Anniston Gets Front Page Notice," *Anniston Evening Star*, November 4, 1915; *Anniston Evening Star*, September 7, September 29, and October 21, 1915; "Birth of a Nation Spectacular Production," *Anniston Evening Star and Daily Hot Blast*, April 26, 1915; Rev. Dr. Charles H. Parkhurst, "On 'The Birth of a Nation,'" *Anniston Evening Star*, April 25, 1915.

21. Lewis Hine Photographs, Nos. 3805, 3807, 3842, 3843, Anniston, Ala., October 1914, http://memory.loc.gov/cgi-bin/query (June 24, 2006).

22. Interview with Henry Givahn by Grace Hooten Gates, February 29, 1980, Audiotape Collection, PLACC.

23. Ibid.; interview with Dr. Gordon Rodgers Jr., February 5, 2005.

24. "Weevil Reaches Calhoun County," *Anniston Evening Star*, October 26, 1915; "The Iron and Steel Trade," *Anniston Evening Star*, October 31, 1915; "The Hog Industry," *Anniston Sunday Star and Daily Hot Blast*, November 14, 1915; "Anniston Pipe Seeks Foreign Markets," *Anniston Evening Star*, November 10, 1915; "Moonshiners Are Fined Very Heavily," *Anniston Star*, November 3, 1915; "Anniston People Are Pleased at Prospect of Munition Plant," *Anniston Evening Star*, November 17, 1915.

25. "The Story of Monsanto," 1946, 6, series 10, box 3, Monsanto Company History (Historical Accounts), Monsanto Records; Monsanto, "History of the Anniston Plant," 1987, 1, CHEMEWG; Atkins, *"Developed for the Service of Alabama,"* 87; "Story of Munitions Plant Is Prematurely Published," *Anniston Evening Star*, November 16, 1915; "New Name Given to Munitions Company," *Anniston Sunday Star and Daily Hot Blast*, December 5, 1915; Atkins, *"Developed for the Service of Alabama,"* 124.

26. "Committee on Industrial Preparedness of the Naval Consulting Board of the U.S.," box 96, folder 5, Herty Collection; Griffith and Satterfield, *Triumphs and Troubles*, 28–30.

27. "Munition Plant and Electric Furnace Employing 300 Skilled Mechanics Are Assured for Anniston," *Anniston Evening Star*, November 24, 1915; "Steel Furnace Is Ordered for Anniston," *Anniston Evening Star*, November 24, 1915; "Anniston People Are Pleased at Prospect of Munition Plant," *Anniston Evening Star*,

November 17, 1915; "Our Fortune and Our Aims," *Anniston Evening Star*, November 25, 1915.

28. Richard H. Edmonds, "Anniston Is Congratulated," *Anniston Sunday Star and Daily Hot Blast*, November 21, 1915; Schlesinger, Gaventa, and Merrifield, *Our Own Worst Enemy*, 18; "Work Is Started on Army Camp Location," *Anniston Evening Star*, June 21, 1917; "Anniston Certain to Become Great Military Center," *Anniston Evening Star*, May 19, 1917; *Complete History of Fort McClellan, 1917–1999*, 1, Fort McClellan Records, U.S. Army Military History Institute, Carlisle, Penn., January 2002, http//www.mcclellan.army.mil/complete.htm (September 6, 2003).

29. Griffith and Satterfield, *Triumphs and Troubles*, 35; "Southern Manganese Company Workers Cottages," file no. 4881, negative no. 636, September 12, 1923, Russell Brothers Photo Collection, PLACC.

30. Interview with Henry Givahn by Grace Hooten Gates, February 29, 1980, PLACC; Rev. Harry E. Jones, "Remarkable Speech by Negro at Patriotic Mass Meeting Gives Insight to Race Loyalty," *Anniston Evening Star*, April 21, 1917.

31. Fries and West, *Chemical Warfare*, 13, 1–4, 6; Brophy, Miles, and Cochrane, *Chemical Warfare Service: From Laboratory to Field*, 1–2; "Chemical Corps Lesson Plan, Army Organization: History, Organization, Mission, and Activities of CmlC [Chemical Corps], course for Chemical Staff Specialists at the U.S. Army Chemical Corps School, Fort McClellan, Alabama," February 10, 1961, file 1508-A-534.1, Records of the Chemical School, Fort McClellan, Ala., Records of the Chemical Warfare Service, 1917–63, RG 175, NARA-CP; Harris and Paxman, *Higher Form of Killing*, 5.

32. Fries and West, *Chemical Warfare*, ix; "Chemists Talk of National Defense," *Anniston Evening Star and Daily Hot Blast*, September 22, 1915; "Chemical History of the U.S.: Two Wars Turned Tiny Industry into 16-Billion-a-Year Business," *New York Herald Tribune*, September 2, 1951, 7.

33. Aftalion, *History of the International Chemical Industry*, 124; Speech by General Sibert reported by Ben Jenkins, Captain C.W.S., U.S. Army, December 13, 1918, 30, box 101, folder 1, Herty Collection.

34. Griffith and Satterfield, *Triumphs and Troubles*, 37; Penning, "Swann Corporation," 150; Harry A. Kuhn, Captain, Chemical Warfare Service, through the Chief of the CWS, to Executive Officer, Pittsburgh C. W. Procurement District, June 1, 1935, Index Briefs 400.123/2014, Records of the Chemical School, Fort McClellan, Ala., Records of the Chemical Warfare Service, 1917–63, RG 175, NARA-DC; "Phosphoric Acid to be Discussed," *Birmingham News*, April 2, 1922; Brophy, Miles, and Cochrane, *Chemical Warfare Service: From Laboratory to Field*, 14.

35. Aftalion, *History of the International Chemical Industry*, 126; Forrestal, *Faith, Hope, and $5,000*, 30, 28.

36. Reed, *Crusading for Chemistry*, 162–63; Steen, "Patents, Patriotism," 91; H. E. Howe to Dr. Wilder D. Bancroft and Dr. Charles H. Herty, June 28, 1926, box 120, folder 2, Herty Collection.

37. Francis J. Curtis, "Twenty Years of the American Chemical Industry," *Monsanto Current Events*, 1937, 9, Monsanto Records; Dr. Lloyd F. Nickell, "Coal-Tar," 1916, series 3, box 1, 10, Products (Coal Tar), Monsanto Records.

38. Du Pont, "Human Wants," 489; Amos A. Fries, "Chemical Warfare and Its Effects on Strategy and Tactics," 19, box 101, folder 4, Herty Collection.

39. Fries and West, *Chemical Warfare*, 13; Russell, *War and Nature*, 2–3; Harris and Paxman, *Higher Form of Killing*, 34; Charles Sellers, *Field Notes and Diary*, 28, courtesy of Carolyn Merchant; "Ease and Economy of Preparing for Chemical Warfare," box 101, folder 5, Herty Collection; Amos A. Fries, "Chemical Warfare Strategy and Tactics," 7, box 101, folder 4, Herty Collection.

40. Amos A. Fries, "Chemical Warfare Strategy and Tactics," 7, box 101, folder 4, Herty Collection; General Amos A. Fries, "Making America Safe for the Reds," 2–3, box 101, folder 6, Herty Collection; "Swords or Science," box 101, folder 6, Herty Collection; Speech by General Sibert reported by Ben Jenkins, Captain C.W.S., U.S. Army, December 13, 1918, 30, box 101, folder 1, Herty Collection.

41. "A Dinner in Honor of Major General William L. Sibert," Washington, D.C., December 13, 1918, box 101, folder 3, Herty Collection; Harry Mell Ayers to Captain Elbert "Happy" J. Lyman Jr., February 3, 1943, box 138, folder 12, Ayers Papers, also cited in Stoker, "Harry Mell Ayers," 161–62.

42. "Seating Arrangements, Third Annual Chemical Warfare Dinner," box 101, folder 3, Herty Collection.

43. Handwritten note on Charles Herty's Chemical Warfare Service dinner program, December 13, 1918, box 101, folder 1, Herty Collection; "Report of Chief of Chemical Warfare Service," 1921, 40, box 101, folder 3, Herty Collection.

44. For accounts of the Caldwell incident, see Mark Schneider, *"We Return Fighting,"* 92–97; Lentz-Smith, *Freedom Struggles*, 169–205; Sullivan, "'To Make America Safe for Democracy,'" 76; and Sprayberry, "'Town among the Trees,'" 93–96.

45. Mark Schneider, *"We Return Fighting,"* 93; interview with Henry Givahn by Grace Hooten Gates, February 29, 1980, PLACC; Mark Schneider, *"We Return Fighting,"* 97; *Caldwell v. Parker* (1920); Sullivan, "'To Make America Safe for Democracy,'" 76.

46. At least eight NAACP branches existed in Alabama after World War I, the strongest in Birmingham, Montgomery, Mobile, and others in Selma, Unionton, Blocton, Florence, and Anniston. Mark Schneider, *"We Return Fighting,"* 97, 239; Fosl, *Subversive Southerner*, 63; "Pastors and Manufacturers Make Protest against Rumors," *Anniston Star*, October 26, 1919; Sprayberry, "'Town among the Trees,'" 98.

47. Dr. Charles E. Thomas, "Anniston Is Best City in U.S. for Negro Development," Club and Industrial Edition, *Anniston Star*, March 5, 1924. "White power crushed the Alabama NAACP branches or drove them underground" in the 1920s. Mark Schneider, *"We Return Fighting,"* 239.

48. *Edgewood Arsenal*, photo opposite page 64, box 101, folder 2, Herty Collection; Hale, *Making Whiteness*, 252; General Amos A. Fries, "The Relation of Chemistry to National Peace," speech delivered to the National Association of Cotton Manufacturers, 9, box 101, item 12, Herty Collection.

49. Hale, *Making Whiteness*, 252; Amos A. Fries, "Chemical Warfare and Its Effect on Strategy and Tactics," 9, box 101, folder 4, Herty Collection.

50. "Epistemology is a problem at the heart of American race-thinking," wrote Patricia Yaeger in *Dirt and Desire*, 58. General Amos A. Fries, "The Relation of Chemistry to National Peace," Speech delivered to the National Association of Cotton Manufacturers, 9, box 101, item 12, Herty Collection; Amos A. Fries, "Chemical Warfare and Its Effect on Strategy and Tactics," 9, box 101, folder 4, Herty Collection.

51. Charles Holmes Herty Daybook, box 142, folder 5, Daybooks: 1929–30, Herty Collection; "Swords or Science," 3, box 101, folder 6, Herty Collection; Charles H. Herty, "The Reserves of the Chemical Warfare Service," February 21, 1921, box 144, folder 2, Herty Collection.

52. Brophy and Fisher, *Chemical Warfare Service: Organizing for War*, 151.

53. On white ideas about differential vulnerability to disease, see, for example, Valenčius, *Health of the Country*, 237; Downs, *Sick from Freedom*, 34–35; Karen Kruse Thomas, *Deluxe Jim Crow*, 12, 16; Washington, *Medical Apartheid*, 41; and Vedder and Walton, *Medical Aspects*, 150.

54. Dr. Charles H. Herty, "Chemistry and National Defense," *Chemicals*, September 26, 1927, 11, box 101, folder 7, Herty Collection; General Amos A. Fries, "Making America Safe for the Reds," 2–3, box 101, folder 6, Herty Collection; Hale, *Making Whiteness*, 252.

55. Ellis Island Passenger Arrival Records, American Family Immigration History Center, New York, http://www.ellisisland.org (June 26, 2005); Forrestal, *Faith, Hope, and $5,000*, photo inset following page 96; Griffith and Satterfield, *Triumphs and Troubles*, 99.

56. Reed, *Crusading for Chemistry*, xi.

57. Agriculture remained the dominant economic driver with 55.6 percent of employment in farming and forestry in 1920. T. D. Johnson, "The New Industries Division of Alabama Power Company: Its Purpose and Functions," ca. 1940 (accession no. 5.1.1.98.237): 4, courtesy of Alabama Power Company Corporate Archives; Vance et al., "Education and the Southern Potential," *Regionalism and the South*, 276; Kirby, *Rural Worlds Lost*, 275–76; Swann, "Manufacture of Phosphoric Acid."

58. Penning, "Swann Corporation," 152.

59. "Without the American Chemical Society Industrialists Would Stumble Blindly," *Birmingham News*, April 2, 1922.

60. Dr. Charles Holmes Herty, box 142, folder 2, Daybooks, 1921–22, January 25, 1922, Herty Collection; Dr. Charles Holmes Herty, box 142, folder 6, Notebooks: Notes to Accounts, 1916, Herty Collection (emphasis in original); *Exhibitors, Southern Exposition, May 11–23, 1925* (Greenville, S.C.: Southern Exposition, 1925), box 70, folder 3, Herty Collection; W. G. Sirrine to Dr. Charles Holmes Herty, May 28, 1925, box 70, folder 1, Herty Collection.

61. J. E. Mills, "Statistical Information," in NRC, Division of Chemistry and Chemical Technology, *Chemical Progress*, 199.

62. Hersey, *"My Work Is That of Conservation."* Two African American chemists earned Ph.D. degrees in chemistry in the mid-1910s: St. Elmo Brady earned the first from the University of Illinois in 1916, followed by Edward Marion Augustus

Chandler at the same institution the following year. Burkett, Burkett, and Gates, *Black Biography*, 135; Quay and Denison, *Negro in the Chemical Industry*.

63. The Swann Chemical Company brought together the Southern Manganese Corporation, the Southern Manganese Mining Corporation, the Southern Manganese Land Company, the Federal Carbide Company, the Jax Plant Food Company, and the Federal Phosphorus Company. "Chemical Kaleidoscope for 1930," 7; Forrestal, *Faith, Hope, and $5,000*, 30.

Chapter Three

1. Interview with Opal Scruggs, September 25, 2003; "Mitchell Hill Area," Model City–Anniston Photos, donated by Opal Scruggs, PLACC; Monsanto, "Plant History—Anniston," ca. 1986, PLACC; *Alabama City Directory*, 1931 (Birmingham: R. L. Polk and Co., 1931), 1; Penning, "Swann Corporation," 151; interview with Opal Scruggs, September 25, 2003.

2. Griffith and Satterfield, *Triumphs and Troubles*, 52–55. The second version comes from Chester H. Penning, a chemist at Swann Research Inc., Birmingham, Ala., "Diphenyl and Diphenyl Derivatives."

3. Griffith and Satterfield, *Triumphs and Troubles*, 54.

4. Hubert Kay, "Monsanto and the American Idea," June 1958, C-40, series 6, box 1, Hubert Kay (first draft), Monsanto Records. German chemists Gustav Schultz and H. Schmidt described the synthesis of chlorinated biphenyl compounds in "Ueber Diphenylbasen." Translation by Emory University research chemist Stefan Lutz, personal communication, December 27, 2004. In patent no. 2,034,580, "Chlorinated Diphenyl-Sulphur Mixtures" (filed April 21, 1930), Russell L. Jenkins and Glennon Hardy state that "other methods of producing chlorinated diphenyl are described in Liebig's *Annalen der Chemie*," 189 (1877): 135–45.

5. Jenkins, McCullough, and Booth, "Syntheses in the Diphenyl Series," 32; Thomas J. Scott of Foley, Ala., assignor to Swann Research Inc., "Process and Apparatus for the Production of Diphenyl" (filed June 2, 1928), no. 1,894,283; Russell L. Jenkins, assignor to Swann Research Inc., "Process for the Production of Chlorinated Diaryls" (filed September 28, 1929), no. 1,892,397.

6. Penning, "Diphenyl and Diphenyl Derivatives," 153; "Contributions of the Monsanto, Illinois, Plants of the Monsanto Chemical Company to the War Effort," talk given at the East St. Louis Forum, City Club, April 29, 1943, by William G. Krummrich, 7–8, Monsanto Business, series 10, box 3A, Monsanto Records; Penning, "Physical Characteristics and Commercial Possibilities."

7. Griffith and Satterfield, *Triumphs and Troubles*, 55. The trade name "Aroclor" appears in Russell L. Jenkins and Glennon Hardy, "Chlorinated Diphenyl-Sulphur Mixtures" (filed April 21, 1930), no. 2,034,580. Analysis of Aroclors shipments using figures from "Operating Costs at Anniston," series 10, box 31, Monsanto Records; Jonathan Sapers, "Monsanto: The Wizard Now Sleeps," *Anniston Star*, October 27, 1985; "Operating Costs at Anniston," series 10, box 31, Monsanto Records.

8. Federal Phosphorus Company vice president B. G. Klugh to Dr. Charles H. Herty, February 21, 1929, box 94, folder 13, Herty Collection.

9. The percentage of weekly payroll paid to hourly employees declined from 53 percent of the total in 1928 to 40 percent in 1930. Analysis using figures from "Operating Costs at Anniston," series 10, box 31, Monsanto Records.

10. Foster Eaton, "Glowing Picture of Industrial Dixie Painted by Scientists," *Anniston Star*, April 10, 1930.

11. Griffith and Satterfield, *Triumphs and Troubles*, 41–42.

12. Ibid., 32, 115, 16. According to historian J. Wayne Flynt, Governor Bibb Graves coined the term "Big Mules." Flynt, *Alabama in the Twentieth Century*, 63.

13. Forrestal, *Faith, Hope, and $5,000*, 81; Griffith and Satterfield, *Triumphs and Troubles*, 74–75; Penning, "Swann Corporation," 151; H. C. Godt Jr., "Organizational Chronology of Monsanto Domestic Operating Units Including Major Acquisitions and Divestitures," August 1997, Oversize materials, Monsanto Records.

14. Forrestal, *Faith, Hope, and $5,000*, 81; Griffith and Satterfield, *Triumphs and Troubles*, 88.

15. J. Ralph McNaron, "Industries in Anniston Are Vital Factors," *Anniston Times*, June 4, 1935; Griffith and Satterfield, *Triumphs and Troubles*, 88–89; Forrestal, *Faith, Hope, and $5,000*, 79; "Swann Merger Near: Federal Body Must Okay," *Anniston Star*, Sunday, May 5, 1935, 1; Griffith and Satterfield, *Triumphs and Troubles*, 89–90. Along with Swann Mining in Tennessee, the research arm appears also to have been absorbed into the Monsanto structure in the latter half of the decade. H. C. Godt Jr., "Organizational Chronology of Monsanto Domestic Operating Units Including Major Acquisitions and Divestitures," August 1997, Oversize materials, Monsanto Records; Griffith and Satterfield, *Triumphs and Troubles*, 110.

16. Hubert Kay, "Monsanto and the American Idea," June 1958, F-56, C-40, series 6, box 1, Hubert Kay (first draft), Monsanto Records; Francis J. Curtis, "Early Days," December 9, 1950, 3, series 10, box 3, folder: Monsanto Company History (Historical Accounts, Gaston DuBois), Monsanto Records; Aftalion, *History of the International Chemical Industry*, 176.

17. Interview with Howard K. Nason by James E. McKee, July 24, 1981; Forrestal, *Faith, Hope, and $5,000*, 48.

18. Cobb, *Selling of the South*, 1; Forrestal, *Faith, Hope, and $5,000*, 79; Edgar M. Queeny, "The Chemical Industry Turns to the South," *Manufacturers Record*, August 1933, 19.

19. Edgar M. Queeny, "The Chemical Industry Turns to the South," *Manufacturers Record*, August 1933, 18; Monsanto Chemical Company, "How Monsanto Serves: The Story of the Monsanto Chemical Company" (St. Louis, 1938): 12, Anniston—Monsanto, PLACC; Cobb, *Selling of the South*, 229.

20. Jonathan Daniels, "A Native at Large," *The Nation*, August 14, 1940, 135; Federal Writers' Program (Alabama), *Alabama: A Guide to the Deep South*, 159; Daniels, "A Native at Large," *The Nation*, August 14, 1940, 135.

21. "Queeny Thanks Local Group for Welcome," *Anniston Star*, May 17, 1935; "Swann Company Name Is Changed," *Anniston Star*, August 7, 1935; Harry A. Kuhn, Captain, Chemical Warfare Service, through the Chief of the CWS, to Executive Officer, Pittsburgh C. W. Procurement District, June 1, 1935, Index Briefs 400.123/2014, Records of the Chemical School, Fort McClellan, Ala., Records of

the Chemical Warfare Service, 1917–63, RG 175, NARA-DC; Forrestal, *Faith, Hope, and $5,000*, 79; Griffith and Satterfield, *Triumphs and Troubles*, 93.

22. Price, "Health Problems," 1159; Colten, "Historical Questions," 8; Haynes, *Men, Money, and Molecules*, 63.

23. Christopher Sellers, *Hazards of the Job*, 42; Baskerville, "American Chemist," 768; Edsall, "Diseases"; Christopher Sellers, *Hazards of the Job*, 53.

24. Christopher Sellers, *Hazards of the Job*, 61; Baskerville, "American Chemist," 768; Charles Baskerville to A. G. Howe, July 6, 1916, 1, MSS 8, box 20, item 39, Herty Collection; Christopher Sellers, *Hazards of the Job*, 138–40.

25. Baskerville, "Symposium on Occupational Diseases."

26. Ibid.

27. Ibid.

28. Hubert Kay, "Monsanto and the American Idea," June 1958, F-46–47, C-40, series 6, box 1, Hubert Kay (first draft), Monsanto Records.

29. Ibid.

30. Nickell, "Coal-Tar," 9, Monsanto Records (my emphasis).

31. Ibid. (my emphasis). Nickell left Sauget to head Monsanto Chemicals Ltd. before Monsanto began producing PCBs there in 1936. Forrestal, *Faith, Hope, and $5,000*, 90; "John F. Queeny's Office," series 1, box 1, Queeny Room, Monsanto Records.

32. Griffith and Satterfield, *Triumphs and Troubles*, 43; Steen, "Patents, Patriotism," 91; Hubert Kay, "Monsanto and the American Idea," June 1958, C-31 C-40, series 6, box 1, Hubert Kay (first draft), Monsanto Records; Griffith and Satterfield, *Triumphs and Troubles*, 43; National Agricultural Safety Database, http://www.cdc.gov/nasd/docs/d001501-d001600/d001519/d001519.html (July 24, 2006); Penning, "Swann Corporation," 150.

33. Interview with Dr. Gordon Rodgers Jr., February 5, 2005.

34. Matson, "Polychlorinated Biphenyl (PCB) Emissions from Monsanto Anniston," 1; Dr. Charles Holmes Herty, box 142, folder 2, Daybooks, 1921–22, November 14, 1922, Herty Collection.

35. Tarr, *Search for the Ultimate Sink*, 344, 345; Melosi, *Sanitary City*, 162; Besselievre, "Statutory Regulation of Stream Pollution," 225. Prompted by a typhoid outbreak, Alabama's 1907 stream pollution law focused on sewage in the greater Birmingham area, Public Affairs Research Council of Alabama, *The History of the Jefferson County Sanitary Sewer System* (Birmingham, Ala.: Jefferson County Commission, 2001), 19.

36. A "sanitary survey" of conditions in nearby Birmingham carried out in 1918 yielded the following advice under the heading "Industrial Hygiene": "Inspection should not be limited to the detection of gross unsanitary conditions but should be done by trained individuals who can detect the different hazards peculiar to a given plant. This would prevent many cases of industrial accidents and industrial sickness." Kennedy, "Sanitary Survey of Birmingham"; Alabama State Board of Health, *Annual Report*, 19.

37. "Health Week's Structure Is Revamped," *New Journal and Guide*, November 22, 1930; "Negro Health Service Work Is Begun Here," *Anniston Star*, December 4, 1930.

38. "Colored People Make Plans for Raising Own Food," *Anniston Star*, March 16, 1932; "Negroes Will Begin Clean-up Drive Sunday," *Anniston Star*, April 1, 1932; "First Report Made in Chest Canning Drive," *Anniston Star*, August 26, 1931; "Canvass Made of Houses for Canned Goods," *Anniston Star*, September 27, 1931; "C. Jacob Jones Makes Appeal to Colored People," *Anniston Star*, April 30, 1933; "Negro Health Worker Faces an Operation," *Anniston Star*, December 10, 1931; "Vets Registered at Legion Hall," *Anniston Star*, September 27, 1931; C. Jacob Jones, in "Negro Health Service Leader Moves Office," *Anniston Star*, February 26, 1931.

39. Medical Association of the State of Alabama, *Transactions*, 38, 37.

40. "Diphenyl and Chlorinated Diphenyl Derivatives" (1935), Plaintiff's Exhibit 4A002, 114, *Abernathy* documents; R. Williams to B. O. Severson, January 20, 1971, Plaintiff's Exhibit 4A12, *Abernathy* documents. Williams lists the workers who sued as Craig Slaughter, Ollie Slaughter, James Hartsfield, and a man named Henderson. The 1935 Anniston City Directory lists Hugh L. Henderson and Hugh L. Henderson Sr. of 1628 Cooper Street both as laborers at Monsanto and designates them "C" for "Colored."

41. "Diphenyl and Aroclor Organization Chart," appendix to "Diphenyl and Chlorinated Diphenyl Derivatives," June 1935, *Abernathy* documents. Relative to other industries, "labor was not a major component of the chemical industry's production costs," wrote Fred Aftalion in 1991 (*History of the International Chemical Industry*, 169).

42. Jones and Alden, "Acneform Dermatergosis," 1027. The workers examined by Jones and Alden in 1932 and 1933 would have worked at Monsanto's Anniston plant, the only U.S. producer of PCBs at the time. Monsanto did not begin making PCBs at Sauget, Illinois, until after 1935. Mark H. Hermanson, "Polychlorinated Biphenyls in Tree Bark near the Former Manufacturing Site in Sauget, Illinois, USA," Presentation at the VI International PCB Workshop, Visby, Sweden, June 1, 2010.

43. Jones and Alden, "Acneform Dermatergosis," 1024.

44. Ibid., 1033–34. See also Sulzberger, Rostenberg, and Sher, "Acneform Eruptions." Hormone research, mainly directed at developing inexpensive synthetic estrogens, intensified in the late 1930s (see Langston, *Toxic Bodies*, 31) but not until Theo Colborn and colleagues published *Our Stolen Future* in 1996 did awareness reach a broader public of the potential for chlorinated hydrocarbons to disrupt hormone function. Colborn, Myers, and Dumanoski, *Our Stolen Future*.

45. Frederick B. Flinn, "Report of Dr. Frederick B. Flinn of patch tests made on material received from Swann Research, Inc." (1934), 1, *Abernathy* documents. In a 1936 published report, Frederick Flinn and N. E. Jarvik concluded that "certain chlorinated naphthalenes or impurities contained within them" were "a possible etiologic agent in the factory cases." Flinn and Jarvik, "Action of Certain Chlorinated Naphthalenes."

46. "Diphenyl and Chlorinated Diphenyl Derivatives," June 1935, 114, *Abernathy* documents. For accounts of the Gauley Bridge incident, see Gottlieb, *Forcing the Spring*, 236–40; and Cherniack, *Hawk's Nest Incident*, 104. "Diphenyl and Chlorinated Diphenyl Derivatives," June 1935, 114, *Abernathy* documents.

47. Drinker, Warren, and Bennett, "Problem of Possible Systemic Effects," 283.

48. Bowen, *Family Portrait*; "Dr. C. K. Drinker: A Health Expert," *New York Times*, April 16, 1956.

49. See Christopher Sellers, *Hazards of the Job*, for a detailed account of these developments in the field of industrial medicine.

50. Nash, *Inescapable Ecologies*, 211; Curran, *Founders of the Harvard School of Public Health*, 200.

51. Walter B. Cannon to Harvard president A. Lawrence Lowell, June 14, 1920, box 1, folder 29, Cecil Kent Drinker Papers, 1898–1958, H MS c165, HML; Christopher Sellers, *Hazards of the Job*, 153; George E. Vincent, president of the Rockefeller Foundation, to David L. Edsall, dean of the Harvard Medical School, December 11, 1919, E72.5.A1, box 1, folder: Letters and Papers, 1918–20, Harvard School of Public Health, Industrial Hygiene Dept., HML.

52. Sandford Brown to Dr. Cecil K. Drinker, October 25, 1937, E72.A2, box 2, folder: Industrial Hygiene Dept., Halowax Gift, 1937, and Sandford Brown to Dr. Cecil K. Drinker, April 30, 1936, E72.A2, box 3, folder: Physiology Dept., Halowax Gift, 1936–37, both in Harvard School of Public Health, Dean's Files, 1922–49, HML; Sicherman and Hamilton, *Alice Hamilton*, 283.

53. Drinker, Warren, and Bennett, "Problem of Possible Systemic Effects."

54. Ibid., 285, 298.

55. Ibid., 296.

56. Report to the Monsanto Chemical Company, 5, 7, 8, *Abernathy* documents.

57. Drinker, Warren, and Bennett, "Problem of Possible Systemic Effects," 298–99, 296. Also see Drinker, *Report to Monsanto*. This report to Monsanto was published in two sections (September 15, 1938, *Abernathy* documents).

58. Christopher Sellers, *Hazards of the Job*, 179; Drinker, Warren, and Bennett, "Problem of Possible Systemic Effects." Halogenated compounds refer to combinations with any of the elements in the chemical table in the halogen family, including fluorine, chlorine, bromine, iodine. Regarding brand names, see Drinker, Warren, and Bennett, "Problem of Possible Systemic Effects," 283n; Greenburg, "Chlorinated Naphthalenes," 521; and Carson, *Silent Spring*, 304.

59. Drinker, Warren, and Bennett, "Problem of Possible Systemic Effects," 311. At least two other papers based on the studies in Drinker's lab also appeared in the *Journal*: Bennett, Drinker, and Warren, "Morphological Changes"; and Yaglou, Sands, and Drinker, "Ventilation of Wire."

60. Drinker, Warren, and Bennett, "Problem of Possible Systemic Effects," 307.

61. Ibid.; Emmet Kelly to Louis Spolyar, February 14, 1950, CHEMEWG.

62. Tebbens, "Portable Combustion Apparatus"; Drinker, Warren, and Bennett, "Problem of Possible Systemic Effects," 303.

63. L. A. Watt, Memo, October 11, 1937, CHEMEWG (my emphasis).

64. *Gentry v. Swann* (1937) (emphasis in original).

65. Ibid. (my emphasis).

66. Drinker, "Further Observations on Possible Systemic Toxicity," 157; R. Emmet Kelly to J. W. Barrett, September 20, 1955, CHEMEWG; Mark Hermanson, *Abernathy* transcript, January 16, 2002.

67. Monsanto Chemical Company, *1944 Monsanto Salesmen's Manual*, 5, *Aberna-thy* documents.

68. Ibid., 6–8, 19.

69. "Diphenyl and Chlorinated Diphenyl Derivatives," June 1935, 115, *Abernathy* documents; E. Mather, "Process for the Production of Aroclors, Pyranols, etc., at the Anniston and at the W. G. Krummrich Plant" (St. Louis: Monsanto, 1955), Plaintiff's Exhibit 3E1, XI-4, *Abernathy* documents.

70. "A. C. W. Pennington of Newport, Reporting on His American Tour," December 29, 1950, 5;. E. Mather, "Process for the Production of Aroclors, Pyranols, etc., at the Anniston and at the W. G. Krummrich Plant" (St. Louis: Monsanto, 1955), Plaintiff's Exhibit 3E1, XI-4, *Abernathy* documents.

71. Foristall, "Merit of Monsanto," 6; Monsanto Annual Report, 1937, PLACC; Forrestal, *Faith, Hope, and $5,000*, 59.

72. Dan Forrestal describes the 1939 formation of the new public relations unit, the Department of Advertising and Monsanto Practice (*Faith, Hope, and $5,000*, 59).

73. "It's Plastics Picking Time down South," *Fortune*, September 1939, 13, artwork by Felix Schmidt.

74. Monsanto Chemical Works, "The Downfall of a Popular Misconception," December 4, 1930, series 3, box 1, Products (Coal Tar), Monsanto Records; Hubert A. Kay, "Meaning of Monsanto," 9; "It's Plastics Picking Time down South," *Fortune*, September 1939, 13, artwork by Felix Schmidt.

75. "It's Plastics Picking Time down South," *Fortune*, September 1939, 13, artwork by Felix Schmidt.

76. Colborn, Myers, and Dumanoski, *Our Stolen Future*, 89; Minutes of the Monsanto Research Directors Meeting, St. Louis, November 14–15, 1940, 26, 1, series 10, box 1, Monsanto Records (emphasis in original).

Chapter Four

1. "Chemicals Just Coming into Own, Says Monsanto Official," *Anniston Star*, July 25, 1943.

2. "General Summerall Will Read Order Promoting Post," *Birmingham News-Herald*, June 30, 1929; H. Brandt Ayers, *In Love with Defeat*, 17; Stoker, "From Prohibitionist to New Deal Liberal," 263; Forrestal, *Faith, Hope, and $5,000*, 82–83.

3. Interview with Georgia Calhoun, June 10, 2005; Miles Denham, "Anniston Still Growing as Military Installations Expand," *Birmingham Post-Herald*, February 4, 1953; ADPH, *Annual Report*, 350–51.

4. Brophy, Miles, and Cochrane, *Chemical Warfare Service: From Laboratory to Field*, 52; "Chemical Division (Monsanto Chemical Co.)," July 3, 1936, Index Briefs, box 488, entry no. 2, NARA-DC; "Chemical History of the U.S.," *New York Herald Tribune*, September 2, 1951, 7.

5. Edgar Queeny, "Says War Will Hurt Chemical Industry Here: Monsanto Head Declares Contrary Public Belief Is Erroneous," *Baltimore Evening Sun*, April 17, 1939.

6. *General History of Monsanto Chemical Company*, part 8, "Actions under Antitrust Laws," 1945, 22, indictments no. 1267 and no. 1269, series 10, box 3, Monsanto Records.

7. Monsanto news release, August 17, [1942,] series 10, box 4, Monsanto Records.

8. Brophy, Miles, and Cochrane, *Chemical Warfare Service: From Laboratory to Field*, 254–55, 328–29, 451.

9. Charles Belknap to Henry L. Stimson, December 8, 1941, series 10, box 4, Monsanto Records; Forrestal, *Faith, Hope, and $5,000*, 95; Charles Belknap to James W. Irwin, June 30, 1942; E. W. Reid, War Production Board chief, Chemicals Branch, to Charles Belknap, July 27, 1942, series 10, box 4, Monsanto Records.

10. Forrestal, *Faith, Hope, and $5,000*, 103; Brophy, Miles, and Cochrane, *Chemical Warfare Service: From Laboratory to Field*, 53, 374. Monsanto continued to supply white phosphorus after the war. Procurement Objective Information on Lists I & II Principal Items, schedule no. 5846, Atlanta Chemical Procurement, October 4, 1950, folder CPD, Production Objective Info., Records of the Atlanta Chemical Procurement District, RG 156, NARA-Morrow.

11. Interview with Howard K. Nason by James E. McKee, July 24, 1981, 15, series 10, box 3, Monsanto Co. History (Oral History Project), Monsanto Records.

12. Brophy, Miles, and Cochrane, *Chemical Warfare Service: From Laboratory to Field*, 92; Allan D. Farquhar, assistant director of naval intelligence, to Charles Belknap, November 9, 1937, series 10, box 3A, Monsanto Records.

13. "Monsanto Chemical Company's Part in the War Effort," February 5, 1943, 5, series 10, box 3A, Monsanto Business, Monsanto Records; William G. Krummrich, "Contribution of the Monsanto, Illinois Plants of the Monsanto Chemical Company to the War Effort," April 29, 1943, 7–8, series 10, box 3A, Monsanto Business, Monsanto Records.

14. Rear Admiral H. A. Wiley, USN, to E. M. Queeny, April 21, 1942, series 10, box 3A, Monsanto Records; "Awarding of 'E' Is Impressive Ceremony Here," *Anniston Times*, January 23, 1942; "Monsanto Chemical Company's Part in the War Effort," February 5, 1943, 15, series 10, box 3A, Monsanto Business, Monsanto Records.

15. Monsanto press release, January 14, 1942, series 10, box 3A, Monsanto Records; "Awarding of 'E' Is Impressive Ceremony Here," *Anniston Times*, January 23, 1942; "Silent Shrapnel," *Monsanto Magazine*, October 1942, 4–7; Telegram from James W. Irwin to Ensign Thad Brown, January 17, 1941, series 10, box 4, Products, War-Related, Monsanto Records; "Monsanto Chemical Company's Part in the War Effort," February 5, 1943, 6, series 10, box 3A, Monsanto Business, Monsanto Records; "Contributions of the Monsanto, Illinois, Plants of the Monsanto Chemical Company to the War Effort," talk given at the East St. Louis Forum, City Club, April 29, 1943, by William G. Krummrich, 8, series 10, box 3A, Monsanto Business, Monsanto Records.

16. "A. C. W. Pennington of Newport, Reporting on His American Tour," December 29, 1950, 5; E. Mather, "Process for the Production of Aroclors," XI-4, *Abernathy* documents; Van Strum, *Bitter Fog*, 69–70; Monsanto Chemical Company, 1944 Monsanto Salesmen's Manual, Army-Navy Aeronautical Specification, prepared October 8, 1943, 27, *Abernathy* documents; Greenburg, "Chlorinated

Naphthalenes"; P. G. Benignus to T. K. Smith (Monsanto, St. Louis), February 29, 1952, 2, CHEMEWG.

17. Greenburg, "Chlorinated Naphthalenes," 520–22; Bowen, *Family Portrait*, 257.

18. Major General Alden H. Waitt, chief, Chemical Warfare Service to Charles Belknap, July 26, 1946, series 10, box 3, Monsanto Company History (World War II) (Commendatory letters), Monsanto Records. For the year ending May 31, 1945, Monsanto ranked fifth by sales volume, behind DuPont, Union Carbide, Allied Chemical, and Dow, "Monsanto's Place in the Chemical Industry," I-7, Monsanto, General to 1947, series 10, box 4, Monsanto Records; Forrestal, *Faith, Hope, and $5,000*, 81–82, 102.

19. "The Chem World This Week," *Chemical and Engineering News*, 31, no. 22 (June 1953): 2281; Weiss, *Manpower, Chemistry and Agriculture*, 2.

20. Thornton, *Pandora's Poison*, 237.

21. Jack House, "War Role of Ft. McClellan," *Birmingham News-Age-Herald*, September 9, 1945; Camp Sibert, Parsons Environmental Services, "Former Camp Sibert CWM Site, Engineering Evaluation/Cost Analysis," http://www.projectost.com/sibert/public/index.shtml (August 16, 2004).

22. Hugh E. Rozelle, clerk, to Senator Lister Hill to Dwight T. Raff, president, Kiwanis Club of Talladega, August 21, 1946, box 184, folder 124, Hill Papers; Vance Johnson and Carroll Kilpatrick, "Future of Ft. McClellan Depends Largely on Army's Appropriation," *Birmingham News-Age-Herald*, May 18, 1947; Harry M. Ayers to Hon. John Sparkman, March 23, 1951, box 186, folder 132, Hill Papers.

23. "Report of Survey Team for Relocation of Chemical Corps School and Replacement Training Center," October 1950, School Relocation, Records of the Chemical School, Fort McClellan, Ala., Records of the Chemical Warfare Service, 1917–63, RG 175, NARA-CP.

24. Frederick W. Gerhard to Commanding General, Chemical Corps, November 1, 1950, and Colonel Geoffrey Marshall to Chief Chemical Officer, Department of the Army, October 9, 1950, School Relocation, Records of the Chemical School, Fort McClellan, Ala., Records of the Chemical Warfare Service, 1917–63, RG 175, NARA-CP; Memorandum from J. G. Cohen to Major Ellicott, Edgewood Arsenal, "Industrial Development of the Chemical Warfare Service Organization," November 1918, box 96, folder 8, Herty Collection.

25. Herb Tittel to Colonel Harry M. Ayers, February 19, 1951, box 174, folder 402, Ayers Papers; Monsanto Chemical Company, Detail Listing of All Charges, Letter Contract DA-18-108-CML-1879, General Correspondence, Commercial Series, 1955–58, folder 161, Monsanto Chemical Company, Records of the Chemical School, Fort McClellan, Ala., Records of the Chemical Warfare Service, 1917–63, RG 175, NARA-CP; Universal Oil Processes Inc., Lehman Brothers Collection, Twentieth Century Business Archives, Harvard Business School Baker Library Historical Collections, http://www.library.hbs.edu/hc/lehman/chrono.html?company=universal_oil_processes_inc (May 17, 2012). Chemical engineer Jim Tarr, a PCB plaintiffs' witness who had worked at Monsanto's Chocolate Bayou, Texas, plant from 1969 to 1972, cited as his authority Army document

4790-T, "Statement of Significant Steps in the Development and Production of E101 Clusters." Jim Tarr, deposition in *Owens v. Monsanto* (2001), March 8, 2001, 188–89.

26. *Monsanto Record Buster*, June 1953, E4.

27. Thomas F. Hill, "Chemical Corps 'Breaks' Ground for New Training Center—and It's All Quite a Show," *Birmingham News*, November 27, 1952.

28. The Fort McClellan Records (Carlisle, Penn.: U.S. Army Military History Institute, 2002), http//www.mcclellan.army.mil/complete.htm (September 6, 2003); Miles Denham, "Anniston Still Growing as Military Installations Expand," *Birmingham Post-Herald*, February 4, 1953.

29. "List of Current School Publications," Chemical Corps School, Chemical Corps Training Command, Fort McClellan, Ala., revised September 2, 1952, 6, 16, 20, 23, box 4, mimeo no. 8, Records of the Chemical School, Fort McClellan, Ala., Records of the Chemical Warfare Service, 1917–63, RG 175, NARA-CP.

30. Mauroni, *America's Struggle with Chemical-Biological Warfare*, 47, 52. Fort McClellan's commander in 1969, Colonel William McKean, maintained that no open air tests were conducted: "The post uses small amounts of mustard gas in training operations. Mustard is not a nerve gas." "Army Says No Open Air Nerve Gas Tests Held at McClellan," *Birmingham News*, July 13, 1969. Interview with John Lawry, November 19, 2004.

31. Colonel Richard R. Danek, deputy commander, Report of Inspection to Commanding Officer, January 26, 1953, 1–2, 12–13, quoted in Colonel John R. Burns, commandant of the Chemical Corps School, Report of Inspection to the Commandant at the Chemical Corps School at Fort McClellan, prepared January 31, 1953, box 6, "Environmental Surveys," Records of the Chemical School, Fort McClellan, Ala., Records of the Chemical Warfare Service, 1917–63, RG 175, NARA-CP.

32. Thomas A. Mitchell, Major, Cml C, Secretary to Commanding Officer, Cml C Tng Comd, May 4, 1953, Chemical Corps—Project 845: 1, Records of the Chemical School, Fort McClellan, Ala., Records of the Chemical Warfare Service, 1917–63, RG 175, NARA-CP.

33. "Paper Claims Germ Attack on McClellan," *Birmingham News*, December 22, 1976; "Army Germ Warfare Tests Conducted in Eight Areas," *Birmingham Post-Herald*, December 23, 1976. The State Bureau of Vital Statistics showed that pneumonia cases in Calhoun County "jumped from 42 in 1950 to 98 in 1951 and to 333 in 1952, before dropping to 139 in 1953 and 98 in 1954." "Calhoun [Gets] Pneumonia When Army 'Germ Tests,'" *Birmingham News*, December 23, 1976; Frederick Burger, "Fort Site of Germ Warfare Tests," *Anniston Star*, March 9, 1977.

34. Forrestal, *Faith, Hope, and $5,000*, 113; Minutaglio, *City on Fire*; Stephens, *Texas City Disaster*.

35. *Dalehite v. United States* (1953), 51.

36. Ibid., 52.

37. Van Strum, *Bitter Fog*, 69–70; Zack and Suskind, "Mortality Experience." For an account of Agent Orange production and litigation, see Martini, *Agent Orange: History, Science, and the Politics of Uncertainty*. Health studies of the Nitro workers conducted by researchers hired by Monsanto and published in the 1980s showed

"no apparent increase in total mortality" in the dioxin-exposed workers. These studies were later found to be flawed. EPA chemist Cate Jenkins identified several methodological flaws in the Monsanto-sponsored studies of 2, 4, 5-T: exclusion of workers with no obvious chloracne from the study population, failure to exclude workers with other chemical rashes from the exposed group, and including as "non-exposed" workers from the same plant. EPA, "Cate Jenkins, Ph.D., . . . to John West, Special Agent." A later study found cancer mortality to be "slightly but significantly elevated in the overall cohort." Fingerhut, Halperin, et al., "Cancer Mortality."

38. "Queeny Is King: Monsanto Board Chairman Spurs Firm to New Peaks," *Forbes*, May 15, 1949, 20.

39. Federal Writers' Program (Alabama), *Alabama: A Guide to the Deep South*, 160; interview with Georgia Calhoun, June 10, 2004; Deed record, *Owens* Archive; Marshall, Kinney, and Hudson, "Incineration of Chemical Weapons in Anniston," 150.

40. Robert Brown, "Toxicity of the 'Arochlors,'" 35, 33.

41. "On October 27, 1947 Mr. Barbre of the Krummrich plant sent a copy of the journal to Dr. Jenkins at Anniston for comment"; "Aroclors: Toxicity," E. Mather to Mr. P. J. C. Haywood, December 11, 1951, E. Mather, "Process for the Production of Aroclors, Pyranols, etc., at the Anniston and at the W. G. Krummrich Plant" (St. Louis: Monsanto, 1955), Plaintiff's Exhibit 3E1, XI-2, *Abernathy* documents; *Monsanto Record Buster*, June 1953, E4, PLACC.

42. P. G. Benignus to T. K. Smith (Monsanto, St. Louis), February 29, 1952, 2, CHEMEWG; E. Mather, "Process for the Production of Aroclors," VI-35, XI-5, *Abernathy* documents.

43. E. Mather, "Process for the Production of Aroclors," XI-5, *Abernathy* documents.

44. Dr. Emmet Kelly to Dr. J. W. Barrett in London, September 20, 1955, 1, *Abernathy* documents.

45. "Many of Monsanto's Top Men Got Early Training at Plant; Instrument Failure Blamed for April Monsanto Blast," *Charleston (W.Va.) Gazette*, June 14, 1957; Michael Gordon, "Monsanto: The Continent's Parathion Capital," *Anniston Star*, January 23, 1983; interview with Glynn Young, July 15, 2004; ATSDR, *Toxicological Profile for Methyl Parathion*, 4; "Parathion by Monsanto at Anniston."

46. "Many of Monsanto's Top Men Got Early Training at Plant in City," *Anniston Star*, n.d., ca. July 1957; Rob Jordan, "Maker of 1080 May Face Time of Change," *Anniston Star*, August 8, 2005; interview with Edmund Greene by James E. McKee, December 31, 1981, 33, series 10, box 3, Monsanto Co. History (Oral History Project), Monsanto Records.

47. Forrestal, *Faith, Hope, and $5,000*, 58–59, 170; "Plastics Fair," *Monsanto Annual Report*, 1955, 20.

48. Forrestal, *Faith, Hope, and $5,000*, 252–53.

49. Ibid., 79; Griffith and Satterfield, *Triumphs and Troubles*, 93.

50. Interview with Ralph C. Piper by James E. McKee, September 11, 1981, 32–33, series 10, box 3, Monsanto Co. History (Oral History Project), Monsanto Records; Forrestal, *Faith, Hope, and $5,000*, 81, 257.

51. Interview with Ralph C. Piper by James E. McKee, September 11, 1981, 34–36, series 10, box 3, Monsanto Co. History (Oral History Project), Monsanto Records.

52. Ibid.

53. Ibid.

54. Monsanto Chemical Company, "How Monsanto Serves: The Story of the Monsanto Chemical Company" (St. Louis, 1938), 12, Anniston—Monsanto, PLACC; Forrestal, *Faith, Hope, and $5,000*, 48; interview with Howard K. Nason by James E. McKee, July 24, 1981, 15, series 10, box 3, Monsanto Co. History (Oral History Project), Monsanto Records, 9; Hubert Kay, "Monsanto and the American Idea," June 1958, P-1, C-40, series 6, box 1, Hubert Kay (first draft), Monsanto Records; Monsanto Annual Report, 1960, 14.

55. Forrestal, *Faith, Hope, and $5,000*, 98; Christensen, *Dictionary of Missouri Biography*, 634–35; Queeny, *Spirit of Enterprise*, 241, 76.

56. Forrestal, *Faith, Hope, and $5,000*, 65.

57. Queeny, *Latuko* (1951); Queeny, *Pagan Sudan* (1952); Queeny, *We Saw Primeval Man* (1951). For a detailed discussion of Edgar Queeny's films, see Staples, "Safari Ethnography," 173–258, 214.

58. Queeny, *Spirit of Enterprise*, 37–38.

59. "Chemical Corps Lesson Plan, Army Organization: History, Organization, Mission, and Activities of Chemical Corps, Course for Chemical Staff Specialists at the U.S. Army Chemical Corps School, Fort McClellan, Alabama," February 10, 1961, 5, file I508-A-534.1, Records of the Chemical School, Fort McClellan, Ala., Records of the Chemical Warfare Service, 1917–63, RG 175, NARA-CP; "The Atom: The Peril of Strontium 90," *Time*, May 6, 1957; Souder, *On a Farther Shore*, 294–95; Harris and Paxman, *Higher Form of Killing*, 186–87, 204.

60. Schneir, "Campaign to Make Chemical Warfare Respectable,"; Harris and Paxman, *Higher Form of Killing*, 204–6.

61. Harris and Paxman, *Higher Form of Killing*, 206.

62. "Ft. McClellan Unit Observes Anniversary," *Montgomery Advertiser*, April 8, 1960; "Ft. McClellan Schedules Big 'Dixie Day,'" *Birmingham News*, July 1, 1960.

63. "Chemical Corps Command United with McClellan," *Birmingham News*, June 2, 1962; interview with ANCDF public affairs officer Michael Abrams, August 20, 2003.

64. Charlie Grainger, "Some Grumbling, of Course, but Morale Mostly Good," *Birmingham News*, December 3, 1961; Dwight D. Eisenhower, "Farewell Address," January 17, 1961, http://www.eisenhower.archives.gov/farewell.htm (July 16, 2006); Mauroni, *America's Struggle with Chemical-Biological Warfare*, 50, 25.

Chapter Five

1. Interview with Imogene Baker, September 17, 2003.

2. The outcome in Winnsboro could have been much worse, Thomas recounted later. Released from jail, he escaped a waiting mob thanks only to the aid of a passing black motorist. Interview with Hank Thomas, March 8, 2013. For detailed chronicles of the Freedom Riders in Anniston, see Arsenault, *Freedom Riders*, 135, 140–49; and Sprayberry, "'Town among the Trees,'" 236–71.

3. Thomas Noland, "Freedom Ride: FBI Papers Indicate City Police Didn't Act When Violence Started aboard a Trailways Bus," *Anniston Star*, September 26, 1978; Arsenault, *Freedom Riders*, 143.

4. Sam Jones, "Investigator Hero in Attack on Bus," *Anniston Star*, May 15, 1961; Hank Thomas, at the ground-breaking for the Freedom Riders Park, Anniston, October 18, 2012.

5. Interview with Imogene Baker, September 17, 2003.

6. Janie Forsyth remembers being taunted by her high school peers for having helped the Riders. Interview with Janie Forsyth McKinney, May 11, 2011; Cooper, "They Had a Dream"; Arsenault, *Freedom Riders*, 146.

7. "Mob Rocks, Burns Big Bus in County Racial Incidents: Four Hospitalized after Disorders," *Anniston Star*, May 15, 1961; Thomas Noland, "Freedom Ride," *Anniston Star*, September 26, 1978.

8. Arsenault, *Freedom Riders*, 149–50; Sprayberry, "'Town among the Trees,'" 271.

9. In *NAACP v. Alabama* (1958), the U.S. Supreme Court overturned an Alabama court's ruling that blocked the NAACP from functioning in the state. Subsequent legal battles kept the organization from regaining its footing until 1964, though its members continued their advocacy. Rogers et al., *Alabama: History of a Deep South State*, 569.

10. Sprayberry, "'Town among the Trees,'" 224–25.

11. Ibid., 223–25; interview with Rev. Nimrod Q. Reynolds, November 4, 2003; Sprayberry, "'Town among the Trees,'" 305; Phil Noble, *Beyond the Burning Bus*, 144. Rev. J. Phillips Noble is not related to the Nobles who cofounded Anniston.

12. Interview with Imogene Baker, September 17, 2003.

13. Ibid.

14. Ibid.; Molders Union, Local 414 Minutes, 1962–64, box 177, SLA.

15. Interview with Imogene Baker, September 17, 2003; interview with David Baker, March 26, 2004.

16. Interview with Imogene Baker, September 17, 2003; interview with David Baker, March 26, 2004.

17. Interview with Imogene Baker, September 17, 2003.

18. "Soldiers Patrol Streets of Alabama Town," *Pittsburgh Courier*, July 25, 1960.

19. James Chisom, "On-Base School Is Scheduled for Fort McClellan Students," *Anniston Star*, February 22, 1963; "Probe Pushed into Crowd Violence at Ft. McClellan," *Anniston Star*, November 15, 1971; J. Gregory Spoon, "Protestors Complete First Leg AAD March," *Anniston Star*, May 30, 1987; "Protestors March over Alleged Bias at Anniston Army Depot," *Birmingham News*, May 30, 1987.

20. "Oral History Interview of Aaron E. Henry," interview by T. H. Baker, conducted in Clarksdale, Miss., September 12, 1970, accession no. 78–108: 3, General Services Administration, National Archives and Records Service, Lyndon Baines Johnson Library, http://www.lbjlib.utexas.edu/johnson/archives.hom/oralhistory.hom/Henry-A/Henry.asp (April 28, 2004); Henry and Curry, *Aaron Henry*, 59.

21. Rogers et al., *Alabama: History of a Deep South State*, 62–63.

22. Davidson and Grofman, *Quiet Revolution*, 378–79. On the impact of international pressure on U.S. civil rights policy, see Dudziak, *Cold War Civil Rights*.

23. Morgan McVicar, "Some Bitterness in Those Indicted after Bus Burning," *Anniston Star*, May 14, 1981.

24. Jim Lowrey, "Adams Freed, Jury Eyes Fate of 7 in Bus Trial," *Anniston Star*, November 3, 1961; Sam Jones, "'No Contest' Pleas Made," *Anniston Star*, January 16, 1962; Sprayberry, "'Town among the Trees,'" 353–54; "Annistonian Shot, Listed Fairly Good," *Anniston Star*, November 10, 1969; Will Jones, "Victim Heard in Adams Trial," *Anniston Star*, April 23, 1970; Will Jones, "Adams Sentenced to Two-Year Term," *Anniston Star*, April 25, 1970.

25. Phil Noble, *Beyond the Burning Bus*, 51; Nan Woodruff, introduction to Phil Noble, *Beyond the Burning Bus*, 26; Dan Carter, *Politics of Rage*, 106–7, 139.

26. Braden, *Wall Between*, 24–25.

27. Ibid.

28. H. Brandt Ayers, *In Love with Defeat*, 105; Sprayberry, "'Town among the Trees,'" 188–91, 195, 189. Also see Pitts, *Problems of Journalism*, 72–98.

29. Stoker, "Harry Mell Ayers," 558.

30. Atlanta's path of "negotiated settlement" is detailed by George King in the radio documentary *Will the Circle Be Unbroken? A Personal History of the Civil Rights Movement and the Music of Those Times*, Atlanta: Southern Regional Council, 1997. Ron Gibson, "Seek Racial Answer, Rooster Club Advised," *Anniston Star*, May 18, 1961; Crespino, *In Search of Another Country*, 4.

31. Tyson, *Blood Done Sign My Name*, 268.

32. Anniston Chapter, Southern Christian Leadership Conference, 1, box: Chapters and Affiliated Chapters Files, folder: Alabama: Anniston/Calhoun County Chapter, circa 1980–96, MSS 1083, SCLC Papers.

33. Fosl, *Subversive Southerner*, 62–63; interviews with Gordon Rodgers Jr., February 5, 2005, and Representative Barbara Bigsby Boyd, February 25, 2005.

34. Molders Union, Local 414 Minutes, 1962–64, box 177, SLA; Sprayberry, "'Town among the Trees,'" 278, 398; Phil Noble, *Beyond the Burning Bus*, 89.

35. Phil Noble, *Beyond the Burning Bus*, 77, 88–89; Sprayberry, "'Town among the Trees,'" 286–87.

36. Sprayberry, "'Town among the Trees,'" 302.

37. Phil Noble, *Beyond the Burning Bus*, 36, 103–4; Sprayberry, "'Town among the Trees,'" 290.

38. "News Editor Has a New Job," *Jacksonville (Ala.) News*, June 11, 1969; Sprayberry, "'Town among the Trees,'" 188–90; H. Brandt Ayers, *In Love with Defeat*, 44.

39. Interview with Cleophus Thomas, July 15, 2003.

40. Interview with Rev. Nimrod Q. Reynolds, November 4, 2003.

41. Rev. William B. McClain, foreword to Phil Noble, *Beyond the Burning Bus*, 9–10.

42. Interview with Rev. Nimrod Q. Reynolds, November 4, 2003; interview with Rev. J. Phillips Noble, June 5, 2006; Phil Noble, *Beyond the Burning Bus*, 109.

43. Interview with Rev. Nimrod Q. Reynolds, November 4, 2003; Phil Noble, *Beyond the Burning Bus*, 112; H. Brandt Ayers, *In Love with Defeat*, 95.

44. Interview with Rev. Nimrod Q. Reynolds, November 4, 2003; author's notes, Fortieth Anniversary Commemoration, PLACC, September 13, 2003.

45. Author's notes, Fortieth Anniversary Commemoration; Sprayberry, "'Town among the Trees,'" 295.

46. Phil Noble, *Beyond the Burning Bus*, 117; See also H. Brandt Ayers's account of these events in *In Love with Defeat*, 93–96.

47. "The Anniston Manifesto," *Anniston Star*, September 13, 1964.

48. "Bomb Rips Interior of a Negro Church near Anniston, Ala.," *New York Times*, May 14, 1965.

49. John McCaa Jr., "Bullet Hits Negro Driving in County," *Anniston Star*, July 16, 1965. See accounts in Phil Noble, *Beyond the Burning Bus*, 131–33; and Sprayberry, "'Town among the Trees,'" 305, 314–25.

50. Jean Quillen, "Bullet from Body May Provide Clue in Ambush Killing," *Anniston Star*, July 19, 1965.

51. George Wallace gave $1,000 to the reward fund. Sprayberry, "'Town among the Trees,'" 333.

52. Sprayberry, "'Can We Say We Are All Innocent?'"; Sprayberry, "'Town among the Trees,'" 306–8; Sara Bullard, *Free at Last*, 20–21; Phil Noble, *Beyond the Burning Bus*, 134; John Neary, "Unprecedented Turn of Justice in the South," *Life*, December 17, 1965, 34.

53. Sprayberry, "'Town among the Trees,'" 304–52; Sherry Kughn, "Sprayberry Says Brewster Murder Shaped Local History," *Anniston Star*, January 11, 2006; U.S. Department of Justice, Federal Bureau of Investigation, Willie Brewster file, part 2, 123, copy in author's possession.

54. Rev. William B. McClain, foreword to Phil Noble, *Beyond the Burning Bus*, 9–10; interview with Rev. J. Phillips Noble, June 5, 2006.

55. U.S. Department of Justice, Federal Bureau of Investigation, Willie Brewster file, Memo to FBI, August 5, 1965, 3, copy in author's possession.

56. Rodgers received 1,101 of the 7,000 votes cast on March 20, 1962. On September 2, 1969, Rodgers later became the first African American elected to municipal office in Anniston, winning a seat on the city council by 3,429 votes to 2,433 for his opponent. Sprayberry, "'Town among the Trees,'" 278, 398; Phil Noble, *Beyond the Burning Bus*, 89.

57. Thomas S. Potts, "The Donoho School (formerly the Anniston Academy): The First Twenty Years, 1963–1983" (Anniston: Donoho School, 1983), 8, Subject Files, Anniston, Education, The Donoho School, PLACC; interview with Cleophus Thomas, July 15, 2003.

58. Egerton, "Profiles of Change," 8–10, 26–28; Sprayberry, "'Town among the Trees,'" 326 (n. 27).

59. Interview with Rev. Nimrod Q. Reynolds, November 4, 2003; "Talks in Doubt," *Anniston Star*, November 3, 1971. Janice Baker and Johnnie Mae Elston were the first black students to graduate from Wellborn High School in 1967. But discrimination continued, escalating as the number of black students slowly increased. Interview with Imogene Baker, September 17, 2003; interview with David Baker, March 26, 2004.

60. Interview with David Baker, March 26, 2004.

61. Ibid.

62. Ibid.

63. Interview with Rev. Nimrod Q. Reynolds, November 4, 2003; Frank Denton, "Violence Follows Nightrider Attack," *Anniston Star*, October 30, 1971; Jennie Cromie, "Nettles Honored for Years of Service," *Anniston Star*, March 27, 1993.

64. Hoyt W. Howell to Thomas S. Potts, April 26, 1972, COUL Papers.

65. COUL Annual Report, November 1972 to October 1973, 65, COUL Papers.

66. Interview with Rev. Nimrod Q. Reynolds, February 23, 2013; Anne Plott, "More than 20 Negroes Protest Hiring Practices," *Anniston Star*, March 10, 1969; "Picketers Continue," *Anniston Star*, March 17, 1969; "COUL to Tackle Community Problems," *Anniston Star*, November 21, 1971.

67. Interview with Henry Givahn by Grace Hooten Gates, February 29, 1980. For a detailed account of the 1969 city election, see Sprayberry, "'Town among the Trees,'" 398.

68. Frank Denton, "Trial Judge Supports Mass Arrests at Fort," *Anniston Star*, December 22, 1971; Beverly Bradford, "Jury Finds GI Innocent," *Anniston Star*, January 14, 1972; Bragg, *All Over but the Shoutin'*, 5; Anniston Chapter, Southern Christian Leadership Conference, 1, box: Chapters and Affiliated Chapters Files, folder: Alabama: Anniston/Calhoun County Chapter, circa 1980–96, MSS 1083, SCLC Papers.

69. Representative Johnny Ford, speech at CAP banquet, Anniston City Meeting Center, November 1, 2003; interview with David Baker, March 26, 2004.

70. Interview with David Baker, October 15, 2004; Love, *My City Was Gone*, 30–31.

71. The transition to racial hegemony after World War II is described in Winant, *World Is a Ghetto*. Nixon, *Slow Violence*; Ford, "Boundaries of Race."

Chapter Six

1. "The Nature of the Poison," in LKB Produkter, "Poison: KLB Helps to Make a Safer World," press release, January 10, 1967, *Owens* Archive; Jim Lowrey, "U.S., State Are Investigating Choccolocco Creek Fish Deaths," *Anniston Star*, May 20, 1961.

2. Jim Lowrey, "U.S., State Are Investigating Choccolocco Creek Fish Deaths," *Anniston Star*, May 20, 1961.

3. "Monsanto Expanding," *Anniston Star*, January 19, 1961; "Calhoun and Anniston: Depressed Area Designation Seen," *Anniston Star*, February 2, 1961; "Monsanto Moves Up," *Anniston Star*, February 25, 1961; Monsanto Chemical Company, Monsanto Annual Report 1960, 10; "Monsanto Optimistic Despite National Economy: Present Level to Stay Here," *Anniston Star*, March 21, 1961.

4. Monsanto Chemical Company, "Salesmen's Manual, Aroclors Description and Properties," October 1, 1944, 6, *Abernathy* documents; E. Mather, "Process for the Production of Aroclors, Pyranols, etc. at the Anniston and at the W. G. Krummrich Plant, XI. Hazards, Toxicity," 3–7 (April 1955), *Abernathy* documents; *Ex parte Monsanto and Solutia (Abernathy v. Monsanto)*, February 26, 2003; Jack T. Garrett to S. Facini, Chicago Pneumatic Tool Company, August 29, 1960, *Abernathy* documents.

5. Special meeting notice, *Anniston Star*, April 15, 1958; D. B. Hosmer, "To the People of Anniston: Progress Report," *Monsanto v. Fincher* (1961), 535–38, 536, 537, 538.

6. Jim Lowrey, "U.S., State Are Investigating Choccolocco Creek Fish Deaths," *Anniston Star*, May 20, 1961.

7. Interview with Shirley McCord, August 26, 2004; interviews with Arthur and Bettye Bowie, September 29, 2003.

8. "200 Employes [*sic*] Strike Local Monsanto Plant," *Anniston Star*, October 16, 1969; EPA, *Superfund Proposed Plan*, 19. One part per million (ppm) is 1,000 times greater concentration than one part per billion (ppb). One part per million (1 ppm) can also be expressed as one milligram per kilogram (1 mg/kg) or, in liquids, one milligram per liter (1 mg/L); one part per billion (1 ppb) is one microgram per gram (1 μg/g) or one microgram per liter (1 μg/L). http://www.nesc.wvu.edu/ ndwc/articles/ot/fa04/q&a.pdf (May 12, 2013).

9. Bill Hughes, deposition in *Owens v. Monsanto* (2001), October 21, 1999.

10. Hermanson and Johnson, "Polychlorinated Biphenyls in Tree Bark."

11. H. B. Richards Jr., report no. 2970, Final Report on Aroclor in Gases, job no. 17101089, file no. 141, March 15, 1954, Research Department, Phosphate Division, Anniston, Ala.; Charles Chatman, deposition in *Owens v. Monsanto* (2001), November 4, 1999, 26; Jack T. Garrett to H. B. Patrick, Department 246 (Aroclors), November 14, 1955, CHEMEWG.

12. Don Robertson believed that he was the first white laborer hired in September 1966. Don Robertson, deposition in *Owens v. Monsanto* (2001), November 3, 1999, 10; Charles Chatman, deposition in *Owens v. Monsanto* (2001), November 4, 1999, 35; Quay and Denison, *Negro in the Chemical Industry*, 16; Dr. John Daniel Cotman, "Recent Accessions," *Amistad Reports* 14, no. 7 (Fall 2003): 3.

13. Meigs, Albom, and Kartin, "Chloracne from an Unusual Exposure to Aro-chlor"; "Seven Workers Develop Chloracne in Plant Using Arochlor," *Chemical and Engineering News* 32, no. 20 (1954): 2038–39 (my emphasis). According to the second article, the recommended maximum allowable concentration at the time was 1.0 mg. per cubic meter of air.

14. Meigs, Albom, and Kartin, "Chloracne from an Unusual Exposure to Arochlor."

15. Bill Hughes, deposition in *Owens v. Monsanto* (2001), October 21, 1999, 21–24, 34, 39; William B. Papageorge, deposition in *Owens v. Monsanto* (2001), March 31, 2001, 58; E. G. Wright to P. B. Hodges et al., "Aroclor Losses at the Anniston Plant," Technical Services Department Progress Report, July 21, 1970, 1.

16. In the *Owens* opening statements, Monsanto attorney Jere White repeated Monsanto's frequent claim: "We had no reason to want to lose PCBs from our plant. PCBs are what we were making to sell, not to lose and waste and have get out away from us." *Owens* transcript, April 4, 2001, 453–54. Interview with Jack Matson, July 28, 2010; William B. Papageorge, deposition in *Owens v. Monsanto* (2001), March 31, 2001, 58.

17. Interview with Mark Hermanson, June 2, 2010; Carl Smith, deposition in *Owens v. Monsanto* (2001), October 27, 1999, 13.

18. Anne Plott, "Agenda," *Tuscaloosa News*, June 27, 1971.

19. Ferguson, *Final Report*, 6, 13–14.

20. Michael Grunwald, "Monsanto Hid Decades of Pollution," *Washington Post*, January 1, 2002; Ferguson, *Final Report*, 14.

21. Ferguson, *Final Report*, 6, 14, 9, 6.

22. Ibid., 8; interview with Jack Matson, July 28, 2010.

23. "In Fish Kill Suit: Anniston Groups Back Monsanto," *Anniston Star*, September 19, 1967; Anne Plott, "Agenda," *Tuscaloosa News*, June 27, 1971.

24. E. G. Wright to W. F. Taffee, "New Sump below Plant Dump," October 29, 1970, *Abernathy* documents; interview with Cassandra Roberts, September 3, 2003.

25. Interview with Opal Scruggs, September 25, 2003; interview with Arthur Bowie, September 29, 2003.

26. Monsanto Annual Reports, 1970, 11; Forrestal, *Faith, Hope, and $5,000*, 191.

27. Aftalion, *History of the International Chemical Industry*, 252–53; Garcia-Johnson, *Exporting Environmentalism*, 85. The number of company-wide employees had risen from 11,523 in 1944 to 34,889 in 1959 to 64,604 in 1969. Monsanto Company, *1969 Annual Report*, 23. Forrestal, *Faith, Hope, and $5,000*, 181; "Facts about Monsanto," Monsanto Company, St. Louis, 1969; Monsanto Company, *1970 Annual Report*, 1–2; Monsanto Company, *1971 Annual Report*, 1; PCB Presentation to Corporate Development Committee, n.d., ca. 1970, CHEMEWG.

28. Nisbet and Sarofim, "Rates and Routes of Transport of PCBs." Monsanto downplayed its role in using PCBs as pesticide extenders to prolong the persistence of pesticide applications, but a 1947 termite ad indicates their use for that purpose. W. B. Papageorge to Dr. S. G. Herman, at UC Santa Barbara, April 6, 1971, 2. "This Was Adam's Bug Killer," *Fortune*, February 1946, 17; PCB Committee, "Scott Analysis—Electrosol [*sic*] 5 ppm—Detergent," August 25, 1969, handwritten notes attached to second draft of Aroclors minutes, October 15, 1969.

29. Profits for calendar year 1958 and first quarter 1959 are reported in "Confidential Report to C. A. Thomas," July 7, 1959, series 1, box 5, Organic Chemicals Division (History), Monsanto Records. Worldwide Aroclors sales and profits figures are taken from "PCB Presentation to Corporate Development Committee," n.d., ca. 1970, Risebrough Papers.

30. P. G. Benignus to T. K. Smith (Monsanto, St. Louis), February 29, 1952, CHEMEWG; Lloyd B. Shone, acting director, Preventive Medicine Division, to Emmet Kelly, medical director, Monsanto Chemical Company, September 1, 1955, CHEMEWG.

31. Meigs, Albom, and Kartin, "Chloracne from an Unusual Exposure to Arochlor," 1418. "We have had no experience with any regulatory agency concerning the discharge of these materials," the hygiene department wrote in 1960. Jack T. Garrett to Mr. S. Facini of the Engineering Department of the Chicago Pneumatic Tool Company in Franklin, Penn., August 29, 1960.

32. D. F. Smith to R. D. "Bob" Minteer, December 5, 1958, *Abernathy* documents.

33. Besselievre, "Statutory Regulation of Stream Pollution," 217, 225. Successful Refuse Act suits included *U.S. v. Republic Steel* (1960) and *U.S. v. Standard Oil*

(1966). See Percival, *Environmental Regulation*, 881–82; and Melosi, *Sanitary City*, 233, 315.

34. Lear, *Rachel Carson*, 118–19; Hays and Hays, *Beauty, Health, and Permanence*, 174, 205.

35. Langston, *Toxic Bodies*, 26–27, 82; Food Additives Amendment of 1958, P.L. 85-929, 72 Stat. 1784.

36. Besselievre, "Statutory Regulation of Stream Pollution," 225; Alabama Department of Conservation and Natural Resources (ADCNR), *Encyclopedia of Alabama*, http://www.encyclopediaofalabama.org/face/Article.jsp?id=h-2453 (May 11, 2013); Myers, "Alabama Water Improvement Commission Responsibilities," 149.

37. "Pollution Action Due," *Anniston Star*, July 16, 1965.

38. Brickman, *Controlling Chemicals*, 243; "Chemicals Just Coming into Own, Says Monsanto Official," *Anniston Star*, July 25, 1943.

39. Carson, *Silent Spring*; Lear, *Rachel Carson*, 374, 358–60, 411–12; Souder, *On a Farther Shore*, 293–95, 303–5, 342.

40. Carson, *Silent Spring*, 25, 304n; "This Was Adam's Bug Killer," *Fortune*, February 1946, 17; W. B. Papageorge to Dr. S. G. Herman, at UC Santa Barbara, April 6, 1971, 2, Risebrough Papers.

41. Lear, *Rachel Carson*, 412; Stauber and Rampton, *Toxic Sludge Is Good for You*, 123–24; "The Desolate Year," *Monsanto Magazine*, October 1962, 4–9. Environmental historian Joshua Blu Buhs suggests that Carson herself was partly responsible for limiting the focus to "nature" and wildlife. Buhs, "Fire Ant Wars." Phone communication with Eric Francis, June 9, 2005.

42. EPA, "DDT Ban Takes Effect," press release, June 14, 1972, http://www.epa.gov/history/topics/ddt/01.htm (November 18, 2010).

43. Gerald W. Miller, deposition in *Sewell v. Monsanto*, March 15, 1995, 17; interview with Søren Jensen, May 31, 2010; e-mail communication with Søren Jensen, August 16, 2011.

44. Interview with Søren Jensen, May 31, 2010.

45. Ibid.; Jensen et al., "Effects of PCB and DDT," 239, http://www.jstor.org/stable/4312286 (May 19, 2010).

46. E-mail communication with Søren Jensen, September 21, 2010.

47. Jensen, "PCB Story," 124; "Report of a New Chemical Hazard," 612.

48. Colborn, Myers, and Dumanoski, *Our Stolen Future*, 280; "Report of a New Chemical Hazard," 612.

49. "Report of a New Chemical Hazard," 612; Jensen, "PCB Story," 130; interview with Søren Jensen, May 31, 2010.

50. D. Wood to G. R. Buchanan, St. Louis, December 1, 1966, CHEMEWG; Henry Strand, Rising & Strand, to David Wood, Monsanto Europe, November 28, 1966, CHEMEWG.

51. This information came to light during testimony in one of the major PCB trials. See memo from William Papageorge to Dr. Robert George Kaley, *Abernathy* transcript, January 30, 2002.

52. Interview with Jack Matson, July 28, 2010; D. Wood to G. R. Buchanan, St. Louis, December 1, 1966, CHEMEWG; Henry Strand, Rising & Strand, to David

Wood, Monsanto Europe, November 28, 1966, CHEMEWG; William B. Papageorge, deposition in *Pennsylvania v. U.S. Mineral Products*, April 28, 1998, 132. Widmark had visited Monsanto in St. Louis in 1965 on a different project. Gunnar Widmark to Mr. Ford, December 29, 1966, CHEMEWG.

53. Sulzberger, Rostenberg, and Sher, "Acneform Eruptions"; Carson, *Silent Spring*, 76; Risebrough et al., "Polychlorinated Biphenyls," 1102.

54. David Perlman, "A Menacing New Pollutant," *San Francisco Chronicle*, February 24, 1969.

55. Interview with Robert Risebrough, December 6, 2010.

56. W. R. Richard, Research Center, to W. A. Kuhn, December 30, 1968, *Abernathy* documents.

57. Notes on meeting, March 6, 1969, Industrial Bio-Test Laboratories Inc., Aroclor—Wildlife, March 10, 1969, *Abernathy* documents; E. Scott Tucker to W. R. Richard and E. P. Wheeler, "Aroclor—Wildlife," February 25, 1969, *Abernathy* documents.

58. "Jessee New Manager of Monsanto Plant," *Anniston Star*, December 30, 1969, 6A; "Outline—CMC Presentation PCB Environmental Problem," April 15, 1970, 3, Risebrough Papers.

59. Phone communication with Robert Risebrough, September 17, 2010; William B. Papageorge, deposition in *Owens v. Monsanto* (2001), March 31, 2001, 92–94; Edward D. Goldberg to William B. Papageorge, November 10, 1971; R. W. Risebrough, "Suggested Questions to Be Posed to the Monsanto Company," 1; Edward D. Goldberg to William B. Papageorge, January 12, 1972; Robert W. Risebrough to William B. Papageorge, April 17, 1972; 1960–71 Production figures calculated from Monsanto, "Monsanto Releases Production Figures to Department of Commerce," press release, 2, November 30, 1971, all in Risebrough Papers.

60. Elmer P. Wheeler to Richard Davis, September 3, 1965, 1, *Abernathy* documents (my emphasis).

61. J. Roach and I. Pomerantz, FDA, "Kanechlor 400 was ingested by several hundred Japanese in the Yusho incident [1968] as reported by Kurastune," Association of Analytical Communities (AOAC), October 1974, Plaintiff's Exhibit 4B06, *Abernathy* documents; Kuratsume et al., "Epidemiologic Study on Yusho." Some researchers later suggested that furans in the rice oil, released as PCBs were heated, caused the illnesses, though that is not what observers, including Monsanto, believed at the time. "PCB Environmental Pollution Abatement Plan," October 15, 1969, 7, *Abernathy* documents.

62. "Minutes of Meeting of the Corporate Development Committee," April 28, 1969, CHEMEWG; "Meeting of the Board of Directors," May 22, 1969, CHEMEWG.

63. P. B. Hodges, "Minutes of Aroclor 'Ad Hoc' Committee, First Meeting, Confidential," September 5, 1969, 1, *Abernathy* documents.

64. Ibid., 3: W. R. Richard, Research Center, to W. A. Kuhn, December 30, 1968, *Abernathy* documents.

65. W. R. Richard, Research Center, to W. A. Kuhn, December 30, 1968, *Abernathy* documents; W. R. Richard to E. Wheeler, "Defense of Aroclor—F. [Functional] Fluids," September 9, 1969, 6, *Abernathy* documents.

66. "PCB Environmental Pollution Abatement Plan," October 15, 1969, 7, *Abernathy* documents; P. B. Hodges, "Minutes of Aroclor 'Ad Hoc' Committee, First Meeting, Confidential," September 5, 1969, 3, *Abernathy* documents.

67. "PCB Environmental Pollution Abatement Plan," October 15, 1969, 7, *Abernathy* documents; M. N. Farrar et al. to Rodney Harris, "Report of the Aroclors 'Ad Hoc' Committee, Second Draft," October 15, 1969, *Abernathy* documents.

68. E. G. Wright to P. B. Hodges et al., "Aroclor Losses at the Anniston Plant," Technical Service Department Progress Report, July 21, 1970, 1, *Abernathy* documents. Dumping returned to 88 pounds a day in August 1970. W. B. Papageorge to D. S. Cameron, "PCB Environmental Problem," September 8, 1970, 9, CHEMEWG. Dr. Ian C. Nisbet, *Owens* transcript, April 11, 2001, 1319–20. Nisbet reviewed an internal memo from E. S. Tucker to W. B. Papageorge, "PCB Content of Choccolocco Creek Fish," August 6, 1970, Table 1, CHEMEWG.

69. "PCB Environmental Pollution Abatement Plan," October 15, 1969, 3, *Abernathy* documents; P. B. Hodges, "Minutes of Aroclor 'Ad Hoc' Committee, First Meeting, Confidential," September 5, 1969, 1, *Abernathy* documents.

70. Forrestal, *Faith, Hope, and $5,000*, photo caption opposite page 97; phone communication with Neal Dillard, ICWU, June 13, 2013. Meetings of Swann Chemical Co. employees, including a separate session for "Colored employees," had been held by Federal Labor Union no. 18317 and no. 18401 ten years earlier. *Anniston Star*, April 20, 1934. Hubert Kay in Princeton, N.J., to Dorothy Brockhoff in St. Louis, August 1, 1953, series 6, box 1, Hubert Kay (Correspondence with Brockhoff), Monsanto Records; Frank Curtis, October 2, 1951, series 12, box 1, Labor Unions, Monsanto Records.

71. Basil Penny, "200 Employes [*sic*] Strike Local Monsanto Plant," *Anniston Star*, October 16, 1969.

72. "PCB Environmental Pollution Abatement Plan," October 15, 1969, 7, *Abernathy* documents; "Profit and Liability vs. Time," PCB Environmental Pollution Abatement Plan, October 15, 1969, 19, *Abernathy* documents; N. T. Johnson to P. Craska et al., "Pollution Letter," February 16, 1970, *Abernathy* documents.

73. P. B. Hodges, "Minutes of Aroclor 'Ad Hoc' Committee, First Meeting, Confidential," September 5, 1969, 1; meeting of the Board of Directors, May 22, 1969, CHEMEWG; handwritten note on August 25, 1969 memo, M. N. Farrar et al. to Rodney Harris, "Report of the Aroclors 'Ad Hoc' Committee, Second Draft," October 15, 1969, *Abernathy* documents.

74. Robert H. Boyle, "Poison Roams Our Coastal Seas," *Sports Illustrated*, October 26, 1970, 71, 81, 84.

75. Richard Lyons, "If You Think DDT's a Problem, Meet PCB," *New York Times*, September 26, 1971.

76. Francis, "Conspiracy of Silence"; "U.S. Fears Poison in Some Chicks," *New York Times*, July 24, 1971; Outline CMC Presentation PCB Environmental Problem, April 15, 1970, 4; "List of Customers Buying Fish Meal from East Coast Terminals, Inc. (Wilmington, Delaware), ca. 1971"; W. B. Papageorge to F. G. Jenkins, July 8, 1970, all in Risebrough Papers.

77. E. G. Wright to W. F. Taffee, "New Sump below Plant Dump," October 29, 1970, *Abernathy* documents; Jack T. Garrett to J. C. Landwehr, August 17, 1970, CHEMEWG; E. G. Wright to W. F. Taffee, "New Sump below Plant Dump," October 29, 1970, *Abernathy* documents.

78. Jesse Abernathy, deposition in *Owens v. Monsanto* (2001), October 27, 1999, 36–37.

Chapter Seven

1. Nancy Beiles, "What Monsanto Knew: Outraged by PCB Contamination, an Alabama Town Unearths a Company's Past," *The Nation*, May 29, 2000, http://www.thenation.com/doc/20000529/beiles (October 11, 2003); Environmental Working Group, "Anniston, Alabama, In-Depth: Pollution, Contamination, Betrayal," CHEMEWG, last updated January 9, 2002, http://chemicalindustryarchives.org/dirtysecrets/annistonindepth/indepth.pdf (May 17, 2011).

2. Monsanto Company, Organic Chemicals Division, Research Department, "Aroclors Analysis: Hog Analysis Results," December 24, 1970, *Abernathy* documents; E. S. Tucker to William B. Papageorge, "PCB Content of Hog Fat and Liver Samples Sent from Anniston," December 21, 1970, CHEMEWG; Judy Johnson, "Chemicals above Acceptable Amounts," *Anniston Star*, November 22, 1970; NRC, Committee on Remediation of PCB-Contaminated Sediments, *Risk Management Strategy*, 32. "The types of PCBs that tend to bioaccumulate in fish and other animals and bind to sediments happen to be the most carcinogenic components of PCB mixtures." EPA, *Health Effects of Polychlorinated Biphenyls (PCBs)*.

3. "Monsanto Records Sales Hike," *Anniston Star*, January 29, 1969; Forrestal, *Faith, Hope, and $5,000*, 215–17. The 1973 OPEC oil embargo would exacerbate this problem. Chandler, *Shaping the Industrial Century*, 28–29. Monsanto had witnessed the power of the new environmental lobby in the battle over cyclamates, which the company produced from 1965 to 1967; the FDA banned the artificial sweeteners in 1969. Forrestal, *Faith, Hope, and $5,000*, 197–98. See also Tinker, "PCB Story," 17.

4. David Bird, "Curb Urged in Use of PCB Chemical," *New York Times*, April 11, 1970.

5. Gottlieb, *Forcing the Spring*, 180.

6. Russell E. Train, "Environmental Protection, Rx for Public Health," *National Conference on Polychlorinated Biphenyls*, November 19–21, 1975, Conference Proceedings 560/6-75-004, Environmental Protection Agency Office of Toxic Substances, Washington, D.C., March 1976, 7; Edward D. Goldberg to William B. Papageorge, November 10, 1971, Risebrough Papers. Train summarized the OECD agreement in "Environmental Protection: Rx for Public Health," in EPA, *National Conference on Polychlorinated Biphenyls (1975)*, 7.

7. J. R. Savage to T. L. Gossage et al., "Minutes—12/4/70 Meeting on Aroclor Manufacturing Sites," December 9, 1970, 3, *Abernathy* documents.

8. D. B. Hosmer, meeting at Southwest [Southeast] Regional Office of EPA Atlanta, "PCB Effluents from Anniston Plant to Snow Creek, Choccolocco Creek,

etc.," November 11, 1971, 2, *Abernathy* documents. In early 1970, Monsanto reduced the 50 ppb target to 10 ppb, to be achieved by the third quarter of 1971. W. B. Papageorge to J. Savage, "PCB in Plant Effluent," January 29, 1971; Monsanto Company, "Performance Review 1970, Objectives: Polychlorinated Biphenyl Environmental Problem," 1, *Abernathy* documents.

9. Judy Johnson, "Chemicals above Acceptable Amounts," *Anniston Star*, November 22, 1970; Judy Johnson, "Choccolocco 'Dead Creek' in Stretch Past Oxford," *Anniston Star*, July 30, 1971.

10. COUL Annual Report, November 1972 to October 1973, 42–45, 36, COUL Papers; Community Affairs Committee Report, Agenda, ca. May 1972, COUL Papers; COUL Annual Report, November 1972 to October 1973, 36–37, 45, COUL Papers.

11. Monsanto, "Outline—CMC Presentation, PCB Environmental Problem," April 15, 1970, 3, Risebrough Papers (my emphasis); Elmer P. Wheeler to Don Otto, "PCB Literature Search," August 6, 1971, CHEMEWG; "Monsanto Replies to Charge That PCB Threatens Environment," news release, April 10, 1970, 2, http://www.chemicalindustryarchives.org/search/pdfs/anniston/19700410_209.pdf (June 22, 2006).

12. W. B. Mullally to J. L. Corder, "Recommendations of the Task Force on Plant Dump," March 31, 1970, 1, *Abernathy* documents; Paul B. Hodges, St. Louis, to Toby Bell, Anniston, September 18, 1970, "PCB Environmental Problem, September Status Report," October 6, 1970, 1 (my emphasis); Monsanto-Sangamo Electric Company Indemnity Agreement: "Special Undertaking by Purchasers of Polychlorinated Biphenyls," January 14, 1972, box 13, folder 381, Silbergeld Papers. Also see Edmund Greene to J. P. Berndt et al., January 14, 1972, CHEMEWG. According to Nancy Beiles, most of the damages lawsuits brought by companies that purchased PCBs from Monsanto were dismissed on the grounds that "these companies knew what they were getting into." Beiles, "What Monsanto Knew: Outraged by PCB Contamination, an Alabama Town Unearths a Company's Past," *The Nation*, May 29, 2000. H. C. Godt, "Organizational Chronology of Monsanto Domestic Operating Units Including Major Acquisitions and Divestitures," August 1997, Monsanto Records.

13. "PCB Problem Unfolded as Environment Hazard," *Anniston Star*, November 22, 1970.

14. E. V. John at World Headquarters to W. B. Papageorge, "November PR Report: Polychlorinated Biphenyl," November 30, 1970, Plaintiff's Exhibit 1A3, *Abernathy* documents; W. B. Papageorge to D. S. Cameron, "PCB Environmental Problem, August Status Report," September 8, 1970, 3–4, CHEMEWG.

15. Royal D. Suttkus and Gerald E. Gunning, Biological Consultants, to Eugene Wright, August 15, 1971, 3, *Abernathy* documents; Congressional Record, PCBs, Environmental Poison, House, 7136–38, July 26, 1971.

16. Monsanto, "Monsanto Cites Actions Taken on Environmental Issue," press release, July 16, 1970, Risebrough Papers.

17. Drinker, *Report to Monsanto*, 6; Birnbaum, "Third Biannual International PCB Workshop," 1.

18. W. B. Papageorge to D. S. Cameron, PCB Environmental Problem, August Status Report, September 8, 1970, 1, CHEMEWG.

19. Monsanto, "Keeping PCBs Out of the Environment: A Status Report," October 1972, CHEMEWG. Aroclor 1016 was distributed to several customers in 1970. W. B. Papageorge to D. S. Cameron, "PCB Environmental Problem, August Status Report," September 8, 1970, 5, CHEMEWG. Mark H. Hermanson, "Polychlorinated Biphenyls in Tree Bark near the Former Manufacturing Site in Sauget, Illinois," Sixth International PCB Workshop, Visby, Sweden, June 2, 2010. Mitchell Erickson disputes the claim that this confusion in name was intentional on Monsanto's part. Erickson, "Applications of Polychlorinated Biphenyls," 139.

20. E. Scott Tucker to W. R. Richard and E. P. Wheeler, "Aroclor—Wildlife," February 25, 1969, *Abernathy* documents; Monsanto, "Monsanto Cites Actions Taken on Environmental Issue," press release, July 16, 1970, Risebrough Papers; Tinker, "PCB Story," 16; Monsanto, "Schedule for Discontinuing Aroclor Applications," in "Outline—CMC Presentation, PCB Environmental Problem," April 15, 1970, 9, Risebrough Papers.

21. Ecologists were critical at the time of the assertion that PCBs could be "sufficiently contained." Hays and Hays, *Beauty, Health, and Permanence,* 195; David Perlman, "A Menacing New Pollutant," *San Francisco Chronicle,* February 24, 1969. Numerous PCB-containing transformer fires in New York, New Jersey, San Francisco, Quebec, and elsewhere between 1981 and 1991 heightened concern about PCBs, and dioxins released during burning. One of the worst of the fires was a February 5, 1981, fire that shut down the eighteen-story State Office Building in Binghamton, New York. Paul L. Montgomery, "PCB Cleanup Shuts Upstate Tower for Months," *New York Times,* February 21, 1981; "Pollutants Still in Building Despite Cleanup," *New York Times,* June 18, 1990. Because of the contamination, the building remained unoccupied until 1994. Francis, "Conspiracy of Silence"; William B. Papageorge, deposition in *Pennsylvania v. U.S. Mineral Products,* April 28, 1998, 162. The "closed use" exclusion continues to play a role in PCB regulation in 2013.

22. Ellen K. Silbergeld, "Draft Conclusions," 1, October 4, 1983, box 4, folder 114, Silbergeld Papers.

23. J. R. Savage to T. L. Gossage et al., "Minutes—12/4/70 Meeting on Aroclor Manufacturing Sites," December 9, 1970, 3, 2 *Abernathy* documents; Congressional Record, PCBs, Environmental Poison, House, 7136–38, July 26, 1971; W. B. Papageorge to J. Savage, "PCBs in Plant Effluent," January 29, 1971, *Abernathy* documents; E. G. Wright, Progress Report, Technical Services Department, Anniston, Alabama Plant, "Aroclor Losses at the Anniston Plant," July 21, 1970, *Abernathy* documents; Forrestal, *Faith, Hope, and $5,000,* 198.

24. "Jury Verdict," *Abernathy v. Monsanto,* February 22, 2002; *Ex parte Monsanto and Solutia* (*Abernathy v. Monsanto*), February 26, 2003, 4; George J. Levinskas to Dr. J. C. Calandra, "AROCLOR 2-Year Rat Feeding Studies," July 18, 1975, 1, *Abernathy* documents.

25. W. R. Richard to E. Wheeler, "Defense of Aroclor—F. [Functional] Fluids," September 9, 1969, 1, *Abernathy* documents. For a discussion of "manufacturing doubt" as central to corporations' strategies for defending their products, see Oreskes and Conway, *Merchants of Doubt.* "Report of Aroclor 'Ad Hoc' Committee

(Second Draft)," October 15, 1969, 8, CHEMEWG. I am indebted to an anonymous reader for this insight about the industrial idea of contamination. The *New Oxford American Dictionary*, 3rd ed. (Oxford: Oxford University Press, 2012), defines *to contaminate* as to "make (something) impure by exposure to or addition of a poisonous or polluting substance." "Questions and Answers for ANSI," attachment to W. B. Papageorge to A. Posefsky, E. L. Raab, General Electric Company, February 2, 1972, *Abernathy* documents.

26. P. B. Hodges to M. W. Farrar et al., "Minutes of Aroclor 'Ad Hoc' Committee, First Meeting," September 5, 1969, 1, *Abernathy* documents.

27. W. R. Richard to E. Wheeler, "Defense of Aroclor—F. [Functional] Fluids," September 9, 1969, 1, *Abernathy* documents; Christopher Sellers, *Hazards of the Job*, 200; P. B. Hodges to M. W. Farrar et al., "Minutes of Aroclor 'Ad Hoc' Committee, First Meeting," September 5, 1969, 2, *Abernathy* documents; M. N. Farrar et al. to Rodney Harris, "Report of Aroclor 'Ad Hoc' Committee (Second Draft)," October 15, 1969, 23, *Abernathy* documents.

28. Fagin, Lavelle, and Center for Public Integrity, *Toxic Deception*, 33.

29. "Industrial Bio-Test" (Monsanto), box 13, folder 381, Silbergeld Papers. The IBT studies for Monsanto began as early as 1963, with several studies that year by Richard J. Palazzalo and John H. Kay of "Subacute Dermal Toxicity of Aroclor," using Aroclors 4465, 1254, and 1268. A meeting with Joe Calandra, president of IBT Labs, occurred in March 1969. W. R. Richard, memo to file, "Notes on Meeting 3/6/69 Industrial Bio-Test Laboratories, Inc. Aroclor—Wildlife," March 10, 1969, 1, *Abernathy* documents.

30. Francis, "Conspiracy of Silence." Also see Keith Schneider, "Faking It." The IBT investigation began in 1975. The trials were held in 1983, sentencing in April 1984. "Three Receive Prison Terms for Falsifying Chemical Tests," *New York Times*, April 10, 1984. The only Monsanto product tests investigated in the IBT Labs cases were those conducted on trichlorocarbanilide (TCC), an antibacterial agent used in deodorant soap. Eliot Marshall, "Murky World," 1131.

31. E. S. Tucker, R & D Laboratories, South Second Street, to E. G. Wright, Anniston Plant, January 19, 1970, 2, *Abernathy* documents; "Monsanto Replies to Charge That PCB Threatens Environment," news release, 2, April 10, 1970, CHEMEWG; E. S. Tucker, R & D Laboratories, South Second Street, to E. G. Wright, Anniston Plant, January 19, 1970, 2, *Abernathy* documents.

32. Handwritten memo from "Otis" to Don, Industrial Bio-Test Laboratories, January 14, 1972, 1, 2, *Abernathy* documents; George J. Levinskas to Dr. J. C. Calandra, "AROCLOR 2-Year Rat Feeding Studies," July 18, 1975, 1, *Abernathy* documents.

33. "Three Receive Prison Terms for Falsifying Chemical Tests," *New York Times*, April 10, 1984; Fagin, Lavelle, and Center for Public Integrity, *Toxic Deception*, 35.

34. Gottlieb, *Forcing the Spring*, 360; Francis, "Conspiracy of Silence"; "Outline—CMC Presentation PCB Environmental Problem," April 15, 1970, 4, Risebrough Papers; H. Blumenthal to Dr. Leo Friedman, July 30, 1971, 3–4, CHEMEWG; "FDA Defends Handling of Chemical, Opposes Call for Outright Ban," *Wall Street Journal*, September 30, 1971, 18; "FDA Studying Chance of PCB Contamination in Containers for Food," *Wall Street Journal*, September 28, 1971, 4.

35. "Report of Aroclor 'Ad Hoc' Committee (Second Draft)," October 15, 1969, 8, CHEMEWG; *Ex parte Monsanto and Solutia* (*Abernathy v. Monsanto*), February 26, 2003, 4. "The Hog Analysis Results," for example, did not become available to regulators or to the public until many years later. "Monsanto Replies to Charge That PCB Threatens Environment," news release, April 10, 1970, 2, CHEMEWG; George J. Levinskas to Dr. J. C. Calandra, "AROCLOR 2-Year Rat Feeding Studies," July 18, 1975, 1, *Abernathy* documents; Christopher Sellers, *Hazards of the Job*, 179.

36. Forrestal, *Faith, Hope, and $5,000*, 257.

37. W. B. Papageorge to D. S. Cameron et al., "PCB Environmental Problem: August Status Report," September 8, 1970, 1, *Abernathy* documents. A nongovernmental organization, ANSI was founded in 1918 by electrical and engineering business associations to set voluntary norms and guidelines for commercial products.

38. Michael Grunwald, "Monsanto Hid Decades of Pollution," *Washington Post*, January 1, 2002; D. B. Hosmer, "PCB Effluents from Anniston Plant to Snow Creek, Choccolocco Creek, Etc.," meeting at Southwest [Southeast] Regional EPA, November 11, 1971, 1–2, *Abernathy* documents.

39. ADPH/ATSDR, *Cobbtown/Sweet Valley Health Consultation No. 2*, June 26, 1996, 1; Judy Johnson, "Chemicals above Acceptable Levels," *Anniston Star*, November 22, 1970; W. B. Papageorge to D. S. Cameron et al., "PCB Environmental Problem: August Status Report," September 8, 1970, 9, *Abernathy* documents; "Engineer: Monsanto Knew PCB Danger," *Birmingham News*, January 12, 2002; "Monsanto: Verdict Is Just the Beginning," *Anniston Star*, February 23, 2002; Paul B. Hodges to H. S. Bergen Jr., Anniston PCB Cleanup Program, August 7, 1970, 4, CHEMEWG; G. W. Miller to G. W. Jessee, "Aroclor Pollution—AWIC Contact," May 7, 1970, CHEMEWG.

40. "I believe they will use our data," wrote D. B. Hosmer. "PCB Effluents from Anniston Plant to Snow Creek, Choccolocco Creek, Etc.," meeting at Southwest [Southeast] Regional EPA, November 11, 1971, 3, *Abernathy* documents.

41. EPA, "Proposed Rules: Water Pollution Prevention and Control," *Federal Register* 38, no. 129 (July 6, 1973): 10844; Federal Water Pollution Control Act (FPCWA, commonly known as the Clean Water Act), Section 101(a)(3) of the FWPCA, 33 U.S.C. §1251(a)(3) (1976). FWPCA also required the EPA to list and establish standards for toxic chemicals, Section 307(a) of FWPCA, 33 U.S.C. §1317(a) (1976). See *Environmental Defense Fund (EDF) v. EPA* (1978), 72. "Regulatory steps that Congress expected to take little more than *one year* took *four years*." *EDF v. EPA* (1978), 67 (emphasis in original); *EDF v. EPA* (1978), 62 (n. 18).

42. *EDF v. EPA* (1978), 99.

43. EPA, "Toxic Pollutant Effluent Standards, List of Toxic Pollutants," *Federal Register* 38, no. 173 (September 7, 1973): 24342–44; EPA, "Proposed Toxic Pollutant Effluent Standards for Polychlorinated Biphenyls," 40 CFR Part 129, *Federal Register* 41, no. 143 (July 23, 1976): 30470, 30473. EPA issued the final rule the following February. EPA, "Standards for Polychlorinated Biphenyls (PCBs), Final Decision," 40 CFR Part 129, *Federal Register* 42, no. 22 (February 2, 1977): 6531–55; phone interview with Wendy Pearson, June 14, 2013.

44. Elmer P. Wheeler to W. R. Richard, May 26, 1969, 1–2, *Abernathy* documents.

45. Ibid., 2.

46. Monsanto issued the defense that PCBs were not a household product a few days after Congressman Ryan held his press conference announcing plans to introduce legislation regulating toxic chemicals. "Monsanto Replies to Charge That PCB Threatens Environment," news release, April 10, 1970, CHEMEWG; Cumming Paton to W. B. Papageorge, "Aroclor Plasticizer Survey," marked "Personal and Confidential," April 13, 1970, 1–3, *Owens* Archive. PCBs were also reportedly used in at least eight brands of insecticides in 1970. David E. Rosenbaum, "Monsanto Plans to Curb Chemical," *New York Times*, July 15, 1970. Monsanto acknowledged that PCBs had been used as pesticide extenders in a memo on plans to discontinue uses. "Outline—CMC Presentation, PCB Environmental Problem," April 15, 1970, 9, Risebrough Papers. Paul B. Hodges to W. A. Kuhn, "Aroclors Cleanup from Plant Effluents," May 12, 1969, 3, *Abernathy* documents.

47. Bill Cambron, deposition in *Owens v. Monsanto* (2001), October 22, 1999, 83–86; Judy Johnson, "Cleanup Group Examines Problems of Environment," *Anniston Star*, April 18, 1971.

48. Judy Johnson, "Monsanto Emissions Watched," *Anniston Star*, July 4, 1973; Howard Miller, "Legal Action Considered on Monsanto Emissions," *Anniston Star*, September 11, 1973.

49. Communications with Henry Caddell, September 12, 2003, May 21, 2013; Cobb, *Selling of the South*, 236. For a discussion of the changing state-federal regulatory relationships in environmental policy, see Dewey, "Fickle Finger of Phosphate." Monsanto also had chosen to construct an incinerator to burn PCB wastes at the Krummrich plant in Sauget. Phone interview with Wendy Pearson, June 14, 2013.

50. Frank Denton, "Three Local Industries Accused of Pollution," *Anniston Star*, July 12, 1970; "Deadline Extended in Pollution Suits," *Anniston Star*, August 14, 1970; "All but 14 Companies Dismissed," *Anniston Star*, August 29, 1970.

51. W. B. Papageorge to Mr. Dan A. Albert, March 18, 1975, CHEMEWG.

52. William B. Papageorge, deposition in *Owens v. Monsanto* (2001), 71; William B. Papageorge, deposition in *Mars Hill Missionary Baptist Church v. Monsanto*, March 31, 1998, 45.

53. Within a few days after Representative Ryan held a press conference in early April 1970 announcing plans to introduce legislation regulating toxic chemicals, Monsanto issued a press release defending Aroclors. See "Monsanto Replies to Charge That PCB Threatens Environment," press release, April 10, 1970, CHEMEWG; and Environmental and Natural Resources Policy Division, *Legislative History of TSCA*, 210.

54. First enacted in 1947 and updated in 1972, the Federal Insecticide, Fungicide, and Rodenticide Act (FIFRA) provided for the registration of pesticides with "unreasonable adverse effects on the environment." Percival, *Environmental Regulation*, 522.

55. William M. Blair, "Senate Unit Told of Fish Tainting," *New York Times*, August 5, 1971; "Senate Consideration of S. 3149," *Congressional Record*, March 26, 1976,

Senate, S4397–S4432; Environmental and Natural Resources Policy Division, *Legislative History of TSCA*, 209–10. The section banning PCBs is 15 U.S.C. §2605, sect. 6(e).

56. Tony Mazzocchi, quoted in Druley and Ordway, *Toxic Substances Control Act*, 19.

57. John J. Sheehan, quoted in Druley and Ordway, *Toxic Substances Control Act,* 15.

58. Representative John Murphy, "Showdown on Toxins," *New York Times*, August 25, 1976. Sen. Gaylord Nelson introduced the amendment that banned PCBs by name. Section 6(e), 14 U.S.C. §2605 (e) (1976), Senate Hearing, March 26, 1976; Environmental and Natural Resources Policy Division, *Legislative History of TSCA*, 236.

59. Russell Train, in EPA, *National Conference on Polychlorinated Biphenyls (1975)*, 7; Summary Session, in EPA, *National Conference on Polychlorinated Biphenyls (1975)*, 457–71. As EPA administrator, Train bore some responsibility for the EPA's long delay in setting PCB standards under the Clean Water Act. The delay added to frustration that spurred Congress to include the PCB ban in TSCA. A federal district court in Washington, D.C., called the EPA's inaction on PCB regulation in the mid-1970s "a failure indicating a need for new preventive regulation." *EDF v. EPA* (1978), 62 (n. 11).

60. Kimbrough, "Induction of Liver Tumors," 1455, 1454; Kimbrough, Linder, and Gaines, "Morphological Changes in Livers."

61. Kuratsune, Masuda, and Nagayama, "Some of the Recent Findings Concerning Yusho," in EPA, *National Conference on Polychlorinated Biphenyls (1975)*, 14; Kimbrough, "Toxicity of Polychlorinated Polycyclic Compounds," 467; R. E. Keller to R. Baxter, "Chlorinated Dibenzofurans," August 15, 1975, CHEMEWG; Bowes et al., "Identification of Chlorinated Dibenzofurans." See also statement by J. Roach and I. Pomerantz: "Kanechlor 400 was ingested by several hundred Japanese in the Yusho incident [1968] as reported by Kuratsune," Association of Analytical Communities (AOAC), October 1974, Plaintiff's Exhibit 4B06, *Abernathy* documents; and Roach and Pomerantz, "Finding of Chlorinated Dibenzofurans."

62. Dr. J. G. Vos, "Summary of Session I," in EPA, *National Conference on Polychlorinated Biphenyls (1975)*, 459.

63. Forrestal, *Faith, Hope, and $5,000*, 256; interview with Winthrop R. Corey by James E. McKee, December 30, 1981, 1–2, series 10, box 3, Monsanto Co. History (Oral History Project), Monsanto Records; R. T. Phelps to Hon. Strom Thurmond, January 19, 1976, in Environmental and Natural Resources Policy Division, *Legislative History of TSCA*, 244–45.

64. Forrestal, *Faith, Hope, and $5,000*, 198; Monsanto, "Outline—CMC Presentation, PCB Environmental Problem," April 15, 1970, 5, Risebrough Papers.

65. Environmental and Natural Resources Policy Division, *Legislative History of TSCA*, 210.

66. Toxic Substances Control Act 15 U.S.C. §2622; Environmental and Natural Resources Policy Division, *Legislative History of TSCA*, 231–33.

67. EPA, "Proposed Toxic Pollutant Effluent Standards for Polychlorinated Biphenyls," 40 CFR Part 129, *Federal Register* 41, no. 143 (July 23, 1976): 30470, 30473. EPA issued the final rule the following February. EPA, "Standards for Polychlorinated Biphenyls (PCBs), Final Decision," 40 CFR Part 129, *Federal Register* 42, no. 22 (February 2, 1977): 6531–55; Environmental and Natural Resources Policy Division, *Legislative History of TSCA*, v.

68. Hays and Hays, *Beauty, Health, and Permanence*, 194. DDT was banned not by Congress but by the EPA. Administrator William D. Ruckelshaus cancelled the federal registration of DDT products in June 1972, effectively limiting legal uses to "public health, quarantine, and a few crop uses, as well as export." EPA, "DDT Ban Takes Effect," press release, June 14, 1972, http://www.epa.gov/history/topics/ddt/01.htm (November 18, 2010); Toxic Substances Control Act, 15 U.S.C §2605 6(e)1B; EPA, "Polychlorinated Biphenyls (PCBs): Reassessment of Use Authorizations, Advance Notice of Proposed Rulemaking," 40 CFR 761 (EPA-HQ-OPPT-2009-0757; FRL-8811-7), *Federal Register* 75, no. 66 (April 7, 2010), Proposed Rules, 17647; Ellen K. Silbergeld, "Draft Conclusions," 18, October 4, 1983, box 4, folder 114, Silbergeld Papers.

69. Forrestal, *Faith, Hope, and $5,000*, 198.

70. Hays and Hays, *Beauty, Health, and Permanence*, 195; NRC, *Polychlorinated Biphenyls*, 117; Cranor, *Regulating Toxic Substances*, 105.

71. Yueliang Leon Guo and Chen-Chin Hsu, "Yucheng and Yusho," 137. Dibenzofurans appeared with repeated reheating of the PCB-containing cooking oil. Chang et al., "Immunologic Evaluation of Patients with Polychlorinated Biphenyl Poisoning," 62, linked depressed immune function with the *yucheng* exposures. Chen et al., "Cognitive Development."

72. Commoner, "Let's Get Serious." A report from the Alabama Department of Conservation on fish contamination in Choccolocco had been presented in 1971 to the Senate subcommittee considering the bill. William M. Blair, "Senate Unit Told of Fish Tainting," *New York Times*, August 5, 1971.

73. D. B. Hosmer, "PCB Effluents from Anniston Plant to Snow Creek, Choccolocco Creek, Etc.," meeting at Southwest [Southeast] Regional Office of EPA, November 12, 1971, 2, *Abernathy* documents. Plant manager Jessee explained that "current PCB emissions in the liquid effluents primarily resulted from our inability to make a complete separation of biphenyl from other polyphenyls." E. G. Wright to P. B. Hodges et al., "Aroclor Losses at the Anniston Plant," Technical Service Department Progress Report, July 21, 1970, 1, *Abernathy* documents; D. B. Hosmer, "PCB Effluents from Anniston Plant to Snow Creek, Choccolocco Creek, Etc.," meeting at Southwest [Southeast] Regional Office of EPA, November 12, 1971, 1–2, *Abernathy* documents.

74. Jack Anderson and Les Whitten, "Pro-Chemicals Campaign Outlined," *Anniston Star*, December 15, 1977.

75. Randy Henderson, "Anniston an All-America City," *Anniston Star*, April 13, 1978.

76. Darrell A. Baker, *EPA Potential Hazardous Waste Site Inspection Report*, March 5, 1980, 4. Monsanto sought a permit in 1972 for disposing up to 3 million

pounds of Montars. J. T. Bell, "Permit Application for Manufacturing or Processing Operation," April 4, 1972, *Abernathy* documents; Hermanson and Johnson, "Polychlorinated Biphenyls in Tree Bark."

77. H. C. Godt Jr., "Organizational Chronology of Monsanto Records," Monsanto Annual Review, St. Louis, 1970, 11; Forrestal, *Faith, Hope, and $5,000*, 199.

78. Forrestal, *Faith, Hope, and $5,000*, 257.

79. Clarence Thomas, *My Grandfather's Son*, 114.

80. Ibid.

81. Royal G. Suttkus and Gerald E. Gunning to J. T. Bell, June 9, 1972, 4, *Abernathy* documents. The commission's six industry representatives, who voted in a block with three government officials, had long dominated the fourteen-member board. Steve Traylor, "State Water Commission Dies Quietly," *Anniston Star*, October 10, 1971. The industry representatives came from the mining, textile, chemical, lumber, paper, and metals industries. Sam L. Spencer, chief, Fisheries Section, Game and Fish Division, Alabama Department of Conservation, "Alabama Program for the Investigation of Fish Kills," n.d., *Owens* Archive, 26. The commission was abolished by the state legislature effective October 1, 1971. Daniel E. Cooper to Gene L. Jessee, November 13, 1972, CHEMEWG.

82. George J. Levinskas to Dr. J. C. Calandra, "AROCLOR 2-Year Rat Feeding Studies," July 18, 1975, 1, *Abernathy* documents. Environmental engineer Jack Matson credits the 1972 Clean Water Act, not TSCA, as the driving force in shutting down PCB production in Anniston. Interview with Jack Matson, July 28, 2010. Vicki McClure, "Jury: Spread of PCBs Created Public Hazard," *Birmingham News*, February 26, 2002; Henry Hudson to file, "Monsanto/Snow Creek PCBs— Anniston, AL," September 9, 1985, *Abernathy* documents, 1.

83. Interview with R. Emmet Kelly by James E. McKee, September 2, 1981, 3, 10, series 10, box 3, Monsanto Co. History (Oral History Project), Monsanto Records.

84. Interview with Winthrop R. Corey by James E. McKee, December 30, 1981, 35, series 10, box 3, Monsanto Co. History (Oral History Project), Monsanto Records; interview with William A. Daume by James E. McKee, November 17, 1981, 30, series 10, box 3, Monsanto Co. History (Oral History Project), Monsanto Records.

85. J. Gregory Spoon, "Plant Appears Stable," *Anniston Star*, August 6, 1987; Darrell A. Baker, *EPA Potential Hazardous Waste Site Inspection Report*, March 5, 1980, 3–4; Michael Gordon, "Monsanto: The Continent's Parathion Capital," *Anniston Star*, January 23, 1983.

86. "Preparedness Statement, Anniston Plant PCB Incident," March 16, 1983, 1, *Abernathy* documents; Elizabeth Bluemink, "The Evolution of Anniston's 72-Year PCB History," *Anniston Star*, February 25, 2001; Sean Reilly, "PCBs: The Persistent Problem, Officials Doing Little about Choccolocco Creek Pollution," *Anniston Star*, July 10, 1994; Henry Hudson to file, "Monsanto/Snow Creek PCBs—Anniston, AL," September 9, 1985, Plaintiff's Exhibit 6A5, 1, *Abernathy* documents; Jerry L. Brown to James M. Moore, "Snow Creek Tributary Sediment Removal," 1, May 15, 1986; Vicki McClure, "Jury: Spread of PCBs Created Public Hazard," *Birmingham News*, February 26, 2002; Charles A. Graddick to Richard J. Mahoney, January 22, 1985, CHEMEWG.

87. J. Gregory Spoon, "Plant Appears Stable," *Anniston Star*, August 6, 1987; Darrell A. Baker, *EPA Potential Hazardous Waste Site Inspection Report*, March 5, 1980, 3–4.

88. Nash, *Inescapable Ecologies*, 128; interview with Glynn Young, July 15, 2004.

89. Sheila Mullan, "Citizens Reject Landfill," *Anniston Star*, August 8, 1986; twelve hundred signers, Sean Reilly, "Landfill Offers Area Uncertain Legacy," *Anniston Star*, September 18, 1994; "Mercury Rising at Monsanto," *Anniston Star*, July 20, 2001; W. B. Papageorge responses to questionnaire to Earl J. Stephenson, director, EPA Enforcement Division, December 11, 1975, *Abernathy* documents.

Chapter Eight

1. Jim Harmon, *Speak Out* letter to *Anniston Star*, September 17, 1992.

2. "Final Report Adds 35 Chemical Sites," *Anniston Star*, November 24, 1993.

3. U.S. Army Chemical Materials Agency, "M-55 Rocket Operations at the Anniston Chemical Agent Disposal Facility," presentation at the Anniston Outreach Center, January 15, 2004; Anniston Chemical Activity (ANCA), http://www.globalsecurity.org/wmd/facility/anniston.htm (March 26, 2013).

4. Centers for Disease Control and Prevention, "Facts about Sarin," http://emergency.cdc.gov/agent/sarin/basics/facts.asp (August 1, 2012). Sarin was used in the Tokyo Metro assault of 1995, which killed thirteen people and injured thousands. Tom A. Peter, "Japan Catches Final Fugitive in 1995 Nerve Gas Attack," *Christian Science Monitor*, June 15, 2012. "Sarin is said to be 500 times more toxic than cyanide gas, which is used to execute people in gas chambers in American penitentiaries." Nicholas D. Kristof, "Hundreds in Japan Hunt Gas Attackers after 8 Die," *New York Times*, March 20, 1985, 1. Centers for Disease Control and Prevention, "Facts about VX," http://emergency.cdc.gov/agent/vx/basics/facts.asp (August 1, 2012); Centers for Disease Control and Prevention, "Facts about Mustard," http://emergency.cdc.gov/agent/sulfurmustard/basics/facts.asp (August 1, 2012).

5. U.S. Bureau of the Census, *Alabama Population of Counties*.

6. Fries and West, *Chemical Warfare*, ix; Durant, *Greening of the U.S. Military*, 178.

7. "Toxic Terror," *Anniston Star*, March 22, 1995; *Arms Control: Status of U.S.-Russian Agreements and the Chemical Weapons Convention* (chapter report, 03/15/94, GAO/NSIAD-94-136), http://www.gpo.gov/fdsys/pkg/GAOREPORTS-NSIAD-94-136/html/GAOREPORTS-NSIAD-94-136.htm (August 2, 2012). The convention did not enter into force until April 29, 1997. Organisation for the Prohibition of Chemical Weapons, Technical Secretariat, "Status of the Convention on the Prohibition of the Development, Production, Stockpiling and Use of Chemical Weapons and on Their Destruction," August 4, 1997, Incineration Archive.

8. NRC, Panel on Review and Evaluation of Alternative Disposal Technologies, *Review and Evaluation*, 10. The Army's Programmatic Record of Decision on incineration was issued in February 1988. Pierce, "Citizen Resistance to Chemical Weapons Incineration," 460 (n. 5).

9. Interview with Brenda Lindell, July 30, 2003.

10. Jim Harmon, "Our Region's Depot Debate Is on Common Ground," *Anniston Star*, October 1, 1992.

11. U.S. Representative Glen Browder, "What Should We Do after the BRAC Decision?," *Anniston Star*, July 5, 1995.

12. Rick Bragg, "Poison or Poverty?," *St. Petersburg Times*, September 13, 1992; Anniston Ordnance Depot, Calhoun County, Ala., entry 0002, box 2, Records of the Atlanta Chemical Procurement District, RG 156, Office of the Chief of Ordnance, Anniston Ordnance Depot, Anniston, Ala., General Administration Files, 1944–46, Memorandums—Historical Reports, 1, NARA-Morrow; Sean Reilly, "Again, Area Awaits Words on Fort's Fate," *Anniston Star*, January 4, 1993; Sean Reilly, "400 Jobs to Be Lost at Depot," *Anniston Star*, June 24, 1993.

13. U.S. Bureau of the Census, *1990 Census of Population and Housing*, Table 19, Income and Poverty Status in 1989:1990; interview with Chris Waddle, November 19, 2003; Cobb, *Selling of the South*, 229.

14. Frank M. Drendel interview by Jim Keller, March 16, 2000, Cable Center, http://www.cablecenter.org/barco-library-hauser-oral-history/item/drendel-frank.html (December 19, 2012).

15. Frank Sikora, "McClellan Says Its Use of Nerve Gas Not Risky," *Birmingham News*, July 14, 1969; "At Ft. McClellan: Gas Use to Resume," *Birmingham Post-Herald*, October 18, 1969.

16. "The 50th Anniversary of the Army Chemical Center and School at Ft. McClellan Was Marked Monday," *Birmingham News*, June 16, 1970; Sean Reilly, "In 70, Chemical Weapons Disposed of Much Differently," *Anniston Star*, June 28, 1992; Mike Lewis, "Army Stresses Safety as Nerve Gas Is Loaded," *Birmingham Post-Herald*, August 8, 1970.

17. "The Green Dragon," photo, *Birmingham News*, May 29, 1973.

18. "Move by Army Will Boost Anniston's Economic Life," *Birmingham News*, November 30, 1979.

19. Schlesinger, Gaventa, and Merrifield, *Our Own Worst Enemy*, 200; Charles P. Dean, "First in New Line of Updated Army Tanks Brings VIPs to Anniston," *Birmingham News*, August 29, 1981; "Tanks Roll into Depot for Powerful Rebirth," *Birmingham News*, September 15, 1981.

20. Interview with Charles Sherrer, June 6, 2011.

21. Interview with Chris Waddle, November 19, 2003. Anniston activists learned the numbers from their Russian counterparts. Interview with Suzanne Marshall, May 28, 2013.

22. Interview with Brenda Lindell, July 30, 2003.

23. Seager, *Earth Follies*, 14; *Alabama v. Seeber* (1974). The U.S. Supreme Court vacated this decision two years later with its ruling in *Hancock v. Train* (1976). Congress amended the Clean Air Act two years later to require federal facilities to comply with state air pollution permit requirements. Henry H. Caddell, correspondence with author, September 25, 2003. During the George W. Bush administration, the military again sought immunity, this time from the Comprehensive Environmental Response, Compensation, and Liability Act (CERCLA), the Superfund law. Townsend, "Military Exemptions," 67.

24. Robert B. McNeil, "Depot Site Put on Priority Cleanup List," *Anniston Star*, March 31, 1989; Bullard et al., *Environmental Justice and Superfund Sites Workshop*, 4; U.S. Army Environmental Center, Fort McClellan, Ala., *Final Environmental Baseline Survey*, contract no. DACA 31-94-D-0065, Task Order Number 0001, January 1998, 3–13. Trichloroethylene (TCE) was endangering the water supply and had to be monitored vigorously. U.S. Army Corps of Engineers, Mobile District, "Protectiveness Statement," in EPA, *Five-Year Review Report*; Eric Larson, "Depot Research Seeking Contaminated Water," *Anniston Star*, January 30, 1994.

25. Interview with David Christian, September 2, 2003; interview with Alice Donald, August 21, 2003.

26. Durant, *Greening of the U.S. Military*, 180–81; Richard Cockle, "Group Accuses Army of Exaggerating M55 Risk," *Oregonian*, January 14, 1994.

27. Sean Reilly, "Burning Questions Remain," *Anniston Star*, June 17, 1992.

28. NRC, Committee on Review and Evaluation of the Army Chemical Stockpile Disposal Program, *Recommendations*, 3; Committee on Review and Evaluation of the Army Chemical Stockpile Disposal, 17, Alternative Technologies Public Forum, June 30, 1993, Incineration Archive.

29. Richard Cockle, "Group Accuses Army of Exaggerating M55 Risk," *Oregonian*, January 14, 1994.

30. Interview with Brenda Lindell, July 30, 2003.

31. Suzanne Marshall, *"Lord, We're Just Trying to Save Your Water"*; Sean Reilly, "'Burn Busters' Take Incineration Debate to Capitol," *Anniston Star*, June 21, 1994; interview with Suzanne Marshall, October 23, 2003.

32. Interview with Suzanne Marshall, October 23, 2003.

33. Linda Kanamine and Paul Hoverstein, "EPA Cracks Down on Incinerators with Moratorium," *USA Today*, May 19, 1883, 12A; Peter Montague, "EPA Announces New Incinerator Policies," *Rachel's Hazardous Waste News*, May 20, 1993; interview with Suzanne Marshall, October 23, 2003.

34. Ronald Smothers, "Plan to Destroy Toxic Weapons Polarizes a City," *New York Times*, September 24, 1992; Citizens for SPRING newsletter, *What We Believe* 1, no. 1 (September 1992), Incineration Archive; interview with Suzanne Marshall, October 23, 2003; Jim Harmon, "Our Region's Depot Debate Is on Common Ground," *Anniston Star*, October 1, 1992.

35. Rick Bragg, "Poison or Poverty?," *St. Petersburg Times*, September 13, 1992; John Street to Brenda Dozier, September 22, 1992, Incineration Archive.

36. Eric Larsen, "Browder Seeks Incineration Safeguards," *Anniston Star*, August 6, 1993; Sarah Pekkanen, "Browder Urges Chemical Hearings," *Anniston Star*, November 4, 1993.

37. NRC, Committee on Review and Evaluation of the Army Chemical Stockpile Disposal Program, *Recommendations*, executive summary, 1.

38. "Not So Fast: Hold Up Anniston Incinerator," *Montgomery Advertiser*, September 12, 1992; "The Time to Be Sure," *Anniston Star*, September 20, 1992.

39. Randy Noll, Friends of SPRING (Supporting Proven Reliable Incineration of Nerve Gas), "Speak Out: Support the Incinerator," *Anniston Star*, May 20, 1993.

40. "Congress Approves Funding for a Study of Possible On-going Use of the Incinerators after the Nerve Agent Is Burned," *Common Ground* (Berea, Ky.), November 1989, Incineration Archive; William Kresnak, "Inouye Meets Johnston Isle Protester," *Honolulu Advertiser*, August 17, 1990; GAO, "Chemical Warfare: DOD's Successful Effort to Remove U.S. Chemical Weapons from Germany," GAO/NSIAD-91-105, February 1991, Incineration Archive.

41. Spears, "Reducing Environmental Burdens," 205.

42. Eric Larson, "Browder Seeks Incineration Safeguards," *Anniston Star*, August 6, 1993.

43. Eric Larson, "Incinerator Panel's Makeup Raises Eyebrows," *Anniston Star*, November 30, 1993.

44. "Accident Shuts Down Army Weapons Disposal Plant in Pacific," *Anniston Star*, January 4, 1993; Johnson Atoll Chemical Agent Disposal System (JACADS), *Report of the 23 March 1994 Chemical Agent (GB) Release from the Common Stack*, Department of the Army, U.S. Army Chemical Materiel Destruction Agency, Aberdeen Proving Ground, MD 21010-5401, March 23, 1994, 15–17, 20, Incineration Archive.

45. Richard D. Magee and Elisabeth M. Drake, National Research Council's Committee on Review and Evaluation of the Army Chemical Stockpile Disposal Program, "Statement in Regards to Concerns about Storage Risks Associated with the Nation's Stockpile of Chemical Agents and Munitions," August 15, 1994, Incineration Archive; Sean Reilly, "Incineration Opponents Getting Ready for Fight," *Anniston Star*, April 29, 1993; Sarah Pekkanen, "Mom Takes Incineration Fight to D.C.," *Anniston Star*, May 4, 1993; interview with Suzanne Marshall, October 23, 2003.

46. "Browder Wants Assurance of Safe Depot Destruction," *Birmingham News*, July 17, 1993.

47. NRC, Committee on Review and Evaluation of the Army Chemical Stockpile Disposal Program, *Recommendations*, 2, 6–7, 10; U.S. Government Accounting Office, *Chemical Weapons Destruction*.

48. NRC, Committee on Review and Evaluation of the Army Chemical Stockpile Disposal Program, *Recommendations*, 12, 11, 3.

49. Interview with Suzanne Marshall, October 23, 2003.

50. NRC, Committee on Review and Evaluation of the Army Chemical Stockpile Disposal Program, *Recommendations*, 12, 5–6, 13, 14.

51. Pat Costner, Greenpeace, "The Incineration of HD Agent at JACADS: MPF [Metal Parts Furnace] Trial Burn and LIC Demonstration Burn," March 17, 1994, Incineration Archive.

52. Craig Williams, "NRC Stockpile Committee Telephone Conversations of July 25–28," July 29, 1994, Incineration Archive.

53. Interview with Chris Waddle, November 19, 2003; Eric Larson, "AAD Facility Won't Be Slowed: Browder," *Anniston Star*, December 30, 1994.

54. Eric Larson, "Protesters Say No to Incineration: About 300 March to Express Opposition," *Anniston Star*, April 18, 1994; Eric Larson, "Neutralization Process Nearer Than Some Think," *Anniston Star*, April 19, 1994.

55. Scott C. Mohr, Physicians for Social Responsibility, "Critique of Incineration Proposal for Destruction of Chemical Warfare Agents," Boston, March 18, 1994, Incineration Archive.

56. Ibid., 3 (emphasis in original).

57. Jim Harmon, co–vice chairman of the CDCAC, to the Honorable Sam Nunn, June 10, 1994, ALA CAC folder, Incineration Archive.

58. Jim Harmon, of the Alabama Chemical Demilitarization Citizens Advisory Commission, to Congressman Glen Browder, "U.S. Army Report of March 1994 JACADS Agent Release," June 24, 1994; Jim Folsom to the Honorable Ronald V. Dellums, July 6, 1994, ALA CAC folder, Incineration Archive.

59. Glen Browder to Dr. Doris L. Gertler, June 21, 1994, ALA CAC folder, Incineration Archive; Jim Harmon to Chris Waddel (sic), letter to *Anniston Star*, August 24, 1994, Incineration Archive.

60. Defense Environmental Alert, August 10, 1994, folder: M-55, Incineration Archive; U.S. Army Chemical Material Destruction Agency, Aberdeen Proving Ground, Md., "Risk Assessment Study," press release, August 9, 1994, Incineration Archive; Travis Flora, "Army Admits Mistake; Accused of Lying to NRC," *Berea Citizen* 95, no. 7 (August 11, 1994): 1; Walter L. Busbee, brigadier general, U.S. Army commander/director, to Dr. Doris Gertler, August 19, 1994, Incineration Archive.

61. Sam Nunn to Jim Harmon, August 18, 1994, Incineration Archive; *Report on the National Defense Authorization Act for Fiscal Year 1995*, June 14 (legislative day June 7), 1994 (Washington, D.C.: U.S. Government Printing Office, 1994), 47–49.

62. Commander, U.S. Army Chemical Demilitarization and Remediation Activity, "Final Screening Risk Assessment, RCRA Part B, no. 39-26-1399-95, Anniston Chemical Demilitarization Facility, Anniston Army Depot, Anniston, Alabama," Table 1, Aberdeen Proving Ground, Md., March 27, 1995; Mick Harrison, "Green Law Preliminary Risk Analysis of the Army Chemical Weapon Incineration Program," Washington, D.C., September 1996; EPA, *Health Assessment Document for TCDD (1994)*; "Study Heightens Dioxin Alarm," *Anniston Star*, September 12, 1994.

63. Rufus Kinney, "No, Let's Try Something Safer," *Birmingham News*, May 24, 1994.

64. Families Concerned about Nerve Gas Incineration, press release, August 10, 1994, Incineration Archive; Jim Harmon to Chris Waddel (sic), Exchange Page, *Anniston Star*, August 24, 1994.

65. Common Ground, "Local Citizens Gear Up for Richmond March for Safe Disposal of Nerve Gas," press release, September 12, 1994, Incineration Archive.

66. Steve Jones to Henry Silvestri, "Internal Audit Executive Summary," August 2, 1994, 1, Incineration Archive.

67. Craig Williams, Chemical Weapons Working Group, "Interview with Steve Jones," September 19, 1994, 2, Incineration Archive; John Thompson, "Safety Manager Blows Whistle on Chemical Burner," *Tooele (Utah) Transcript-Bulletin*, September 20, 1004; Sen. Orrin Hatch, "Possible Chemical Weapons Leaks in Utah under Investigation," press release, September 20, 1994, Incineration Archive.

68. The Defense Authorization Act, PL 104-208, Sec. 8065, September 30, 1996 awarded the funds for ACWA.

69. Eric Larson, "Incinerator Bid Awarded," *Anniston Star*, March 1, 1996; Representative Bob Riley to Carrie N. Baker, July 22, 1998, CRBI Archive; Elizabeth Pezzulo, "Permit Contains No Big Surprises," *Anniston Star*, June 25, 1997; Sen. Richard Shelby to Carrie Baker, June 3, 1998, CRBI Archive; interviews with David Christian, September 9, 2003, February 22, 2013; Durant, *Greening of the U.S. Military*, 189.

70. John H. Hankinson Jr., EPA regional administrator, to Sen. Max Cleland, August 3, 1998, enclosure A-1, A-2, Incineration Archive.

71. Craig Williams to Listserv, December 7, 2000, Incineration Archive.

72. Suzanne Marshall, *Chemical Weapons Disposal and Environmental Justice*, http://cwwg.org/ej.html (May 15, 2013); Marshall, Kinney, and Hudson, "Incineration of Chemical Weapons in Anniston," 151, 153.

73. Marshall, Kinney, and Hudson, "Incineration of Chemical Weapons," 160–61; interview with Rufus Kinney, July 15, 2003.

74. Marshall, Kinney, and Hudson, "Incineration of Chemical Weapons," 164, 162, 164, 167.

75. Interview with Brenda Lindell, July 30, 2003.

76. Interview with Rufus Kinney, July 15, 2003. Kentucky and Indiana passed laws imposing tough regulatory standards on the Army that effectively precluded incineration. Sean Reilly, "Depot Boss Calls Incineration Safe," *Anniston Star*, August 21, 1992. Maryland eventually did so as well. Pierce, "Citizen Resistance to Chemical Weapons Incineration," 477; interview with David Christian, February 22, 2013; interview with Suzanne Marshall, October 23, 2003.

77. Errin Haines, "Rash of Noose Incidents Reported," *USA Today*, October 10, 2007. In 2012, the American Federation of Government Employees represented roughly 4,000 depot employees. Cameron Steele, "Depot Union Leader Everett Kelley Wins National Spot," *Anniston Star*, May 30, 2012.

78. Elizabeth Pezzullo, "EPA Dismisses Racism Complaint," *Anniston Star*, January 29, 1998.

79. The official closing ceremony took place on May 20, 1999. History of Fort McClellan, 1917–99, Transition Force, United States Army Garrison, Fort McClellan, Ala., http://www.mcclellan.army.mil/Info.asp (May 30, 2013).

80. *Families Concerned v. U.S. Department of the Army*, March 18, 2005; Jay Reeves, "Alabama Files Suit to Block Chemical Weapons Incinerator," *Gadsden (Ala.) Times*, February 15, 2002; Matthew Creamer, "Siegelman Raises Issues with FEMA," *Anniston Star*, February 23, 2002.

81. Interview with Rev. Henry Sterling, November 4, 2003.

82. "America's Cold War Remnant, Folly, in Praise of Protest," *Anniston Star*, April 18, 1993; interview with Chris Waddle, November 19, 2003.

Chapter Nine

1. Sweet Valley/Cobbtown Environmental Justice Taskforce, *Justice Track*, Fall 1998, 1.

2. Communication with Sylvester Harris, July 14, 2003; Elizabeth Pezzullo, "Choccolocco Creek Fish Is Contaminated," *Anniston Star*, November 4, 1993;

Alabama Department of Environmental Management, Special Studies Section, Field Operation Division, "Draft Choccolocco Creek Watershed Study Proposal," 1993, 1; ATSDR, *Public Health Assessment for Monsanto*, 25; Alabama Department of Public Health, "Alabama Fish Consumption Advisory Guidelines," http://www.adph.org/tox/assets/FishAdv2011.pdf (April 28, 2012). The Sewells filed suit against Monsanto in early April 1994. Sean Reilly, "Third Suit Filed against Monsanto," *Anniston Star*, April 6, 1994; Mike Bolton, "Late Warning: Don't Eat Fish from Lay Lake," *Birmingham News*, September 17, 2000.

3. ADPH/ATSDR, *Monsanto Company*, 4; "Discovery of Contamination at Anniston Transmission Substation," April 23, 1993, *Abernathy* transcript, January 14–18, 2002; Donald Stewart, *Abernathy* transcript, January 28, 2002; Laura Howard, "PCB Level Probed," *Anniston Star*, April 4, 1993, quoting power company spokesperson Buddy Eiland. Paradoxically, Alabama Power had been a driving force behind the early manufacture of chlorinated diphenyls, and electrical companies had been vocal opponents of banning Aroclors production. Robert T. Jones, "Memorandum for Record Stormwater Permit Application," January 30, 1995, 1.

4. George J. Tanber and Sean Reilly, "Contaminated Ditch: PCB Find Put Residents on Alert," *Anniston Star*, March 23, 1995; Elizabeth Pezzullo and Thomas Spencer, "PCB-Affected Area Should Be Tested, Residents Are Told," *Anniston Star*, October 20, 1995.

5. Interview with Cassandra Roberts, September 3, 2003.

6. ADPH/ATSDR, *Cobbtown/Sweet Valley Health Consultation No. 2*, June 26, 1996, 13.

7. Elizabeth Pezzullo, "Towns Await Results of Tests to Determine PCB Levels," *Anniston Star*, January 21, 1996; Elizabeth Pezzullo, "Meeting on PCBs Leaves Residents Still Uncertain," *Anniston Star*, January 24, 1996.

8. Phil Brown, *Toxic Exposures*, 33.

9. Isaac, "Movement of Movements." Payne, *I've Got the Light of Freedom*, and John Dittmer, *Local People*, are examples of this approach. Sweet Valley/Cobbtown Environmental Justice Taskforce, *Justice Track*, Fall 1998, 3. HBCU-based centers include the Deep South Center for Environmental Justice (DSCEJ), established by Beverly Wright at Xavier University in 1992, now housed at Dillard University, and the Environmental Justice Research Center (EJRC) launched by Robert Bullard at Clark-Atlanta University in 1994.

10. Rev. Joseph Lowery, "Statement by Rev. Joseph Lowery on PCB Dumping Protest in North Carolina," September 15, 1982; Dale Roussakoff, "Tiny Community Stirs Fuss over Waste Dump," *Atlanta Constitution*, October 17, 1982; "39 Juveniles, 44 Adults Arrested in PCB Protests," *Durham (N.C.) Morning Herald*, October 5, 1982.

11. The Warren County PCB struggle also stimulated voter registration drives that led to significant black empowerment locally. See McGurty, *Transforming Environmentalism*, 90–93.

12. Commission for Racial Justice, *Toxic Wastes and Race*; Bullard, *Dumping in Dixie*.

13. Taylor, "Environmentalism and the Politics of Inclusion," 57.

14. Environmental Justice Act of 1992, H.R. 2105, 103rd Congress (1993–94).

15. EPA administrator William Reilly had established an Environmental Equity Work Group in 1990. Environmental Justice Resource Center, *Second National People of Color Summit: Celebrating Our Victories, Strengthening Our Roots*, http://www.ejrc.cau.edu/summit2/%20EJTimeline.pdf (April 28, 2012); "Clinton Executive Order 12898: Federal Actions to Address Environmental Justice in Minority Populations and Low-Income Populations," February 11, 1994, *Federal Register* 59, no. 32 (February 16, 1994): 7629–33.

16. Isaac, "Movement of Movements," citing Goodwin and Jasper, *Social Movements Reader*, 3; Mueller, "Building Social Movement Theory," 22; interview with David Baker, March 26, 2004.

17. Interview with Kay Beard, July 16, 2003; interview with James Hall, July 8, 2004; interview with Bessie Jones, October 15, 2004.

18. Sean Reilly, "PCBs Linger in Area," *Anniston Star*, January 11, 1995; Sean Reilly, "Tests Show PCB Levels in Fish Still Too High," *Anniston Star*, March 24, 1995; Auyero and Swistun, "Social Production."

19. "Environment, tort reform, and trade were the three public policy issues I focused on" (Mahoney, *In My Opinion*, 227). Opheim, "Five Years after the Pledge," reprinted in Mahoney, *In My Opinion*, 228–33; "Monsanto Training Manual on Synergy '94: The Community Responsibilities of Sustainable Development," 1, series 11, box 2, Monsanto Records.

20. Opheim, "Five Years after the Pledge."

21. Mahoney, *Commitment to Greatness*, 9, 7, 10. Industry historian Alfred du Pont Chandler has also made this point in *Shaping the Industrial Century*, 49–50. Loeb, "Hendrick Verfaille."

22. Opheim, "Five Years after the Pledge," 231; interview with Howard K. Nason by James E. McKee, July 24, 1981, 1–2, series 10, box 3, Monsanto Co. History (Oral History Project), Monsanto Records.

23. The American Chemistry Council (successor to the Chemical Manufacturers Association) still maintains the Responsible Care approach. http://responsiblecare.americanchemistry.com/ (April 15, 2012). Chemical Manufacturers Association Public Outreach Program, December 10, 1990, 3, Chemical Industry Archives, http://chemicalindustryarchives.org/dirtysecrets/responsiblecare/pdfs/CMA083581.pdf#page=2 (January 4, 2012).

24. Interview with Kay Beard, July 16, 2003; Jonathan Sapers, "Monsanto: The Wizard Now Sleeps," *Anniston Star*, October 27, 1985.

25. Interview with Glynn Young, July 15, 2004; Sandman and American Industrial Hygiene Association, *Responding to Community Outrage*, 113. Also see Bob Burton, "Advice on Making Nice": Peter Sandman Plots to Make You a Winner," PR Watch, Center on Media and Democracy, *PR Watch: Public Interest Reporting on the PR/Public Affairs Industry* 6, no. 1 (First Quarter 1999): 1–6, Center on Media and Democracy, http://www.prwatch.org/files/pdfs/prwatch/prwv6n1.pdf (December 12, 2005).

26. "How Dick Mahoney Aced Retirement," *Inside PR's Magazine of Reputation Management*, November/December 1996, reprinted in Mahoney, *In My Opinion*, 12; Tokar, *Earth for Sale*, 35.

27. The Emergency Planning and Community Right-to-Know Act of 1986 established the TRI as a national database of toxic chemical releases as reported by industry. Public Law 99-499, 100 Stat. 1613 (1986), 42 U.S.C. §§11001–50. Mahoney recalled "vividly when I first looked at the [TRI] numbers, it was a shock to me. They were quite large, . . . I didn't like them and I was sure that the public was going to hate them" (quoted in Opheim, "Five Years after the Pledge," 232). Interview with Glynn Young, July 15, 2004. Robert McGough reported Monsanto's 1987 releases in "A Matter of Perception," *Financial World*, January 23, 1990, 43. "EPA's Inventory of Toxic Trouble" ranked Monsanto number five among parent corporations with the highest total emissions for 1991. *USA Today*, May 26, 1993. "How Dick Mahoney Aced Retirement," *Inside PR's Magazine of Reputation Management*, November/December 1996, reprinted in Mahoney, *In My Opinion*, 11; "Monsanto Training Manual on Synergy '94: The Community Responsibilities of Sustainable Development," series 11, box 2, Monsanto Records; Mahoney, *Commitment to Greatness*, 4.

28. Birnbaum, "Third Biannual International PCB Workshop," 1; U.S. Attorney, Southern District of New York, "United States Announces Approximately $773 Million Settlement with GM to Resolve Environmental Liabilities," press release, October 10, 2010, 1–2; EPA, "Hudson River PCBs." See also David Gargill, "The General Electric Superfraud: Why the Hudson River Will Never Run Clean," *Harper's Magazine*, December 2009, 41–51; Francis, "Conspiracy of Silence"; EPA National Priorities List, "NPL Site Narrative for Fox River NRDA/PCB Releases," http://www.epa.gov/superfund/sites/npl/nar1515.htm (April 28, 2012); *Transwestern Pipeline v. Monsanto* (1996); "EPA Superfund Explanation of Significant Differences: Commencement Bay, Near Shore/Tide Flats, Pierce County, Washington, July 28, 1997," 4–5, http://www.epa.gov/superfund/sites/rods/fulltext/e1097059.pdf (November 21, 2011).

29. For corporate sustainability practices, see, for example, Anderson, *Midcourse Correction: Toward a Sustainable Enterprise*. Tokar, *Earth for Sale*, 21.

30. "Monsanto Training Manual on Synergy '94: The Community Responsibilities of Sustainable Development," 1, series 11, box 2, Monsanto Records.

31. *Environmental Equity Vulnerability Analysis*, Monsanto Company, 1994, series 11, box 2, Monsanto Records.

32. Interview with David Baker, March 26, 2004.

33. Monsanto Pledge, 1990, *Abernathy* documents; interview with David Baker, March 26, 2004.

34. Interview with David Baker, March 26, 2004.

35. Quoted in Elizabeth Pezzullo and Thomas Spencer, "PCB-Affected Area Should Be Tested, Residents Are Told," *Anniston Star*, October 20, 1995.

36. *Monsanto Property Purchase Program*, prepared by Prudential Relocation Services, October 1995, 3, in author's possession; EPA Proceedings: Superfund Relocation Roundtable Meeting, May 2–4, 1996, Pensacola Civic Center, Pensacola, Fla.; Solid Waste and Emergency Response, 9378.0-03, EPA 540-K-96-010, PB96-963254, December 1996.

37. *Monsanto Property Purchase Program*, prepared by Prudential Relocation Services, October 1995, 8, in author's possession.

38. Interview with Eloise Mealing, February 22, 2004; Elizabeth Pezzullo, "Families Packing Homes, Memories for PCB Cleanup," *Anniston Star*, October 20, 1996; interview with Cassandra Roberts, September 3, 2003.

39. U.S. Bureau of the Census, Table 19, "Income and Poverty Status in 1989,"1990, 64. In 1989, 2,180 persons living in Tract 13, which covered most of West Anniston, of which Sweet Valley and Cobbtown were a part, 440, or 20.2 percent, had incomes below poverty level. Fifteen percent of the West Anniston population was elderly; 7 percent were children ages five and younger, based on 1990 figures, ATSDR, *Public Health Assessment for Monsanto*, 5. Lythcott, *Sweet Valley/Cobb Town Relocation Study*, 4, 7–8.

40. Sweet Valley/Cobbtown Environmental Justice Taskforce, *Justice Track*, 1; Bill Wilson, "Monsanto Corp., you have made our life so complicated," photo, *Anniston Star*, February 8, 1996.

41. Lythcott, *Sweet Valley/Cobb Town Relocation Study*, 4.

42. Interviews with Arthur and Bettye Bowie, September 29, 2003.

43. Interview with Arthur Bowie, September 29, 2003.

44. Amended Complaint, *Owens v. Monsanto* (2001), 13; Lythcott, *Sweet Valley/Cobb Town Relocation Study*, "Community Relocation Update," draft, September 24, 1996.

45. Fullilove, *Root Shock*; interview with Salle Bowie Franklin, September 29, 2003; testimony by Sallie Bowie Franklin, *Abernathy* transcript, January 15, 2002.

46. Erik Eckholm, "Clay Eating Proves Widespread but Cause Is Uncertain," *New York Times*, July 22, 1986; Flynt, *Poor but Proud*, 178; interview with Bettye Bowie, September 29, 2003.

47. Interview with Jacqueline Brown, September 25, 2003; Thomas Spencer, "PCBs High in Soil Dug near Monsanto," *Anniston Star*, April 5, 1996.

48. Erikson, "Trauma at Buffalo Creek," 153; Stephen R. Couch and Anne Mercuri, "Toxic Water, Toxic Knowledge, and a Subculture of Distress," talk at the Eastern Sociological Association, noted in *BSED in Touch* 3, no. 1 (Fall 2001): 3; Couch and Kroll-Smith, "Patterns of Victimization."

49. Interview with Opal Scruggs, September 25, 2003.

50. Ibid.; *Abernathy* transcript, January 25, 2002; Kroft, "Toxic Town"; Dr. David O. Carpenter, *Owens* transcript, April 9, 2001, 929.

51. Interview with Opal Scruggs, September 25, 2003.

52. Ibid.

53. ADPH/ATSDR, *Cobbtown/Sweet Valley Health Consultation No. 2*, June 26, 1996, 13, 9, 8, 3–4 (my emphasis).

54. Interview with Jacqueline Brown, September 25, 2003.

55. Interviews with Arthur and Bettye Bowie, September 29, 2003.

56. ADPH/ATSDR, *Cobbtown/Sweet Valley Health Consultation No. 2*, June 26, 1996, 10, 2, 11, 13.

57. Ibid., 10, 12, 11; Pavuk et al., "Assessment of Human Exposure to PCBs in Anniston," 1084; handwritten note on ADPH/ATSDR, *Cobbtown/Sweet Valley Health Consultation No. 2*, June 26, 1996, 11.

58. Alabama Department of Environmental Management, *In the Matter of Monsanto Company*, Anniston, Calhoun County, Ala., I.D. no. ALD 004 019 048, consent order no. 96-054-CHW, 3. An earlier consent order dated April 5, 1995, with ADEM outlined a sampling plan for the Monsanto site. ATSDR, *Public Health Assessment for Monsanto*, May 17, 2001, 3; ADPH/ATSDR, *Cobbtown/Sweet Valley Health Consultation No. 2*, June 26, 1996, 9–10, 15, 16.

59. Interview with Eloise Mealing, February 22, 2004; Elizabeth Pezzullo, "Families Packing Homes, Memories for PCB Cleanup," *Anniston Star*, October 20, 1996.

60. A broad cross-class and interracial left-liberal alliance against Jim Crow, the SCHW attracted everyone from Communist Party mine worker organizers to Eleanor Roosevelt, who famously defied segregation at the organization's 1938 founding meeting in Birmingham. Fosl, *Subversive Southerner*, 44; Egerton, *Speak Now Against the Day*, 193–94; Robin D. G. Kelley, *Hammer and Hoe*, 186; Spears, "Freedom Buses Rolling"; phone interview with Connie Tucker, December 4, 2008.

61. Interview with Cassandra Roberts, March 18, 2013.

62. Ibid.

63. EPA Proceedings: Superfund Relocation Roundtable Meeting, May 2–4, 1996, Pensacola Civic Center, Pensacola, Fla.; Solid Waste and Emergency Response, 9378.0-03, EPA 540-K-96-010, PB96-963254, December 1996.

64. Interview with Cassandra Roberts, March 18, 2013; phone interview with Suzanne Marshall, March 17, 2013.

65. Brown, *Toxic Exposures*, 17; Brown and Mikkelson, *No Safe Place*, 2.

66. McCord's Grocery was among the stores exempted from the 1971 boycott of Anniston retail outlets because the McCords hired black workers. "Blacks Call for Broad Boycott; 13 Stores Exempt," *Anniston Star*, November 10, 1971; "Deaths," McCord Papers.

67. Alaimo, *Bodily Natures*, 20, citing Steingraber, *Living Downstream*, 102; EPA, *Polychlorinated Biphenyls: Health Effects*.

68. Sean Reilly, "Officials Doing Little about Choccolocco Creek Pollution," *Anniston Star*, July 10, 1994; Elizabeth Bluemink, "Testimony Begins Today in *Owens vs. Monsanto* Lawsuit," *Anniston Star*, April 5, 2001; Jennifer McCullars, "Stored PCB-Laden Dirt Said No Threat," *Anniston Star*, April 8, 2001; Elizabeth Bluemink, "Jury Rules against Monsanto," *Anniston Star*, February 23, 2002; Lythcott, *Sweet Valley/Cobb Town Relocation Study*, March 15, 1997.

69. Interview with Cassandra Roberts, September 3, 2003; *Monsanto Property Purchase Program*, prepared by Prudential Relocation Services, October 1995, 5, in author's possession.

70. Donald Stewart, University of Alabama School of Law lecture, April 11, 2012.

71. Elizabeth Pezzullo, "Church Members Not Swayed by Padlock," *Anniston Star*, January 26, 1998; Vandana Shiva, interview, *UNESCO Courier* 45, no. 3 (March 1992): 8; Elizabeth Pezzullo, "Chapel Controversy: Mars Hill Congregation Attempts to Fire Lawyer, Pastor and Deacon," *Anniston Star*, July 21, 1997; Elizabeth Pezzullo, "Mars Pastor Keeps Job," *Anniston Star*, October 23, 1997. The Alabama Supreme Court upheld Judge Laird's ruling that the insurgent group

could not contest the settlement. *Mars Hill Baptist Church v. Mars Hill Missionary Baptist Church*, November 12, 1999.

72. Jonathan Lifland, "Laird Says Mars Hill Case Closed," *Anniston Star*, August 6, 1998.

73. Testimony by Cassandra Roberts, in *Mars Hill Missionary Baptist Church v. Monsanto*, September 3, 1998, 66.

74. Goulden, *Jerry Wurf*, 293.

75. Interview with Andrew Bowie, October 14, 2003.

76. Interview with David Baker, March 26, 2004.

77. Shirley Baker was later appointed to the ATSDR's Tribal and Community Affairs Committee.

78. The West Anniston Environmental Justice Task Force, later referred to as CAP, was distinct from the Sweet Valley/Cobbtown Environmental Justice Taskforce.

79. ADPH/ATSDR, *Cobbtown/Sweet Valley Health Consultation No. 2*, June 26, 1996, 9; EPA Potential Hazardous Waste Site Investigation and Preliminary Assessment, Eckhardt Report, October 5, 1979, *Abernathy* documents.

80. U.S. Senate, Committee on Appropriations, *PCB Contamination in Anniston*, 30–31; John A. Poole Jr., to Juan Reyes and Richard Green, February 29, 1996; Sean Reilly, "Officials Doing Little about Choccolocco Creek Pollution," *Anniston Star*, July 10, 1994; letter from Myron D. Lair, chief, Emergency Response and Removal Branch of the U.S. Environmental Protection Agency, Region IV, to Mr. Dan Cooper, chief of special projects for the Alabama Department of Environmental Management, March 19, 1996, *Abernathy* documents; Elizabeth Bluemink, "The Evolution of Anniston's 72-Year PCB History," *Anniston Star*, February 25, 2001.

81. Laura Nation, "Class Action Suit against Monsanto Proceeds," *Anniston Star*, September 29, 1998; U.S. Senate, Committee on Appropriations, *PCB Contamination in Anniston*, 31.

82. Interview with David Baker, February 27, 2012; EPA, "Environmental Justice Small Grants Program"; *United States v. Pharmacia* (2003); EPA Fact Sheet: Anniston Site, Anniston, Calhoun County, Ala., February 13, 2001; EPA Office of Environmental Justice, National Environmental Justice Advisory Council, executive summary, May 23–26, 2000, ES-1; Eddie Motes, "Kids and PCBs Don't Mix," photo, *Anniston Star*, November 7, 2000.

83. Elizabeth Bluemink, "Five Anniston Anti-pollution Groups Seek to Link Causes," *Anniston Star*, January 17, 2001.

84. Solutia director of environmental affairs Robert G. Kaley II to Dr. Jeffrey P. Koplan, ATSDR, May 2, 2000, 2; Robert G. Kaley to ATSDR, "Re: Public Health Assessment for Monsanto Company," February 8, 2000, 1–23, CHEMEWG.

Chapter Ten

1. *Owens v. Monsanto* (2001); *Abernathy v. Monsanto*; *Tolbert v. Monsanto*.

2. *Dyer v. Monsanto*; *Shelter Cove Management v. Monsanto*. Heard by St. Clair Circuit Court Judge Bob Austin, these cases were settled in 1999 for $22.7 million

in payments to 4,300 landowners and $21 million for waterway cleanup. Associated Press, "Former Monsanto Corp. Offers $43.7 Million in Pollution Case," *Times Daily*, June 18, 1999.

3. Donald Stewart, *Abernathy* transcript, February 20, 2002; Dr. Robert George Kaley, *Abernathy* transcript, January 31, 2002.

4. Jones, "Explosion in Toxic Torts"; Jasanoff, *Science at the Bar*, 118.

5. Jasanoff, *Science at the Bar*, 119; Dr. Ian C. Nisbet, *Owens* transcript, April 11, 2001, 1355.

6. Zaillian, *Civil Action*; Soderbergh, *Erin Brockovich*.

7. Jones, "Explosion in Toxic Torts."

8. *Daubert v. Merrell Dow Pharmaceuticals* (1993); Shields and Bryan, "Georgia's New Expert Witness Rule," 22 (n. 29).

9. Jasanoff, *Science at the Bar*, 40; Stephen Breyer, introduction to Federal Judicial Center, *Reference Manual*; Shields and Bryan, "Georgia's New Expert Witness Rule." For a discussion of *Daubert*'s impact on environmental health regulation and litigation, see *American Journal of Public Health*, Suppl. 1, 95 (July 2005).

10. On "The Limits of Litigation," see Cole and Foster, *From the Ground Up*, 121–30; and Cole, "Environmental Justice Litigation."

11. For an early review of potential legal claims of environmental injustice, see Godsil, "Remedying Environmental Racism"; Cole, "Environmental Justice Litigation," 121–30; and Ford, "Boundaries of Race."

12. Dr. Emmet Kelly to Dr. J. W. Barrett in London, September 20, 1955, 1, *Abernathy* documents; Paul B. Hodges to Toby Bell, "Confidential," September 18, 1970; D. B. Hosmer, "PCB Effluents from Anniston Plant to Snow Creek, Choccolocco Creek, Etc.," meeting at Southwest [Southeast] Regional EPA, November 11, 1971, 2, *Abernathy* documents.

13. Interview with Cassandra Roberts, September 3, 2003; interview with Ralph Knowles, October 16, 2008.

14. Interview with Jacqueline Brown, September 25, 2003.

15. The *Owens* complaint was initially filed on February 22, 1996, by Frank Davis and Selma, Alabama, civil rights attorney J. L. Chestnut. Named plaintiff and lake property landowner Walter Owens, Walter Frazier, and Clay Albright were severed from the claims of the other plaintiffs. Final Judgment and Order of Dismissal, U.S.D.C. N. D., Ala., Eastern Division, Judge Inge Johnson, April 26, 2001, 1.

16. Interview with Cleophus Thomas, July 15, 2003; David Scott, Associated Press, "Old Chemical History Dogs Monsanto's Efforts to Reinvent Itself," *Anniston Star*, January 19, 2002; Toni Clarke, "Solutia Sees Monsanto's Shares Rise," *Bloomberg News*, September 8, 1997.

17. Interview with Glynn Young, July 15, 2004; Dr. Robert George Kaley, *Abernathy* transcript, January 31, 2002. Solutia declared itself "a totally separate business entity." ATSDR, *Public Health Assessment for Monsanto*, May 17, 2001, 40. Monsanto stockholders retained ownership shares in Solutia. See testimony by John Hunter, *Abernathy* transcript, March 12, 2002.

18. For a chronology of the corporate restructuring, see the Monsanto Company 2003 Form 10K filed with the U.S. Securities and Exchange Commission for the

fiscal year ended December 31, 2000. David Scott, Associated Press, "Old Chemical History Dogs Monsanto's Efforts to Reinvent Itself," *Anniston Star*, January 19, 2002. Also see Desiree J. Hanford, Dow Jones Newswires, "Solutia Says Ala. Residents Aren't Owed More Money," http://www.prophet.net/quotes/stocknews.jsp?symbol=SOI&article+20031204460_29b2001c795d6eaf (May 5, 2006).

19. "Monsanto Clarifies Issues Related to Anniston, AL and PCB Cleanup," *Monsanto Imagine*, http://www.monsanto.com/monsanto/layout/pf.asp?pf (April 12, 2004) (my emphasis); Moyers, "Toxic Communities"; Kroft, "Toxic Town."

20. Settlement talks had been abandoned on February 2, 2001. Ralph Knowles, *Owens* transcript, April 10, 2001, 1059.

21. Jack Matson, "Death Sentence: PCBs on Trial," unpublished manuscript, 4.

22. Bob Shields, *Owens* transcript, April 4, 2001, 425, 448, 438; M. N. Farrar et al. to Rodney Harris, "Report of the Aroclors 'Ad Hoc' Committee, Second Draft," October 15, 1969, *Abernathy* documents.

23. Jere White, *Owens* transcript, April 4, 2001, 463, 459, 476, 464.

24. Oreskes and Conway, *Merchants of Doubt*; Littlemore, "Manufacturing Doubt," 41; Case, "Manufacturing Doubt in Product Defense"; "PCBs: Just How Dangerous?"; Dr. Robert D. Kaley II, "Chemical Studies Are Flawed and Inconclusive"; John Peterson Myers, "The Evidence Is There—Corporations Ignore It" *Anniston Star*, March 30, 2001.

25. Quoted in Elizabeth Bluemink, "Monsanto Reports Available Online," *Anniston Star*, March 29, 2001.

26. Ruth Mims, *Owens* transcript, April 5, 2001, 497, 565–67; Michael Grunwald, "In Dirt, Water and Hogs, Town Got Its Fill of PCBs: Unknowing Residents Have Little Left but Lawsuits," *Washington Post*, January 1, 2002.

27. *Owens v. Monsanto* (2001), filed February 22, 1996. The cases were mass toxic torts, "aggregate non-class" cases, as opposed to class action lawsuits. Interview with Ralph Knowles, October 16, 2008; Gentle, "Administration of the 2003 Tolbert PCB Settlement," 1251; Dr. David O. Carpenter, *Owens* transcript, April 9, 2001, 940, 540, 994; SESD Surface Soil Sampling, Anniston, Ala., USEPA Region Four, Science and Ecosystem Support Division, Hazardous Waste Section, *Owens* transcript, April 5, 2001, 534; Plaintiffs exhibit 1038, June 18, 1999; Bob Shields, *Owens* transcript, April 3, 2001, 10; Ruth Mims, *Owens* transcript, April 5, 2001, 549.

28. Ralph Knowles, *Owens* transcript, April 5, 2001, 564, citing Denzel Ferguson, "Partial Report to Monsanto," November 2, 1966.

29. Ruth Mims, *Owens* transcript, April 5, 2001, 582, 571, 588–89.

30. Ibid., 551; Nancy Beiles, "What Monsanto Knew," *The Nation*, May 29, 2000; Michael Grunwald, "In Dirt, Water and Hogs, Town Got Its Fill of PCBs: Unknowing Residents Have Little Left but Lawsuits," *Washington Post*, January 1, 2002; "Hog Analysis Results," December 24, 1970, *Abernathy* documents; interview with Ralph Knowles, October 16, 2008.

31. George Ford, *Abernathy* transcript, February 20, 2002; Jere White, *Abernathy* transcript, January 14, 2002.

32. Jack Matson, *Owens* transcript, April 6, 2001, 741–42; interview with Jack Matson, July 28, 2010; Jack Matson, *Owens* transcript, April 5, 2001, 596.

33. Jack Matson, *Owens* transcript, April 6, 2001, 726; Jack Matson, *Abernathy* transcript, January 14, 2002.

34. Nisbet and Sarofim, "Rates and Routes of Transport of PCBs"; Dr. Ian C. Nisbet, *Owens* transcript, April 11, 2001, 1272–1462, at 1357, 1366 (my emphasis).

35. Dr. David O. Carpenter, *Owens* transcript, April 9, 2001, 875; Carpenter, "Polychlorinated Biphenyls and Human Health"; Michael Grunwald, "Monsanto Hid Decades of Pollution," *Washington Post*, January 1, 2002.

36. Dr. David O. Carpenter, *Owens* transcript, April 9, 2001.

37. Brown and Jones, "Mortality and Industrial Hygiene Study of Workers Exposed to PCBs"; David Brown, "Mortality of Workers Exposed to PCBs: An Update"; Gustavsson, Hogstedt, and Rappe, "Short-Term Mortality."

38. Loomis et al., "Cancer Mortality among Electric Utility Workers"; Rothman et al., "Nested Case-Control Study of Non-Hodgkin Lymphoma."

39. The North Carolina study is Millikan et al., "DDE, PCBs and Breast Cancer." For more on breast cancer etiology, see Moysich, "Environmental Exposure to Polychlorinated Biphenyls and Breast Cancer Risk"; and Krieger et al., "Breast Cancer and Serum Organochlorines."

40. Jacobson and Jacobson, "Intellectual Impairment in Children Exposed to PCBs." Such relationships might be quite causally complex; see Longnecker et al., "Polychlorinated Biphenyl Serum Levels in Pregnant Subjects with Diabetes."

41. Dr. David O. Carpenter, *Owens* transcript, April 9, 2001, 982–83; Sulzberger, Rostenberg, and Sher, "Acneform Eruptions"; Colborn, Myers, and Dumanoski, *Our Stolen Future*, 87–109, 111. See also Langston, *Toxic Bodies*, 9–10. Dr. David O. Carpenter, *Owens* transcript, April 9, 2001, 929. Ian Nisbet also noted PCB effects on the endocrine system. *Owens* transcript, April 11, 2001, 1391.

42. Dr. David O. Carpenter, *Owens* transcript, April 9, 2001, 929, 936–37, 939.

43. Warren Lightfoot, *Owens* transcript, April 10, 2001, 1245–46, 1261–62; Dr. David O. Carpenter, *Owens* transcript, April 10, 2001, 1125; Warren Lightfoot, *Owens* transcript, April 11, 2001, 1262, 1261.

44. Associated Press, "Monsanto Agrees to Settle PCB Lawsuit," April 25, 2001. Mims eventually received $32,000. Michael Grunwald, "In Dirt, Water and Hogs, Town Got Its Fill of PCBs," *Washington Post*. The average "per capita gross cash recovery," before attorneys' fees, just under 40 percent, and trial expenses were deducted, would be $20,676.69. Settlement agreement, *Owens v. Monsanto* (2001), April 26, 2001, 15, 17.

45. West Anniston Foundation, Mission, http://westannistonfdn.org/ (September 10, 2013).

46. Interview with Ralph Knowles, October 16, 2008.

47. Interview with Robert B. Roden, May 21, 2004.

48. *Garrett v. Raytheon* (1979); *Hinton v. Monsanto* (2001), 828, 831–32; Robert Leslie Palmer, "Alabama's Court System Shuts Out Toxin Victims," *Birmingham News*, April 30, 2006. In a 2008 decision, *Griffin v. Unocal* (2008), the Alabama Supreme Court overruled the 1979 decision, ruling that the two-year limit for filing suit begins to run only when the illness manifests, not when the exposure to toxic substances from which that illness stems ends. Philip Rawls, Associated

Press, "Alabama Supreme Court Reverses Course, Offers Hope to Ill Workers," January 30, 2008. The change applied only prospectively. *Jerkins v. Lincoln Elec.* (2011).

49. Dr. David O. Carpenter, deposition in *Long v. Monsanto, Abernathy v. Monsanto, Abbott v. Monsanto,* December 16, 1998, School of Public Health in Rensselaer, N.Y. ("a very, very extremely exposed population," 31); Dr. David O. Carpenter, in Kroft, "Toxic Town."

50. Michael Grunwald, "Monsanto Hid Decades of Pollution," *Washington Post,* January 1, 2002; S. Kaplan and J. Morris, "Kids at Risk," *U.S. News and World Report,* June 19, 2000, 47–53; Nancy Beiles, "What Monsanto Knew," *The Nation,* May 29, 2000; Elizabeth Bluemink, "Judgment Day in Sight: Court Case against Monsanto Co. Begins Monday," *Anniston Star,* January 6, 2002; "EPA Orders Dredging of New York's Hudson River," December 5, 2001, http://articles.cnn.com/2001-12-05/us/hudson.cleanup_1_pcb-contamination-dredging-highly-toxic-chemicals?_s=PM:US (July 15, 2012).

51. Elizabeth Bluemink, "Judge Dismisses Healthy Plaintiffs," *Anniston Star,* January 9, 2002; Tom C. Ford, manager of divisional public relations for Monsanto, to Robert Hoving of Booth Newspapers, September 13, 1969, *Abernathy* transcript, January 14, 2002; Tom C. Ford to Phillip Yaffee, *Wall Street Journal,* June 13, 1969, *Abernathy* transcript, January 14, 2002.

52. Interview with Sallie Bowie Franklin, September 29, 2003; Harlan Prater, *Abernathy* transcript, January 14, 2002.

53. Philip Rawls, Associated Press, "Alabama Supreme Court Reverses Course, Offers Hope to Ill Workers," January 30, 2008.

54. Interview with Ralph Knowles, October 16, 2008.

55. Mark Hermanson, *Abernathy* transcript, January 16, 2002. See Hermanson and Johnson, "Polychlorinated Biphenyls in Tree Bark." EPA Region 3 had developed guidelines of 3.3 ng/m^3, a standard later reduced to 3.1 ng/m^3 in 2001. *Abernathy* transcript, January 16, 2002. Mark Hermanson, *Abernathy* transcript, January 16, 2002; Buddy Cox, *Abernathy* transcript, January 16, 2002.

56. Mark Hermanson, *Abernathy* transcript, January 16, 2002.

57. Harlan Prater, *Abernathy* transcript, January 22, 2002.

58. Dr. Richard W. Clapp, *Abernathy* transcript, January 22, 2002; Hill, "Environment and Disease: Association or Causation?"; Rothman et al., "Nested Case-Control Study of Non-Hodgkin Lymphoma."

59. Dr. Robert George Kaley, *Abernathy* transcript, January 31, 2002.

60. William Papageorge, *Abernathy* transcript, January 16, 2002.

61. Richard Allen Maloy, *Abernathy* transcript, January 5, 2002.

62. N. T. Johnson to P. Craska et al., "Pollution Letter," February 16, 1970, *Abernathy* documents; Jimmie Curvin, *Abernathy* transcript, January 29, 2002; J. Wray Pearce, *Abernathy* transcript, January 29, 2002.

63. Dr. Robert George Kaley, *Abernathy* transcript, February 4, 2002; Kimbrough, "Induction of Liver Tumors," 1455, 1454; Kimbrough, Linder, and Gaines, "Morphological Changes in Livers"; Renate D. Kimbrough, *Abernathy* transcript, February 12, 2002.

64. Kimbrough, "Human Health Effects"; Renate D. Kimbrough, *Abernathy* transcript, February 12, 2002.

65. Papageorge to Dr. R. Emmet Kelly, February 13, 1967, cited by Donald Stewart during Dr. Robert George Kaley's testimony, *Abernathy* transcript, January 31, 2002.

66. George Ford, *Abernathy* transcript, February 20, 2002.

67. Dr. Robert George Kaley, *Abernathy* transcript, January 31, 2002.

68. Jerry Brown, *Abernathy* transcript, February 11, 2002.

69. William Papageorge, *Abernathy* transcript, January 16, 2002; George Ford, *Abernathy* transcript, February 20, 2002.

70. Ishmael Ransaw, *Abernathy* transcript, February 12, 2002.

71. Robert Cheever, *Abernathy* transcript, January 30, 2002. At the time of the trial, both the EPA and Solutia complained of not being able to get access to all the properties to test for PCBs, stalled by Stewart's admonishment to the plaintiffs not to allow access for fear that Monsanto would then argue that no injury was present. Author's notes on the trial, July 2003.

72. Elizabeth Bluemink, "Judgment Day in Sight: Court Case against Monsanto Co. Begins Monday," *Anniston Star*, January 6, 2002; Michael Grunwald, "Monsanto Hid Decades of Pollution," *Washington Post*, January 1, 2002.

73. George Ford, *Abernathy* transcript, February 20, 2002.

74. Donald Stewart, *Abernathy* transcript, February 20, 2002.

75. Ibid.

76. Ibid.

77. David Cain, *Abernathy* transcript, February 14, 2002.

78. Judge Joel Laird, *Abernathy* transcript, February 5, 2002.

79. *Ex parte Monsanto and Solutia (Abernathy v. Monsanto)*, February 26, 2003, 4; Restatement of the Law, Second, Torts, §46, American Law Institute, 1965; Vicki McClure, "Monsanto, Solutia Liable, Verdict Means Companies Face Hundreds of Millions in PCB Claims," *Birmingham News/Birmingham Post-Herald*, February 23, 2002; interview with Bettye Bowie, September 29, 2003.

80. Interview with Bettye Bowie, September 29, 2003.

81. Michael Grunwald, "Monsanto Held Liable for PCB Dumping," *Washington Post*, February 23, 2002.

82. Elizabeth Bluemink, "Judgment Day in Sight: Court Case against Monsanto Co. Begins Monday," *Anniston Star*, January 6, 2002; *Ex parte Monsanto and Solutia (Abernathy v. Monsanto)*, February 26, 2003.

83. Elizabeth Bluemink, "Judgment Day in Sight: Court Case against Monsanto Co. Begins Monday," *Anniston Star*, January 6, 2002; EPA, "Region 4 Briefing on Anniston"; *United States v. Pharmacia*, statement of David Baker, in U.S. Senate, Committee on Appropriations, *PCB Contamination in Anniston*, 39.

84. Interview with David Baker, March 26, 2004.

85. Statement of David Baker, in U.S. Senate, Committee on Appropriations, *PCB Contamination in Anniston*, 37, 42, 44.

86. Statement of Sen. Richard C. Shelby, in U.S. Senate, Committee on Appropriations, *PCB Contamination in Anniston*, 3, 25, 17; statement of Sen. Barbara A. Mikulski, in U.S. Senate, Committee on Appropriations, *PCB Contamination in*

Anniston, 3; Sen. Barbara A. Mikulski to the Honorable Christie Whitman, April 30, 2002.

87. The recusals were discussed at the hearing. U.S. Senate, Committee on Appropriations, *PCB Contamination in Anniston*, 21–22. Peter Overby, National Public Radio, "Christine Todd Whitman Ends Her Tenure as Chief of the EPA Leaving Unanswered Questions about a Controversial Case of Industrial Pollution," June 27, 2003; Sara Clemence, "Anniston Attorney Accuses EPA Head of Conspiracy with Solutia," *Anniston Star*, February 7, 2003; Sara Clemence, "EPA Denies Conspiracy Alleged by Anniston Attorneys," *Anniston Star*, February 12, 2003; David Baker and Kenneth Cook to Christine Todd Whitman, June 18, 2003, http://www.ewg.org/research/monsanto-alabama/ewg-letter-whitman-18-june-03 (August 31, 2013).

88. Sen. Barbara A. Mikulski, in U.S. Senate, Committee on Appropriations, *PCB Contamination in Anniston*, 56.

89. Dr. Henry Falk, in U.S. Senate, Committee on Appropriations, *PCB Contamination in Anniston*, 11–15.

90. *In re Solutia, Inc. et al.*, chapter 11, case no. 03-17949, Wilmington Trust Company, as Successor Indenture Trustee to J. P. Morgan Chase Bank, N.A. Adv. Pro. no. 05-01843, 9; author's notes on the trial, July 2003.

91. Interview with Robert B. Roden, May 21, 2004. The *Tolbert* docket gives a filing date of June 6, 2001, though many of the cases were filed in January 2002. Elizabeth Bluemink, "15,000 Additional Plaintiffs File Another PCB Lawsuit," *Anniston Star*, January 24, 2002.

92. "Boycott Planned by Black Groups," *Anniston Star*, November 5, 1971.

93. An Agent Orange lawsuit, in which Monsanto was ordered to pay $16.2 million for failing to warn residents of dioxin in Sturgeon, Mo., lasted longer, from February 1984 to October 1987. *Kemner v. Monsanto* (1987); Ed Schafer, "$16 Million Awarded in Chemical Spill Suit," *Columbus (Ga.) Ledger*, October 23, 1987; settlement agreement, *Abernathy v. Monsanto*, September 10, 2003.

94. Interview with Judge U. W. Clemon, November 15, 2013.

Chapter Eleven

1. Rick Bragg, with Glynn Wilson, "Burning of Chemical Arms Puts Fear in Wind," *New York Times*, September 15, 2002; Bill Hewitt, with Linda Trischetta and Siobhan Morrissey, "Living on Poisoned Ground," *People*, March 25, 2002, 60; Sesno and Guarino, *Avoiding Armageddon*.

2. Press conference, author's notes, August 21, 2003.

3. The consent decree on cleanup was finalized as part of the global settlement of the federal and state toxic tort lawsuits. *United States v. Pharmacia* (2003); press conference, author's notes, August 21, 2003.

4. Press conference, author's notes, August 21, 2003; settlement agreement, *Abernathy v. Monsanto*, *Bowie v. Monsanto*, September 10, 2003; *Tolbert v. Monsanto* (2003).

5. Press conference, author's notes, August 21, 2003.

6. Ibid.; "Solutia Stock Rises 344 Percent Thursday," *Anniston Star*, August 22, 2003. The share price rose $3.10, from $.90 to $4.00. Monsanto shares also rose

6 percent, from $22.69 to 24.12. Solutia stock had been valued at $12.55 per share before the *Abernathy* trial began in 2002. "Solutia Stock Takes a Dive," *Anniston Star*, January 4, 2002.

7. Press conference, author's notes, August 21, 2003.

8. Ibid.; interview with Jacqueline Brown, September 25, 2003; interview with Andrew Bowie, October 19, 2003. Andrew Bowie died on November 9, 2005.

9. Brandon Tubbs, "Protestors March against the Incinerator," *Anniston Star*, August 17, 2003; "Incineration Resumes after 1-Week Shutdown," *Anniston Star*, March 8, 2004.

10. ANCDF (Anniston Chemical Agent Disposal Facility) Army project site manager Tim Garrett, press conference, October 29, 2003; ANCDF, "ANCDF Disposal Operations Resume," press release, April 27, 2005.

11. Elizabeth Bluemink, "Mercury Pollution: Monsanto Contamination Now Gets Scrutiny after 30 Years," *Anniston Star*, July 20, 2001. The EPA had been looking at multisource modeling for exposure to pesticides for roughly ten years. EPA, "Guidelines for Exposure Assessment," *Federal Register* 57, no. 104 (1992): 22888–938; EPA, *General Principles for Performing Aggregate Exposure.*

12. Sara Clemence, "Cleaning Up Chalk Line," *Anniston Star*, July 9, 2003; EPA, *Five-Year Review Report for Southeast Industrial Area Groundwater.*

13. Author's notes, July 23, 2003; Sara Clemence, "System to Remove TCE from Anniston's Water Supply," *Anniston Star*, December 9, 2003; Brandon Tubbs, "Treatment System to Remove TCE from Anniston Water," *Anniston Star*, June 6, 2004; Rob Jordan, "Monday Meeting to Answer Water Questions," *Anniston Star*, June 13, 2004; Jim Morris, "Widely Used Chemical Might Have Cancer Link," *Boston Globe*, January 11, 2005; "Shoddy UXO Cleanup," *Anniston Star*, September 1, 2004; Sara Clemence, "The Creek's Sorrow: 55-Gallon Drums Build a Mystery," *Anniston Star*, November 5, 2003; Katherine Bouma, "Incinerator Barrels Found in Rural Creek Bed Again," *Birmingham News*, August 12, 2004.

14. Brooks Fahy, presentation at Anniston City Meeting Center, February 21, 2004, EPA Integrated Risk Information System, "Sodium Fluoroacetate (CASRN 62-74-8)," last revised July 1, 1993, http://www.epa.gov/iris/subst/0469.htm (July 22, 2006); Charlotte Tubbs, "EPA Tests for Lead Contamination in Hobson City, Western Anniston," *Anniston Star*, February 26, 2004.

15. EPA, "EPA to Begin Second Phase of Superfund Removal Site Assessment at the Anniston Lead Site, Anniston, Calhoun County, Alabama," press release, March 7, 2002, http://www.epa.gov/region4/foiapgs/readingroom/anniston/, http://yosemite.epa.gov/opa/admpress.nsf/8b770facf5edf6f185257359003fb69e/7e5de42365fa89998525733300447dc5!OpenDocument&Highlight=2,Anniston,Alabama (June 18, 2013)

16. "As Many as Thirty Lawsuits," *Solutia Bankruptcy News*, Bankruptcy Creditors' Service, 1, no. 1 (December 18, 2003), http://bankrupt.com/solutia.txt (June 5, 2006); Sara Clemence, "Hundreds Want in on New PCBs Suit," *Anniston Star*, November 19, 2003. Birmingham attorney Robert Roden filed suit on behalf of approximately 4,500 plaintiffs. Interview with Robert B. Roden, January 28, 2006.

17. David Barboza, "Monsanto Struggles Even as It Dominates," *New York Times*, May 31, 2003; "Monsanto Posts a $188 Million Fourth-Quarter Loss," *Anniston Star*, October 16, 2003.

18. *In re Solutia, Inc. et al.*, chapter 11, case no. 03-17949, Wilmington Trust Company, as Successor Indenture Trustee to J. P. Morgan Chase Bank, N.A. Adv. Pro. No. 05-01843, 10; Edgar Gentle, author's notes on the CAP Annual Awards Dinner, October 29, 2004.

19. Interview with Peter Montague, June 3, 2004. A consultant for Monsanto sued Montague in a $4 million libel action for reporting in *Rachel's Weekly* that Monsanto falsified studies about links between dioxins and cancer, studies that the EPA had relied on to establish health standards for dioxin. The suit was dismissed in 1995. Peter Montague, "Part I: Dioxins and Cancer: Fraudulent Studies," *Rachel's Health and Environment Weekly*, no. 171 (March 7, 1990); "Chemicals and Health: Part 2 and SLAPPed," *Rachel's Health and Environment Weekly*, no. 370 (December 30, 1993); Thornton, *Pandora's Poison*, 481 (n. 183); *In re Solutia, Inc. et al.*, chapter 11, case no. 03-17949, Wilmington Trust Company, as Successor Indenture Trustee to J. P. Morgan Chase Bank, N.A. Adv. Pro. No. 05-01843, 9; author's notes, October 29, 2004; "Solutia Stock Rises 344 Percent Thursday," *Anniston Star*, August 22, 2003.

20. Author's notes, October 29, 2004.

21. Interview with Cassandra Roberts, September 3, 2003; *Owens v. Monsanto* (2004).

22. Jessica Centers, "PCBs Plaintiffs Demand Answers," *Anniston Star*, March 23, 2004; "PCB Case Payouts Roil Alabama City," *Washington Post*, March 24, 2004.

23. Interview with U. W. Clemon, November 15, 2013; Sara Clemence, "PCBs Settlement: A New Twist," *Anniston Star*, November 6, 2003; Susan Kitchens, "Money Grab," *Forbes*, November 15, 2004, 162–68; Jessica Centers, "Outburst Erupts at PCB Hearing," *Anniston Star*, November 24, 2004; Jessica Centers, "Laird Bars Further Lawsuits in Settled PCBs Case," *Anniston Star*, December 17, 2004; Jessica Centers, "Laird Order Will Stand," *Anniston Star*, December 17, 2004; Jay Reeves, "PCB Case Payouts Roil Alabama City," *Washington Post*, March 24, 2004. Susan Kitchens of *Forbes* magazine placed the Cochran firm's fees even higher, at $40 million, and estimated that Donald Stewart and the other firm in the *Abernathy* case split $114 million. Kitchens, "Money Grab," 168. Cochran died March 30, 2005, of an inoperable brain tumor. Alabama Civil Justice Foundation, "History of the Alabama Civil Justice Foundation," http://www.acjf.org/About_Us.htm (May 8, 2006); *Bates v. Stewart* (2012); "PCB Pollution Case Settlement Protest," September 19, 2012, ABC 33/40 News. A raucous May 31, 2013, demonstration linked continued protest of Stewart with an antifluoride message. Nathan Young, "Monsanto Protest in Anniston," June 1, 2013, http://www.youtube.com/watch?v=8Gk3NEIwKvA (September 13, 2013).

24. Interview with Shirley Baker, April 21, 2004.

25. Robert B. Roden to Claimants, March 18, 2004, in Gentle, "Administration of the Tolbert Settlement," 1257.

26. Author's notes, March 22, 2004.

27. Jessica Centers, "Waiting for Answers," *Anniston Star*, June 15, 2005; Jessica Centers, "PCB Settlement Perplexing to Some Area Tax Preparers," *Anniston Star*, February 22, 2004; Jessica Centers, "Physical Injury, Punitive Damages Off Limits to IRS," *Anniston Star*, February 22, 2004; interview with Myrtle Joshua, August 26, 2004.

28. "Questions and Answers," Tolbert Qualified Settlement Fund, http://www.tolbertqsf.com/q_as.120803.htm (May 22, 2013).

29. Brandon Tubbs, "PCB Town Meetings Delayed until Summer," *Anniston Star*, March 6, 2004; Stephen Gross, "Monsanto Money Welcome!," photo, *Anniston Star*, December 19, 2003.

30. Author's notes, March 22, 2004.

31. Attorney Earl Underwood filed suit on behalf of additional plaintiffs in October 2004. Interview with Robert B. Roden, January 28, 2006; Silverstone et al., "Polychlorinated Biphenyl (PCB) Exposure and Diabetes," 732; Goncharov et al., "Blood Pressure and Hypertension in Serum PCBs in Residents of Anniston"; Erin Stock, "A Jefferson County Jury Rules in Favor of the Former Monsanto Co. in PCB Suit," *Birmingham News*, Wednesday, April 15, 2009.

32. Jessica Centers, "PCBs Cleanup: Concerns Raised at Meeting," *Anniston Star*, April 20, 2004; Rachel Melcer, "Anniston Cleanups Wait as Companies Debate Liability," *St. Louis Post-Dispatch*, February 4, 2004; interview with Glynn Young, July 15, 2004; *In re Solutia*, chapter 11, case no. 03-17949 (PCB), May 5, 2007.

33. Reuters, "Monsanto to Pull Solutia from Bankruptcy," June 7, 2005, http://news.moneycentral.msn.com/provider/providerarticle.asp?feed=OBR&Date=20050607&ID=4874323 (June 7, 2005); discussions at CAG meetings, February 16 and March 16, 2004; Solutia Inc., 10-K for March 15, 2006, http://www.sec.gov/Archives/edgar/data (May 16, 2006).

34. Young felt that the companies had handled cleanup operations more effectively at Sauget than at Anniston. Interview with Glynn Young, July 15, 2004. EPA, "Superfund Update"; "Stipulation on Liability of Defendants Pharmacia, Solutia, et al., under Section 107 of CERCLA," *EPA v. Pharmacia*, October 3, 2003, 12; *EPA v. Monsanto*, January 28, 1999, 3, 5; "Plaintiff United States of America's Memorandum in Support of Its Motion for Ruling on the Appropriate Scope and Standard of Review of Agency Remedy Selection and for Protective Order," *EPA v. Pharmacia*, August 26, 2002, 6; Daniel Kelley, "Federal, State Officials Gauge Cost of Cleaning Up Contaminated Land in Sauget," *Belleville (Ill.) News-Democrat*, August 7, 2013.

35. Rachel Melcer, "Anniston Cleanups Wait as Companies Debate Liability: Monsanto, Pharmacia, Pfizer, Solutia," *St. Louis Post-Dispatch*, February 7, 2004; Solutia Inc., 8-K for March 31, 2006—EX-99 SEC file 1-13255, accession no. 1068800-6-238, 12, SEC Info, http://www.secinfo.com/dlzJxf.v71.d.htm (May 16, 2006).

36. Sara Clemence, "Solutia Sues Other Companies," *Anniston Star*, June 6, 2003.

37. Rachel Melcer, "Anniston Cleanups Wait as Companies Debate Liability: Monsanto, Pharmacia, Pfizer, Solutia," *St. Louis Post-Dispatch*, February 7, 2004;

interview with Shirley Baker, April 21, 2004; ATSDR, *Health Consultation: Evaluation of Lead in Residential Surface Soil from Anniston,* August 7, 2000; *Solutia and Pharmacia v. McWane,* June 5, 2003; Sara Clemence, "Solutia Sues Other Companies," *Anniston Star,* June 6, 2003. The foundry cleanup was outlined in the U.S. EPA, *Administrative Agreement,* signed by the EPA on July 27, 2005. ATSDR, *Health Consultation: Assessment of Four Activities Addressing Childhood Blood Lead Levels in Anniston,* June 26, 2003, 6–7; Charlotte Tubbs, "EPA Tests for Lead Contamination in Hobson City, Western Anniston," *Anniston Star,* February 26, 2004.

38. Editorial, "PCBs and the EPA," *Anniston Star,* June 27, 2003; EPA Quarterly Meeting, author's notes, April 11, 2006. Senator Mikulski had discussed the question of Superfund designation at the Senate hearing. *PCB Contamination in Anniston,* April 19, 2002, 25. The Comprehensive Environmental Response, Compensation, and Liability Act of 1980, 42 U.S.C. §9601 et seq. (1980), or CERCLA, established the federal "Superfund," as the law is popularly known. The law required polluting companies to pay for cleanup when found liable. The law was amended in 1986 by the Superfund Reauthorization and Amendment (SARA), 42 U.S.C. §9601 et seq. (1986). Interview with Leslie Leahy, June 2, 2004; EPA, "Anniston PCB Site."

39. Guidance for Community Advisory Groups at Superfund Sites (EPA 540-K-96-001), December 1995, http://www.epa.gov/superfund/tools/cag/resource/guidance/caguide.pdf (May 18, 2006). NEJAC Model Plan for Public Participation, Public Participation and Accountability Subcommittee of the National Environmental Justice Advisory Council and the EPA Office of Environmental Justice, http://www.epa.gov/projctxl/nejac.htm (May 18, 2006).

40. The National Environmental Policy Act of 1969, as amended (Pub. L. 91-190, 42 U.S.C. 4321-4347, January 1, 1970). The Federal Advisory Committee Act, PL 92-463, October 6, 1972, covered advisory committees to a variety of government agencies.

41. Author's notes on the meeting, July 15, 2003.

42. In addition to its work for Solutia, the Ross Public Affairs Group has created and facilitated community advisory panels for the U.S. Department of Energy, the Army Corps of Engineers, other corporations such as Roche, Witco, PSE&G, and GPU, and county governments in Ocean County, New Jersey, and Rockland County, New York. Ross Public Affairs Group website, http://www.rosspag.com/practice.shtml (March 3, 2006). Ross Public Affairs Group Inc., "Practice Specialties," http://www.rosspag.com/practice2.shtml (May 17, 2004); interview with Stephen B. Ross, May 17, 2004.

43. Ross Public Affairs Group Inc., "Practice Specialties," http://www.rosspag.com/practice2.shtml (May 17, 2004); interview with Stephen B. Ross, May 17, 2004.

44. Interview with Stephen Ross, May 17, 2004; Ross Public Affairs Group website, http://www.rosspag.com/practice.shtml (March 3, 2006).

45. Ibid.

46. Lawyer-scholars Luke Cole and Sheila Foster suggest that the very informality of the selection processes for community advisory groups can work against effective democratic representation, undermining genuine democracy, especially

among already marginalized groups. Cole and Foster, *From the Ground Up*, 2001, 110–11.

47. Interview with Stephanie Yvette Brown, EPA community involvement coordinator for Anniston, November 6, 2003.

48. Ibid. Lea Cheatwood, who represented Oxford, and Shirley McCord, who lived in Golden Springs, have both passed away.

49. Interview with Shirley Baker, July 18, 2006.

50. Interview with David Baker, July 18, 2006.

51. EPA, "Proposed Plan Fact Sheet," 3.

52. EPA, "Interim Record of Decision"; Bullard and Wright, *Wrong Complexion for Protection*, 103–4.

53. Interview with Shirley Baker, July 18, 2006; Jessica Centers, "EPA Is Criticized for Miscommunication about Miller Property," *Anniston Star*, November 16, 2004; Joseph Lord, "Anniston City Council Wants PCB Dump Site Researched," *Anniston Star*, March 1, 2006; Dan Whisenhunt, "Independent PCB Testing May Begin This Month," *Anniston Star*, May 3, 2006. The independent testing registered 0.34 ppm, under EPA recommended guidelines. Community Advisory Group Report, July 17, 2006.

54. Wayne Carmello-Harper to Judge U. W. Clemon, November 2, 2004; Jessica Centers, "Fired Technical Adviser Returns to Fight for Job," *Anniston Star*, November 10, 2004.

55. Long and Beierle, "Federal Advisory Committee Act and Public Participation in Environmental Policy," ii.

56. Rev. Thomas Long, Community Advisory Group meeting, author's notes, July 17, 2006.

57. ATSDR, *Evaluation of Soil, Blood, and Air Data from Anniston, Alabama, Calhoun County, Alabama*, public comment release, February 14, 2000, executive summary, 1; interview with Max McCombs, July 14, 2004; interview with Craig Branchfield, November 5, 2003.

58. From 1971 through October 1975, "5,764,000 pounds of PCBs were landfilled at the Monsanto Anniston Plant. Records are not complete at Anniston." "Polychlorinated Biphenyl (PCB) Compounds or Mixtures," Response to Questionnaire, Item 5, Plaintiffs Exhibit 1C01C, attached to letter from W. B. Papageorge to Earl J. Stephenson, December 11, 1975, *Abernathy* documents. EPA granted approval of the South Soil Management Area (SSMA) in 2006.

59. An interim record of decision for the plant site itself was issued in September 2011. EPA, "Interim Record of Decision." However, the residential and downstream RODs were still pending, anticipated in 2013 and 2015, respectively. EPA, "Anniston PCB Site."

60. Robert Pear, "Romney Aide Advises on State Health Plans," *New York Times*, July 22, 2012.

60. Foreword to Oquirrh Institute, *Enlibra Toolkit*.

61. The Enlibra principles are spelled out in Oquirrh Institute, *Enlibra Toolkit*. Michael Janofsky, "Nominee for E.P.A. Defends His Job as Utah Governor," *New York Times*, August 14, 2003.

62. Office of the Administrator, U.S. Environmental Protection Agency, "The Enlibra Principles," http://www.epa.gov/adminweb/administrator/enlibra.htm (July 27, 2006).

63. Hirschhorn, "Enlibra"; "Lessons Learned," in Oquirrh Institute, *Enlibra Toolkit*, 80; Keith Rogers, "'Enlibra' Seeks End to Pattern of Disputes," *Las Vegas Review Journal*, December 6, 1998; Office of the Administrator, U.S. Environmental Protection Agency, "The Enlibra Principles," http://www.epa.gov/adminweb/administrator/enlibra.htm (July 27, 2006).

64. Administrator Steve Johnson, "The Enlibra Principles," http://www.epa.gov/adminweb/administrator/enlibra.htm (June 5, 2006).

65. Concurrent with the global settlement, the consent decree in *United States v. Pharmacia* (2003), the EPA enforcement action for the Anniston PCB site, required the $3.2 allocation for the educational foundation.

66. *United States v. Pharmacia*; author's notes from monthly CAG meetings.

67. Anniston High School, High-Schools.com, http://high-schools.com/schools/509/anniston-high-school.html (June 16, 2013); Wellborn High School, High-Schools.com, http://high-schools.com/schools/2210/wellborn-high-school.html (June 16, 2003).

68. Brandy Warren, "Tolbert Patients to Be Charged Co-payment for Costly Prescription Drugs," *Anniston Star*, November 16, 2005.

69. U.S. Department of Health and Human Services, "Community Health Status Indicators Report," http://wwwn.cdc.gov/CommunityHealth/MeasuresOfBirthAndDeath.aspx?GeogCD=01015&PeerStrat=6&state=Alabama&county=Calhoun (April 20, 2013).

70. Interview with Martha Lavender, July 30, 2003; interview with Jane Cash, July 8, 2004.

71. Author's notes on the Anniston Environmental Health Research Consortium conference call, May 24, 2004.

72. Author's notes on the Anniston Environmental Health Research Consortium conference call, May 11, 2006; Pavuk et al., "Assessment of Human Exposure to PCBs in Anniston."

73. Author's notes on the CAC meetings, 2003–4.

74. Marian Pavuk, ATSDR/CDC, "Anniston Community Health Survey: Update of Results," public meeting, March 7, 2011, reporting on F. Biasini et al. for the Anniston Environmental Health Research Consortium, "A Study of Neurocognitive Function in Children following PCB Exposure."

75. African Americans in the study lived closer to the plant (median distance of 2.19 km) than whites (3.83 km). Pavuk et al., "Assessment of Human Exposure to PCBs in Anniston," 1084.

76. Silverstone et al., "Mono-ortho and Di-ortho Substituted PCB Congeners and Type 2 Diabetes in Anniston," 270; Silverstone et al., "Polychlorinated Biphenyl (PCB) Exposure and Diabetes," 732; Fred Biasini, Alan Percy, Jane Lane, Jerry Childers, and Richard Rector, "A Study of Neurocognitive and Neurobehavioral Function in Children following PCB Exposure," presentation at the Fifth International PCB Workshop, University of Iowa, May 21, 2008; Goncharov et al., "Blood

Pressure in Relation to Concentrations of PCB Congeners." This finding proved true even after adjusting for the effects of BMI, gender, race (African American, Caucasian), smoking status, and level of exercise. CDC, "Anniston Community Health Survey, Follow-Up and Dioxin Analyses (ACHS II) Background and Brief Description," *Federal Register* 78, no. 77 (April 22, 2013): 23766–67.

77. Rhoda E. Johnson, Shirley Baker, and Christie Shelton, "Living with Chemical Contamination: West Anniston Speaks Out," presentation, Greater Thankful Baptist Church, Anniston, Ala., April 1, 2008.

78. Ibid.

Epilogue

1. Interview with Opal Scruggs, September 25, 2003.

2. Alabama Department of Environmental Management, legal notice, *Anniston Star*, October 30, 2007; Chemical Materials Activity (CMA), "ADEM Cites, Fines ANCDF for Rules Violations," press release, October 30, 2007; CMA, "ADEM Reviews ANCDF Self-Reported Concerns, Issues Notice," press release, September 19, 2012; Cameron Steele, "Anniston Chemical Demil Facility Cited for Environmental Violations," *Anniston Star*, September 20, 2012. Steele also reports on violations that occurred in September 2010. Interview with David Christian, February 22, 2013; Cameron Steele, "Chemical Incinerator's Work to Extend into September," *Anniston Star*, May 26, 2011.

3. Laura Camper, "Army Report Looks at Possible New Uses for Incinerator," *Anniston Star*, September 26, 2011; Rufus Kinney, "Poisoning Our Community," *Anniston Star*, November 11, 2011; U.S. Army Chemical Materials Agency, *Anniston Chemical Agent Disposal Facility Overarching Facility Closure Requirements and Potential Reuse Report, Phase II Technical Assessment*, Final, July 2011; Cameron Steele, "International Observers, Others Watch Chemical Weapon Burn Process," *Anniston Star*, September 23, 2011.

4. Darrell A. Baker, *EPA Potential Hazardous Waste Site Inspection Report,* March 5, 1980, 4.

5. Bob Davis, "Image Doesn't Define Us," *Anniston Star*, May 12, 2013; U.S. Bureau of the Census, *State and County QuickFacts*, "Anniston, Alabama: 2010," "Calhoun County, Alabama: 2010"; Federal Writers' Program (Alabama), *Alabama: A Guide to the Deep South*, 159; U.S. Bureau of the Census, *Alabama Population of Counties*.

6. Interview with Bettye Bowie, March 18, 2013; interview with Opal Scruggs, February 22, 2013.

7. Laura Johnson, "EPA Tests City's Ditches for Contaminants," *Anniston Star*, August 1, 2012; U.S. Environmental Protection Agency, "Anniston PCB Air Study, Anniston, Calhoun County, Alabama, October 23–25, 2012," 7, March 13, 2013, http://www.annistoncag.org/uploadedFiles/File/REPORT_Anniston_2012_PCB_Air_Study.pdf (November 13, 2013); Franklin Hill, deputy director EPA Region 4, author's notes from Anniston PCB Site CAG meeting at Carver Community Center, March 18, 2013.

8. David Baker, author's notes from Anniston PCB Site CAG meeting, Carver Community Center, March 18, 2013.

9. Representative Barbara Bigsby Boyd, author's notes from Anniston PCB Site CAG meeting, Carver Community Center, March 18, 2013.

10. Interview with Craig Branchfield, November 5, 2003; Veronica MacDonald, "Solutia to Build New Aviation Fluid Unit in Anniston, AL," *Chemical Week*, March 9, 2005; Mark Scott, "Eastman Chemical to Buy Solutia for $3.4 Billion," *New York Times*, January 27, 2012. Eastman estimates Solutia's value even higher, at $4.8 billion. Eastman, "Eastman Completes Acquisition of Solutia," press release, July 2, 2012.

11. U.S. Bureau of the Census, *State and County QuickFacts*, "Anniston, Alabama: 2010," data derived from Population Estimates, American Community Survey, Census of Population and Housing; Megan Nichols, "Dominating the Polls," *Anniston Star*, August 28, 2008; Laura Camper, "Stewart Wins Anniston Mayor Race; Voters Reject Incumbents," *Anniston Star*, August 28, 2012.

12. John Miller, "Fourteen States Want U.S. Bio-agro Lab," *Scientist*, April 3, 2006, http://www.the-scientist.com/news/display/23263/ (May 5, 2006); "Get Behind Biotech Lab," *Anniston Star*, May 8, 2006; Matt Kasper, "Chamber of Commerce Stands Behind Bio Lab," *Anniston Star*, May 18, 2006.

13. Pew Center on the States, *Impact of the Fiscal Cliff*, 23; EPA, *Five-Year Review Report for Southeast Industrial Area, Anniston Army Depot*; Matthew Korade, "JPA Wants to Determine Feasibility of Creating McClellan Research Park," *Anniston Star*, July 20, 2005. Matthew Korade, "Depot's Future Looks Bright: Chamber's Military Liaison Working to Protect Anniston Facility," *Anniston Star*, September 19, 2005; Steve Ivey, "Construction to Begin on New Powertrain Facility at Anniston Army Depot," *Anniston Star*, April 4, 2006; Kate Brannen, "U.S. Army to Congress: No New Tanks, Please," *Defense News*, May 7, 2012, http://www. defensenews.com/article/20120307/DEFREG02/303070011/U-S-Army-Congress-No-New-Tanks-Please (September 6, 2012).

14. Jessica Centers, "Environmental Duo at McClellan in for the Long Haul," *Anniston Star*, November 4, 2004; Steve Ivey, "Senate Committee to Vote on Funding for CDP Today," *Anniston Star*, June 29, 2006; Matthew Korade, "Center for Domestic Preparedness Will Expand," *Anniston Star*, September 21, 2005; Jessica Centers, "ADEM Cites Hazardous Waste Violations at McClellan," *Anniston Star*, August 3, 2004.

15. Interview with Sherri Sumners, October 16, 2003; Elizabeth Bluemink, "A Master Plan to Recovery: Area Looks to Rediscover Its Environmental Identity," *Anniston Star*, October 5, 2003.

16. Restoration Advisory Board Minutes, January 23, 2012, http://www. mcclellan.army.mil/Documents/Restoration%20Advisory%20Board%20Transcripts/2012/RAB%20trans%201-23-12.pdf (May 31, 2013); Darryl Fears, "Officials Want to Turn World War II Nuclear-Weapon Development Sites into National Parks," *Washington Post*, July 28, 2012; Brian Anderson, "Mountain Longleaf Refuge Celebrates 10 Years Saturday," *Anniston Star*, May 31, 2013.

17. Interview with Pete Conroy, August 13, 2004.

18. Ibid.; interview with Rev. Nimrod Q. Reynolds, November 4, 2003.

19. Harvey, *Spaces of Hope*, 31; author's notes from Anniston PCB Site CAG meeting, Carver Community Center, March 18, 2013.

20. "Wellborn Cabinet," *Anniston Star*, March 3, 2004; interview with Sherri Sumners, October 16, 2003; interview with David Cain, August 20, 2003.

21. Speech by Trey Glenn to the Environmental Law Section of the Alabama Bar, June 30, 2006, 3 (my emphasis); Katherine Bouma, "Remarks Anger Some Environmentalists," *Birmingham News*, June 28, 2006; Desiree Hunter, "Environmental Justice Unit in Works," *Montgomery Advertiser*, July 5, 2006; Conservation Alabama, "Discrimination Complaint Filed with the EPA," January 3, 2012, http://conservationalabama.wordpress.com/tag/david-a-ludder/ (May 2, 2013).

22. Patrick McCreless, "Talladega Forest Drilling Could Boost Economy—If There's Anything down There," *Anniston Star*, April 24, 2012; Wayne Ruple, "Some 200 Gather to Protest Fracking," *Cleburne (Ala.) News*, May 17, 2012.

23. "The Wingspread Statement," in Tickner, Raffensperger, and Myers, *Precautionary Principle*, 19.

24. Nicholas Varchaver, "Chemical Reaction," *Fortune*, April 2, 2007, 57.

25. EPA, "Polychlorinated Biphenyls (PCBs): Reassessment of Use Authorizations, Advance Notice of Proposed Rulemaking," 40 CFR 761 (EPA-HQ-OPPT-2009-0757; FRL-8811-7), *Federal Register* 75, no. 66 (April 7, 2010), Proposed Rules, 17645–66, at 17647; Safe Chemicals Act of 2010, http://lautenberg.senate.gov/assets/SCA2010.pdf (May 27, 2010); Chemical Safety Improvement Act of 2013, http://www.gpo.gov/fdsys/pkg/BILLS-113s1009is/pdf/BILLS-113s1009is.pdf (November 18, 2013).

26. U.S. Department of Health and Human Services, *Reducing Environmental Cancer Risk*, 31. This study suggests disparate impact may occur even with equivalent exposure. Toxic Substances Control Act of 1976, 15 U.S.C. §2601 et seq.; Safe Chemicals Act of 2010, http://lautenberg.senate.gov/assets/SCA2010.pdf (May 27, 2010); Toxic Chemicals Safety Act of 2010, House "Discussion Draft," http://energycommerce.house.gov/Press_111/20100415/TCSA.Discussion.Draft.pdf (May 27, 2010); EPA, "Polychlorinated Biphenyls (PCBs): Reassessment of Use Authorizations, Advance Notice of Proposed Rulemaking," 40 CFR 761 (EPA-HQ-OPPT-2009-0757; FRL-8811-7), *Federal Register* 75, no. 66 (April 7, 2010), Proposed Rules, 17645–66, at 17648; Naiki, "Assessing Policy Reach," 92; United Nations Environment Program, Stockholm Convention on Persistent Organic Pollutants, *Report on Progress in Establishing the Polychlorinated Biphenyls Elimination Network*, January 15, 2011, http://chm.pops.int/Implementation/PCBs/DecisionsRecommendations/tabid/692/Default.aspx (May 31, 2013).

27. Edward Ball, "An American Tragedy," *New York Times*, April 11, 2011.

28. Alex Boraine, vice-chair of the South African Truth and Reconciliation Commission, Comparative Human Relations Initiative, Emory University, April 4–7, 1997; Fullilove, *Root Shock*; Anniston Environmental Health Research Consortium Community Advisory Council, author's notes, October 20–21, 2005.

29. "Healing Wounds in Anniston," *Anniston Star*, September 20, 2007; author's notes, September 23, 2007; Dan Whisenhunt, "Soothing Words: Group Begins Dialogue on Healing Anniston," *Anniston Star*, September 24, 2007.

30. Interview with Sallie Bowie Franklin, September 29, 2003.

31. Phone communication with Betsy Bean, May 26, 2009.

32. Marisol Bello, "An Uneasy Past Meets an Uneasy Future: Alabama Town Faces Its History and New Challenges 50 Years after Freedom Rides," *USA Today*, June 10, 2011; Brian Anderson, "Freedom Riders Park Sign Damaged by Fire," *Anniston Star*, November 4, 2012.

33. Nick Cenegy, "Anniston Residents Forced Out by PCBs Have Reunion," *Anniston Star*, September 2, 2007; Bill Wilson, "Third Annual PCB Victims Reunion Picnic," photo, *Anniston Star*, August 5, 2012; interview with David Baker, July 18, 2006.

BIBLIOGRAPHY

Manuscript Collections

Alabama Power Company, Corporate Archives, Birmingham, Ala.
Alabama Room, Public Library of Anniston–Calhoun County, Anniston, Ala.
    Biographical Files
    Grace Hooten Gates Records and Recordings
Birmingham Public Library, Birmingham, Ala.
    Vertical Files
Chemical Industry Archives, Environmental Working Group,
    www.chemicalindustryarchives.org
Committee of Unified Leadership Papers, private collection, Anniston, Ala.
Alice Donald Papers, private collection, Anniston, Ala.
    Incineration Archive
Etowah County Courthouse, Gadsden, Ala.
    Records and other documents from *Abernathy v. Monsanto*
Georgia State University Special Collections, Atlanta, Ga.
    Southern Labor Archives, International Molders and Allied Workers Union of
        North America, Local 324 (Anniston, Ala.)
Harvard Medical Library in the Francis A. Countway Library of Medicine, Harvard
    University, Boston, Mass.
    Cecil Kent Drinker Papers, 1898–1958 (H MS c165)
    Harvard School of Public Health, Dean's Files, 1922–49 (E72.A2)
    Harvard School of Public Health, Industrial Hygiene Department, papers se-
        lected by Drs. Frederick and George Shattuck, 1918–34 (E72.5.A1)
Jacksonville State University, Jacksonville, Ala.
    Oral History Collection
Manuscript, Archives and Rare Book Library, Emory University, Atlanta, Ga.
    Charles Holmes Herty Collection
    Southern Christian Leadership Conference Papers
National Archives and Records Administration, College Park, Md., and
    Washington, D.C.
    Records of the Chemical School, Fort McClellan, Alabama, 1949–63 (RG 175)
National Archives and Records Administration, Morrow, Ga.
    Records of the Atlanta Chemical Procurement District, 1942, 1949–50 (RG 156)
Robert W. Risebrough Papers, private collection, Berkeley, Calif.
Schlesinger Library, Radcliffe Institute, Harvard University, Cambridge, Mass.
    Ellen K. Silbergeld Papers
University Archives, Department of Special Collections, Washington University
    Libraries, St. Louis, Mo.
    Monsanto Company Records

W. S. Hoole Special Collections Library, University Libraries Division of Special Collections, The University of Alabama, Tuscaloosa, Ala.
Harry Mell Ayers Papers
Lister Hill Papers

Interviews

Abrams, Michael. Interview by author, Anniston, Ala., August 20, 2003.

Ayers, H. Brandt. Interview by author, Anniston, Ala., October 13, 2003.

Baker, David. Interviews by author, Anniston, Ala., June 16, 2003; March 26, 2004; July 17, 2006; July 18, 2006; February 27, 2012; March 18, 2013.

Baker, Imogene. Interview by author, Anniston, Ala., September 17, 2003.

Baker, Shirley, see Carter, Shirley Baker.

Barksdale, Scott. Interview by author, Anniston, Ala., October 16, 2003.

Bates, Rev. George. Interview by author, Anniston, Ala., April 6, 2004.

Beard, Kay. Interviews by author, Anniston, Ala., July 16, 2003; February 22, 2013.

Bowie, Andrew. Interview by author, Anniston, Ala., October 14, 2003.

Bowie, Arthur. Interviews by author, Anniston, Ala., September 29, 2003; July 17, 2006.

Bowie, Bettye. Interviews by author, Anniston, Ala., September 29, 2003; July 17, 2006; March 18, 2013.

Boyd, Rep. Barbara Bigsby. Interview by author, Anniston, Ala., February 25, 2005.

Braden, Anne McCarty. Interview by author, Louisville, Ky., July 25, 2004.

Branchfield, Craig. Interview by author, Anniston, Ala., November 5, 2003.

Brown, Jacqueline. Interview by author, Anniston, Ala., September 25, 2003.

Brown, Stephanie Yvette. Interview by author, Atlanta, Ga., November 6, 2003.

Cain, David. Interview by author, Anniston, Ala., August 20, 2003.

Calhoun, Georgia. Interviews by author, Choccolocco, Ala., June 10, 2005; February 25, 2013.

Carpenter, David O. Interview by author, Anniston, Ala., July 17, 2004.

Carter, Shirley Baker. Interviews by author, Anniston, Ala., June 16, 2003; April 21, 2004; July 18, 2006; March 11, 2013.

Cash, Jane. Interview by author, Anniston, Ala., July 8, 2004.

Cheatwood, Lea. Interviews by author, Oxford, Ala., November 5, 2003; phone follow-up, August 21, 2005.

Cherry, Timothy, and Kama Cherry. Interviews by author, Anniston, Ala., July 16, 2003.

Christian, David. Interviews by author, Anniston, Ala., September 2, 2003; September 9, 2003; February 22, 2013.

Clemon, U. W. Interview by author, Birmingham, Ala., November 15, 2013.

Conroy, Pete. Interview by author, Jacksonville, Ala., August 13, 2004.

Corey, Winthrop R. Interview by James E. McKee, Monsanto Oral History Project, transcript, December 30, 1981.

Daume, William R. Interview by James E. McKee, Monsanto Oral History Project, transcript, Naples, Fla., November 17, 1981.

Drendel, Frank M. Interview by Jim Keller, March 16, 2000, Cable Center (accessed December 19, 2012).

Donald, Alice. Interview by author, Anniston, Ala., August 21, 2003.

Fahy, Brooks. Interview by author, Anniston, Ala., February 21, 2004.

Franklin, Salle Bowie. Interview by author, Anniston, Ala., September 29, 2003.

Gentle, Edgar C., III. Interview by author, Anniston, Ala., March 19, 2004.

Givhan, Henry. Interview by Grace Hooten Gates, tape recording, Anniston, Ala., February 29, 1980.

Greene, Edmund. Interview by James E. McKee, Monsanto Oral History Project, transcript, December 31, 1981.

Hall, James. Interview by author, Anniston, Ala., July 8, 2004.

Hermanson, Mark. Interview by author, Visby, Sweden, June 2, 2010.

Howell, Hoyt "Chip," Jr. Interview by author, Anniston, Ala., January 13, 2004.

Jensen, Søren. Interview by author, Visby, Sweden, May 31, 2010.

Jones, Bessie. Interview by author, Golden Springs, Ala., October 15, 2004.

Joshua, Myrtle. Interview by author, Anniston, Ala., August 26, 2004.

Kelly, R. Emmet. Interview by James E. McKee, Monsanto Oral History Project, transcript, September 2, 1981.

Kinney, Rufus. Interview by author, Jacksonville, Ala., July 15, 2003.

Knowles, Ralph. Interview by author, Atlanta, Ga., October 16, 2008.

Lavender, Martha. Interview by author, Jacksonville, Ala., July 30, 2003.

Lawry, John. Interview by author, Anniston, Ala., November 19, 2004.

Leahy, Leslie. Interview by author, Washington, D.C., June 2, 2004.

Lindell, Brenda. Interview by author, Anniston, Ala., July 30, 2003.

Marshall, Suzanne. Interview by author, Rome, Ga., October 23, 2003; phone follow-up, March 17, 2013; May 28, 2013.

Matson, Jack. Interviews by author, Visby, Sweden, June 2, 2010; State College, Pa., July 28, 2010; July 30, 2010.

McCombs, Max. Interview by author, St. Louis, Mo., July 14, 2004.

McCord, Shirley. Interview by author, Golden Springs, Ala., August 26, 2004.

McCrory, Rev. Alberta. Interviews by author, Hobson City, Ala., November 19, 2004; October 21, 2005.

McKinney, Janie Forsyth. Interview by author, Anniston, Ala., May 11, 2011.

Mealing, Eloise. Interview by author, Anniston, Ala., February 22, 2004.

Michael, Max. Interview by author, Birmingham, Ala., May 21, 2004.

Montague, Peter. Interview by author, Metro Park, N.J., June 3, 2004.

Munford, Rose Mary Tolliver. Interview by author, Anniston, Ala., June 19, 2004.

Nason, Howard K. Interview by James E. McKee, Monsanto Oral History Project, transcript, July 24, 1981.

Noble, Rev. J. Phillips. Interview by author, Decatur, Ga., June 5, 2006.

Pearson, Wendy. Interviews by author, Visby, Sweden, June 2, 2013; State College, Pa., July 29, 2010; phone follow-up, May 31, 2013; June 14, 2013.

Piper, Ralph C. Interview by James E. McKee, Monsanto Oral History Project, transcript, September 11, 1981.

Reynolds, Rev. Nimrod Q. Interviews by author, Anniston, Ala., November 4, 2003; February 22, 2013.

Risebrough, Robert. Interviews by author, Berkeley, Calif., September 17, 2010 (phone interview); December 6, 2010; January 30, 2011.

Roberts, Cassandra. Interviews by author, Anniston, Ala., August 21, 2003; September 3, 2003; February 22, 2013; March 18, 2013.

Roden, Robert B. Interviews by author, Birmingham, Ala., May 21, 2004; Anniston, Ala., January 28, 2006.

Rodgers, Dr. Gordon, Jr. Interview by author, Douglasville, Ga., February 5, 2005.

Ross, Stephen B. Interview by author, Anniston, Ala., May 17, 2004.

Scruggs, Opal. Interviews by author, Anniston, Ala., September 25, 2003; February 22, 2013.

Scully, Pam. Interview by author, Atlanta, Ga., May 19, 2004.

Sherrer, Charles. Phone interview by author, June 6, 2011.

Silverstone, Allen. Interview by author, Atlanta, Ga., November 22, 2003.

Sterling, Rev. Henry. Interview by author, Oxford, Ala., November 4, 2003.

Stewart, Donald. Interview by author, Anniston, Ala., July 31, 2003.

Sumners, Sherri. Interview by author, Anniston, Ala., October 16, 2003.

Thomas, Cleophus. Interview by author, Anniston, Ala., July 15, 2003.

Thomas, Hank. Interview by author, Stone Mountain, Ga., March 8, 2013.

Tucker, Connie. Phone interview by author, December 4, 2008.

Waddle, Chris. Interview by author, Anniston, Ala., November 19, 2003.

Williams, Craig. Interview by author, Oxford, Ala., August 16, 2003; phone follow-up, February 2, 2004.

Young, Glynn. Interview by author, St. Louis, Mo., July 15, 2004.

Government Documents

Agency for Toxic Substances and Disease Registry (ATSDR). *Draft Toxicological Profile for Lead.* September 2005. http://www.atsdr.cdc.gov/toxprofiles/tp13.html (June 12, 2006).

———. *Evaluation of Soil, Blood, and Air Data from Anniston, Alabama, Calhoun County, Alabama.* Atlanta: U.S. Department of Health and Human Services, Public Health Service, ATSDR Division of Health Assessment and Consultation, 2000.

———. *Health Consultation: Assessment of Four Activities Addressing Childhood Blood Lead Levels in Anniston, Alabama.* Anniston Lead Site. Anniston, Calhoun County, Ala. EPA Facility ID: ALN000407242. Atlanta: U.S. Department of Health and Human Services, Public Health Service, ATSDR Division of Health Assessment and Consultation, June 26, 2003.

———. *Health Consultation: Evaluation of Lead in Residential Surface Soil from Anniston, Alabama.* Atlanta: U.S. Department of Health and Human Services, Public Health Service, ATSDR Division of Health Assessment and Consultation, Public Comment Release, August 7, 2000.

———. "Potential Exposure Pathways." Table 2 in *Public Health Assessment, Anniston Army Depot, Anniston, Alabama*. http://atsdr.cdc.gove/HAC/PHA/anniston/ann_p4.html (July 22, 2006).

———. *Public Health Assessment for Monsanto Company/Solutia Incorporated (aka Anniston PCB Site [Monsanto Company])*. Anniston, Calhoun County, Ala. EPA Facility ID: ALD004019048. Atlanta: U.S. Department of Health and Human Services, Public Health Service, ATSDR, Final Release, May 17, 2001.

———. *Toxicological Profile for Methyl Parathion*. September 2002. http://www.atsdr.cdc.gov/toxprofiles/tp48.html (June 12, 2006).

———. *Toxicological Profile for Polychlorinated Biphenyls (PCBs)*. November 2000. http://www.atsdr.cdc.gov/toxprofiles/tp17.html (June 12, 2006).

Alabama Department of Environmental Management. *In the Matter of Monsanto Company*. Anniston, Calhoun County, Ala. Consent Order No. 960-54-CHW.

Alabama Department of Public Health (ADPH). *Annual Report of the State Department of Public Health of Alabama, 1942*. Wetumpka, Ala.: Wetumpka Printing, 1943.

Alabama Department of Public Health under Cooperative Agreement with the Agency for Toxic Substances and Disease Registry (ADPH/ATSDR). *Health Consultation No. 2, Cobbtown/Sweet Valley Community PCB Exposure Investigation, Anniston, Calhoun County, Ala.*, June 26, 1996.

———. *Health Consultation, Monsanto Company*. Anniston, Calhoun County, Ala. CERCLIS No. ALD004019048, January 1996.

Alabama State Board of Health. *Annual Report of the State Board of Health of Alabama: 1936*. Montgomery, Ala.: State Printers and Binders, 1936.

Baker, Darrell A. *EPA Potential Hazardous Waste Site Inspection Report*. Montgomery: Alabama Department of Public Health, Division of Solid Waste, March 5, 1980.

Centers for Disease Control and Prevention. *Third National Report on Human Exposure to Environmental Chemicals*. 2005. http://www.cdc.gov/exposurereport/3rd/ (July 25, 2006).

Environmental and Natural Resources Policy Division. *Legislative History of the Toxic Substances Control Act* (TSCA), 94th Congress, 2nd session, edited by House Committee on Interstate and Foreign Commerce. Washington, D.C.: Library of Congress, 1976.

Federal Judicial Center. *Reference Manual on Scientific Evidence*. 2nd ed. Washington, D.C.: Federal Judicial Center, 2000. http://www.fjc.gov/public/pdf.nsf/lookup/scimanoo.pdf/$file/scimanoo.pdf (July 26, 2006).

Medical Association of the State of Alabama. *Transactions of the Medical Association of the State of Alabama, 1938*. Montgomery, Ala., 1938.

National Research Council (NRC), Committee on Remediation of PCB-Contaminated Sediments. *A Risk Management Strategy for PCB-Contaminated Sediments*. Washington, D.C.: National Academies Press, 2013.

———, Committee on Review and Evaluation of the Army Chemical Stockpile Disposal Program. *Recommendations for the Disposal of Chemical Weapons and Munitions*. Washington, D.C.: National Academies Press, 1994.

————, Committee on the Assessment of Polychlorinated Biphenyls in the Environment. *Polychlorinated Biphenyls*. Washington, D.C.: National Academies Press, 1979.

————, Division of Chemistry and Chemical Technology. *Chemical Progress in the South*. New York: Chemical Foundation, 1930.

————, Panel on Review and Evaluation of Alternative Disposal Technologies. *Review and Evaluation of Alternative Disposal Technologies*. Washington, D.C.: National Academies Press, 2006.

Official Proceedings of the Constitutional Convention of the State of Alabama, May 21, 1901 to September 3, 1901. http://www.legislature.state.al.us/misc/history/constitutions/1901/proceedings/1901_proceedings_vol1/1901.html (January 16, 2006).

Public Affairs Research Council of Alabama. *The History of the Jefferson County Sanitary Sewer System*. Birmingham, Ala.: Jefferson County Commission, 2001.

United Nations Environment Program, Stockholm Convention on Persistent Organic Pollutants. *Report on Progress in Establishing the Polychlorinated Biphenyls Elimination Network*, January 15, 2011. http://chm.pops.int/Implementation/PCBs/DecisionsRecommendations/tabid/692/Default.aspx (May 31, 2013).

U.S. Bureau of the Census. *Alabama Population of Counties by Decennial Census: 1900 to 1990*, compiled and edited by Richard. L. Forstall. Washington, D.C.: U.S. Bureau of the Census, 1995. http://www.census.gov/population/cencounts/al190090.txt (May 30, 2013).

————. *Profile of General Demographic Characteristics: 2000, American Factfinder*. Washington, D.C.: U.S. Bureau of the Census, 2001. http://factfinder2.census.gov/faces/tableservices/jsf/pages/productview.xhtml?src=bkmk (May 30, 2013).

————. *1990 Census of Population and Housing*. Population and Housing Characteristics for Census Tracts and Block Numbering Areas, Anniston, AL MSA. Washington, D.C., U.S. Bureau of the Census, 1990.

————. *State and County QuickFacts*. "Anniston, Alabama: 2010." "Calhoun County, Alabama: 2010." Data derived from Population Estimates, American Community Survey, Census of Population and Housing. http://quickfacts.census.gov/qfd/states/01/0101852.html (March 26, 2012).

U.S. Department of Health and Human Services, President's Cancer Panel. *Reducing Environmental Cancer Risk: What We Can Do Now*. Annual Report, 2008–9. Washington, D.C., April 2010.

U.S. Environmental Protection Agency (EPA). *Administrative Agreement and Order on Consent for Removal Action*. Region 4. Docket No.: CERCLA-04-2005-3777. Anniston Lead Site and Anniston PCB Site. Anniston, Calhoun County, Ala. DII Industries, L.L.C.; FMC Corporation; Huron Valley Steel Corporation; McWane, Inc.; MW Custom Papers, L.L.C.; MeadWestvaco Corporation; MRC Holdings, Inc.; Phelps Dodge Industries, Inc.; United Defense, L.P.; United States Pipe and Foundry Company, Inc.; and Walter Industries, Inc., July 27, 2005. http://www.epa.gov/Region4/waste/sf/AnnistonLeadPCB-AOC-0805.pdf (June 12, 2006).

———. "Anniston PCB Site." http://www.epa.gov/region4/superfund/sites/npl/ alabama/anpcbstal.html (June 18, 2013).

———. *Drinking Water Criteria Document for Polychlorinated Biphenyls (PCBs) (Final)*. Washington, D.C.: U.S. Environmental Protection Agency, April 1988.

———. "Environmental Justice." http://www.epa.gov/environmentaljustice (August 24, 2012).

———. "Environmental Justice Small Grants Program." http://www.scribd. com/doc/1549075/Environmental-Protection-Agency-ej-smgrants-emerging- tools-2nd-edition (November 21, 2011).

———. *Five-Year Review Report for Southeast Industrial Area Groundwater and Soils and Ammunition Storage*. Anniston Army Depot, Calhoun County, Ala. EPA ID: 321002027, U.S. Environmental Protection Agency, Region 4. Atlanta, Sep- tember 2010. http://www.epa.gov/superfund/sites/fiveyear/f2010040003795. pdf (May 31, 2013).

———. *General Principles for Performing Aggregate Exposure and Risk Assessments*. Office of Pesticide Programs, 2001. http://www.epa.gov/pesticides/trac/sci- ence/aggregate.pdf (May 5, 2013).

———. *Health Assessment Document for 2,3,7,8-Tetrachlorodibenzo-P-Dioxin (TCDD) and Related Compounds (1994 Final Report)*. Washington, D.C., PA/600/BP-92/001a (NTIS PB94205465), 1994.

———. "Hudson River PCBs: Project Background." http://www.epa.gov/hudson/ (April 28, 2012).

———. "Interim Record of Decision, Summary of Remedial Alternative Selection, Region 4." Atlanta, September 29, 2011.

———. "Jenkins, Cate, Ph.D. Chemist Regulatory Development Branch (OS 332) Characterization and Assessment Division, to John West, Special Agent in Charge Office of Criminal Investigations Center, U.S. Environmental Protection Agency: Criminal Investigation of Monsanto Corporation, Cover-Up of Dioxin Contamination in Products, Falsification of Dioxin Health Studies; Kanawha River Site." U.S. EPA Mid-Atlantic Superfund, December 2004.

———. *National Conference on Polychlorinated Biphenyls (1975: Chicago)*. Wash- ington, D.C.: Environmental Protection Agency Office of Toxic Substances, 1976.

———. *PCBs: Cancer Dose-Response Assessment and Application to Environmen- tal Mixtures. National Center for Environmental Assessment Office of Research and Development*. Washington, D.C.: U.S. Environmental Protection Agency, 1996.

———. *Polychlorinated Biphenyls: Health Effects of PCBs*. Washington, D.C.: En- vironmental Protection Agency. http://www.epa.gov/pcb/pubs/effects.html (July 26, 2006).

———. "Proposed Plan Fact Sheet: Update on Long-Term Response Plan Activities— No. 2, Anniston PCB Site." http://www.epa.gov/region4/superfund/images/ nplmedia/pdfs/anpcbstalpplan.pdf (June 18, 2013).

———. "Region 4 Briefing on Anniston." Administrator's briefing, March 6, 2002, http://static.ewg.org/files/foia_response.pdf (September 2, 2013)

————. *The Removal Administrative Record for the Anniston Polychlorinated Biphenyl Site, Anniston, Calhoun County, Alabama.* Washington, D.C.: Environmental Protection Agency, 2001.

————. *Superfund Proposed Plan, Operable Unit 3 of the Anniston PCB Site.* Anniston, Calhoun County, Ala., August 2010.

————. "Superfund Relocation Roundtable Meeting, May 2–4, 1996." Pensacola Civic Center, Pensacola, Fla., Solid Waste and Emergency Response, 9378.0-03, EPA 540-K-96-010, PB96-963254, December 1996.

————. "Superfund Update: Cleanup Progressing and Future Plans, Sauget Area 1 and Area 2 Superfund Sites." Sauget, Ill., November 2009. http://www.epa.gov/region5/cleanup/saugetarea2/pdfs/sauget1_fs_200911.pdf (September 6, 2012).

U.S. General Accounting Office. *Siting of Hazardous Waste Landfills and Their Correlation with Racial and Economic Status of Surrounding Communities.* Washington, D.C.: U.S. Government Printing Office, 1983.

U.S. Government Accounting Office. *Chemical Weapons Destruction: Advantages and Disadvantages of Alternatives to Incineration.* Report to the Chairman, Subcommittee on Environment, Energy, and Natural Resources, Committee on Government Operations, House of Representatives. Washington, D.C., March 18, 1994.

U.S. House of Representatives, Committee on Government Reform, Minority Staff Special Investigations Division. *The Chemical Industry, the Bush Administration, and European Efforts to Regulate Chemicals.* Prepared for Rep. Henry A. Waxman. Washington, D.C.: U.S. House of Representatives, 2004.

U.S. Senate, Committee on Appropriations, Subcommittee on VA-HUD-Independent Agencies. *PCB Contamination in Anniston, Alabama: Hearing before a Subcommittee of the Committee on Appropriations.* 107th Congress, 2nd session, Special Hearing, April 19, 2002, Anniston, Ala. Washington, D.C.: U.S. Government Printing Office, 2003.

Weiss, Francis Joseph. *Manpower, Chemistry and Agriculture* [Humphrey Report]. Staff Report to the Subcommittee on Labor and Public Welfare. U.S. Senate, 82nd Congress, 1st session, presented by Mr. [Hubert H.] Humphrey, February 20 (legislative day, January 10, 1952). Washington, D.C.: U.S. Government Printing Office, 1952.

World Health Organization, International Agency for Research on Cancer (WHO/IARC). *IARC Monographs on the Evaluation of Carcinogenic Risks to Humans, Overall Evaluations of Carcinogenicity: An Updating of IARC Monographs,* vols. 1–42, suppl. 7 (1987).

Legal Sources

Abbott v. Monsanto, No. CV-97-967 (Ala. Cir. Ct. Etowah County), consolidated with *Abernathy. Abernathy v. Monsanto,* No. CV-96-269 (Ala. Cir. Ct. Etowah County, September 10, 2003), renamed *Bowie v. Monsanto.*
Alabama v. Seeber, 502 F.2d 1238 (5th Cir. 1974).

Bates v. Stewart, 99 So. 3d 837 (Ala. 2012).

Bowie v. Monsanto, No. CV-01-832 (Ala. Cir. Ct. Etowah County, September 10, 2003), consolidated with *Abernathy*.

Caldwell v. Parker, 252 U.S. 376 (1920).

Dalehite v. United States, 346 U.S. 15 (1953).

Daubert v. Merrell Dow Pharmaceuticals, Inc., 509 U.S. 579 (1993).

Dyer v. Monsanto, No. CV-93-250 (Ala. Cir. Ct. St. Clair County, June 9, 1999), aff'd, *Ex parte Anderson*, 807 So. 2d 505 (Ala. 2000).

Environmental Defense Fund v. EPA, 598 F.2d 62 (D.C. Cir. 1978).

EPA v. Pharmacia Corporation (f/k/a Monsanto), No. CV 99-63-DRH (S.D. Ill., August 26, 2002).

Ex parte Monsanto Company and Solutia, Inc. (In re Abernathy v. Monsanto), 862 So. 2d 595 (Ala. 2003).

Ex parte Monsanto Company (In re Long v. Monsanto and Abernathy v. Monsanto), 794 So. 2d 350 (Ala. 2001).

Families Concerned about Nerve Gas Incineration v. United States Department of the Army, 380 F. Supp. 2d 1233 (N.D. Ala. 2005).

Garrett v. Raytheon Company, 368 So. 2d 516 (Ala. 1979).

Gentry v. Swann Chemical Company, 174 So. 530 (Ala. 1937).

Griffin v. Unocal Corporation, 990 So. 2d 291 (Ala. 2008).

Hancock v. Train, 426 U.S. 167 (1976).

Hinton, Travis v. Monsanto, 813 So. 2d 827 (Ala. 2001).

Jerkins v. Lincoln Electric Company, 103 So. 3d 1 (Ala. 2011).

Kemner v. Monsanto, 492 NE 2d 1327 (Ill. 1986).

Ladiga v. Roland, 43 U.S. 581 (1844).

Long v. Monsanto, No. CV-96-268, (Ala. Cir. Ct. Etowah County), consolidated with *Abernathy*.

Mars Hill Baptist Church of Anniston v. Mars Hill Missionary Baptist Church, 761 So. 2d 975 (1999).

Mars Hill Missionary Baptist Church v. Monsanto, No. CV-96-243 (Ala. Cir. Ct. Calhoun County, June 25, 1998).

Monsanto Chemical Company. v. Fincher, 133 So. 2d 192 (Ala. 1961).

NAACP v. Alabama, 357 U.S. 449 (1958).

Owens v. Monsanto, No. CV-96-J-0440-E (N.D. Ala. 2001).

Owens v. Monsanto, No. 05-13258-B (11th Cir., August 19, 2004).

Pennsylvania v. U.S. Mineral Products Co., 809 A. 2d 1000 (Pa. Commw. Ct. 2002).

Sewell v. Monsanto, No. CV-94-00778-WMA (N.D., Ala., January 25, 1996).

Shelter Cove Management, Inc. v. Monsanto, No. CV-94-50 (Ala. Cir. Ct. St. Clair County), aff'd, *Ex parte Anderson*, 807 So. 2d 505 (Ala. 2000).

Solutia and Pharmacia v. McWane, CV-03-PWG-1345-E (N.D., Ala. filed June 5, 2003).

Suggs v. Monsanto, No. CV-01-0874 (Ala. Cir. Ct. Calhoun County), consolidated with *Abernathy*.

Swift v. Monsanto., No. CV-97-02430 (N.D. Ala., September 10, 1997).

Tolbert v. Monsanto, No. CV-01-C-1407-UWC (N.D. Ala., 2003).

Transwestern Pipeline Company v. Monsanto, 53 Cal. Rptr. 2d 887 (Cal. Ct. App. 1996).

United States v. Pharmacia Corporation (f/k/a Monsanto Company and Solutia Inc.), No. 02-CV-0749-E, 2003 WL 22319070 (N.D. Ala., August 4, 2003).

United States v. Republic Steel Corporation, 362 U.S. 482 (1960).

United States v. Standard Oil Company, 384 U.S. 224 (1966).

Van Valkenberg v. Brown, 43 Cal. 43, 13 Am Rpts. 142 (1872).

Depositions and Expert Testimony

Abernathy, Jesse. Deposition in *Owens v. Monsanto*, CV-96-J-0440-E, October 27, 1999.

Cambron, Bill. Deposition in *Owens v. Monsanto*, CV-96-J-0440-E, October 22, 1999.

Carpenter, David O. Deposition in *Long v. Monsanto*, CV-96-268; *Abernathy v. Monsanto*, CV-96-269; and *Abbott v. Monsanto*, CV-97-767, December 16, 1998.

———. Deposition in *Swift v. Monsanto*, CV-97-AR-2430-E, July 12, 1999.

Chatman, Charles. Deposition in *Owens v. Monsanto*, CV-96-J-0440-E, November 4, 1999.

Hughes, Bill. Deposition in *Owens v. Monsanto*, CV-96-J-0440-E, October 21, 1999.

Matson, Jack. "Polychlorinated Biphenyl (PCB) Emission from the Monsanto Anniston, Alabama Manufacturing Facility." Supplemental expert report in *Owens v. Monsanto*, CV-96-P-0440-E, February 28, 2001.

Miller, Gerald W. Deposition in *Sewell v. Monsanto*, No. CV-94-AR-778-E, March 15, 1995.

Papageorge, William B. Deposition in *Mars Hill Missionary Baptist Church v. Monsanto Company*, CV-96-243, March 31, 1998.

———. Deposition in *Owens v. Monsanto*, CV-96-J-0440-E, March 31, 2001.

———. Deposition in *Pennsylvania v. U.S. Mineral Products Co. et al.* (No. 284 MD 1990), April 28, 1998.

Smith, Carl. Deposition in *Owens v. Monsanto*, CV-96-J-0440-E, October 27, 1999.

Tarr, Jim. Deposition in *Owens v. Monsanto*, CV-96-J-0440-E, March 8, 2001.

Newspapers and Periodicals

American Journal of Public Health
Anniston Evening Star
Anniston Evening Star and Hot Blast
Anniston Hot Blast
Anniston Star
Anniston Sunday Star and Daily Hot Blast
Anniston Times
Anniston Weekly Hot Blast
Anniston Weekly Times
Anniston Weekly Watchman
Antipode: A Radical Journal of Geography
Archives of Dermatology and Syphilology
Atlanta Constitution
Atlanta Journal
Baltimore Evening Sun
Bankruptcy News
Birmingham Age-Herald
Birmingham News

Birmingham News-Herald
Birmingham Post-Herald
Bloomberg News
BSED in Touch
Charleston (W.Va.) Gazette
Chemical and Engineering News
Chemical Week
Cleburne (Ala.) News
Columbus (Ga.) Ledger
Creative Loafing
Defense News
Durham (N.C.) Morning Herald
EHS Today: The Magazine for
    Environment, Health and Safety
    Leaders
Environmental Ethics
Environmental Health News
Environmental Health Perspectives
Environmental History
Environmental Science and Technology
Federal Register
Financial World
Forbes
Gadsden (Ala.) Times
Harper's Magazine
Honolulu Advertiser
ISIS: Journal of the History of Science in
    Society
Jacksonville (Ala.) News
Jacksonville (Ala.) Republican
Joliet (Ill.) Olympian
Journal of Agricultural and Food
    Chemistry
Journal of Business
Journal of Industrial and Engineering
    Chemistry
Journal of Industrial Hygiene and
    Toxicology

Journal of Negro History
Journal of the American Medical
    Association (JAMA)
Journal of the National Cancer Institute
Las Vegas Review Journal
Life
Manufacturers Record
Monsanto Imagine
Monsanto Magazine
Monsanto Record Buster
Montgomery Advertiser
The Nation
New Scientist
Newsday
Newsweek
New York Herald Tribune
New York Times
Oregonian
People
People's Journal (Jacksonville, Ala.)
Pittsburgh Courier
Rachel's Health and Environment Weekly
    (Rachel's Weekly, Rachel's Hazardous
    Waste News)
San Francisco Chronicle
Science News
Sierra
Sports Illustrated
St. Louis Post-Dispatch
St. Petersburg Times
Time
Tooele (Utah) Transcript-Bulletin
Tuscaloosa News
UNESCO Courier
USA Today
U.S. News and World Report
Washington Post

Books and Pamphlets

Aftalion, Fred. *A History of the International Chemical Industry*. Philadelphia: University of Pennsylvania Press, 1991.

Alaimo, Stacy. *Bodily Natures: Science, Environment, and the Material Self*. Bloomington: Indiana University Press, 2010.

Allen, Barbara L. *Uneasy Alchemy: Citizens and Experts in Louisiana's Chemical Corridor Disputes*. Urban and Industrial Environments. Cambridge, Mass.: MIT Press, 2003.

Anderson, Ray C. *Mid-course Correction: Toward a Sustainable Enterprise—The Interface Model*. Atlanta: Peregrinzilla, 1998.

Anniston in North Alabama: The Model City of the South. Baltimore: Record Printing House, 1885.

Armes, Ethel. *The Story of Coal and Iron in Alabama: Big Business, Economic Power in a Free Society*. New York: Arno, 1973.

Arsenault, Raymond. *Freedom Riders: 1961 and the Struggle for Racial Justice*. Pivotal Moments in American History. Oxford: Oxford University Press, 2006.

Atkins, Leah Rawls. *"Developed for the Service of Alabama": The Centennial History of the Alabama Power Company, 1906–2006*. Birmingham: Alabama Power Co., 2006.

Ayers, Edward L. *The Promise of the New South: Life after Reconstruction*. New York: Oxford University Press, 1992.

Ayers, H. Brandt. *In Love with Defeat: The South's Undying Affair with Bad Choices*. Montgomery, Ala.: NewSouth, 2012.

Baldwin, Joseph G., and James H. Justus. *The Flush Times of Alabama and Mississippi: A Series of Sketches*. Library of Southern Civilization. Baton Rouge: Louisiana State University Press, 1987.

Balshem, Martha. *Cancer in the Community: Class and Medical Authority*. Washington, D.C.: Smithsonian Institution Press, 1993.

Blackmon, Ross. *A Story of the Progress and Achievements of the Negro Race in the Art of Self-Government*. Anniston, Ala.: Stephens, 1947.

Bowen, Catherine Drinker. *Family Portrait*. 1st ed. Boston: Little, Brown, 1970.

Braden, Anne. *The Wall Between*. Knoxville: University of Tennessee Press, 1999.

Bragg, Rick. *All Over but the Shoutin'*. 1st ed. New York: Pantheon, 1997.

Brewer, Willis. *Alabama: Her History, Resources, War Record, and Public Men—From 1540 to 1872*. Montgomery, Ala.: Barrett and Brown, 1872.

Brickman, Ronald. *Controlling Chemicals: The Politics of Regulation in Europe and the United States*. Ithaca, N.Y.: Cornell University Press, 1985.

Brophy, Leo P., Wyndham D. Miles, and Rexmond Canning Cochrane. *The Chemical Warfare Service: From Laboratory to Field*. Washington, D.C.: Office of the Chief of Military History, Department of the Army, 1959.

Brophy, Leo P., and George J. B. Fisher. *The Chemical Warfare Service: Organizing for War*. Washington, D.C.: Office of the Chief of Military History, Department of the Army, 1959.

Brown, Phil. *Toxic Exposures: Contested Illnesses and the Environmental Health Movement*. New York: Columbia University Press, 2007.

Brown, Phil, and Edwin J. Mikkelson. *No Safe Place: Toxic Waste, Leukemia, and Community Action*. Berkeley: University of California Press, 1997 [1990].

Bullard, Robert D. *The Black Metropolis in the Twenty-First Century: Race, Power, and Politics of Place*. New York: Rowan and Littlefield, 2007.

———. *Dumping in Dixie: Race, Class, and Environmental Quality*. Boulder, Colo.: Westview, 1990.

Bullard, Robert D., ed. *Confronting Environmental Racism: Voices from the Grass-roots.* Boston: South End, 1993.

———. *Unequal Protection: Environmental Justice and Communities of Color.* San Francisco: Sierra Club Books, 1994.

Bullard, Robert D., Glenn S. Johnson, Angel O. Torres, and DeLane Garner. *Environmental Justice and Superfund Sites Workshop in EPA Region IV, Anniston Army Depot (ANAD).* Atlanta: Environmental Justice Resource Center, Clark Atlanta University, November 14, 1996.

Bullard, Robert D., and Beverly Wright. *The Wrong Complexion for Protection: How the Government Response to Disaster Endangers African American Communities.* New York: New York University Press, 2012.

Bullard, Sara. *Free at Last: A History of the Civil Rights Movement and Those Who Died in the Struggle.* New York: Oxford University Press, 1993.

Burkett, Randall K., Nancy Hall Burkett, and Henry Louis Gates Jr., eds. *Black Biography, 1790–1950.* Alexandria, Va.: Chadwyck-Healey, 1990.

Carson, Rachel. *Silent Spring.* Boston: Houghton Mifflin, 1962.

Carter, Dan T. *The Politics of Rage: George Wallace, the Origins of the New Conservatism, and the Transformation of American Politics.* New York: Simon and Schuster, 1995.

Carter, Hodding. *Lower Mississippi.* New York: Farrar and Rinehart, 1942.

Cash, Wilbur Joseph. *The Mind of the South.* New York: A. A. Knopf, 1941.

Chandler, Alfred du Pont. *Shaping the Industrial Century: The Remarkable Story of the Evolution of the Modern Chemical and Pharmaceutical Industries.* Harvard Studies in Business History. Cambridge, Mass.: Harvard University Press, 2005.

Cherniack, Martin. *The Hawk's Nest Incident: America's Worst Industrial Disaster.* New Haven, Conn.: Yale University Press, 1986.

Christensen, Lawrence O. *Dictionary of Missouri Biography.* Columbia: University of Missouri Press, 1999.

Cobb, James C. *The Selling of the South: The Southern Crusade for Industrial Development, 1936–1990.* 2nd ed. Urbana: University of Illinois Press, 1993.

Colborn, Theo, John Peterson Myers, and Dianne Dumanoski. *Our Stolen Future: Are We Threatening Our Fertility, Intelligence, and Survival? A Scientific Detective Story.* New York: Dutton, 1996.

Cole, Luke W., and Sheila R. Foster. *From the Ground Up: Environmental Racism and the Rise of the Environmental Justice Movement.* Critical America. New York: New York University Press, 2001.

Collins, Patricia Hill. *Fighting Words: Black Women and the Search for Justice.* Contradictions of Modernity, vol. 7. Minneapolis: University of Minnesota Press, 1998.

Commission for Racial Justice (United Church of Christ). *Toxic Wastes and Race in the United States: A National Report on the Racial and Socioeconomic Characteristics of Communities with Hazardous Waste Sites.* New York: United Church of Christ, 1987.

Coppin, Clayton A., and Jack C. High. *The Politics of Purity: Harvey Washington Wiley and the Origins of Federal Food Policy.* Ann Arbor: University of Michigan Press, 1999.

Cowdrey, Albert E. *This Land, This South: An Environmental History*. Rev. ed. Lexington: University Press of Kentucky, 1996.

Cranor, Carl F. *Regulating Toxic Substances: A Philosophy of Science and the Law*. New York: Oxford University Press, 1993.

Crespino, Joseph. *In Search of Another Country: Mississippi and the Conservative Counterrevolution, Politics and Society in Twentieth-Century America*. Princeton, N.J.: Princeton University Press, 2007.

Cronon, William. *Changes in the Land: Indians, Colonists, and the Ecology of New England*. 1st ed. New York: Hill and Wang, 1983.

———. *Uncommon Ground: Rethinking the Human Place in Nature*. New York: W. W. Norton, 1996.

Cuesta Camacho, David E. *Environmental Injustices, Political Struggles: Race, Class, and the Environment*. Durham, N.C.: Duke University Press, 1998.

Curran, Jean Alonzo. *Founders of the Harvard School of Public Health, with Biographical Notes, 1909–1946*. [New York]: Josiah Macy Jr., 1970.

Daniel, Pete. *Toxic Drift: Pesticides and Health in the Post–World War II South*. Walter Lynwood Fleming Lectures in Southern History. Baton Rouge: Louisiana State University Press in association with Smithsonian Institution, 2005.

Davidson, Chandler, and Bernard Grofman. *Quiet Revolution in the South: The Impact of the Voting Rights Act, 1965–1990*. Princeton, N.J.: Princeton University Press, 1994.

Davis, Devra Lee. *When Smoke Ran Like Water: Tales of Environmental Deception and the Battle against Pollution*. New York: Basic Books, 2002.

Davis, Donald Edward. *Where There Are Mountains: An Environmental History of the Southern Appalachians*. Athens: University of Georgia Press, 2000.

Dittmer, John. *Local People: The Struggle for Civil Rights in Mississippi*. Urbana: University of Illinois Press, 1994.

Douglas, Mary. *Purity and Danger: An Analysis of Concepts of Pollution and Taboo*. Routledge Classics. London: Routledge, 2002 [1966].

Downs, Jim. *Sick from Freedom: African-American Illness and Suffering during the Civil War and Reconstruction*. New York: Oxford University Press, 2012.

Dracos, Ted. *Biocidal: Confronting the Poisonous Legacy of PCBs*. Boston: Beacon, 2010.

Drinker, Cecil K., M.D. *Report to the Monsanto Chemical Company*. Boston: Harvard School of Public Health, 1938.

Druley, Ray M., and Girard Lanterman Ordway. *The Toxic Substances Control Act*. Rev. ed. Washington, D.C.: Bureau of National Affairs, 1981.

Duck, Leigh Anne. *The Nation's Region: Southern Modernism, Segregation, and U.S. Nationalism*. New Southern Studies. Athens: University of Georgia Press, 2006.

Dudziak, Mary L. *Cold War Civil Rights: Race and the Image of American Democracy, Politics and Society in Twentieth-Century America*. Princeton, N.J.: Princeton University Press, 2000.

Durant, Robert F. *The Greening of the U.S. Military: Environmental Policy, National Security, and Organizational Change*. Washington, D.C.: Georgetown University Press, 2007.

Egerton, John. *Speak Now against the Day: The Generation before the Civil Rights Movement in the South*. 1st ed. New York: Knopf, 1994.

Environmental Defense Fund, Joseph H. Highland, and Robert H. Boyle. *Malignant Neglect*. 1st ed. New York: Knopf, 1979.

Fagin, Dan, Marianne Lavelle, and Center for Public Integrity. *Toxic Deception: How the Chemical Industry Manipulates Science, Bends the Law, and Endangers Your Health*. 2nd ed. Monroe, Me.: Common Courage, 1999.

Federal Writers' Program (Alabama). *Alabama: A Guide to the Deep South*. American Guide Series. New York: R. R. Smith, 1941.

Feldman, Glenn. *The Disfranchisement Myth: Poor Whites and Suffrage Restriction in Alabama*. Athens: University of Georgia Press, 2004.

Ferguson, Denzel E. *A Final Report: Investigations of Certain Pesticide-Wildlife Relationships in the Choccolocco Creek Drainage*. Contract between the Monsanto Chemical Company and Mississippi State University (September 1, 1966, through August 31, 1967), 1967, 1–22.

Finseth, Ian. *Shades of Green: Visions of Nature in the Literature of American Slavery, 1770–1860*. Athens: University of Georgia Press, 2009.

Fischer, Frank. *Citizens, Experts and the Environment: The Politics of Local Knowledge*. Durham, N.C.: Duke University Press, 2000.

Flynt, J. Wayne. *Alabama in the Twentieth Century*. Edited by Glenn Feldman and Kari Frederickson, Modern South Series. Tuscaloosa: University of Alabama Press, 2004.

———. *Poor but Proud: Alabama's Poor Whites*. Tuscaloosa: University of Alabama Press, 1989.

Foner, Eric. *A Short History of Reconstruction, 1863–1877*. 1st ed. New York: Harper and Row, 1990.

Forrestal, Dan J. *Faith, Hope, and $5,000: The Story of Monsanto—The Trials and Triumphs of the First 75 Years*. New York: Simon and Schuster, 1977.

Fosl, Catherine. *Subversive Southerner: Anne Braden and the Struggle for Racial Justice in the Cold War South*. 1st ed. New York: Palgrave Macmillan, 2002.

Foucault, Michel. *Power/Knowledge: Selected Interviews and Other Writings, 1972–1977*. Edited by Colin Gordon. 1st U.S. ed. New York: Pantheon, 1980.

Fries, Amos A., and Clarence J. West. *Chemical Warfare*. 1st ed. New York: McGraw-Hill, 1921.

Fullilove, Mindy Thompson. *Root Shock: How Tearing up City Neighborhoods Hurts America, and What We Can Do about It*. 1st ed. New York: One World/Ballantine, 2004.

Garcia-Johnson, Ronie. *Exporting Environmentalism: U.S. Multinational Chemical Corporations in Brazil and Mexico*. Cambridge, Mass.: MIT Press, 2000.

Gaston, Paul M. *The New South Creed: A Study in Southern Mythmaking*. 1st ed. New York: Knopf, 1970.

Gates, Grace Hooten. *The Model City of the New South—Anniston, Alabama, 1872–1900*. Huntsville, Ala.: Strode, 1978.

Gaventa, John. *Power and Powerlessness: Quiescence and Rebellion in an Appalachian Valley*. Urbana: University of Illinois Press, 1980.

Gibbs, Lois Marie. *Love Canal: The Story Continues*. Gabriola Island, B.C.: New Society, 1998.

Glave, Dianne D., and Mark Stoll. *To Love the Wind and the Rain: African Americans and Environmental History*. Pittsburgh: University of Pittsburgh Press, 2006.

Godshalk, David Fort. *Veiled Visions: The 1906 Atlanta Race Riot and the Reshaping of American Race Relations*. Chapel Hill: University of North Carolina Press, 2005.

Goodwin, Jeff, and James M. Jasper, eds. *The Social Movements Reader: Cases and Concepts*. Malden, Mass: Wiley-Blackwell, 2009.

Gotham, Kevin Fox. *Race, Real Estate, and Uneven Development: The Kansas City Experience, 1900–2000*. Albany: State University of New York Press, 2002.

Gottlieb, Robert. *Forcing the Spring: The Transformation of the American Environmental Movement*. Washington, D.C.: Island, 1993.

Goulden, Joseph C. *Jerry Wurf: Labor's Last Angry Man*. 1st ed. New York: Atheneum, 1982.

Griffith, Edward, and Carolyn Green Satterfield. *The Triumphs and Troubles of Theodore Swann*. Montgomery, Ala.: Black Belt, 1999.

Griffith, Lucille. *Alabama: A Documentary History to 1900*. Rev. and enl. ed. Tuscaloosa: University of Alabama Press, 1972.

Hackney, Sheldon. *Populism to Progressivism in Alabama*. Princeton, N.J.: Princeton University Press, 1969.

Hale, Grace Elizabeth. *Making Whiteness: The Culture of Segregation in the South, 1890–1940*. 1st ed. New York: Pantheon, 1998.

Hall, Bob. *Environmental Politics: Lessons from the Grassroots*. Durham, N.C.: Institute for Southern Studies, 1988.

Harden, Victoria Angela. *Inventing the NIH: Federal Biomedical Research Policy, 1887–1937*. Baltimore: Johns Hopkins University Press, 1986.

Harlan, Louis R., Pete Daniel, Stuart B. Kaufman, Raymond Smock, and William M. Welty, eds. *The Booker T. Washington Papers*. 14 vols. Vol. 2, *1860–1889*. Urbana: University of Illinois Press, 1972.

Harr, Jonathan. *A Civil Action*. New York: Vintage, 1995.

Harris, Robert, and Jeremy Paxman. *A Higher Form of Killing: The Secret Story of Chemical and Biological Warfare*. 1st U.S. ed. New York: Hill and Wang, 1982.

Harvey, David. *Justice, Nature and the Geography of Difference*. Malden, Mass.: Blackwell, 1996.

———. *Spaces of Hope*. California Studies in Critical Human Geography 7. Berkeley: University of California Press, 2000.

Hayden, Dolores. *The Power of Place: Urban Landscapes as Public History*. Cambridge, Mass.: MIT Press, 1995.

Haynes, Williams. *Chemical Pioneers: The Founders of the American Chemical Industry*. New York: D. Van Nostrand, 1939.

———. *Men, Money, and Molecules*. Garden City, N.Y.: Doubleday, Doran, 1936.

Hays, Samuel P., and Barbara D. Hays. *Beauty, Health, and Permanence: Environmental Politics in the United States, 1955–1985*. Studies in Environment and History. Cambridge: Cambridge University Press, 1987.

Henry, Aaron, and Constance Curry. *Aaron Henry: The Fire Ever Burning*. Margaret Walker Alexander Series in African American Studies. Jackson: University Press of Mississippi, 2000.

Hersey, John. *Hiroshima*. New York: A. A. Knopf, 1946.

Hersey, Mark D. *"My Work Is That of Conservation": An Environmental Biography of George Washington Carver*. Environmental History and the American South. Athens: University of Georgia Press, 2011.

Hounshell, David A., and John K. Smith. *Science and Corporate Strategy: DuPont R&D, 1902–1980*. Cambridge: Cambridge University Press, 1988.

Howard, Gene L. *Death at Cross Plains: An Alabama Reconstruction Tragedy*. Tuscaloosa: University of Alabama Press, 1984.

Howard, R. A. *1887–88 Anniston City Directory*. Atlanta: Byrd and Patillo, 1887.

Hunter, Tera W. *To 'Joy My Freedom: Southern Black Women's Lives and Labors after the Civil War*. Cambridge, Mass.: Harvard University Press, 1997.

Hurley, Andrew. *Environmental Inequalities: Class, Race, and Industrial Pollution in Gary, Indiana, 1945–1980*. Chapel Hill: University of North Carolina Press, 1995.

Institute of Continuing Legal Education in Georgia. *Toxic Torts*. Athens: ICLE in Georgia, March 17, 2005.

Institute of Medicine. *Toward Environmental Justice: Research, Education, and Health Policy Needs*. Washington, D.C.: National Academy Press, 1999.

Jackson, Harvey H. *Inside Alabama: A Personal History of My State*. Tuscaloosa: University of Alabama Press, 2003.

Jasanoff, Sheila. *Science at the Bar: Law, Science, and Technology in America*. Cambridge, Mass.: Harvard University Press, 1995.

Kay, Terry. *The Year the Lights Came On: A Novel*. Athens: University of Georgia Press, 1989.

Kelley, Robin D. G. *Hammer and Hoe: Alabama Communists during the Great Depression*. Chapel Hill: University of North Carolina Press, 1990.

Kelley, William D. *The Old South and the New: A Series of Letters*. New York: G. P. Putnam, 1888.

Kelly, Brian. *Race, Class, and Power in the Alabama Coalfields, 1908–21*. Urbana: University of Illinois Press, 2001.

Kimball, Solon Toothaker, and Marion Pearsall. *The Talladega Story: A Study in Community Process*. Tuscaloosa: University of Alabama Press, 1954.

Kirby, Jack Temple. *Rural Worlds Lost: The American South, 1920–1960*. Baton Rouge: Louisiana State University Press, 1987.

Kolodny, Annette. *The Lay of the Land: Metaphor as Experience and History in American Life and Letters*. Chapel Hill: University of North Carolina Press, 1975.

Kousser, J. Morgan. *The Shaping of Southern Politics: Suffrage Restriction and the Establishment of the One-Party South, 1880–1910*. Yale Historical Publications: Miscellany. New Haven, Conn.: Yale University Press, 1974.

Kozol, Jonathan. *Savage Inequalities: Children in America's Schools*. 1st ed. New York: Crown, 1991.

Lacefield, Jim. *Lost Worlds in Alabama's Rocks: A Guide to the State's Ancient Life and Landscapes*. Tuscaloosa: Alabama Geological Society, 2000.

LaHaye, Tim F., and Jerry B. Jenkins. *Armageddon: The Cosmic Battle of the Ages.* Left Behind Series. Wheaton, Ill.: Tyndale, 2003.

Langston, Nancy. *Toxic Bodies: Hormone Disruptors and the Legacy of DES.* New Haven, Conn.: Yale University Press, 2010.

Lear, Linda J. *Rachel Carson: Witness for Nature.* 1st ed. New York: Henry Holt, 1997.

Lentz-Smith, Adriane Danette. *Freedom Struggles: African Americans and World War I.* Cambridge, Mass.: Harvard University Press, 2009.

Lipsitz, George. *Time Passages: Collective Memory and American Popular Culture.* Minneapolis: University of Minnesota Press, 1990.

Love, Dennis. *My City Was Gone: The Poisoning of a Small American Town.* 1st ed. New York: William Morrow, 2006.

Mahoney, Richard J. *A Commitment to Greatness.* Springfield, Mass.: Monsanto Co., 1988.

———. *In My Opinion: Writings on Public Policy, 1995–2002.* St. Louis: Center for the Study of American Business, 2003.

Markel, Howard. *Quarantine! East European Jewish Immigrants and the New York City Epidemics of 1892.* Baltimore: Johns Hopkins University Press, 1997.

Markowitz, Gerald E., and David Rosner. *Deceit and Denial: The Deadly Politics of Industrial Pollution.* Berkeley: University of California Press, 2002.

Marshall, Suzanne. *"Lord, We're Just Trying to Save Your Water": Environmental Activism and Dissent in the Appalachian South.* Southern Dissent. Gainesville: University Press of Florida, 2002.

Martin, Thomas Wesley. *The Story of Electricity in Alabama since the Turn of the Century, 1900–1952.* 1st ed. Birmingham, Ala.: Birmingham Publishing, 1952.

Martini, Edwin A. *Agent Orange: History, Science, and the Politics of Uncertainty, Culture, Politics, and the Cold War.* Amherst: University of Massachusetts Press, 2012.

Mauroni, Albert J. *America's Struggle with Chemical-Biological Warfare.* Westport, Conn.: Praeger, 2000.

McGurty, Eileen Maura. *Transforming Environmentalism: Warren County, PCBs, and the Origins of Environmental Justice.* New Brunswick, N.J.: Rutgers University Press, 2007.

McSpirit, Stephanie, Lynne Faltraco, and Conner Bailey. *Confronting Ecological Crisis in Appalachia and the South: University and Community Partnerships.* Lexington: University Press of Kentucky, 2012.

McWhorter, Diane. *Carry Me Home: Birmingham, Alabama: The Climactic Battle of the Civil Rights Revolution.* New York: Simon and Schuster, 2001.

Melosi, Martin V. *The Sanitary City: Urban Infrastructure in America from Colonial Times to the Present.* Creating the North American Landscape. Baltimore: Johns Hopkins University Press, 2000.

Merchant, Carolyn. *Reinventing Eden: The Fate of Nature in Western Culture.* New York: Routledge, 2003.

Minutaglio, Bill. *City on Fire: The Forgotten Disaster That Devastated a Town and Ignited a Landmark Legal Battle.* 1st ed. New York: HarperCollins, 2003.

Moore, Glover. *A Calhoun County, Alabama, Boy in the 1860s*. Jackson: University Press of Mississippi, 1978.

Morris, Sylvia Jukes. *Edith Kermit Roosevelt: Portrait of a First Lady Morris*. Kindle ed. New York: Coward, McCann and Geoghegan, 1980.

Morrison, Toni. *Playing in the Dark: Whiteness and the Literary Imagination*. Cambridge, Mass.: Harvard University Press, 1992.

Mumford, Lewis. *The City in History: Its Origins, Its Transformations, and Its Prospects*. 1st ed. New York: Harcourt Brace and World, 1961.

Nash, Linda Lorraine. *Inescapable Ecologies: A History of Environment, Disease, and Knowledge*. Berkeley: University of California Press, 2006.

Nixon, Rob. *Slow Violence and the Environmentalism of the Poor*. Cambridge, Mass.: Harvard University Press, 2011.

Noble, David F. *America by Design: Science, Technology, and the Rise of Corporate Capitalism*. 1st ed. New York: Knopf, 1977.

Noble, Phil. *Beyond the Burning Bus: The Civil Rights Revolution in a Southern Town*. Montgomery, Ala.: NewSouth, 2003.

Oquirrh Institute. *The Enlibra Toolkit: Principles and Tools for Environmental Management*. 1st ed. http://www.oquirrhinstitute.org/em_toolkit.html (May 12, 2006).

Oreskes, Naomi, and Erik M. Conway. *Merchants of Doubt: How a Handful of Scientists Obscured the Truth on Issues from Tobacco Smoke to Global Warming*. 1st U.S. ed. New York: Bloomsbury, 2010.

Oxford English Dictionary. Compact ed. Oxford: Oxford University Press, 1982 [1971].

Payne, Charles M. *I've Got the Light of Freedom: The Organizing Tradition and the Mississippi Freedom Struggle*. Berkeley: University of California Press, 1995.

Percival, Robert V. *Environmental Regulation: Law, Science, and Policy*. 2nd ed. Law School Casebook Series. Boston: Little Brown, 1996.

Pew Center on the States. *The Impact of the Fiscal Cliff on the States*. Washington, D.C.: Pew Charitable Trusts, November 2012.

Pitts, Alice Fox, ed. *Problems of Journalism: Proceedings of the 1956 Convention of the American Society of Newspapers Editors*. Washington, D.C.: ASNE, 1956.

Porter, Dorothy. *Health, Civilization, and the State: A History of Public Health from Ancient to Modern Times*. London: Routledge, 1999.

Pulido, Laura. *Environmentalism and Economic Justice: Two Chicano Struggles in the Southwest*. Society, Environment, and Place. Tucson: University of Arizona Press, 1996.

Quay, William Howard, and Marjorie C. Denison. *The Negro in the Chemical Industry: The Racial Policies of American Industry*. Philadelphia: Industrial Research Unit, Wharton School of Finance and Commerce, 1969.

Queeny, Edgar M. *The Spirit of Enterprise*. New York: Scribner's Sons, 1943.

Queeny, Edgar M., and Richard E. Bishop. *Prairie Wings; Pen and Camera Flight Studies*. New York: Ducks Unlimited, 1946.

Reed, Germaine M. *Crusading for Chemistry: The Professional Career of Charles Holmes Herty*. Durham, N.C.: Forest History Society; Athens: University of Georgia Press, 1995.

Robertson, Larry W., and L. G. Hansen, eds. *PCBs: Recent Advances in Environmental Toxicology and Health Effects.* Lexington: University Press of Kentucky, 2001.

Rogers, William Warren, Robert David Ward, Leah Rawls Atkins, and Wayne Flynt. *Alabama: The History of a Deep South State.* Tuscaloosa: University of Alabama Press, 1994.

Russell, Edmund. *War and Nature: Fighting Humans and Insects with Chemicals from World War I to "Silent Spring."* Studies in Environment and History. Cambridge: Cambridge University Press, 2001.

Sandman, Peter M., and American Industrial Hygiene Association. *Responding to Community Outrage: Strategies for Effective Risk Communication.* Fairfax, Va.: American Industrial Hygiene Association, 1993.

Sanguinetti, Elise. *The Last of the Whitfields.* Tuscaloosa: University of Alabama Press, 1986 [1962].

Schlesinger, Tom, with John Gaventa and Juliet Merrifield. *Our Own Worst Enemy: The Impact of Military Production on the Upper South.* New Market, Tenn.: Highlander Research and Education Center, 1983.

Schneider, Mark R. *"We Return Fighting": The Civil Rights Movement in the Jazz Age.* Boston: Northeastern University Press, 2002.

Seager, Joni. *Earth Follies: Coming to Feminist Terms with the Global Environmental Crisis.* New York: Routledge, 1993.

Seagrave, Sterling. *Yellow Rain: A Journey through the Terror of Chemical Warfare.* New York: M. Evans, 1981.

Sellers, Charles G. *Field Notes and Diary.* Vol. 2, unpublished, in author's possession, 1917–18.

Sellers, Christopher C. *Hazards of the Job: From Industrial Disease to Environmental Health Science.* Chapel Hill: University of North Carolina Press, 1997.

Shabecoff, Philip. *A Fierce Green Fire: The American Environmental Movement.* 1st ed. New York: Hill and Wang, 1993.

Sicherman, Barbara, and Alice Hamilton. *Alice Hamilton: A Life in Letters.* Cambridge, Mass.: Harvard University Press, 1984.

Smith, Henry Nash. *Virgin Land: The American West as Symbol and Myth.* Cambridge, Mass.: Harvard University Press, 1950.

Smith, Kimberly K. *African American Environmental Thought: Foundations.* American Political Thought. Lawrence: University Press of Kansas, 2007.

Smith, Neil. *Uneven Development: Nature, Capital, and the Production of Space.* New York: Blackwell, 1984.

Souder, William. *On a Farther Shore: The Life and Legacy of Rachel Carson.* 1st ed. New York: Crown, 2012.

Spears, Ellen Griffith. Photographs by Michael Schwarz. *The Newtown Story: One Community's Fight for Environmental Justice.* Atlanta: Center for Democratic Renewal, 1998.

Stauber, John C., and Sheldon Rampton. *Toxic Sludge Is Good for You: Lies, Damn Lies, and the Public Relations Industry.* 1st ed. Monroe, Me.: Common Courage, 1995.

Steinberg, Theodore. *Down to Earth: Nature's Role in American History.* New York: Oxford University Press, 2002.

Steingraber, Sandra. *Living Downstream: An Ecologist Looks at Cancer and the Environment*. Reading, Mass.: Addison-Wesley, 1997.

Stephens, Hugh W. *The Texas City Disaster, 1947*. 1st ed. Austin: University of Texas Press, 1997.

Tarr, Joel A. *The Search for the Ultimate Sink: Urban Pollution in Historical Perspective*. 1st ed. Technology and the Environment. Akron, Ohio: University of Akron Press, 1996.

Tesh, Sylvia Noble. *Uncertain Hazards: Environmental Activists and Scientific Proof*. Ithaca, N.Y.: Cornell University Press, 2000.

Thomas, Clarence. *My Grandfather's Son: A Memoir*. 1st ed. New York: Harper, 2007.

Thomas, Karen Kruse. *Deluxe Jim Crow: Civil Rights and American Health Policy, 1935–1954*. Athens: University of Georgia Press, 2011.

Thornton, Joe. *Pandora's Poison: Chlorine, Health, and a New Environmental Strategy*. Cambridge, Mass.: MIT Press, 2000.

Thorsheim, Peter. *Inventing Pollution: Coal, Smoke, and Culture in Britain since 1800*. Ecology and History. Athens: Ohio University Press, 2006.

Tickner, Joel A. *Precaution, Environmental Science, and Preventive Public Policy*. Washington, D.C.: Island, 2003.

Tickner, Joel, Carolyn Raffensperger, and Nancy Myers. *The Precautionary Principle in Action: A Handbook*. Windsor, N.D.: Science and Environmental Health Network, 1999.

Tokar, Brian. *Earth for Sale: Reclaiming Ecology in the Age of Corporate Greenwash*. Boston: South End, 1997.

Tyson, Timothy B. *Blood Done Sign My Name: A True Story*. 1st ed. New York: Crown, 2004.

Valenčius, Conevery Bolton. *The Health of the Country: How American Settlers Understood Themselves and Their Land*. 1st ed. New York: Basic Books, 2002.

Vance, Rupert Bayless, John Shelton Reed, and Daniel Joseph Singal. *Regionalism and the South: Selected Papers of Rupert Vance*. The Fred W. Morrison Series in Southern Studies. Chapel Hill: University of North Carolina Press, 1982.

Van Strum, Carol. *A Bitter Fog: Herbicides and Human Rights*. San Francisco: Sierra Club Books, 1983.

Vedder, Edward B., and Duncan Cameron Walton. *The Medical Aspects of Chemical Warfare*. Baltimore: Williams and Wilkins, 1925.

Waid, John S. *PCBs and the Environment*. 3 vols. Boca Raton, Fla.: CRC Press, 1986.

Walters, Ronald G. *Scientific Authority and Twentieth-Century America*. Baltimore: Johns Hopkins University Press, 1997.

Warren, Christian. *Brush with Death: A Social History of Lead Poisoning*. Baltimore: Johns Hopkins University Press, 2000.

Washington, Harriet A. *Medical Apartheid: The Dark History of Medical Experimentation on Black Americans from Colonial Times to the Present*. 1st ed. New York: Doubleday, 2006.

Wexler, Alice. *Mapping Fate: A Memoir of Family, Risk, and Genetic Research*. Berkeley: University of California Press, 1995.

Williams, Bruce Alan, and Albert R. Matheny. *Democracy, Dialogue, and Environmental Disputes: The Contested Languages of Social Regulation*. New Haven, Conn.: Yale University Press, 1995.

Winant, Howard. *The World Is a Ghetto: Race and Democracy since World War II*. 1st ed. New York: Basic Books, 2001.

Woodward, C. Vann. *The Burden of Southern History*. 3rd ed. Baton Rouge: Louisiana State University Press, 1993.

———. *Origins of the New South, 1877–1913*. Baton Rouge: Louisiana State University Press, 1951.

Wright, J. Handly, and Byron H. Christian. *Public Relations in Management*. New York: McGraw-Hill, 1949.

Wynne, Brian. *Risk Management and Hazardous Waste: Implementation and the Dialectics of Credibility*. Berlin: Springer, 1987.

Yaeger, Patricia. *Dirt and Desire: Reconstructing Southern Women's Writing, 1930–1990*. Chicago: University of Chicago Press, 2000.

Young, Alvin L. *The History, Use, Disposition, and Environmental Fate of Agent Orange*. New York: Springer, 2008.

Young, Iris Marion. *Inclusion and Democracy*. Oxford Political Theory. Oxford: Oxford University Press, 2002.

———. *Justice and the Politics of Difference*. Princeton, N.J.: Princeton University Press, 1990.

Articles and Essays

Auyero, Javier, and Debora Swistun. "The Social Production of Toxic Uncertainty." *American Sociological Review* 73, no. 3 (June 2008): 357–79.

Baskerville, Charles. "The American Chemist and Occupational Disease." *Medicine and Surgery* 1 (1917): 767–71.

———. "Occupational Diseases in the Chemical Trades." *Journal of Industrial and Engineering Chemistry* 8, no. 11 (November 1916): 1054–55.

———. "Symposium on Occupational Diseases in Chemical Trades." *Journal of Industrial and Engineering Chemistry* 8, no. 10 (October 1916): 946.

Been, Vicki. "What's Fairness Got to Do with It? Environmental Justice and the Siting of Locally Undesirable Land Uses." *Cornell Law Review* 78, no. 6 (1993): 1001–85.

Bennett, Granville A., Cecil Drinker, and Madeleine Field Warren. "Morphological Changes in the Livers of Rats Resulting from Exposure to Certain Chlorinated Hydrocarbons." *Journal of Industrial Hygiene and Toxicology* 20 (1938): 97–123.

Besselievre, E. B. "Statutory Regulation of Stream Pollution and the Common Law." *Transactions* (American Institute of Chemical Engineers), June 24, 1925, 217–30.

Bird, Elizabeth Ann R. "The Social Construction of Nature: Theoretical Approaches to the History of Environmental Problems." *Environmental Review* 11, no. 4 (1987). 255–63.

Birnbaum, Linda. "The Third Biannual International PCB Workshop." In *PCBs: Human and Environmental Disposition and Toxicology*, edited by Larry G. Hansen and Larry W. Robertson, 1–6. Urbana: University of Illinois Press, 2008.

Bond, Horace Mann. "Social and Economic Forces in Alabama Reconstruction." In *Reconstruction: An Anthology of Revisionist Writings*, edited by Kenneth M. Stampp and Leon F. Litwack, 370–40. Baton Rouge: Louisiana State University Press, 1969. Originally published in *Journal of Negro History* 23 (1938): 377–81.

Bowes, C. W., M. J. Mulvihill, B. R. Simoneit, A. L. Burlingame, and R. W. Risebrough. "Identification of Chlorinated Dibenzofurans in American Polychlorinated Biphenyls." *Nature* 256, no. 5515 (July 24, 1975): 305–7.

Broadbank, Roy. "The PCB Peril in Perspective." *Process Engineering* 72 (1991): 41–42.

Brown, David P. "Mortality of Workers Exposed to Polychlorinated Biphenyls: An Update." *Archives of Environmental Health* 42, no. 6 (1987): 333–39.

Brown, David P., and Mark Jones. "Mortality and Industrial Hygiene Study of Workers Exposed to Polychlorinated Biphenyls, *Archives of Environmental Health* 36, no. 3 (1981): 120–29.

Brown, Robert M. "On the Toxicity of the 'Arochlors,'" *Chemist Analyst* 36, no. 2 (September, 1947): 33–35.

Buhs, Joshua Blu. "The Fire Ant Wars: Nature and Science in the Pesticide Controversies of the Late Twentieth Century." *Isis: Journal of the History of Science in Society* 93 (2002): 377–400.

Carpenter, David O. "Polychlorinated Biphenyls and Human Health." *International Journal of Occupational Medicine and Environmental Health* 11, no. 4 (1998): 291–303.

Case, David. "Manufacturing Doubt in Product Defense." *Fast Company*, February 1, 2009. http://www.fastcompany.com/1139299/manufacturing-doubt-product-defense (September 1, 2013).

Cha-Jua, Sundiata Keita, and Clarence Lang. "The 'Long Movement' as Vampire: Temporal and Spatial Fallacies in Recent Black Freedom Studies." *Journal of African American History* 92, no. 1 (2007): 265–88.

Chang, King-Jen, Kue-Hsuing Hsieh, Tee-Ping Lee, Shu-Ying Tang, and Ta-Cheng Tung. "Immunologic Evaluation of Patients with Polychlorinated Biphenyl Poisoning: Determination of Lymphocyte Subpopulations." *Toxicology and Applied Pharmacology* 61 (1981): 58–63.

"The Chemical Kaleidoscope for 1930." *Journal of Industrial and Engineering Chemistry* 23, no. 1 (1931): 4–9.

Chen, Yung-Cheng Joseph, Yue-Liang Guo, Chen-Chin Hsu, and Walter J. Rogan. "Cognitive Development of Yu-Cheng ('Oil Disease') Children Prenatally Exposed to Heat-Degraded PCBs." *JAMA* 268, no. 22 (December 9, 1992): 3213–18.

Coates, Peter, Tim Cole, Marianna Dudley, and Chris Pearson. "Defending Nation, Defending Nature? Militarized Landscapes and Military Environmentalism in Britain, France, and the United States." *Environmental History* 16, no. 3 (2011): 456–91.

Cobb, James C. "The Price of Progress." In *The Selling of the South: The Southern Crusade for Industrial Development, 1936–1990*, by James C. Cobb, 2nd ed., 229–53. Urbana: University of Illinois Press, 1993.

Cole, Luke W. "Environmental Justice Litigation: Another Stone in David's Sling." *Fordham Urban Journal* (Fordham University School of Law) 21, no. 523 (1994): 523–45.

Colten, Craig E. "Historical Questions in Hazardous Waste Management." *Public Historian* 10, no. 1 (1988): 6–20.

Commoner, Barry. "Let's Get Serious about Pollution Prevention." *EPA Journal*, July–August 1989, 15.

Cooper, William B. "They Had a Dream: The Freedom Rides Remembered." *Commonweal*, August 14, 1992, 13.

Couch, Stephen R., and J. Stephen Kroll-Smith. "Patterns of Victimization and the Chronic Technological Disaster." In *The Victimology Handbook: Research Findings, Treatment, and Public Policy*, edited by Emilio Viano, 159–76. Garland Reference Library of Social Science, vol. 605. New York: Garland, 1990.

DeMelle, Brendan, and Environmental Working Group. "Anniston in Depth." *Chemical Industry Archives*, 2002. http://chemicalindustryarchives.com/dirtysecrets/annistonindepth/intro.asp (May 20, 2006).

Dewey, Scott Hamilton. "The Fickle Finger of Phosphate: Central Florida Air Pollution and the Failure of Environmental Policy, 1957–1970." In *Other Souths: Diversity and Difference in the U.S. South, Reconstruction to Present*, edited by Pippa Holloway, 344–80. Athens: University of Georgia Press, 2008.

Diez Roux, Ana V. "Investigating Neighborhood and Area Effects on Health." *American Journal of Public Health* 91, no. 11 (2001): 1783–89.

Drinker, Cecil K. "Further Observations on the Possible Systemic Toxicity of Certain of the Chlorinated Hydrocarbons with Suggestions for Permissible Concentrations in the Air of Workrooms." *Journal of Industrial Hygiene and Toxicology* 21, no. 5 (May 1939): 155–59.

Drinker, Cecil K., M.D., Madeleine Field Warren, and Granville A. Bennett. "The Problem of Possible Systemic Effects from Certain Chlorinated Hydrocarbons." *Journal of Industrial Hygiene and Toxicology* 19 (1937): 283–311.

Du Pont, Lammot. "Human Wants and the Chemical Industry." *Journal of Industrial and Engineering Chemistry* 27, no. 5 (1935): 485–93.

Edsall, David. "Diseases Due to Chemical Agents." In William Osler and Thomas McCrae, *Modern Medicine: Its Theory and Practice*, 1:83–155. Philadelphia: Lea Brothers, 1907.

Egan, Michael. "Toxic Knowledge: A Mercurial Fugue in Three Parts." *Environmental History* 13, no. 4 (October 2008): 636–42.

Egerton, John. "Profiles of Change." *Southern Changes* 1, no. 8 (1979): 8–10, 26–28.

Erickson, Mitchell. "Applications of Polychlorinated Biphenyls." *Environmental Science and Pollution Research* 18 (2011): 135–51.

Erikson, Kai T. "Trauma at Buffalo Creek." *Society* 35, no. 2 (January–February 1998): 153–61.

Fields, Barbara J. "Ideology and Race in American History." In *Region, Race and Reconstruction*, edited by J. Morgan Kousser and James M. McPherson, 143–77. New York: Oxford University Press, 1982.

Fingerhut, M. A., W. E. Halperin, et al. "Cancer Mortality in Workers Exposed to 2,3,7,8-Tetrachlorodibenzo-P-Dioxin." *New England Journal of Medicine* 324, no. 4 (1991): 212–19.

Flinn, Frederick B. and N. E. Jarvik. "Action of Certain Chlorinated Naphthalenes on the Liver." *Proceedings of the Society for Experimental Biology and Medicine* 35 (1936): 118–20.

Ford, Richard Thompson. "The Boundaries of Race: Political Geography in Legal Analysis." *Harvard Law Review* 107, no. 8 (1994): 1841–921.

Foristall, T. M. "The Merit of Monsanto: The Company's Status in the Expanding Chemical Industry." *Barron's*, July 3, 1933, 6.

Francis, Eric. "Conspiracy of Silence." *Sierra*, September–October 1994. http://www.sierraclub.org/sierra/200103/conspiracy.asp (April 9, 2004); originally published as Eric F. Coppolino, "Pandora's Poison."

Frumkin, Howard. "Healthy Places: Exploring the Evidence." *American Journal of Public Health* 93, no. 9 (2003): 1451–56.

Frumkin, Howard, and Warren Kantrowitz. "Cancer Clusters in the Workplace: An Approach to Investigation." *Journal of Occupational Medicine* 29, no. 12 (1987): 949–52.

Gates, Paul Wallace. "Federal Land Policy in the South, 1866–1888." *Journal of Southern History* 6 (1940): 303–30.

Gentle, Edward C., III. "Administration of the 2003 Tolbert PCB Settlement in Anniston, Alabama: An Attempted Collaborative and Holistic Remedy." *Alabama Law Review* 60, no. 5 (2009): 1249–64.

Godsil, Rachel D. "Remedying Environmental Racism." *Michigan Law Review* 90, no. 2 (1991): 394–427.

Goldstein, Bernard D., and Mary Sue Henifin. "Reference Guide on Toxicology." In Federal Judicial Center, *Reference Manual on Scientific Evidence*, 2nd ed., 403–38. Washington, D.C.: Federal Judicial Center, 2000. http://www.fjc.gov/public/pdf.nsf/lookup/scimanoo.pdf/$file/scimanoo.pdf (July 26, 2006).

Goncharov, A., M. Bloom, I. Birman, and D. O. Carpenter. "Blood Pressure and Hypertension in Relation to Levels of Serum Polychlorinated Biphenyls in Residents of Anniston, Alabama." *Journal of Hypertension* 28, no. 10 (October 2010): 2053–60.

Goncharov, Alexey, Marian Pavuk, Herman R. Foushee, and David O. Carpenter, for the Anniston Environmental Health Research Consortium. "Blood Pressure in Relation to Concentrations of PCB Congeners and Chlorinated Pesticides." *Environmental Health Perspectives* 119, no. 3 (March 2011): 319–25.

Greenburg, Leonard. "Chlorinated Naphthalenes and Diphenyls." *Industrial Medicine*, August 1943, 520–22.

Gustavsson, P., C. Hogstedt, and C. Rappe. "Short-Term Mortality and Cancer Incidence in Capacitor Manufacturing Workers Exposed to Polychlorinated Biphenyls (PCBs)." *American Journal of Industrial Medicine* 10, no. 4 (1986): 341–44.

Halfacre, Angela C., and Albert R. Matheny. "The Grassroots at Risk: Local Perceptions and Environmental Injustice." In *Locality and Identity: Environmental Issues in Law and Society*, edited by Jane Holder and Donald McGillivray, 151–67. Aldershot: Ashgate/Dartmouth, 1999.

Hall, Jacquelyn Dowd. "The Long Civil Rights Movement and the Political Uses of the Past." *Journal of American History* 91, no. 4 (March 2005): 1233–63.

Haraway, Donna. "Situated Knowledges: The Science Question in Feminism and the Privilege of Partial Perspective." In *Human Geography: An Essential Anthology*, edited by David N. Livingstone, John Agnew, and Alisdair Rogers, 111–28. Malden, Mass.: Blackwell, 1996.

Harding, Sandra. "Gender, Development, and Post-Enlightenment Philosophies of Science." *Hypatia* 13, no. 3 (1998a): 146–67.

———. "Who Knows? Identities and Feminist Epistemology." In *(En)Gendering Knowledge: Feminists in Academe*, edited by Joan E. Hartman and Ellen Messer-Davidow, 100–115. Knoxville: University of Tennessee Press, 1991.

Hermanson, Mark H., and Glenn W. Johnson. "Polychlorinated Biphenyls in Tree Bark near a Former Manufacturing Plant in Anniston, Alabama." *Chemosphere* 68 (2007): 191–98.

Hermanson, Mark H., Cheryl A. Scholten, and Kevin Compher. "Variable Air Temperature Response of Gas-Phase Atmospheric Polychlorinated Biphenyls near a Former Manufacturing Facility." *Environmental Science and Technology* 37 (2003): 4038–42.

Hill, Austin Bradford. "The Environment and Disease: Association or Causation?" *Proceedings of the Royal Society of Medicine* 58, no. 5 (1965): 295–300.

Hirschhorn, Joel S. "Enlibra: A New Shared Doctrine for Environmental Management." Natural Resources Policy Studies Division, National Governors' Association, Washington, D.C. http://www.nga.org/nga/legislativeUpdate/1,1169, C_POLICY_POSITION%5ED_625,00.html (August 29, 2004).

Hunold, Christian, and Iris Marion Young. "Justice, Democracy, and Hazardous Siting." *Political Studies* 46 (1998): 82–95.

Hurley, Andrew. "Fiasco at Wagner Electric: Environmental Justice and Urban Geography in St. Louis." *Environmental History* 2, no. 4 (1997): 460–81.

Isaac, Larry. "Movement of Movements: Culture Moves in the Long Civil Rights Struggle." *Social Forces* 87, no. 1 (2008): 33–63.

Jacobson, J. L., and S. W. Jacobson. "Intellectual Impairment in Children Exposed to Polychlorinated Biphenyls in Utero." *New England Journal of Medicine* 335 (1996): 783–89.

Jenkins, Russell L., Rogers McCullough, and C. F. Booth. "Syntheses in the Diphenyl Series." *Industrial and Engineering Chemistry* 22, no. 1 (1930): 31–34.

Jensen, Søren. "The PCB Story." *Ambio* 1 (1972): 123–31.

Jensen, Søren, J. E. Kihlström, M. Olsson, C. Lundberg, and J. Örberg. "Effects of PCB and DDT on Mink (*Mustela vision*) during the Reproductive Season." *Ambio* 6, no. 4 (1977): 239.

Jewkes, Rachel, and Anne Murcott. "Community Representatives: Representing the 'Community'?" *Social Science and Medicine* 46, no. 7 (1998): 843–58.

Jones, Jack W., and Herbert S. Alden. "An Acneform Dermatergosis." *Archives of Dermatology and Syphilology* 33 (1936): 1022–34.

Jones, Rhon E. "The Explosion in Toxic Torts." *Alabama State Bar Environmental Law Section Program.* http://www.beasleyallen.com/publications/rej/toxic_torts.pdf (March 11, 2006), 1–21.

Jones, Rhon E., and Mark Englehart. "Litigating Toxic Torts." http://www.beasley-allen.com/publications/rej/toxic_torts.pdf (March 11, 2006), 1–28.

Kay, Hubert. "The Meaning of Monsanto." *Monsanto Magazine*, December 1951, 4–17.

Kennedy, B. Hughes. "A Sanitary Survey of Birmingham, Alabama." Department of Preventive Medicine and Hygiene, Harvard Medical School, December 1920.

Kimbrough, Renate D. "Human Health Effects of Polychlorinated Biphenyls (PCBs) and Polybrominated Biphenyls (PBBs)." *Annual Review of Pharmacology and Toxicology* 27 (April 1987): 87–111.

———. "Induction of Liver Tumors in Sherman Strain Female Rats by Polychlorinated Biphenyl Aroclor 1260." *Journal of the National Cancer Institute* 55, no. 6 (1975): 1453–59.

———. "Toxicity of Polychlorinated Polycyclic Compounds and Related Chemicals." *CRC Critical Reviews in Toxicology* 2, no. 4 (1974): 445–98.

Kimbrough, Renate D., Ralph E. Linder, and T. B. Gaines. "Morphological Changes in Livers of Rats Fed Polychlorinated Biphenyls." *Archives of Environmental Health* 25 (1972): 354–61.

Krieger, N., M. S. Wolff, R. A. Hiatt, M. Rivera, J. Vogelman, and N. Orientreich. "Breast Cancer and Serum Organochlorines: A Prospective Study among White, Black, and Asian Women." *Journal of the National Cancer Institute* 86 (1994): 589–99.

Kriess, Kathleen. "Studies on Populations Exposed to Polychlorinated Biphenyls." *Environmental Health Perspectives* 60 (1985): 193–99.

Kuratsume, Masanori, Takesumi Yoshimura, Junichi Matsuzaka, and Atsuko Uamaguchi. "Epidemiologic Study on Yusho: A Poisoning Caused by Ingestion of Rice Oil Contaminated with a Commercial Brand of Polychlorinated Biphenyls." *Environmental Health Perspectives* 1, no. 1 (April 1972): 119–28.

Kuratsune, Masanori, Yoshito Masuda, and Junya Nagayama. "Some of the Recent Findings Concerning Yusho." In U.S. EPA, *National Conference on Polychlorinated Biphenyls (1975: Chicago)*, 14–29. Washington, D.C.: Environmental Protection Agency Office of Toxic Substances, 1976.

Lambert, Thomas, and Christopher Boerner. "Environmental Inequity: Economic Causes, Economic Solutions." *Yale Journal on Regulation* 14 (1997): 195–234.

Lavelle, Marianne, and Marcia Coyle. "Unequal Protection: The Racial Divide in Environmental Law—A Special Investigation." *National Law Journal*, September 21, 1992, S1ff.

Lazarus, Richard. "Pursuing 'Environmental Justice': The Distributional Effects of Environmental Protection." *Northwestern University Law Review* 87, no. 3 (1993): 787–859.

Lipsitz, George. "The Racialization of Space and the Spatialization of Race: Theorizing the Hidden Architecture of Landscape." *Landscape Journal* 26, no. 1 (January 1, 2007): 10–23.

Littlemore, Richard. "Manufacturing Doubt." *New Scientist* 206, no. 2760 (May 12, 2010): 41.

Loeb, Marshall. "Interview with Hendrick Verfaille, President and Chief Operating Officer: Monsanto, Stern Chief Executive Series." *Stern* (Spring/Summer): 7.

Long, Rebecca J., and Thomas C. Beierle. "The Federal Advisory Committee Act and Public Participation in Environmental Policy." In *Resources for the Future*. Discussion paper no. 99-17, January 1999.

Longnecker, Matthew P., John W. Brock, Mark A. Klebanoff, and Haibo Zhou. "Polychlorinated Biphenyl Serum Levels in Pregnant Subjects with Diabetes." *Diabetes Care* 24, no. 6 (June 2001): 1099–1101.

Loomis, D., S. R. Browning, A. P. Schenck, E. Gregory, and D. A. Savitz. "Cancer Mortality among Electric Utility Workers Exposed to Polychlorinated Biphenyls." *Occupational and Environmental Medicine* 54, no. 10 (1997): 720–28.

Lythcott, Michael. *Sweet Valley/Cobb Town Relocation Study. Anniston, Alabama, Final Report, Significant Findings, Issues and Recommendations, March 15, 1997.* Oak Bluffs, Mass.: Lythcott Company, 1997.

Marchand, Roland, and Michael L. Smith. "Corporate Science on Display." In *Scientific Authority and Twentieth-Century America*, edited by Ronald G. Walters, 148–82. Baltimore: Johns Hopkins University Press, 1997.

Marshall, Eliot. "The Murky World of Toxicity Testing." *Science* 220, no. 4602 (June 10, 1983): 1130–32.

Marshall, Suzanne, Rufus Kinney, and Antoinnette Hudson. "The Incineration of Chemical Weapons in Anniston, Alabama: The March for Environmental Justice." In *Confronting Ecological Crisis in Appalachia and the South: University and Community Partnerships*, edited by Stephanie McSpirit, Lynne Faltraco, and Conner Bailey, 147–70. Lexington: University Press of Kentucky, 2012.

Meigs, J. Wister, Jack Jonathan Albom, and Bernard L. Kartin. "Chloracne from an Unusual Exposure to Arochlor." *Journal of the American Medical Association* 154, no. 17 (1954): 1417–18.

Melosi, Martin V. "Equity, Eco-Racism and Environmental History." *Environmental History Review* 19, no. 3 (1995): 1–16.

Merchant, Carolyn. "Shades of Darkness: Race and Environmental History." *Environmental History* 8, no. 3 (2003): 380–94.

Millikan, Robert, Emily DeVoto, Eric J. Duell, Chiu-Kit Tse, David A. Savitz, James Beach, Sharon Edmiston, Susan Jackson, and Beth Newman. "DDE, PCBs and Breast Cancer among African American and White Residents of North Carolina." *Cancer Epidemiology Biomarkers and Prevention* 7 (2000): 1233–40.

Mitman, Gregg. "In Search of Health: Landscape and Disease in American Environmental History." *Environmental History* 10, no. 2 (2005): 184–210.

Moysich, Kirsten B. "Environmental Exposure to Polychlorinated Biphenyls and Breast Cancer Risk." In *PCBs: Recent Advances in Environmental Toxicology and*

Health Effects, edited by Larry W. Robertson and L. G. Hansen, 119–26. Lexington: University Press of Kentucky, 2001.

Mueller, Carol McClurg. "Building Social Movement Theory." In *Frontiers in Social Movement Theory*, edited by Aldon D. Morris and Carol McClurg Mueller, 3–25. New Haven, Conn.: Yale University Press, 1992.

Murdocca, Carmela. "'There Is Something in That Water': Race, Nationalism, and Legal Violence." *Law and Social Inquiry* 35, no. 2 (Spring 2010): 369–402.

Myers, Ira L. "Alabama Water Improvement Commission Responsibilities, Activities and Accomplishments." *Journal of the Medical Association of the State of Alabama* (Alabama Department of Public Health) 34, no. 5 (November 1964): 148–50.

Naiki, Yoshiko. "Assessing Policy Reach: Japan's Chemical Policy Reform in Response to the EU's Reach Regulation." *Journal of Environmental Law* 22, no. 2 (2010): 171–93.

Nisbet, Ian C. T., and Adel F. Sarofim. "Rates and Routes of Transport of PCBs in the Environment." *Environmental Health Perspectives*, no. 1 (April 1972): 21–38.

Opheim, Teresa. "Five Years after the Pledge." *Environmental Forum* 12, no. 6 (November–December 1995): 30–36.

Oser, Bernard L. "Highlights in the History of Saccharin Toxicology." *Food and Chemical Toxicology* 23, no. 4–5 (1985): 535–41.

"Parathion by Monsanto at Anniston." *Journal of Agricultural and Food Chemistry* 5, no. 6 (1957): 395.

Pavuk, Marian, J. R. Olson, A. Sjödin, M. Bonner, S. M. Dearwent, W. J. Turner, and L. L. Needham for the Anniston Environmental Health Research Consortium. "Assessment of Human Exposure to PCBs in the Anniston Community Health Survey." *Organohalogen Compounds*, 2009, 1083–86.

Penning, Chester H. "Diphenyl and Diphenyl Derivatives." In *Chemical Progress in the South*, by National Research Council, Division of Chemistry and Chemical Technology, 153–55. New York: Chemical Foundation, 1930.

———. "Physical Characteristics and Commercial Possibilities of Chlorinated Diphenyl." *Industrial and Engineering Chemistry* 22, no. 11 (1930): 1180–82.

———. "The Swann Corporation." In *Chemical Progress in the South*, by National Research Council, Division of Chemistry and Chemical Technology, 150–52. New York: Chemical Foundation, 1930.

Pierce, Heather. "Citizen Resistance to Chemical Weapons Incineration: Can NEPA Give Local Communities Leverage over Military Arms Decommissioning Programs?" *Boston College Environmental Affairs Law Review* 32, no. 2 (January 2005): 459–91.

Price, George M. "Health Problems in the Chemical Industries." *Journal of Industrial and Engineering Chemistry* 2, no. 12 (December 1916): 1159–60.

Radway, Janice. "What's in a Name? Presidential Address to the American Studies Association." *American Quarterly* 51, no. 1 (March 1999): 1–32.

"Report of a New Chemical Hazard." *New Scientist*, December 15, 1966, 612.

Risebrough, R. W., P. Reiche, S. G. Herman, D. B. Peakall, and M. N. Kirven. "Polychlorinated Biphenyls in the Global Ecosystem." *Nature* 220 (1968): 1098–102.

Roach, John A. G., and Irwin H. Pomerantz, "The Finding of Chlorinated Dibenzo-furans in a Japanese Polychlorinated Biphenyl Sample." *Bulletin of Environmental Contamination and Toxicology* 12, no. 3 (September 1974): 338–42.

Rome, Adam. "What Really Matters in History? Environmental Perspectives on Modern America." *Environmental History* 7, no. 2 (2002): 303–18.

Rothman, Nathaniel, Kenneth Cantor, Aaron Blair, David Bush, Kathy Helzlsouer, Shelia Zahm, Robert Hoover, George Comstock, and Paul Strickland. "A Nested Case-Control Study of Non-Hodgkin Lymphoma and Serum Organochlorine Residues." *Lancet* 350 (July 26, 1997): 240–44.

Schneider, Keith. "Faking It: The Case against IBT Labs." *Amicus Journal* (Natural Resources Defense Council), Spring 1983, 14–26.

Schneir, Walter. "The Campaign to Make Chemical Warfare Respectable." *Reporter: The Magazine of Facts and Ideas*, October 1959, 24–28.

Schultz, Gustav, and H. Schmidt. "Ueber Diphenylbasen." *Annalen der Chemie* 207 (1881): 311–69. Translated by Stefan Lutz.

Shields, Robert E., and Leslie J. Bryan. "Georgia's New Expert Witness Rule: *Daubert* and More." *Georgia Bar Journal* 11, no. 2 (October 2005): 16–23.

Showers, Kate B., and Gwendolyn M. Malaleha. "Oral Evidence in Historical Impact Assessment: Soil Conservation in Lesotho in the 1930s and 1940s." *Journal of Southern African Studies* 18, no. 2 (1992): 276–96.

Silverman, Jason H. "The 'Divided Mind of the New South' Revisited: Richard Hathaway Edmonds, the *Manufacturers' Record*, and the Immigrant." *Southern Studies* 26, no. 1 (1987): 41–51.

Silverstone, Allen E., Paula F. Rosenbaum, Ruth S. Weinstock, Scott M. Bartell, Herman R. Foushee, Christie Shelton, and Marian Pavuk, for the Anniston Environmental Health Research Consortium. "Polychlorinated Biphenyl (PCB) Exposure and Diabetes: Results from the Anniston Community Health Survey." *Environmental Health Perspectives* 120, no. 5 (2012): 727–32.

Silverstone, Allen E., Ruth S. Weinstock, Paula F. Rosenbaum, Herman R. Foushee, and Marian Pavuk for the Anniston Environmental Health Research Consortium. "Mono-ortho and Di-ortho Substituted PCB Congeners and Type 2 Diabetes in the Anniston Community Health Survey." *Organohalogen Compounds* 71 (2009): 1059–63.

Smith, Kimberly K. "What Is Africa to Me? Wilderness in Black Thought, 1860–1930." *Environmental Ethics* 27 (2005): 279–97.

Spears, Ellen Griffith. "Freedom Buses Rolling on Cancer Alley." *Southern Changes* 15, no. 1 (Spring 1993): 1–11.

———. "Making Illnesses Visible: The Newtown Florist Club and the Quest for Environmental Justice in Gainesville, Georgia." In *Emerging Illnesses and Society: Negotiating the Public Health Agenda*, edited by Randall M. Packard, Peter J. Brown, Ruth L. Berkelman, and Howard Frumkin, 171–90. Baltimore: Johns Hopkins University Press, 2004.

———. "Reducing Environmental Burdens: A Southern Agenda." In *American Crisis: Southern Solutions*, edited by Anthony Dunbar, 200–211. Montgomery, Ala.: NewSouth, 2008.

Sprayberry, Gary S. "'Can We Say We Are All Innocent?' The 1965 Murder of Willie Brewster and the Limits of Political Violence." *Paisano*, no. 4 (Winter 2002), http://www.la.utexas.edu/research/paisano/GGStext.html (September, 11, 2005).

Steen, Kathryn. "Patents, Patriotism and 'Skilled in the Art.'" *ISIS: Journal of the History of Science in Society* 92, no. 1 (2001): 91–123.

Stewart, Mart A. "Southern Environmental History." In *A Companion to the American South*, edited by John B. Boles, 409–23. Malden, Mass.: Blackwell, 2002.

Stoker, Kevin. "From Prohibitionist to New Deal Liberal: The Political Evolution of Colonel Harry Mell Ayers of the *Anniston Star*." *Alabama Review*, October 2009, 262–96.

Sullivan, Patricia. "'To Make America Safe for Democracy': Black Freedom Struggles in the World War I Era." *Reviews in American History* 32, no. 1 (2004): 76–83.

Sulzberger, Marion B., Adolph Rostenberg Jr., and J. J. Sher. "Acneform Eruptions: With Remarks on Acne Vulgaris and Its Pathogenesis." *New York State Journal of Medicine* 34, no. 21 (1934): 899–908.

Swann, Theodore. "Manufacture of Phosphoric Acid in the Electric Furnace by the Condensation and Electric Precipitation Method." *Journal of Industrial and Engineering Chemistry* 14, no. 7 (1922): 630–31.

Taylor, Dorceta E. "Environmentalism and the Politics of Inclusion." In *Confronting Environmental Racism: Voices from the Grassroots*, edited by Robert D. Bullard, 53–61. Boston: South End, 1993.

———. "The Rise of the Environmental Justice Paradigm: Injustice Framing and the Social Construction of Environmental Discourses." *American Behavioral Scientist*, 43, no. 4 (2000): 508–80.

Tebbens, B. D. "Portable Combustion Apparatus for Field Determinations of Chlorinated Hydrocarbons." *Journal of Industrial Hygiene and Toxicology*, May 1937, 204.

Terrie, Philip G. "Recent Work in Environmental History." *American Studies International* 27, no. 2 (1989): 43–64.

Tinker, Jon. "The PCB Story: Seagulls Aren't Funny Anymore." *New Scientist and Science Journal* 50 (1971): 16–18.

Townsend, Martha. "Military Exemptions from Environmental Laws." *Natural Resources and Environment* 19, no. 4 (Spring 2005): 65–67.

Tullos, Allen. "The Great Hookworm Crusade." *Southern Exposure* 6 (Summer 1978): 40–49.

Walters, Ronald G. "Uncertainty, Science, and Reform in Twentieth-Century America." In *Scientific Authority and Twentieth-Century America*, edited by Ronald G. Walters, 1–12. Baltimore: Johns Hopkins University Press, 1997.

Wilson, Charles Reagan. "American Regionalism in a Postmodern World." *American Studies* 42, no. 2 (1997): 145–58.

Yearley, Steven. "The Environmental Challenge to Science Studies." In *Handbook of Science and Technology Studies*, edited by Gerald E. Markle Sheila Jasanoff, and James C. Petersen, 457–79. Thousand Oaks, Calif.: Sage, 1995.

Yaglou, C. P., F. W. Sands, and Philip Drinker. "Ventilation of Wire Impregnating Tanks Using Chlorinated Hydrocarbons." *Journal of Industrial Hygiene and Toxicology* 20, no. 6 (1938): 401–18.

Young, Iris Marion. "Harvey's Complaint with Race and Gender Struggles: A Critical Response." *Antipode: A Radical Journal of Geography* 30, no. 1 (January 1988): 36–42.

Yueliang Leon Guo and Chen-Chin Hsu. "Yucheng and Yusho: The Effects of Toxic Oil in Developing Humans in Asia" In *PCBs: Recent Advances in Environmental Toxicology and Health Effects*, edited by Larry W. Robertson and L. G. Hansen, 137–41. Lexington: University Press of Kentucky, 2001.

Zack, J. A., and R. R. Suskind. "The Mortality Experience of Workers Exposed to Tetrachlorodibenzodioxin in a Trichlorophenol Process Accident." *Journal of Occupational Medicine* 22 (January 22, 1980): 11–14.

Dissertations and Theses

Coffin, Thomas Allen. "First Generation Land Management Planning on the Chattahoochee-Oconee National Forests/A Case Study of Forest Service/Environmentalist Interaction in an Era of Change (1960–1986)." Ph.D. diss., University of Georgia, 1995.

Cook, Jennifer Michelle. "What Industry and Government Knew about the Hazards and Effects of Polychlorinated Biphenyls." MEng thesis, University of Louisville, 2000.

Kurtz, Hilda Elizabeth. "The Politics of Environmental Justice as a Politics of Scale: The Case of the Shintech Controversy, St. James Parish, Louisiana." Ph.D. diss., University of Minnesota, 2000.

Laska, Mary Katherine. "Neighborhood Leaders and Their Role in Mediating Community Response to a Chemical Disaster (Alabama)." Ph.D. diss. University of Alabama, 2001.

Maher, Francis Joseph. "Risk Perception of Chemical Weapons Storage and Disposal." Ph.D. diss., University of Alabama at Birmingham, 1999.

Spears, Ellen Griffith. "Toxic Knowledge: A Social History of Environmental Health in the 'New South's Model City,' Anniston, Alabama, 1872–present." Ph.D. diss., Emory University, 2006.

Sprayberry, Gary S. "'Town among the Trees': Paternalism, Class, and Civil Rights in Anniston, Alabama, 1872 to Present." Ph.D. diss., University of Alabama, 2003.

Staples, Amy Jane. "Safari Ethnography: Expeditionary Film, Popular Science and the Work of Adventure Tourism." Ph.D. diss., University of California, Santa Cruz, 2003.

Stoker, Kevin. "Harry Mell Ayers: New South Community Journalism in the Age of Reform." Ph.D. diss., University of Alabama, 1998.

Williams, Gertrude. "The Origin and Early Development of Anniston." Research paper, Jacksonville State College, 1959.

Films

Achbar, Mark, Jennifer Abbott, and Joel Bakan. *The Corporation*. Based on the book *The Corporation: The Pathological Pursuit of Profit and Power*, by Joel Bakan. Vancouver, B.C.: Good Company Communications, 2003.

Kroft, Steve. "Toxic Town." *60 Minutes*. CBS, November 10, 2002.

Moyers, Bill. *Toxic Communities: NOW with Bill Moyers*. PBS, June 21, 2002.

———. *Trade Secrets: A Moyers Report*. PBS, March 26, 2001.

Queeny, Edgar M. *Latuko*. New York: American Museum of Natural History, 1951.

———. *The Pagan Sudan*. New York: American Museum of Natural History, 1952.

———. *We Saw Primeval Man*. New York: American Museum of Natural History, 1951.

Robin, Marie-Monique. *The World According to Monsanto*. Paris: Image and Compagnie, Productions Thalie, ARTE France, National Film Board of Canada and WDR, 2008.

Sesno, Frank, and Chris Guarino, producers. Walter Cronkite, host. *Avoiding Armageddon*. PBS, August 14, 2003.

Soderbergh, Steven. *Erin Brockovich*. Hollywood, Calif.: Universal Pictures, 2000.

Zaillian, Steven. *A Civil Action*. Based on the book *A Civil Action*, by Jonathan Harr. Burbank, Calif.: Touchstone Pictures, 1998.

INDEX

contamination by lead, 269–70; technical documents by, 231; toxicological profile on PCBs by, 247

Agent Orange, 88, 327 (n. 37)

Agriculture: and boll weevil, 39–40; cotton production, 27, 28, 59–60, 75–77; employment in, 28, 76, 100, 318 (n. 57); fertilizers for, 50; herbicide for, 88; linking of industry and, 59–60; and sharecropping system, 100; in South generally, 36, 38, 51

Air pollution: and climate warming, 293; federal legislation for control of, 161–62; health impact of airborne PCBs, 124–25; and incinerating PCBs, 160; by iron industry, 9, 25–26; levels of PCBs in, 252, 282, 292, 293; and maximum allowable PCB concentration, 334 (n. 13); by Monsanto Anniston plant, 64, 88, 126, 161, 252; by Swann Chemical Company, 63, 88; and tree bark with PCBs, 124, 252, 363 (n. 55)

Alabama. See Anniston, Ala.; Calhoun County; and other cities and towns

Alabama African American Environmental Justice Action Network, 206, 298

Alabama Air Pollution Control Commission, 161

Alabama Attorney General's Office: environmental enforcement, 161–62, 172, 181; NAACP ban, 106

Alabama Board of Health, 65–66

Alabama Chemical Demilitarization Citizens Advisory Commission (CDCAC), 187, 190, 191

Alabama Civil Justice Foundation, 272

Alabama Conservancy, 193

Alabama Constitution (1901), 11, 29–30, 313 (n. 38)

Alabama Department of Conservation, 119, 127, 131, 346 (n. 72)

Alabama Department of Environmental Management (ADEM): and Anniston Army Depot incinerator, 194, 197, 291; and drums containing hazardous materials from Anniston Army Depot, 269; Environmental Justice Unit at, 298; and EPA, 232, 233; and fish contamination in Snow and Choccolocco creeks, 220–21; and Fort McClellan, 181; and landfill permit for Monsanto Anniston plant, 173; mediocre job of, 12–13, 232–33, 261; and mercury pollution in Anniston, 269; Monsanto's reports to, 257; oversight group for, 298; and PCB contamination in Anniston, 203; Reform Coalition, 298; and relocation plan by Monsanto, 224, 228; and soil sampling in

Anniston, 232. See also Alabama Water Improvement Commission

Alabama Department of Public Health (ADPH): Division of Solid Waste, 169; and Fort McClellan, 79; "no-consumption" fish advisory by, 5, 203, 210; on PCB health assessments in West Anniston, 204, 222–23, 224, 251; and PCB soil sampling by ADEM, 232; and sewage in Choccolocco Creek, 79

Alabama Division of Industrial Hygiene, 65–66

Alabama Game and Fish Division, 172

Alabama Historical Commission, 302

Alabama National Guard, 78, 101

Alabama Power Company, 36, 38–41, 46, 51, 203–4, 257, 264, 354 (n. 3)

Alabama Supreme Court: and Abernathy case, 249, 259, 272; on "duty to warn," 10, 73; and Hinton case, 249; and lawsuit against Monsanto for pollution from its parathion operation, 120; and Stewart's legal fees for PCB lawsuit, 273; and Ten Commandments monument at state capitol, 265

Alabama Water Improvement Commission (AWIC): changes in, after 1971, 162; composition of, 347 (n. 81); creation of, 131; failures of, regarding PCB pollution in Anniston, 12, 119, 232; and fish contamination in Choccolocco Creek, 119, 146; lawsuit against Monsanto by, 126–27; and PCB level in discharge, 158; and reporting/underreporting of PCB releases by Monsanto, 244, 257. See also Alabama Department of Environmental Management

Albright, Clay, 360 (n. 15)

Alden, Herbert S., 66–67, 322 (n. 42)

All-America City, 115, 169

Allen, James Browning, 166

Alternatives to incineration. See Anti-incinerator campaign; Chemical weapons; Incineration of chemical weapons; Neutralization technologies

American Chemical Society (ACS): and chemical industry in South, 45, 50, 56; Committee on Occupational Diseases in the Chemical Trades, 61–62; Herty as leader of, 38, 42; meetings of, 42, 50, 56; membership statistics of, 50; and national defense linked with chemistry, 42–44; and occupational diseases in chemical industry, 61–62; political power of, 79; Wiley as leader of, 46

American Chemistry Council, 254, 278, 299,

building for, 295; on PCB lawsuits and trials, 241, 242, 259, 272; on pollution from Monsanto Anniston plant, 119, 161, 215, 301; on Robinson's mayoralty, 294; on soil contamination from PCBs, 204; and support for military installations, 83; Waddle as executive editor of, 179, 181, 190, 201; on World War I, 41

ANSI. *See* American National Standards Institute

Anti-incinerator campaign: and African Americans, 195, 198–99; and alternatives to incineration, 186–90, 192–94, 198; in Anniston, 15–16, 177–78, 182–85, 187, 190–201, 268–69; and anti-PCB campaign, 233; Army's Assembled Chemical Weapons Assessment, 193–94, 196; by Burn Busters, 184–85, 193, 196; congressional focus on, 185–86, 190–92, 194, 196; demonstrations and other protest tactics by, 15–16, 184, 190, 192–93, 195, 196, 199–200, 268; and emergency management plan, 192, 195–201, 268; and environmental justice, 15–16, 195–201; and fear of procedural failures or accidents, 5, 184, 188, 221, 268; lawsuits in, 194, 198–99; media coverage of, 184, 185, 186, 188, 190, 192, 195, 201; and National Research Council Stockpile Committee report on disposal of chemical weapons, 177, 186, 188–90; and neutralization technologies, 183, 184, 188, 190–93; and problems at incinerator sites, 183, 187–88, 190–93; regional and national support for Anniston activists, 182–83, 185, 186, 188, 190–94; and repurposing of chemical weapons incinerators, 187–88, 201, 291–92; by Serving Alabama's Future Environment, 184, 189, 193, 196, 197; and social class, 15, 182, 196; successes of, 196, 201, 291–92; and temporary moratorium on chemical weapons incineration, 185, 186. *See also* Families Concerned about Nerve Gas Incineration; Incineration of chemical weapons

Antinuclear lobby, 93–94

Anti-PCB campaign: in Anniston, 202, 204–5, 217, 218, 219, 225–34; and anti-incinerator campaign, 233; biracial cooperation in, 230; and churches, 204, 207, 214, 228–29; and cleanup by Monsanto, 231–33; and contamination at Alabama Power substation, 203–4; demonstrations and other protest tactics by, 217, 218, 219, 226, 233; and destruction of contaminated homes in West Anniston, 225, 226; and

environmental justice, 15–16, 205–10; and EPA, 205, 217, 226, 231, 233; and fish contamination, 202–3; and founding of local groups in Anniston, 202, 205; and government testing of PCB contamination in Anniston, 204–5; and health impact of PCBs, 223–25; and ineffectiveness of federal and state authorities, 231–33; and Mars Hill controversy, 228–29; media coverage of, 226; Monsanto's approach to environmental movement before, 210–14; and Monsanto's buyout offers and relocation of West Anniston residents, 215–22, 228–29, 232, 234, 235, 257; nonviolent tactics of, 15–16; regional and national support for Anniston activists, 205, 226–27, 231; and social class, 15; success of, 291; and "toxic uncertainty," 210, 227. *See also* PCB lawsuits and trials; Sweet Valley/Cobbtown Environmental Justice Task Force

ARCH. *See* "Anniston Reconnecting: A Catalyst for Healing"

Archives of Dermatology and Syphilology, 66–67

ARCO, 212

Army. *See* U.S. Army

Army Corps of Engineers, 175, 182, 369 (n. 42)

Aroclors. *See* PCBs

Arsenault, Ray, 98

Arsenic, 269

Artificial sweeteners, 34–35

ASNE. *See* American Society of Newspaper Editors

Assembled Chemical Weapons Assessment (ACWA), 193–94, 196

Association of Minority Racing Fans, 6

Astor, John Jacob, 23

Atlanta, Ga., 5, 56, 99, 107

Atlanta Constitution, 18, 20

Atom bomb, 80, 84, 93. *See also* Nuclear weapons

ATSDR. *See* Agency for Toxic Substances and Disease Registry

Austin, Bob, 232–33, 359–60 (n. 2)

Avian reproduction, 137–39, 156

Avoiding Armageddon, 7, 264

AWIC. *See* Alabama Water Improvement Commission

Ayers, Harry Mell: in Alabama National Guard, 78; and Alzheimer's disease, 105; as *Anniston Star* editor and publisher, xiv, 104; and chemical industry and military installations in Anniston, xiv, 78, 83–84,

churches and ministers; Civil rights movement; Desegregation; Race; Racism; Residential segregation; Segregation

Blevins, Lewis, 112

Blue Cross Association, 163

Bluemink, Elizabeth, 259

Blumenthal, H., 157

Bock, Edward J., 91

Body. *See* Toxic bodies

Boll weevil, 39–40

Booth, C. F., 55

Boraine, Alex, 301

Bowie, Andrew, 228, 230, 249, 268, 293, 366 (n. 8)

Bowie, Arthur and Bettye, xv–xvii, 128, 218, 220, 221, 223–24, 228, 251, 259

Boyd, Barbara Bigsby, 24–25, 106, 285, 293, 313 (n. 34)

Boyle, Robert H., 143, 145

Boynton v. Virginia, 96

BRAC commissions. *See* Base Realignment and Closure commissions

Braden, Anne Gambrell McCarty, 104, 225–26

Bradley, H. A., 142

Brady, St. Elmo, 318 (n. 62)

Bragg, Rick, 8, 116, 178–79, 185

Branchfield, Craig, 271, 282

Breastfeeding, 2, 215, 223, 245

Brewster, Lestine, 111

Brewster, Willie, 111–13, 182, 264

Breyer, Stephen, 237

Brockovich, Erin, 236–37

Browder, Glen, 186, 187, 188, 191

Brown, David P., 245

Brown, Jacqueline, 217, 220, 223, 239, 248, 268, 285, 286; photograph of, 286

Brown, Jerry, 256

Brown, Phil, 205

Brown, Robert M., 78, 88–89

Brown, Sandford, 70, 71–72

Brown, Stephanie, 280

Browner, Carol, 231, 233

Brown v. Board of Education, 99

Buhs, Joshua Blu, 336 (n. 41)

Bullard, Robert, 207, 208, 227, 354 (n. 9)

Bunnett, Joe, 190

Burn Busters, 184–85, 193, 196

Bush, George H. W., 254

Bush, George W., 6, 16, 259, 283, 284, 299, 349 (n. 23)

CAC. *See* Community Advisory Committee

Caddell, Henry "Hank," 161–62

Caffeine, 35

CAGs. *See* Community advisory groups

Cain, David, 258, 266–67, 297

Calandra, Joe, 155–56, 342 (n. 29)

Caldwell, Edgar, 46–47, 101, 102

Calhoun, Georgia, 79, 302

Calhoun, John C., 21

Calhoun County: economy of, 39–40; ecotourism for, 296–97; location of, 19; lynchings in, 22–23; naming of, 21; natural resources of, 19–20; population of, 5, 176, 293; poverty in, 179; railroads in, 22; removal of Creek Indians from, 20; and secession, 21. *See also* Anniston, Ala.

Calhoun County Chamber of Commerce, 291–92, 296

Calhoun County Clean Up the Environment (CUE), 150, 161

Calhoun County Improvement Association (CCIA): and Anniston Manifesto, 110, 264; civil rights campaigns of, 106, 108, 112, 113, 116, 117; founding of, 106; lawsuits by, 263

Calhoun County Negro Veterans Organization, 102

Calhoun County Training School, 29, 115, 313 (n. 34)

Calhoun County Voters League, 263

California, 86, 92, 113, 236–37, 238

Cambron, William "Bill," 142, 161

Camp McClellan, 7, 41, 78. *See also* Fort McClellan

Camp Shipp, 27–28

Camp Sibert, 83, 175

Cancer: and cigarette smoking, 242; and dioxin exposure, 328 (n. 37), 367 (n. 19); Obama administration's report on, 300; and PCBs, 1, 53, 165, 221–22, 224, 227, 245–46, 287, 339 (n. 2); and TCE, 269; and toxic substances generally, 164

Cannon, Walter B., 69

CAP. *See* Community Against Pollution

Cardiovascular disorders, 245, 275, 287, 288, 289

Carmichael, Beverly, 272

Carpenter, David, 243, 245–47, 250, 287

Carson, Rachel, xiii, xvi, 71, 130–33, 137, 210, 336 (n. 41)

Carter, Asa Earl, 103

Carter, Dan, 103

Carter, Jimmy, 263

Carter, Shirley Baker. *See* Baker, Shirley

Carver, George Washington, 51

Cash, Jane, 287

Causation: and latency, 62; and "manufacturing doubt," 16, 242; proof of, 246–47,

Chemical Weapons Working Group (CWWG): and Army reports on stockpile leaks, 191–92; and demonstrations in anti-incinerator campaign, 192–93, 199, 268; and discrimination complaint against Anniston incinerator, 197; founding of, 182; and Johnston Atoll incinerator, 190; and meeting with representatives from incineration sites, 188, 190; and safer alternatives to incineration, 182–83, 186; and Southern Christian Leadership Conference, 195, 268; success of, in anti-incinerator campaign, 196

Chemist Analyst, 88

Cherry, Kama and Timothy, xvi

Chestnut, J. L., 360 (n. 15)

Chevron, 212

Children: birth defects in, 140; lead screening for, 230; learning disabilities of, 285, 288, 289; PCBs' health impact on, 1, 2, 117–18, 128, 140, 168, 215, 223–24, 245, 246, 285, 288, 289

China, 27; PCB exposures in, 168, 255. See also *Yucheng*

Chloracne, xvi, 66–68, 72–74, 82, 124–25, 129, 139–40, 245

Chlorinated diphenyls: animal studies on, 70, 72, 74, 89, 134–35; commercial possibilities, 55–56; early manufacture of, 51–52, 54–56, 354 (n. 3); health impact of, 66–75, 82; labeling of, 82, 88–89; marketing of, as Aroclors, 1, 56; permissible exposure limit for, 73–74, 89; research on toxicity of, 67–74, 82. See also PCBs

Chlorine, 79–80, 82, 83, 89–90

Choccolocco Creek: FDA findings on fish contamination in, 150, 151–52; fish contamination and fish kills in, 5, 119, 126, 141, 150, 151–52, 172, 202–3, 221, 346 (n. 72); hazardous materials in drums found in, 269; meaning of name of, 20; Monsanto's testing of, 138, 172; PCB contamination of, 119, 126–28, 131, 141, 146, 172, 203; sewage in, from Fort McClellan, 79

Christian, David, 182, 194, 291

Christian, John L., 91

Churches. See Black churches and ministers; *and specific churches*

Citigroup, 261

Citizens Against Pollution, 230. See also Community Against Pollution

Citizens' Clearinghouse on Hazardous Wastes (CCHW), 227

Citizens Councils, 103

Citizens for Environmental Justice (CEJ): founding of, 205; protest by, 233

Civil Action, A (Harr), 236

Civilian Conservation Corps (CCC), 79

Civil Rights Act: of 1957, 102; of 1960, 102; of 1964, 114, 197

Civil rights movement: and African American leaders in Anniston, 106–18; and Anniston Manifesto, 110; and armed self-defense, 101; and biracial cooperation in Anniston, 105–8, 115–18; and bombing of Birmingham church, 108, 109, 110; Cold War's impact on, 102–3; and Congress of Racial Equality, 96, 99; and desegregation of public schools and public libraries, 108–10; and desegregation of public transportation, 22, 106; environmental justice movement compared with, 208; and fire-bombing of Freedom Riders' bus in Anniston, xiv, 14, 96, 98, 99, 100, 112, 302–3; and Freedom Riders, xiv, 14, 96–100, 112, 121–22, 329 (n. 2), 330 (n. 6); "long civil rights movement," 14–15, 99, 102–3; ministers' involvement in, 106–10; moderate southern whites' responses to, 105–8; and nonviolence, xiv, 15, 96, 99, 117; police response to, 97, 98, 110, 113; and Selma to Montgomery voting rights march, 111; and Southern Christian Leadership Conference, 106, 112, 116; and "strategic accommodation" by moderate whites, 105–6; and Student Nonviolent Coordinating Committee, 99, 105; and student sit-ins, 99; violence and threats against activists in, xiv, 14, 96–101, 103–4, 107, 108–11, 283, 301. See also Desegregation

Clapp, Richard W., 252–53

Clark-Atlanta University, 354 (n. 9)

Class. See Social class

Clay eating by pregnant women, 128, 220

Clean Air Act, 161–62, 181

Cleanup. See Environmental cleanup

Clean Water Act, 159, 171, 189, 343 (n. 41), 345 (n. 59), 347 (n. 82), 349 (n. 23)

Cleland, Max, 194

Clemon, U. W., 263, 264, 265, 270, 272

Clinton, Bill, 187, 208–9, 231, 233, 300, 313 (n. 34)

Closed-uses strategy for PCBs, 152–54, 162, 167

Coalition of Black Trade Unionists (CBTU), 231, 260

Coal tar and coal-tar products, 19, 33, 35, 54, 62, 63, 77. See also PCBs

Cobb, James, 8–9, 12

Endocrine disruption, 67, 137, 194, 247, 362 (n. 41). *See also* Hormonal disorders

Enlibra strategy, 16, 283–85

Environmental Action, 163

Environmental cleanup: and bankruptcy by Solutia, 275–77; community advisory group on, 272, 277–82; cost of, 257; and destruction of PCB-contaminated homes in Sweet Valley/Cobbtown, 225, 226, 277; engineering problems of, 277; EPA's consent decree on, 257–62, 265, 277, 285, 365 (n. 3); EPA's monitoring of and responsibility for, 276–77, 281–83, 293, 298; and EPA's Technical Assistance Grant program, 281; as euphemistic misnomer, 277; of Fort McClellan, 295–97; of military's hazardous waste, 7; by Monsanto Anniston plant, 172, 214–15, 231–33, 257; and Monsanto Enviro-Chem Systems, 169; Monsanto's financial responsibility for, 16, 275; negative impact of, 292–94; and "outrage reduction" strategy, 278–79, 283; problems with and delays in, 276–83; refuse fires from cleanup at defunct Chalk Line textile plant, 269; Senate subcommittee hearings on Anniston PCB cleanup, 260–62, 265; of Snow Creek, 172, 257; of soil contamination, 281–83, 293; and Solutia, 257, 258, 259–61, 275–83. *See also* Superfund program

Environmental Defense Fund (EDF), 154, 163, 202

Environmental Defense Fund (EDF) v. EPA, 343 (n. 41), 345 (n. 59)

Environmental Equity Vulnerability Analysis, 214

Environmental Equity Work Group, 355 (n. 15)

Environmental illness. *See* Health impact; Health impact of PCBs; *and specific illnesses*

Environmental justice: and anti-incinerator campaign, 15–16, 195–201; and anti-PCB campaign, 15–16, 205–10; and Civil Rights Act (1964), 197; civil rights movement compared with, 208; and Congress, 208; description of environmental injustice, 10–12; and disparagement of West End residents, 222; and Emelle, Ala., hazardous waste facility, 281, 282; and EPA, 208–9; and health impact of PCBs, 223–25; and knowledge, 14, 298; and Monsanto's response to environmental movement, 210–14; National People of Color Environmental Leadership Summit on, 207–8; and Southern Organizing

Committee for Social and Economic Justice, 225–26. *See also* Anti-incinerator campaign; Anti-PCB campaign

Environmental Justice Act, 208, 300

Environmental Justice Research Center (EJRC), 227, 354 (n. 9)

Environmental Justice Small Grants Program, 217, 233, 261

Environmental Lobby, 163

Environmental Policy Center, 163

Environmental Protection Agency (EPA): and anti-PCB campaign, 205, 217, 226, 231, 233; and cleanup at Sauget, Ill., Krummrich plant, 275–76; and cleanup of Anniston, 257–62, 265, 276–77, 281–83, 285, 293, 298, 365 (n. 3); and community advisory groups, 278; creation of, 148–49; DDT banned by, 346 (n. 68); and dioxin health standards, 367 (n. 19); Emergency Response and Removal Branch, 233; enforcement action by, for Anniston PCB site, 371 (n. 65); Enlibra strategy of, 16, 283–85; on environmental contamination by PCBs, 165; and Environmental Equity Work Group, 355 (n. 15); and environmental justice complaints, 197–98; Environmental Justice Small Grants Program, 233; and Federal Water Pollution Control Act, 343 (n. 41); guidelines for exposure assessment by, 366 (n. 11); and hazardous waste incinerators, 185; on health impact of PCBs, 1, 160, 165, 227–28, 300; inaction of, on PCB regulation, 159, 232, 345 (n. 59); on limits on PCB levels in wastes, 167; list of toxic pollutants from, 159, 160; and military installations, 181–82; mission of, 159; on Monsanto's toxic emissions, 356 (n. 27); National Environmental Justice Advisory Council, 208–9, 233, 277; Office of Environmental Justice, 209; and soil contamination in Anniston, 269–70; and Solutia, 259–61; on standard for PCB discharges, 150, 158, 159; support by, for Monsanto's production of PCBs, 158, 159; Technical Assistance Grant program, 281; technical documents from, 231; on threshold for PCB contamination, 122; and Toxic Substances Control Act, 167–68, 300; and water pollution in Calhoun County, 150. See also *EPA v. Pharmacia*; Superfund program; *United States v. Pharmacia*

Environmental protest. *See* Anti-incinerator campaign; Anti-PCB campaign

Environmental racism, 10–12, 14, 64, 207. *See also* Environmental justice; Racism

Environmental Working Group (EWG), 231, 242, 249, 259, 260, 276

EPA. *See* Environmental Protection Agency

EPA v. Pharmacia (Sauget, Ill.), 275–76, 368 (n. 34)

Epidemiology: and Hill Principles, 252–53; "popular epidemiology," 227

Episcopal Church, 23

Epistemology, 318 (n. 50). *See also* Knowledge; Toxic knowledge

Equal Protection Clause, 238

Erlinghaus, J. C. B., 108

European Union's REACH protocol, 299, 300

EWG. *See* Environmental Working Group

Expertise. *See* Knowledge

Exposure pathways, 5, 134, 147, 223, 236. *See also* Health impact: of biological agents; Health impact of PCBs

Falk, Henry, 261

Families Concerned about Nerve Gas Incineration, 178, 182–87, 190, 192, 194–99, 233, 291

Farming. *See* Agriculture

FBI: and Klan violence, 97, 112

FDA. *See* Food and Drug Administration

Federal Abrasives, 43

Federal Advisory Community Act, 277

Federal Electro-Chemical Company, 43

Federal Fertilizer, 43

Federal Insecticide, Fungicide and Rodenticide Act (FIFRA), 344 (n. 54)

Federal Phosphorus Company, 43, 51, 56, 58, 307 (n. 3), 319 (n. 63)

Federal Refuse Act, 130, 145, 158, 162, 335–36 (n. 33)

Federal Safe Drinking Water Act, 269

Federal Water Pollution Control Act (FWPCA). *See* Clean Water Act

Federal Water Pollution Control Authority (FWPCA), 160

Federal Water Quality Administration, 147

Federal Writers' Program, 21

Fell, Charlie, 253

Ferguson, Denzel, 126–27, 243

Ferguson, Jefferson A., 53

Ferguson, Opal. *See* Scruggs, Opal

Fertilizers, 50, 86

Field-of-movements, 205

FIFRA. *See* Federal Insecticide, Fungicide and Rodenticide Act

Films. *See* Movies and movie theaters

Fincher, Joe, 120

Finley, Mack, 126–27

Fischer, Frank, 13, 36–37

Fish contamination and fish kills: and breast cancer, 246; and carcinogenic nature of PCBs, 339 (n. 2); in Choccolocco Creek, 5, 119, 126, 141, 150–52, 172, 202–3, 221, 346 (n. 72); and elevated PCB blood levels, 224; FDA findings on, 150, 151–52; FDA guidelines on acceptable PCB level in fish, 146, 147; Jensen on, 134; lawsuit against Monsanto for, 126–27; media coverage of, 143, 210; in New York State, 213; "noconsumption" fish advisory due to, 5, 203, 210; as spark for local anti-PCB campaign, 202–3; sports fishermen's concern for, 162; and state regulation of water pollution, 130, 131; in Sweden, 134; and Toxic Substances Control Act hearings, 168; in Washington State, 213. *See also* Water pollution

Fisher, Linda, 261, 299

Flinn, Frederick B., 67, 322 (n. 45)

Flooding, 128, 150, 282–83, 293

Florida, 86, 146, 180, 226

Folsom, Big Jim, 182

Folsom, Jim, Jr., 187, 191

Food and Drug Act, 130–31

Food and Drug Administration (FDA): and chemicals in food products and packaging, 130–31, 163; criticisms of, 163–64; cyclamates banned by, 339 (n. 3); and environmental contamination by PCBs, 165; forerunner of, 35; and John F. Queeny, 35; and limits on PCB content of foodstuffs, 157, 203; and PCB levels in fish, 146, 147, 150, 151–52, 203; on pesticides and rodenticides, 163; reluctance of, to ban PCBs, 157; and thalidomide, 132

Food contamination: and contaminated livestock, 145–46, 147, 148; FDA regulation of chemicals in food, 157, 163; and food packaging, 145; and hogs purchased by Monsanto, 147, 148, 149, 154, 243–44; media coverage of, 145; of milk, 146; and PCB blood levels, 224; of seafood, 141, 146; of vegetables from home gardens, 220, 223, 224; *yucheng* (oil disease), 168, 255; *yusho* in Japan, 139–40, 165, 255, 337 (n. 61). *See also* Fish contamination and fish kills

Forbes magazine, 8, 88, 367 (n. 23)

Ford, George P., 255, 256, 257

Ford, Johnny, 117

Ford, Richard Thompson, 12

Ford, Tom, 251

Forever Wild, 258

Forrestal, Daniel J. (Dan), 1, 35, 43, 58, 60, 91, 324 (n. 72)

and water pollution, 119, 121, 130–31, 150. *See also* Water pollution; *and specific environmental laws and state and federal agencies*
GPU corporation, 369 (n. 42)
Graddick, Charlie, 172
Grady, Henry, 18, 20
Graesser-Monsanto Chemical Works Ltd., Ruabon, Wales, 50
Graham, Bob, 6
Grandcamp (ship), 86–87
Graves, Bibb, 58, 78
"Great Saccharin War," 34–35, 211
Green, Karen, 301
Greenburg, Leonard, 82
Greenpeace, 183, 189–91
Griffin v. Unocal, 362 (n. 48)
Griffith, D. W., 39
Grooms, Hobart, 103
Gunning, Gerald E., 152, 171

Hague Congress (1907), 42
Hague Declaration (1899), 42
Hale, Grace, 27
Hall, James, 209
Halliburton, 276
Halogenated compounds, 68, 323 (n. 58)
Halowax Corporation, 68–72, 82
Hamilton, Alice, 61, 62, 68, 69–70
Hancock v. Train, 349 (n. 23)
Hankins, Grover, 238
Hankinson, John, 194
Hanna, Charles Edgar, 29
Harmon, Donna, 177–78, 182
Harmon, Jim, 177–78, 182, 184, 185, 187, 191–92
Harr, Jonathan, 236
Harris, Sylvester, 202, 214–15, 226, 230
Hartsfield, James, 322 (n. 40)
Harvard Medical School, 68
Harvard School of Public Health, 61, 68–72, 82
Hatch, Orrin, 193
Hawks Nest Incident, 67–68
Hays, Samuel and Barbara, 167–68
Hazardous waste industry, 186–87
HCl. *See* Hydrochloric acid
Head, Aaron, 195
Health clinics, 16, 263, 265, 270, 273, 285, 286–87
Health impact: of biological agents, 86; of chemical weapons and their disposal, 1, 44–45, 49, 175–76, 183, 189–90, 192, 194; Clarence Thomas on effects of exposure to toxic wastes, 170–71; of creosote, 171;

of dioxins, 88, 328 (n. 37), 367 (n. 19); of iron manufacturing, 25–27; knowledge about effects of exposure to chemicals in early twentieth century, 60–63; of lead, 269; of mercury, 269; of nerve agents, 175–76; of parathion, 90, 120, 173; of phenacetin manufacturing, 62–63; at Swann Chemical, 9. *See also* Health impact of PCBs; Industrial hygiene; Industrial responses to chemical harm; Toxic knowledge
Health impact of PCBs: on African Americans, xv–xvii, 11, 66–68, 117–18, 125, 288, 289; and age, 289; Anniston Environmental Health Research Consortium on, 287–90, 301; bioaccumulation and biomagnification of PCBs, 2; on children, 1, 2, 117–18, 128, 140, 168, 215, 223–24, 245, 246, 285, 288, 289; deaths, xvi, 82, 89, 117–18, 129, 132, 139–40, 243; Drinker's research on, 2, 68–74, 132; early accounts of, 9, 56–57; and environmental justice movement, 223–25; EPA on, 160, 227–28; and exposure routes and transmission of PCBs, 70, 147, 215, 245; and gender, 288, 289; intergenerational effects, 2, 223, 289; Jensen's research on, 2, 133–37; knowledge of, in 1930s, xvi; labeling on, 82, 88–89; lawsuits focusing on, with research to support, 236, 241, 244–47, 249–50, 252–53; McCord's documentation of, xvi, 227, 294, 358 (n. 66); media coverage of, 7; medical monitoring of, 249, 260, 261, 262; Monsanto's research on, 155–57; and "popular epidemiology," 227; on pregnant women, 128, 220, 223, 245; Risebrough's research on, 137–39, 154, 156. *See also* Industrial responses to chemical harm; Toxic bodies; Toxic knowledge
—specific diseases and disorders: birth defects, 140; cancer, 1, 53, 165, 221–22, 224, 227, 245–46, 287, 339 (n. 2); cardiovascular disorders, 245, 275, 287, 288, 289; chloracne, xvi, 66–68, 72–74, 82, 124–25, 129, 139–40, 245; diabetes, 275, 288, 289; hormonal disorders, 245, 246–47; immune disorders, 1, 192, 245; liver ailments, xvi, 1, 70, 74, 82, 125, 132, 135, 139, 165, 245; reproductive system disorders, 165, 192, 246; respiratory ailments, 161; *yucheng* (oil disease), 168, 255; *yusho* incident in Japan, 139–40, 165, 255, 337 (n. 61)
Health studies of Anniston residents, xv, 5, 227, 260, 261, 270, 287–90
Heflin, Ala., 298

Helms, Jesse, 166

Henderson, Hugh L., 322 (n. 40)

Henry, Aaron, 102

Hermanson, Mark, 252, 322 (n. 42)

Herty, Charles Holmes, 38, 42, 45–46, 49–51, 56, 64

Highlander Research and Education Center, 185

Hill, Austin Bradford, 252–53

Hill, Franklin, 293

Hill, Lister, 78, 83

Hill Principles, 252–53

Hine, Lewis, 39

Hinton, Nona, 249

Hinton, Travis, 249

Hinton v. Monsanto, 249, 250, 262, 362 (n. 48)

Historically Black College and University-based centers, 354

Hobson City, Ala., 28–31, 111, 115, 269, 279, 301

Hochwalt, Ted, 211

Hodges, Paul B., 140

"Hog Analysis Results," 147, 148, 149, 154, 243–44

Hooker, A. H., 45

Hooker Chemical, 45

Hookey, John A., 70

Hoover, Herbert, 91

Hoover, Herbert Clark, Jr., 90–91

Hoover, J. E., 46

Hormonal disorders, 67, 137, 194, 245, 322 (n. 44). *See also* Endocrine disruption

Hosmer, D. B. 343 (n. 40)

Hot Blast, xiv, 45. See also *Anniston Star*

Houston, George S., 22

Howe, Harrison, 56

Howell, Hoyt "Chip," Jr., 267, 294, 296, 301; photograph of, 267

Hudson, Antoinette, 195

Hudson, Henry, 172

Hughes, Bill, 122

Hughes, Dolly, 110

Human exposure to PCBs. *See* Health impact of PCBs; Toxic bodies

Hunter, John, 266–67

Hydrochloric acid (HCl), 54, 66, 122, 124, 125, 127, 140. *See also* Muriatic acid

IARC. *See* International Agency for Research on Cancer

IBT Labs. *See* Industrial Bio-Test Laboratories

ICWU. *See* International Chemical Workers Union

Illness. *See* Health impact; Health impact of PCBs; *and specific illnesses*

Incineration of chemical weapons: at Anniston Army Depot, xiii, xiv, xv–xvi, 5, 195, 196, 197, 264, 268–69, 291–92; Army arguments for, 186–87; Army's risk assessment of, 192; Assembled Chemical Weapons Assessment by Army, 193–94, 196; congressional focus on, 185–86, 190–92, 194, 196; cost of incinerator, 187; economic impact of Anniston Army Depot incinerator, 291–92; emergency management plan for, 192, 195–201, 268; fears accompanying, 5, 184, 188, 221, 268; funding for, 192; health risks of, 175–76, 183, 189–90, 192, 194; at Johnston Atoll, 175, 177, 183, 186–90, 192, 193; lawsuits on, 194, 198–99; media coverage of, 184, 185, 186, 188, 190, 192, 195, 201; and National Research Council Stockpile Committee report on, 177, 186, 188–90; neutralization technologies versus, 183, 184, 188, 190–93; problems at incinerator sites, 183, 187–88, 190–93; pro-incineration campaign, 185, 186–87; and real estate near incinerator, 185; and repurposing of incinerators, 187–88, 201, 291–92; and Talladega Speedway, 268–69; temporary moratorium on, 185, 186; at Tooele, Utah, 175, 176, 187, 190, 193. *See also* Anniston Army Depot; Anti-incinerator campaign

Incineration of PCBs, 160, 344 (n. 49)

India, 173

Indiana, 196, 353 (n. 76)

Industrial Bio-Test Laboratories (IBT Labs), 155–57, 342 (nn. 29–30)

Industrial hygiene, 61–63, 65–66, 68–71, 73–74, 82, 120, 129

Industrialization. *See* Southern industrialization

Industrial paternalism: Anniston Manifesto's challenge to, 110; of Anniston's founders, 9, 23–24; and community advisory groups, 212, 280; compared with military discipline, 180; and health of workers, 26–27; and labor relations, 30; and Monsanto's buyout plan, 217; and Monsanto's denial of PCB toxicity, 121; and racism, 23–24, 30, 312 (n. 21); and whites' moderate course for civil rights, 106, 107

Industrial responses to chemical harm: alteration of PCB research results by Industrial Bio-Test Laboratories, 155–57; appeal to scientific uncertainty, 14, 16, 71, 157, 159, 166, 210, 227, 241–42, 253; attacks

Marvinny, Mike, 184
Maryland, 196, 246
Masry, Ed, 236
Massachusetts, 236
"Massive resistance," 107
Mather, E., 89
Matson, Jack, 244, 250–51, 347 (n. 82)
Maximum allowable concentrations, 74, 89, 125, 157, 334 (n. 13)
Mayausky, Jack, 210, 215
Mazzocchi, Tony, 164
McClain, Rev. William B., 106–11, 113, 116
McCombs, Max, 282
McCord, Shirley, xvi, 227, 294, 358 (n. 66), 370 (n. 48)
McCown, John, 195
McCrae, Thomas, 61
McCrory, Rev. Alberta, 301
McCullough, Rogers, 55
McGough, Robert, 356 (n. 27)
McKean, William, 327 (n. 30)
McKee, James E., 91–92, 172
McKinney, Janie Forsyth, 98, 330 (n. 6)
Mealing, Eloise, 216, 217, 225, 226, 228
Mealing, Frank, 216, 277
MECSI. See Monsanto Enviro-Chem Systems Inc.
Media coverage: of anti-incinerator campaign, 184, 185, 186, 188, 190, 192, 195, 201, 264; of anti-PCB campaign, 226; of fish contamination, 151–52, 210; of nineteenth-century Anniston, 18, 20, 25; of PCB lawsuits and trials, 241, 250, 265; of PCB toxicity, 143, 145, 154; of stock values of Solutia and Monsanto, 240; of toxic contamination in Anniston, 7–8. See also specific newspapers
Medical Association of the State of Alabama, 66
Medical Aspects of Chemical Warfare, The (Vedder and Walton), 49
Medical monitoring, 249, 260, 261, 262
Medical treatment. See Health clinics; Public health
Meigs, J. Wister, 125
Melosi, Martin, 64–65
Merck drug firm, 32
Mercury, xiii, 127, 143, 269
Methodist Church, 109, 111, 301
Meyer Brothers Drug Company, 32
Michael, Max, 287
Michigan, 252
Mikulski, Barbara, 260–61, 369 (n. 38)
Military-industrial complex. See Anniston Army Depot; Chemical industry;

Chemical weapons; Fort McClellan; Monsanto Chemical Company/Monsanto Company; U.S. Army; War
Military Toxics Project of National Toxics Campaign, 183
Miller, Zell, 194
Mills, J. E., 51
Mims, Ruth, 217, 243–44, 248
Mining, 139
Minkler, Howard L., 152
Mississippi, 98, 102
Mississippi River, 276
Mississippi State University, 126
Mitchell, James, 40–41
Mitchell, Thomas A., 86
Mithoff and Jacks, 239
Mitman, Gregg, 147
Mitre consulting firm, 191
Model City, 8, 19, 20, 21, 23, 110, 291, 294, 295
Mohr, Scott C., 190–91
Monsanto, Olga Mendez, 32
Monsanto Ag Company, 240
Monsanto Anniston plant: African American employees at, 66–67, 124, 258; chloracne in workers at, 66–68, 72–74, 82; chlorine production at, 89–90; citizen complaints about odors from, 88, 161; and civil rights movement, 113; Compound 1080 rodenticide discontinued at, 90; description of, 122; employment statistics at, 60, 122, 320 (n. 9); end of production of PCBs at, 154, 162, 168–69, 347 (n. 82); environmental cleanup by, 214–15, 231–33; expansion of PCB production at, in 1969, 140; labor union and strike at, 142, 164; location of, 121–22; parathion production at, 90, 120, 127, 173; PCB concentration level at, 122; PCB-containing waste buried near, 292; PCB exposure treated as matter of individual hygiene at, 73, 74–75; PCB levels in effluent from, 146, 150, 151, 346 (n. 73); PCB production at, 3, 35, 122–26, 139, 140; PCB spills at, 146; photographs of, 60, 121, 123, 149; pollution-control equipment at, 126, 150, 154, 162, 169, 172, 244; pollution from generally, xiv, 3–5, 64, 120, 121; pollution of Choccolocco Creek by, 119, 126–28, 131, 141, 146, 172, 203; pollution of ditches in West Anniston by, 118, 125, 127–28, 141, 146, 150, 204, 223, 281; production statistics for, 120, 139; sale of, attempted by Monsanto, 173; segregation of, 124; silence, denials, and minimization of PCB toxicity by, xvi, xvii, 210, 214, 215,

OPEC, 210–11

Operation CHASE, 179–80

OREPA. *See* Oak Ridge Environmental Peace Alliance

Organization for Economic Cooperation and Development (OECD), 149

Organization for the Prohibition of Chemical Weapons, 292

Organochlorines, 83, 132, 242, 247

OSHA. *See* Occupational Safety and Health Act

Osler, William, 61

Our Stolen Future (Colborn), 247

"Outrage reduction," 212, 278–79, 283, 284

Owens, Walter, 360 (n. 15)

Owens v. Monsanto: and attorneys for plaintiffs, 238–39, 252; defense attorney's opening statement in, 241–42, 334 (n. 16); expert witnesses in, 244–47; filing of, 239, 360 (n. 15); financial settlement of, 248, 268, 271, 362 (n. 44); local residents as witnesses in, 243–44; plaintiffs in, 235, 242–43, 360 (n. 15); trial of, 241–48, 254; West Anniston Foundation funded by, 271, 285, 286

Oxford, Ala.: Anniston's founders in, 19; advisory against fish consumption in, 203; and community advisory group for PCB cleanup, 279, 370 (n. 48); creation of Hobson City from, 28; and financial settlement of PCB lawsuit, 274; mall in, 297; and PCB contamination, 119, 150, 173; racial discrimination in, 28, 103; Tull Chemical Company in, 90, 269, 276

Pacific Gas and Electric, 236–37

Pagnol, Marcel, xvi

Palazzalo, Richard J., 342 (n. 29)

Palmer, A. Mitchell, 43, 47

Palmer, Jimmy, 261

Palmore, Herbert, 301

Palmore, Lula, 301–2

Papageorge, William, 125, 138–39, 151, 154, 162–63, 253, 255, 256

Paper products, 145

Parathion, xiii, 90, 120, 127, 173, 211

Parker, Mike, 194

Paternalism. *See* Industrial paternalism; White paternalism

PCB cleanup. *See* Environmental cleanup

PCB contamination of fish. *See* Fish contamination and fish kills

PCB Environmental Pollution Abatement Plan (Monsanto), 140, 142–43

PCB lawsuits and trials: by Alabama Water Improvement Commission for water pollution, 126–27; announcement of settlement accord for, 264, 265–68; by Bass Anglers Sportsman Society for water pollution, 162; and losses of local businesses, 254; on chloracne suffered by Monsanto employees in 1930s, xvi, 66–67, 245, 322 (n. 40); cleanup required of Monsanto following, 16; and *Daubert* rules for toxic torts, 237; defense by Monsanto in, 2, 236, 241–42, 254–57; disparities in financial settlements from, 270–71, 273–75, 289; distancing of new Monsanto Company from, 240–41; and drawbacks of toxic tort litigation, 237–38; educational foundation as part of settlement, 285, 371 (n. 65); expert testimony during, 244–47, 250–55; financial settlements from, 16, 248, 263, 264, 265, 270–75, 289, 359–60 (n. 2), 362 (n. 44); health clinics as part of settlement of, 16, 263, 265, 270, 273, 285, 286–87; and health impact of PCBs, 236, 241, 244–47, 249–50, 252–53; health studies as part of settlement of, 260, 261, 270, 288; *Hinton v. Monsanto*, 249, 250, 262, 362 (n. 48); jury decision against Monsanto in *Abernathy* case, 1, 16, 258–59, 262; legal fees for, 272–73, 367 (n. 23); and Mars Hill controversy, 229; as mass toxic torts, 236–39, 275, 361 (n. 27); media coverage of, 241, 250, 265; and "most favored nation clause," 248, 271; number of plaintiffs in, 16, 235, 259, 262, 263; penalty phase of *Abernathy* case, 5, 16, 262–63; per capita gross cash recovery by plaintiffs, 248, 273, 362 (n. 44); property damage verdicts from *Abernathy* case, 262; and real estate values, 251, 254; testimony by Anniston residents in, 243–44, 251; testimony by Monsanto employees in, 84, 253–58; on water pollution in Jefferson, Talladega, and St. Clair counties, 235–36. See also *Abernathy v. Monsanto*; *Owens v. Monsanto*; *Tolbert v. Monsanto*

PCB manufacturing: chemistry behind, 54–55; commercial possibilities of new chlorinated diphenyls, 55–56; early period of, 354 (n. 3); end of, 2, 154, 162, 167, 168–69, 275, 347 (n. 82); Monsanto's monopoly for, in U.S., 1, 129, 153; in North Wales, 50; process of, 122–26; statistics on, 56, 120, 139–40, 154; by Swann Chemical, 1, 51–52, 54–56. See also Monsanto Anniston plant; Sauget, Ill., Krummrich plant

of, 240; landholdings of, 292; and PCB lawsuits, 236, 240, 262, 266–67; products manufactured by, 293–94; purchase of, by Eastman Chemicals, 294; stock prices of, 240, 267, 271, 365–66 (n. 6)

"Sound science," 284, 298. See also Scientific authority

South African Truth and Reconciliation Commission (TRC), 301

South Carolina, 96, 97, 182, 278, 329 (n. 2)

Southern Christian Leadership Conference (SCLC): and anti-incinerator campaign, 195, 198, 199, 268; and anti-PCB campaign, 207, 209; and civil rights movement, 106, 112, 116, 117

Southern Conference on Human Welfare (SCHW), 225, 358 (n. 60)

Southern Expositions, 51

Southern industrialization, xiii, 18, 36, 38, 50–52. See also Anniston, Ala.; New South; Swann Chemical Company

Southern Manganese Company, 41

"Southern Manifesto," 110

Southern Munitions Corporation, 40–41

Southern Organizing Committee for Social and Economic Justice (SOC), 218, 225–26, 238

Southern Research Institute, 190–91

South Landfill. See Landfills

Soviet Union/Russia, 5, 49, 94, 177, 181, 183, 188

Spanish-American War, 7, 27–28

Sparkman, John, 83

Spirit of Anniston, 302

Spirit of Enterprise, The (Queeny), 92, 93

Sports Illustrated, 143, 145

Sprayberry, Gary, 107, 112, 333 (n. 67)

Sproull, Miller, 110

"Standard of care," 244

Standards of proof, 247

Staples, Amy Jane, 93

Stauber, John, 133

Steele, Charles: photograph of, 199

Sterling, Rev. Henry, 199–200

Stewart, Donald: and Abernathy v. Monsanto, 235, 249–51, 253, 255, 257–58, 261, 266, 272–73, 364 (n. 71), 367 (n. 23); and anti-PCB campaign, 204–5, 228, 229, 231; demonstrations against, 273, 367 (n. 23); on EPA's approach to cleanup of Anniston, 261; legal fees for, 272–73, 367 (n. 23); and Mars Hill controversy, 228, 229; on Monsanto's defense, 236; photograph of, 266; in U.S. Congress, 166–67

Stewart, Vaughn, 294

Stimson, Henry L., 80

Stockpile Committee, 177, 186, 188–90

Stoker, Kevin, 105

Stone, John, 288

Stoner, J. B., 98, 112

Stop the Pollution (STP), 185

STP. See Stop the Pollution

Strange, Hubert Damon, 112

"Strategic accommodation," 105–6

Stream pollution law, 321 (n. 35)

Streetscape project, 294

Strontium 90, 93–94

Stroud, Sarge, 230

Structural inequalities: and violence, 14, 15, 113, 115, 118

Student Nonviolent Coordinating Committee (SNCC), 99, 105

Students Concerned about the Future, 207

Sulfuric acid, 80, 81, 88

Sulzberger, Marion B., 67

Summerall, Charles P., 78

Sumners, Sherri, 295, 296

SUNY, 245, 287

Superfund program: and Anniston Army Depot, xiii, 181, 269; and Anniston PCB cleanup, 232, 233, 276–77; at Commencement Bay, Washington, 213; laws on, 349 (n. 23), 369 (n. 38); meetings and workshops on, 226–27

Superfund Reauthorization and Amendment (SARA), 369 (n. 38)

Suttkus, Royal D., 152, 171

Swann, Theodore: as advocate for industrial development in South, 50–52, 58; birth date of, 40; chemical companies owned by, 40–42, 50–51, 307 (n. 3); chemical research funded by, 50–53; entrepreneurship of, 56–58; financial worth of holdings of, 58; home of, 57; loan from Monsanto to, 57; and PCB production at Anniston chemical plant, 18–19, 36, 52–56; photograph of, 37; and race relations in Anniston, 47; rail expedition to Rose Bowl by, 57, 92; and takeover of Swann Chemical by Monsanto, 57–58; wife and daughter of, 57; and World War I, 42–43. See also Swann Chemical Company

Swann, Virginia, 57

Swann Chemical Company: acquisitions by, 319 (n. 63); customers of, 166; employees of, 9, 56, 338 (n. 70); financial loan to, 57; first attempt to produce biphenyl at, 34, 54, 55; investors in, 56–57; and labor union, 338 (n. 70); managers of, 91; and munitions company during World War I,

about PCBs, 120–21, 124, 129, 139–43, 146, 151, 155, 162, 242, 250–51, 255, 257, 259; Monsanto's and Solutia's denial, minimization, and underreporting of, 75, 119, 121, 127, 151–52, 155, 157, 160, 162–63, 215, 242, 244, 250–51, 253, 257; of Monsanto's customers, 129, 151, 162; and Monsanto's defense of PCBs, 2, 140–45, 154, 155–57, 236, 241–42, 254–57, 344 (nn. 46, 53); and Monsanto's research, 155–57; questions on, 13–14; and Risebrough's research, 137–39, 154, 156; stress from, xvii, 13; trauma of, on the public, 221, 251–52, 257, 259; withholding of, from the public, 129, 151–52, 158–59, 162–63, 171, 214–16, 218, 220, 289. *See also* Health impact; Health impact of PCBs
Toxicology, 61. *See also* Industrial hygiene
Toxic Release Inventory (TRI), 213, 356 (n. 27)
Toxic Substances Control Act (TSCA): on "confidential business information," 168, 299–300; and EPA, 167–68, 300; and incineration of chemical weapons, 189; industry lobby against, 163, 165–66, 172, 300; legislative debate on, 164–67; PCB ban in, 167–68, 171, 275, 345 (n. 59), 347 (n. 82); provisions of, 167–68, 299–300; reform of, 299–300; supporters of, 163–64
Toxic torts, 236–39, 275, 361 (n. 27). *See also* PCB lawsuits and trials; *and specific lawsuits*
"Toxic uncertainty," 71, 157, 159, 166, 210, 227, 241–42, 253
Toxic Wastes and Race, 207
Train, Russell, 149, 165, 345 (n. 59)
Trammell, Rev. Raleigh: photograph of, 199
Transparency, 180–81, 213, 215, 291, 299, 303
Transwestern Pipeline Company, 213
Travolta, John, 236
TRC. *See* South African Truth and Reconciliation Commission
Tree bark containing PCBs, 124, 252, 363 (n. 55)
Trials. *See* PCB lawsuits and trials
Trichloroethylene. *See* TCE
Trisodium phosphate. *See* TSP
Truman, Harry S., 91, 102
Truth and Reconciliation paradigm, 301
TSCA. *See* Toxic Substances Control Act
TSP (trisodium phosphate), 64, 73
Tucker, Connie, 226
Tucker, Scott, 138, 156
Tull Chemical Company, 90, 269, 276
Tunney, John V., 166
Turner, Alma: photograph of, 286

Tuskegee Institute/University, 51, 288
Tyler, Alfred Leigh, 20
Tyler, Anne Scott, 20, 23
Tyler, Daniel H., 19, 21, 23, 30
Typhoid, 321 (n. 35)
Tyson, Timothy B., 106, 291

UNCED. *See* U.N. Conference on Environment and Development
Underwood, Earl, 368 (n. 31)
Union Carbide, 67–68
United Church of Christ, 207
United Nations, 149, 177
United States v. Pharmacia: and EPA cleanup enforcement in Anniston, 259, 260, 261, 277, 285, 365 (n. 3), 371 (n. 65)
United States v. Republic Steel, 335 (n. 33)
United States v. Standard Oil, 335–36 (n. 33)
U.N. Conference on Environment and Development (UNCED), 149
U.S. Army: and Assembled Chemical Weapons Assessment, 193–94, 196; biological agents tested by, 85, 86; Chemical-Biological Radiological Corps Command of, 94, 120, 179; Chemical Corps and Training School of, 7, 45, 83–86, 93, 94, 120, 179, 180; Chemical Corps Command of, 94; Chemical Demilitarization Unit of, 194; Chemical Warfare Service of, 42–46, 48–49, 56, 60, 81–84, 177; cutbacks in, and base closures during 1990s, 178, 198; desegregation of, 102; and environmental laws and EPA regulations, 7, 181, 189. *See also* Anniston Army Depot; Camp McClellan; Chemical weapons; Incineration of chemical weapons; *and specific wars*
U.S. Department of Agriculture (USDA): Bureau of Chemistry, 35, 46, 130, 163–64
U.S. Department of Energy, 369 (n. 42)
U.S. Department of Homeland Security, xv, 86, 295–96
U.S. Department of Interior, 130, 141
U.S. Fish and Wildlife Service, 130, 296–97
U.S. General Accounting Office (GAO), 188–90
U.S. Justice Department, 46, 117, 158
U.S. Navy, 80, 81–82, 89, 129
U.S. Public Health Service, 65, 70, 82, 89, 119, 130
U.S. Supreme Court: on ban on segregation in interstate public transportation, 96; on "duty to warn," 87–88; on Texas City explosion, 87–88; on toxic torts, 237
U.S. War Department, 79, 80. *See also* U.S. Army

United Steelworkers of America, 164
Universal Oil Products Company, 84
University of Alabama, 57, 109, 287–89
University of California, 137–38, 143
University of Massachusetts, 210
University of North Carolina, 38
University of Pennsylvania, 252
University of Wisconsin, 136, 143; Alumni
    Research Foundation (WARF Institute),
    143
Upjohn, 240
Urban Environmental Conference, 163
Urban environments, 11, 20, 23, 25, 26, 64,
    208. See also specific cities and towns
USA Today, 226
USDA. See U.S. Department of Agriculture

Vandalism, 293
Van den Bosch, Robert, 143
Vedder, Edward, 49
Verfaille, Hendrik, 211
Vietnam War, 88, 179, 180
Violence: and Alabama Constitutional
    Convention of 1901, 30; in "Battle of
    Anniston," 27–28, 101; against civil rights
    activists, xiv, 14, 96–101, 103–4, 107,
    108–11, 283, 301; against Freedom Riders,
    xiv, 14, 96–100, 112; hanging of Edgar
    Caldwell in death of white streetcar con-
    ductor, 46–47; lynchings, 22–23, 101, 104,
    311 (n. 17); murders of blacks by whites,
    111–13, 264; personal violence, 15; racial
    violence, xiv, 14, 27–28, 46–47, 99–105,
    107–12, 115, 158; "slow violence" of pollu-
    tion, 15, 118, 221, 283, 292, 301; and Watts
    riots in Los Angeles, 113. See also Ku Klux
    Klan; War
Virginia, 99
Vos, J. G., 165
Voting rights, 111, 113, 264, 354 (n. 11)
Voting Rights Act (1965), 113, 264
VX nerve gas, xiii, 175, 176, 181, 187

WACs. See Women's Army Corps School
Waddle, Chris, 179, 181, 190, 201
WAF. See West Anniston Foundation
Wallace, George, 103, 105, 262, 332 (n. 51)
Wall Between, The (Braden), 104
Wall Street Journal, 157
Walters, Ronald G., 37
Walter Wellborn High School: desegrega-
    tion of, 114–15, 116, 117, 158, 230, 263;
    racial composition in 2013, 286
Walton, Duncan, 49
War: and chemical industry, 7, 36, 38, 41–49,

78–83; and environment, 5, 7. See also
    Chemical weapons; and specific wars
WARF Institute. See University of Wisconsin:
    Alumni Research Foundation
War Production Board, 80
Warren County, N.C., 207
Washington, Booker T., 29, 65
Washington, D.C., 226
Washington, Judy: photograph of, 286
Washington Post, 250
Washington State, 213
Water pollution: in California, 236–37;
    control of, for public health, 64–65; of
    ditches in West Anniston, 118, 125, 127–28,
    141, 146, 150, 204, 223, 281; and drinking
    water, 181–82, 269; federal legislation
    on, 159, 171, 269, 343 (n. 41), 345 (n. 59),
    347 (n. 82), 349 (n. 23); and flooding,
    128; ignorance of, claimed by Monsanto
    Anniston plant, 119; by industrial wastes
    generally, 64–65, 126; lawsuits against
    Monsanto for, 126–27, 162, 235–36; legal
    rationales for regulation of, 130; by
    mercury, arsenic, and selenium, 269;
    by Monsanto Anniston plant, 3–5, 64,
    119, 120, 121, 141, 161, 253; Monsanto's
    awareness of, 138, 141, 253; of oceans, 149;
    penalties for, in Alabama, 162; regulation
    and investigation of, 119, 121, 130–31, 150,
    162, 167, 171; from Sauget, Ill., Krummrich
    plant, 276; by TCE, 269; in Woburn,
    Mass., 236. See also Choccolocco Creek;
    Fish contamination and fish kills
Watt, L. A., 73
Watts riots, 113
Weapons. See Biological weapons; Chemical
    weapons; Nuclear weapons
Weatherly, Pastor Morris, 228, 229
Weatherly, W. H., 47
Welch, Jack, 210
West Africa, 93
West Anniston, Ala. See Anniston, Ala.;
    Sweet Valley/Cobbtown, Ala.
West Anniston Environmental Justice Task
    Force, 231, 359 (n. 78)
West Anniston Foundation (WAF), 248, 271,
    281, 285, 286, 298
Westinghouse, 162, 194, 291
West Landfill. See Landfills
Wheeler, Earl G., 158
Wheeler, Elmer P., 139, 160
Whisenhunt, Dan, 301
Whistle-blower provision, 166
White, C. E., 172
White, Jere, 241–42, 244, 334 (n. 16)